Nicholas Patrick Wiseman

The Dublin Review:

Third Series, Volume XI, January-April 1884

Nicholas Patrick Wiseman

The Dublin Review:
Third Series, Volume XI, January-April 1884

ISBN/EAN: 9783741182334

Manufactured in Europe, USA, Canada, Australia, Japa

Cover: Foto ©Andreas Hilbeck / pixelio.de

Manufactured and distributed by brebook publishing software (www.brebook.com)

Nicholas Patrick Wiseman

The Dublin Review:

THE DUBLIN REVIEW

THIRD SERIES.—No. XXI.

JANUARY, 1884.

CONTENTS.

I. Secular Education.
II. Wycliffe and his Teaching concerning the Primacy. By the Rev. L. Delplace, S.J.
III. Liberty, Laisser-Faire and Legislation. By N. J. Synnott.
IV. Alexander Farnese.
V. The Copts.
VI. Madagascar; Past and Present. By Miss E. M. Clerke.
VII. The City of Our Martyrs. By the Rev. J. B. Mackinlay, O.S.B.
VIII. New Testament Vaticanism.
Science Notices.
Notices of Catholic Continental Periodicals.
Notices of Books.

LONDON: BURNS & OATES.
DUBLIN: M. H. GILL & SON.
NEW YORK: CATHOLIC PUBLICATION SOCIETY CO.
9, BARCLAY STREET.

Price Six Shillings.

to be brought into the Church.

ST. JOSEPH'S
FOREIGN MISSIONARY COLLEGE
OF
THE SACRED HEART.
MILL HILL, N.W.

PLEASE help us to educate Priests for the Foreign Mission
No work lies nearer to the Heart of Our Lord.

ROWLANDS' ODONT

Is the purest and most fragrant dentifrice ever made; it whitens the te
prevents decay, and gives a pleasing fragrance to the breath. All den
will allow that neither washes nor pastes can possibly be as efficacion
polishing the teeth and keeping them sound and white as a pure
non-gritty tooth powder; such Rowlands' Odonto has always pr
itself to be.

ROWLANDS' MACASSAR O

Has been known for the last 80 years as the best and safest preserver
beautifier of the hair; it contains no lead or mineral ingredients; an
especially adapted for the hair of children. It can now also be had
golden colour as well as in the ordinary tint. Sold in usual four s

In bringing this ingenious [novel]ty before the Public, the [paten]tees desire to state their [belief] that it creates a new era in [penc]il-making, being the most [impo]rtant improvement in pocket [penc]ils since the introduction of [the] famous Perryian propelling [and] withdrawing motion, more [than] a quarter of a century ago.

[The] action is simple and [effec]tive; when not in use the [poin]t is concealed in the tube, [thus] protecting the lead and [shor]tening the pencil to a con[venien]t size for the pocket. If [requi]red for use, press on the [top] or seal, holding the pencil [down]wards; to close, reverse [the p]encil, press against the seal [with] the forefinger.

CLOSED. OPEN. CLOSED.

PRICES.

	EACH.	£	s.	d.
Aluminium Gold plain, or engine turned		0	2	6
Aluminium Gold with seal or ball top		0	4	0
Aluminium Gold, richly engraved		0	5	0
Aluminium Gold, with mother-o'-pearl tube		0	7	6
Hall-marked Silver, plain		0	6	0
Hall-marked Silver, richly engraved		0	7	6
Hall-marked Silver, barleycorn pattern		0	10	6
15ct. GOLD SERIES.				
Engine cut		3	0	0
Barleycorn pattern		4	10	0
18ct. GOLD SERIES.				
Engine cut		3	15	0
Barleycorn pattern		5	5	0
Pearl tube, mounted in 18ct. gold		3	10	0

SOLD BY ALL STATIONERS & DEALERS IN FANCY GOODS.

IF YOU WANT [a] really good Steel Pen, [ask] your Stationer, or [sen]d 7/2in Stamps [for] a sample box [cont]aining [a] dozen of

PERRY PENS

STEEL, Nickel, and Gilt, of assorted patterns, in a metal box. Sold by all Stationers. Wholesale, HOLBORN VIADUCT, LONDON.

PERRY & CO.'S
[Pa]tent Nickel Silver Pens.

[T]he great success and favour these Pens [are fi]nding with the public have induced the [paten]tees to publish the following patterns; the [one] of soft and quill-like action; the Nickel, J.

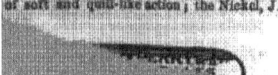

PERRY & CO.'S
Royal Aromatic Elastic Bands

The universal favour that these assorted boxes of Bands have met with from the public fully justifies us in stating that they are one of

PERRY & CO.'S JOHN BULL KNIVES.
THE CHEAPEST IN THE WORLD.

Two good Blades highly finished 5 inches long

COLLEGE OF BEAUCAMPS, PRÈS LILLE, FRANCE. Conducted by the Marist Brothers. Under the Patronage of his Eminence the Cardinal Archbishop of Cambrai. Established 1842. Pension, £26. No extras. For Prospectus, &c., apply to the Superior as above, or 9, Polygon, Clarendon Square, London, N.W.

ST. JOSEPH'S COLLEGE, WESTON HALL, near RUGBY.

This School is intended to afford to Catholic youth the advantages of a good education at a moderate pension (£7 per quarter, no extras). Since June, 1879, 22 Certificates have been gained at the Public Examinations. For particulars address the Principal.

CONVENT SCHOOL, MARK CROSS, TUNBRIDGE WELLS.

Conducted by the SISTERS of the HOLY CHILD JESUS from St. Leonards-on-Sea.

The pension is £18 per annum, inclusive terms.

Music, 15s. per quarter. Entrance Fee, £1 1s.

W. GARSTIN & SONS,

Catholic Undertakers,

5, WELBECK STREET, CAVENDISH SQUARE.

Funerals furnished agreeably to modern taste and requirements. Terms extremely moderate. Choice equipages and appointments. Monumental Works at Kensal Green, opposite All Souls' Cemetery. A Private Mortuary, also Reception Rooms can be engaged where removals from hotels, &c., are necessary.

INSTITUTION OF STE. CATHERINE.

Près Arras (Pas de Calais), France, at three hours express from Calais.

Under the Patronage of His Grandeur the Bishop of Arras.

The Course of Instruction is particularly calculated for boys destined to teaching, business, agriculture, finance, and different branches of administration.

ST. MARY'S LODGE, PEVENSEY ROAD, ST. LEONARD'S-ON-SEA.

PREPARATORY SCHOOL for the Sons of Gentlemen. Under the Patronage of the Right Rev. the Lord Bishop of Southwark. The educational course is specially designed to prepare the pupils for College. The healthy climate of St. Leonard's renders this school very desirable.

For Prospectus and further particulars apply to Miss Stevens, as above.

LIFE OF

ST. JOHN BAPTIST DE ROSSI.

Translated by LADY HERBERT.

INTRODUCTION

ON ECCLESIASTICAL TRAINING

AND

THE SACERDOTAL LIFE.

BY THE

BISHOP OF SALFORD.

Price Six Shillings.

THOS. RICHARDSON & SON, 26, KING EDWARD STREET, LONDON, E.C., and DERBY.

CARLOW LAY COLLEGE.

RESULTS OF PAST YEAR.

LONDON UNIVERSITY.

One passed the examination for the Degree of B.A.

ROYAL UNIVERSITY.

31 entered for the Matriculation Examination; 30 Matriculated.

INTERMEDIATE EXAMINATIONS.

20 Pupils were examined; 70 per cent. passed; 3 gained Exhibitions; three First-class Prizes, and one a Second-class Prize.

Classes have been formed this year in preparation for Matriculation in the London University, and for Matriculation and First University Examination in the Royal University. The Intermediate Classes continue as heretofore.

ST. MARY'S PREPARATORY SCHOOL, KNOCKBEG.

For Military Education Candidates for Sandhurst, Woolwich, and Commissions through the Militia.

BLENHEIM HOUSE,
9, Leyland Road, Lee, Blackheath, S.E.

Rev. E. VON ORSBACH, late Tutor to their Highnesses the PRINCES OF THURN and TAXIS, assisted by a Staff of able and experienced Masters, prepares Gentlemen for Military examinations, viz.—
(a.) For admission to the Royal Military College, Sandhurst; and for First Appointments to the Royal Marine Light Infantry.
(b.) For admission to the Royal Military Academy, Woolwich; and for First Appointments in the Royal Marine Artillery.
(c.) Of Lieutenants of Militia recommended for Commissions in the Regular Army.

TUTORIAL STAFF.

PRINCIPAL	Rev. E. VON ORSBACH.
Preliminary Subjects	The Principal and L. Davies, Esq.
Higher Mathematics	G. Merrit Reeves, Esq., M.A.; 13th Wrangler, 1873; late Scholar of St. John's College, Cambridge.
Trigonometry	J. A. Pease, Esq.
Algebra	J. A. Pease, Esq. and L. Davies, Esq.
Euclid	J. A. Pease, Esq. and L. Davies, Esq.
English Literature and History	L. Davies, Esq., and J. A. Prout, Esq., B.A. Oxon.
Latin and Greek	The Principal.
French Language	Mons. Victor Lemaire, Bachelier es Sciences et es Lettres.
German Language	The Principal.
Experimental Science and Geology	J. Morris, Esq.
Physical Geography	J. Morris, Esq.
Political Geography	The Principal.
Geometrical Drawing	J. A. Pease, Esq.
Freehand Drawing	J. A. Pease, Esq.
Drill and Fencing	Serjeant J. Myre, B.A., Woolwich.

Rev. E. VON ORSBACH receives no Gentleman into his Establishment without a Testimonial of good conduct from his last place of education, a rule which he has adopted as much for the benefit of his Pupils as for himself.
Pupils have the privilege of Daily Mass in the house.

NEW ILLUSTRATED CATHOLIC PERIODICAL.
PUBLISHED QUARTERLY.
ST. JOSEPH'S
FOREIGN MISSIONARY ADVOCATE.

It contains five beautiful and striking illustrations—16 pages. Price 1½d., by post 2d. Order copies at once direct from the EDITOR, ST. JOSEPH'S COLLEGE, MILL HILL, LONDON, or through your bookseller.

# DR. J. COLLIS BROWNE'S
ORIGINAL AND ONLY GENUINE.
CHLORODYNE.

Coughs, Colds, Asthma, Bronchitis.

DR. J. COLLIS BROWNE'S CHLORODYNE.—This wonderful remedy was discovered by Dr. J. COLLIS BROWNE, and the word CHLORODYNE coined by him expressly to designate it. There never has been a remedy so vastly beneficial to suffering humanity, and it is a subject of deep concern to the public that they should not be imposed upon by having imitations pressed upon them on account of cheapness, and as being the same thing. Dr. J. COLLIS BROWNE'S CHLORODYNE is a totally distinct thing from the spurious compounds called Chlorodyne, the use of which only ends in disappointment and failure.

DR. J. COLLIS BROWNE'S CHLORODYNE.—Vice Chancellor Sir W. PAGE WOOD, STATED PUBLICLY in Court that Dr. J. COLLIS BROWNE was UNDOUBTEDLY the INVENTOR of CHLORODYNE, that the whole story of the defendant was deliberately untrue, and he regretted to say it had been sworn to.—See *The Times*, July 13th, 1864.

DR. J. COLLIS BROWNE'S CHLORODYNE is a LIQUID MEDICINE which ASSUAGES PAIN of EVERY KIND, affords a calm, refreshing sleep WITHOUT HEADACHE, and INVIGORATES the NERVOUS SYSTEM when exhausted.

DR. J. COLLIS BROWNE'S CHLORODYNE is the GREAT SPECIFIC FOR CHOLERA, DYSENTERY, DIARRHŒA.

The GENERAL BOARD of HEALTH, London, REPORT that it ACTS as a CHARM, one dose generally sufficient.

Dr. GIBBON, Army Medical Staff, Calcutta, states: "TWO DOSES COMPLETELY CURED ME of DIARRHŒA."

DR. J. COLLIS BROWNE'S CHLORODYNE rapidly cuts short all attacks of EPILEPSY, SPASMS, COLIC, PALPITATION, HYSTERIA.

COUGHS, COLDS, &c.

From W. VESALIUS PETTIGREW, M.D., formerly Lecturer at St. George's Hospital, LONDON.

"I have no hesitation in stating that I have never met with any medicine so efficacious as an Anti-Spasmodic and Sedative. I have used it in Consumption, Asthma, Diarrhœa, and other diseases, and am perfectly satisfied with the results."

From W. C. WILKINSON, Esq. F.R.C.S., Spalding.

"I consider it invaluable in Phthisis and Spasmodic Cough; the benefit is very marked indeed."

DR. J. COLLIS BROWNE'S CHLORODYNE is the TRUE PALLIATIVE in NEURALGIA, GOUT, CANCER, TOOTHACHE, RHEUMATISM.

From Dr. B. J. BOULTON and Co., Horncastle.

"We have made pretty extensive use of Chlorodyne in our practice lately, and look upon it as an excellent direct Sedative and Anti-Spasmodic. It seems to allay pain and irritation in whatever organ, and from whatever cause. It induces a feeling of comfort and quietude not obtainable by any other remedy, and it seems to possess this great advantage over all other Sedatives, that it leaves no unpleasant after effects."

IMPORTANT CAUTION. The IMMENSE SALE of this REMEDY has given rise to many UNSCRUPULOUS IMITATIONS.

N.B.—EVERY BOTTLE of GENUINE CHLORODYNE BEARS on the GOVERNMENT STAMP the NAME of the INVENTOR,

DR. J. COLLIS BROWNE.

SOLD IN BOTTLES, 1s. 1½d., 2s. 9d., 4s. 6d., by all Chemists.

SOLE MANUFACTURER, J. T. DAVENPORT, 33, GREAT RUSSELL STREET, W.C.

SECULAR SCHOOL for the Daughters of Gentlemen, ABBEY HOUSE, KENILWORTH.

Highest References, both clerical and secular. For particulars apply to the Principal,

Mrs. CASSERA (diplômée).

PAX.

ST. AUGUSTINE'S BENEDICTINE COLLEGE, RAMSGATE, KENT. Complete Collegiate Course. ST. PLACID'S HOUSE for the younger boys under an experienced Lady Matron.

URSULINE CONVENT (from HANOVER), CROOM'S HILL, GREENWICH, S.E. (on Blackheath). Inclusive Terms from £45 per Annum.

See Prospectus and Letter of the late KING OF HANOVER.

CONVENT OF NOTRE DAME DE SION, WORTHING, SUSSEX.

Under the Patronage of his Lordship the BISHOP OF SOUTHWARK.

A superior School for Young Ladies is conducted at this healthy watering-place by the Religious of Notre Dame de Sion. Large house and gardens attached.

For particulars apply to the Rev. Mother Superior or to the Rev. J. Purdon, St. Mary of the Angels,

ST. BEDE'S COLLEGE.

ALEXANDRA PARK, MANCHESTER.

UNDER THE DIRECTION OF THE BISHOP OF SALFORD.

RECTOR:
Very Rev. MONSIGNOR CANON WRENNALL.

PREFECT OF STUDIES:
Rev. L. C. CASARTELLI, M.A.

This College is designed to prepare the sons of gentlemen directly for business and for various professions.

Applications for prospectus, terms, and admission to be made to the Rector. They may also be made direct to his Lord-

The Works of S. Francis De Sales,

TRANSLATED INTO THE ENGLISH LANGUAGE BY THE

REV. H. B. MACKEY, O.S.B.,

UNDER THE DIRECTION AND PATRONAGE OF

THE RIGHT REV. DR. HEDLEY, O.S.B.,

Bishop of Newport and Menevia.

We propose, under the title "Library of S. Francis de Sales," to publish an English translation of the chief works of this great Doctor. This will form, as nearly as is demanded in the present state of ascetical literature in this country, an English "Complete Works" of the Saint.

The Bull, *Dives in Misericordiâ*, by which S. Francis was declared *Doctor Ecclesiæ*, supersedes all need of praise. And, indeed, his writings are in veneration with all the faithful. They are, however, with the exception of the *Introduction*, more highly venerated than fully or exactly known. Persons are familiar with quotations from them, which occur abundantly in most of the spiritual writers of the last three centuries. But we wish to make accessible to English readers the whole works from which the extracts are taken, the treasures of which these are but samples. S. Francis is called, and he is, the *Doctor of Devotion*. "Other Doctors," as Bourdaloue says, "have excelled in their kind, but to form the moral character of the faithful, and to establish in souls a solid piety, none have had the same gift as the Bishop of Geneva."

His two great controversial works, *The Controversies* and the *Standard of the Cross*, with his sermons and many of his shorter works, have never been translated at all. We have fair translations only of the *Introduction* and the *Conferences*.

The great mine of his letters may be said to have no shaft from English soil. An Anglican lady has translated a sixth part of them, or rather extracts from a sixth part of them. She uses her own spiritual light and her own authority. The most important and distinctive Catholic truths are calmly omitted or slurred over; what is worse, the doctrine is sometimes most erroneously stated. Even from a literary point of view the work is not recommendable, for though we willingly concede it the praise of being good English, it fails, most importantly, in being a faithful rendering of the Saint's language or expression of his thoughts. The meaning is not exactly given, the difficulties are baulked, the delicate shading and the individuality of style are almost obliterated.

The current English edition of *The Love of God* does not deserve to be called a

TRÜBNER AND CO.'S LIST.

MR. ARNOLD'S POPULAR POEM ON BUDDHA AND BUDDHISM.

THE LIGHT OF ASIA; or, the Great Renunciation. Being the Life and Teaching of Gautama, Prince of India and Founder of Buddhism. Told in Verse by an Indian Buddhist. By EDWIN ARNOLD, C.S.I., &c. Crown 8vo, limp parchment wrapper, 2s. 6d. Also, now ready, in post 8vo, cloth, 7s. 6d.
"The most sympathetic account ever published in Europe of the life and teaching of the Sakya Saint."—*Times.*

NEW WORK BY MR. EDWIN ARNOLD.

INDIAN IDYLLS. From the Sanskrit of the Mahâbhârata. By EDWIN ARNOLD, C.S.I., &c., Author of "The Light of Asia," &c. Post 8vo, cloth, 7s. 6d.

INDIAN POETRY. From the Sanskrit of the "Gita Govinda" of Jayadeva; "Proverbial Wisdom" from the Shlokas of Hitopadesa, and other Oriental Poems. By EDWIN ARNOLD, C.S.I., &c., Author of "The Light of Asia," &c. Third Edition. Post 8vo. cloth, 7s. 6d.

PEARLS OF THE FAITH; or, Islam's Rosary. Being the Ninety-nine Beautiful Names of Allah. With Comments in Verse from various Oriental sources, as made by an Indian Mussulman. By EDWIN ARNOLD, C.S.I., &c., Author of "The Light of Asia," &c. Crown 8vo, cloth, 7s. 6d.
"Really displays an astonishing wealth and variety of mystical and devotional imagery and allegory."—*Daily News.*

THE WORLD AS WILL AND IDEA. By ARTHUR SCHOPENHAUER. Translated from the German by R. B. HALDANE, M.A., and JOHN KEMP, M.A. Vol. I. containing Four Books Post 8vo, cloth 18s.
Forms Vol. XXII. of "The English and Foreign Philosophical Library."

CREEDS OF THE DAY; or, Collated Opinions of Reputable Thinkers. By HENRY COKE. In Three Series. 2 vols. demy 8vo, cloth, £1 1s.

THE EARLY HISTORY OF LAND-HOLDING AMONG THE GERMANS. By DENMAN W. ROSS, Ph.D. Demy 8vo, cloth, 12s.

HOW TO USE THE OPHTHALMOSCOPE. Being Elementary Instructions in Ophthalmoscopy, adapted to the wants of Students. By EDGAR A. BROWNE, Surgeon to the Liverpool Eye and Ear Infirmary, &c. With Thirty-five Figures. Second Edition. Crown 8vo, cloth, 3s. 6d.

SPANISH AND PORTUGUESE SOUTH AMERICA DURING THE COLONIAL PERIOD. By R. G. WATSON. 2 vols. post 8vo. [*In the Press.*

DARLOW & CO.'S
IMPROVED PATENT MAGNETINE CURATIVE APPLIANCES

These Appliances are recommended and used by the Profession for the Cure of

Gout	Asthma	Chest Weakness	Sore Throat
Sciatica	Rheumatism	Spinal Affection	Heart Affections
Lumbago	Rheumatic Gout	Bronchitis	Liver Complaint
Neuralgia	Lung Affections	Winter Cough	General Debility

And every other form of Nervous and Rheumatic Affection.

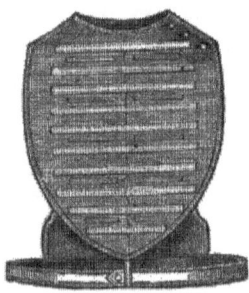

25s., 30s., 35s. each.

LUNG INVIGORATOR.

This is recommended in cases of incipient consumption, obstinate cough, weakness of the lungs, asthma, and bronchitis. It covers the entire surface of the lungs, back and front, and forms an excellent appliance as a Lung Protector, especially for winter use and night travelling.

The magnetic influence of this appliance, which penetrates the tubes and tissues of the Lungs, has in many cases given almost immediate relief, and effected rapid cures.

On the 3rd October, 1883, the Rev. J. CHARLESWORTH writes:—"Will you be good enough to forward one of your Chest Protectors? I have worn one during several winters with great benefit."

PAMPHLET] **DARLOW & CO.** [POST FREE

443, WEST STRAND, LONDON, W.C., 443.

B. HERDER, libraire-éditeur à Fribourg (Bade).

Vient de paraître et en vente chez MM. BURNS & OATES, 28, ORCHARD STREET, LONDON, W.

Lehmkuhl, A., S. J., THEOLOGIA MORALIS. Vol. 1

continens theologiam moralem generalem et ex speciali theologia morali tractatus de virtutibus et officiis vitae christianae. Cum approbatione Archiep. Friburg. et Super. Ordinis. In 8°. (XIX et 783 p.) Prix: Frcs. 11.25. (Le second et dernier volume est sous presse.)

---

3 vols. demy 8vo, cloth.

ROSMINI'S ORIGIN OF IDEAS.

Translated from the Fifth Italian Edition of the Nuovo Saggio *Sull' Origine delle Idee.*

VOLS. I. and II. NOW READY, 16s. each.

BURNS & OATES'
Christmas & New Year's List.

Cardinal Newman's Works. Complete in 36 volumes, Half-bound in Calf. The set £14 0s. 0d. net.

Cardinal Manning's Works. Complete in 14 volumes, Half-bound in Calf. The set £6 0s. 0d. net.

Faber's (Father) Works. Complete in 12 volumes, Half-bound in Calf. The set £5 0s. 0d. net.

Bishop Ullathorne's Works. GROUNDWORK OF THE CHRISTIAN VIRTUES, 10s. 6d. ENDOWMENTS OF MAN, &c., new and revised edition, 10s. 6d.

The New Parish Priest's Practical Manual: A Work useful also for other Ecclesiastics, especially for Confessors and Preachers. By JOSEPH FRASSINETTI, Prior of St. Sabina, Genoa. Translated from the Italian by WILLIAM HUTCH, D.D., President of St. Colman's College, Fermoy. Crown 8vo, printed on extra superfine paper, price 6s.

Spiritual Exercises according to the Method of St. Ignatius of Loyola. By Father ALOYSIUS BELLECIO, S.J. Translated from the Italian Version of Father ANTHONY BRESCIANI, S.J., by WILLIAM HUTCH, D.D., President of St. Colman's College, Fermoy; Author of "Nano Nagle: Her Life, Her Labours, and their Fruits," &c., &c. Second edition, 18mo, cloth, gilt lettered, 2s. 6d.

Lacordaire's Conferences:—Jesus Christ—God—God and Man. Translated from the French, with the Author's permission. New edition, 1 vol., 6s.

Sermons for the Spring Quarter. By the late Very Rev. CHARLES MEYNELL, D.D. Edited by H. I. D. RYDER, of the Oratory. Cloth extra, bevelled boards, 6s.

Lacordaire (Henri Dominique). Life of Saint Dominic. Translated from the French. Cloth extra, bevelled boards, red edges, 6s. 6d.

The Parochial Hymn-Book. Containing Music and Words. Compiled by the Rev. A. POLICE. Demy 8vo, Cloth, 6s. 6d. net. Words for ditto, price 1s. net.

Growth in the Knowledge of Our Lord. Meditations for Every Day of the Year, exclusive of those for Festivals, Days of Retreat, &c. Adapted from the Original of ABBÉ DE BRANDT. By a "Daughter of the Cross." This work bears the "Imprimatur" of his Eminence the Cardinal Archbishop of Westminster, and has received the approbation of his Lordship the Bishop of Salford. Complete in 5 vols., 7s. each.

The Works of St. Francis de Sales. Vol. I. **Letters to Persons in the World.** With Introduction by Dr. HEDLEY. Translated into the English Language by the Rev. H. B. MACKEY, O.S.B. Cloth, 6s.

A LARGE ASSORTMENT OF HANDSOMELY BOUND PRAYER BOOKS FOR PRESENTS.

Quarterly Series.

Colombière, Life of the Ven. Claude de la. By EUGENE SEGUIN, S.J. 5s.

Dialogues of St. Gregory the Great: an Old English Version. Edited by the Rev. H. J. COLERIDGE, S.J. 6s.

History of the Sacred Passion. By Father LUIS DE LA PALMA, of the Society of Jesus. Translated from the Spanish. With Preface by the Rev. H. J. COLERIDGE, S.J. Third edition. 7s. 6d.

Life and Letters of St. Francis Xavier. By the Rev. H. J. COLERIDGE, S.J. 2 vols., 15s. Cheap edition, 2 vols. in 1, 9s.

Life of Anne Catharine Emmerich. By HELEN RAM. With Preface by the Rev. H. J. COLERIDGE, S.J. 5s.

Life and Teaching of Jesus Christ, in Meditations for every Day in the Year. By P. N. AVANCINO, S.J. 2 vols., 10s. 6d.

Life of Margaret Mostyn (Mother Margaret of Jesus), Religious of the Reformed Order of our Blessed Lady of Mount Carmel (1625-1679). By the Very Rev. EDMUND BEDINGFIELD, Canon of the Collegiate Church of St. Gomar, and Confessor to the English Teresians at Lierre. Edited from the Manuscripts preserved at Darlington, by the Rev. H. J. COLERIDGE, S.J. 6s.

Life of our Life: The Harmony of the Gospel, arranged, with Introductory and Explanatory Chapters, Notes, and Indices. By the Rev. H. J. COLERIDGE, S.J. 2 vols., 15s.

Life of the Blessed John Berchmans. Second edition. By the Rev. F. GOLDIE, S.J. 6s.

Life of the Blessed Peter Favre, First Companion of St. Ignatius Loyola. From the Italian of Father BOERO. With Preface by the Rev. H. J. COLERIDGE, S.J. 6s. 6d.

Pious Affections towards God and the Saints. Meditations for every Day in the Year, and for the principal Festivals. From the Latin of the Venerable NICHOLAS LARCINIUS, S.J. With Preface by GEORGE PORTER, S.J. 7s. 6d.

Public Life of our Lord Jesus Christ. By the Rev. H. J. COLERIDGE, S.J. 6 vols. Each, 6s. 6d. Others in preparation.

Story of St. Stanislaus Kostka. With Preface by the Rev. H. J. COLERIDGE, S.J. 3s. 6d.

Life of Mother Mary Teresa Ball. By Rev. H. J. COLERIDGE, S.J. With Portrait. 6s. 6d.

Life and Letters of St. Teresa. Vol. I. By Rev. H. J. COLERIDGE, S.J. 7s. 6d.

The Life of Mary Ward. By MARY CATHERINE ELIZABETH CHAMBERS, of the Institute of the Blessed Virgin. Edited by HENRY JAMES COLERIDGE, of the Society of Jesus. Vol. I. 7s. 6d.

The Return of the King. Discourses on the Latter Days. By the Rev. H. J. COLERIDGE, S.J. 7s. 6d.

Granville Popular Library.

All handsomely bound in Cloth, extra gilt.

	s.	d.
Tales of Kings and Queens	1	0
Tales of Naval and Military Life	1	0
Tales of France	1	0
Manor of Mount Cruel	1	0
Vessels of the Sanctuary	1	0
Joe Baker	1	0
James Chapman	1	0
The Poor Man's Child	1	0
Clare Maitland	1	0
Monks of Lerins	1	0
Amusements of Travel	1	0
Tales of Land and Sea	1	0
Little Snowdrop	1	0
Cardinal d'Amboise	1	0
Footsteps of Spirits	1	0
Andersen's Popular Tales	1	0
Lucy Ward	1	0
Madeleine the Rosiere	1	0
Tales of Enterprise and Peril	1	0
Life of S. Margaret, &c.	1	0
Tales of Daring and Peril	1	0
Saints of the Working Classes	1	0
Catholic Legends and Traditions	1	0
Conversion of Ratisbonne	1	0
Emma's Cross, and other Tales	1	0
Winefride Jones	1	0
Tales of Bandits, &c.	1	0
Tales of the French Revolution	1	0
Arctic Voyages and Discoveries	1	0
Afternoons with Mrs. Maitland	1	0
Book of 300 Anecdotes	1	0
Life of St. Elizabeth of Hungary	1	0
Blind Rosa	1	0
Conscript	1	0
Count Hugo	1	0
Poor Gentleman	1	0
Ricketicketack	1	0
Rich and Poor	1	0
Robert May	1	0
George Morton	1	0
Kate Kavanagh	1	0
Suffering for the Faith	1	0
Parables and Stories of Père Bonaventure	1	0
Christian Heroism	1	0
Historical Tales and Legends	1	6
Lives of St. Francis & St. Clare	1	6
Lives of Pious Youth	1	6
Tales of Catholic A...	1	6
Tales of Celebrate...	1	6

	s.	d.
Tales of Celebrated Women	1	6
Tales of the Crusades	1	6
Tales and Traditions	1	6
Twelve Stories for Children	1	6
Fireside Stories	1	6
Tales for the Home Circle	1	6
Tales of Faith and Loyalty	1	6
Miser	1	6
Scenes and Incidents at Sea	1	6
Missions in the West	1	6
Heath House Stories	1	6
Adventures at Sea	2	0
Heroines of Charity	2	0
Tales of Duty and Affection	2	0
Life of S. Ignatius	2	0
Tales of Bandits	2	0
Children of Mary, The: containing Narratives of Lives of Young Ladies	2	0
Anecdotes and Incidents	2	0
Breton Legends	2	0
Tales of Remarkable Men	2	0
Tales for the Festivals	2	0
Tales for the Young	2	0
Monks of Lorins, and other Legends	2	0
Lives of Sainted Queens	2	0
Twelve Tales for the Young:		
1st Series	2	0
2nd Series	2	0
Historical Tales, Legends and Traditions	2	6
Witch of Melton Hill	2	6
Luisa de Carjaval	2	6
Tales of Celebrated and Remarkable Men	3	0
History of France	3	0
By Hendrick Conscience.		
Curse of the Village	3	0
Tales of Flanders	3	0
Veva, or the War	3	0
Demon of Gold	3	0
Lion of Flanders	3	0
Pictures of Christian Heroism	3	0
Miser, and other Stories	3	0
Romantic Tales of Great Men	3	0
Never Forgotten	3	6
Our Sunday Fireside	4	6
Bertha	6	0

Granv... ...ns, 28, Orchard Street, London, W.

Christmas Books—Suitable for Presents.

Wild Birds of Killeevy, The. By Miss ROSA MULHOLLAND. Cloth, extra gilt, 5s.
"Full of high and pure purpose, and distinguishing by its perfect grace and refinement of style."—*Irish Monthly.*
"The book has many merits, and some vivid bits of description—notably an appreciative sketch of Verona."—*Academy.*
"A simple but most pleasing tale, with much local colouring about it to give it freshness and interest."—*Month.*
"No one will find 'The Wild Birds of Killeevy' tedious, and no one, we think, will fail to recognise in it an elevating and purifying influence."—*Spectator.*

Our Little Ones and the Nursery: Illustrated Stories and Poems for Little People. Embellished with 370 original Illustrations, and beautifully bound in fancy cover, gilt edges, 6s.

Golden Sands. Translated from the French by ELLA MCMAHON. Fancy cover, 6s.

Twit Twats: A Christmas allegorical Story of Birds. By Rev. AUG. J. THÉBAUD, S.J. Illustrated, fancy cover, gilt edges. 3s. net.

Law, Rev. A. H. (S. J.), Memoir of the Life and Death of. The set of three volumes now completed. Part I., cloth, 4s. 6d; Part II., cloth, 4s. 6d.; Part III., cloth, 5s. 6d.

"Merry England," Vol. I. of. Containing the first six parts and upwards of 50 stories, essays, and poems; also 15 full page Etchings and other Illustrations by Sir Frederick Leighton, P.R.A., Mrs. Butler, and Tristam Ellis. Cloth, 7s. 6d.

Pocket Prayer-book. Cloth, extra, red edges, 9d.; calf, red edges, 2s. 6d.; calf, round corners, 3s.

Baby: A Study of Baby Life. Cloth, fancy cover, 2s.

Little Hinges to Great Doors. And other Tales. By Miss AMES, Author of "Marion Howard," and "Maggie's Rosary." Cloth extra, bevelled boards, 3s. 6d.

Through Thorny Paths. A New Novel by Miss NOBLE, Author of "Gertrude Mannering." 7s. 6d.

My Story. Cloth, extra gilt, 5s.

National Pictures; From the Spanish of FERNAN CABALLERO. 5s.

Ancilla Domini; or, May Carols. By AUBREY DE VERE. Beautifully Illustrated. 7s. 6d.

I Promessi Sposi; or, the Betrothed. By MANZONI. New edition. Cloth, 3s. 6d.

Roman Violets and Where They Blossom. A Story for Young and Old. By THEODORA LANE CLARKE. Beautifully bound in cloth, bevelled edges, 4s.

Tales from Twelve Tongues. Translated by a British Museum Librarian. Cloth extra, gilt lettering, 4s. 6d.

Among the Lilies and other Tales, with a Sketch of Nazareth and Loretto, drawn from ancient and other authentic sources. By Miss E. M. SHAPCOTE. Cloth, fancy cover, 4s.

Ethna; or, Etchings in Black and White. By Mrs. STUART LAIDLAW. 4s. 6d.
"It is a very touching tale, and one specially well fitted for Christmas gifts and prizes."—*Tablet.*

[SELECT LIST.] [JANUARY, 1884.

Catholic Publications Recently Issued by
THOMAS RICHARDSON & SON,
3, KING EDWARD STREET, CITY, LONDON, E.C.; & DERBY.

☞ NEW BOOKS JUST PUBLISHED.

Now Ready, crown 8vo, elegantly bound in superfine cloth, with beautiful design on cover in black, and gold lettering, price 3s. 6d.

CONRAD VALLENROD
AN HISTORICAL POEM.
BY ADAM MITSKIEVITCH.
Translated from the Polish by **MICHAEL HENRY DZIEWICKI**.

"This Poem holds the highest rank among the creations that enrich Polish poetry. It came from the pen of the very first poet, not only of Poland, but of all Sclavonian countries, and its place among its works is one of the first. Half a century and more has gone by since it was written; times and circumstances are changed; but 'Conrad Vallenrod' charms us still, as it charmed our fathers; it is to-day, and will remain for ever, one of the brightest jewels of Polish literature."—*Sketch by Dr. Iickowski.*

Small crown 8vo, cloth elegant, inked design on cover, lettered in gold, price 2s.

MAUD HAMILTON,
OR, SELF-WILL AND ITS CONSEQUENCES.
BY MARY AGATHA PENNELL,
Author of "Elsie McDermott;" "Bertram Eldon;" "Agnes Wilmott," &c.

LIFE OF ST. JOHN BAPTIST DE ROSSI, translated from the Italian, by LADY HERBERT. With an **Introduction on Ecclesiastical Training and the Sacerdotal Life**, by the BISHOP OF SALFORD. Demy 8vo, with Portrait of the Saint, superfine cloth, lettered in gold, price **6s.**

LIFE of DOM BARTHOLOMEW OF THE MARTYRS, Religious of the Order of St. Dominic, Archbishop of Braga, in Portugal. Translated from his Biographies. By LADY HERBERT. In one thick volume, demy 8vo, price **12s. 6d.**

LIGHTS AND SHADOWS OF HOME AFFECTIONS. A Moral Tale for the present epoch. Humbly Dedicated to her virtuous Queen, by the authoress of "Footsteps through Life," &c. Crown 8vo, elegantly bound in cloth, price **7s.**

A

RICHARDSON AND SON'S PUBLICATIONS.

THE STIGMATA: a History of Various Cases. Translated from the "Mystik," of Görres. By the Rev. H. Austin. Foolscap 8vo, neat cloth binding, price 3s. 6d.

FATHER MILLERIOT, the Ravignan of the Working Men of Paris. From the French of the Rev. Pere Clair, S.J., with the special permission of the author, by Mrs. F. Raymond-Barker. Foolscap 8vo, extra cloth, inked design on cover, lettered in gold, price 2s.

SHORT SERMONS, CHIEFLY on DOCTRINAL SUBJECTS. Preached in the Chapel of S. Mary's College, Oscott. By the Rev. Charles Meynell, D.D., Professor of Theology and Literature at the same College. Second edition, post 8vo, cloth, price 4s.

> The Sermons have this one general aim and character, of TEACHING, rather than exhortation, and may be regarded as exhibiting the results of theological reading, in a popular form, and clear of technicalities.

The **HOLY SACRIFICE** of the **MASS**, in which the Holy Sacrifice, and its Liturgy, Rites, and Ceremonies, are explained, in a Dialogue between a Catholic and a Protestant. To which is added, Devotions for Mass, compiled by the Venerable Bishop Challoner, taken from the Garden of the Soul. Crown 16mo, cloth, red edges, price 6d.

THERE IS A GOD. A reply to Mr. Bradlaugh's "Plea for Atheism." By Francis Winterton. Price 4d.

THE CHRISTIAN SCHOOLS OF ENGLAND, and Recent Legislation concerning them. By Mr. Charles Russell, Q.C., M.P. Price 1d.

COMPLIN; BENEDICTION; QUARANT' ORE; with a Selection of Psalms and Hymns. Extra cloth, gold lettering, red edges, price 1s.

VIRGIN MARY ACCORDING to the GOSPEL. By Nicolas. Edited by the Rev. H. Collins. Post 8vo, superfine cloth, 6s. 6d.

GRAZIELLA; or the History of a Broken Heart. An Episode of my Life. By A. De Lamartine. Translated from the French by J. B. S. Foolscap 8vo, cloth elegant, 2s. 6d.

LIFE of S. ANTHONY OF PADUA, Friar Minor. Translated from the French. Second edition, foolscap 8vo, cloth, 3s. 6d.

MIDDLEFORD HALL. A Tale for Children. Edited by the Authoress of "Ellerton Priory," "Claire Maitland," &c. Second edition, foolscap 8vo, handsome cloth binding, price 3s.

MANUAL of the LIVES of the POPES, from St. Peter to Pius IX. For the use of Students. By John Charles Earle, B.A. Foolscap 8vo, price 3s. 6d.

ENGLISH POPE ADRIAN IV. An Historical Sketch. By Richard Raby. Octavo, superfine paper, cloth, gilt, price 3s.

The **Apostolic See.** A Concise Sketch of Church History, with a List of the Popes, price 1d.

NEW WORKS BY DR. WENINGER, S.J.

Demy 8vo, strongly bound in cloth, price 10s. per Vol.

Original, Short, and Practical CONFERENCES, intended as a Three Years' Course. In two volumes.

Vol. I.—Conferences for Married Men and Young Men. Thirty-six Conferences for each.

Vol. II.—Conferences for Married Women and Young Maidens. Thirty-six Conferences for each.

Original, Short, and Practical SERMONS for EVERY SUNDAY of the Ecclesiastical Year. Three Sermons for every Sunday. By F. X. Weninger, S.J., Doctor of Theology. SECOND English Edition. 10s.

"The book is a very handsome one, and the three Sermons for every Sunday in the Year will be very useful to Priests. They appear to me to be very well done."—*Bishop of Nottingham.*

Original, Short, and Practical SERMONS for EVERY FEAST of the Ecclesiastical Year. Three Sermons for every Feast. By F. X. Weninger, S.J., Doctor of Theology. English Edition, price 10s.

MANUAL of the CATHOLIC RELIGION, for Catechists, Teachers and Self-Instruction. By Rev. F. X. Weninger, D.D., S.J. 12mo, 410 pp. Cloth. Price 4s. 6d.

*** *This Work, because of the PRACTICAL INSTRUCTION IT CONTAINS, has no parallel in English literature.*

LIFE of S. JOHN OF GOD. By Eleanor Baillon. Foolscap 8vo, handsomely bound in cloth, 1s.; in paper cover, 8d.

SNARES of the DEVIL. By John Gerson, Chancellor of Paris. With Life of the Author. Demy 18mo, handsomely bound in cloth, price 6d.

COMFORT and CONSOLATION for the SICK and AFFLICTED. With Mass and Prayers for the Sick and for the Dead. Crown 16mo, with Frontispiece, cloth, blocked black, red edges, lettered in gold, price 2s.

HEAVEN OPENED: or our Home in Heaven, and the Way Thither. A Manual of Guidance for Devout Souls. By Rev. Father Collins. Post 8vo, handsomely bound, 5s.

FRANCIS WILLINGTON; or a Life for the Foreign Missions. By Weston Reay. With Preface by Rev. Isaac Moore, S.J. Dedicated by permission to the Bp. of Salford. Crown 8vo, elegantly bound in cloth, 5s.

LIFE of VENERABLE JOHN EUDES, with a sketch of the HISTORY OF HIS FOUNDATIONS, from A.D. 1601 to 1874. By M. Ch. de Montzey. With a Brief of Approval from His Holiness Pope Pius IX. Second edition, post 8vo, cloth, price 4s. 6d.

SHORT LIFE of VENERABLE FATHER EUDES. From the French. By Father Collins. Demy 18mo, ornamental cloth binding, price 6d.

SHORT MEDITATIONS FOR EVERY DAY IN THE YEAR, according to the Method of St. Ignatius. Revised by a Jesuit Father. For pupils in Convent and other Schools.
In two vols. post 12mo, cloth, price 6s. the two vols.
Also in 12 monthly parts, paper wrapper, 4d. each part.

BERNADETTE.—Sister Marie-Bernard. The Sequel to "Our Lady of Lourdes." By HENRI LASSERRE. Translated with the special permission of the author, by MRS. F. RAYMOND-BARKER. Foolscap 8vo, ornamental cloth, price 4s.

SILENCE IN LIFE, and FORGIVENESS IN DEATH. From the Spanish of Fernan Caballero. By Rev. J. J. Kelly, O.S.F. Foolscap 8vo, handsome cloth binding, price 1s.

LASSIE, AND HER GUARDIAN ANGEL. By Charlotte Dean, authoress of "May Templeton." Foolscap 8vo, price 1s., handsomely bound in cloth.

EVA; or, as the Child so the Woman. By A. I. O'Neill Daunt. Foolscap 8vo, price 1s., handsomely bound in cloth.

LEGEND of the BLESSED VIRGIN MARY, Mother of Christ our Lord. By Michael Henry Dziewicki. In wrapper, price 6d.

⁕THE PROBLEM SOLVED. Edited by LADY HERBERT. Crown 8vo, 450 pp., extra cloth, blocked black, with gold lettering, price 6s.

NUN OF THE ORDER OF THE VISITATION, Anne Madeleine de Remusat, of Marseilles, called the Second Margaret Mary of the Sacred Heart. Foolscap 8vo, superfine cloth, 3s. 6d.

PRIMACY OF ST. PETER demonstrated from the Liturgy of the Greco-Russian Church. With several Documents and the Russian Text of all the passages quoted from the Slavonic Liturgy. By the REV. C. TONDINI DE QUARENGHI, Barnabite. Demy 8vo, price 3s.

MEDIÆVAL LEGENDS, from Cesar of Heisterbach. Translated by Henry Collins. With a Steel Engraving of the Abbey of Mount St. Bernard, Leicestershire. Foolscap 8vo, cloth extra, price 3s.

LIFE of the VEN. F. LOUIS DE PONTE, S.J. Post 8vo, extra cloth, blocked black, lettered in gold, price 4s.
May also be had uniform with his MEDITATIONS, paper wrapper, price 3s.; dark cloth, red edges, 5s.

Meditations on all the Mysteries of the Faith, together with a Treatise on Mental Prayer. By the Ven. F. Louis de Ponte, S J. To which are added, the Meditations on the Sacred Heart of Jesus. By the Ven. F. C. Borgo, S.J., Complete in six vols. 8vo, superfine paper, printed wrapper, price 18s. Any vol. may be had separately, price 3s. The six vols. bound in cloth, red edges, £1. 10s. 0d.

Instructions and Devotions for Mass. By Bishop Challoner. A large type edition. In paper wrapper, 2d.

Sacramentals of the Holy Catholic Church; being Instructions on the Prayers and Benedictions of the Church. By the Rev. W. J. Barry. Royal 32mo, handsome cloth binding, red edges. Price 1s. 6d.

Visits to the Most Holy Sacrament, for every Day in the Month; also Preparation for and Thanksgiving after Communion. By St. Alphonsus Liguori. With Benediction of the Blessed Sacrament. Cloth, price 6d.

RICHARDSON AND SON'S PUBLICATIONS.

BOOKS FROM OUR LADY'S LIBRARY.

The Loves which Reign in the HEART OF MARY. For our Lady's true Lovers, showing how they may increase their love, and live in still closer union with their sweet Mother. Post 12mo, cloth, blocked black, gold lettering, price 3s.

Mary's Conferences to her Loving CHILDREN, both in the World and in the Cloister. Post 12mo, bound in cloth, price 2s. 6d.

Our Lady's Comfort to the Sorrowful. New edition, enlarged and revised. Price 8d.—Cloth, gilt, 1s.

Mary's Call to her Loving Children; or, Devotion to the Dying. By the Authoress of the "Path of Mary." Post 12mo., bound in cloth, price 2s. 6d.

Spiritual Exercises of Mary. A Sequel to the "Path of Mary." Royal 32mo, superfine cloth, lettered, price 2s.

The Path of Mary. A new edition, with additions. Approved by the Bishop of Nottingham. Royal 32mo, price 8d.; bound in cloth, lettered, 1s.

A Message from the Mother-Heart of MARY. New and enlarged edition. Price 4d.; bound, 6d.

Efficacious Prayer, known to produce Special Graces. Price 1d.; 9d. per doz.

Indulgenced Prayers to be said at MASS, in honour of the Precious Blood. Price 4d. per dozen.

Indulgenced Prayers for the Holy SOULS AND FOR THE DYING. From "Our Lady's Comfort to the Sorrowful." Price 6d. per dozen.

Act of Consecration, and Morning OFFERING, for those who enter on the Path of Mary. From the "Spiritual Exercises of Mary." Price 1d.; 9d. per dozen.

MINIATURE WORKS OF DEVOTIONAL AND PRACTICAL PIETY.

Demy 18mo, handsome cloth binding, price Sixpence each.

Meditations on the Seven Gifts of THE HOLY GHOST. By Father Pergmayer, S.J.

Communion Prayers for Every Day of the Week. By Canon A. C. Arvisenet.

Heavenward. From "Heaven Opened." By Rev. Father Collins.

Comfort for Mourners. By S. Francis de Sales. From his Letters. Translated by E. M. B.

Holy Will of God: a Short Rule of Perfection. By Father Benedict Canfield, Capuchin Friar. Translated by Father Collins.

Month of Jesus Christ. By Saint Bonaventure.

Stations of the Passion, as made in Jerusalem; and Select Devotions on the Passion, from the Prayers of St. Gertrude. Translated by Father Collins.

The Our Father: Meditations on the Lord's Prayer. By St. Teresa. Translated by E. M. B.

Quiet of the Soul. By Father John de Bovilla. To which is added, THE CURE FOR SCRUPLES. By Dom Schram, O.S.B. Edited by the Rev. H. Collins.

Little Manual of Direction, for Priests, Religious Superiors, Novice-Masters and Mistresses, &c. By Dom Schram, O.S.B. Translated by Father Collins.

RICHARDSON'S POPULAR CATHOLIC MANUALS.

Devotions for the Forty Hours' Adoration, or Quarant' Ore; Solemn Exposition; and Benediction of the Blessed Sacrament. Compiled by a Catholic Priest. Price One Penny.

Story of St. ; the "Good Thief." By a Catholic Priest. Crown 16mo, with frontispiece. (second) One Penny.

Mass for the Dead; Dies Iræ, and Prayers for the Departed. One Penny.

Marriage, and Family Duties in GENERAL. By Archbishop Purcell, of Cincinnati, America. Adapted for English readers by a Catholic Priest. Price 1d.

Life of our Lord. Reprinted from "Religious Instruction for Standard 3." Price One Penny.

Sanctification of Sickness; Practical Instructions for the Comfort of the Sick. Price One Penny.

CLASSIFIED LIST OF
ENTERTAINING AND INSTRUCTIVE BOOKS,
CONSISTING OF LIVES OF SAINTS, BIOGRAPHICAL WORKS AND POPULAR TALES.

Suitable for Presents, School-Prizes, and for School and Parochial Libraries.

☞ The Books in this List, unless otherwise described, are in small 8vo, handsomely bound in cloth.

At Sixpence each,
Demy 18mo, handsomely bound in cloth, black printing on side.

Morning and Evening Star.
Christmas Dinner.
Hawthorn Bush.
Pearl Lost and Found.
The Holy House.
Altar Flowers; a Story of the Blessed Sacrament.
Maurice's Trial.
Carry's Trials.
A Tale of the Crusaders.
Life of Freddy Wragg, Brother M. Aloysius, a Dominican Tertiary.
Augustine Mc'Nally, Tertiary O.S.D.
Willie and his Sisters.

At One Shilling each.

The Queen's Confession; or the Martyrdom of St. John Nepomucene.
Child Life and its Lessons. Poetry, Original and Selected.
Elsie Mc'Dermott, the Little Watercress Girl.
Little Flower Basket.
Hilda's Victory; and Una's Repentance.
Little Musicians who became great Masters. First Series.
Little Musicians. Second Series. Together with Flowers of Childhood.
Ellerton Priory.
Search for Happiness, and other Tales.
Marie, the Fisherman's Daughter.
Godfrey, the Little Hermit.
Forest Pony, Gipsy Boy, and other Tales.
The Gift: three interesting Tales.
Miracle at Lourdes, September 16th, 1877.
Martha Blondel, the Factory Girl, *super royal 32mo. cloth lettered.*
Life of Maria Bonneau de Miramion, *32mo, cloth lettered.*

At One Shilling and Sixpence each.

Life of St Patrick.
Life of Anna Maria Taigi, *super royal 32mo, cloth, gilt edges.*
Diamond or Glass, *super royal 32mo.*
Chinese Mother, a Drama, *paper cover.*

At Two Shillings each.

Holy Mountain of La Salette, 18mo, *superfine cloth, gilt edges.*
Hidden Gem.
Julian Watts Russell, Pontifical Zouave.
Christian Instructions for Youth, *super royal 32mo, cloth, lettered.*
Children of Mary Instructed, *demy 18mo, cloth, gilt edges.*
Marcion, the Magician of Antioch. A Drama. cloth.
Life of Dame Gertrude More, *demy 18mo, cloth, lettered.*
Louise Lateau, the Ecstatica of Bois d'Haine; her Life, Stigmata, and Ecstasies.
Farm Boys of Rockstone.

At Two Shillings and Sixpence each.

The Green Island, a Tale for Boys.
Roman Catacombs: Part I.—Their Importance for the Teaching of the Catholic Church. Part II.—The Cata-
The Lost Found; Magdalen, or the Governess.
Heiress of Morden; a Tale of our own Times, or God's Will and Man's Ways.

At Three Shillings each.

Middleford Hall, a Tale for Children.
Irish Diamonds, or a Chronicle of Peterstown.
Disappointed Ambition, or Wedded and Caswall's Poems. [Single.
Roman Martyrology.
Lily of Israel.

Abbé Zouave: or Life of Joseph Louis Guerin, a Volunteer in the Pontifical Corps.
In re Garland, a Tale of a Transition Time.
Lady May. A Pastoral, *crown 8vo, superfine cloth.*

At Three Shillings and Sixpence each.

Diamonds from the Waverley Mines, or Maxims selected from the Novels of Sir Walter Scott.
Manual of the Lives of the Popes from St. Peter to Pius IX.
Avice Arden, the Old Man's Romance.
Life of St. Anthony of Padua.
Spiritual Conferences of St. Francis of Sales.

Evelyn Clare, or the Wrecked Homesteads: an Irish Story of Love and Landlordism.
Revelations of S. Bridget, Princess of Sweden.
Inheritance of Lynch Morgan's Heir.
The Rosary; a Legend of Wilton Abbey, *crown 8vo, gilt edges.*

At Four Shillings each.

Spiritual Consolation, a Treatise on the Peace of the Soul.
Old Village Church.
May Carols.
Calvary and the Altar; or Devotions for the Octave of the Blessed Sacrament.
Lætare, or the Bell-Ringer of Louville.
Apostleship of Prayer: a Holy League of Christian Hearts united with the Heart of Jesus.
Divinity of our Lord.

St. Francis and the Franciscans
Earlscliff.
The Divine Cloud, with Notes and a Preface.
Destiny, or the Priest's Blessing.
Chieftain's Daughter, a Legend of Sybil Head, and other Poems.
Revelations of Rome; Sketches of the Past and Present.
Florence Danby.
Meynell's Sermons, *post 8vo, superfine cloth.*

At Four Shillings and Sixpence each.

Spiritual Letters of Father Surin.
New Glories of the Catholic Church, *post 8vo, superfine cloth.*

Story of Fordington Hall.
Mary Herbert; or the Fallible World.

At Five Shillings each.

Leaflets of Promise. Poems.

Life and Select Writings of Louise

Life and Letters of Frederick William Faber,
D.D., Priest of the Oratory of St. Philip Neri. By John Edward Bowden, of the same Congregation. One vol., demy 8vo, price 10s. 6d. Full gilt sides 1s. 6d. extra.

Brief Sketch of the Early Life of the late F. W. Faber, D.D. By his only surviving Brother. Post 8vo, price 2s. 6d.

Works by the Very Rev. Dr. Faber.

Notes on Doctrinal and Spiritual Subjects. Selected from the Papers of the late Very Rev. Father Faber, D.D., Priest of the Oratory of St. Philip Neri. Edited by John Edward Bowden, Priest of the same Congregation. Complete in two volumes. Price 10s.

All for Jesus: or the Easy Ways of Divine Love. With a copious Index. (Eighth Edition, Fifteenth thousand.) Price 5s.

The Precious Blood; or the Price of our Salvation. (Second Edition, Fourth thousand.) Price 5s.

Bethlehem. With a copious Index, (Second Edition,) 7s.

The Blessed Sacrament; or the Works and Ways of God. With a copious Index. (Third Edition, Sixth thousand.) Price 7s. 6d.

The Creator and the Creature; or the Wonders of Divine Love. (Fourth Edition, Fifth thousand.) Price 6s.

Spiritual Conferences. (Third Edition, Fourth thousand.) With a copious Index. Price 6s.

Growth in Holiness; or the Progress of the Spiritual Life. (Third Edition, Sixth thousand.) With a copious Index. Price 6s.

Hymns, hitherto scattered in different Publications, together with Fifty-Six New Hymns. (Second Edition.) Price 6s.

The Foot of the Cross; or the Sorrows of Mary. With a copious Index. (Fourth Edition, Sixth Thousand.) Price 6s.

Ethel's Book; or, Tales of the Angels. (Second Edition.) Price 2s. 6d.

Sir Lancelot. A Tale of the Middle Ages. (Second Edition.) Price 5s.

Poems. (Fourth Edition.) Price 7s. 6d.

An Essay on Canonization and Beatification. 3s.

An Essay on the Interests and Characteristics of the Lives of the Saints. Price 2s.

An Essay on Catholic Home Missions. Printed wrapper. Price 1s. 6d.

Devotion to the Pope. Price 4d.

Devotion to the Church. Price 4d.

A Letter to the Members of the Confraternity of the Most Precious Blood. Eight pages 8vo, fine paper, ½d.

Thanksgiving after Communion. From "All for Jesus." Price 1d. in wrapper.

Three beautiful Prints of the Holy Souls in Purgatory. With Verses. Price 1d. each.

Scheme of Intercessory Prayer for the Month. For the Use of the Confraternity of the Precious Blood. Price 1d.

The London Oratory and the Union Newspaper. Being Three Letters on the Respect Due to Our Blessed Lord. Price 1d.

The Month of Mary Conceived Without Sin. Translated from the French of A. Gratry, Priest of the Oratory of the Immaculate Conception. With an Introduction by the Very Rev. F. W. Faber, D.D., of the London Oratory. Superfine paper, cloth lettered. Price 3s.

The New Glories of the Catholic Church. Translated from the Italian, by the Fathers of the London Oratory, at the request of the Cardinal Archbishop of Westminster, with a Preface by His Eminence. Superfine paper. Price 4s. 6d.

Devotion to the Heart of Jesus. With an Introduction on the History of Jansenism. By the Rev. Father Dalgairns, Priest of the Oratory. Superfine cloth, lettered, price 3s. 6d.

Medals of the Precious Blood, price 1d.

Medals of St. Philip Neri, price ½d. and 1d.

Edited by the Very Reverend Dr. Faber.

Oratorian Lives of the Saints, translated from various languages, for spiritual reading, with Prefaces, post 8vo, cloth lettered, price 4s. per vol.
Companions of St. Philip Neri, 1 vol.—Fathers of the Oratory, B. Sebastian Valfre, De Santi, Matteucci, 1 vol.—B. Sebastian of Apparizio, 1 vol.—St. Alphonso Liguori, 5 vols.—Companions of St. Alphonso, 1 vol.—F. Anchieta, Alvera Von Virmundt, V. John Berchmans, 1 vol.—B. Benedict Joseph Labre, 1 vol.—Fathers of the Oratory, V. Fabrizio Dall' Aste. V. Mariano Sozzini, 1 vol.—St. Joseph Calasanctius, B. Ippolito Galantini, 1 vol.—St. Camillus of Lellis, V. Louis da Ponte, and F. La Nuza, 2 vols.—Fathers of the Oratory, Talpa, Eustachio, and Prever, 1 vol.—Fathers Segneri, Pinamonti, and V. John de Britto, 1 vol.—St. Catherine of Ricci, 1 vol.—B. Paul of the Cross, 3 vols.—St. Peter of Alcantara, and Ven. F. Ignatius Azevedo, 2 vols.

ST. PHILIP NERI, 1 vol., price 5s.
B. MARGARET MARY ALACOQUE, 1 vol., price 5s.
ST. ROSE OF LIMA, B. COLUMBA OF RIETI, AND ST. JULIANA FALCONIERI, complete in 1 vol., price 4s.
ST. FRANCIS OF SALES, complete in 2 vols., price 8s.
POPE BENEDICT XIV. ON HEROIC VIRTUE. The Three vols., price 12s.

Any volume may be had separately.

CROWN OF JESUS. A Complete Manual of Prayers, Devotions, 214 Hymns, Instructions for the Public, Private, or Domestic use of all the Faithful. With the special recommendation of all the Archbishops of Great Britain and Ireland; also honoured with the Approval and Blessing of our Holy Father Pope Pius IX.

	s.	d.
Cloth, lettered, sprinkled edges	2	0
Strong leather, lettered, sprinkled edges	3	0
Strong roan, ditto ditto	3	0
Roan, lettered, gilt or red edg., flexible back	4	0
Persian leather, very strong, gilt or red edges	5	0
Morocco plain, gilt or red edges, flexible back	6	0
Morocco extra, gilt or red edges, flexible back	6	0
Strong calf plain, gilt or red edges ditto	6	0
Calf extra, gilt or red edges	7	0
Best Turkey morocco, plain, gilt edges, do.	9	0
Best Turkey morocco elegant, gilt edges, flexible back	11	0
Best Turkey morocco plain, gilt edges, flexible back, bevelled boards, ornamental tooled edges	13	0
The same, elegant	15	0
Best Turkey morocco plain, gilt edges, flexible back, gilt rims and clasp	11	0
The same, elegant	13	0

The Little Crown, a beautiful miniature Prayer Book, containing the Devotions and Instructions most frequently required. Approved by Ecclesiastical Authority.

	s.	d.
Cloth, red edges	0	6
Cloth, red edges, rims and clasp	1	0
Roan, gilt edges	1	0
Calf plain, gilt edges	1	6
Calf extra, gilt edges	2	0
Morocco plain, gilt edges	1	6
Morocco extra, gilt edges	2	0
Rich Velvet, rims and corners	4	0

Crown of Jesus Music. Approved by Ecclesiastical Authority. In Four Parts. Price of each Part, 2s. 6d. in paper wrapper; in stiff cover, 3s.; half-bound, 4s.—Parts I., II., and III., half-bound, red edges, price 10s.—The Four Parts complete, half-bound, red edges, price 13s.

PART I. contains English Hymns, Children's Mass, Hymns for Missions and Retreats, &c, Nos. 1 to 94.

PART II. contains English Hymns, Litany and Hymns to the Saints and B. V. Mary; Hymns to the B. Sacrament, and for Christmas, &c., Nos. 95 to 182.

PART III. contains Vesper Chants, Complin and Benediction Music, Latin Hymns, 20 Benediction Services, Litanies B. V. Mary for Processions, &c. Nos. 183 to 277.

PART IV. contains Gregorian and English Masses, Requiem Mass, &c.

Crown Hymn Book, containing 240 English and Latin Hymns, forming the most complete collection of Hymns for Churches, Private Chapels, Colleges, Convents, Schools, Confraternities, and for all the Festivals, Seasons, and Novenas of the Year. Price 3d. Cloth, 6d.

Crown Hymn Book Music. Containing simple and beautiful Music for all the Hymns in the Crown Hymn Book; also Gregorian Tones and one Benediction Service. Adapted for either the Organ, Harmonium, or Pianoforte, and embraces 310 Airs. Price 6s.

Rosary Book. New and Revised Edition. Most useful to the Clergy and Laity; containing every information as to the Rosary, and Our Lady's "Guard of Honour," i.e. the "Perpetual Rosary." 1d.

BEADS—Dominican Beads for use of Rosary Confraternities, and Perpetual Rosary.—Ditto, with the 15 Decades.—Tertiary Office Beads.

"Penny Prayer Book" for Singing of Mass for Children, Benediction, Rosary, Missions, and Sunday Schools. Selected from the "Crown of Jesus" as a Companion for Missions.

Living Rosary Circles, with Engraving of each Mystery and Patron Saint, printed on 12 sheets, for each month of the year, price 4s. per 100.

Medals of Rosary and Angelic Warfare, large size, 1s. 6d. per dozen—small, 4d. per dozen.

MEDIÆVAL LIBRARY OF MYSTICAL AND ASCETICAL WORKS.

Post 8vo, superfine cloth, lettered.

VOLUMES ALREADY PUBLISHED.

Revelations of Divine Love, shewn to a Devout Anchoress, by name, MOTHER JULIAN OF NORWICH. With Preface by Henry Collins. Price 4s.

Select Revelations of S. Mechtild, Virgin, taken from the Five Books of her Spiritual Grace, and translated from the Latin by a Secular Priest. Price 8s. 6d.

Meditations on the Life and Passion of our Lord Jesus Christ. By Dr. John Tauler, Dominican Friar. Translated from the Latin by a Secular Priest. Price 6s.

The Fiery Soliloquy with God, of the Rev. Master Gerlac Petersen, throwing light upon the solid ways of the whole Spiritual Life. Translated from the Latin by a Secular Priest. Price 3s.

Book of the Visions and Instructions of B. Angela of Foligno, as taken down from her own lips, by Brother Arnold of the Friars Minor. Now first translated into English, by a Secular Priest of the Third Order of S. Dominic. Price 4s.

Life and Select Writings of the Venerable Servant of God Louis Marie Grignon de Montfort, Missionary Apostolic, Dominican Tertiary, and Founder of the Missionaries of the Holy Ghost, and of the Daughters of Wisdom. From the French. By a Secular Priest of the Third Order of St. Dominic. Post 8vo, pr

RICHARDSON AND SON'S PUBLICATIONS.

PAROCHIAL REGISTER BOOKS.

Liber Baptizatorum (five forms on a page.)

Liber Confirmatorum (a page contains spaces for thirty-four names.)

Liber Matrimoniorum (four forms on a page.)

Liber Defunctorum (five forms on a page.)

☞ Very strongly half-bound in red Basil, cloth sides and joints, red edges, lettered in gold, various thicknesses, to suit all Missions.

PRICES PER SET OF FOUR BOOKS.

No. ½. (18 pages in each book) ... £1 0 0
1. (72 pages in each book) ... 1 8 0
2. (168 pages in each book) ... 2 0 0
3. (264 pages in each book) ... 2 12 0
4. (360 pages in each book) ... 3 4 0
5. (456 pages in each book) ... 4 0 0
6. (552 pages in each book) ... 4 8 0
7. (648 pages in each book) ... 5 0 0
8. (744 pages in each book) ... 5 12 0

District and Street Register Books for PRIESTS. Bound in leather, price 2s.

Sacramental Register, for Children and Young People, and for Confraternities. Ruled, with headings for every month.
No. 1, for 100 names, wrapper 6d., cloth 8d.
No. 2, for 180 names, wrapper 6d., cloth 8d.
No. 3, for 200 names, wrapper 8d., cloth 10d.

Mission Cash Book, for Large and Small Missions. Arranged under various Headings, in a concise and convenient form. No. 1, estimated to last for Two Years, 2s. 6d.—No. 2, for four Years, 4s. 6d.

Rite of Administration of Holy Orders. In English and Latin. From the Roman Pontifical. Crown 8vo, printed red and black, price 1s. 0d.

Discourses on the Holy Sacrifice of the Mass, and on the Divine Office, with a Preparation and Thanksgiving before and after Mass for every Day in the Week. By St. Alphonsus Liguori. New edition, with Appendix, containing Indulgenced Prayers.—Cloth, 2s.

Praxis Synodi Dioecesanæ Celebrandæ. Ex opere D. B. Gavanti redacta. Editio Altera. Permissu Superiorum. Cloth lettered, red edges, price 8s.

Altar Cards, printed red and black, in large clear type. Size of centre card, 17½ inches, by 12½ inches, exclusive of margin. Price on cardboard 4s.—on paper 2s. 6d.
Complaints have often been made by priests about the smallness of the type, and the consequent difficulty of reading the Altar Cards in common use. This New Set of Large Type Altar Cards has been expressly designed by a priest, and will be found superior to anything hitherto published.

Ritus Servandus in Expositione et Benedictione Sanctissimi Sacramenti. Adjectis Hymnis, Litaniis, et Orationibus, quæ in ipsa Expositione et in aliis Sacris Ritibus adhiberi solent. New edition, carefully revised, and approved by the Bishop of Nottingham. Price in wrapper, 2s. 6d. Roan, gilt edges, 7s. Intermediate morocco, 10s. Super morocco, 15s.

Ordo Administrandi Sacramenta, et alia quædam Officia Ecclesiastica Rite Peragendi in Missione Anglicana: ex Rituali Romano, Jussu Pauli Quinti Edito Extractus; nonnullis adjectis ex Antiquo Rituali Anglicano. Approved by His Eminence the Cardinal Archbishop, and the Bishops of England. Foolscap 8vo, printed wrapper, price 2s. 6d.
ALSO a Large fine Edition, post 8vo, printed wrapper, price 3s. 6d.
ALSO an Edition in 4to, for use at the Altar, in intermediate morocco, gilt edges, price 16s.
All the above may be had in various bindings.

Manuale Officiorum Quorundam ex ordine Administrandi Sacramenta Excerptorum. New Edition. Wrapper 1s. 3d.—Embossed Roan, red or gilt edges, price 1s. 6d.

Ordo Baptismi Plurium Parvulorum. Post 8vo, price 6d.

The Following of Christ, translated out of Latin into English, A.D. 1556, by Father Richard Whytford, Brigittine of Syon House, edited, with Historical Introduction, by Dom Wilfred Raynal, O.S.B., Canon Penitentiary of Newport and Menevia. Post 8vo, superfine cloth, price 5s.

The Ordinal of King Edward VI. its History, Theology and Liturgy. By Dom Wilfrid Raynal, O.S.B., Canon Penitentiary of Newport and Menevia. Post 8vo, super fine cloth, price 4s.

Lectures on Catholic Faith and Practice. By the Right Rev. J. N. Sweeney, O.S.B. Complete in three vols., price 9s.

Manual of Devotion to the Sacred Heart of Jesus. By the Rev. Father Gautrelet, S.J. Translated from the French. A NEW EDITION, considerably enlarged, containing all the approved popular Devotions to the Sacred Heart. Cheap Edition, price 2s.—Superfine cloth, lettered, price 3s.

Month of the Sacred Heart of Jesus. Translated from the French by the Rev. George Tickell, S.J. Post 12mo, superfine cloth, lettered, price 2s.

Dr. Dollinger's Appeal to the Fathers. A Commentary, by writers of the First Five Centuries, on the Place of St. Peter in the New Testament, and that of St. Peter's Successors in the Church. By the Very Rev. J. Waterworth, D.D., Provost of Nottingham. Demy 8vo, price 7s. 6d.

The Inquirer's Instructor at the Catholic Church. Price 4d.

Stranger's Guide at Vespers and Benediction of the B. Sacrament. Uniform with the "Stranger's Guide at High Mass." In paper wrapper, price 2d.—in cloth, 4d.

Stranger's Guide at High Mass. Frontispiece by A. W. Pugin. Royal 32mo, printed wrapper, price 2d.—bound in cloth, 4d.

Practice of Christian and Religious Perfection, by Father Alphonsus Rodrigues, S.J. Three vols. 8vo, cloth, price 12s. the three vols.

The Difficulties and Dangers of the Conscientious Protestant. By Henry John Pye, Esq. Price 4d.

Revelations of S. Bridget, Princess of Sweden. With a Preface by the Cardinal Archbishop of Westminster. Foolscap 8vo, price 3s. 6d.

Glories and Privileges of S. Joseph. Abridged from the French of Father Ambroise Potton, O.P. Royal 32mo, cloth, red edges, price 1s.

Life of St. Juliana of Cornillon. By George Ambrose Bradbury, O.C., Mount St. Bernard's Abbey, Leicestershire. Post 8vo, price 4s.

Christian Trumpet; or, Previsions and Predictions about impending General Calamities, the Universal Triumph of the Church, the Coming of Antichrist, the Last Judgment, and the End of the World. Compiled from the Writings of the Saints and Eminent Servants of God, and other approved ancient and modern sources, by a Missionary Priest. With Superior's Permission. Post 8vo, price 5s.

Meditations on the Life of the B. VIRGIN, for every day in the Month, suitable for all Seasons, and especially for the MONTH OF MAY. Preceded by a Letter from Mgr. Dupanloup, Bishop of Orleans, translated from the French. With a Preface by the Cardinal Archbishop of Westminster. Superfine cloth, post 8vo, price 6s.

Meditations on the Way of the Cross. By L'Abbe H. Perreyve. Edited in English by a Priest of the Diocese of Birmingham. Cloth, foolscap 8vo, 2s.

Imitation of Christ. Translated by Bishop Challoner. To which are added, Practical Reflections and a Prayer at the end of each chapter, from the French of the Rev. F. Gonnelieu, S.J. Improved edition, with Life of the Author. Royal 32mo, cloth, red edges, price 1s. Also in various bindings, at 1s. 6d.; 2s. 6d.; 3s.; 4s.

The Catholic Church in England and the Anglicans. An Historical Sketch. Foolscap 8vo, cloth, price 2s.

Devotions to St. Joseph, Spouse to the B. V. Mary, Mother of Jesus. With a choice engraving. Reprinted from the English Edition of 1790. Edited by the Rev. George Tickell, S.J. Price 2s.

God's Safe Way of Obedience. A Treatise on the Blind Obedience of a Humble Penitent By the Rev. Silvester Jenks, D.D., Missionary in England in the 17th Century. Revised and Edited by a Priest, with an account of the Author. 2s.

Butler's Lives of the Saints. 12 volumes, royal 32mo, with frontispiece to each volume. ...... cloth, blocked black, gold lettering, ... edges, suitable for presentation, pric...... er set of 12 volumes. The same, plai...... 12s. per set of 12 vols.

Life and M...... of St. Wenefride, Vir...... tyr, and Abbess, Patroness of ...... with an historical description o...... anefride's Well, at Holywell, Fl...... To which is added, the Litanies o...... Saint. Price 6d.

Heart to ?...... ith Jesus, or Pious Affecti...... ing Soul, in tender intimacy wi...... y Hubert Lebun. Superfine clo...... price 1s. 6d.

RICHARDSON AND SON'S PUBLICATIONS.

NEW WORKS FOR CATHOLIC SCHOOLS.

Bible History, containing the most Remarkable Events of the Old and New Testaments. Cheap edition—without illustrations—containing the full course of Sacred History for the Higher Standards in Catholic Schools. Price 1s. bound in cloth.

Old Testament History: being Part I. of the above. Price 4d. in paper cover; in cloth, 6d.

New Testament History; being Part II. of the above. Price 4d. in paper cover; in cloth 6d.

Bible History, beautifully Illustrated, containing the most remarkable events of the Old and New Testaments. With 140 Woodcuts and Map of the Holy Land. By Right Rev. R. Gilmour, Bishop of Cleveland. Over 30 Archbishops and Bishops of the United States have approved of and recommended this book to Catholic Schools. 2s.

Easy Lessons on the Sacraments AND ON GRACE. For Children who are preparing for the Sacraments. Price 2d. in printed cover.

Catholic Religious Instruction for Standards 1, 2, and 3, in accordance with the REVISED CATECHISM of 1883. Containing all that Children are required to learn for the Examinations in Religious Knowledge in Catholic Schools.
  Standard 1, ... price 1d.
  Standard 2, ... price 2d.
  Standard 3, ... price 2d.

Concise Notes on the Acts of the Apostles, to assist Pupil-Teachers and Students in preparing for the Bishops' Examinations. By C. H. Poole, Principal of St. Joseph's School, Pailton, Rugby. Paper wrapper, price 3d.—cloth cover, 4d.

Catholic Penny Prayer Book, designed for the Use of Schools. New Edition, Revised and Enlarged. ...ed by the Bishop of Nottingham. ...d, in paper cover; in cloth, 2d.

S. Mary's Catholic ...a Book, containing 55 Popular F... d Benedic- tion of the B. Sacrament ; cloth, 2d.
The Penny Prayer Boc ...rnn Book together, paper cove; ...t, 3d.

Sacred History, c/ ...the lead- ing facts of the Ol... .w Testa- ment. Edited by t... Rev. Dr. Goss, Bishop of L... ntispiece, superfine cloth, lett... d.

Catholic Pupil Teachers' Examinations.—QUESTIONS IN CHRISTIAN DOCTRINE AND SACRED HISTORY, given at the Religious Examinations held during the Four Years ending March, 1881. Also QUESTIONS GIVEN AT THE EXAMINATIONS OF STUDENTS IN THE TRAINING COLLEGES. By a Diocesan Inspector. Foolscap 8vo. 6d.

Life of our Lord. Reprinted from "Catholic Religious Instruction" of Standard 3. Paper cover, 1d. ; cloth, 2d.
The same, with Catechism of Christian Doctrine, in paper cover, 2d. ; in cloth, 3d.

Illustrated Manual of Bible History, with Parables of our Lord. Embellished with 81 woodcuts. Compiled by a Priest. In stiff paper cover, price 2d.

Select Hymns for Catholic Schools. Approved by the Bishop of Salford. New Edition, *greatly enlarged*, price 1d.

Catechism of Christian Doctrine, (No. 2.) Approved by the Cardinal Archbishop and Bishops of England and Wales, and directed to be used in all their Dioceses. Price One Penny.
THE SAME, in cloth cover, price 2d.

School Attendance Tickets. By a Diocesan Inspector. No. 1, Religious Instruction. No. 2, Mass. No. 3, Catechism—Present. No. 4, Catechism—Merit. No. 5, Attendance. Printed on cardboard. In Threepenny Packets, each Packet containing one gross of Tickets.

RICHARDSON AND SON'S PUBLICATIONS.

Price 6d. cloth red edges.

GARDEN OF THE SOUL,

With Popular Hymns, approved Devotions, the Asperges, &c. Printed from good bold type. **THE BEST AND CHEAPEST EDITION HITHERTO PUBLISHED.**

THE SAME Book, with Epistles and Gospels and Ordinary of the Mass:

	s.	d.
Cloth, red edges, cut flush	0	8
Cloth, squares	0	6
Cloth, rims and clasp	1	0

PAROCHIAL

GARDEN OF THE SOUL.

New Large Type 18mo edition.

PRICE ONE SHILLING.

SAME Book, with Epistles and Gospels, 1s. 6d.

The cheapest and most complete edition of the Garden of the Soul, and the one best adapted for general use.

All Messrs. Richardson and Son's Editions of the GARDEN OF THE SOUL *are still in print, and may be had as usual.*

FORTHCOMING WORKS.

WHISPERS OF OUR LADY, DURING A NINE DAYS RETREAT. *Ready shortly.*

The Words of the INTROITS, GRADUALS, OFFERTORIES and COMMUNIONS, from the "Epitome ex Graduali Romano." *Nearly ready.*

HISTORY OF ST. MONICA. By the Abbé Bougaud, Vicar-General of Orleans. Translated by Mrs. E. A. Hazeland.

PRACTICAL GUIDE TO SPIRITUAL PRAYER. By John Gerson, Chancellor of Paris. Literally translated by the Rev. H. Austin.

LIBRARY EDITION OF DERBY REPRINTS. Crown Octavo. The First Volume will be ready shortly.

ALTAR BREADS

Made by Sisters of Mercy.

ROSARY BEADS.

Rosary Beads with strong chain, at 1s., 2s., 3s., 4s., per dozen.

Ditto, better quality, at 5s., 7s., 8s., up to 25s. per dozen.

Beads of the Five Wounds, at 2s., 3s. 6d., 4s. per dozen.

Ditto, St. Thomas Aquinas, 4s. per dozen.

INCENSE,

As used and recommended by His Eminence the late CARDINAL WISEMAN.

Prepared from the Purest Frankincense and Aromatic Gums. In 1 lb. and 2 lb. cans.

	s.	d.	
Extra Superior Siam Incense	7	6	per lb.
Superior Siam Incense	5	0	,,
Best Incense No. 2	3	6	,,
Fine Incense No. 3	2	6	,,
Do. No. 4	2	0	,,
Do. No. 5	1	6	,,

Complete Catalogue of Catholic Publications, also List of Prayer Books in various Bindings, may be had on application to

Messrs. Richardson and Son,

PUBLISHERS,

23, King Edward Street, City, LONDON, E.C.;

and DERBY.

SPECIAL NOTICE.

NEW WORK IN THE PRESS.

MESSRS. RICHARDSON AND SON

Have had placed in their hands for Publication,

THE NEW

MANUAL OF PRAYERS
FOR PUBLIC USE.

VERSION AUTHORISED AND PRESCRIBED

BY THE

Cardinal Archbishop and Bishops of England.

This book of devotion will be issued in various sizes, printed from good bold type.

NOTICE.—All MESSRS. RICHARDSON & SON'S editions of the Garden of the Soul, and THEIR other Catholic Prayer Books, will be altered in strict conformity with the NEW MANUAL of PRAYERS for PUBLIC USE, authorised and prescribed by the Cardinal Archbishop and Bishops of England.

THOMAS RICHARDSON AND SON,

Publishers, Wholesale and Export Booksellers,

23, King Edward Street, City, London, E.C.;

AND DERBY.

NOW READY, REVISED EDITION OF 1883.

N.B.—This Revised Edition may be at once known by the two questions on Character, given in Chapter vi., page 49.

A CATECHISM
OF
Christian Doctrine.
No. II.

Approved by the Cardinal Archbishop and Bishops of England and Wales, and directed to be used in all their Dioceses.

Crown 16mo, 80 pages, Large Clear Type, and strong stiff cover, <u>superior to any other Edition</u>. Price One Penny. Special quotations given for 5000 and upwards, and 10,000 and upwards. Orders should be sent at once to MESSRS. RICHARDSON AND SON.

The same book, in cloth cover, price 2d.

Fifth Edition, Enlarged, price 1d. in paper wrapper.

THE CHILDREN'S MASS.

With the Approbation of the late RIGHT REV. J. CHADWICK, D.D., Bishop of Hexham and Newcastle.

CATHOLIC ALMANACKS FOR 1884.

PRICE ONE PENNY.

Catholic Almanack, and Guide to the Service of the Church.
Catholic Almanack, and Guide to the Services in Churches served by **FATHERS OF THE SOCIETY OF JESUS.**
Either of the above Almanacks, with Illustrations, and interleaved with writing paper, Sixpence each.—In Pocket Book form, with tuck, One Shilling.

1884. An Almanack for Time and Eternity. Price 9d.

THOMAS RICHARDSON & SON,
23, King Edward Street, City, London, and Derby.

THE DUBLIN REVIEW.

THIRD SERIES.

VOL. XI.

JANUARY—APRIL.
MDCCCLXXXIV.

LONDON: BURNS & OATES.
DUBLIN: M. H. GILL & SON.
BALTIMORE: JOHN B. PIET.

1884.

Ballantyne Press
BALLANTYNE, HANSON AND CO., EDINBURGH
CHANDOS STREET, LONDON

CONTENTS.

	PAGE
ART. I.—SECULAR EDUCATION	1

Growth of Governmental measures for elementary education and disregard of Catholic claims—Right of school inspection extended to control of subjects taught—Not safe to trust any Government with education—Claim of State to right of educating, equal to slavery; evil results consequent on its exercise—Arguments for State interference; and replies.

ART. II.—WYCLIFFE AND HIS TEACHING CONCERNING THE PRIMACY 23

Common hatred of heretics for authority—Duty of Christians towards sins of those in authority—Was Wycliffe a Protestant?—Certain Papal claims and dispositions of Church property had long been unpopular in England in Wycliffe's time—Wycliffe turns this circumstance to account; his false theory of dominion—An examination of some of his writings which enforced his views that the spiritual power had no direct claim on temporalities—He attacks the Pope's Bulls—Election of an Anti-Pope favourable to Wycliffe's errors—He still acknowledges the Pope's authority—His doctrines condemned; he withdraws from Oxford; writes the "Trialogus"—He never held the Bible to be the Rule of Faith—Reconciliation of his contradictory statements regarding the Primacy—His last writings—Distinction laid down by Luther between Wycliffe and the Reformers.

ART. III.—LIBERTY, LAISSER-FAIRE, AND LEGISLATION . . 62

Liberty no longer the watchword of Democrats—Doctrine of "liberty" and "laisser-faire" dormant, not dead; signs of awakening—Instances quoted of Governmental interference with liberty; this inconsistently denounced in the abstract and called for in concrete cases—Uses and various meanings of word "liberty"—No special meaning solves political and economic difficulties—The demand for "freedom of contract" used for a purpose—Principles on which society is based not explained by any natural law of liberty.

ART. IV.—ALEXANDER FARNESE 81

Loyalty of Farnese to Philip II.—Contrast between him and Don John; their close friendship—Farnese, after death of his wife, joins Don John in Netherlands—Death of Don John; Farnese succeeds him; his successes—He strongly objects to Philip's ban against Orange—Farnese's loyalty and Philip's persistent suspicions—His attitude towards the Armada—His devotion unto death.

ART. V.—THE COPTS 93

Recent expressions of interest in the Copts—Sketch of Egyptian Church history to Council of Chalcedon—Chalcedon to the Mahommedan conquest: a time of strife—Mahommedan persecutions of the Native Christians—The Copt of to-day; his social status and intelligence—Rome respects the Coptic rite—The Coptic Mass—Their belief in the Real Presence; in seven Sacraments—Peculiarities in regard to Extreme Unction—Their Lents and Fasts—Celibacy of their Monks and Bishops—Franciscan and Jesuit educational efforts—Their Monks and Monasteries.

ART. VI.—MADAGASCAR, PAST AND PRESENT. . . . 117

Geographical details—The flora and fauna of the island—The discovery of Madagascar in 1506—French occupation—The island becomes the abode of pirates—The native races—English colonies—Captain Le Sage's embassy to King Radama I.—English missionaries permitted to establish themselves—Queen Ranavàlona: her ferocious disposition—Her love of her son—Europeans expelled by the Queen and Christians persecuted—Accession of King Radama II.; his letter to the Pope—His mistakes and murder—M. Lambert and French claims—Queen Rasohèrina baptized and encourages Christianity—Constitutional balance nicely adjusted—Food, drink, dwellings of the Malagasy—Their language and customs—Their many superstitions—Toleration of Catholicity : its progress—Present political crisis.

ART. VII.—THE CITY OF OUR MARTYRS 149

The geographical and physical situation of the town of Douai—Its connection with England and our English martyrs the reason of this sketch—The early history of Douai—Its saints—St. Adalbald—St. Rictrude—St. Maurand—St. Amé—Douai under the Counts of Flanders—Its ecclesiastical and material growth—Its trade and commerce—Its connection with England in the Middle Ages—Its social position in the 14th century—Its decay under the Dukes of Burgundy (A.D. 1384–1529)—The Spanish rule (A.D. 1529–1667)—The University of Douai—The town's scholastic life—The French possession—The town's military character developed—Bird's-eye view of Douai previous to the French Revolution.

ART. VIII.—NEW TESTAMENT VATICANISM 196

The new Vaticanism English : meaning of the term—Large acceptance of this extravagant opinion—In differences between manuscripts, who is to decide ?—History of the Vatican manuscript : its recent publication—The Sinait   ex—The writer of the one, one of the four scrib   the other: among those which Eusebius prep   or Constantine—The value of Eusebius's auth   Arian opinions prevalent—Difficulties raised by   Testament Revisers.

SCIENCE N   218
   Profe   rici on Mathematical Teaching—The Im-
   pe   of Euclid—Electrical Progress—Prehistoric

Footprints—The Persistency of Animalcules—Science and Religion.

NOTICES OF CATHOLIC CONTINENTAL PERIODICALS . . . 222

Katholik — Historisch-politische Blätter—Jahrbuch der Görres-Gesellschaft—Stimmen aus Maria Laach—La Civiltà Cattolica — Œuvre des Ecoles d'Orient—La Controverse.

NOTICES OF BOOKS 218

Cardinal Manning's Eternal Priesthood—Dr. A. Bellesheim's Church History of Scotland—Canon Doyle's Principles of Religious Life—Abbé Le Camus's Vie de Jesus-Christ—Brownhill's Principles of English Canon Law—Palmer's Narrative of Publication of Tracts for the Times—Dr. C. Germanus's Reformers and Luther—Cochin's Espérances Chretiennes—La Marquise de Forbin d'Oppède's Delphine de Sabran—Father Mackey's Four Essays on St. Francis de Sales—The Parochial Hymn Book—Rev. E. MacCartan's Reminiscences of Rome—Tickel's Privilegium Otto I.—Devas's Groundwork of Economics—Stock's Attempts at Truth—Schopenhauer's World, or Will an Idea—Barry O'Brien's Fifty Years of Concession to Ireland—Forster's Law of Compensation under Agricultural Holdings Act—Merry England.

LIST OF BOOKS RECEIVED 244

THE
DUBLIN REVIEW.

JANUARY, 1884.

ART I.—SECULAR EDUCATION.

The Elementary Education Acts, 1870—1880, with Notes, Cases, Index, and Appendix. Containing the Incorporated Statutes and Official Documents relating to the Acts. By W. CUNNINGHAM GLEN, Barrister-at-Law. Sixth Edition, by R. CUNNINGHAM GLEN, B.A., LL.B., Barrister-at-Law. London: 1881.

ELEMENTARY Education has made progress; it has called forth the erudition of men learned in the law, has exercised the minds of the judges, and has certainly disturbed the conscience and lightened the purses of many. The London School Board spends about a million, considerably more, in the year, and the public is eminently gratified. Nevertheless education does not seem to be much desired, for that Board spends, within fifty pounds, £27,000 a-year in bringing children to school, and nearly half a million upon teachers. Other boards are equally munificent in spending other men's money, and if this goes on as it has done during the last ten years we shall spend as much on education as we do on the army, which keeps the peace.

When the Government, now fifty years ago, undertook to meddle with the education of children, it made no claim to the powers it has since assumed, and it did not suggest that the expense would be so great. In the year 1833 it came forward, in the erson of Lord Althorp, as a modest subscriber for building schoolrooms, the annual subscription was in proportion to the dignity of the subscriber, which was £20,000 a-year, given away on the recommendation of two voluntary societies which had been formed for the education of the poor.

The first of these societies was the National Society, the members of which were of the established religion, professing to bring up children in the principles of that religion. The other was the British and Foreign School Society, professing another, and an opposing principle. This Society had a religion without definite doctrines, but it had a respect for the Protestant tradition, and had the Bible read in its schools. But the Bible must be read only, nothing more; it was the Bible "without note or comment." This was regarded as a safeguard against the Established Church, and also against Popery. The members of that Society, whether rightly or wrongly, were considered to be extreme Protestants, as they certainly were, and also with suspicion generally, for many of them were very keen politicians, unfriendly to the established religion.

The Government, notwithstanding its adoption of the principle of indifferentism, professed to be very zealous for the religious education of the people, and would help to build no school which should not be religiously maintained. It distinguished between a secular school and an unsectarian school; the first was not tolerated, but the second was encouraged, and the great principle was the communication of religious truth from "the authorized version of the Holy Scriptures without any sectarian interpretation," the non-sectarian interpretation, being of necessity, nothing but heresy.

The interference of the Government was not regarded by all men as a lawful exercise of its powers, and Lord Althorp, to conciliate opponents, professed that this act was an experiment, and that the contribution of the Government was not to be perpetual. But the promises of politicians are not to be depended on always. It was also promised in 1870 that the school rate would not go beyond threepence in the pound, and they who made that promise seem to have forgotten it. It is now a matter for laughter.

In 1839 the Government went a step further; it proposed to establish and endow out of the taxes a normal school for the education of teachers, thereby implying that the promise made in 1833 was no longer binding on those who made it; the temporary experiment was to be perpetual. The teachers were to "be practised in the most approved methods of religious and moral training and instruction," and were to have the further advantage of being employed in a model school into which children were to be admitted "of all ages from three to fourteen."

In this year, 1839, the Treasury was relieved of the duty of apportioning the grant of £20,000, and a committee of the Privy Council was created to "superintend the application of any sums of money voted by Parliament for the purpose of promoting public education." This committee was created on the 10th of April, and the minute of the committee for the creation of the normal school was dated April 13; but it is perfectly plain that the minute had been considered and settled long before the day assigned for its birth.

People who had retained the religious impressions of their childhood were very much alarmed at the conduct of the Government, and were most hostile to the attempt made by the State to obtain possession of the schoolmaster's rod. Lord John Russell was regarded generally as the active and most earnest promoter of public education; he was suspected of being under the dominion of singular prejudices and of most unsound notions of the Christian religion, nor was that suspicion dissipated four-and-thirty years afterwards when he published his "Essays on the Rise and Progress of the Christian Religion in the West of Europe."

So strong was the opposition to the scheme of the Government, that the Parliamentary grant of 1839—raised to only £30,000—was carried in the House of Commons by a majority only of two, and the Archbishop of Canterbury moved and carried an address to the Queen against it, having with him a majority of 110 in the Upper House.

Good people were alarmed, and not without cause. Sir James Kay-Shuttleworth, the active propagator of the new doctrine, confesses that there were grounds of uneasiness for every religious mind. These are his words:—

On the other hand, there was much in the opinions of a certain class of politicians to justify the suspicions with which the clergy and a large body of the laity regarded proposals for the interference of Government in the education of the people. Among such politicians it was a favourite doctrine to represent the certainty of the exact sciences .... and to contrast these conditions of scientific investigation with the almost endless diversities of opinion on morals and religion. Some went so far as to assert that it was obvious that religion ought to be excluded altogether from the education of the young, and to be examined only by a mature and vigorous intellect. . . . .

Leave, then, said they, the dogmas of churches and sects to be examined by an intellect matured in the study of an exact philosophy, and present, for the first time, the choice of a religion to those whom you have thus taught to discriminate between falsehood and truth.—*Four Periods of Public Education*, 1862, pp. 496, 7.

"There were others," says Sir James, "whose views were more superficial. These men proposed the 'diffusion of useful knowledge,' but were not, however, very few in number, notwithstanding the foolishness of their doctrine and the absence of all reasonableness. They 'appeared to rely upon this diffusion of useful knowledge as a moral panacea by teaching men how prudent it was to be wise, how useful to be virtuous, how politic to be honest, and that the greatest happiness of the greatest number was a condition certain to be attained by proving the convenience of virtue and the suicidal tendencies of vice."—*Ibid.*, p. 497.

The third class of doctors held and taught that education was a function of Government which it must discharge, and inasmuch as religion stood in the way, to these "the establishment of schools on a simply secular basis appeared the only practicable solution of the difficulties with which the question was encumbered."—*Ibid.*

Even these men must be now looked on as having fallen in one point short of political perfection, for they proposed to admit the "ministers of the different communions at periods set apart for that purpose." Here Sir James is himself at fault, for he adds: " Such politicians did not appear to foresee that a religious country could not tolerate a body of schoolmasters without religion." Those schoolmasters have since made their appearance, and the country tolerates them, and is proud of them.

At this time, certainly, the Government had not made up its mind to give up religion to be thrown like a dead dog into the nearest ditch, for these subversive and abominable "opinions were never entertained by the leading statesmen," says Sir James, of either of the two great parties in Parliament. Lord John Russell, in his letter to Lord Lansdowne, in 1839, had declared that it is " Her Majesty's wish that the youth of this Kingdom should be religiously brought up, and that the rights of conscience should be respected."—*Ibid.* p. 499.

Thus it was admitted that the education of the people must be religious; but of the nature of that religiosity very little was said, because among those who used it no two persons, probably, had ever learned the meaning of the word. The religion, or religious instruction, which the Government proposed to give was very scanty, very ill-defined, and certainly heretical in principle, though it may not always have run against defined dogma. "It was intended," says Sir James Kay-Shuttleworth, its earnest promoter and defender, "that the general religious instruction should resemble that given in British and Foreign schools, from the Holy Scriptures, without peculiar interpretation, and that such doctrinal instruction should be given only at times set apart." In the House of Lords the Archbishop of Canterbury asked the Government to explain the meaning of " general instruction in Christianity." He wanted to know what the Committee of the Privy Council meant when it inserted in its minute these words: " Religious instruction to be considered as general and special." The answer given was not clear, but time has revealed the meaning—namely, none.

In 1839 also, the Government relaxed one of the rules laid

down for the distribution of the Annual Grant, and promised to
help schools that had no relations with the National Society or
with the British and Foreign School Society; but the offer was
very vague, and for some years no one took advantage of the
relaxation. The Minute of the Committee of Council on Education, of the 3rd day of June of that year, was as follows:—

> The Committee do not feel themselves precluded from making grants
> in particular cases, which shall appear to them to call for the aid of
> Government, although the application may not come from either of the
> two mentioned societies.

In this year the Government instituted the potent army of
Inspectors, and laid its plans for greater works than the
simple distribution of the Annual Grant; but it made no claim
to interfere with the instruction or education of the people.

In 1846 the Catholics, who had hitherto received neither
money nor recognition from their friends in power, nor from
their supposed enemies, who then were driven into Opposition
again, made an attempt to enlist Sir Robert Peel on their side.
The right hon. baronet was on the eve of his downfall, and could
not find time even to see Mr. Langdale on the matter. Mr.
Langdale then waited till the new Ministry had begun its
task, and applied to Lord John Russell, who got rid of him by
sending his letter to Lord Lansdowne, the President of the
Council. Mr. Langdale's patience was sorely tried, but at last,
on the 18th of December, 1847, the Committee of the Council
resolved to recognize Catholics as claimants for their share of the
Annual Grant, on the condition of inspection "respecting the
secular instruction only," but the inspectors were to be appointed
with the sanction of the Poor School Committee. Then, too, it
was resolved in the Privy Council:—

> That no gratuity, stipend, or augmentation of salary be awarded to
> schoolmasters or assistant-teachers who are in holy orders; but that
> their lordships reserve to themselves the power of making an exception in the case of training-schools and of model-schools connected
> therewith.

This was the first act of interference with the education of the
people; the refusal to acknowledge schoolmasters in holy orders.
Catholics were to be dealt with differently from the sects; the
ministers of the Establishment and Dissent were not touched;

they should fall under the inspection of the Government. The Lords of the Council were ready enough to give us a share of the grants on their terms, but the terms were such as could not be accepted. Thus, on the 21st of April, wrote Mr. Langdale in reply:—

In the alteration proposed by the Lords of Council in the Clause, as prepared by the Poor School Committee, touching matters where religion may be directly or indirectly involved, which substitutes simple "superintendent" for "sole and exclusive charge," a Roman Catholic principle is involved which cannot be conceded without a violation of an imperative dictate of their religion which, it is well known, reserves to their clergy alone the sole and exclusive right of teaching in matters of religion, and to their ecclesiastical authorities of prescribing what may, and may not, involve such matters of religion.—*Minutes of Committee of Council, Correspondence*, 1848–9, p. 99.

The Government was hard, but then it had no desire to see the Catholics admitted to a share in the grant. The money was in the hands of the Government, and could be had only on the terms of that Government. The Catholics might have so many schools as they pleased, and teach whatever they pleased; Government did not meddle with them nor control them in any way, and it was therefore difficult to convince the Lords of the Council that they were unjust. They had never been instructed to give any money to the Catholics, and they would give none but upon conditions.

Again, on the 14th of July in the same year, Mr. Langdale thus sums up the question—he is writing to his own political friends:—

If, then, the Lord President of the Council, or of Parliament, intends admitting Roman Catholics to a participation of the aid which they are prepared to afford to other classes of Her Majesty's subjects, surely it is no measure of justice to say to the Catholic: "We have insisted upon certain terms with others, which they could admit without any violation of conscience; therefore, you must submit to the same, though they may violate your conscience, or remain excluded still, as you have hitherto been, though upon a different ground of conscientious scruple." —*Minutes*, 1850–51, p. 30.

Mr. Langdale, the Chairman of the Poor School Committee, was a very prudent man, not given to rash judgments, or to intemperateness of speech; nevertheless he was constrained to write as he did, and his words are the more important because addressed to his own political friends then in power, the most conspicuous advocates of civil and religious liberty. He charges them with an intolerable act of tyranny; dealing with all the sects upon the principles of the sects, and refusing to deal with Catholics as Catholics. The money which the Government refused was the money of the Queen's subjects, and some of it came out of the purses of the Catholics.

In the same letter, Mr. Langdale told the Government that its proposals could not be admitted by the Catholics, because the admission " would deprive their schools of the first principles of a Roman Catholic school—the being wholly subject in religion and morals to its ecclesiastical superiors."

Now at this time the Government did not pretend to any right to control the education of the people, not even to direct it in any form. All that it did was to subscribe money towards the maintenance of schools. Anybody may do that, and anybody who subscribes may make his terms. The Government made its terms, but they were at variance with the Catholic religion, and accordingly Mr. Langdale denounced them. The Government wished to have some control over our schools, and was ready to pay the price, and in offering to pay the price, admitted that it had no other right but the right obtained by purchase.

Before April 15, 1850, the Government waived some of its more serious demands, and as it appears from a letter of Mr. Langdale, written on that day, the Catholic Poor School Committee waived some of the rights of the Catholics. These are Mr. Langdale's words:—

In admitting the principle of lay management, even in the temporal affairs of their schools, the Poor School Committee wished it to be understood that they do so under protest, and only because it was a principle that had been insisted upon in the cases of all other classes of their fellow-countrymen, and which is not containing anything actually contrary to Catholic doctrine, they yielded, though most unwillingly, under the pressure of the requirements of their lordships. —*Ibid.* p. 35.

This concession, unwillingly made, was not, after all, a very great one, now that we have been accustomed to the yoke. No priest has probably had any trouble in managing his schools, because he is supposed to have a committee to help him; in fact, this committee, which the Government insisted upon, has hardly

Nevertheless, it must be admitted with Mr. Langdale, who
admits it with sorrow, that a breach was made in the fortress;
the Government obtained a positive advantage, bought with
money, and not claimed as a right. The schools were to be open
at all times to the Inspectors sent by the Government; and
Catholic education lay at the mercy of the State. The State
indeed claimed no right to control our education, and it would
gladly have left us alone, but we were poor, and the rest
of the people received money contributed by us; we were
damnified in two ways, refused our share of the public money, and
the share refused to us helped our enemies to destroy us.

In that letter of April 15, Mr. Langdale, as the Chairman of
the Poor School Committee, refused to acknowledge any right in
the State to control education, saying on behalf of himself and
the other members of the committee, that:

> They feel it the more incumbent to repeat these observations, as
> they are aware that a large and influential body of their countrymen,
> with whom they must express their concurrence, entertain similar
> sentiments—that security for the perpetuation of a school for the
> purposes of education and the inspection of the mode of con-
> ducting its secular instruction, should be the limit of Government
> interference.

Certainly at this time the Government claimed no more than
was conceded by Mr. Langdale. It gave money for the building of
schools, and it was a fair claim on its part to make when it asked
for security that the money was spent on the object for which it
was given, and that the building, towards the erection of which it
contributed, was used as a school, and that children were educated
in it.

Though Mr. Langdale conceded the claim of the Government
to inspect "the mode of conducting" the secular instruction, he
admitted no claim of the Government to control the instruction
given, and the Government made none at the time.

Thus the entrance of the Government into the schools was a
purchased entrance; the Government paid for it in money, and
the managers of the schools throughout the country sold that
entrance for money. The Government never said that it had any
right to enter any school whether Catholic or heretic, for it had
none, and it knew it; and to this day the Government has never
ventured to say that it has any right at all in any school except
the right which it has bought and paid for with the money of the
people who are subject to it. Moreover at this t̶ ̶ ̶ the Government, at least in words, insisted upon a religiou   ̶ing up of
the youth, and professed to be utterly intoler   ̶ll schools
that were simply secular. Even Lord John   the great

doctor of toleration, was on this point as intolerant as Sir Robert Inglis. "To omit any inculcation of the duties of religion, to omit instructing the children in the principles of the love of God and love to their neighbour, would be a grave and a serious and an irreparable fault."—Hansard, vol. xii. 1847.* Those are words of that noble Lord.

However sincere the profession thus made the Government could not observe it. The men who were most busy about public education were men whose aim was uniformity in all schools, and religion stood in their way. Nor can it be said that the Government itself cared much about the means it used for "inculcation of the duties of religion." The Lords of the Council held very vague notions of these duties, for according to Sir James Kay-Shuttleworth the intention was "that the general religious instruction should resemble that given in British and foreign schools from Holy Scriptures without peculiar interpretation, and that such doctrinal instruction should be given only at times set apart."—*Four Periods*, p. 501. Thus from the first the scheme of the Government was all that its enemies said of it—a scheme for the destruction of dogma.

Now the Lords of the Council having bought the inspection of "the mode," proceeded to make their bargain profitable. Their next step was to control the subjects taught. This they effected by their Conscience Clause, not, however, without much opposition and earnest remonstrance on the part of those who saw that there was danger in it. As usual with all dangerous schemes it was defended by good men. It was said that the acceptance of the clause would be a defence of education in religion, and would hinder the Government from adopting certain opinions which were becoming common in favour of purely secular instruction to the seclusion of all distinctive teaching of sacred truth. The result falsified the prophecy. The Conscience Clause once accepted, paved the way for those who were bent on banishing all religion from all schools in the three kingdoms. They knew their business too well.

In the year 1870 these men and their friends were in power, their adversaries were blind or worn out, for they did not seem

been praised before as being one of its most perfect safeguards.

The Government not only founded new schools at the public cost which were to be schools without religion, but also forbade all religious teaching during four hours every day in all schools which received any part of the parliamentary grant. In other words, the Government endowed every irreligious or non-religious school out of the rates which people must pay, but gave no such advantage to those schools which professed to give a religious education to the children in them. This was not all. The Government assumed the power to prescribe the time for religious instruction in schools maintained by voluntary contributions, if they obtained any part of the grant. Into the schools it founded in 1870 it allows no religion to enter, and controls the teaching of it in all others. At this moment all instruction in all schools is controlled by the State, and no religion can be taught in any of them except at those times which are allowed by the Government through its Inspectors, and never in what is called the school-hours of a child.

This jurisdiction of the State over the schools has been bought with money. The Government purchased the "mode" of instruction first, and then seized upon the teaching, paying the price. It has never yet asserted a right other than a right bought and paid for. It has made a bargain or a contract, and if any school were to decline the grant the Government cannot enter it. That school may be religious all the day, and the Government will have nothing to say to it, for the State has not yet said that education is a function of civil government, though its conduct implies that it is.

The Government subsidizes all public elementary schools, and every school subsidized is a public elementary school, and open to every one. During four hours of the day the instruction is alike in all, and the former practice is done away with under which the scholars might be taught religiously at all times, and in all their lessons. Now, the religious instruction, if any, must be given separately from the secular, at a time allowed by the Inspector of the Government. For that power over the schools the Government pays. It has not yet claimed it as a right belonging to it otherwise than by purchase.

Before the year 1870 the Government did not forbid, but rather insisted upon, the teaching of all things religiously. In that year it put religion on one side, for it changed the old practice of giving help only to schools that were religious, by giving it to schools the instruction in which was to be purely secular. While doing this it professed (:pect religion, and still professes, for in the instruction to t spectors, January

16, 1878, the Lords of the Council say that they will not have it that "the State is indifferent to the moral character of the schools, or in any way unfriendly to religious teaching."

Here is the wonder: the Government is not unfriendly to religious teaching, and the law it has made and enforces declares that "no religious catechism or religious formulary, which is distinctive of any particular denomination, shall be taught in the school." By this clause all the schools which the Government founded are stripped of all religious disguises; they are brought back to the simplicity of natural religion, for if the Bible be taught in them according to even the Protestant sense, that becomes distinctive against the Catholic and the Jew, as well as against the heathen. Though the sacred writings can hardly be called either catechism or formulary, they are nevertheless "distinctive," and must remain excluded under the operation of the grand invention called the Conscience Clause.

It will be said probably in reply to this, that the Government could not do otherwise than interdict catechisms; perhaps not, but then it may be said that the interdiction shows the incapacity of the Government, and that it is not its business to meddle with education. The education it furnishes is incomplete and delusive; it does not bring up the child as the child ought to be brought up, even according to the confession of Lord John Russell. That which the Government has done is this: it has obtained the power of suppressing all religious teaching, whether true or false. It has compelled the voluntary schools to descend to the level of the Board Schools, and to put the religious teaching in a corner, by prescribing the time during which it may be given, and by so doing, it cannot be doubted, that it really claims the power to prescribe as well.

But many will say that the English Government will never venture to forbid all religious instruction in the schools it subsidizes. That is easily said, and it is generally a waste of time to contradict prophets, but it is surely not unreasonable to observe that fifty years ago nobody imagined that the Government would ever do that which it did in the year 1870, and is doing still with the applause of the whole nation.

The Government has constituted itself the schoolmaster of the country, and they who defend its conduct say it has done nothing amiss, and   it has a natural right to teach the Queen's subjects. Ed   n is one of the functions of Civil Government. That is th   rine now too commonly held.

The pe   o say this are, for the most part, those who scoff and jeer   ternal Governments. It is true those paternal Governr   ere not ordered on the principles of these gentlemen. That probably made those Governments so distasteful to them. But then no Government is ever trusted by these people if it be not what they call a Liberal Government, and it may be safely said that they would trust no Government with the education of the people which is not liberal. In other words, education must be confided to them or left alone. Some sixty years ago it was proposed in this country to educate everybody on one plan; but the plan, though proposed by a liberal, was itself not liberal. The account of it shall be taken from a liberal and dissenting authority.

The Dissenters were alarmed, in 1820, by the Bill which Mr. Brougham brought into the House of Commons, to create a national system of education. To reward the clergy [of the Establishment] for communicating information, he proposed to trust them with the execution of his plan. Schools were to be established all over the country, and the schoolmasters were to be of the Established Church, of which they were to give proof by having taken the Sacrament within six months previously. This proposal of a new Sacramental test filled the Dissenters with astonishment and roused them to oppose the scheme, which, however, was postponed for six months, and finally dropped.—*History of Dissenters from 1808 to 1838*, by JAMES BENNETT, D.D., pp. 54, 55.

There have been Governments in the world which have been what is called patrons of learning, founders of schools and universities, but they have not, all of them, meddled with learning itself; that they left to its learned professors. There have been, also, and there are, Governments which meddle with learning, and these Governments were, and are, enemies of the Faith, in spite of the plausible professions which some of them made. It is not very safe to trust any Government with education.

Louis XIV. entered the episcopal seminaries with the four articles of Bossuet, but it was not in the interest of the Faith. Joseph II. founded ecclesiastical seminaries to supersede those of the bishops, and that was to teach Jansenism. The first of the Buonapartes founded schools in order to keep souls out of the jurisdiction of the Pope, and all the world knows the good intentions of Frère-Orban in Belgium, and of Gambetta and Paul Bert in France. Our own legislation in 1870 was confessedly directed by those whose purpose was to put all religion out of the schools. The Gallican Jurisconsult, M. Troplong,* a vehement defender of the State's claims to control education, could not find his doctrine anywhere but in a decree of Julian the Apostate, who, according to him, was the first to meddle with education, and he

---

* "Du Pouvoir de l'Etat sur l'Enseignement," ch. iv., Paris, 1844.

meddled with it for the express purpose of destroying the Faith.* Perhaps it may be said that no State meddled with education for any other purpose, whatever may have been the ostensible object set forth to silence the doubts of some, and help others to shut their eyes.

Now, the end of Civil Government is, in short, the preservation of life and property. Civil Government, or the State, is not the giver of life, nor is it the giver of property. Men entered into political or civil society in order to obtain security for their lives and their possessions; they are not indebted to the State for one more than for the other. Life and property exist before the State. The property of John Roe was his property prior to, and independent of, the civil law, and if John Roe invaded or claimed it from him, he went before the judge, who said, not that John Roe shall not have it, but that John Roe had no right to it. The judge did not give John Roe his property, but protected him, and maintained him in possession. The State, too, may have property, as any person may have, and then the title of the State comes under the conditions of all other titles.

If, then, our possessions are our own, so are our lives. Men do not give themselves to be killed at pleasure, but to be protected. They do not give up their wills or their understanding to the Government of the State. Their souls are their own for the service of God, who made them; even slaves retain the dominion of their own minds: that was said by Seneca, and St. Thomas quotes him with approbation.† Much more may free men claim to be respected and treated as reasonable creatures, and not as clay in the hands of the potter, to be moulded into any form that may please the imagination of other men in power, because they are in possession of the offices of the State.

Ignorance is a danger to the State, so men say, and the State has a right to protect itself against everything that threatens to weaken or destroy it. Certainly it has, for it is not reasonable to suppose that men enter or live in a political society unable to protect them; and the State cannot protect them if it cannot protect itself. But, after all, this right of the State to protect itself is neither more nor less than the right of a private person to protect himself, for the State among States is as the subject of one State to his fellow-subjects in the same State. The State must protect itself lawfully by lawful means, for the natural law must be respected by all persons, whether governors or governed.

But further, they say the State is liable to be endangered from within, and the safest protection is education—as well as the least costly. Now, admitting that education is the best protection, it does not therefore follow that the State has any right over it. Then, again, it may be doubted that education will do all that is assigned to it. We ought to be told of some one State, at least, that perished through the ignorance of the people. It is not ignorance that imperils States, but rather the so-called education of the day. The men who disturb and ruin States are the men of education and culture—the men of ideas and ambition, who resent with indignation the charge of ignorance. Here is an honest and unexpected confession of this, made by no less an authority than the *Times* newspaper on the 15th day of October, 1883:—

We are not writing [says the great defender of education] in irony when we say that the disturbances of Hayti and her sister State may be ascribed, in a large measure—like those of some of the South American Republics—to the high standard of education among some of the men of the upper classes. These have, in many cases, been sent to Europe for education, and have imbibed liberal ideas there.

That is a very creditable confession, and none the less to be accepted gladly because it is founded on facts. The authors of the French revolution were learned and scientific men—men of the highest culture; so were they who conspired against Charles X., and those who got rid of Louis Philippe. It certainly was not by ignorant men that the Second Empire was done to death. Orsini was a highly scientific man, with one very accomplished friend at least in London. Then there is no want of education among the Nihilists, some of them being highly cultured and accomplished men. In our own country we have not been disturbed by ignorance, even in the famous dark ages; Wycliffe was a great preacher of revolution, and in modern times the Whigs of 1688 were able to read and write, and the Invincibles are scientific chemists.

If the Government has the right to educate the people, then the people are in a condition worse than that of slaves, whose souls are still their own. This claim on the part of the State is

The doctrine would never have been heard of if a faction at war with the Church did not see its way to make use of it. The doctors of this school will never admit that a Catholic Government can have any right of the kind. Justinian and his lawyers did not insert the law of Julian the Apostate in the "Pandects," but admitted, on the contrary, both in the "Pandects" and the "Institutions," that the bringing up of children belonged to the parent of the natural law prior to all civil legislation. Nevertheless, five years afterwards, meddling with ecclesiastical matters, he inserted in his Code the iniquitous law of the Apostate.

If one Government has the right to educate the subjects, all Governments must have it; but no Liberal has ever admitted that a Catholic Government has the right. If the Tories were in power, and strong enough to carry their measure, it may be fairly questioned whether the Whigs would submit their children to the discipline of the Tory schoolmasters. The doctrine of the State's right is really a dishonest doctrine; its professors maintain it, not because they think it true, but because of its convenience and usefulness. The doctrine is scouted; if it cannot be used in one special way—that is, against the Faith, it is not considered true under other conditions.

If the State has a right to educate the poor it has the right to educate the rich, and if it insists on educating the layman, it may insist also on educating the priest. The State may enter the seminaries of the bishops, and determine the nature of the teaching there. They who admit the claims of the State must admit that. The French lawyer, Dupin, has drawn that consequence from the claims of the State. He held that the seminaries are like the other schools, subject to the control of the Government, and he insisted on his doctrine because he saw that it was fatal to the Faith. Even here in England we have not been without experience of the doctrine and of the watchfulness of the Government in checking the spread of true doctrine where it can. The Government has entered our schools, but not the seminaries at present, and its doings in part are thus described by the Cardinal Archbishop of Westminster in his speech at St. James's Hall, on Tuesday, July 11, 1876. He is speaking of the objection by the Government, through the inspectors, to the books for the instruction of Catholic boys and girls in what we or schools. These are his words:—

---

* "M Droit publique ecclésiastique," p. 341, 2 édit. Paris, 1844. "les ordonnances qui précèdent . . . . montrent que les écoles e ies, aussi bien que les autres, sont assujetties à l'action de ce p ımentaire."

These school-books used in our schools, under the Statute of 1870, were carefully revised. They were revised, not under my eye, but with my cognizance, by persons whom I believed to be most competent to revise them in conformity with the law. After they were revised, they were printed; they were put into use shortly afterwards, and a new objection arose that these books still retained religious and Catholic matter. I had them revised again. I had many pages cut out altogether. These books were examined with very great diligence, and, in my belief, these books were not fairly open to challenge, unless there shall have escaped me—which, I must say, is a very possible thing, for I was not able to revise the books in person—here and there an expression.

It is perfectly clear from this history that the Government will not tolerate Catholic teaching, and if Governments have a right to teach, they have a right to do what the Government of England has done, and is doing. What the Government is doing may be learned from the same authority, for His Eminence, in St. James's Hall, on another Tuesday, June 14, 1881, said before a large congregation:—

They [that is, the Government] founded a secular system of education from which religion is absolutely excluded. Moreover, they then proceeded to exclude the teaching of religion in our own voluntary schools, and shut it up in half an hour before or after school-hours. And more than this, they forbade the use of any book, during the four hours of school-time, in which the name of our Divine Master, or God, should be found.

That is the way in which the State exercises its right, if right it has. The spirit of Julian the Apostate is the spirit of the State, and his legislation is revived and made active and strong. If the State has a right to control education, it has a right to do all it has done both in this country and on the Continent, for the State is supreme in its own affairs, and education is an affair of State; that is the doctrine of the day, and seemingly by few disputed.

This difficulty is supposed to be overcome by saying that all this is an abuse of the right. But the answer is not to the purpose, if the right be admitted. If the State has a right to educate, we must accept the education it gives, because there is no appeal to a higher authority recognized by the State. The Catholic will say that the State ought to accept the doctrines of the Church, which in this matter is above the State. Even that is not a good answer, for the State refuses everywhere to accept the doctrines of the Church, and yet it claims the right to educate. And certainly if it has the right, it has it independent of the Church, had it always, and the Church has not taken it away or denounced it, if it be its right. It makes no difference whether the State be Pagan or Christian, the right, if it exists, belongs as much to the Pagan as to the Christian. It certainly does not belong to the Christian State as such, for if that were true, the authority of bishops and priests is denied, and we must accept the condemned doctrine of Marsilius of Padua.

Then again, some say it is very true that the education of the child belongs to the father, but if the father neglects his duty, the State steps in and does it for him. That is simply begging the question, for there can be no right founded on a wrong. The exercise of a right may follow upon the wrong, but the right must exist before the wrong is done. The magistrate sentences a thief, but he had the right to pronounce sentence before the thief took his neighbour's goods. So if the State has a right to educate a neglected child, it must have that right over all children, for wrong-doing gives no jurisdiction. The right of the State then must be sought for in some other quarter than in the father's neglect to educate his child.

The true account of this claim of the State is this: the notion that the subject is the property of the State. People do not like to say so in so many words, but that is the major premiss of their syllogism. There are people who say that all property belongs to the State, and are called Communists; and there are people who think that all persons belong to the State; and they, without a name, are very busy in Board Schools and kindred institutions, striving continually to bring about a uniform system of education, and hinting plainly that the education of all must be controlled and directed by the State. If these people prevail, they will not confine their attentions to lay schools, for they will see, as Prince von Bismarck saw, that the priests were not properly, but imperfectly, educated in the episcopal seminaries; and they will also see, as he did, that the proper place to educate them are the schools and the universities in which the doctrines of the State are taught, and the knowledge of God passed by.

If the Government has a right to educate, it must have some doctrine to teach, some rule of life to enforce, and some habits to form. It would be well if we could learn what the aim of the Government is; what is the character it wishes to impress on the minds of the children whose education it claims as its own work. There ough some security that this education shall not be at the discr successive Ministers of State, for if it be not a uniform e, it cannot be that of the State, but the whims of eac er. There is an instance, and a very serious one, brou he notice of us in the Report of the Diocesan Insper estminster of 1883. Lord Sandon, as the chief instructor of the kingdom, required in his Code that the Inspectors should be satisfied that "reasonable care is taken in the ordinary management of the school to bring up the children in habits of punctuality, of good manners and language, of cleanliness and neatness, and also to impress upon the children the importance of cheerful obedience to duty, of consideration and respect for others, and of honour and truthfulness in word and act." All this is good in itself, and, so far as it reaches, most desirable; but it is not education. Lord Sandon's successor, Mr. Mundella, either despises or objects to this instruction, for the Inspector has to record his sorrow that Mr. Mundella has not inserted it in his Code. Thus, we must be at the mercy of the Ministers of the day, and the education furnished by the State is the education that pleases him, whoever he may be, who, in the contests of faction, can compel his allies to make him Vice-president of the Council. We may have Mr. Bradlaugh before long directing the education of England.

Surely it is not unreasonable to deny this claim of the State, seeing that the State does not know what to teach. The teacher knows nothing and believes nothing. It does not know the end for which men are created, and therefore can teach him nothing to the purpose. It cannot direct him to his end, and therefore ruins him body and soul for ever. That is what the State has always done when it meddled with the souls of men.

There are those who say that Governments may compel the subject to learn how to read and write. If it has the right to do that, it has the right to do more. Reading and writing are weapons of extreme delicacy and sharpness, and if people do not learn the right use of them, they will be in worse case than if they were ignorant. The Government cannot, and will not, tell us how we are to use these weapons. It professes complete ignorance, and leaves us to find out for ourselves how to handle them. It is indifferent; and so far as the Government is concerned, he who has learned to read may read Rousseau and Voltaire; and that alone is fatal to the claim set up on behalf of the civil power.

In the Elementary Education Act of 1876, 39 and 40 Vic., c. 79, Parliament has said that—

> It shall be the duty of the parent of every child to cause such child to receive efficient elementary instruction in reading, writing, and arithmetic; and if such parent fail to perform such duty, he shall be liable to such orders and penalties as are provided by this Act.

Mr. Glen, as a lawyer, is struck by eclaration of Parliament, and observes upon it as follo Previously to the passing of the present Act there was no statutory decla-

ration as to the duty of a parent." If the Act is declaratory of a duty, and not the imposition of an obligation, there must be some previous Act or declaration in existence, or the duty must stand on the law of Nature. The words of the Act, if taken strictly, suggest that Parliament laid this duty on parents in the year 1876, and the Act is therefore nothing but the expression of the right of the State over education. But if the duty is a duty prior to, and independent of, the Act, it must be a duty everywhere and at all times; but undoubtedly a duty most utterly neglected in all ages and among all nations ever since the world began.

It would be just as reasonable to say that it shall be the duty of the parent to cause his child to be an athlete, or a boxer or pugilist, or a good shot. The child is not the property of the State, but, if the expression may be allowed, the property of the father; and the duty of the father towards the child is to bring it up himself for the service of God, who gave the child to him. The State has nothing to do with the child till he comes to man's estate, and the child is not responsible even for wrong acts till it arrives at years of discretion; nevertheless, the father must begin its education even before it has come to the age of reason. The State does not ordinarily undertake duties which are neglected, nor does it punish all transgressions or non-observances of the natural law. If a father refuses to have his child taught how to write, can it be said that this is an affair of State? Governments do not supply all non-observance of duties; if a man refuses to pay his debts, which by the natural law he ought to do if he has the means, the State will not pay them for him, and if the creditor is silent will not force him to pay them.

Here comes the next defence—namely, that children are helpless, and if the father is careless of their welfare the State most charitably comes forth as the legal father, and compels the true father to make the proper intellectual provision for his children. But the State will not interfere with a spendthrift father, who wastes his patrimony, and who will leave his children in poverty. It will not interfere with the lazy father who makes no attempt to provide for them, nor with the father of vicious life who corrupts them. Fathers of this kind are as bad, at least, and as hurtful to the State, as the fathers who do not send their children to school; they ruin their children quite as effectually, and the State has nothing to say to them. Then it is said that education is so great a blessing that some means must be found by which all may obtain it, and there is no other way but compulsion on the part of the civil Government.

If that be so, let us see what the blessing is. First of all, the education is simply secular; if it is not openly ungodly, it is none the less detestable, seeing that it keeps back from the child the very matters which most concerns it to know. The education is of the world worldly, for worldly ends on worldly motives. It ruins souls before children learn that they have souls to be ruined. Politicians who rule States have never been commissioned to teach men how to serve God; if they have they have always betrayed their trust. It cannot be otherwise, for the State has no doctrine, and if it has no doctrine it has no right to teach.

The education of the child, by the law of God, belongs to the parent; and the parent of the child may teach himself his child, or may use the services of another, or may send his child to a school. He is responsible for the domestic teaching, and for the teaching in the school. As the father may send his child to be taught in any school he likes, as any one is free to keep a school, for that is a part of the freedom of the father. If the State, in imitation of Julian the Apostate, allowed no teachers but such as satisfied the demands of the Government, it would thereby wrong the father, and deprive him of a clear right, which does not belong to him by the municipal law, and is therefore beyond the reach of the State. But it is said that the State stands in the place of the father when the father cannot discharge his obligations in the matter of his child's education, and may on that ground educate the child. If the State stands in that relation to the child, it ought to educate the child, as the father is bound to educate it, and not in its own way. If the State be Pagan, it would not be possible for it to educate a Christian child. If it be a heretical State, it would refuse to bring up the child in the faith; and if the State were Catholic, it would be bound to bring up the child in the Church. Thus there is no uniform exercise of this pretended right possible in the present condition of the world.

At this time it is not lawful for any one to give up his child to be educated by the State, for the State does not educate Christians. The father who may trust his child to the care of another to supply the father's incapacity, must, if he be a Christian, keep him out of the reach of the State. Fathers are expressly commanded, not counselled, to bring up their children in the Catholic faith: *Educate illos in disciplina et correptione Domini* (Eph. vi. 4). The civil State, then, that undertakes to educate children without the knowledge of God, is a State that sets up a false religion, and offers the children to Moloch.

Moreover, the right of the Christian State, if we could find one, does not extend to education. It is not a thing created for that purpose, nor are its powers different from those of a Pagan State. It is bound to use its powers according to the Christian law, but the Christian law gives it none. All the power it has, as a State, is the power belonging to all States, Pagan or Turkish. If the State has any right over the mind of man, and especially this right to educate him, the Pagan States would have been within their rights if they had taken the baptized children and brought them up in the heathen schools, and made them worship idols. States that call themselves Christian act upon the same principle when they throw the images of Christ and His saints out of the schools they have founded. If the State has any right at all, it has a right to the whole substance of education in virtue of its sovereignty, and they who admit the right of the State, are unconsciously the disciples of Hobbes, who has laid it down as a certain truth that all teaching belongs to the State, saying,

> It belongeth, therefore, to him that hath the sovereign power, to be judge, or constitute all judges of opinions and doctrines, as a thing necessary to peace; thereby to prevent discord and civil war.—*Leviathan*, pt. ii. ch. 18.

Hobbes was a Liberal in advance of his age, and if he had not been the Liberal he was, it is not quite certain that Sir William Molesworth would have spent so much time and money in reprinting his dismal works.

It is of no use in this matter to say that the State ought to do this or leave that undone, or that the State should only supply deficiencies and minister assistance where it is needed. No State has ever denied itself in the use of power, and there is no State disposed to do so. Governments aim at absolute power; if they set up schools they will control and direct them, they will listen to no remonstrance, and as they are doing that which they ought not to do, and meddling with matters not within their jurisdiction, they are the more likely to go astray. It is waste of words to say that they ought to hear the Church, for that is the last thing they propose to themselves. They are setting themselves up as the enemies of the Church, and do not hesitate to say they are her masters; she must serve them.

It is possible that some one may say that the State may educate, if only it would respect the Church, and that surely the Christian State has a right in the matter. The answer is very short: the ⟨...⟩ s of a Christian State are identical with the rights of a Stat⟨...⟩ ⟨wh⟩ich no one has submitted to be baptized. Civil States st⟨...⟩ ⟨t⟩he law of Nature. A Pagan prince loses no right by his ⟨...⟩ and he gains no right. He was a sovereign prince ⟨...⟩ accepted the faith, and he is a sovereign prince when h⟨...⟩ ⟨m⟩ember of the Church. The jurisdiction of his Govern⟨ment⟩ ⟨re⟩mains the same. As he had no right to educate

his subjects in Paganism because that education was against the
natural law, so by his conversion he acquires no right to educate
them in the faith, because our Lord has not given the faith to him
to teach. The State, therefore, has nothing to do with education.
The doctrine is most clearly expressed by Suarez.* He says that
Christian States are, as States, not different from Pagan States,
having the same end and the same matter for their jurisdiction.
Now it cannot possibly be true that education was a function of
Pagan Governments, for if it was once it must always be, and
thus those who say that the State may interfere with the rights
of a father, presumed to be negligent, must admit that the Pagan
State could control and direct Christian education. More than
this, they must admit, too, that the State could interdict that
education, because the State having decided that the father who
brought up his children Christians neglected his duty, took
possession lawfully upon this principle of the children, and made
them, if it so pleased, burn incense to Jupiter and Juno. The
interference of the State with education once admitted, all
education belongs to the State, because the State insisting on its
supposed rights declines to be guided by any authority beyond
itself. Again, if the State has this right, it has the right to
mould men's minds, to discipline their understanding, and to
direct and control their wills. The claim set up is a claim to
direct the whole man, and to fashion him, as they say, into a
good citizen or subject. That is education, but the education is
for this world only, not at all for the next; it is an education
which is false, because it at best pretermits the truth, and brings
men up on merely natural principles, and without the true
meaning of those principles besides, because it will not and cannot
teach them in the light of the faith. Surely it is not reasonable
to admit this pretended right; the very greatness of it is enough
to discredit it, for it makes men slaves, or rather reduces them to
a state worse than slavery. If the Government insisted upon
depriving every child of its eyes, it would not commit greater
tyranny, and possibly that tyranny might be infinitely less
hurtful, provided the understanding was not corrupted. If the
State is to form the minds of the subject, there is no room left for

---

* "De Legibus," lib. iii., c. xi., n. 9. "Quarto, dico potestatem hanc civilem—etiam prout est in principibus Christianis fidei conjuncta—non extendi in materia vel actibus suis ad finem supernaturalem, seu spiritualem vitæ futuræ, vel præsentis, licet legislatores fideles in suis legibus ferendis, intueri possint, et ex debeant supernaturalem finem et actum ipsum ferendi legem in naturalem finem referre. Utraque pars assertionis manifesta videt ıa quidem, quia potestas hæc, ut nunc est in principibus Christi se non est major, nec alterius naturæ quam fuerit in principibu ; ergo ex se non habet alium finem nec aliam materiam."

the Church. The State will accept of no catechism, no supernatural truth. Even if the State allowed instruction in religion that would not mend the matter, because religious instruction is placed thereby on a level with any other learning, such as astronomy or botany. The civil Government cannot surely have any right of this kind,* seeing that it is a right by which it can destroy the Christian religion by sowing tares in a soil which it has made incapable of receiving good seed to any good purpose. It cannot be repeated too often the child belongs to the parent by the law of God, and by the law of God also the parent is bound to bring up the child in the knowledge of God, and he cannot discharge that grave obligation by giving it up to be educated in the schools of the State, for unto them the knowledge of God enters not.

D. L.

Art. II.—WYCLIFFE AND HIS TEACHING CONCERNING THE PRIMACY.

TAKEN FROM STATE PAPERS.

Rerum Britannicarum Medii Ævi Scriptores.

AT no period of her existence has the Church of Christ been free from the attacks of error, and those who have severed themselves from the centre of Christian unity have generally fallen victims to this foe. Every teacher of error bears the common stamp of hatred of spiritual authority, especially of that wielded by the Pope; and this hatred each teacher seeks to instil into the hearts of the faithful in order to alienate them from the Church and bind them to his own sect. He seldom hesitates to speed the shaft of calumny, whilst occasionally, alas! the conduct

be forgiven in the representatives of sovereign power; whilst if they are met with in the delegates of the higher spiritual authority in the world, then, indeed, is the scandal greater, and men but too inclined to cast aside the yoke of that authority altogether.

Without going further back than the Middle Ages, and without entering into a detailed account of the numerous sects which, under the name of Albigenses, Cathares or the Pure, Waldenses, &c., ravaged Europe during several centuries, we shall only quote the words of Bossuet,* that:—

> The bait they most generally threw out to allure weak souls into their nets was the hatred they instilled for the pastors of the Church. Struck by the disorders they saw reigning in the Church, chiefly in the lives of Her ministers, they did not believe that the promise of everlasting life made to Her could survive in the midst of such abuses. Inflated with pride, and thereby rendered weak, they yielded to the temptation prompting them to hate the office in their hatred of the person holding it.

The true children of the Church, on the contrary, whilst deploring the disorders of their brethren and the scandal resulting therefrom, looked upon rupture with authority as the last and worst of evils. Alain of Lisle† wrote at the beginning of the thirteenth century: "We must obey the Bishops, not only such as are good men, but such also as are bad; for the wicked lives of the bad does not deprive them of their authority: the prerogative of ordination, of binding and loosing, of teaching and commanding was granted to their sacred office and not to their personal merit." Saint Bernard pointed out and regretted this deplorable confusion, natural enough to the vulgar mind between the unassailable rights of authority and the personal merits of its representatives. He says the erroneous doctrine of the heretics of his time was, that popes, archbishops and priests lost the power belonging to their order directly they fell away into sin.‡ Yet he mourned grievously over the disorders and relaxed morals of the clergy, and in a letter to Pope Eugenius III. he wrote: "Would that before I die, I could see the divine Church like to what it was in its early days." Firm in his faith and strong in the promise of Jesus Christ, he never believed that the human element could destroy in the Church or in her pastors the supernatural character of divine authority.

In all ages society as well as individuals have stood in need of reform; the struggle against evil tendencies and sinful disorders

---

* "Histoire des Variations," book i. No. 5.
† Book II., Migne, Patrologia Latina, 210, p. 305.
‡ Serm. 65 in Cantic. Cant.

is one of the conditions of mankind's existence. Providence has not excepted from this law those men whom it has appointed to guide others: should they prove faithless to their private duties they are no less entitled to command, and to receive obedience. Paternal and civil authority are viewed in this light, and spiritual authority established in favour of Christian society should also be independent of personal virtue or vice. History bears witness that the ignoring of these self-evident principles and the skill which party leaders have shown in working up false notions in this matter of authority, have been the cause of those revolutions, civil and religious, that have upheaved society.

Towards the end of the fifteenth century there arose a teacher in England, who, like many other heresiarchs, was a victim to foiled ambition, and who, under the specious guise of reform, sowed broadcast in Church and State the seeds of revolt. Protestants count him among their ancestors; intent on claiming for their Church that apostolicity, so essential to a Christian Church, they assert that the fundamental elements of their doctrine are to be found in the teaching of Wycliffe, and writers are not wanting in these days who, like Thomas James,* look upon him as one of the precursors of the great "Reform" of the sixteenth century. Melanchthon was not of this opinion; for judging Wycliffe by his teaching on Justification, on Church property, on Transubstantiation, and on civil power, he finds him full of error, and far removed from Protestant ideas.† We will not take up the question of dogma, which, to us, appears a secondary one. The essence of Protestantism may be reduced to a single principle: the negation of authority in matters of religion, and principally the negation of the Primacy or supreme spiritual authority. Does Wycliffe's teaching on this subject agree, if not with Luther's views, who had no definite theory on this point,‡ at least with those of subsequent Reformers? This is the question to be elucidated; a question which, considered from the standpoint of Protestant controversy, is not an uninteresting one, and from that of general history borrows importance from one of the greatest events of modern times, since it has to do with the origin of the Reformation.

Wycliffe has left behind him numerous works on Philosophy and Theology, and collections of sermons. Posterity has scarcely deemed them worthy of publication,§ and they lay buried for

---

* "An Apology of John Wycliffe." Oxford, 1608.
† Bossuet, "Variations," book ix. n. 160.
‡ "Variations," book i., n. 26.
§ "Trialogus," his last work, was printed (at Basle?) in 1525, and at Frankfort in 1753. "The Wicket," 1546, at Nuremberg, and, 1612, at Oxford; the short treatises against the Orders of Mendicant Friars,

years in libraries known only to a few scholars, whence we may infer that they contained nothing very wonderful; some only were published in the sixteenth and seventeenth centuries. In 1851, J. H. Todd, D.D., printed at Dublin some short treatises by Wycliffe against the Church,* and to celebrate the fifth centenary of his death (1884) a society has been founded for collecting, annotating, and editing what is styled the Wycliffian Literature. These publications are interesting from a philological point of view, but to historical criticism they present great difficulties; for, following the example of Bale, most of the religious treatises written in the fourteenth and fifteenth centuries have been assigned without discrimination to Wycliffe.† Mr. Matthew has edited the English works of this Reformer.‡ Lastly, Mr. Buddensieg published lately the treatise: "De Christo et Antichristo," from a manuscript in the Vienna Library; and he offered to continue his publication of the Latin works, but the University of Oxford has shown small sympathy with his project, and it seems likely to prove futile. The published portions of Wycliffe's works are sufficient to afford an idea of his system. To analyze them in detail would be long and useless. Any one courageous enough to peruse them would arrive at the same conclusion drawn by Cave, an admirer of Wycliffe,§ that variations and even contradictions are to be found in his teaching: "diversa sæpe ac nonnunquam contraria dogmata." We would only ask them not to seek therein any pretext for praising the innovator. Whatever Cave may say, it is impossible to admit that these variations show that maturity of judgment and calmness of reason with which Wycliffe should have sought out and combated the errors of the Church. Variations imply uncertainty and doubt; truth is unchangeable. When Protestantism can produce a reliable history of "Variations of the Catholic Church" they may have some claim to pride themselves on the pretended progress of ideas and of evolution to be found in Wycliffe's teaching and in that of the numberless sects of the Reformation. If Wycliffe be guilty of change, of teaching at one time one thing, at another the contrary, it is because he did not listen to

---

1608, at Oxford. His translation of the New Testament, 1731, at London. The "Prologue to the Bible," 1536 and 1550, is the work of Purvey, one of his disciples.

* "Three Treatises by John Wycliffe." 1851.

† Todd, "An Apology for Lollard Doctrines." Camden Society. London, 1842, p. 17. Shirley, "Fasciculi Zizr------n." London, 1851, p. xiii.

‡ "The English Works of Wycliffe, hither   rinted." London, 1881.

§ Cave, "Scriptorum Eccles. Historia Litte   Coloniæ Allobrogum, 1720. Appendix, 41.

the voice of Him who said: "I am the Way and the Truth." To us it has seemed more interesting to seek out the origin of his errors, and, without attempting to epitomize all his works, we have traced throughout them the development of his views on the Papacy.

I.

About the year 1370, John Wycliffe was Doctor of Theology and Professor of Holy Scripture at Oxford. He was the author of several treatises on "Universals," on "Materia prima," and other questions of a similar nature, much debated in his day. He was ambitious, and his ambition had been thwarted. According to Thomas of Walden,* a contemporary, the See of Worcester becoming vacant, Wycliffe was disappointed at being judged less worthy than others of enjoying the dignity and revenues of this bishopric; according to other writers, his application for the Wardenship of Canterbury Hall at Oxford had been rejected, and the Pope having ratified the decision of the Bishop, Simon Langham, had aroused the strong hatred Wycliffe afterwards bore to Rome. This foiled ambition was hereafter to become the most fiery adversary of ambition, the enemy of dignities and authority, the apostle of Evangelical poverty.

To understand Wycliffe's teaching in connection with the Catholic thesis of the Roman Primacy, it is necessary to glance at the difficulties which had for some time existed between the See of Rome and England.

As early as the days of the Norman Kings the English people and clergy had turned restive under certain rights claimed by the Pope, and which remotely, or nearly, concerned the royal prerogative. To define clearly the limits of these two powers would be no easy matter, and if dissensions arise when it was believed they would be impossible because of the separating of Church and State, they must have happened when the two were united and yet not fused. St. Anselm and St. Thomas of Canterbury had distinguished themselves in defending the liberties of the Church against William Rufus and the first two Henries. History in the eleventh century offers more than one example of the difficulties which arose concerning temporalities between Bishops and Princes. The latter, after generously endowing churches and monasteries, declared themselves protectors of the same, and eccle[siastical] authority recognizing their claims, granted them cons[iderable] rights. Princes abused them; and the influence they [had] in the nomination of Abbots and Bishops too often

---

* [Doctrin]ale Fidei," lib. ii. cap. 60; lib. iv. cap. 33. He quotes the [epistle of] Robert, Bishop of Salisbury, at the Synod of Canterbury.

opened the sanctuary doors to simonniacal prelates more devoted to the person of their Sovereign than to the interests of their flock. Similar occurrences were the cause of the great quarrel about investitures, in which that glorious Pope, Gregory VII., showed the immovable firmness that has rendered his name for ever famous. His successors were no less energetic in asserting the independence of the Church. In 1103, Pascal II., opposing the cupidity of Henry I., said to his ambassador: "Your King, as you say, would sooner lose his crown than his rights over church benefices; know then that I would sooner lose my life than allow him to dispose of them at his good pleasure."* The revenues of vacant bishoprics were the cause of endless contests between the Crown and the Holy See, and the subsidies raised in the name of the Sovereign Pontiffs, whether to organize a crusade, or for some less popular object, raised a keen opposition amongst the clergy as well as amongst the laity.† The chroniclers of the twelfth and thirteenth centuries, especially Matthew of Paris, give us proofs of this.‡ Now, though we must not lose sight of the exactions and cupidity of the civic power, still it is conceivable that the pecuniary demands of the Popes were considered more grievous burdens, because they were often turned to profit by a clergy who, although devoted to the court of Rome and interests of the Church, were strangers to the temporal interests and nationality of the English people. Referring to a benefice which Pope Innocent IV. claimed of the Abbey of St. Albans in favour of a nephew, the chronicler writes :§ " We have cited these facts that our readers may know to what extent the Court of Rome oppresses and enslaves us, and how the hearts of many are being turned away, and are failing in their love for our Lord the Pope, *though we ought to love him with our whole heart*, as we love a father." Robert Grosseteste,‖ the famous Bishop of Lincoln, who admitted that the Pope and holy Roman Church had the right to dispose freely of all ecclesiastical benefices, and who

---

* Matth. of Paris, "English History" (Madden's edition). London, 1866, i. p. 192.
† Fr. Stevenson, S.J., "The Precursors of the Reformation." *The Month*, 1882, i., p. 46.

opposed the King when the latter wanted to impede the levying of subsidies in favour of an exiled and persecuted Pope, himself complained that the legates of the Holy See, and even Innocent IV., disposed of English Church property without consulting the temporal patrons, giving it, sometimes, to foreigners of little worth. No incident is better known or more frequently quoted in Protestant controversial works than the letter in which this great Bishop protests vigorously against the collation of a canonry to a nephew of Innocent IV. Protestants have extolled this letter, declaring it sufficient in itself to immortalize this Prelate's name; they have even, after somewhat altering the text,* declared that it constituted him a herald of revolt, a precursor of the Reformation,† and this because they pretend not to understand the intrepidity of Christian obedience, of episcopal submission, of how Robert, whilst bowing respectfully to supreme authority, could at the same time uphold with boldness and courage the liberties guaranteed to the English Church by the Popes in the great Charter.‡ In this very letter, so often quoted, so highly praised, he says:—

Your prudence knows that I obey with filial affection, respect, and devotedness every truly apostolic command, but from zeal for the honour of the Holy Father I oppose and resist all that is contrary to this spirit: in both cases I am bound by the law of God. In truth, apostolic commands are not and cannot be but in conformity with the doctrine of the Apostles and of their Lord and Master, Jesus Christ, whose special representative and imitator in the Church-hierarchy our lord the Pope is. For our Lord Jesus Christ Himself said: "He who is not with me is against me;" but there is not and cannot be anything against Him that proceeds from the divine holiness of the Apostolic See.

Proceeding, then, to prove that it is contrary to the duty of a true shepherd to fleece and milk the flocks of the Lord in order to squander their milk and wool on his relations, he ascribes the abuses, the peculations of clergy, bishops, and Roman Pontiffs to the suggestions of Lucifer and Antichrist. But he soon acknowledges fully the pre-eminence of the Apostolic See: "The plenitude of power consists in exercising every power for building up: hæc est plenitudo potestatis, omnia posse ad ædificationem." It cann[ot be de]nied that this letter (a private one, let us note) is full of [force]and vehemence; but it pays a splendid homage to the Pri[macy a]nd affords us an insight into those ages characterized by an [earnest t]hough rugged faith. Christian obedience is not self-annihi[lating o]r slavery; it is not a blind and passive submission;

---

* Matthew of Paris, ed. cit. iii., p. 140.
† I[bid.,] f. xiii. xiv.   ‡ Ibid., pp. 230, 265, 272.

it is, on the contrary, a devoted and filial respect for authority within the limits of divine justice. At the present time, when respect for authority is limited to mere exterior forms, a protest like that of the Bishop of Lincoln would be considered rebellious; but Innocent IV. acknowledged his mistake, and promised to reform the abuses of which the prelate complained.* Bold at need against the exactions of kings,† as well as popes, Robert of Lincoln's writings contain remarkable passages on the distinction of the two powers,‡ and others not less explicit on the prerogatives of the spiritual power.§

Much evidence might be collected to prove that when difficulties arose between the Holy See and the Crown, especially during the reign of Innocent IV., no question was ever raised as to the spiritual authority of the Roman Pontiff: "That which pertaineth to our crown and royalty we will and ought to keep intact, and we desire that our Lord the Pope and the Church would help us in this matter; on our side, rest assured, that we will always yield obedience, fidelity, and devotedness to our Lord the Pope as to our spiritual Father, and to the Holy Roman Church as to our mother." Such was the sentiment expressed by Henry III.‖

The gravity of the situation increased in the fourteenth century. Unfortunately for the Church, her supreme head, during this period, resided at a distance from the centre of Christianity where St. Peter had inaugurated the series of martyr-popes; where, since Constantine, the Pontiffs had reigned free and respected, the possessors of a rich patrimony; where, lastly, since Gregory II. (730), by a wise disposition of Providence, they had occupied an honourable political status worthy of their elevated position.¶ The circumstances that caused the removal of the Papacy from the Eternal City are well known. That great Pope, Boniface VIII., had maintained the rights of the Primacy and Temporal Power with a courage which Philip the Fair strove vainly to shake; in the Holy One overwhelmed with outrages, insults, and blows at Anaqui, even Dante, a Ghibellin and personal enemy of Boniface, recognized and worshipped Jesus Christ, a prisoner in the person of his Vicar.** The perfidious King thought that French Popes would prove more subservient to him, and so with the election of Clement V. was opened this sad

---

* Waterworth, "England and Rome," p. 311.
† Luard, p. 277. ‡ Ibid., pp. 348, 349.
§ Ibid., 369, cfr. 390. ‖ Ibid., p. 338.
¶ Fr. Colombier, S.J. "On Roman Church Property:" *Etudes Religieuses.* Lyons, 1872, ii. p. 25.—Bartolini, di S. Zacharia Papa, 1879, p. 441.
** Tosti, in his "Life of Boniface VIII."

epoch in history known as the Exile at Avignon, the Captivity of Babylon. Whatever may have been the personal merits and virtues of the popes at Avignon, their political situation could not but prove injurious to the prestige of the Papacy. The French element predominated in the Roman Court; the Cardinals, naturally, were devoted to the French cause. Now this was the period of the great national wars between England and France.

With the Popes resident at Avignon, and no longer enjoying, in the esteem of the English, that character for political neutrality which had made the Roman Pontiff the natural arbitrator of Christendom, we may conceive of the opposition they were likely to meet with. Edward III., who styled himself "King of France and England," addressed a letter (1343) "full of respect to the Most Holy Father and Lord, Clement VI., Sovereign Pontiff of the Universal Church," complaining that 2,000 marks taken from Church revenues had been demanded in favour of two French Cardinals;* they were it is true, natives of Aquitaine, which belonged to the English Crown. In virtue of an agreement concluded formerly between John Lackland and Innocent III., the Popes at Avignon, following the example of their predecessors, sought to raise in England an annual tribute of a thousand marks; it was not often that their efforts proved successful; so seldom, indeed, that in 1366 Urban V. had occasion to claim arrears extending over thirty-three years.† The English bishops had frequently protested that they did not admit the validity of this tribute;‡ indeed, they declared that "neither the said King John nor any other could place himself or his kingdom or his people under such subjection without their consent and agreement." The nobles and commons joined with the prelates, and proclaimed that the deed of John Lackland was not binding on them, being contrary to the oath sworn by this king at his coronation.§

The situation of England after the Treaty of Bretigny (1360), the imminent danger of war being renewed, the heavy taxes that Edward III. had been obliged to levy, all tended to make the demands of the Court at Avignon most unpopular.

---

* Thomas Walsingham, "Historia Anglicana," edited by Henry Thomas Riley, M.A., 1863, i. 255–260.

† "Fasciculi," preface, xix. Neither Thomas of Walsingham, so hostile

II.

Wycliffe knew how to turn circumstances to account. By his skilful representation of the national causes for complaint he won such favour that he was appointed, first royal chaplain* and afterwards a member of the deputation sent to Bruges in 1374 to negotiate with the envoys of Pope Gregory XI. on the points in dispute.† It is probable that he remained till the conclusion of the negotiations, which lasted two years.‡ It is evident that Wycliffe's fame was raised by this mission, and that his influence in the University increased: but it would appear also that these negotiations resulted in deepening his animosity against Rome. In fact, the first article of the long-disputed Concordat, running counter to the law of 1363, stipulated that the Pope should retain his right to dispose of the benefices of vacant Sees, and moreover Wycliffe was not appointed to one.§

Before this Conference Wycliffe had, in his writings, been the mouthpiece of the national grievances against the power of the Holy See. In a public discussion which he held with a Carmelite named Cuningham, he had attacked the validity of charters and deeds of perpetual endowment on which were based certain recognized rights of the Pope.‖ His chief argument was the comparatively recent date of these deeds; but it is the age, the antiquity of a deed that lends it authority. Pressed hard by his opponent he advanced, and wished to prove the theory that a perpetual gift or endowment is null and void unless it is eternal in its origin, that is to say, unless it is made by God Himself. "God," said he, "could give to Abraham and his seed, to true believers, the land of Channan till the end of time; Peter has not the like power or right."¶ The Carmelite objected that this theory, based on the literal meaning of the word "perpetual" in the gift made to Abraham, endangered the rights of churches, and particularly those of the Roman Church, to certain possessions bequeathed by Constantine, and specially to the city of Rome which King Louis had granted to, or recognized as belonging to, Pope Pascal and his successors.** What answer did Wycliffe make? It is not to be found in the documents published by

---

* "Peculiaris regis clericus."
† "Ut ea qua honorem Sanctæ Ecclesiæ et conservationem inrium

Shirley,* but what has been said above allows one to suppose that this discussion led him to make a sketch, to be filled in later on, of his theory on this subject. We will now examine more closely this theory as set forth by Shirley in the preface to the "Fasciculi."†

1. God alone is universal Lord and Master. He alone has an essential, eternal and inalienable right to exact service and obedience. He holds sovereign dominion over consciences as well as over the possessions of this world. This dominion He transfers freely to His creatures, as does a suzerain to his vassals, on condition that they be faithful to Him; hence ownership and authority are lost by sin; this twofold right can only be vested in a man living in the grace of God.

The falseness and danger of this theory, as well from the civil as religious point of view, must be apparent to all. It would place in constant jeopardy and doubt the rights of ownership and authority. Would it be possible to maintain order in society were it not based on social rights independent, to a certain extent, of the individual merit of those in whom they are vested? Authority, for example—not to speak in this place of rights of ownership—is evidently established by God, not for the advantage and honour of its representatives, but for the good of those subject to them and with a view to maintaining order. Authority, therefore, is always real, always living, and if cases occur in which an unworthy man forfeits his rights to command, such cases should be adjudicated by him through whom the right is transmitted, but are not to be submitted to arbitrary criticism.

---

* Cuningham's answer seems noteworthy. That Constantine the Great had granted to the Roman Church the site most adapted to her, and that, renouncing Rome, he had transferred the seat of the empire to Byzantium—this is a fact known to history; but that, besides the right to the possession of Rome, which the Emperor admitted, and to the wealth with which he endowed the See of Peter, and which is known under the name of Peter's Patrimony (from the custom of calling the property of individual churches by the name of their patron saint), he also constituted the Pope Emperor of the West—is a statement that will always meet with contradiction. Whilst some discuss the validity of this pretended gift of Constantine, others deny its authenticity; it only

Under the feudal system, treason deprived a vassal of all his rights; but unless the contrary can be clearly proved from a text in the Gospel, no one has a right to lay down the principle that sin, which is treason to God, deprives a superior of his legitimate claim to authority.

When the disastrous consequences of his doctrine were laid before Wycliffe, he set them aside, it would seem, by the following distinction:—

2. The unworthy master has no authority and has no claim to any respect; nevertheless we should yield him submission in act, a passive obedience, because God, who permits evil, wills that we should endure it; thus if the evil principle is personified in a wicked superior, we are obliged to tolerate him; this, said he, was the reason why our Lord, whilst refusing to adore Satan, allowed Himself to be ill-used by him; and why, with no esteem for Judas, He yet endured his treachery. The man possessed by the devil went so far as to say that God obeyed the devil.* To obey Satan, or a sinner, or Antichrist, is to serve God.

This explanation, more absurd even than the principle stated above, would serve to ratify every excess and abuse of power, and lead to hopeless slavery.

All right, all power in the temporal as in the spiritual order, emanates from God and resides in God; this cannot be contested: there cannot exist between the two orders so wide a separation as to prevent all relations between the two powers. In handling the question of the relations between Church and State, Wycliffe was betrayed into fresh paradoxes. St. Thomas à Becket, the martyred Archbishop of Canterbury, had taught that, in governing, the Crown was not utterly independent of spiritual authority, and, making use of the famous metaphor of the two swords, he said: "One is from above, and comes directly from God; the other is from below, and comes from God, but indirectly in the sense that it is the people who place it in the hands of a man or dynasty. Spiritual authority teaches and rules the children of the Church and all nations who acknowledge her for their mother; temporal authority is guided by the law of Jesus Christ, of which the Pope is the highest interpreter." Was this theory, true in every age, rejected by Wycliffe? No; this is fully conceded by Shirley,† but during the Middle Ages its limits had been extended as required by circumstances, and it would be as repugnant as it would be unjust to judge of this extension by the standard of our modern ideas.

---

* "Fasciculi," lxiii. 899. Shirley here quotes an extract from a sermon: "Obedientia facienda, latria neganda."

† *Ibid.*, lxv.

The union of Church and State admitted, in theory, by the Civil power since the time of Constantine, and acknowledged, with various limits, by different legislations and in international claims, had procured for the Papacy a transient position most beneficial to States; for the kind of suzerainty which it exercised, whether personally or through the medium of emperors, formed in those barbaric ages a rampart against the despotism of princes and the revolt of subjects.* The feudal *régime* had been placed under the protection of the head of the Church. The Emperor was the highest representative of the Holy See, and even after several princes had been created electors of the Empire, it was the pontifical ratification and consecration that alone constituted the legitimacy of the Emperor. Every Christian king was linked politically with the Papacy, but it is absurd to pretend that the Popes ever nourished the ambition of reducing the various kingdoms to so many fiefs, and their kings to vassals revocable at pleasure. During the disputes between John Lackland and Philip Augustus, Innocent III. declared that he did not assume the right of deciding on a question as to the validity of a feudal claim, but that he only sat in judgment on infractions of the moral law.†

That certain abuses arose, that some Popes, or, much oftener, their legates (sometimes false legates),‡ put forward excessive pretensions, are facts that no Catholic theologian need be eager to deny. The Church has her vulnerable side—that, namely, on which she comes in close contact with humanity—and if she has not always been holy in the person of the Sovereign Pontiffs, neither has she the prerogative of having been always above reproach in the exercise of her political authority. To judge impartially in this matter, it would here be necessary to look upon the Popes as temporal sovereigns and to establish a comparison between them and the princes of their day; but, where is the reader, however little versed in history, who will not admit that such a comparison would prove altogether to the glory of the Church and of her Pontiffs?

As we have already stated, complaints waxed louder in England in proportion as the guardianship of the Papacy seemed less needed; the English clergy themselves were of opinion that the share of the Papacy in questions relating to politics required to be restricted, and without contesting its spiritual claims, they

---

* Hergenröther, "Handbuch der Kirchengeschichte," periode v., chap. i. § i. h.
† Philips, "Handbuch des Kirchenrechts," book i. § 122–133.
‡ Lingard (Boston edition, 1853, iv. p. 156, note): "In the preamble of a statute of Edward III. we read: 'Le Pape y meist volontiers convenable remedie, si sa Segntete estoit sur ces choses enfourmee.'"

often gave their support to the protests of King and Parliament against its interference in temporal matters.* Wycliffe, falsely deducing the illicitness of a thing from the existence of an abuse of it, and the negation of a right from the violation of a duty in connection with it, thought to strike the evil at the root by denying that the spiritual power had any direct claim on temporalities. This thesis, in our opinion, resumes all the errors of this sectarian concerning the question now under consideration. We will follow him in the development of his views, to which at first he did not give a very definite utterance, and examine some writings which he published about the year 1377.†

III.

The first of these writings was addressed to King Richard's Parliament. After declaring that he is a Christian, and that if in this pamphlet he be guilty of error, he retracts it beforehand, "submitting himself humbly to correction from his holy Mother the Church," Wycliffe puts forward eighteen propositions‡—on the right of property, on excommunications, on the rights pertaining to Holy Orders, on the rights of kings and suzerains in respect to ecclesiastical benefices, and, lastly, on the charges brought against the clergy and the Pope. What do they contain that is opposed to the sovereign rights of the Primacy—that is to say, to the *spiritual* authority of the Roman Pontiff? Let us briefly analyze this document :—

No one except Christ can invest Peter and his successors with perpetual political sovereignty over the world, for all sovereignty will cease at the Last Judgment. Hence charters granting perpetual endowments are of human invention and worthless. . . . . A right of property given for a certain time, however, does not offend against this principle, and the Pope, as the minister of Jesus Christ, can use it, if, following the example of Jesus Christ and conforming to the spirit of the Gospel, he act as the servant of the servants of God; for forgetfulness of the Gospel and a worldly ostentation seem to lead him only too easily to blasphemy and to exalt himself like Antichrist,—especially in the case in which these leaders (*capitanei*) who pretend to oblige one in all matters of faith, in spite of their own ignorance of Holy Scripture,§—would look upon the truths of faith of our holy books as cockle, destructive of Christian Faith (" lollium, fidei

The outrageous boldness of this language, scandalous even in the mouth of a man prepared to retract, does not appear to us, however, as a negation of authority : the rebellious spirit hesitates and brings forward a supposition injurious to the prerogative of the Vicar of Jesus Christ, but admits implicitly that Catholic belief in all ages has acknowledged the teaching authority of the Vicar of Christ, and does not deny that the teaching is binding on the faithful.

"The temporal lords have a right, and do well to deprive a church of its property when wrong-doing or abuses take place within it." He adds, however, that they may only do this with the permission of the Church.*

The Vicar of Jesus Christ can neither confer nor abrogate a right, except only in the name of God ("vicariè, in nomine Dei"), in whose name he notifies to the Church the man whom God has invested with a right. Excommunication, to be valid, presupposes sin in the person excommunicated; the power to excommunicate is not absolute, the Vicar of Christ may not use it as an end to obtain temporal goods.

He admits that the Pope has the right to nominate or approve of bishops, but not to dispose of benefices; this latter belongs to kings, yet only within the limits of justice. "An ecclesiastic, even the Roman Pontiff, may, for the good of the Church, be reprimanded and accused by the clergy, and even by the laity." Wycliffe here stands on the rule for brotherly correction laid down in St. Matthew xviii. 15, the application of which, however, he restricts to opportuneness, according to the example of St. Paul's reproof to St. Peter (Galat. ii. 11). Then, recalling the fact that several Popes of disorderly life had been deposed by the Emperors, he adds :

The Church is above such a pontiff ("supra istum pontificem"); to say that he should not be reprimanded by a man, but only by God, whatever sin he may have committed, implies, apparently, that he is above the Church, and that, like Antichrist, he is exalted above Christ. Yet Christ, all sinless though He was, chose to submit to princes, even when they deprived Him of His temporal goods.

It is to be remarked that Wycliffe's concern is the question of benefices and of taxes, at that time in dispute between the Pope and the King. Is there here any question of ecclesiastical authority? None whatever. As to the supposed consequence that if the Pope owe submission to none he would therefore be

---

* "Auctoritate Eccles ecclesiasticus corripiendu proposition, Wycliffe da make ill use of her poss‹ lefectu spiritualis propositi et in casu quo a fide devius." In Walsingham's seventh lecide if, in point of fact, the Church does

above the Church, who does not see how absurd it is? What Catholic is not aware that the Pope, in order to obtain forgiveness for his sins, must bow down in the Sacrament of Penance before a minister of God's mercy, that, like St. Peter, he may see himself reproved and corrected without any detriment to the authority he exercises over the faithful? The right to accuse publicly and to depose a Pope, the validity of whose election was open to doubt, was a question more or less contested in Wycliffe's time, and which was brought forward some years later in the Council of Constance.

Wycliffe is not long content with argument; his impetuous spirit soon carries him away, and leads him into war against the abuses he sought to reform. His pamphlet ends as follows:

These conclusions are, in my opinion, the seed of Faith separated from the chaff with which, at the harvest and day of vengeance, the cockle will be burned ("ingratum lollium"). The infallible sign by which this cockle, the food of Antichrist, can be recognized is that the clergy are dominated by the venomous pride of Lucifer, the passion for ruling; the desire for earthly riches, wedded to passion for power, brings forth children of the devil, and the children of evangelical poverty perish. The power of this diabolical race has even reduced the degenerate sons of apostolical poverty to a cowardly silence; even they are fearful of losing the temporal advantages they possess.

Gregory XI. had hardly returned to the Eternal City before he sent a triple Bull to the King, the bishops, and the University of Oxford;* he reproached this learned body for having by its supineness allowed the cockle ("lollium") to develop and increase; it is to this expression that the innovator alludes at the end of his pamphlet.†

Wycliffe soon openly attacked the Pope's Bulls in an anonymous work, which he dedicated the same year to the Doctors of Divinity.‡ He advised them to be firm in defending the faith. He writes: "Now, Christian faith is Holy Scripture, and many enemies attack it in these days by word and by deed." We must not too hastily detach this fragmentary phrase from its surroundings, otherwise we might run the risk of turning Wycliffe into a perfect Protestant. He goes on to say:—

---

* Walsingham, i., 346–352, Anno Septimo, Mai 22, 1377; cfr. "Fasciculi," xxviii., note.
† This is the origin of the term "Lollard." Cunningham is styled

In truth, in these days the error is gaining ground that he who becomes Pope is impeccable, or, at least, that he cannot sin mortally, consequently that all he ordains and thinks is right, that the Gospel is only to be accepted through his medium, that he is above the Gospel, and that his life and his words form the rule of our faith. If he do not conform his life to that of Jesus Christ and His Apostles, that is, they say, because times are changed; that he has the power to dispense us from imitating Christ and His Apostles, or else that he alone can interpret Scripture.

The ordinary result of discussions is to push certain minds into exaggeration.* Did the opponents of Wycliffe stretch Papal prerogative beyond just limits? Whether this accusation is to be believed or not, our readers will find in it one more testimony to the rule of Catholic faith—to the existence of a living authority, whose representatives, alas! through the frailty of human nature, do not always live in that conformity with the Gospel which they teach others. But let us hear the prophet resuming his *rôle* of reformer, repeating these s me charges against the clergy:—

Lately, however, a professor of Holy Scripture, predestined by the grace of God (he is alluding to himself) has proved by this same Scripture that priests should in all humility administer the Sacraments and preach the true and literal doctrine of the Gospel of peace, and that in the greatness of this humble ministry resides all their worth before God. Thus, they should live without possessions, a life poor as that of Jesus Christ. . . . . No change of the times, no dispensation of the Pope, can exempt them from this duty; they are not the real owners, but only the dispensers, of the goods belonging to the poor. But the disciples of Antichrist have interpreted St. Luke (xxii. 25) and the Doctors, especially St. Chrysostom and St. Bernard, in the sense that they were forbidden to seek to rule after the manner of the Pagans, but not to acquire wealth for the advantage of the Church, and so they have had recourse to the Roman Pontiff. The latter has sent several Bulls, in which the nineteen propositions are condemned. Two propositions in particular are strongly condemned—those concerning the right of Kings over the temporalities of the clergy, and the right of the laity to correct ecclesiastics and the Roman Pontiff.

We will not follow him in his diatribe against Rome's censure; our separated brethren do not admit Wycliffe's theories on church property any more than we do; and yet in this exactly lies the gist of all Wycliffe's error:—

Jesus Christ will never be delivered from her bitterness until the reign of the Prince of Peace is restored and the worldly spirit of Antichrist destroyed. .... The faithful ought unanimously to resist, that the faith may be saved.

Then he falls into absurd exaggerations: "The Pope will anathematize all who oppose his ambition; he will take possession of every kingdom; he will overthrow the world; he will revive the excesses of the Bégards"—language more suited to fanaticism than reason, and worthier of the leader of a faction than of a Doctor of Divinity. But once more, even in the midst of these exaggerations, we will hear what this pretended precursor of the great Reformation has to say: "Non resistatur igitur tali ut Papæ vel clerico. We must resist such a man, and not look upon him as Pope or cleric; but, if he be obstinate, we must oppose him as the worst of Antichrists, as the great beast of Pharaoh's chariot, rushing to plunge headlong into the Red Sea." After continuing in this strain, he adds:—

Jesus Christ gave Peter *supreme authority* and *the keys of the Kingdom of Heaven* ("capitale privilegium clavium regni cælorum"), and declared him blessed. Directly, however, that Peter strove to oppose His Will and the work of our salvation, his meek and gentle Master called him "Satan." Scripture has bequeathed us such incidents in order to teach us to be prudent and reserved in the respect due to the Vicars of Jesus Christ ("ut quilibet christianus caveat cultu sapiente vicarios adorari").* Here is the right rule given us by the most holy Pope Peter: "If any man minister ("servus servorum Christi"), let him do it as of the power which God administereth, so that this *God*, who *gives His Vicars the light wherewith to understand the Scriptures* ("Deus qui concedit ejus vicariis lumen intelligentiæ Scripturæ") may be honoured by all men, and that these should imitate the customs of their forefathers."

Any one with a grain of good faith cannot but acknowledge that Wycliffe in this pamphlet admits the supreme spiritual authority of the Papacy. If a little consideration be given to the italicised passages above, it will easily be seen that he did not consider the Bible, and the Bible alone, to be the rule of faith: "Christ's vicar," he says, " has received the mission and the light to understand and interpret it."

Under a somewhat different form, Wycliffe published some declarations in defence of his teaching against the decision of Gregory XI.,† and this work confirms the conclusions we have drawn from the former one. After maintaining that the Pope has not an arbitrary power to bind and loose,‡ he says: "I do

---

* In two other MSS. these words are indistinct. Probably, some Protestant reader, being scandalized, obliterated them.
† Walsingham, i., 357.　　　　　　　‡ Proposition XIII.

not wish to detract from his authority or that of any other
prelate, for by the power of the Head (Jesus Christ) they can
bind and loose. But I restrict this power in the sense that it is
not admissible it should be always and "in all cases efficacious
and necessarily ratified by heaven." Concerning Proposition
XVIII., on the right of correction belonging to the laity, he
says : " This assertion is evident, since the Pope can commit sin,
excepting, however, the sin against the Holy Ghost; this last
sin must be excluded, I suppose, by the holiness, humility, and
respect due to such a father. But if he commit other sins, and
his college (Cardinalice) neglect to reprove him, the Universal
Church, and the laity, who constitute the larger part of it, may
take it upon themselves." Then, quoting the text of Canon Law,
" Si papa fuerit devius a fide," he remarks that, except the proof
be incontestable, so great a fall as heresy must not be supposed,
and that, were it to occur, it was not to be inferred that the Pope
would persist so obstinately in it as not to accept with humility
the remedy from the hands of his superior in God, (his confessor ?)

On this subject we are almost tempted to consider Wycliffe
reasonable enough. For that the Pope—infallible as Pope—may,
as a private individual, fall into heresy is a doctrine contrary
neither to the Gospel, to tradition, nor to scholastic theology.*
Turrecremata, even whilst admitting that the Pope has no judge
except God, whose chief vicar he is, maintains nevertheless that
in the event of his lapsing into heresy, he thereby forfeits the
Primacy. Now Wycliffe tells us that on this point we should give
in only to irrefragable proof. Several cardinals at the Council of
Constance showed themselves less exacting when, thirty years
later, they deposed two competitors for the Pontifical throne, declaring them heretics merely on the ground of their obstinacy in
believing themselves to be legitimate Popes, and hindering the
reunion of their divided jurisdiction.

IV.

a regulation which proves the contrary. It is there laid down that, in case of appeals, the hierarchical order is to be observed, and that in all religious matters the final appeal must be to the Pope.* What, then, can have been the cause of this hesitation on the part of the University authorities? Was it the fear of supporting the exercise of Pontifical authority? Political circumstances, it seems to us, give the explanation of this hesitation. In the difficulties that arose between the Duke of Lancaster, then acting as Regent, and the House of Commons, the Duke sought the adhesion of Wycliffe's numerous partisans. When the innovator was summoned to appear before Bishop Courtney and the Houses of Convocation, sitting within Old Saint Paul's, Lancaster did not hesitate to stand at his side.† The Bishops themselves were obliged to yield before the tumultuous manifestations of the Lollards and the influence of the Regent.‡ We shall see, later on, the position taken up by the University.

The question of Papal dues had ever been one giving rise to animated discussion and to much irritation. At the beginning of Richard II.'s reign the Council of Regency§ believed that Wycliffe had been authorised to solve it. This we need not regret, since it led to the production of a fourth document which confirms our views on the errors taught by the Reformer.

The question submitted to Wycliffe's decision was: "May the kingdom of England, in spite of the censure and commands of the Pope, prevent its revenues being withdrawn to foreign lands when it is threatened with proximate war?" The arguments with which he supports his answer‖ are drawn from principles laid down in the law of Christ, and from some writings of St. Bernard and St. Gregory against simony, but he completely ignores both the Canon Law and the Civil law of the land, which contained, however, the real key to the solution. Any one who examines this document carefully cannot but call it violent; at one moment, the vehemence of the sectarian exceeding all bounds, the King and his counsellors silenced him. Yet we find nothing in it which implies negation of the Primacy. That "the Pope is

---

* "Munimenta Academica," edited by Anstey, London, 1869, i. p. 132. "In causa civili dominus noster rex, sed in causa spirituali dumtaxat

not above the law of Jesus Christ" is evident to every Christian mind; that "the commands of Christ's Vicar are not binding, should they be contrary to the law of the Gospel," is true enough. Wycliffe holds that "the law of conscience compels temporal lords to respect the intentions of donors who have founded endowments and benefices; to infringe on them and misapply the bequest is to enfeeble the clergy, who form the chief link between the kingdom and God." He adds: "Let the clergy be faithful in executing the obligations imposed on them by our forefathers; these latter from within the flames of Purgatory reproach their descendants with their disloyalty." He wantonly exaggerates abuses and the use made by the Pope of the riches of the world in order that he might live like the princes of his day. In this matter he might have been reminded of his own past life, which had not been as austere as his adherents believed.* He is unjust when he takes upon himself to lash the nepotism of the Popes; for, if Clement VI. deserved reproach on this point, neither Urban V. (1362–1370), nor Gregory XI. (1370–1378) deserved it. Walsingham tells us that: "Gregory was a just and good man;† he was distressed at the evils which afflicted France and England, and strove to restore a good understanding between the two kingdoms." But the sectarian's hatred knew not the bounds of truth and justice, and the holiest of pontiffs was in his eyes but a son of Antichrist unless he accepted his own chimerical theories.

"Antichrist!" This had been the war-cry of the Waldenses;‡ later on it became the enraged cry of the Reformers. Luther and his adepts did not use it sparingly. How many simple souls, how many nations, alas! have been drawn away into apostasy by talismanic words of this kind! Wycliffe's expression, " the Pope is Antichrist," has, however, by most authors been taken in too extended a sense; this proposition can nowhere be found used in a universal sense. Because he calls certain individual Popes by this hateful name are we to conclude that he recognizes neither Pope nor Papacy?

Great misfortunes were about to overwhelm the Church of Jesus Christ, and to imperil the principle of Her Unity, the divine authority of Her visible Head. Gregory XI. died at Rome, March 27, 1378, after having by his Bull, "Periculis et detrimentis," determined the rights of the future Conclave. By the unanimous votes of the sixteen cardinals present in Rome,§ the Archbishop of Bari was elected, and ascended the throne of

---

* *Cfr.* " Fasciculi,"   ce xlv., notes.
† " Hist. Angl." (e   iamed above), i., 368.   ‡
‡ Cæsarius, " Dia¹   raculorum" (Strange's edition), i. 305.
§ Baronius, 1378,

Saint Peter under the name of Urban VI. Now were to be gathered in the bitter fruits of the captivity of Babylon. His severity, whether rightly or wrongly, soon irritated the members of the Sacred College; eleven French and one Spanish Cardinal (this included the two future Anti-Popes) rebelled and left Rome; and on September 20 they elected another Pope, Robert of Geneva, a scion of the royal family of France. It appears that Robert, after having voted a few months previously for the election of Urban, had officially notified the choice to Louis de Maele, Count of Flanders,* and to the Parliament sitting at Gloucester.† Zealous as was the King of France to bring about the recognition of the French Pope, he even went the length of awarding the penalty of death to the adherents of Urban VI.‡ England and the northern States of Europe were equally earnest in supporting the claims of the Roman Pontiff. "Urban is the true Pope," wrote the English King, "and every one should acknowledge him as Pope and Head of the Holy Church."§ The Archbishop of Canterbury, in answer to the ambassadors of Clement VII.‖ said, with much warmth of protestation, "Unus erit pastor noster" (Ezech. xxxiv. 23.) This was to be the final outcome of the deplorable division which had occurred and over which the Unity of the Church and Her monarchical constitution were to triumph after half a century of internal struggle.

In proportion as the election of Clement VII. was grievous to the Church in England, so did it bring joy to Wycliffe; he wrote, "Now is the favourable time; put your trust in Christ, for already the head of Antichrist is divided in two; the sins of the Popes have caused this division." Here, then, was a precious opportunity for the heresiarch, supported by Lancaster, to abjure the Roman Church, and found a reformed Church independent of the Pope, whom Wycliffe had grown into the habit of calling by the odious name of Antichrist. We have heard him preaching the doctrine of the pure Gospel: was that not because the Bible is all sufficient and the true rule of our faith? No thought of such a thing is to be found in his life or works. In the same passage he urges kings to help in the re-establishment of peace and the destruction of simony.¶

From 1378 to 1379 he was engaged on his work, "On the Truth of Scripture." What is the aim of this book? All we

---

* Walsingham, i., 393. The name to be inserted in the next page is Theruannensem.
† Ibid., 380, and "Fasciculi," 506.   ‡ Walsingham, i. 391.
§ Rymer, "Fœdera," iv. p. 85.   ‖ Walsingham, i. 381.
¶ This passage is quoted from a MS. in De Ruever-Groneman, "Diatribe, &c." 1837, p. 165.

know of it is derived from some extracts published by Shirley. As Protestants have been in no hurry to publish it, we infer that it does not treat of their thesis on the Rule of Faith; probably Wycliffe, in this work, expounded the literal meaning of the text of the Scriptures.* Whatever the case, here are two passages which we submit to the attention of our readers.† He w.ites: "I protested in my writings (and this protestation has been sent by the hands of two Bishops to the court of our lord the Pope) that in explaining my views, I wish to seek support from the manner of speech used in the Bible and by the Holy Fathers." A Catholic would not speak otherwise: Wycliffe acknowledges the living authority to which he appeals, and the twofold anthority of Holy Scripture and Tradition, of which the Head of the Church is the trustee. He tells us himself that some had said to him : "If you look upon your conclusions as Catholic and useful to the Church of God you would not hesitate to submit them to the Sovereign Pontiff, and to allow them to be examined by the Roman Church." What answer does he make to this? He begins by invective; he says: "The reasoning here is defective, because a false principle is laid down; it might so happen that our lord the Pope be ignorant of the law of Holy Scripture, and that it be better known in England than in the whole of that Roman Church composed of such a Pope and of such Cardinals." We see here that he throws a doubt on the legitimacy of the Pope. This is the first reply which occurred to the mind of the rebellious Doctor. When he has relieved his hatred for his judges, reason and faith once more reassert themselves, and he continues:—

> The action I have taken in this matter proves that I cannot be suspected of fear on account of my theses, for I have spread them abroad over most of England and Christendom, and lately I have forwarded them to the Roman Court for examination. When the above-named Doctor shall have read my protestation he will, by the grace of God, see that I am not afraid to defend them; he will see that I am ready to submit them to the judgment, not only of the Roman Court, but even to the entire Church militant and triumphant; I have submitted myself humbly to our Mother the Church, and God preserve me from excluding therefrom the Roman Church, for *I believe her to be the Mother of all the Militant Churches.*

With full confidence in the answer we ask, Is such a proposi-

---

* *Cfr.* " Fasciculi," pp. 20, 457.
† Bodleian MS., 924; *cfr.* "Fasciculi," xxxiii., 899 sqq. the date, "Hodie in vigiliæ Annunciationis MCCCLXXVIII."—p. 119, of the MS.—and the mention of the cardinals created by Urban VI. (1379 ?), may be made to agree if we suppose that the author took a year to complete his work.

tion as this last compatible with a supposition that Wycliffe
sought to evolve a theological system which should supplant the
spiritual authority of the Sovereign Pontiff? And if it were
true that in other works he puts forward the Protestant principle
that the Bible is the only rule of faith, we should then have to
resign ourselves to finding in his teaching utterly incompatible
doctrines. Were all his manuscripts published, we might then
form a better judgment on him. A Protestant writer* observes
that it would not be just to judge the teaching of a man merely
on those points which have been condemned by prejudice or ill-
informed judges. We are far from consenting to the insinuation
conveyed in the latter part of the above sentence. We are still
less willing to accept as true the various propositions condemned
by the Council of Constance. The thirty-seventh and the forty-
first, which bear upon our present subject,† are manifestly
heretical in the absolute sense they at first convey to the mind;
in whatever relative and restrictive sense they may be taken they
are seditious and scandalous.‡ What meaning did they bear in
Wycliffe's context? Were they intended as rejecting in general
and universal terms the authority of the Vicars of Jesus Christ
and the supremacy of the Roman Church? Before we could
assert this in the face of the explicit quotations we have given, it
would be necessary to have proofs drawn from the context of
these propositions. Most writers, whether Catholic or Protestant,
have only been able to form an opinion of Wycliffe's system on
the strength of extracts taken from his works,§ and often they
have interpreted his doctrines according to their private views.
We know how frequently it happens that an historian not
burdened with scruples has, in drawing up a body of doctrine
from the scattered errors of a writer, set aside principles not
agreeing with his preconceived plan, and has succeeded in
offering the theories of the author under a totally false aspect.

We will not examine Wycliffe's teaching concerning the Holy
Eucharist (1381), but content ourselves with quoting a few
details. He did not deny the Real Presence, but the mode of
presence by Transubstantiation. To prove the possibility of the
simultaneous coexistence of the bread and the Body of Jesus
Christ (it is not the possibility, but the fact, which is in question),

---

* Lenfant, "Histoire du Concile de Constance," liv. ii., n. 59.
† Denzinger, "Enchiridion," n. 513, 517.
‡ Cfr. Denzinger, n. 555.
§ It was John Lucke, Bachelor of Divinity, Oxford, who drew up, in
1413, the 260 or 2.. ..icles laid before the Council of Constance. (Cfr.
Duplessis D'Arge.... "Collectio Judiciorum de novis Erroribus," vol. i.
part ii. p. 29.

he made use of this comparison :* " A sinner is converted, and becomes a just man, nevertheless he remains the same man as before. Gregory or Innocent is changed into a Pope because he has been created Pope, and he remains the same man as before." Had Wycliffe followed up his idea of the Papal election, which effects no change in the nature of the person elected, he would have deduced from it that as the pontifical dignity does not destroy either good or evil qualities, it, in itself, claims respect and obedience irrespective of the personal merits of its representative. In the decree of condemnation promulgated in the name of the University, William Berton, the chancellor, accuses the innovator of wishing by his errors in dogma to rend the Lord's tunic—that is to say, the unity of our holy mother the Church.† Wycliffe made a kind of retractation,‡ in which he pretended that his doctrine did not differ from that of Scripture, or of the holy Fathers, or of the decrees of the Roman Church. The Franciscan, Tysington, made answer to him that—

The opinion held by the children of Holy Church can produce many witnesses in its favour, and possesses this advantage, that it repudiates the doctrine of no Pope, Bishop, or Doctor, who has flourished since Christ down to the present Pope: it only repudiates the teaching of those whom the Church has publicly denounced, of Berengarius, Abelard, and their modern disciples.

Tysington develops this statement, and shows the absurdity of Wycliffe's views, which, resting on the testimony of the first ten centuries, rejected the numerous witnesses of the Catholic faith during the last 380 years, on the pretext that, after the first decade of centuries, Satan had been loosed, and had set up his kingdom in the Church. It is worthy of note that among the rejected witnesses to the truth, St. Bernard, St. Anselm, Hugh of St. Victor, and others, are to be found to whose authority the heresiarch had often referred; but contradiction is the characteristic feature of error.

V.

Whilst Wycliffe was writing his various works, his subversive doctrines relating to authority and property were bringing forth fruit according to their kind. The popular mind, which is scarcely adequate to the discussion of abstract principles, soon jumps to the more practical conclusions they lead to, and its logic is terrible. The Reformation of the sixteenth century was

---

* "Fasciculi," p. 107
† "Molientes tuni   )omini, scilicet sanctæ matris Ecclesiæ scindere unitatem."
‡ "Fasciculi," 11

followed by the Peasants' War, and the hideous outrages of the Anabaptists; the teaching of Wycliffe, John Ball, Jack Straw, and of other followers of Wycliffe, led to civil dissensions and broils far and wide. The Archbishop of Canterbury, together with some members of the Royal Council, were murdered; the king and queen-mother imprisoned in the Tower of London, and civil war in all its fury of pillaging and burning threatened the fair realm of England, showing that the sacred rights of authority, whether civil or religious, cannot with impunity be tampered with. Wycliffe's share in these disorders has been repudiated as a hateful calumny; but that his teaching fostered the revolt appears to us most evident from the nature of things, and the testimony of contemporary writers. John Ball, one of the leaders of the insurrection, had, according to his own statement made before his execution, been for two years Wycliffe's disciple.*
Two poems of the time make Wycliffe responsible for the excesses of the populace.†

To return to the doctrine of the heresiarch, which forms the subject of this notice. Simon of Sudbury's successor in the See of Canterbury, William of Courtney, had no sooner received the pallium from Rome, than at the entreaties of King and Parliament,‡ he resolved to condemn publicly the errors that had been the cause of so many disorders. On this occasion the King was willing to lend his countenance. The Archbishop convoked a synod, to be held at the Dominican Convent in London, May 21, 1382. Ten bishops, and a great many doctors in divinity and Canon Law were present. After discussing twenty-four propositions from Wycliffe, they condemned them—some as being erroneous, others as being heretical and opposed to the decisions of the Church.§ Only some of these bear upon the subject now in hand; the eighth treats of the Pope's divine authority over the faithful. According to the heresiarch, the Pope and the clergy, deprived of all temporal possessions, were to live quite beyond the ordinary conditions of human life, in complete poverty. Pushing a theory conceived by fanatic zeal to its furthest limits, it would appear that he affected thereby to reduce them to a state of impeccability and confirmed holiness. According to Wycliffe, the validity of the sacraments is essentially dependent on the state of grace in the priest administering them, and the Pope is the legitimate head of the Church only on the condition that he is holy, and numbered among the elect; "if he be a sinner and

---
* " Fasciculi," 273.
† " Political Poems and Songs," edited by Thomas Wright, Esq., i. 231-252, 258.—Articles, by F. Stevenson, in *The Month*, 1882, January—June, treat of this question.
‡ " Fasciculi," 272.   § *Ibid.*, p. 277.

a member of the devil, he has no power over the faithful of Christ, or at most only the power conferred upon him by Cæsar." A most absurd doctrine, one manifestly opposed to common sense and to our Lord's institution, since He has never promised that His vicar should be impeccable. Such a characteristic could not possibly be consistent with the frailty of human nature in a long line of Pontiffs. On the contrary, Jesus Christ has taught us the distinction which right reason commands us to draw between the unassailable rights of authority and the personal merits of its representatives :* "The scribes and pharisees have sitten on the chair of Moses. All things, therefore, whatsoever they shall say to you, observe and do; but according to their works do ye not."† The very limits he assigns to legitimate authority presuppose the existence of Divine right in this authority.

The ninth proposition ran thus: "After Urban VI. none must be recognised as Pope, but we must live, like the Greeks, under our own laws." It is difficult to decide whether the heresiarch attached an absolute and definite meaning to this proposition : it would be necessary to see the context before making any assertion; not having it, we reserve our judgment. We would, however, here remind our readers that at this period Christendom was already threatened with schism. In England, and the French provinces belonging to England, a faction was formed favourable to the Anti-Pope, Clement VII., and it reached such proportions that Urban VI. in 1382 sent a Bull to the Bishop of Norwich,‡ conferring on him considerable powers to be used against the partisans of the Anti-Pope. Wycliffe§ alludes to these dissensions, and he accuses the Religious Orders of favouring the claims of the French Pope. His want of good faith is very evident. He says: "Not content with having condemned as heretics Christ and all true Christians, they strive to make men think that the King of England, his ancestors, and his kingdom are heretical, and to deprive them of their rights in order that they may bring Robert of Geneva, with his body of heretical partisans, into England." The Bishop of Norwich met with opposition from the Parliament, which hesitated to recognise the ample powers granted him by the Pope in view of a crusade against Clement VII.|| Was it the fear of seeing the

---

* St. Matth. ch. x 3.
† This same thec Wycliffe had been formerly brought forward by William II. of Er his contest with St. Anselm. *Cfr.*, "Historia Anglorum," Matthew ris (edited by Madden), London, 1866, i. p. 50:
"Rex allegavit . . . Walsingham,
‡ "Trialogus," i Fasciculi," p. 285.
§ Walsingham.

party of Robert of Geneva triumphant that led Wycliffe to proclaim that it were best to acknowledge no Pope after the death of Urban VI. rather than accept his adversary? Until the meaning of the proposition can be better elucidated, this explanation seems as probable as any other.*

On the very day when the Council met to condemn Wycliffe's doctrines an earthquake was felt at London; according to Wycliffe,† the earth was crying for vengeance because the members of Christ did not raise up their voice. On the 28th of the same month the Primate deputed a Carmelite of the name of Stokes, Professor of Holy Scripture, to publish the sentence in the University of Oxford.‡ Here some opposition awaited him, for though Wycliffe's teaching had been discountenanced by most of the Professors,§ yet it found some adherents, to whom Chancellor Rygge showed too much favour. He told Stokes that the Archbishop infringed the rights of the University, that neither bishop nor archbishop held any jurisdiction over this learned body, even in the matter of heresy;‖ he appointed Philip Repyngdon, a disciple of Wycliffe, as preacher for the solemnity of Corpus Christi; however, he submitted, June 12,¶ and two Royal decrees, dated Westminster, July 14, put an end to the quarrel.

After these events Wycliffe withdrew from Oxford, and spent the last two years of his life in his rectory at Lutterworth. It was here he wrote his most important work, "Trialogus;" it is in the form of a dialogue between Truth, Error, and Prudence on the philosopical subjects he had blundered against in the course of his sad career. In it he states his views on God, the Creation, and loses himself, as so many others before and since have done, in the mystery of Predestination; doubtless he prided himself on having understood and fathomed, on this question, the "Doctor of Grace;" his disciples were wont to call him "Master John of St. Augustin."** How much wiser are they who, imitating the prudence of Holy Church, refrain from investigating that which our Lord has not been pleased to reveal to us, and who make use of the grace given in this life in the firm confidence that it will help them, if they co-operate with it, to

---

* The Council of Constance (1415), in condemning this proposition, took advantage of the fact that the bishops assembled at Pisa had put an end to the schism by electing Alexander V. (Vonder Hardt, iii. 175). This refutation could not have been occasioned by Wycliffe, who had been dead thirty years.

† "Trialogus," iv. 36.   ‡ "Fasciculi," 275–282.
§ Mansi, "Sacrorum Conciliorum nova . . . . Collectio," xxvi. 721. Letter to the Primate.
‖ "Fasciculi," 299.   ¶ Ibid., 308.
** Thom. Walden., "Doctrinale," l. i. c. 34.

reach the kingdom of the Church triumphant! Like Jansenius, later on, he went so far as to deny free will. He has little cause for sarcastic jeering at his opponents; he says: "Their arguments amount simply to this—the Roman Court, or the Doctors approved by it, speak thus, therefore it is true."* One need only examine their writings to feel convinced that their theological knowledge was far superior to his own,† and that if they always kept in view the infallible authority established by Jesus Christ they knew how to extend their horizon and to labour for the real advancement of learning without indulging in wild speculations or violating the store-house of revelation. The works of the Carmelite, Thomas of Walden,‡ and those of the Dominican Turrecremata,§ are not unworthy of the glorious age that produced St. Thomas; modern theologians may consult them with profit.

The "Trialogus" merely contains a repetition of the views we have already noticed, clothed in the trivial and vituperative language natural to all false reformers. In it Wycliffe admits the cultus of the Saints, though the people then, as now, in their childlike simplicity, sometimes exceeded the just limits, and he wisely acknowledges that the Church in Her liturgical prayers addresses Her praises directly to Jesus Christ and indirectly to the Saints as to mediators and intercessors.‖ He says: "Our holiness consists in imitating in our life the life of Jesus Christ, as it is shown to us in the Holy Scripture." This is quite true; so also is the following: "The Holy Scripture is above all other books, because a book deserves the greater reverence as its author is higher in sanctity."¶ The Catholic Church indeed teaches that the Scriptures are the very Word of God, whilst she does not characterize the definitions of the Holy See as Divine inspirations, properly so called, but teaches that by a simple divine assistance they are preserved from error in the interpretation of the deposit of Faith. He quotes St. Augustine in support of a truth which we admit:—"All truth is contained either explicitly or implicitly in Holy Scripture,"** yet is the ministry of preaching†† needful, that it may be set before the ignorant multitude and all the children of the Church, and it is necessary,

* "Trialogus," iii. chap. lxxxi.
† Cfr. "Fasciculi," 1–104, and especially 133–181.
‡ The "Doctrinale" was written before 1422, as proved by the mention it makes of Henry V., then reigning. Book ii. chap. 46.
§ "Summa de Ecclesia."
‖ "Trialogus" (Venice edition 1525, p. xcvi.)
¶ Ibid., xcvii.
** S. Augustini, "De Doct. Christiana," lib. ii.—"Trialogus," lib. iii. cap. 31.
†† "Quomodo prædicabunt nisi mittantur."—Rom. x. 15.

before believing the Gospel, to have the certainty that it is a book inspired by God, and that Jesus Christ, whose doctrine and life it treats of, is the Man-God.

Wycliffe admits "that the foundation of our reverence for Holy Scripture is the Faith of the Church, which teaches us to believe that Christ, God and Man, became incarnate."* It is evident that Wycliffe is far from considering the Bible as the foundation and sole rule of Faith, but he maintains what he has repeated to satiety, that the Church and the Pope have abandoned true Christian morality, apostolic poverty, and that charters and ecclesiastical laws favourable to ambition and to anti-Christian dignities are esteemed more highly than the law laid down in the Gospel; he does not reject all the laws of the Church and of the Pope, but those which he affects to think are contrary to the Gospel.† According to him (and he is for ever reverting to the same idea) Antichrist is desirous of giving preponderance to worldly maxims; he has at his command twelve emissaries—the Cardinals, Patriarchs, Bishops, Canons, Monks, and more especially the false Friars or Mendicant Friars,‡ recently introduced. Towards the last-named, who were the most valiant champions of the Faith and his most zealous opponents, he bore a hatred so inveterate that the vilest abuse could not satisfy it. He says: "the four begging Orders are the personification of Cain." Let us see the fine proof which he gives for this:—

The Carmelites, the Augustinians, the Jacobins, and the Friars Minor, whose initials form this hateful name [Caim or Cain], pretend, in vain, to trace back their origin to the first ages of the Church, and to have received their rule from the great Saint Augustin or the patriarch Elias; they descend from Satan. Since Satan has been loosed, the faith of Scripture has been cast aside, and the friars go defending heresy, blaspheming Jesus Christ and the law of His Gospel, debasing, in our esteem, the Pope and Court of Rome, infecting prelates, nobles, priests, and all the people.§

Wycliffe accuses them of fostering the spirit of domineering and acquisition in the Vicars of Jesus Christ. He says:—

They transfer the possession of their wealth and convents to the Roman Pontiff as to him who is nearest to Christ; thus do they develop in the Church the spirit of the world, contrary to that of Christ, and they are dar‑‑‑‑‑us to States, and especially to England; for

---

* "Fundamentum is Christus Deus et homo
† "Tunc Scriptura debent, forent postposi sententiæ . . . . forer
‡ Book iv. chap. 26

·riæ est fides Ecclesiæ qua credimus quia ·natus."
in reverentia et bullæ papales, sicut ·ges papales quam doctorum novorum ibus veneratæ."
§ *Ibid.*, p. cii.

if a more evil Antichrist, such as Robert of Geneva, should succeed in bringing under his sway a greater number of friars than belong to the true Pope, what is there to hinder him from invading the Kingdom and taking it for himself?*

VI.

Clearly Wycliffe is a man of one idea, and if he have no system of theology capable of being compared with that of the Reformers of the sixteenth century, if he do not reject the doctrine of the Primacy, he overwhelms the Popes with a torrent of the low-tongued eloquence which has ever characterized the rebellious children of Holy Church. There is not a single passage to be found throughout the "Trialogus," Wycliffe's principal work, from which Protestants can infer that he ever considered the Bible as the Rule of Faith. This assertion is important.

The whole Reformation is based on the fundamental principle that Holy Scripture requires no authoritative interpretation whatever, and that in itself it is all-sufficient for the faithful. It is true, as proved by history, that it was not till much later that this principle was adopted; even the Confession of Augsburg (1530), drawn up ten years after the revolt of Luther, does not mention it. The necessity of fixing a base in discussions with Catholic theologians, and the hope of securing unity of doctrine amongst Protestants, were the real causes which led the Reformers to bring forward this theory, the weakness of which was so soon to be demonstrated by the religious dissensions it bred. The historical origin of this theory has not, as far as we know, attracted sufficient notice; it can by attentive study be found in the works and life of Wyckliffe; and from this study we may draw the conclusion that, from an historical point of view, the whole Reformation is based on a wretched equivocation: *it took for a Rule of Faith that which fifteen centuries had accepted only as a Rule of Morals.* The law of Christianity is the law of the Gospel; no one denies this. The Bible is the rule of our conduct; this, again, no one doubts. The faithful ought to know and reverence—above all, they ought to observe—this divine law. On all this Protestants and Catholics alike agree. The point on which they disagree is: Is the Bible not only the rule for our conduct, but is it likewise the rule, and only rule, of our faith? Catholics deny this, and for nineteen cen-

testants assert it, and within three centuries they have split into innumerable sects, through private interpretation of the Bible.

Had Protestantism any precursors during the fifteen preceding centuries? Can its fundamental dogma be traced back through these to the Apostles? This most interesting question finds, in part, an answer in our present study of Wyckliffe. Under pretext of affording a remedy to the woes of the Church, which they did but aggravate, sects had arisen who made a parade of commending the Word of God and the pure Gospel; it was an attempt made with good intentions perhaps, but which could only succeed if the claims of authority were guaranteed, and the project itself placed under the control of that same authority. Too often it was accompanied by deplorable disturbances. Since the time of Innocent III.* copies of the Bible had been distributed with a view to reform, and, as Latin had ceased to be the vulgar tongue, translations—and not very exact ones—were made. Waldenses, Albigenses, Fraticellis devoted themselves to the triumph of the pure Gospel, and it is most remarkable that all these sects came to discover in the Gospel the absolute condemnation of riches, and the dangerous errors of the Manichæans. They declared "that it was the evil principle which had introduced into the Church the thirst for earthly possessions and the abuse of the world condemned by Jesus Christ. Neither Jesus Christ nor his disciples possessed anything in private: to possess is to be guilty of evil." What did the Church do? Did she condemn the Bible, as has been pretended by certain leaders of the Reformation? Did she condemn the translation of the Bible into the vulgar tongue, and the reading of the Bible? No; she only condemned translations made without the sanction of pastors, and such false interpretations as were the outcome of private opinion.

In England, also, the teaching of Christian morality by the clergy had seemed inadequate to a certain number of over-excited minds, and, before Wycliffe's time, portions of the Bible had been translated into English. These renderings were rather paraphrases than translations†, and Wycliffe tells us that they provoked the censure of the Bishops.‡ The latter, as a measure of prudence, prohibited them, and roused Wycliffe's indignation. He writes:—

Who has least love for Christ, who is an object of detestation in the

---

* Lib. ii. "Epistol.," 141, 142 (Baluze's edition), i., pp. 432, 435.—Migne, P. L., 214, p. 695.
† Lewis, "History of the English Translations," 1739, p. 12.
‡ Wycliffe, "In Prologo Explic. Orat. Domin. apud Usserum Armacanum, de Script. vernac. auctarium,"

sight of God, if not the man that hinders the translation of the Bible? Such an one is Satan, the enemy of Christ. .... Worldly priests pretend that the Bible, read in English, leads to discord in the Christian Republic, and incites subjects to take up arms against their Princes, and that for this reason it is not to be allowed to the laity. Alas! how can they calumniate more shamelessly the authority of God and the peace and holiness of the Law!

His indignation notwithstanding, the pure Gospel, and the dogma of ecclesiastical poverty which was supposed to be therein inculcated, gave rise to only too many disorders in England. In his turn he published a translation of the New Testament, fully persuaded that it would lead to the triumphant realization of his dreams of reform, and the guidance of morality.* This translation was condemned and prohibited in 1408 by the Council of Oxford, as having been made without the sanction of the proper authorities.†

Any one desirous of forming an exact idea of the teaching of this Reformer in relation to Catholic doctrine respecting the Primacy, yet wishing to reconcile, as far as possible, the contradictions into which he fell, would have to keep in mind the keynote to all his works: "The maxim of the Gospel has been cast aside, the clergy and the Pope no longer being solicitous of imitating the poverty and humility of the Saviour, and giving themselves up to the world and to all things condemned by Jesus Christ; let us lead back the Church to the Gospel." We will, from this point of view, take a brief survey of the other treatises written by Wycliffe against the Church and the Pope; an explanation can be found for all they contain.

"De Christo et Antichristo," cap. v.* we read :—

Jesus Christ is, according to the testimony of Holy Scripture, the Head of the Church, and this name was given to Him for His own; usurpers, blinded by their pride, wish to give this name to Peter and the Popes; not only do they style them Head of the militant Church, but they rank them higher than the angels by declaring them Head of the triumphant Church. Simon received the name of Cephas: by what right is the interpretation of St. Jerome rejected in order to

---

* *Cfr.* Todd, "Apology for Lollard Doctrines," p. xx.—Shirley, "Fasciculi," p. 530

† Mansi, 1784, . 1038. "Statuimus .... et ordinamus ut nemo deinceps ali: :tum Sacræ Scripturæ *auctoritate sua* in linguam Anglicana iam transferat .... nec legatur aliquis hujusmodi liber riter tempore dicti Joannis Wyclif sive citra compositus aut is .... quoadusque .... translatio fuerit approbata."

‡ Buddens· Dresden: Teubner, p. 41.

maintain that this word signifies head? It symbolizes strength, stability, but in no wise elevation, sovereignty.*

If we were to separate the above from its context, we should naturally be led to misapprehend his opinions, and to infer from the audacious tone of his language that Wycliffe denied that the Pope was Head of the Church; elsewhere, as Thomas of Walden remarks,† he has declared him to be Head of the Church,‡ but at that moment he was doubtless in a calmer mood and less preoccupied with false humility; now, filled with the idea of leading back the Pope to the Gospel-law, he rejects a title which, to his mind, savours of domination;§ he reserves this name for Our Lord, and neither Peter nor his successors may assume it.

Again (*ibid.*, cap. vi.) after acknowledging that Peter was the Vicar of Jesus Christ, he hesitates at some difficulties which have perplexed several Fathers of the Church and afforded much satisfaction to disingenuous heretics: all the Apostles owned the prerogative of personal infallibility and a jurisdiction extending over the whole earth; St. Paul opposed St. Peter to his face on a matter of practical discipline; St. James was Bishop of Jerusalem, that See being reckoned the highest, &c. What does he conclude from all this? The negation of the Primacy? No, at the end of the chapter he returns to the point, and owns that St. Peter was in some respects superior to the other Apostles, but this excellence had been conferred on him as a pure gift, and by reason of his remarkable humility.‖ Refusing, as he does, the title of Head of the Church to the Pope, he will end by rejecting the word "Pope." This word seems to convey an idea of power and dignity that might induce pride; he says: "Pope and Cardinals, these are not of divine institution; they are not in the Gospel [as though *Papa* were not derived from "*pasce oves meas*"] they are diabolical inventions dating from the donation of

---

* Isidore, "Etymol.," lib. vii. cap. 9, putting aside the explanation of St. Jerome (in "Epist. ad Gal.," lib. i., cap. 2), who translates κηφᾶς and the corresponding Syriac word as *petra*, confounds it with κεφαλή.

† "Doctrinale," lib. ii. c. 1.

‡ "De Dotatione Ecclesiæ," cap. v. "Pasce oves meas: Quod quia Petrus fecit excellentius, fuit constitutus Caput Ecclesiæ."

§ More than one Wycliffite or Hussite writer of this time was affected by the same folly (Von der Hardt, i. p. 70): "Nec istius ecclesiæ papa potest dici caput, sed solum vicarius Christi." The treatise, "De Modis Uniendi" (*Ibid.*, 74–78) is full of these notions of Wycliffe: "Papa non est supra Evangelium—Papa est deponendus." According to Schwab, this has been attributed w— ⸺y to Gerson.

‖ *Ibid.*, p. 42. The⸺ ⸺n Thomas Waldensis runs: "Petrus alios in aliquo excedebat cum⸺ sit quod verbum Christi singulariter dictum Petro, fuit doctrina e⸺ ⸺r sequenti Ecclesiæ militanti. Sed si fuit Petri excellentia simp⸺ per alios, hoc fuit ex Dei gratia et propter meritum humilitatis.

Constantine,* and if the term 'pope' implies the idea of this donation it must be rejected."

Lastly (*ibid.*, cap. vii.) in accepting Constantine's gift, Pope Sylvester sinned, because he departed from the spirit of the Gospel and, in opposition to the intention of Jesus Christ, laid the foundation of an earthly power. Elsewhere he says there is nothing to justify the rule that Christ's Vicar should reside in Rome unless indeed it be that there he slays souls, as tyrants formerly killed the bodies of the martyrs, and that there dwelt the Cæsar who, in spite of the law of Christ, endowed the Church and the Popes.† It is true, he hesitates somewhat: he declares himself ready to retract, if required,‡ but soon his mania for apostolic poverty seizes him, and impels him to fresh denunciations against Antichrist; nothing will content him but a Pope like to those who governed the Church before the gift of Constantine. In truth the pen refuses to epitomize the rest of this treatise, and to reiterate twenty times the same denunciations; one seeks in vain for some fruitful idea, some sound doctrine amidst this tissue of exaggeration and hateful falsehood. We will explore no further, lest our readers weary of listening to the croakings of this ill-boding raven, "Antichrist reigns; cockle abounds in the field of the Lord; scarcely can one find one just man among thousands of reprobates." Evidently he believed himself at the end of the world!

VII.

Before Luther's time, about half a century after Wycliffe had worked out his scheme for a spurious reformation and published his absurd pretensions of leading Christendom back to the law of the Gospel and the imitation of Jesus Christ by the paths of criminal revolt, a man, humble and simple, whose name was to be blessed by future generations, was also working with his pen in favour of a reform in morals; Thomas à Kempis wrote in his first chapter of the "Imitation" §: "If thou didst know the whole Bible by heart what would it profit thee without the love of God and His grace?" And he made the title of the second chapter: "Of having a humble opinion of oneself." He also recommended the reading of Holy Scripture, but he added: "It is a very great

in thine own sentiments, but be ready also with pleasure to hear those of others."* He advocated self-denial, poverty, and the imitation of our Lord Jesus Christ; but he knew how to distinguish between the state of perfection—that is, practice of the evangelical counsels—and the ordinary Christian life, or keeping the Commandments. How much more did not the humble brother of common life contribute towards a reform of morals in the members of the Church than did Wycliffe!

The last document of the heresiarch is deserving of the attention of our readers. In 1384 he was summoned to Rome to justify himself before Pope Urban VI. Already struck with paralysis,† he was soon to appear before his Supreme Judge, and he was unable to attempt the journey. We have the letter he wrote on this occasion,‡ and doubtless he bestowed on it that mature reflection absent from so many of his other writings. If we examine it we shall find there the substance and epitome of his teaching :—

I take much pleasure in manifesting my faith to the whole world and especially to the Roman Pontiff, because I hold (" suppono," I lay down as basis; this is also the meaning of the word later on) that if my faith be orthodox, he will ratify it humbly, and if it be erroneous, he will correct it.

This introduction is not written by a man rebelling against Pontifical authority. Who does not see in the words "fidem confirmabit" an allusion to the promise made to St. Peter : " I have prayed for thee that thy faith fail not, and thou, being once converted, confirm thy brethren, ' confirma fratres tuos.' "§ He does not miss the opportunity of reminding the Pope of the virtue of humility.

Now I hold that the Gospel is the substance of the law of God, and I believe that Christ, who Himself gave us this Gospel, is true God and true Man, and that, therefore, the law of the Gospel is greater than all other Scripture.

Does Wycliffe here accept the Bible as the sole rule of Faith? Not at all: such is not his meaning, for he says: " Christ did not write or give the *Book* of the Bible, He gave His Gospel"— that is to say, the New Law: a law that in Wycliffe's eyes is above all a law of self-denial and poverty—a law, according to him, above all charters, all written endowments, all Papal Bulls. The Reformer affects to condemn contempt for and neglect of the Gospel. This the Catholic Church condemns as much as he, but without deducing the exaggerated conclusions to which his

---

* Chapter ix. † " Fasciculi," xlv.
‡ *Ibid.*, p. 341. § S. Luke xxii. 32.

indiscreet zeal led him. This explanation is borne out by the sequel.

I hold, secondly, that the Roman Pontiff, being the supreme Vicar of Christ on earth, is required, more than other men, to keep this law of the Gospel. For among the disciples of Christ greatness is not reckoned by the standard of earthly greatness, but by the imitation of the life of Christ. Moreover, from the very heart of the law of God I deduce this evident truth, that during His life on this earth Christ was a very poor man, rejecting all worldly sway. This is evident on the faith of the Gospel (Matt. viii. 20 ; 2 Cor. viii. 9).

I conclude from the above that no Christian should imitate the Pope or any Saint except inasmuch as they imitate the Lord Jesus Christ, for Peter, Paul, and the sons of Zebedee sinned by coveting—contrary to this law of imitation—wordly dignities, and for this reason they are not to be imitated in the above error.

From all this I conclude, by way of counsel,* that the Pope should leave all temporal government to the Secular Power, and efficaciously persuade his clergy to do the same : for it was thus Christ explicitly taught his apostles.

It is evident that Wycliffe does not dream of denying the Spiritual Authority; he does not even deduce the necessity of depriving the Pope and clergy of all benefices or worldly possessions ; he restricts himself to wishing that the Spiritual Power should deprive itself, not of the enjoyment of earthly goods, but of proprietorship and temporal sway. His language is more measured; reflection and the approach of death have brought calm. He concludes this exposition of his doctrine as follows :—

If in this I have erred, I wish, with all humility, to be punished even with death. And if, in accordance with my desire, I might set forth on a journey, I would humbly go to the Roman Pontiff. But God has made this thing impossible, and has taught me to obey, generally, God rather than men. Since God has given to our Pope desires that are right and in conformity with the Gospel, we would beg of him that these desires should not be stifled by traitorous counsels, and that neither Pope nor Cardinals should be impelled to do aught against the law of the Lord. We pray, then, to the Master of all creatures, that He would excite our Pope, Urban VI., with his clergy, to the imitation of the life of Jesus Christ, that they may effectually teach the people to imitate them in this. In spirit we ask the Pope to withhold himself f   il counsel, for we know that the enemies of man dwell within h   od does not allow us to be tempted beyond our strength, mu·   loes He exact from any creature more than they are able to   : this is evidently the characteristic of Antichrist.

---

elicio tanquam consilium."

These last lines are sufficiently incoherent. On the 29th of December, 1384, as he was hearing Mass in his church at Lutterworth, Wycliffe was struck with death. Paralysis deprived him of speech, and he died two days later, carrying with him into eternity the responsibility of the riots which his teaching had helped to foment, and of the disturbances which his disciples were soon to cause in Bohemia.

VIII.

It has been said that Wycliffe was the precursor of Luther, and the morning star of the Reformation; to an earnest and Christian mind, seeking seriously the true Church, these are but deceitful words. The morning star makes not the day; the light—the true light of the Sun of Justice—dates from the foundation of the Church on Pentecost Day, and the preaching of the Prince of the Apostles, to whom our Lord had said, "Feed My sheep." If the Reformed Church is content with looking upon itself as a sect risen in revolt against the true Church of Jesus Christ, we allow it to claim Wycliffe, and many other so-called reformers; for such have risen up in all ages; and all heretics who, after appealing to the Apostolic See, have refused to submit themselves to this highest tribunal of the Militant Church might be claimed by the Reformation just as well as Wycliffe. But if our separate Protestant brethren pretend to be the true Church of Jesus Christ, reaching back by an uninterrupted succession in unity of faith to her divine Founder, and built up on the basis of private interpretation of the Bible, then Wycliffe does not belong to them. In the midst of much error, blasphemy, and fanatic revolt, he extolled the Holy Gospel and did not reject tradition. He attacked authority in its representatives, but not in its principle; he denied that the Pope and clergy had a right of property in the riches of this world; he never contested the existence of the Spiritual Authority. His chief error as to the incompatibility of authority with sin led him to contest the legitimacy of the Popes and Bishops of his time; carried away by this illusion, he strove to recall them to the poverty he considered essential to their character as successors of the Apostles, he never put forward the principle that forms the basis of Protestantism.

Luther himself has made this remark in his "Table-Talk:" "Wycliffe attacked the morals, the Reform has attacked the doctrine of the Roman Church." This distinction is a true one. As it is a leading one in the matter of the sources of the Reformation, we will support it by a rapid sketch of the doctrines professed by the Wycliffites:—

1. The conclusion to suppress all authority in the Church

might be legitimately drawn from several of the propositions of their Master. They rejected this conclusion as exceeding the aim and intentions of Wycliffe, who, they said, had no wish to destroy the divine order of things, but only to condemn abuses.*

2. In an apology for the Lollards which Todd attributed to Wycliffe,† and which is certainly contemporary with him, the sectarian's doctrine is explained in the sense we have assigned to it: the Pope is the Vicar of Christ or of Peter, but only when he does not act in contradiction to the law of God. The writer strives to prove this proposition, which, to say the least, is suspicious, by the teaching of the Fathers; to support this view he quotes the text in St. John: "Feed My sheep;" he maintains that the Popes then reigning were Antichrists. In no work of his do we find the Protestant error as to the Rule of Faith.

3. John Huss, the leading disseminator of Wycliffe's teaching in Bohemia, does not deny the Primacy, but, like his master, refused to style the Pope Head of the Church (a title which he reserved for Our Lord), allowing him merely that of Vicar of Christ. When attacked at the Council of Constance for his proposition asserting that the Papal power was derived from the Roman Emperors, he brought forward his writings to prove that he alluded only to the outward dignity and temporal authority, that he had not denied the Divine source of the Spiritual power.‡ He even admitted that God continues to act through the medium of the Pope, however unworthy he may be, because he is the legitimate Vicar of Jesus Christ. This was the teaching of the disciples, this had been the teaching of their master.

A century and a half was to elapse before this conservative dogma of Christianity, this principle of Spiritual Authority or Papal Primacy, was to be swept away by the Reformers; but experience has shown that no Christian Church can find a firm basis outside that fundamental rock on which Jesus Christ built His Church. Whilst sects, treading the paths of dogmatic reform, have condemned themselves to overthrow every tenet of Christian faith, the Catholic Church, under the authoritative guidance of her Pontiffs, has brought about a reform in morals which has increased Her lustre and, in certain respects, Her strength, so that she is more resplendent and powerful than she ever was before the time of Wycliffe and Henry VIII. Even in the present day, when States ignore Her and persecute Her in the persons of Her Head and clergy, she grows and flourishes. Never

---

* "Patronum antistitum quos Thom. Wald.,] Wycliffe nolle exterminium sacrorum Christi itantiam ordinis sed ad damnationem abusus."— p. 57.

† "Apology , pp. 1 and 5. Cfr. Introduction, xix., lxi.
‡ Von der . . 316.

was Her divine character of unity more distinctly apparent, never was the authority of the Sovereign Pontiff more revered and respected by Her children. It would seem that God had chosen an epoch when sectarianism betrays its incurable weakness to make manifest Papal authority in all its splendour, in order to clearly prove that the safeguard and permanence of Christianity rest on reverence for the Primacy. The more Christianity enlarges its sphere the deeper-rooted grows its centre. Our hope for the future of the Holy Church of Jesus Christ revives in seeing that the principle and centre of unity grow stronger in the Christian world. "There shall be one fold and one Shepherd." A day will dawn when there will be in all Christendom but one fold and one shepherd.

L. DELPLACE, S.J.

ART. III.—LIBERTY, LAISSER-FAIRE, AND LEGISLATION.

1. *Essays in Political Economy, Theoretical and Applied.* By J. E. CAIRNES. 1873.
2. *The Principles of Political Economy.* By HENRY SIDGWICK, author of "The Methods of Ethics." London: Macmillan & Co. 1883.
3. *Laissez-Faire and Government Interference.* The Opening Address of the Edinburgh Philosophical Institution. By the Right Hon. G. J. GOSCHEN, M.P. Macmillan & Co.
4. *Lord Bramwell on Liberty.* London: 1883.

IT has been generally felt that Lord Salisbury in his recent article on the housing of the poor, has brought to the front problems of far greater scope and importance than the special subject-matter of his contribution to the *National Review.*

I am not regarding the political aspect of the new departure, which enemies style "the Conservative plunge;" nor the anxious fears of orthodox Tories, who suddenly and without preparation were thus summoned to cross the Rubicon—with the particular evil there discussed, and the special remedies suggested, it is not my purpose here to deal. My subject has rather to do with the almost hidden assumption underlying Lord Salisbury's reasonings, than with those reasonings themselves. That assumption comes to light for a moment when he declares that the principle of "laisser-faire" cannot be pleaded in bar of Government interference; that "laisser-faire" must be applied on both sides. But without seeking to twist phrases, it would not be unfair to say that Lord Salisbury's arguments are entirely based on expediency. He sets up no law of natural liberty against State action, if, on the whole, State action is likely to do good. He would appear to think, with Buret, that when the doctrine of "laisser-faire" is advanced to obstruct measures for the relief of squalor and penury, it should be held equivalent to "Laissez faire la misère, laissez passer la mort." Mr. Goschen in like manner recognizes the hopelessness nowadays of advancing any such principle against paternal legislation. The doctrine he seems to imply, in the striking address delivered in October last at the Edinburgh Philosophical Institution, became defunct after the golden age of the eighteenth-century physiocrats, and its attempted revival by English economists was too ghostlike and sepulchral to stand in the way of bustling philanthropists backed up by the moral sympathies of the masses.

It seems hardly necessary to quote from advanced Liberals for the purpose of showing that the old cry of "Liberty" is no longer the watchword of the Democratic camp. Their support of "Free Trade" and denunciations of Protection form only an apparent exception, for it is very plain that trade is free, and our ports are open in England solely because upon balancing the contentions for and against, we are content to believe that such a system conduces either to a greater production, or a more equable distribution, of wealth; certainly not because freedom in this respect, apart from its advantages, is *per se* to be desired. Mr. Cobden and Mr. John Bright knew far too well the temper of the English people to advance arguments of that kind; both in the House of Commons and on provincial platforms the battle was fought and won without a solitary appeal to the abstract principle of natural liberty. Apparently, as I have said, the Radicals are satisfied they need no longer take their stand on such high ground. Their performances, their projects, their prophecies all point in quite another direction: to a tendency to make little of vested rights or of individual responsibility if they stand in the way of a scheme for promoting the *general good* of the community or of a class. All the more important legislative acts of the past few years are of this stamp. The Irish Land Acts, the Education Acts, the Merchant Shipping Acts (better known when associated with the name of Plimsoll), the Employers' Liability Act, and a host of minor measures. It is true that "Free Land, Free Labour, Free Schools" is the programme of ad\   d Liberals; but, as I hope to show later on, this is the w   abuse of the primary meaning of the term "free." It is   ient for the present to point out that the tendency of pu   pinion expressed by men of rival political camps is to place a robust faith in the efficacy of State action, to extend the sphere of Government interference not merely into new fields of business—such, for instance, as telegraphy and electric lighting—but into the relations of classes, and the private transactions of individuals; to hold that self-interest must be made subject to the aggregate moral sense and sympathies of the nation.

The individual withers and the world is more and more.

An extended franchise gives expression to feelings which it is not paradoxical to say have in combination a far greater force than the mere sum of individual opinions would seem to warrant.* Time was when the saying, "in corruptissimâ reipublica plurimæ leges" would have been a fair measure of average British political opinion; now-a-days, to judge from fierce complaints about "obstruction," and the common type of criticism used on public platforms, a Government is praised or blamed as the number and extent of its Bills passed is greater or less. Are, then, the old allied cries of "liberty" and "laisser faire" really extinct; have they passed to the limbo of forgotten phrases? Have they shared the fate, the natural fate, of all appeals to the practical, shall we say Philistine, mind of the British electorate, when founded on an abstract idea, and not plainly concerning the near and dear claims of health, pocket, or prejudice? The truth probably is that the doctrine is rather dormant than dead. Signs of awakening are even now not absent. Here and there is heard the still small voice of the political economist, struggling again to raise the old watchword; at intervals there appears in the *Pall Mall Gazette* or the *Times* a letter signed significantly " B.," or with some other easily deciphered anonym; and within the last few months we have had addressed to us the solemn warnings of an independent statesman at Edinburgh. But this is by no means all. The friends of liberty have lately not been content with isolated efforts, and being men of intelligence, and conscious of the advantages of united action, they have endeavoured to give

---

* Add to this a consideration not to be lost sight of, which is put forward in a recent article in this REVIEW on "County Administration:" "With the increased rapidity of communication there has come not only the possibility of knowing the difficulties and burdens of far-off heathen, but a strange quickening of human sympathies. The tale of distant disaster which once would have fallen on careless ears, now rouses the same angry impatience to help the suffering or to strike down the wrongdoer as though it were close to our doors. This willingness on the part of the public to take up every difficulty as their own, and as something calling directly for the intervention of the State, leads naturally to a gradual narrowing of the sphere of individual freedom and the sure sacrifice of local liberties."—*County Administration*, DUBLIN REVIEW, April, 1882, p. 322.

their views a corporate life and a corporate dignity. They observe that the dissociated efforts of individuals to check the tyranny of majorities, and the thoughtless intermeddling of Parliament with private rights, may reach the height of heroism, but are plainly ineffectual to stem the tide. Wisely, therefore, have they ceased to wail and prophesy in loneliness, but, combining their forces, they have founded a "Liberty and Property Defence League," whose mission is to preserve individual rights and individual freedom from the assaults of an overweening Legislature.

The League purports to represent every class and creed of the social and political world—the poor and the rich, the employers and the employed, Tories militant and Tories old-fashioned and immovable, Radicals philosophic and Radicals philanthropic, city and county potentates, lawyers, and even champions of the rights of labour. I have before me a list of members; it includes the Chairman of the Pawnbrokers' National Defence Association, the Parliamentary Agent of the Licensed Victuallers' National Defence League, the Chairman of the Music Hall Proprietors' Protection Association, and a hundred other important functionaries. Their principles are summed up in a phrase which has recently acquired a certain fame, "freedom of contract." The origin of this watchword appears to be wrapt in obscurity. Probably economists and lawyers have an equal share in its invention. There is no doubt that it was effectually used by the so-called "orthodox" economists of the school of Adam Smith, who, in the first half of this century, preached the pure and unadulterated doctrine of "laisser-faire." It is to be noticed that "freedom of contract" has little in common with the social contract doctrine of Rousseau, or the "natural liberty" of Locke. The term in its modern use is not at all meant to give an explanation of the development of civilized society. The Liberty and Property Defence League, it is fair to say, does not profess any abstract views on the rights of man, and claims no kinship with the French philosophers of the eighteenth century. The economists, I have said, brought the doctrine into prominence, but it is probable that "freedom of contract" first appeared as a tenet of jurisprudence. In the mouth of a jurist it would mean that within the limits of decency and morality adult men should be allowed to ··· upon what bargains they pleased, and should be held to su ·rgains. I have said that the cry has been raised with new r in the last few years; perhaps its use may be said to e with the first public measures of the present Govern· The existing Liberal Ministry (so the champions of free lare) have given us the most signal examples of libert\ ed rights disregarded and violated and sacrificed to class interests. The reader will remember how during the debates in Parliament within the last three years on the Employers' Liability Act, the Ground Game Act (known in its embryo stage as the Hares and Rabbits Bill), and, above all, the Irish Land Act, a strenuous and unrelenting opposition was given to these measures, based solely on their supposed interference with vested rights of property or with "freedom of contract," quite apart from considerations of expediency. From the same standpoint Professor Bonamy Price declared that to adopt the doctrine of the three F's in the projected Irish land reform would be to banish political economy to Jupiter and Saturn. Year by year we have evidence, it is said, of the savage and unscrupulous violation of the fundamental principle of liberty in the measures of the present Government, and never, perhaps, so openly cast aside as in the last session. I have the volume of Statutes for 1883 before me, and it is not to be denied that the list is formidable. It includes the Payment of Wages in Public Houses Prohibition Act, 1883, which met with the scathing sarcasm of Lord Bramwell; the Merchant Shipping (Fishing Boats) Act, 1883, regulating not only the apprenticeship of boys in the fishing trade, but making elaborate provisions for the payment of wages of adult fishermen, the methods of engaging and discharging them from service, and for enforcing discipline and obedience on board fishing-boats, of inquiry in cases of death, injury, ill-treatment, punishment, and casualty. There is, again, the Factory and Workshop Act of this year, which, for instance, makes it a condition to certain kinds of factories being certified as fit for use "that there be provided for the use of persons employed in the factory sufficient means of frequently washing hands and feet with a sufficient supply of hot and cold water, soap, towels, and brushes . . . ."

Finally, and above all, the Agricultural Holdings Act, 1883, is cited as an open and undisguised interference with the free action of men under no duress, imposition, or compulsion. It is to be noticed that complaints of legislation of this kind are sometimes not in terms founded on an asserted breach of the doctrine of "liberty," or "freedom of contract," but take a more popular shape. They are not unfrequently summed up in those cant commonplaces which govern the political instincts of ruder minds, and sometimes satisfy intelligent men who dislike the trouble of thinking. Such is the familiar saying that you cannot make men virtuous by Acts of Parliament, and such the growling diatribes against "paternal" and "grandmotherly" legislation that are so appreciated in provincial political gatherings. Apart from a burning question of the hour, no topic is so generally certain to "go down" at a public meeting as a condemnation of too dominant State-power. References, full of pity and disdain, to the despotic and centralized Governments of France and Germany never fail to provoke applause. Mr. Matthew Arnold has, to his own satisfaction at least, measured the length and breadth of the stereotyped opinions of the middle classes of the country, and his explanation on this head is curious. After noticing that Protestant Dissenters form the kernel of the English middle class, he states that—

> In the minds of that class State-action in social and domestic concerns became inextricably associated with the idea of a Conventicle Act, a Five-Mile Act, an Act of Uniformity. Their abhorrence of such a State-action as this they extended to State-action in general; and having never known a beneficent and just State-power they enlarged their hatred of a cruel and partial State-power, the only one they had ever known, into a maxim that no State-power was to be trusted, that the least action in certain provinces was rigorously to be denied to the State whenever the denial was possible."—*Mixed Essays*, p. 31.

If one might be disrespectful to so great an authority this would be styled wild reasoning; but this I leave for the present. What I am upon is to show the curious inconsistency of public opinion upon this question. In the abstract, the meddlesomeness of Government is heartily denounced; but it needs only an explosion, a wreck, a railway accident, to rouse loud calls for State supervision. Perhaps this apparent contradiction and looseness of thought may be explained by examining the uses and meanings put upon the term "liberty." Of "laisser-faire" as involving any fundamental principle it is not necessary to treat separately, as the larger term "liberty" includes its main features. A very slight and brief examination will show that a multitude of distinct, independent, and even contradictory ideas have been covered by the word "liberty," a fact largely explaining its present shifty and indeterminate denotation. There can be little doubt that we must look back a hundred years for the period when the theory and cry of liberty had the largest sphere of action and vitality. Then it was the grand maxim appealed to by our colonists in America during their struggle for independence; in F   ، it helped to the overturning and reconstruction of Go   ent, laws, and society; in our own country foreign abuse   cry stirred up Burke, by speech and letter and pamphle   ierely to denounce in gorgeous, undying rhetoric the   is of Rousseau and his school, but to employ his weight   in delaying Parliamentary reform a half-century; it   ;e place in the speculations of philosophers who woul   y on self-interest; and, in another shape, was the most popular and effective doctrine of the economic school of Adam Smith.

On the surface, the rising in America was but a struggle for a dry constitutional right, and the Revolution in France merely the wild, aimless answer of the oppressed masses to the exactions of a tyrannous caste; but events proved that in both countries the contention was, in great part, for the realization of a definite idea. In each case the struggle in the end was quite as pointedly aimed at individual liberty, the enforcing of the rights of man, as at freeing of class or country from servitude or exaction. The Declaration of Independence in America was prefaced by the grand principle that "all men are born free;" and it may be said that the new Constitution of the States is soaked with this idea; whilst it appears as the governing and inspiring principle in the universal suffrage and new code of laws in Republican France.

I am not forgetting that at the end of last century the cry of liberty was inseparable from that of equality, and considered complementary to it, though, as I hope to show later on, the two dogmas are in many respects inconsistent. Perhaps they came to be used together owing to their common origin and common use as judicial maxims in Imperial Rome—a source from which the French propagandists freely borrowed. Sir Henry Maine has pointed out that the grand maxim, " omnes homines naturâ æquales sunt," was a fundamental dogma of mature Roman jurisprudence, which ignored the old privileges of citizenship, and recognized the claims of foreigners to civil and legal rights.

It is not improbable that the doctrine of individual freedom had a similar legal origin, expressing the disregard of Roman tribunals for commands, or threats, or penalties which possessed no legal sanction, not without reference to the removal of restraints then imposed upon the servile class respecting contract and ownership.

In our own time no writer has reasoned out the theory of liberty with such plausibility and earnestness as J. S. Mill, whose form of the doctrine is thus summed up :—" That the individual is not accountable to society for his actions so far as they concern the interests of no person but himself, and that he may be subjected to social or legal punishments for such actions only as are prejudicial to others."

The days of force and of compulsion, to his mind, have passed away, and the controlling weapons of society should be reason and persuasion. Here let it suffice to say, that Mill's theory ignores admitted rights of individuals in modern society—rights which extend far beyond protection from injury; that it does not accord with Mr. Mill's own views on utilitarianism; that it takes far too little account of the effects of ignorance, prejudice, or blind adherence to routine; that it is a bare assumption to declare that the greatest average individual development will follow from the greatest freedom from restraint; that such a theory has no place for the important virtues of obedience, deference to authority, and self-discipline.

Moreover, Mill's qualification of his thesis which admits the influence of social restraints—"the unfavourable judgment of others"—merely substitutes one form of coercion for another: a coercion intermittent, undefined, and unprincipled, for one fixed, visible, and defined.

Mr. Herbert Spencer has expressed the doctrine of liberty in a formula which is compact, terse, and to all appearance very simple. As stated by him in his "Social Statics," this "first principle" runs thus: "Every man has freedom to do all that he wills provided he infringes not the equal freedom of any other man."* To attempt a full criticism of this dogma in all its aspects would be to exceed my purpose and space-limits. It will occur, however, at once to the reader that this theory does not fit in with the facts. No form of civilization that ever yet has appeared could have endured for a day if Mr. Spencer's principle were applied to the full, whatever may happen when "the completely-adapted man in the completely-evolved society comes into existence." Take, for instance, a man's right to his fair fame or his freedom from personal assault. Neither of these undeniable rights can be allowed or justified upon Mr. Spencer's simple doctrine, which must go to this extent, that a man may take away my character by every form of malicious libel, because I am "equally free" to retort upon him with like weapons; further, that I have no right to complain if I am knocked down in the street by a bully, if he is pleased to refrain from totally disabling me, as then I am "free" to get up and do to him as he has done to me. Evidently "the completely adapted man in the completely-evolved society" will not be deterred from committing breaches of the peace through fear of infringing Mr. Spencer's law.

But it is of little purpose dwelling on considerations of this kind, as this first

his fellows. It is only when his action begins to interfere with his neighbour's capacity to do a similar action that it becomes necessary to make a dividing line, to define the neutral territory into which neither A nor B may trespass; and this it is obvious we shall fail to do if A's rights are first determined by the duties of B., and then *vice versâ*. Mr. Spencer's particular dogma must, of course, not be separated from the broader principles of the evolution theory, which shortly come to this : that a perfect state of society is that in which the members have the greatest average amount of liberty of action. Happiness, it is contended, consists mainly in unfettered *energizing ;* to remove restraints on freedom is, in the general result, equivalent to enlarging the sphere of pleasurable living. It may indeed be necessary, Evolutionists would say, to have checks and restraints on liberty—society could not exist without them; but the grand end and aim of a system of government should be to secure to the greatest possible number the greatest possible freedom of action.

Without attempting to criticize (as beside the present purpose) a doctrine of happiness which makes pleasurable living the "summum bonum," it is sufficient to notice that we are left as far off as ever from a clear insight as to what the doctrine of liberty either is or ought to be. On the other hand, the assumptions and reasoning of Evolutionists seem to open up a mass of nice and intricate problems; one is inclined to wish they would explain their explanation. It may be asked, for instance, when considering the sphere of happiness, to what extent and from what point of view the welfare of future generations is to be regarded, if regarded at all; and, if this is answered, the problem arises as to the chances posterity has of acquiring the benefit we strive to secure them ; and the kind of value they will put upon our endeavours and achievements. A difficult problem will arise, for example, in respect of restraints on freedom of bequest; for it is clear the greater the liberty is allowed to a testator in disposing of his property the more fettered are his successors in their enjoyment of it. And a similar dilemma arises when the proper limits of the power of mortgaging landed property, or of the privilege of pledging the credit (by creating a national debt) of future generations, come under consideration.

And again, " freedom" has itself to be defined. Is it to be mental or physical freedom, or a judicious mixture of both? Or it may be a mere question of balancing one kind of freedom against another. It is common ground that many physical restraints imposed on us by the State in the way of sani and regulations, add far more largely to our individual than they detract from it. As to the principle that l consists in free energizing, it is clearly well to allow f for energy, provided two conditions are secured: first, that the display of energy will follow the granting room and scope for its action, (which is extremely doubtful); secondly, that the energetic action be to some extent beneficial—that it be not directed to, or result merely in, beating down or damaging those who are least able to resist its onslaught (and it would be far within the truth to style this the purest assumption). In spite of what Evolutionists preach, it is an unhappy truth that the way to fame and riches and power largely consists in cutting the ground from under a rival's feet: the battle is to the strong; and, if the fittest survive, it not unfrequently happens they are not the men of worth, but those best fitted and favoured by Nature or art in crushing and extinguishing their neighbours.

It seems impossible, in fact, to frame any simple proposition about liberty in general without descending to trivialities, such as, that it is unpleasant for a man to be prevented from doing what he has a mind to do, or commonplaces concerning the probable abuse of irresponsible power—propositions more calculated to bewilder than to enlighten the legislator. Here, as in many other instances, confusion of thought arises mainly from disregard of the plain ambiguities of words in common use. A man, it is said, has a right to his liberty. Assume for the moment that "liberty" means something accurately definable, we have yet to be told what "right," as used here, means. Is the word "right" used in Austin's sense, when he says "a party has a *right* when another, or others, are bound or obliged by the law to do or forbear towards or in regard to him?" This cannot be, for it begs the whole question. Or is "right" a claim founded on justice and expediency—what is loosely called a "moral" claim; as when it is said that agricultural labourers have a "right" to the franchise? But in this sense a man's right to liberty depends upon, and is measured by, its *proved* expediency. We are thus driven in the end to the basis of Utilitarianism, and the principle of liberty vanishes.*

Leaving out of sight considerations drawn from religion or morals—without discussing, for instance, the sphere of liberty of conscience—the so-called principle of liberty seems to resolve itself in the end into the rough test of expediency, which can be interpreted in a variety of ways, according to the view that is

clusions from the inherent evils of government by force and the natural law of liberty.

Whatever the state of society is, coercion in some shape or other must be one of its chief bonds, as long as men are born with different powers and pursue different ends. And probably the more complex and intricate the social relations the more there is need of coercion. Whether the coercing element be found in the usages of the primitive family and tribe, or public opinion, or legal rules, it is still based on force, though sometimes the working of the regulating machine is not visible. It is no doubt true, as Sir Henry Maine has pointed out, that the great movement of civilization has been from *status* to contract—that in modern society a man's rights and duties are no longer imposed on him at his birth by the rigid customs of family or tribe, or the imperative commands of the head of the clan, but mainly arise from obligations into which he has voluntarily entered with other individuals. But not unfrequently the free contract subjects the individual to the fetters and restraints of a *status*—for instance, in the ordinary agreements for domestic service and those relating to the use and occupation of land. However that may be, we observe that force is the corner-stone of the new as of the old relations. In the village community the head of the tribe, with his power of life and death, was the embodiment of that force; now it is the authority and power of the master or employer; in every case it is finally the strong arm of the State, the sheriff's officer, the bailiff, the gaoler, and the policeman. It is true the working of this sanction of force is not always visible; but its unseen or partially concealed action has probably a much larger sphere than its open interference. For instance, one contract is broken for a hundred that are performed. We see the coercion when the State awards or enforces compensation or penalty; but the force that has induced the performance or prevented the breach of the hundred completed obligations is none the less real. It may, in fact, be said that in the latter case the results show the force to have been more effectual. Nor does the suggested distinction between legal coercion and social restraint, between force and persuasion, seem logically defensible. Whether I am impelled to, or deterred from, a particular course of action by fear of a lawsuit or imprisonment, or by fear of the bad opinions, resentment, or disagreeable remarks of my neighbours, the element of force is seen in each case, the variation being not in the kind but in the amount and direction of the force, whatever particular theory of the effects of motive on the human will is adopted. Cases, moreover, will occur to every one w____ the unfavourable judgment of others is a more powerful ag____ han any dread of legal consequences. Contracts of gan____ and wagering are unenforceable in our tribunals, yet no class of business debts are probably so regularly paid by men who are not professional rogues as losses on the racecourse.

Another strange development of the theory of liberty is that which by implication, rather than in terms, connects the phrase with popular government. Tennyson, in many scattered phrases, seems to give expression to this idea. Freedom no longer stands alone on the heights, she is "broad-based upon the people's will," and "slowly broadens down from precedent to precedent"—

> Then stept she down through town and field
> To mingle with the human race,
> And part by part to men revealed
> The fulness of her face.

A broad representative system may, no doubt, make the poor man's vote equal to that of the rich; but, as long as the rule is that of the majority, those in the minority possess only the contingent freedom of adding to their numbers, turning themselves into a majority and reversing the process of compulsion. Sir James Stephen has some trenchant words on this point which tell the plain truth under a thin veil of paradox:—

Parliamentary government is simply a mild and disguised form of compulsion. We agree to try strength by counting heads instead of breaking heads, but the principle is exactly the same in each case. It is not the wisest side which wins, but the one which for the time being shows its superior strength (of which, no doubt, wisdom is one element) by enlisting the largest amount of active sympathy in its support. The minority gives way, not because it is convinced that it is wrong, but because it is a minority.

Compare Mr. Herbert Spencer,* who cannot be accused of being an enemy of liberty :—

I might dwell on the lesson presented in France, where the political cycle shows us again and again that new Democracy is but old Despotism differently spelt—where now, as heretofore, we find "Liberté, Egalité, Fraternité," conspicuous on the public buildings, and now, as heretofore, have for interpretation of these words the extremest party-hatreds, vituperations and actual assaults in the Assembly, wholesale arrests of men unfriendly to those in power, forbidding of public meetings, and suppression of journals; and where now, as heretofore, writers professing to be ardent advocates of political freedom rejoice in those ac ch shackle and gag their antagonists.

But it lly necessary to dwell upon the absence of connection I democracy and freedom when the most ardent

---

* "Study of Sociology," p. 276.

advocates of freedom give strenuous support to provisions securing what are called the rights of minorities, and shower on ratepayers the blessings of what is curiously styled Free Compulsory Education. How the term "free" ever came to be applied to such a measure as the Education Act of 1870, it is hard to conceive—to an Act which, in the plainest way, interferes with the liberty of everybody concerned, parents, children, and ratepayers. In this country it almost appears as if the epithet "free" must be dragged in *per fas et nefas*, before any proposal can hope for general support. A cry is raised for "free land," which in substance means the most violent form of compulsion; for "free labour," which demands minute supervision and control of the relations between employers and employed; and last, but not least, for "free religion." Now, "free religion," speaking roughly, comes to this (as Sir R. K. Wilson has pointed out): that certain instruction should *not* be provided at the public expense, but be left to the voluntary support of individuals; so that "freedom" here is used in just the opposite sense to that expressed by the term "free schools."

> Indeed it is a strange disposed time,
> But men may construe things after their fashion
> Clean from the purpose of the things themselves.

There is yet another sense in which liberty is advocated against root and branch reformers, on which a few words may be said: I allude to the liberty of acquiring and disposing of property. Not that in this country the acquisition of property by individuals is fettered, except so far as cumbrous and expensive methods of conveyance and taxes on income can be said so to operate; but the doctrine may become a living one if the proposals of Mr. Labouchere to impose a statutory limit to possessing wealth are ever seriously considered. As to the limits of the right to dispose of property once acquired, questions of the greatest possible nicety arise. From one point of view it follows immediately from the doctrine of natural liberty, that no restriction should be imposed to prevent the owner of property directing and stereotyping the channels of its use and enjoyment for all time. But it is obvious that in this respect every extension of freedom of *disposition* is a curtailment of freedom of *enjoyment* on the part of those who succeed to ownership under these conditions. No deductions from a simple doctrine of liberty will solve dilemmas of this kind, which cannot fail to arise in considering the proper limits to put on testamentary power, and the right to alienate lands for charitable purposes; we must have recourse to matter-of-fact arguments which will vary in strength as increase of production, equality of distribution, or some other economic end is first in our thoughts. In the sense now considered it is clear that perfect liberty and perfect equality are irreconcilable ideas. Freedom of acquiring property is the grand cause and justification of inequalities of distributed wealth; to secure an equality of possession and enjoyment, socialistic measures must be adopted which cast liberty of acquisition to the winds.

The inference from the foregoing considerations, whatever view is taken of the doctrine of liberty, seems to be that the solution of economic and political problems does not lie in the application of a hard-and-fast principle concerning individual freedom. The penalty of so doing is that we shall be driven logically into one or other of mutually contradictory poles of thought. In every proposed case of Government interference the questions to be answered are far other, and involve no appeal to a poetic principle. They are of this kind: What is the object aimed at, the evil to be remedied, the good to be attained? is the proposed remedy (whether it be a restraint on freedom or not) likely to secure this end? and, finally, is the interference likely, and how far likely, to bring about evils which may counterbalance the probabilities of a resulting advantage? I leave out of sight the side-question as to what that *good* is which we should adopt as the guiding star of legislation; I only deal with the *method* of attainment. That method is clearly inductive; a careful balance of probabilities is comparative, historical, experimental, but in very small part deductive.

The *conclusion* may point in a particular instance to the net advantage in leaving things in the hands of "vis medicatrix naturæ," and adopting a "laisser-faire" policy, without entangling our *premisses* with the doctrine of "laisser-faire." No doubt the evils of over-government, and the resulting loss of individual energy, the uniformity of a Chinese civilization, are possible dangers to be considered; but they can be accurately appreciated by employing these tentative, inductive methods without the help of a high-sounding dogma. And these dangers are probably exaggerated. Society is day by day being involved in *pleasures* (to use the new standard phrase) of increasing number and intricacy; new forms of property and new contractual relations are recognized with which the slow and cumbersome machinery of State-control can with difficulty keep pace; while th   d principle opposed to non-interference, that each man is t   , judge of his own interests, must every day receive great   ification. Our Statute-books may of late years appear   illed with Acts of Parliament of the protective, meddli   ; but the sphere of interference is as a speck compared t   arged area of uncontrollable voluntary action.

Friendly and benefit societies, trades unions, and joint-stock companies have been regulated by statute within the last quarter of a century, but they are new forms of co-operation, with new aims, owing their very existence to statutory protection; and, as far as the general conduct of their affairs is concerned, they can hardly be said to be more hampered by legislation than a man is hampered by the clothes he wears. The same observations apply to the mass of recent legislation respecting trade-marks, patents, railways, electric lighting, copyright. Nor must it be forgotten how much the functions of the *Central* Government have been enlarged by the decay of local municipal authority and local customs, increased facilities of communication, desire of uniformity. Bearing these facts in mind, we shall not find in the increasing bulk of the volume of statutes serious cause for alarm.

The demand for "freedom of contract" is included in the general advocacy of liberty, but will bear a brief separate treatment. It is true, in a sense, that if the State refuses to recognize the validity of, and will not enforce, a particular kind of contract, and if A and B are both desirous of so contracting, they are not free to do something they both wish to do; but it is equally undeniable that if A and B bind themselves by the terms of a valid contract they are each, to the extent of their mutual obligations, and until these are rescinded or performed, rendered less free. This is plainly seen when, upon a breach by either party, the State is asked and proceeds to visit with penalty or punishment the party in default. There is, in fact, no paradox in the statement that the full application of the principle of "laisser-faire" involves as much interference with freedom as the refusal by the State to recognize a whole army of contracts. Moreover, those who advocate the extension of the sphere of contract should remember how incomplete a remedy the State can afford, and does afford, in obligations of the ordinary business kind. The class of cases in which the Courts will order the specific performances of contractual duties is very small compared to the large number of cases where the only remedy is pecuniary damage awarded to the suitor; and this can hardly be styled complete satisfaction for the wrong done, if we except the peculiar action for breach of promise of marriage.

Bearing the foregoing considerations in mind, we can better appreciate the case that is made for the Agricultural Holdings Act of this year, a measure that, beyond all question, interferes with "freedom of contract" in the popular sense. It seems to be an error to rest that case on the same grounds as those advanced in favour of the recent Fishing Boats Act and the Factory and Workshop Act, where the object mainly is to place employer and employed on an equal footing, to afford protection to the weak and ignorant against something savouring of imposition or undue influence. If it is necessary, in order to justify the Agricultural Holdings Act, to assume that the farmer is a helpless, unforeseeing creature, unable to understand his own interests, in the face of the facts of recent years, which show the tenants to have been the masters of the situation, the less said about the justice of the measure the better. A safer and wiser view of the purport of the Act would appear to be that which sees in it, first and above all, an amendment of those legal presumptions and privileges which the law accorded to the position of the owner of land against the occupier—with that fiction by which everything annexed to the soil became, as it were, part of the soil and the property of the owner of the freehold; with that right of distress which, without stipulation, made every landlord a privileged and secured creditor. Another way of putting the case is, that if the tenant, under the old law, put capital into his business of agriculture, in the interests of good husbandry, by draining, manuring, liming (and I am speaking now only of *tenants'* improvements), he was unable to recover that capital back again in any shape, after the determination of the tenancy, though he had not reaped a penny profit, and though the determination of his tenancy was not his own act, though, as in Cæsar's case, the " good was oft interred with his bones." From this point of view, it is not difficult to understand the expediency of *some* measure of a kind to provide a repayment, or security for repayment, to the tenant of moneys by which the value of the holding had been improved—moneys, so to speak, *lent*, not *given*, to the land, if it is not denied that the fostering of agricultural production is within the functions of a government. It is to be noticed that the Act only secures this return of capital after the contract is determined—after the tenant has quitted his holding; and, in this event, even the old law gave the tenant the right to the emblements—*i.e.*, the crops he had sown and not reaped. Under the new Act, to quote Mr. Shaw-Lefevre's words, "the position of the tenant in respect of moneys which he has put into the soil, or feeding-stuff which has been consumed on the farm and added to its utility, is identical with that in respect of the crops which he has left on the land." The standard answer to these considerations is the argument that it is the tenant's own fault if he has not secured these results for himself by his original contract, that he must have known what the law was when he entered into possession, and the contingency of lo his capital could have been provided against like any oth tingency. To this it is replied, not unreasonably, that r tenant bargains with a landlord about taking a farm, it would be quite the exception for either party to consider what is to be done *after* the expiration of the tenancy; they both contemplate a state of things during which the tenant is the occupier; the relation is, on both sides, intended to be an enduring one, though the tenancy be only from year to year; if the tenant pays his rent and does not commit waste, it is not the desire or interest of either party to sever the relation. In the case of the great mass of tenancies, those from year to year, it would be true to say there have been no contracts at all on the subject of improvements. As a matter of fact, prior express contract can govern but a fractional part of the relations between cultivator and owner, especially in the case of a determinable yearly occupancy. In most cases it would be impossible or prejudicial to frame stipulations as to the amount and kind of improvements, which will depend on the precise nature of the soil, the changes in agricultural methods, the variation of prices, and a hundred like considerations; and it is only after the tenant is in possession and understands his position that his speculations on these heads can approach accuracy. The Act is intended to give the tenant the largest liberty and encouragement to cultivate his holding to the best possible advantage, and it would make the object at once his interest and his duty.

As it stands, the Act is far less compulsory than one would conclude from the strong denunciation it has received in some quarters. In its compensation clauses it is wholly permissive, except in those provisions which relate to the improvements defined in the third part of the Schedule, "boning, chalking, claying, liming, manuring, &c., and even in these cases compensation under the Act is only of right when the landlord has not *agreed* to provide "fair and reasonable" compensation. In every other case any contract as to compensation overrides the statutory provisions. In fact, the main object of the Act (and in this lies its true compulsory character) seems to be to influence landlords to make *some* provisions for recouping to tenants their outlay, leaving in great part all the details to be settled by free bargains between owner and occupier. There is the least possible retrenchment of positive existing rights or contracts.

It is curious, as showing how the cry for freedom of contract is

limit the intended and natural effects of a voluntary agreement, declaring that under certain circumstances the mere inability to pay debts shall operate as a cancellation of the obligation to pay them in full, to allow a man who pays £5,000 when he owes £10,000 to be discharged whitewashed and immaculate and free to begin business again and contract new debts,—casts "Freedom of Contract" to the winds. Nevertheless, it is universally held that the interests of the majority of creditors and of production afford a sufficient justification for such a measure.

So, also, a law which grants a monopoly to the first inventor of a novel and useful process, or to the tradesman who establishes his claim to use a trade-mark or trade design, is plainly a violation of the doctrine of natural liberty. Yet in these cases encouragement to ingenuity and industry, discouragement to deception and fraud have been on all hands recognized as good grounds for a Patent Law and a Trade Marks Act.

The whole course and history of legislation of this country shows how little substance has the doctrine we are discussing. Five centuries ago, as Mr. Thorold Rogers pointed out recently at the Social Science Congress, "freedom of contract was limited by State provisions in the case of the use and exchange of money, of certain kinds of consumable food, of the price of labour," and by every charter and privilege granted to trading corporations. Ever since the process has been continued by the Legislature. It is true that many of these measures have been repealed. The Navigation Laws, the Corn Laws, for instance, are no more; but the reason of their abolition was not their supposed interference with any sentimental principle of liberty, but because, on well-discussed grounds, they were otherwise inexpedient.

Long ago Burke saw the fallacy of striving to explain the principles on which society is based by an appeal to natural laws, and, above all, a natural law of liberty—

> The restraints on men, as well as their liberties [he writes] are to be reckoned among their rights. . . . . Man cannot enjoy the rights of an uncivil and civil state together. That he may obtain justice, he gives up his right of determining what it is in points the most essential to him. That he may secure some liberty, he makes a surrender in trust of the whole of it.

And again—

> The pretended rights of these theorists are all extremes; and in proportion as they are metaphysically true they are morally and politically false he rights of man are in a sort of middle incapable of definition, t impossible to be discerned. The rights of men in government eir advantages, and these are often in balance between diff of good, in compromises sometimes between good

and evil, and sometimes between evil and evil. Political reason is a computing principle—adding, subtracting, multiplying, and dividing, morally and not metaphysically, the moral denominations.[*]

The larger questions of State interference involved in projects for naturalizing land and capital, for limiting the amount of individual incomes, or for providing a compulsory State insurance, are not to be solved, any more than the smaller measures we have considered, by an appeal to any abstract eternal principle. The method in all cases will be a calculus of probable results, and in that calculus no one doctrine or motive will be allowed to assert undivided influence. It may be that our reasonings may not give us any result of sufficiently high probability to warrant a definite course of action, and then the legislative power must have recourse to experiment. The Agricultural Holdings Act of 1875 was, in this sense, an experiment, and the same may be said of all permissive legislation; or the general conclusion, after full balancing of arguments, may be that it was not possible to frame a general rule at all—a course pursued, for instance, in the Irish Land Act of 1881. The Government came to the conclusion, whether wise or not, that what a fair rent is should be undefined; the consequence is the "wilderness of single instances" that the decisions of the Sub-Commissioners present to us. But there is nothing against any inviolate principle in this if, with the best lights the Government had, it was to be deemed just and expedient. Every day our courts of law are doing the same thing. The ruling idea of judge-made law is not an appeal to principle, but an extension of principles by solitary *quasi*-legislative decisions. Principles are not the taskmasters of the courts, but their guides. And so with legislation. Liberty, in this sphere, ought to be expressive of the means rather than of the end, and the work of governing is not to be done by framing deductions from abstract theories—

> Not clinging to some ancient saw,
> Not mastered by some modern term,
> Not swift nor slow to change, but firm
> And in its season bring the law.

N. J. SYNNOTT.

---

[*] "Reflections on the Revolution in France," pp. 88, 89, 92, edition 1791.

Art. IV.—ALEXANDER FARNESE.

1. *Farnese Papers.* MS. in the Museum at Naples.
2. *Correspondence of Philip II.* Archives of Simancas.
3. *Histoire de Philippe II.* Par M. H. FORNERON. Paris:
   Plon et Cie. 1881.

THERE are always in the world men whose actions seem nicely calculated to defeat their own dearest aims, and who are saved from utter ruin only because certain favouring circumstances persist in neutralizing their perversity. To this class of men Philip II. of Spain pre-eminently belonged. Vacillating, tardy, and cumbrous in his policy as never Sovereign was before or after him; fickle in his likings beyond all that poets have unjustly said of woman; given to indulging the darkest suspicions against his lieutenants, and that at the very moment when they were well-nigh accomplishing the impossible on his behalf; he yet had the good fortune to possess a succession of servants so able and so devoted that all his blunders did not suffice to destroy his empire, or even his great name. His officers were well aware of his character and shortcomings; yet he had the gift of throwing over them a glamour which constrained them to undertake all, and to dare all, in his service.

Greatest, most able, and most indispensable to Philip's interests of the many gifted men who were led by this strange attraction, was Alexander Farnese, Prince and Duke of Parma. Farnese was not technically Philip's subject, but was closely allied to him by blood, and received no small measure of favour from the prudent monarch in his youth. Loyalty to Philip ran in Alexander's veins. His mother, Margaret, Duchess of Parma, spent six years of difficulties, terrors, and triumphs in governing the Netherlands for her august half-brother, only to see the Duke of Alva appointed in her stead, Counts Egmont and Horn, who had been her best auxiliaries, decapitated, and the war, which she had just extinguished, lighted up anew. Yet was Margaret ready to return and wear out her strength in the Netherlands at such time as Philip might choose; nor did the king's shabby treatment of his sister diminish the loyal passion of her son, which was almost the only point of resemblance between Margaret and Alexander. In personal appearance they were extremely dissimilar. No one would have believed that the spare, dark man, with his piercing black eyes, keen aquiline face, and aristocratic bearing, was the son of the heavy, fair-haired, thick-featured Margaret, whose every lineament was that of a Flemish peasant. A corresponding difference existed in their characters. Margaret was every whit a Fleming; Alexander a Roman, on whose keen nature Castilian courage had been grafted.

The hero was one of twins, the only children of Ottavio Farnese, by his marriage with the natural daughter of Charles V. The other son died in his infancy; and Alexander's Spanish education was due to the fact that Philip, who had differences with Ottavio on the subject of a claim to Piacenza, desired to keep the heir at Madrid as a hostage for poor Margaret's good behaviour in the Netherlands. The precaution was unnecessary, but to believe that his relations were loyal was an impossibility to Philip. He was kind, however, to his young nephew, and gave him a princely education, in company with Don Carlos and Don John of Austria. Although Alexander was eclipsed in every external quality by the future victor of Lepanto, these two formed a generous and lasting friendship, which no misunderstanding ever crossed. Together they studied at Alcalà, together they rushed from their books to play at tennis and "cañas;" together they read "Captain Girenbert," "Amadis of Gaul," and other specimens of that exciting literature which received its death-blow a little later from the hand of Cervantes. At the age of twenty Alexander bade an eternal farewell to the Spanish Court, and went to join his mother at Brussels, there to wed the fair and saintly Mary, daughter of Don Edward of Portugal. On this occasion Don John, who was then eighteen years old, wrote a nicely worded letter to Margaret, expressing his joy at her son's settlement, and his own feelings of loneliness in this first separation from his friend and companion.*

Alexander is said to have given utterance to some undutiful sentiments with regard to the bride whom his mother and King Philip had chosen for him; but his heart was speedily won by the charming qualities of his young wife. In Mary's piety there was nothing stern or morose; she strove to make her husband love their home, which was fixed at Parma. Alexander was a faithful and affectionate husband, though he chafed somewhat at the inactive life which for six years he was compelled to lead. His pugnacity found vent in nocturnal excursions in the streets, where he would engage in single combat with any gentleman whom he could waylay for that purpose.

These propensities were turned into a more suitable channel in 1571, when he was invited to serve under Don John's command in the great expedition of Christendom against the Turks. Alexander, with a splendid company of noble Italian volunteers, em-

---

* "Don John to Margaret," April, 1565.—Farnese Pa

barked on board the Genoese *Capitana.* He won great praise for his daring exploits at the battle of Lepanto, that extraordinary overthrow of the Turkish naval forces, which, if it produced no positive results, had at least the important negative one of saving Rome from a Mahometan conquest.

Alexander accompanied Don John again on the next year's voyage to the Levant, rendered fruitless by the timid policy of Philip II., who dreaded nothing so much as another battle. At this period of Farnese's career, he shone by personal courage rather than by much promise of the splendid military genius which he afterwards developed. Indeed, when placed in a responsible position, he committed a positive blunder. He had entreated his friend to entrust to him the reduction of Navarino Castle, and then forgot to cut off the enemy's communications with the neighbouring town of Modon. However, no reproach fell from Don John's lips. He continued to besiege the king with requests that some post of honour might be conferred on Farnese, and was never weary of expressing, in his letters to Margaret, the fulness of his affection for her son.*

Philip, however, saw no crying need as yet for his nephew's advancement. Five more years were spent by Alexander at Parma, in the enjoyment of much domestic bliss; and had his wife lived, it is possible that he would never have been Philip's great general, or worn out his life in Philip's service. But in the year 1577 the Princess Mary died; and soon afterwards the question was raised of Farnese going to join Don John in the Netherlands.

It was the moment when the storm of war was about to break once more over the hapless Provinces, after a brief interval of peace and regular government. Don John had been sent there by Philip in the autumn of 1576, to inaugurate a conciliatory policy, and, although every inch a soldier, he sincerely intended to establish quietude, and to reverse the hateful proceedings of the Duke of Alva. He besought Philip to pardon Orange; he restored the Egmont property; he ratified the Pacification of Ghent, and abolished the Inquisition; he sent the Spanish troops away across the Alps, thereby destroying his own favourite chimera of invading England. For the few months that he did govern he governed well. But before Don John's arrival in the Netherlands, William of Orange had acquired immense influence in several of the towns, notably in Brussels; and peace was the last thing that William ˈ ˈ ˈ. The States of the Southern Provinces were all for fˑ ip and accord with the Governor, for Belgium was weary ; but Don John's own temperament

---

'arnese Papers.

played into his antagonist's hands. Because the deputies were rough in manner and naturally distrustful of Spain, he took them to be his enemies and fomenters of plots against his person. Always nervous and impetuous, he was rendered additionally inconsequential by the utter collapse of his health in the ungenial Belgian clime. A riot which certain Dutch agents excited among the Brussels mob threw him into a panic; he committed the error of abandoning the capital, and seized the Castle of Namur, an excellent position if war were intended, but unsuitable as the seat of a pacific Government. King Philip, for once cleverer than his brother, disapproved as much as the States themselves of the *coup d'état* of Namur. At first he refused to send troops to the Governor, and nearly broke his heart by leaving him without letters for four months; but seeing the whole of the Provinces about to follow in the steps of Holland and Zealand, he finally found himself constrained to order back into Belgium the army that had left it in the spring.

Curiously enough, Philip and his brother felt instinctively that Alexander Farnese was a personage whose presence was becoming indispensable in the Netherlands. Philip had a wonderful and saving capacity for knowing where occult genius lay; Don John, oppressed by infinite troubles, longed for the consolation and support of his friend's companionship. He sent off three letters in one week to Alexander, imploring him to hasten to his assistance; the king added his urgent commands; and Farnese, nothing loth, buckled on his armour and bade his native land good-night.

Victory attended his coming. The ill-considered movements of the States troops, under Marshal Goignies, exposed their rear to a disastrous attack from Don John's army near Gemblours, on the 30th of January, 1578. Owing to the sharp-sightedness of Farnese, who discovered a weak place in the enemy's flank, the battle was won by a charge of only twelve hundred horse, and cheaply purchased at the rate of seventy Spanish slain.*

But the overwhelming forces which poured from all sides into the Netherlands, hemming in the diminutive Spanish army, constrained Don John to aim at nothing more than the preservation of a base of operations. This he possessed at Namur, and to Namur he clung with desperate persistence, at the same time writing the most heartrending letters to Philip, requesting immediate supplies of men and money; while the ruthless monarch, characteristically choosing this crisis to punish his brother's

---

* "You had two sons in the battle," Don John wrote to his sister Margaret, whom he dearly loved. He gave her a glowing description of Alexander's prowess at Gemblours, Feb. 2, 1578.—Farnese Papers

imaginary disloyalty, left him to struggle on unaided. The exquisite conduct of Alexander towards his unfortunate kinsman at this terrible time, proves that whatever official faults he may have committed in the service of the king, his heart was generous and tender. Though ever ready to counsel his young commander, and to lighten labours which were beyond his strength, he knew how to avoid the slightest semblance of usurped authority, and to preserve a perfect obedience, even where his own genius pointed out a better way. He opposed Don John's plan of attacking the States' entrenched camp at Rymenant, but when the assault was actually made, he was at the front to minimize the inevitable defeat which ensued. He promptly rejected Philip's heartless proposal that he should supplant Don John in the Government; not for a thousand dignities would Alexander have added to the many sorrows which were bringing the young viceroy to his grave. And when at last Don John was struck down by the pestilence which devastated the Netherlands in 1578, Farnese not only discharged all civil and military affairs, but spent the rest of his time by his friend's sick-bed, soothing his pain with a woman's gentleness. The dying Governor appointed Farnese to be his successor, according to a power which the king, dreading lest another interregnum should occur such as that which followed the demise of Requesens, had conferred upon him; and then, having provided for Philip's interests to the end, the hero of Lepanto peacefully breathed his last in Alexander's arms, on the 1st of October, 1578.

Thus, no sooner did one of this devoted pair fall, than the other stepped into the gap, ready in his turn to be sacrificed in Philip's service. Truly it was a marvellous spectacle to see these two generous and brilliant young men flinging themselves under the wheels of a Juggernaut of whose wooden and painted qualities they were so well aware!

Farnese's extreme grief for his friend was not blunted even by the multitude of his occupations. "I try not to let my sorrow interfere with my labours in his Majesty's service," he wrote to his mother, "but the thought of that blessed soul (*a quella anima benedetta*) is always in my mind."*

To the unsympathetic Philip also he expressed his intense sense of bereavement.† Yet he worked from morning till night, applying himself to make the best of the standing-point he already possessed. Farnese is sometimes spoken of as the sole preserv   Belgium to the Crown of Spain, but he himself

---

*  Margaret," Bouges, Oct. 30, 1578.—Farnese Papers.
  Bouges, Oct. 2, 1578.—Arch. Sim.

would have been the first to admit that his predecessor had broken the neck of his work. Don John had secured the counties of Namur and Luxemburg, and with them the communications with Italy; he had also begun to profit by the discontent of the Walloon Provinces with William's policy. It was this work especially which Farnese strove to perfect. He wrote to the Walloon States, assuring them that their safety depended on reconciliation with Spain, since France on the one hand, and Orange on the other, aimed at the destruction of their rights and privileges. Well did Farnese know that those last words thrilled every Belgian heart like an electric spark; and recent riots, got up by the Dutch faction at Ghent, gave a point to his warnings. A few months later, Hainault, Artois, and the Tournaises fully acknowledged the authority of the Governor-General.

Next year, when the plague had departed and reinforcements arrived, Farnese began to show his mettle as a commander, by taking Limburg and Maestricht. About the same time Margaret of Parma, in accordance with commands from Philip, made a reluctant reappearance in the Netherlands, to resume her old post as Gouvernante, while her son was to act as Captain-General of the Army. But here Alexander showed himself keen-sighted rather than dutiful. Not ambitious, but perceiving at a glance that a divided authority would ruin the Royal cause, he declared that he must have all or none. If he was to be General, he must be Viceroy also. His opposition was the more striking, because Don John had been willing and even anxious to co-operate with Margaret, and the poor Duchess was glad enough to beat a speedy retreat. She never saw her son again.

The duel was now between Farnese and the Prince of Orange. William's influence south of the Scheldt had been diminishing since the battle of Gemblours, but was strong as ever in the north. M. Fornèron, in his work on the reign of Philip II., does justice to Farnese's unwillingness to publish the ban by which Philip made it lawful for all men and any man to take William's life. "Farnese," he says, "was endowed with as much humanity, we may say with as much goodness, as camp life and the manners of his time permitted. He raised objections and difficulties. 'It would seem to many,' he wrote, 'a base falling off in so great a prince as his Majesty, after making war and employing force against Orange, to fall back on such means as these.'"* But "Philip's orders grew pressing; he insisted that the text of the ban, retained by Farnese for ten months, should be published.

---

* "Philippe II.," vol. iii. p. 166.

Farnese did not comply without a protest. 'Never have I approved this placard,' he boldly said."*

Jaurequy's unsuccessful attempt in 1582 was followed by William's elevation to the Countship of Holland; and the fact that he had coins struck in his own effigy gave colour to the report that he aspired to sovereignty. His assassination by the wretched monomaniac, Balthasar Gérard, in August, 1584, cut off his career almost at the apex. The great politician, Alexander's rival in statecraft, though certainly not in generalship, was gone, and Maurice of Nassau was as yet too young to fill up the blank. Thenceforth Farnese advanced with rapid strides. The perplexed States offered themselves first to Henry III. of France, and then to Elizabeth of England; but neither Sovereign cared to accept such troublesome subjects. The inhabitants of those towns and districts which had submitted to Farnese were meanwhile contented enough, for he governed in strict accordance with their precious privileges, and was too wise not to regard their likings. "Farnese," says M. Fornèron, "allowed but little authority in his councils to the Spaniards. An Italian, Çosimo Massi, was his private secretary, and he bestowed his full confidence on Richardot."† Every one understood that he did not wish to be considered a Spaniard; he was affable to the people, gave balls, and won good opinions. Such was his conduct in peace, his prowess in war spoke for itself.

In the year 1585‡ the Duke of Parma's military triumphs culminated in the taking of Antwerp with most inefficient means. And there it was that the genius of the man came out. Philip kept him so short of necessaries that his soldiers were starving and barefoot, and he himself half ruined by supplying these deficiencies out of his own means. Yet the troops fought and conquered under the eye of that unrivalled commander, whose will seemed to annihilate all obstacles. Brussels and Ghent likewise fell into his hands, and Holland and Zealand might possibly have been reconquered, had Philip energetically backed up the "modern Alexander." The Earl of Leicester, whom Elizabeth, according to her usual policy of half-measures, sent over to help and torment the States, was a brave man, and did them some service by bringing to their aid so much of the best blood of England; but he was blown away like a feather whenever he came near the war-worn Duke. For a short time the fate of all the Net' ds seemed to depend on the Spanish King's apprecia†˙ ːrisis.

tendency to persecute his lieutenants was ineradi-

II.," vol. viii. p. 166.   † *Ibid.* vol. iii. p. 203.
in the year 1584. Margaret survived him two years.

cable, and henceforth Alexander's path tended downwards into gloom. It was the epoch of the Invincible Armada which first threw over his career the dread shadow of Philip's suspicion. No doubt the Duke would have preferred that his uncle should never have contemplated the enterprise of 1588. He had too much real work to do—draining marshes, taking cities, and subduing earth, fire, and water, in the reduction of Philip's insurgent Provinces—to delight in a vast expenditure on the conquest of a foreign kingdom; but no sooner did he know that the monarch was resolved than he set all his wisdom to work in the service of the Armada. Alexander, of course, would have had the invasion take place while Mary of Scotland yet lived; but procrastinate as the uncle would, the nephew's invincible patience was never at fault. It was his miserable *rôle* to carry on peace negotiations with Elizabeth, while Philip slowly and cumbrously fitted out an armament to conquer her realms; but where Philip's interests were concerned, Farnese could have outwitted Machiavel himself. He succeeded in so blinding Elizabeth and her Ministers that no troops were under arms in England at the time of the invasion, and he further facilitated matters by the capture of Sluys. Yet the enemies whom his success had raised up were all this time whispering in Philip's ear that Farnese was unfaithful, and was secretly aiming at the coronets of the Netherlands. The Duke was naturally stung to the quick when these slanders came to his knowledge. Bold and open with the master whom he served so well, he complained of them to Philip, who straightway replied with tender assurances that he could never doubt his nephew. "The love which I bear you obliges me to bestow all imaginable favours, according as occasion may offer, on you and on your house. Believe that I will do so, and be quite at ease as to the matter you speak of . . . . I am sure that what was told you must have been a mistake."*

Alexander had known Philip all his life, and was quite aware that his own excessive labours would neither prevent his slanderers from whispering, nor the king from listening to their whispers. Moreover, Philip was convinced that his nephew might very well cross the Channel and occupy London without any help from the fleet at all; in which case it is difficult to see why he was at the trouble of fitting out that armament. In vain Alexander assured him that he had no boats able to make head against an enemy, or even against a troubled sea; while to build proper transports at Antwerp, even if he had the means of so doing, would be to open Elizabeth's eyes at once. The Armada, he told his uncle on

---

* "King Philip to Farnese," Feb. 1587.—MS. Arch. Sim.

the 21st of December, 1587, must clear his way to England. Once landed, he would know how to act. To say nothing of the numerous English fleet, the Dutch rebels had one hundred and thirty sail between the forts of Lillo and Tifscheuser, besides others which had collected daily at Flushing and elsewhere. He added that if the Marquis of Santa Cruz had started, he should send two messengers to meet him, with injunctions to land nowhere save at the point where he could best cover the passage of the troops from Flanders.*

But there was little fear of the Marquis appearing in the Channel in December. Eight months more passed wearily by in preparations before the Armada went forth to conquer, and by that time the Marquis of Santa Cruz was no more. Delays, labours, and the ceaseless harassing directions of Philip, brought the grey head of the old Lepanto warrior to the grave. His place was inefficiently supplied by the Duke of Medina Sidonia, who was quite as fully persuaded as Philip himself that it behoved Parma to help him into an English port. When at last he found himself in the Channel, sorely perplexed by the English "philibotes," and their capacity for taking advantage of the wind, he sent courier after courier off to Alexander with requests for forty or fifty light ships of war, *to be sent at once;* and sorely he complained when he found that they did not come.†

In the meanwhile Parma had been doing his utmost. He made his head-quarters at Bruges, whence he could easily superintend preparations at Sluys, Neiuport, and Dunkerque. On receiving Medina Sidonia's first letter he had the men encamped on the beaches ready to embark, and only waiting till the Armada should have scattered the English navy and the Dutch privateers. Thus the two Dukes were entirely at cross purposes. Parma, when about to mount his horse to go to Dunkerque on the 8th of August, complained almost testily in a letter to the King of the High Admiral's continual demand for naval aid.‡ It was only on this day that he had learnt the arrival of Medina Sidonia in Calais Roads, and the fate of the Armada, though he knew it not, was already decided by the battle of Gravelines.

The loyalty of Parma's conduct in this affair ought to have been as clear as noonday to the king and to the world. Parma had always expressed doubts as to the success of the Armada. " ` ` ody was more fully aware than myself, from the first, that 'ould be much difficulty in gaining an English port, as I

---

na to Philip."—Arch. Sim.
na Sidonia to Parma." Aug. 1588, from off Portland, the Isle
'arwich, and Calais.—M.S. Arch. Sim.
to Philip," Bruges, Aug. 8, 1588.—Arch. Sim.

have told your Majesty many times,"* he wrote to Philip, and great was his indignation at the reflections which were made upon himself. " I am sure that I have served your Majesty with such fidelity, honour and affection, that if I had shown equal zeal in Our Lord's service it would be well for my soul." Thus pathetically did he express his grief to the king.† Philip doubted him, yet went on expecting him to accomplish impossibilities. It was almost enough to make the great soldier weep to be told to go up the Thames and take London !‡ Turning northwards he attempted the capture of Walcheren, but failed even in that. Shadows gathered thickly over his life. Philip did indeed assure him of his undiminished regard, but Alexander was too well acquainted with the Plutonic divinity at Madrid to be at ease. None knew so well as he what had been the sufferings of his predecessor; and it was but to be expected that his own turn would come. A profound melancholy took possession of his soul. He had given up all for Philip—country, health, family ties, the claims of his son to the throne of Portugal; and this was the end. Yet he went on toiling in the gloom, as he had toiled in the sunshine.

Guise and the League, no less than England, had always been a weight round the neck of Parma. Guise was now dead, but the League lived yet, struggling on against Henry IV. with the aid of Spanish ducats. To feed the League, Philip starved the war in the Netherlands. Whenever he sent money to Alexander, at least a third of it always had to go to the League. Philip was likewise in the habit of periodically ordering Farnese over the border into France, to help the unwieldy and incapable Mayenne, when the Duke should have been measuring swords with young Maurice of Nassau. Farnese represented to his master that the Netherlands offered sufficient employment for his actual resources, but finding remonstrance vain, he buckled to the unwelcome work with his usual unfailing obedience. In 1590 he relieved Paris, flying back thence to check the advance of Maurice. In 1591 he raised the siege of Rouen, returning wounded and weary to watch over the Provinces and to drink the waters at Spa; for Farnese was now a worn-out and sickly man. The Hapsburg family had no constitutions, and in the last thirteen years he had done the work of thirty; but, though broken in health, he was

was a favourite axiom of the King. Unfortunately for him, the other two were often his best general and his best opportunity.

He believed in all Farnese's slanderers, one of whom, Commander Moreo, he set about the Duke as a spy. He even grudged him such relief to his physical sufferings as he found in the waters of Spa. When the King's secretary, writing in his name to Farnese, said that "he hoped God would restore the Duke's health through the remedies which he meant to employ," Philip scrawled on the margin of the rough copy, "that if going to the waters of Spa was included among those remedies, the passage had better be struck out, since that excursion was not approved of,"* and the words were omitted. A viceroy who must needs waste time over his own health did not suit the views of the agile Philip. It seemed to him that his nephew cared only for the safety of the Provinces, of which he meant to wear the nine crowns. To remove him from their vicinity was Philip's object now.

In the spring of 1592, he wrote to Alexander, inviting him in kindly terms to pay a short visit to Madrid, that they might confer together on matters of State. About the same time he sent the Marquis of Cerralbo to the Netherlands, to expedite Alexander's departure, and to make him understand, if he refused to go that go he must, but this only in case the Duke were not wanted for the affairs of France. Apparently he was wanted, for in the autumn Philip, postponing his deposition till he should have done one more stroke of work, directed him to march a third time into France to help Mayenne. At this time Parma was almost too ill to mount his horse, but he showed himself obedient to the end. He collected his troops, appointed Count Mansfeld to govern Belgium in his absence, and set out for the frontier.

One who saw him leave Brussels on his last journey has thus described his departure from the Palais de la Cour, in words which convey more pathos than any panegyric. "Although the cold was intense," writes Captain Vasquez, "he was magnificently dressed, and it seemed to me that I had never seen him more gracious in his bearing. This was truly wonderful; for it was not with the heretics of France, but with death itself, that he was about to contend. Without the help of two lackeys, who sustained him on either side, he could not have kept his saddle; yet he succeeded, with that invincible courage which ever distinguished him, in remaining steady in the stirrups, and lifted his hat to the bystanders a   'ing to his usual custom."†

---

* "Correspondance d   ppe II. sur les Affaires des Pays-Bas."
Par M. Gachard. Vol. :   oduction, p. xxxii.
† Quoted in Cor. Phi¹   l. ii., Introduction, p. xxxiii. It was on
the 11th of November t¹   nese left Brussels.

Thus did Alexander's devotion triumph over mortal weakness, almost over death itself; but at Arras he received that summons from the King of kings which saved him from the disgrace already intended for him by his earthly master. On the 2nd of December, 1592, he passed away in a fainting fit, at the age of forty-seven, having governed the Netherlands fourteen years and two months.

Well had he done his work; and, had he done it in his own way, great would have been Philip's glory. Nine Provinces were saved to the Spanish Crown, and, with larger supplies and permission to expend his energies in the Netherlands alone, he might have conquered the other seven as well. Now he was gone, and Philip was rejoiced, because circumstances had removed his disloyal nephew, and made him free to bestow the governorship on one or other of the Archdukes Ernest and Albert of Austria. It was well that neither of them stepped into it till the hard work was done, and the ways made smooth. Alexander Farnese had begun to rule on the strength of two counties and a few scattered towns; he left to his successor the whole of what is now called Belgium, except Ostend. Truly he had traded well with the talents that were given him, and so exclusively for his master's benefit, that hardly enough money was left in his own coffers to transport his body to Parma. He met with no reward on earth save suffering and distrust; but we may hope that his fidelity, mistaken though it sometimes was, and his heroic self-abnegation, received a better recompense elsewhere.

ART. V.—THE COPTS.

1. *A History of the Holy Eastern Church.* By Rev. J. MASON NEALE, M.A. Part I. *General Introduction.* Two vols. 1850.—Part II. *The Patriarchate of Alexandria.* Two vols. London: Masters. 1847.

2. *The Coptic Morning Service for the Lord's Day.* Translated into English by JOHN, MARQUESS OF BUTE, K.T. London: Masters. 1882.

3. *Liturgies, Eastern and Western.* By C. E. HAMMOND, M.A. Oxford: Clarendon Press. 1878.

4. *Liturgicarum Orientalium Collectio.* E. RENAUDOT. Two vols. Paris: 1716.

5. *Lettres Edifiantes et Curieuses: Memoires du Levant.* Tomes IV. et V. Paris: 1780.

6. *Missions Catholiques.* 1882, 1883.

IN fulfilment of the promise made in a former article, in January of last year, we now attempt some account of the Copts, or native Christians of Egypt. Indications of a growing interest in the Copts have been frequent of late in England, a natural consequence of the influential position which this country has taken in that land since the war, a position which recent events will perhaps oblige her to continue holding. The native Copts are Catholics with a flaw of heresy in them, and are not in the obedience of Rome: it is natural that Anglicans should for this reason feel a peculiar sympathy with them. Not to mention the numerous magazine articles which are appearing, we may note that there is somewhere in this country an " Association for the furtherance of Christianity in Egypt;" that the Christian Knowledge Society, which a noble speaker said the other day, at a provincial meeting, had hitherto done little for Egypt, is, as he added, "awakening to the fact that much is to be done, and, having awakened, it will not sleep;" that lastly, an Anglican clergyman, in a lecture delivered in Norwich in May,* says that the needs of the Copts are a "call on the English Church which," he adds, "we may not and dare not, if we hope for God's bless-

---

* "The Ancient Church of Egypt." By Rev. W. Denton, M.A. London: Rivi   1s. 1883.

ing, shrink from obeying." This last speaker also stated that, before leaving London for Norwich, he had assisted at a meeting in the Jerusalem Chamber "for the formation of a committee to make known to the English people the condition of our brethren in Egypt, and to consider the best means by which we may aid the Copts in their endeavours after a higher spiritual life, a better training for their clergy, and a better education for their lay members." The Moravian Brethren, as long ago as 1756, had felt a similar "call" to the Copts, who, however, wanted none of them, and the mission fell through. The American Presbyterian missionaries have been energetically at work in the same vocation ever since 1854, in both Upper and Lower Egypt. Lastly, Catholic missionaries have been in Upper Egypt, where the Copts are most numerous, since the middle of the seventeenth century, and in Lower Egypt, as we saw in January last, from a much earlier date; so that, if the Copt really has aspirations after a higher spiritual life, which we doubt, he certainly cannot complain of a want of variety in his opportunities. In the *Contemporary Review* for November last, Mr. Sheldon Amos struck out a new line by writing on "The Copt as a Political Factor," and he credits them with an importance and latent possibilities which we believe to be ideal. His views on their religious condition, which he did not pass by, are still more peculiar, as we may have occasion to see later on. Let us add to all this that the Copt is the nearest approach to the genuine Egyptian of ancient history, and that his church is the only survival of the glorious patriarchate of Alexandria, the cradle of monastic life, and the bulwark, in the person of Athanasius, against the forces of Arianism, and we have said more than enough to enlist the interest of the reader in the subject of this article.

The history of the Egyptian Church falls easily into three well-divided periods—the first from the Apostolic times to the Council of Chalcedon, in A.D. 451; the next to A.D. 638, the date of the conquest of Egypt by the Mahommedans; whilst the third period extends from that sad event to the present day. The first period is one of the most attractive and glorious pages in the history of Christianity; the next two centuries present a most stirring and dramatic spectacle, oftentimes not very edifying on the one side of the struggle or on the other, but full of interest from the prospect that still survived, that the good might overcome the evil. But the story of the Egyptian Church, from its Mahommedan captivity onwards, is but the mournful record of persecution and degradation, with little to vary its monotony except the inventions with which each ingenious Moslem ruler added new aggravation to old inhumanity—a monotonous and weary record, without crisis and without hope. Religiously, of course, the last two periods have a common claim on our regrets; for we see that the poison of heresy has entered the life-blood of the Egyptian Church, and all energy, vigour, vitality slowly but surely disappearing. The merest glance at the ancient history of the Copts must suffice in this place: but that glance at least is necessary, in order that due interest may be felt in their present condition, and that the lesson which their history points so forcibly may not be altogether lost.

The Church of Alexandria has always prided itself on having been founded by S. Mark the Evangelist—the companion and "son" of S. Peter (1 Pet. v. 13), who perhaps specially sent him as his own representative to the second city of the Gentile world.* However that may be, the Patriarch of Alexandria from the earliest times ranked next to the Pope of Rome, and enjoyed not a few peculiar powers and privileges. Doubtless there were Christians not a few in Egypt long before S. Mark's first visit; doubtless some had been among S. Peter's converts on Pentecost day—"devout men from Egypt and the parts about Lybia" (Acts ii. 10); yet in a true sense S. Mark is the founder of the Church of Alexandria, he gave it form and authority, ordained priests and deacons, and appointed as bishop his first Alexandrian convert, Annianus, a shoemaker, whose hand is said to have been healed by S. Mark of a wound inflicted in using his shoemaker's awl. The Holy Evangelist was martyred in Alexandria, April 25th—his feast-day in both West and East—probably in A.D. 62. Following S. Mark, we have the clear record of an uninterrupted line of Patriarchs, his successors, the first being Annianus, just mentioned, until we reach the twenty-fifth of the line, the infamous Dioscorus, who became the ardent defender of Eutyches and his heresy, and was deposed in A.D. 451, by the Council of Chalcedon. This was a humiliating fall for the Church of so many doctors and holy patriarchs, of SS. Dionysius, Peter Martyr, Alexander, Athanasius and Cyril; for the Church of so many martyrs—which indeed suffered so severely in the persecution, under Diocletian, that the first year of his reign is the Alexandrian "era."†

The error of Eutyches, which sprang from an excessive reaction against Nestorianism, consists essentially in denying the existence of two natures, the human and the divine, in the person of Our Lord ͞s Christ. It strikes one with astonish-

---

* The argument˙ Alexandria, and A et Nova Disciplin

† It is known this year of A.D.

horities for the three Petrine Sees of Rome, stated at length in Thomassinus's "Vetus b. i. c. 7, 8.

of the Martyrs, Aug. 29, A.D. 284, so that ar 1599-1600 of the Era of the Martyrs.

ment that the Alexandria which under S. Athanasius fought for the honour of Christ's divinity against Arius and for the truth of his unique divine personality against Nestorius, under her patriarch Cyril—the battle-cry in the first conflict having been the famous "consubstantial," in the latter "theotokos," or Mary the "Mother of God"—should, with the cry of "one only Nature" in Christ, "monophysis," have become, and that under an immoral patriarch, the champion of heresy. Some have thought to trace this change, as to its root, back to the monotheistic spirit of ancient Egypt; her "many gods" having been in reality but a human attempt to represent the One God, indivisible but manifold in his operations. Without going so far, however, to fetch a doubtful explanation, we may recognize in the Alexandrian Church a disposition to dwell upon the Oneness, the glorious divinity of Christ, rather than upon the twofold aspect of his nature; even in their spiritual life as distinct from dogmatism, dwelling on the divine and conquering, rather than on the suffering Saviour.* Perhaps they imbibed this mental complexion, this one-sided tendency from the Platonic atmosphere of their Schools—an idolon theatri. At least a marked difference can be recognized between the methods of the early Christian Schools of Alexandria and of Antioch. The bent of mind predominant in the former, inherited as it would seem from the influence of Origen, was to speculation and mysticism; they loved to allegorize in interpreting the Holy Scripture. The spirit of Antioch was in theology rationalistic, whilst in hermeneutics it insisted on the plain and literal sense of the words.† When attention was called to the nature of the hypostatic union in Our Lord, the tendency of Alexandrian divines was to dwell upon the divinity, and hence to unite even the natures; of those of Antioch to admit the logical necessity of their distinction. It is easy to see that in giving expression in formulæ of human language, one aspect or the other of that great mystery could be made prominent in either a sound or an heretical sense. Hence it came to pass, that the Church which had repelled Arius and Nestorius felt no horror at the doctrine of Eutyches. It is, however, a much simpler explanation to say that the Egyptians were always (are still) tenacious, persistent, obstinate, blindly so: and that having for a variety of reasons

* Cf. Father Dalgairn's Introduction to "Lives of Fathers of the Desert."

† Hence their divergent opinions as to the extent of inspiration: Alexandrians contending for verbal inspiration, the Antiochenes admitting only that the drift or teaching of each clause or sentence was its inspiration. See the excellent paragraph in Alzog's "Church History," period i. epoch 2, c. 2, § 115.

some of them far removed from the region of dogma, once grown hot in defence of error, they grew only more determined therein with every effort to change them. The Alexandrian tendency was in itself neither good nor bad—under Catholic guidance it had produced both doctors and saints. What was wrong and led them astray was pride, self-sufficient national vanity. Dioscorus was a man of loose morals, proud and passionate, unprincipled; his position as patriarch of Alexandria was a very high and very powerful one: he was not a man, therefore, likely to retract or show humble submission, which alone would have saved him and his city. He had fallen foul of the party which first spoke out against Eutyches's false exaggeration; he sought to ape the part played by his predecessor, St. Cyril, against Nestorius, without having either Cyril's learning or virtue, and when Flavian, the patriarch of Constantinople—that Imperial city which was fast usurping the place so long held by Alexandria—anticipated him, by himself condemning Eutyches, the die was cast. The Robber Synod of Ephesus showed what spirit Dioscorus was of, and how little the honour of Christ was his thought or aim. When, therefore, the Council of Chalcedon assembled, the result was obvious: many erring minds submitted at that assembly, and much confusion of sentiments was cleared and illumined by the celebrated letter, or "tome," of Pope St. Leo the Great, on the Catholic faith in the Incarnation; but Egyptian obstinacy refused to be taught, and from that day the three names of Chalcedon, Marcian (the Emperor), and St. Leo, have shared equally the hatred of the Egyptian Monophysites. True, Dioscorus was deposed by the Council and banished by the Emperor, but the flood he had let loose spread its destruction wider with the years, till Egypt's ancient faith disappeared from the land.

The Imperial minority at Chalcedon dared also, in defiance of the decision of Nicæa, to rank the Patriarch of Constantinople, the New Rome, next to him of Old Rome, thus displacing him of Alexandria from the high and influential position hitherto held. True, the Pope's legates refused to recognize the change, and Pope St. Leo defended the honour and right of Alexandria, and told the Emperor that his New Rome, with whatever grandeur, could not make itself what Alexandria was, an Apostolic See. But the Emperor, after the fashion of Emperors, had might against right, and the humiliated and insulted Alexandrians refused to accept Chalcedon or its faith.

The orthodox Emperor, however, undertook to enforce the faith on Egypt: it would have been better for that faith had St. Leo's exhortation to gentleness been heeded. The Copts have always excu   ir deep hatred of the Court of Constantinople by the severity and cruelty with which it was sought to make them orthodox. Thus it was that the national feeling of the ancient people rose in bitterness against, first the religion and power, and then the very presence, of the Greeks among them. There was, of course, much provocation given to the Greeks; the natives were vindictive, riotous, restless, and also cruel: but the issue gradually simplified itself into the national one of Egyptian or Greek. Thus the growing Monophysite party became known as the Copts or Egyptians: they had long in contempt called their Catholic opponents Melchites, or Royalists, as being the creatures of the Court of Constantinople. Thus was Egypt divided between the State Church and the Church of the people. To the former belonged the secular arm; and it must be confessed that for an irritated and wounded people no agency could have been more prejudicial to the chances of orthodoxy.

We pass over the interval between Chalcedon and the coming of the Moslem. It was a period of struggle and riot. Each party had its patriarch; occasionally an Emperor favoured the heretics, and whichever party was strongest, its own patriarch lorded it at Alexandria, and his rival prudently fled. But the currents of feeling grew deeper and flowed wider apart. Each effort at "union" made union more hopeless,* until at length, when the enemy of Christianity appeared at their doors, they welcomed his advent as a heaven-sent opportunity of rooting the hated Greeks from the face of Egypt.

In the year of the Lord 639, the year of the Hegira of the Prophet 18, Amru, the general of Caliph Omar, entered Egypt. He took Pelusium at a blow; Memphis, the ancient capital, was captured after a seven months' siege; and finally Alexandria itself fell into the conqueror's hands, not, however, without a long struggle on the part of the Imperial garrison. When Amru was despairing of reducing Memphis, it is said that the Imperial governor, an Egyptian named Mokaukas, and a strong Jacobite in religion, took on himself traitorously to negociate with the Saracen. Amru gave him the Prophet's conditions—the Koran, tribute, or the sword. Declining the Koran, he is said to have promised tribute from himself and his people, in order that the Greek might be driven root and branch from the land. "The Greeks," Gibbon reports him as saying, "are determined to abide by the determination of the sword: but with the Greeks I desire no communion, either in this world or in the

---

* Even the "Henoticon" of Zeno only intensified hatreds and multiplied sects.

next, and I abjure for ever the Byzantine tyrant, his synod of Chalcedon, and his Melchite slaves." We may see plainly enough, in after events, that at least the Copts acted up to the spirit of this zealot speech. They fought before Alexandria in the infidel ranks, and more fiercely even than did the Saracen, against the Greek, their common enemy. The city fell, and the Greeks were driven for their lives to the sea. Then the Christian Copts gladly submitted to a tribute of two gold pieces per head—old men, women, and children, and perhaps also monks, excepted. The Copts had an easy triumph, and so complete that for a time we may fancy it even satisfied their uncompromising fanaticism. The Melchites were, as we have said, identified with the Court and power of Constantinople, the great enemy of the Saracen Caliph, so that conqueror and conquered had a common feeling of dislike to the professors of the faith of Chalcedon. When the influence of the Emperors was banished from Egypt, multitudes, from various motives, went over or returned again to the error of the Copts; the wonder indeed is that any Melchite should have remained or ever reappeared in Egypt. Yet they did reappear, and even revive, at one period receiving marked, at another equal favour from the Mahommedan rulers; but they never grew into importance, and became with time more and more Greek in ritual and spirit. It was, as Renaudot thinks, probably now, in the time of Benjamin, the first schismatic patriarch under Moslem rule, that the Alexandrians translated their liturgies from the despised Greek into their vernacular Coptic. But probably enough Coptic liturgies had been long used in Upper Egypt beyond where the refinement and language of the great city was prevalent. St. Anthony did not understand Greek, and doubtless his followers esteemed it as little as he did.*

There is such a thing, to use a vulgar phrase, as to "jump from the pan into the fire;" the unhappy Egyptians soon found that they had done this. The followers of Mahomet despised them not for believing wrongly about the Incarnation, but for believing in it at all, or in the divinity of Christ. "God neither begetteth nor is begotten," was the solemn enunciation of their Koran, and this sentence Abdul-Aziz, the first notorious persecutor of the Christians, had painted up on the doors of their churches, as also this: "Mahomet the Great Apostle of God and Jesus Christ, the Apostle of God." The Mahommedan Emirs of Egypt soon played the *rôle* of the Byzantine Emperors and with a cruelty that Emperors had never dreamed of. The reader must bear in l, as we now glance at the *status* of the

---

* Palmer's "O   Liturgicæ" (Oxford, 1836), vol. i. p. 83.

Copts of the present day, that they have lived under the yoke of the Infidel for twelve hundred years and that, though often enjoying respites of peace, they have been violently and brutally persecuted,* occasionally by outbursts of such violence as marked the early Roman persecutions, and more persistently by a continuance of penal laws that are not without resemblance to those so long in force against Catholics in England and Ireland. They were early forbidden the celebration of the holy mysteries, they were taxed and retaxed until reduced to poverty, whilst defaulters were maimed of a limb or put to death; monks were forbidden to take monastic vows, were heavily taxed, had to wear an iron fetter, and be marked with their letter and number; enormous "donations" were exacted from patriarchs, one of whom had to travel over Egypt begging of his people alms to purchase his ransom, accompanied by a man who was responsible for his return; churches were spoiled, desecrated and ruined; images were destroyed, bells forbidden; their much-loved native tongue was prohibited and grew in time unintelligible to them; they were to wear a peculiar dress as a badge of their Christianity; they were forbidden the use of horses and later on of even mules; professions were also closed to them and also all official positions in the Divan except on previous profession of Mahommedanism. One feature of these persecutions was that money would buy exemption from nearly every penalty, and money was often the only escape from death: gold rose in value, and Christian parents were known to sell their children to escape starvation. Had there been no lulls in this fierce storm the Egyptian Christians must have been swept from the face of their land. Naturally enough the oppressed Copts often rose in rebellion, only to be easily put down, and then treated with increased rigour, and unfortunately too they abused the intervals of peace, and some of them by their arrogance and pride drew forth anew the hatred of the Moslem. It is needless to add that countless numbers of them embraced the religion of their persecutors. It is much the fashion at present to blame the arrogance, violence, treachery and other bad qualities of the Copts as having been the cause of their sufferings. Doubtless they often offended in these ways, but it is plain matter of history that their oppression was due to the hatred of the Moslem for Christianity.

Of late years, however, and particularly since the reign of Mehemet Ali, the Copts have enjoyed the same toleration accorded to all forms of worship by that liberal ruler. A century of immunity has not been enough to undo the effects of the penal times, to rouse them from apathy and timidity, to raise them to anything like the high level of culture they once enjoyed. The long-imposed Moslem yoke has been removed, but the mark of bondage is not yet effaced. This is true to a great extent: yet the Copt is not so black as he is painted. He is represented as morose, sullen, deceitful, unprincipled, repellant of strangers, if not rude; in his dealings avaricious, dishonest, a drunkard, cringing or arrogant as occasion serves, wanting in the manliness of Turk and Arab; in his religion degraded, fanatical, ignorant. This testimony of English, German, and American travellers is for the most part very untrustworthy. The Copt is naturally grave, as was his Egyptian ancestor; he is exclusive and will not unbosom himself to every Cook's tourist who comes to inspect him and suggest his reformation: in fact, he dislikes strangers, is suspicious of Franks and abhors their religions. This conduct the aforesaid travellers resent; are they not by virtue of race and religion the natural superiors of this people? The Copt, too, is a Catholic more pronounced even than the Romanists in such reprehensible matters as Mariolatry, pomp of ceremony, fasting, and other superstitious corruptions—and according to the current logic, not being yet enlightened by Protestantism, he must be more degraded rather than less. This is the tone hitherto much used; but Anglicans are recently fond of speaking very highly of the Coptic Church and its ritual, and very hopefully of the dispositions and capabilities of the people. Lane tells us that he despaired for a long time of learning anything of the Copts, and was surprised at last to find "a Copt of liberal as well as intelligent mind;" and more recent writers generally confirm their special impression about the Copts, or theory as to his needs, by quoting a liberal and intelligent member whom they met! We hardly trust this liberal and intelligent friend; it is suspicious that his opinions are always those of the traveller, however peculiar and recent these may be. Besides, the inner life, the spirit and secret hopes of a people, especially a reserved people, are not got at by the acquaintance of an hour; most of the European and American travellers do not know a word of Arabic, the language of the people!

The Copt is unquestionably of great natural intelligence and aptitude, quick to learn, with a wonderful talent for the science of figures. Copts have always been the scribes, accountants, secretaries, &c., of the Moslem Egyptians. They make excellent artizans, and in Upper Egypt represent skilled labour. Education is not yet compulsory in Egypt, hence we need not refuse to admit that not   Coptic child would pass the most recent

English grade of standards. But they are the best educated portion of the indigenous population. English writers often accuse them of being a race of drunkards, judging perhaps from a short residence among the citizens of Cairo; the truth being that they are not so drunken as the Mahommedans, whose temperance is about as genuine as the modesty of their harems—which English writers have so often had courage to defend of late. In reading, therefore, the frequent opinions put forth about the Copt's religion, or rather want of it, statements that his condition is one of ignorance, that his religious services are empty, frivolous ceremonies, not understood by the people, irreverently conducted and the like, we must remember how our own masses and services have been so often described by English observers in our own literature. One authority here again assures us that *his* intelligent and enlightened Copts agreed with him that the service was neither edifying nor elevating! There is a strong temptation here, which shall be resisted, to divert on the tone frequently assumed by English writers on the matter of religion: their sympathies are with Mahommedanism and its pure monotheism, or they assert the superiority of Moslem morality as quite unquestioned, or they laboriously and *con amore* follow the growth and varieties of the pantheon of pagan Egypt, but have only supercilious indifference or scorn for the protracted theological disputes concerning the divinity of our Lord. The harems have, as we already remarked, found defenders, and polygamy has been pronounced more moral than the *de facto* condition of Europe: Islam has been accepted as an excellent form of monotheism specially adapted to Eastern character. Yet it will presently be thrown at the Copts that they have conformed to Moslem habits, secluded their women and even rigorously veiled them in the streets. It must here be remembered, that living under Moslem rule they have been driven to confirm to such social customs as imply no dereliction of religious principles. What Copt would be enlightened and liberal enough to send his wife abroad unveiled when she by thus appearing would proclaim herself to be what more than all an honest woman abhors the suspicion of? But the rigid veiling of even Turkish and Arab women is giving way before the impact of Western in-attendance of eunuchs, and Coptic ladies of rich families are attended by a man-servant, as is an English lady of like rank.

The Monophysite Copts number at the present day throughout Egypt probably 300,000—about one-tenth of the indigenous population. There are altogether about 5,000 Catholic Copts, of whom about 800 belong to Cairo. It will save time in this rapid sketch, if we mean by Copt the Monophysite, unless the Catholic convert be expressly named. The interest which a study of the Copts has for ourselves is that from their tenacious conservatism, their suspicion of novelty and all foreign influence, and their isolation from the rest of Christianity for nearly twelve centuries, they give testimony to the belief and practices (often here spoiled by puerilities) of a very ancient if not apostolic Christianity. Let us say, however, in this place, that the Catholic Copts do not make use of our ritual and rite—do not, for example, say mass in Latin. Rome not only does not encourage, but expressly forbids, a change by converts from their ancient and venerable rite; and no changes in ritual would be required by Rome, although minor changes and curtailments would be both possible and even demanded, and would certainly be advantageous to priest and worshippers. This is to be noted, because the language of the Coptic ritual is vastly more a dead and unintelligible language to the Copt than Latin is to a European Roman Catholic. The Copt speaks Arabic, like his Turkish neighbour, and does not understand—not all the priests understand—a word of the Coptic; hence one casual observer of their Mass writes that the Arabic portion of the service—the lections are read in Arabic as epistle and gospel with us in English—are the parts which this Scripture-loving people relished: the fact being that with ordinary politeness they listen to what is specially put into the vernacular for their behoof, but esteem the mass proper in its dead tongue as the uneducated but instructed Catholic esteems it in Latin. Unfortunately, instructed Copts are not numerous. The reader who cares to compare the Coptic Mass with his own Latin Mass, and to see for himself what beauty there is in that ancient liturgy of Egypt, can do so by means of a little volume recently published, in which the Marquis of Bute has translated that liturgy into English from the Coptic, which latter he places in parallel columns.* The reader will be able to

---

* This is called "The Coptic Morning Service for the Lord's Day" (Lond--- ˙ ᵀ Masters & Co.), because Lord Bute has also translated the servic rning Incense, which on Sundays usually precedes the Mass. The ı ll find indicated in their places the variations from this form in u ; the Schismatic Copts; they are only two or three. Both Lit۱ d Coptic students owe a debt of gratitude to this oriental sch ⟩rmer more particularly for giving them in English from the

see in the same volume, and in other volumes which refer to the matter,* that the Egyptian Churches are more or less uniformly on a different plan from the Western. The east end of a Coptic church is always apsidal; the high altar is generally flanked on north and south by side-altars. In the eastern apse is the altar, surmounted by a baldaquin, and strictly enclosed from the rest of the church by a high, close screen, called the iconostasis. This altar-enclosure is the Hêkel, or Holy of Holies; within its curtained door enter only the officiating ministers; within its precincts is used only the sacred Coptic—whatever is read in Arabic is read without. This is the first great division of the church; the second is outside this, and is the choir reserved to other ministers, choristers, &c., and containing the lecterns, from which are read the four lections of the Mass and others.† This choir is marked off by an open screen from the third division, which is the nave or body of the church; strictly speaking, it is the men's portion, because women and children are screened off in galleries or other parts of the building. A fourth section, not, however, so unfailingly to be found, is the narthex or outer division, used in ancient times for the catechumens, penitents, and others, and corresponding with the Court of the Gentiles in the Hebrew Temple. As the change of discipline robbed the narthex of its original purpose, it became in some cases the women's division—in many cases it now contains the Epiphany tank or well. When the Copts arrive at church for Mass, they bow or prostrate before the door of the Hêkel, kissing the silk curtain which hangs before it; they then go round paying reverence to the pictures of our Lord, His mother, and the saints, which are numerous in his churches. The Copt does not remove his turban, though frequently he puts off his shoes, and then sits on the floor of the church on a mat. The services are frequently so long, extending over several hours, that the worshippers use a crutch stick, over which they incline and rest as they stand, quite in the opposite way to the use of the "Misereres" in Western choirs.

The celebrating priest is always assisted by at least one deacon, who, however, is often only a little boy, differing from our serving-boy in that he has been ordained a deacon. These boys are ordained deacons as early as seven and eight years of age, and although the deacon always communicates with the priest who

---

old Coptic, not an ancient code but the liturgy in actual use. Our indebtedness to Lord Bute for much information concerning Egyptian matters is very great, and is gratefully acknowledged.

* See particularly four excellent letters in the *Academy*, Nos. 543, 544, 545, 547, for 1882.

† The four lections of the Mass are taken from—1. A Pauline; 2. A Catholic Epistle; 3. The Acts of the Apostles; 4. The Gospels.

offers the Mass, they do not, among the schismatics, go to confession until they arrive at manhood.

The Copts have three liturgies, or ordos of the Mass—one, called St. Gregory's, is used for midnight mass of Easter, Christmas and Epiphany; the other, St. Cyril's, is used once a year only. St. Basil's is used on every other occasion, and the Copts offer Mass every Sunday and feast (these are numerous), every Thursday and Friday in larger churches, and on every day in Lent. They prepare for mass with great care, and frequently spend from midnight in church in chanting psalms &c., in which many devout laity join. There is a long service of Incense now used as immediately preparatory to the Mass, which will be found translated in Lord Bute's book: many of the prayers are of great beauty, and the whole deserves perusal. That portion of the liturgies which precedes the canon is longer than our own, but need not detain us. When we come to the canon of the Mass, the likeness between the Coptic commencement and our own (and the same may be said of the other Oriental liturgies) is strikingly close, pointing to a venerable antiquity—perhaps to a date before the dispersion of the Apostles —for this essential portion of the Christian sacrifice. We have nearly everywhere the "Dominus vobiscum," the "sursum corda," the "Dignum et justum est" &c. We have the Triumphal Hymn embodying our Sanctus, Sanctus, Sanctus. We find, also—what is especially noteworthy—the essential words of consecration so far carefully preserved that the form approved by Rome for the Catholic Copts is unchanged from that used by the schismatics; a peculiarity of the Coptic rite being that deacon and people interrupt the priest with frequent exclamations of "Amen," "we believe, we believe that it is so indeed. Amen." The Copts use the Epiklesis or Invocation of the Holy Spirit after the words of consecration, but apparently not in the erroneous sense adopted by recent Greek schismatics.* The Coptic priest then continues the Canon by praying aloud, and not as with us inaudibly, and at great length for the welfare of the Church, for its prelates and all the hierarchy, for the people and for the fruits of the earth, and for a full rise of the Nile during the season of inundation. The commemoration of the saints follows. It is very much longer than our Latin "Communicantes et memoriam venerantes," and speaks of the blessed Virgin thus:

And chiefly she that is full of glory, that is a virgin unto all times, the Holy Mother of God, the Holy Mary.†

---

* This is well pointed out on p. 88 of "Coptic Morning Service." A good explanation of the Epiklesis and its value may be found in Hurter's "Medulla Theologiæ D   icæ," p. 604.

† Renaudot's Latir   n of the Monophysite text is not easily rendered: "Divæ Sa᷊   im."

Next come the Prayers for the Dead, the fraction of the consecrated bread, the Our Father, and then still other long prayers, in which the living, the sick and the dead are again prayed for. Before the Communion the Confession of Faith is made by both Schismatics and Catholics.

The priest says, Amen. Amen. Amen. I believe, I believe, I believe, and confess till the last breath, that this is the life-giving Flesh which Thy only-begotten Son, Our Lord, and God, and Saviour, Jesus Christ, took from our Lady, the Lady of us all, the Holy Mother of God, the Holy Mary. He united It with His Divinity *without mingling* and *without confusion* and *without alteration*. He witnessed a good confession before Pontius Pilate. He gave it for us upon the holy tree of the Cross, by His Own Will, in very truth for us all. I believe that His Divinity was not separated from His manhood for one moment, or for the twinkling of an eye. Giving it for us, for salvation and remission of sins and eternal life unto them who partake of it; I believe; I believe; I believe that This is It in very deed. Amen.*

The words we have italicised are often adduced as proof that the Copts are orthodox as to the distinction of the two natures, and would be of force if they saw any consequences from them and accepted such consequences. But when pressed therewith, they always fall back on their only formula, that of the one nature.† The Communion which follows is given to the people in both kinds, thus: to the men who come to the door of the Hêkel the particle is dipped into the chalice and administered with a spoon; to the women, who stay behind their grill, the priest takes particles which have been touched by another particle that had been dipped into the chalice: the chalice never leaves the sanctuary. Some post-communion prayers follow, and the mass ends by the priest blessing and dismissing the people—now done in Arabic.

There can be no question of the sound faith of the Copts regarding the Real Presence, nor about their having Catholic sentiments as to the sufficiency of communion in one kind. True it is that they do not now reserve the Blessed Sacrament, and

---

* Lord Bute's translation. Mr. Sheldon Amos considers that our Lord is so prominent in the Coptic liturgy that there is no fear of their placing any mediator above and before Him. The value of this bathos is seen by the language used of the Blessed Virgin in the two above extracts. No mention in the Roman Catholic Canon of the Blessed Virgin is nearly so warm in expression as these.

† That the Coptic Monophysites, or Jacobites, are not thorough-going followers of Eutyches is pointed out by Dr. J. Mason Neale in his "Alexandria," vol. ii. p. 16, and was dilated on two centuries ago by the Jesuit Fathers Bernat and Sicard in their "Lettres edifiantes." They are none the less, however, heretical in their tenets, though practically, and for many generations back, are "more ignorant than heretical."

that when an urgent sick call shows the necessity of viaticum, they say mass at any hour and carry to the dying the consecrated particle touched with the precious blood. But whilst this is manifestly not "the cup to the laity," it is matter of history that long before their schism the Egyptians both reserved the consecrated bread and communicated the people with it alone. They are most careful to prepare the bread for the holy sacrifice, and the oven generally stands in a division of the church itself, as also often does the wine-press. But with regard to wine, the Monophysites were once driven to a peculiar practice which they still continued in the last century. One of the methods of annoying them which their Moslem persecutors invented in the 9th century, was to forbid all buying or selling of wine under severest penalties. The Copts were driven, some think, to use an infusion of vine branches in water.* When the Jesuit Père Bernat lived in Egypt, they still used, as a matter of course, a liquor made by squeezing large raisins in water; and this raisin wine, from the largeness and juiciness of the fruit used, was judged by some French chemist to be really a species of wine. A feature of the Coptic mass and liturgical services is the frequent use of incense: the priest censes not only altar and pictures, but the people, coming down among them and saying prayers, to which they respond in a way that to many western observers savours of familiar chat and absence of religious solemnity. However, people are variously impressed, according to their views on "ritual." An eminent Anglican clergyman, having assisted at the long Easter liturgy in the cathedral at Cairo last Easter, calls it "a gorgeous and interesting service." "What was scriptural and edifying," he adds, "far exceeded what was objectionable,"† and other Anglican visitors recently report in similarly condescending praise: it is generally added, however, that in one way or another the Copts are not as the Romanists are, which is the point to be devoutly noted in these matters.

The Copts believe in seven sacraments, and are in the main correct in their administration of them, although many strange and mistaken details of belief and practice have crept in. Baptism is by triple immersion, first one-third of the child's body being dipped, then two-thirds, and lastly the whole, one person of the Trinity being named at each; and these immersions are preceded by a multitude of anointings, thirty-six with one

---

* This seems the natural reading. Renaudot has "palmites vitis," but says, "per palmites intelligi uvas ex illis pensiles." Vol. i. p. 193.
† Dean Butcher, quoted in Mr. Denton's "Ancient Church of Egypt," p. 20.

kind of oil on as many different parts of the body. The Monophysites are lax as to its necessity, and parents or nurses are said not to dream that they can or ought to baptize a dying child. The administration of baptism is at once followed by that of confirmation, and this even by priests, and without any special need or deputation ; and after confirmation the Holy Eucharist is administered in wine which is conveyed from the chalice on the priest's finger-tip into the child's mouth—manifestly communion in one kind. The necessity of this communion with the Monophysites, and the fact that they do not reserve the Blessed Sacrament, leads to many inconveniences. Perhaps their excessive reverence for the Blessed Sacrament, and the dangers of centuries of persecution, accounts for it, for they certainly used to reserve. Some of their wise men now account for it by reference to the fact that it was forbidden for any of the Paschal Lamb to be left! To the same great reverence we may attribute their careful preparation in the communicant—not only of fasting, but of observance of certain rules concerning personal purity which we should deem excessive; and this as regards the celebrant too, for parochial clergy may be and often are married.

They are lax about the practice of confession, and young people frequently go first when about to be married. Strange to say, the Sacrament of Penance is often followed in the Church by that of Extreme Unction. This seems to be true, though, as Denzinger points out pertinently enough,* not every use of the "oleum infirmorum" in the primitive Eastern Church meant the Sacramental Unction. There was a frequent use of it, as by way of what we call a "sacramental:" thus, *ex. gr.*, the healthy were anointed by way of preservative, and even the dead were marked with it in much the same spirit and intention as our sprinkling of the corpse with holy water. It is true, however, that the Copts do sometimes administer this sacrament after confession to the healthy. They have a peculiar reading of St. James's words. There are three kinds of sickness, say they, that of the body is only one of them: there is also sickness of the soul, which is sin, and of the mind or spirit, which are afflictions: the Unction is good for all of them; those doing penance for apostacy used to be thus anointed. They are also peculiar, not to say humorous, in this, that when they administer Extreme Unction they also anoint the ministers and other bystanders, lest the evil spirit dep⋯⋯ from the sick man should find a "dry place," and take up ⋯de in any of them !

Coptic young men appear to marry ⋯eat a disadvantage as their Moslem fellow-countrymen. ⋯ocial condition of

---

* "Ritus Orientalium," tom. i. I⋯ ⋯ct. § 5.

women in Egypt makes it necessary for him to employ an agent or match-maker, one of his relatives generally, to find him a suitable wife. And the young lady has her "wekil," or agent, a near relative, or, failing that, one of her own appointment, to arrange matters. The bridegroom rarely gets a glimpse of his betrothed till the marriage; but of course this excessive seclusion of women is giving way to Western influence. A good Copt will not marry, except in his own church and with the priest's blessing; indeed, their older writers make the religious rite essential to the contract. But a civil marriage ("marriage à la Turque," as Père Bernat calls it) has always been in vogue when a Copt would marry, in spite of rule and ruler, a Moslem woman or a woman of any other creed than his own. Marriage with a deceased wife's sister is forbidden by an Alexandrian Code of canons still in force.* The canons of the Egyptian Church are against divorce *a vinculo*, even in case of adultery, but their practice has long been somewhat lax. And they can have recourse, not, of course, without sin, to the secular or Moslem tribunal, against the decision of which the threats of their Church avail only in conscience, and can be disregarded with impunity. One cause authorising a new marriage, mentioned by Wansleb, is suggestive of their past sufferings under Mahommedan rule. If man or wife have been led off into slavery, the remaining party may remarry if the absentee is not heard of as alive within a period of five years. Only a virgin bride can be "crowned," which is a special portion of the nuptial benediction with ceremonies peculiar to itself. Only the son of a crowned woman can become the Patriarch of Alexandria. Marriages may not be solemnized in Lent, because it is a penitential season, nor during Easter, because it is unbecoming to share the Paschal joy with any other and more earthly one. Second marriages are not countenanced by the Coptic any more than by the rest of the Oriental Church, but third or fourth marriages are matter for severe and prolonged penances.

So much may be found in any book or article on the Copts about their numerous and rigorous fasts, that we need do no more than say that they have four Lents in each year. The Great Lent is longer than ours by nine days, commencing on the Monday of Sexagesima, though their actual fasting days are not more, since all Saturdays and Sundays are with them as exempt as Sundays in the West. Holy Saturday is the only Saturday

the laity is of thirteen days, but varies for the clergy, who commence it immediately after Pentecost week, and thus get sometimes longer and sometimes shorter measure than the people—sometimes as many as thirty days. The fourth Lent is for fifteen days before the Assumption of our Blessed Lady. The first Lent is a rigorous one, neither meat, fish, eggs, nor white meats being allowed—in fact, only a vegetarian diet, and the first meal not till after None, formerly 3 P.M., now about 1 P.M.

The Copts have bishops, priests, and deacons, in due subordination of grade, all being subject to the Patriarch. The Patriarch, once so powerful politically, has retained his great and absolute importance and power till now. It is the most significant sign of the change coming over the old society of Egypt from Western influences, that this absolute trust of the Copts in their Patriarchs is beginning to be lessened.* The bishops are quite the "creations" of the Patriarch; he consecrates whom he chooses, and none but he can consecrate. He, however, has always two assistant bishops. His suffragans now number just a dozen—the remains of that populous Church which could muster a hundred suffragans of Alexandria in the days of St. Athanasius.

Bishops must live in continence, but may have been the husbands of one wife deceased; but priests who are not monks may marry one wife before receiving priesthood, and may neither marry nor remarry after ordination: it is not true, however, as is frequently asserted, that they *always* marry, much less that they are obliged to do so. Much is being said at present about the ignorance in matters religious of the Coptic clergy and bishops; to a great extent it is but too true. A Coptic monk has no more desire for any acquired science mundane or theological than had SS. Paul or Anthony; and the Patriarch of Alexandria is chosen from their ranks for his piety, and also for a sort of helpless ignorance which will leave him the easy tool of clever advisers. Many of the Alexandrian Patriarchs took for the first time to their school-books after their elevation —much to their credit; it is said that the present one did so, and with success. The patriarchical schools established by the last Patriarch but one have done much to elevate the standard of Coptic education. Among the clergy, those of the Catholic Copts who have been educated at Propaganda show to striking advantage. Four elements of ecclesiastical learning are, however, sadly neglected at present in Egyptian clerical training—thorough study of Coptic, ecclesiastical history, systematic theology, and Sacred Scriptures. Much as we should wish to see this low level of acquirements raised, it need not be said that we regard

---

* See Mr. Sheldon Amos in the *Contemporary*, Nov. 1883.

with more than suspicion the obtrusive efforts made for both laity and clergy by American and English schools. Ignorance may be bad, but the Copt may too easily be educated to the point of sneering at the superstitions of his fathers without acquiring any better thing to venerate and accept. High Anglicans also will at least strengthen that hatred for the Pope which is to our minds his radical defect. Mr. Sheldon Amos is a liberal-minded Englishman, anxious for the elevation of the Coptic clergy; he may be taken as a type of many. "A Church," he says, "with so distinct a theological history and such marked national peculiarities as the Egyptian might well be entitled to fine shades of theological preference in the enunciation of doctrine which only the most tyrannical standards would restrict." All this and much like this uttered in good-natured desire to be wide-minded, we cannot but regard with disapproval, and as of bad augury for the Copt. But there is more to be feared from the energy and active propagandism of such men as the American missionaries, one of whom is of opinion that "the pretended power that the priests have to bind and loose, the invocation of saints and angels, fastings, pilgrimages, &c., are so many false saviours and so many antichrists which the devil has invented to turn weary and heavily-laden souls far away from the true Saviour." These gentlemen and others of like sentiments with them are moving heaven and earth for converts among the Copts. Schools are opened in Upper Egypt; they report themselves in 1880 as having thirty-two schools in their Assiût district, which covers a stretch of 450 miles from Minyeh to Assuan, with 1,343 scholars attending them. Their zeal is backed by abundant means, and the poor class of Copts are in such indigence that wealth exercises a sway among them which they can hardly resist. Their converts are such acquisitions as are the bought converts anywhere else; and a few go over to them to escape the burden of fasts and a burdensome obedience.

The Franciscan Fathers who have had hitherto the sole care of the villages and towns of Upper Egypt, and who in years not far receded have watered the soil with their blood for the faith, have ten houses, including a small one at Cairo, for the Prefect Apostolic of Upper Egypt. Their churches, built by themselves, are frequently in towns where the Catholic Copts have no chapel of their own, and the Franciscan church is used for both rites. The Coptic priest, however, is parish-priest of those of his own rite; the Fathers of those only who are of the Latin rite. The intense poverty of these Franciscan missionaries, raised were in this respect only a degree above the privation of their peasant congregations, is a great drawback to their efficiency in school matters. They cannot pay the masters they would like to have, they cannot multiply schools or increase accommodation. They are sorely pressed as it is to find masters' salaries, books, pens, and even clothes for their wretchedly poor scholars. And this in villages where an active and zealous Protestant agency can build with elegance, and command excellent tuition. For their girls' schools, which might be made a most expeditious and potent means of good, the Fathers much regret their inability to ask the help of any teaching order of nuns. In 1882, in 16 schools in the Nile Valley, they counted 808 scholars, about 300 of whom were schismatic Copts. They have also had the happiness of receiving into the Church small bands of schismatics, twenty in one place, thirty in another, during the past year, but not in such numbers as to indicate a "movement" in the direction of Catholicity.

We must not omit mention of the College at Cairo—attached to which the Jesuit Fathers have the Coptic Seminary of the Holy Family, in which some twenty boys are studying for priests orders in the Catholic Coptic Church. It was established in 1879 by a special order of Pope Leo XIII; but it is, without any secured means of support, dependent on the charity of Europeans. It is scarcely necessary to say that these candidates will have to celebrate according to the Coptic rite; the Holy See not only recognizes these Eastern rituals, but expressly forbids those who submit to Roman authority to leave their native rite. So far, however, is this from being appreciated by the native converts, that the Latin missionaries in Egypt assure us that converts to Roman Catholicism are generally anxious to become Roman thoroughly and entirely; to join Latin rite, devotions, &c. Hence if the clerical students of the Holy Family at Cairo live according to the Latin rite in the Seminary, it is difficult, doubtless, for the Fathers, who are Latins and alone can teach them, to provide any other ritual arrangements for them. They will imbibe too with their years of studentship the piety and devotional practices of their Catholic masters—no small boon and one not likely to be without fruit in after years. It will doubtless need many years and much expense before our standard spiritual works can be rendered into Arabic and popularized.

The College to which the Seminary is attached is, we may say in passing, flourishing. From the 35 pupils of the first year, and the 70 of the second, the number had risen in 1882, soon after the war, to 112, most of them of good families, and thus divided as regards religion :—65 Catholics of various rites, 29 Schismatics, 12 Mussulmen, and 6 Jews.[*] The Rector of the College ex-

---

[*] *Missions Catholiques*, 15 Juin, 1883.

presses in his report the hope that substantial help may enable them to extend their colleges into Upper Egypt, where at the present time numerous scholars, Catholics and schismatics, are driven to the otherwise excellent Protestant schools for want of others. The schismatic Copts, it is his opinion, are as a body giving way to the influence of the modern spirit, and are being visibly disunited (*désagrège*) and *do* show distinct change of feeling towards Rome.

Such are the efforts being made on one hand by the Catholic missionaries, on the other by the Protestant for the benefit of the schismatic Copt. Both the Jesuit and Franciscan appeal for the aid of which they so sorely feel the need. At the same time, though we hope and pray that sufficient means will not be wanting, we regard as the augury of their success, after the goodness of their causes, the blood which Franciscan martyrs have already shed in Egypt, the patronage of that theotokos whom the Copts so warmly love, and their own self-sacrificing devotedness to their poor missions. It was natural to the Franciscan priests and other missionaries to remain at their posts during the late war; the Jesuit Fathers being driven out, took their young clerics with them at great risk and cost to Beyrout. We should not have thought of mentioning this, but we have been perusing a very unctuous account of the American Missions in Egypt, which says as a matter of course that "on the departure of the missionaries and their families on June 19th, 1882 (after the massacre and before the bombardment), to the number of forty-two, the congregations and schools, the outcome of twenty-five years' labour, were left to the tender mercies of Mohammedan fanaticism."*

One feature more of the present *status* of the Coptic Church ought not to be passed over—its monks and monasteries. We shall not need to recall to the reader that this the monastic life was a signal glory of the early Egyptian Church; her deserts, the cradle of monasticism, soon swarmed with so many thousands of penitential anchorites and cenobites, both men and women, that, with some exaggeration of course, the Egypt of the deserts was said to be as populous as the Egypt of the cities. Yet whoever reads Cassian's account of their almost incredible numbers when he visited them, can appreciate the exaggeration. We need not recall eith ﹀w, when heresy disturbed the peace of Alexandria, its poiso ：ad to these deserts and monasteries, and, *corruptio optimi ma*, the monks became as notorious in their reprehensible ⁚es as they had been heroic in the

* "Light in Lands of ss." A Record of Missionary Labour. By
R. Young. London: T Unwin. 1883.
Series.]

extent of their virtue and their orthodoxy. The salt lost its savour, and from the time of Dioscorus onward, the indications of their worldliness and even wickedness multiply. Soon no Alexandrian riot was quite itself until a troop of raving monks rushed in with pandemonic effect, often marking their advent with wanton blood-shedding. Nevertheless, let it be said that there was always at least a minority of good men left in the deserts, who perpetuated with the austerities the spirit and piety of their saintly founders. We shall see that even to-day there are still left among the Egyptian monks some traces of the same fidelity to the past. At a period, however, a little antecedent to the date of Erasmus's anti-monastic witticisms in the West, an Eastern patriarch of humorous turn spoke this fable on a solemn occasion *apropos* of monastic spirit in the East :—

Once on a time, he said, a tanner had a white cat, which was in the habit of taking one mouse daily. But having fallen into the vat of liquor which her master kept for the purpose of blackening his hides, and having thus changed her colour, the mice imagined that she had taken the monastic habit, and would no longer eat meat, and that they might therefore innocently approach her. The consequence of which was, that she made a hearty meal on two of them ; and the others agreed that it was wonderful to find an evil disposition made worse by a religious habit,*

The contrast between this glowing picture and the present ruin of monasticism is one of the most striking in even Egyptian history. A monastery of St. Anthony still stands on Mount Colzim, and in 1716, when Père Sicard visited it, it sheltered a community of only fifteen monks, two of whom were priests. He found four nearly empty monasteries in the desert of Scete, all that remained of at least a hundred ; but the monks assured him that the desert and the adjoining mount of Nitria had boasted as many monasteries as there are days in the year. These four monasteries could not muster altogether two dozen religious inmates ! A quantity of monks are scattered here and there in monasteries along the Nile Valley, but only in numbers equally out of proportion with the ancient multitudes. A glance at those which Père Sicard wrote about nearly two centuries ago in the north-western desert will give the reader a fair idea of the present *status* of Egyptian monks. Curiously enough, another energetic and able priest of the same society† visited the same monasteries two years ago ; yet the two descriptions might with

---

* Neale's " Alexandria." vol. ii. p. 324.

but one exception be substituted the one for the other, so unchanging are these modern Egyptians even in their ruin! That accidental exception we shall presently remark.

There is a striking similarity between all these Egyptian monasteries—the exceptions need not detain us. A high white wall twelve to thirteen yards high forms an enclosed square with sides about 350 feet long, within which are the monastic buildings, tower, church, cells, refectory, kitchen &c. The walls have no outlets except loopholes, and are thus raised and built very thick in protection against enemies, especially Arab robbers. The tower which rises above the walls by about half their height is the last refuge when an invading army has carried the walls and swarm in to pillage or hurt. The tower contains a chapel of St. Michael, library, cells, storerooms, a well—in fact it is a second monastery entered by a drawbridge, wherein in case of invasion the community might hold out for some weeks if necessary. The churches are only slightly different in arrangement from those constructed for parochial use—the essential construction and divisions are the same. The church or churches occupy the centre of the enclosure, and the cells and offices are ranged quite irregularly around in small detached buildings, each such separately built cell having accommodation for two or three monks. Of course not all of them are now occupied; on the contrary many are mere ruins. Père Jullien found twenty religious at El-Baramous, four only of whom were priests, and this total is just about the number distributed over the four monasteries in Père Sicard's time, as we have noted. The monks are clad in a plain tunic of brown wool, girded with a leathern belt, over which they wear a sort of coat of black serge with wide sleeves, a tight fitting black capuce on the head encircled with a white turban; they have no stockings, but wear red or black shoes, which they put off not only at door of church but also of cell, leaving them on the mat. The monks who welcomed Père Jullien at Baramous appear to have been very poorly clad, and the bare legs drew his attention. The reader, however, of Mr. Curzon's sparkling and not very good natured narrative will remember that the monks from a monastery on the Nile swam out to his passing boat quite innocent of any scrap of clothing and squatted on the deck unconscious that apology was called for —living illustrations in a new sense that "habitus non facit monachum!" The Ghomos or superior of Baramous was as poorly clad as his subjects, a man of fifty, cheerfully reserved, self-possessed, and with eyes full of intelligence. The letter of the Monophysite Patriarch, which the Jesuit brought with him, the Ghomos reverently placed on his forehead and on his lips, and then opened read. The brethren regarded the rare visitors with lively curiosity, astonished at everything, especially at note-making in a pocket-book, not quite understanding how one could write from left to right. The water which all the solitaries of this desert drink is so salt as to spoil the flavour of everything it is mixed with. It would seem to us impossible that men could drink nothing else all the year round.

Their food is of the poorest—their whole life extremely simple and severe. The four fasts they keep with great rigour, and even out of these Lent times they touch no meat, drink no wine, rarely indulge in a little coffee. Yet they are neither emaciated nor weak, but strong, healthy and gay. Many hours of both day and night do they spend in their choirs in prayer, and with wonderful virtue obey their superior, who is their living rule. Every evening after the office in choir they fall prostrate at the feet of their superior, accuse themselves of their faults, ask pardon, receive his benediction, reverently kiss his joined hands, kiss one anothers' without interrupting their solemn prayer, and so depart each one for his cell and the mat which forms his bed.

Those ancient and secluded abodes were long the resting-place of Coptic, Arabic, and other MSS., many of them of unique value to the modern scholar—of inappreciable value, unfortunately other than a marketable one, to the disciple of St. Anthony. He has been gradually relieved of them at not exorbitant rates of exchange, and many of them adorn European libraries. Those which remained of any interest have now been conveyed to Cairo by order of the Patriarch. Père Sicard's journey was undertaken in company with the famous Joseph Assemani the elder who gathered the first-fruits of these preserves for the Vatican library. Mr. Curzon followed, a hundred years later, and numerous others since. Here is the one change in the two narratives of nearly two centuries apart from one another. The parchments and papyrus had gone, and in the cupboards and holes Père Jullien saw instead, "heaped up, pell mell, some hundred liturgical volumes, Coptic and Arabic, from the Protestant presses of London, New York, and Beyrouth." There were "many Protestant Bibles" there also. Nevertheless, though denying the Pope's supremacy, the Ghomos prided himself that they were not as Protestants.

We are indebted also to Père Jullien for some very interesting and unique information as to the present *status* of these monks.

if he had been ordained in the monastery, he would become *déprétisé*, and would have to adopt a lay costume and might even marry."

One Mass is offered in the monastery every Sunday, Thursday, and Friday, each priest saying it and each brother serving it in turn, and only the server communicating. In the Great Lent and that preceding the Assumption of Our Lady, a Mass is offered every day, and they rise at midnight to chaunt the office which serves as preparation for the Mass. In spite of all this, how can piety or spirituality thrive among them? They have no notion of mental prayer, they never hear an exhortation or instruction, nor do they read one often, if ever; they even communicate rarely, as we have seen, when their turn comes; and the Blessed Sacrament, the one great joy and stay of the monk or nun, is never there resting with the calm silence of the starry heavens, behind the glimmer of the sanctuary lamp. Schism and self-sufficient national pride have isolated them from the living pulse of life in the body of the Church of the Lord whom they love so much, and have left the very Church robbed of his sustained and sustaining presence—empty, deluding and doomed as the hopes of those who rest on any foothold but the rock which Christ Himself has placed.

ART. VI.—MADAGASCAR PAST AND PRESENT.

1. *Histoire Physique, Naturelle et Politique de Madagascar.* Par ALFRED GRANDIDIER. Paris. 1875.
2. *Voyage à Madagascar.* Par AUGUSTE VINSON. Paris. 1865.
3. *Reise nach Madagaskar.* Von IDA PFEIFFER. Wien. 1861.
4. *L'Ile de Madagascar.* Par E. M. BLANCHARD. *Revue des Deux Mondes,* 1 Juillet, 1 Août, 1 et 15 Séptembre, et 15 Décembre, 1872.
5. *The Great African Island.* By the Rev. JAMES SIBREE, Jun., F.R.G.S. London: Trübner & Co. 1880.
6. *Twelve Months in Madagascar.* By the Rev. JOSEPH MULLENS, D.D. London: James Nisbet & Co. 1875.
7. *Madagascar Revisited.* By the Rev. WILLIAM ELLIS. Lond John Murray. 1867.
8. *Made   r and its People.* By LYONS M'LEOD, F.R.G.S. Lor   Longmans, Green & Co. 1865.

THE   phy of Africa is on so vast a scale as to dwarf our
    i   all adjacent countries, and we scarcely realize
that t   island flanking its eastern seaboard, now menaced

with French aggression or annexation, is in truth a miniature continent equal in area with France itself.

With a major axis of close upon a thousand miles, a lesser diameter of three hundred and fifty, and a surface of over 200,000 square miles, Madagsacar ranks, in point of size, as the second island of the world, being, in this respect, inferior only to Borneo. Rising on the west by a succession of long slopes and steps from the banks of the Mozambique Channel to a central plateau region from 4,000 feet to 5,000 feet above the sea, it plunges on the east in much sharper declivities, like the face of a breaking wave, from its granite crest to the 2,000 fathom soundings of the Indian Ocean. The table-land, a rugged, broken tract, fenced by a low mountain parapet, extends some 200 miles from north to south, and has a width varying from thirty to ninety miles. Near its centre is planted, like a great crown of basalt, the mountain mass of Ankàratra, its four central peaks placed cross-wise, rising from 8,000 to 9,000 feet high, and occupying, with their lower slopes and buttresses, an area of 100 square miles. This pile is evidently the volcanic heart of the island, as a recent traveller, Dr. Mullens, counted as many as a hundred extinct craters on an arc of ninety miles curving round it. Though without an eruptive vent, Madagascar is traversed from north to south by a line of exhausted Plutonic energy, having its terminal outlets in two mildly-active volcanoes on the islands of Réunion to the south-east, and Great Comoro to the north-west of its own shores.

Among its remarkable volcanic monuments is the singular natural fortress of Ambatonga, inhabited by the Antankàrana, or "people of the rocks," to the south-west of Mount Amber, at the northern extremity of the island. Here an extinct crater, covering an area of about eight square miles, forms a sunken floor, girt by a ring of precipices, and communicates with the plain outside through a cavern or fissure resembling a long tunnel, with deep water on either hand the narrow pathway through it. Farther south again, at Mandritsara, is another volcanic depression on a larger scale, forming a valley-pit thirty miles long, 2,000 feet in depth, and studded with beehive-shaped eminences, evidently the product of igneous action.

The rivers of Madagascar, though of considerable size, are not available as water-ways, being for the most part blocked by sandbars at the mouth, and much broken by rapids in their descent from the steeps of the interior. Through the eastern chain they

miles parallel with the coast before making its escape to the sea. The eastern shore is fringed for a like distance by a bar only a few miles across, forming a chain of lagoons which thirty miles of cutting would make available for continuous navigation, and from whose still reaches the surf of the Indian Ocean is heard trampling in thunder on the beach outside.

The northern coast, where the mountains approach the sea, presents bolder outlines than elsewhere, and is indented with deep gulfs and inlets, some of them, notably the bays of Bambetok, Mazembe, Diego Suarez, and Antongil, capable of affording anchorage to considerable fleets.

A forest girdle, from twenty to forty miles in width, sometimes dividing into a double and triple belt of verdure, follows the contour of the shores of Madagascar at some distance from them, and clothes its hanging steeps with tropical vegetation. Conspicuous amid the other foliage is the ravenala, or traveller's tree, its sheaf of enormous banana-like fronds radiating in a single plane, like the spokes of a wheel or the plumes of a peacock's tail. At the base of each, where the channelled mid-rib forms a closed reservoir, the thirsty wayfarer finds a supply of fresh water, which jets out on the puncture of the stalk. Nor does its usefulness end here, for the great leaves not only form a thatch for the native house, but supply its table furniture as well, being converted into mats, dishes, plates, spoons, and goblets. Its flattened bark answers the purposes of planking, and the leaf-rib forms a light, but strong pole, used for rafters, as well as for carrying litters and other burdens. Equally serviceable is the sagus raphia, or sago-palm, whose pith supplies that nutritious starch, while its leaves, sometimes thirty feet in length, make an impermeable roofing, and yield a fibre woven into the coarse cloths commonly used by the natives. The pandanus, or screw pine, whose roots branching from the trunk far above the ground give it the appearance of standing on stilts, abounds especially in the eastern forest, and the mangrove and fan-palm, called in Malagasy be- falatànana, "many palms of the hands," in the western belt of jungle.

Among the flowering shrubs the most conspicuous are the Poinciana regia, called also flamboyant, or mille-fleurs, bearing a flame-coloured mass of blossom, and the Colvillea racemosa, growing to a ˙ ˙ ˙ of fifteen or twenty feet, and covered over with clusters ͺnge-yellow flowers. Of the numerous orchids, the ͱ ͷ sesquipedale, with its blossom-spur forty centimetrͷ s the most striking. More useful, though less ͷᴸ ucts of the jungle are honey, india-rubber, and ͷ hile a sinister interest attaches to a pretty flowe· ːe a cherry tree, whose nut supplies the tanghena poison, celebrated in native jurisprudence. But the most notable of the vegetable wonders of the island is the Ouvirandra fenestralis or lattice-plant, a water-yam with an edible root, whose openwork leaves, like green lace, wave in the running streams.

Separated from Africa only by a comparatively shallow strait, some 300 miles in width, Madagascar might have been expected to form, botanically and zoologically, but an outlying province of that continent. So far, however, is this from being the case, that its vegetation is more nearly allied to that of the Eastern Archipelago, divided from it by an ocean gulf 8,000 miles across, while its animal creation is so unique as to be the wonder and enigma of science. "Here" M. Philibert Commerson writes in 1771 to his friend Lalande, "Nature seems to have retired into a private sanctuary, to work on models different from those she has used elsewhere, and the most wonderful and exceptional forms are to be found at every turn."

But the catalogue of this insular fauna, it has been well observed, is even more remarkable for its omissions than its contents. The great carnivora are entirely absent from it; the ungulates, or solid-hoofed quadrupeds, are unrepresented there; the numerous antelopes thronging the African veldts have not even a remote cousin across the Mozambique Channel, and other ruminants, the wild hogs and cattle which abound there, are believed to be of foreign importation.

Missing species are represented by strange variations on their types: numerous families of agile lemurs, almost exclusively peculiar to Madagascar, take the place of the quadrumana, from whom they are anatomically distinguished; a plantigrade cat presents an unique combination of feline and ursine attributes, and a wart-faced hog adds a fresh deformity to the ugliness of its kind.

Ornithology is no less highly specialized, and M. Grandidier says—"If we except birds of powerful flight, such as the waders, palmipedes, and raptores, most of the species inhabiting the island are not found elsewhere, and there are several genera peculiar to it."

In some cases it would almost seem as if our own feathered friends had resorted thither for a masquerade, and appeared disguised in gay fancy costume. Thus the guinea-fowl enlivens her elegant half-mourning suit of silver spangles with a hood of blue and scarlet patchwork; the homely rustic matron, dame Partridge, vies with the courtly pheasant in the golden glitter of her plumes; and the sober brown bird who, with its chanted

Word in the minor third,

heralds and haunts the northern summer, is replaced by the taitsou, a resplendent cerulean cuckoo flashing like living lapis-lazzuli as it flies.

This zoological isolation has called forth a number of explanatory theories. Some speculators have evolved from their creative fancy an imaginary continent, christened Lemuria, to bridge the abyss of the Indian Ocean, and link the Madagascar group to the Eastern Archipelago. Mr. Alfred Wallace, however, in his "Island Life," has enunciated an hypothesis more in accordance with the present configuration of the sea-bottom. He believes that Madagascar, once part of the adjacent continent, was separated from it by the subsidence of the Mozambique bank, before the present denizens of Africa had migrated thither from their earlier homes in Europe and Asia. The Madagascar fauna would thus be a survival from an earlier phase of animal life, extinguished elsewhere by the advent of more powerful types.

The unhealthiness of its shores early procured for Madagascar the name of the "European's grave," but the highlands are exempt from the malaria fever, to which their inhabitants are equally liable with foreigners in descending to the coast. The summer, from November to May, is the rainy season, the winter six months being dry and clear. The climate of the central province of Imèrina, where snow is unknown, though ice and hail are occasionally seen, is compared to that of Naples and Palermo. Thunderstorms during the rainy season are here of a very destructive character, owing perhaps to the presence of large quantities of iron in the soil, and 300 deaths are calculated to be annually caused by lightning throughout the province. An alternation has been observed between these electrical disturbances and the slight shocks of earthquake which are frequent during the winter. The mountain capital, Antananarivo, now bristles with lightning-conductors, introduced by M. Laborde, a French resident.

A peculiar atmospheric effect visible on the plateaus is described by M. Vinson, a recent traveller.—

From the heights of Antananarivo we often witnessed sunsets of unparalleled magnificence. The luminary sank behind the mountains beyond the Ikoupa on the seaward slope, and his disk, glowing like red-hot iron, seemed at first to hang immovable above the horizon, then slowly to descend, until it finally plunged below it, shedding around an infinity of wonderful lights, and the most brilliant hues in creation, while mounta͏͏͏͏͏͏͏͏͏ lains, and villages were drowned in a sea of crimson and gold ͏͏͏͏͏͏ ery little pond, stream, and watercourse sparkled like a ruby, ͏͏͏͏͏͏ thwart the carmine haze each hill-top seemed on fire. To th͏ l blaze succeeded varying gradations of colour, in shades gro͏ ͏ ͏re and more pale and tender until at last all was quenched, and the picture remained sombre and despoiled of its glory. Then a still more unusual phenomenon displayed itself in the opposite quarter of the heavens. The sky, throughout its entire expanse, assumed a pure green tinge of perfect uniformity and great softness. In the zenith this emerald sky gradually melted off, losing itself in the sapphire which had followed the sunset in the west.

This phenomenon of marvellous beauty, explained by the natives as the reflection on the sky of the great forest of Alanomasoatra, just over the eastern edge of the plateau, is peculiar to Antananarivo.

A great part of the island is still a *terra incognita*, as its northern apex, the main portion of its western seaboard, and large tracts of the interior, have never been visited by Europeans. Much of our recent knowledge of it is due to M. Alfred Grandidier, whose researches there in 1866 and subsequent years, conducted with rare scientific ability, entitle him to be called the Humboldt of Madagascar. The splendid work cited at the head of this article is a worthy monument of his labours, and the coloured plates with which it is profusely illustrated are a revelation of an unknown chapter in natural history, brought before us in all the vivid beauty of tropical life.

The existence of the great African island was first made known to Europe by Marco Polo some six centuries ago, his knowledge of it being derived at second hand from Chinese and Arab traders, accustomed to frequent its shores from a very early period. It figures in his narration under the name of "Madeigascar," as a semi-mythical region—the home of the fabled *rukh*, a bird so powerful as to prey on the elephant by lifting him in its claws, and then dashing him to the earth. Modern discoveries afford a curious explanation of the localization here of this Eastern marvel, for in Madagascar was actually found the so-called "roc's egg," now exhibited at the Natural History Museum at South Kensington, and by its size, represented by a liquid capacity of over two gallons, almost justifying the creations of Oriental fancy. But the æpyornis, the extinct bird hatched from this portentous egg-shell, is believed to have been of the ostrich tribe, and therefore quite unequal to the feats of wing ascribed to Sinbad's aërial carrier.

The first European to catch sight of Madagascar, on February 1, 1506, was Diego Saures, a Portuguese captain, and to a subsequent visit to its western shores in the same year by ships of that nation was due its name of San Laurenço, August 10, St. Lawrence's Day, having been the date of their first glimpse of the island.

All attempts, however, on the part of the Portuguese to occupy the newly-discovered land proved abortive, and the ruins of their fort on the island of Trangoate, on the southern coast, remained for generations a monument of the massacre of their settlers. Abandoned by its first discoverers, the great African island remained, as it were, derelict, on the waters of the Indian Ocean, until it began to attract the attention of other nations.

An English expedition to take possession of it was planned under Charles I., but led to no tangible result, save the publication in 1648 of a poem by Sir William Davenant, entitled "Madagascar," and dedicated to Prince Rupert, the designated Viceroy of the new colony. He is hailed in the following lines as its ruler:—

> And her Cronologers pronounce thy style,
> The first true monarch of the *Golden Isle;*
> An *Isle* so seated for predominance
> Where Navall strength its power can so advance,
> That it may tribute take of what the East
> Shall ever send in traffique to the West.

The treasures which are to reward the followers of the Prince are expatiated on as follows:—

> Some near the deepest shore are sent to dive;
> As with their long retentive breath they strive
> To root up Corall Trees where *Mermaids* lie
> Sighing beneath those Precious boughs, and die
> For absence of their scaly lovers lost
> In midnight storms about the Indian coast.
> Some climbe and search the rocks till each have found
> A *Saphyr*, *Ruby*, and a *Diamond*.
> That which the Sultan's glistrings Bride doth weare,
> To these would but a glowormes eie appear,
> The Tuscan Duk's compared shows sick and dark,
> These living stars, and his a dying spark.

But dazzling visions of the El Dorado of the Indian Ocean were not confined to England, and her rival was already in the field. In 1642 was founded the French Société de l'Orient, empowered to take possession of the island of Madagascar in the name of His Most Christian Majesty, and invested with a commercial monopoly for ten years. In the following year an expedition sailed to give effect to this charter, and planted the French flag on the south-eastern coast of Madagascar, on the wal¹ ?ort Dauphin of lugubrious memory. The infant settlem)on entered on a career of misfortune under the misrul(commandant, Pronis by name, who, having married the daughter of a native chief, distributed the provisions of the colony among his wife's friends, and left his followers to starve. A mutiny was the consequence, and Pronis was placed in irons until released by the arrival of a fresh ship, commanded by Roger de Bourg, with a reinforcement of forty men. The tables being now turned on the mutineers, twelve of the ringleaders were banished to the island of Bourbon with Malagasy wives, and became the progenitors of a race of pirates long the terror of the Indian Ocean.

Pronis used his recovered authority to perpetrate a fresh iniquity, and on the appearance of the Dutch Governor of the Mauritius on a slave hunt in the neighbourhood of Fort Dauphin, willingly undertook to be his purveyor. A number of the unsuspecting natives being engaged as traders, labourers, and servants in the settlement, Pronis, by an act of perfidy, exceptional, one would fain hope, even in the annals of colonial administration, kidnapped and sold to the Dutch seventy-five of their number. Their captors eventually profited little by the bargain, for, under the name of Maroons, apparently derived from the Malagasy "maronita," a cooly or bearer, the descendants of these and other slaves, escaping to the mountains of the Mauritius, rendered the island untenable to the Dutch colonists, and have continued to harass successive generations of French and English settlers down to the present day.

It is not wonderful that at the end of five years of Pronis's administration the whole country round Fort Dauphin should have been in arms against the French, and that he should have left to his successor, Estienne de Flacourt, one of the directors of the Company, a legacy of seven years' incessant warfare. A man of rare energy and ability, the new Governor did much to retrieve the fortunes of the French, and on an island on the north-east coast, called by its inhabitants Nosse Ibrahim, in honour of their claim to be descended from Abraham, but rechristened by its new occupants as Ile Ste. Marie, he established a fresh colony in a most advantageous position. To his pen, too, we owe the most detailed early account of Madagascar, derived from his incessant exploration of its shores.*

In 1665, in emulation of the English and Dutch East India Companies, a new French enterprise was set on foot for the colonization of Madagascar (called in its charter) Eastern France. Despite royal patronage, the "Grand Monarque" himself subscribing a fifth of the capital of 15 millions of francs, the new Society of the East Indies throve no better than its predecessor,

---

* "Histoire de Madagascar." Estienne de Flacourt, Paris, 1658.

and collapsed utterly at the end of five years. Nor were matters mended when the French Crown, in 1670, assumed titular jurisdiction over Madagascar: the massacre of the colonists two years later put an end to its pretensions; and a fresh attempt to colonize Ile Ste. Marie had a like disastrous ending in 1754.

Madagascar figures next as the scene of the closing exploits of a remarkable adventurer. Count Maurice Auguste Beniowsky, a Hungarian magnate of Polish extraction, after a romantic escape from a Siberian prison, organized a private expedition and established himself at Foule Point near the Ile Ste. Marie. An old negress having sworn that he was the son of a Madagascar princess, born in the Mauritius, he was accepted as a sovereign by the neighbouring tribes, and was ultimately killed in resisting an attack by the French in 1786, twelve years after his first arrival on the coast.*

While legitimate commerce was driven from the shores of Madagascar, they became the haunt of all the maritime rascality engaged in piracy and slave-hunting, and it was early known as an ocean Alsatia, the refuge and sanctuary of cosmopolitan crime. Flanking the great traffic route to the East, it afforded a convenient ambush for the sea-vultures gathered from all points of the compass to prey upon its commerce. From the hidden openings of its glass-green lagoons, from the mouths of rivers folded deep in tropical jungle, from creeks where coral reefs parted the blue pool within from the leap and dazzle of the boiling surf outside, stole forth low, dark hulls, smothered under dizzy heights of sail, and displaying the black flag that made them the terror of the deep. Many a Portuguese carrick heavy with the spoil of the Carnatic, many a slow Dutch galleon deep laden with the drugs and spices, the gold and gems of the Eastern Archipelago, was dragged in triumph to the ports of St. Mary's Isle, where her arrival was the signal for a hideous carnival. Hogsheads of spirits were tapped on the beach, around which swarthy Bacchantes flaunted in robes destined as gifts for princesses, and grotesque negresses reeled and sang, their shocks of crisp hair crowned with gems worthy to form an empress's coronet. At night, when blazing torches lit the lurid revel, its fun turned to ferocity, and wild dithyrambs were drowned by wilder curses, and men fought like tigers over their prey, and the beach ran blood into the brine.

dynasties. They surrounded themselves with all the luxury of Eastern sultans, and built lordly dwellings deep in the primæval forest. Captain Misson, a Provençal, erected a fort and town, brought land under cultivation, gave a constitution and code of laws to his settlement, called Libertatia, and, while sending out his ships to scour the seas, traded peaceably with his neighbours on shore. This model corsair colony was nevertheless exterminated by the natives, who suddenly assumed a hostile attitude and massacred their quondam friends.

The notorious Captain Kidd, who, sent out with a roving commission by William III. against the pirates of the Indian Ocean, ended by hoisting the black flag himself, made Madagascar for a time his base of operations.

It was not till 1722, when the capture of a large Portuguese vessel with the Archbishop of Goa on board aroused the indignation of Europe, that the nest of pirates on the northeastern shore of Madagascar was extirpated by a combined expedition. The natives, however, down to the beginning of the present century continued to send out predatory canoe fleets, harassing the Portuguese settlements on the coast of Africa, pillaging the Comoro Islands, and making an occasional prize of a becalmed or helpless vessel; but the establishment of a more regular Government in the island has now put an end to these marauding expeditions.

Piracy left a terrible legacy to Madagascar in the slave trade, resorted to by the ex-corsairs when cut off from their former way of life. Tribal wars were encouraged by the ready sale for prisoners shipped from the ports to Mauritius, Réunion and other islands. The point whence the sea is first visible on the journey from the interior is still called Taniakova, " the weeping place of the Hovas," in memory of the sorrow which tradition says broke forth afresh as the captives, standing on the top of the pass, beheld the black waters and realized the bitterness of exile. The place is now marked by a column inscribed with the name of Radama I., under whose reign the slave trade was abolished.

But before that event took place the history of the island had entered on a new phase, under the impetus of a sudden development of some of the native races.

The ethnology of Madagascar is somewhat of a riddle from the identity of language, apparently in contradiction with diversity of physical type, prevailing throughout its extent. Malay origin is indubitably indicated by the first, while the second may be explained, in regard to the peoples of the coast, as due to subsequent waves of miscellaneous immigration, introducing negro and other elements.

It was exclusively with these coast tribes that Europeans had hitherto come in contact, and of these the Sakalavas were by far the most powerful and energetic. Originally restricted to a small territory in the south-west, they had gradually extended themselves along the whole western and northern coasts, and, subjugating the tribes of the interior, had formed two strong kingdoms whose supremacy endured until the end of the last century. Until then the dominant race in Madagascar, they at last found a rival in an unexpected quarter.

About the date of the Norman Conquest of England, as native tradition tells, a small Malay tribe arrived on the coast of Madagascar from beyond the sea, and, driven by pressure of population towards the rocky plateau of Imerina, possessed themselves there of a district measuring some eighty miles in one direction by sixty in another. Here they attained such relative degree of civilization as is shown by skill in weaving silk and cotton fabrics, in the cultivation of the soil, and the manufacture of metals. The Hovas, however, like the Jews in Europe, were despised by the other races of Madagascar, and perhaps for the same reason—their aptitude for commercial pursuits—but, like the Jews, they too prospered on the antipathy of their neighbours. It was about the beginning of the present century that the appearance among their hereditary rulers of two remarkable sovereigns gave a sudden impulse to their development, and transformed the tribe into a nation.

The first of these leaders, Andrianimpoinimèrina, "the chief in the heart of Imèrina," consolidated his inland kingdom by the subjugation of adjacent provinces; the second, his son and successor, Radama I., carried his victorious arms to the eastern and western seas, reduced the Sakalavas and other tribes to vassalage, and assumed the title of King of Madagascar.

The island had meantime become the battle-field of colonial jealousies between the two great Western Powers of Europe, the English maintaining that it was included in the cession by France, under the Treaty of Paris, of Mauritius and its dependencies. France, which had reoccupied some of her abandoned positions on the Ile Ste. Marie, repudiated this interpretation, and Sir Robert Farquharson, Governor of the Mauritius, conceived the astute idea of playing off the newly-risen force in Madagascar politics against the pretensions of the rival Power. To this epoch, therefore, dates back the long grudge of France against the H(ationality, which her statesmen declare a pure fiction of l diplomacy.

Captain Le S :lected as the English Envoy to Radama I., repaired, in 18 Antananarivo, and was the first European to set foot ii Hova capital. The journey thither of 224 miles, undert 1 the rainy season, when the unbridged torrents were in full flood and the steep paths slippery with mud, was a toilsome one, and its hardships cost the lives of several members of the embassy. Sighted after long days of march, through forest and wilderness, the mountain capital of Imèrina presented a sufficiently imposing aspect to the travellers. Its population of 60,000 or 80,000 justified its name, meaning "the town of a thousand villages," and its situation on a long bluff rising sharply some four or five hundred feet above the plain lends picturesque beauty to the irregular masses of dwellings clinging pell-mell to its narrow ledges, or crowded together on its steep slopes. Its most characteristic feature is derived from the "horns of the houses," the long crossed ends of the gable rafters projecting three or four feet beyond the roof at each end, and giving it the appearance of being terminated by a pair of small windmills. To the end of each of these projections is attached by a wire a small wooden image of the falcon, called voromahery, or "bird of power," the national emblem of the Hovas. Two models of the same bird, in gilt bronze, surmount the Tranovola, the "Silver Palace" of the king, which, built on the highest point of the hill, termed Tampombohitra, "the crown of the town," towers above the mass of houses, with its triple tiers of open galleries and steep slope of roof rising to a height of sixty feet.

As the English visitors approached the capital they were met by a deputation of its noblest inhabitants, male and female, bearing refreshments and offerings—

The women, says M. Blanchard in the interesting series of articles in the *Revue des Deux Mondes* quoted among our headings, dressed in a dark purple lamba (a loose outer garment) fastened at the waist, and falling in graceful folds edged with waving fringes, were adorned with necklaces, silver chains, and rings around the ankles; the men similarly adorned, but distinguished by a sort of silver crown on their heads, wore belts furnished with pockets for amulets, and carried in their hands muskets of elegant construction.

Borne by four stout bearers in a chair of state, around which thousands of native soldiers danced in his honour, Captain Le Sage made his solemn entry into Antananarivo, amid the thunder of cannon, and the acclamations of a vast multitude. As the *cortège* halted, Radama's Minister addressed the people, and announced that the King had given the country to his visitor, appealing to them for assent according to traditional formula, the answering shout of "izay," "it is so," breaking from the throng with a quick, sharp tone like the rattle of musketry. Then, addressing the envoy, the Prime Minister declared to him that he was now King of Madagascar, while

Radama reigned only in the Mauritius. "Such forms of politeness," says the writer just quoted, "might have suggested Persia or India," and they were repeated when Radama himself subsequently received his guest in the royal palace.

The most important provision of the treaty then negotiated was the abolition of the slave trade by the Hova monarch. Its principal agents were the descendants of the former pirates, the most noted of whom, Jean Réné, a French half-caste and chief of Tintingue, paid periodical visits to Antananarivo for the purchase of prisoners of war. In consideration of so costly a concession to humanity, Radama was to receive from England a yearly subsidy of 2,000 dollars, as well as arms, ammunition, and accoutrements for his troops. A temporary difficulty as to the execution of this contract during the absence in England of Sir Robert Farquharson, produced a most unfavourable impression on the monarch's mind, and gave rise to the unflattering simile "false as an Englishman," proverbially current in Madagascar.

The difficulty was eventually surmounted by the despatch of Mr. Hastie, a fresh envoy, and the treaty was finally concluded in 1820.

A magnificent service of plate was among the presents sent to soothe the feelings of the irritated monarch, and a drill-sergeant, sent from the Mauritius to train his army formed another pledge of the amity of his new ally. This man, Brady by name, rose high in the royal favour, and remained a prominent figure at the court of Antananarivo. From his teaching was derived the use of English military terms still employed in Madagascar, though in such corruptions as *Soporitra*, and *Reraiky takopon adrara*, it may not be easy to recognize the familiar words of command, "Support arms!" and " Rear rank take open order!"

But though Radama appreciated the advantages of civilization, he was shrewd enough to dread contact with it, and all Mr. Hastie's persuasions could not prevail on him to permit the construction of a road to his capital. It would soon serve, he said, to bring the English redcoats to Antananarivo, and recent events seem to prove his political sagacity. As a subsequent Prime Minister declared to the French Consul, in reply to a threat of invasion, Generals Hazo and Tazo (forest and fever) enable the Hovas to set such menaces at defiance, and indeed, should these Malagasy equivalents for the "Generals January and February," of Alexander I. of Russia, do their work half as well as their prototypes, Antananarivo has little to fear from an enemy.

No obstacles however, were placed in the way of Christian

teaching in Imèrina, and English missionaries of various sects, but principally of that calling itself Independent, established themselves in the capital. Reducing the Malagasy language for the first time to writing, they prepared translations of the Scriptures, and distributed them extensively, making many converts among the people.

The French, meantime, sought to counterbalance English influence by intrigues against Radama among the coast peoples, and both in the north and south fomented abortive rebellions against his rule. Their attempt to obtain a footing on the mainland, near the Ile Ste. Marie, was likewise frustrated in 1822 by the appearance on the coast of Radama and his victorious army, while at the other extremity of the island the French flag was ignominiously hauled down from the walls of Fort Dauphin, and the settlers driven from the locality.

The Hova conqueror had thus made good his claim to the title of King of Madagascar, but his career was drawing to a close. An abstemious and almost ascetic youth proved no safeguard against temptations to excess in later years, and his death in 1828, at the comparatively early age of thirty-six, was due in great measure to his own intemperance. His barbaric genius has been likened to that of Peter the Great, since he, too, moulded the future of his race by linking it with Western civilization. He proposed, however, a different model for his own imitation, and Napoleon the First, whose picture adorned his palace, was the hero he flattered himself he resembled.

One of his eleven widows, raised to the throne by a court cabal, succeeded him under the title of Ranavàlona I.—a name which may be worthily coupled with those of the most ferocious tyrants in history. The massacre of all her late husband's surviving relatives formed a sanguinary overture to a reign of terror, and was quickly followed by a decree of banishment against all foreigners. The situation was rather aggravated by feeble attempts at intervention on the part of the Western Powers, and the repulse of a combined Anglo-French attack on the forts of Tamatave in 1845 led to the exaction by the haughty Ranavàlona of an indemnity of 15,000 dollars.

The French, meantime, true to their policy of supporting the coast tribes in their resistance to Hova rule, had established that protectorate over the western Sakalavas on which their present claims are based. Isormoumeka, a queen of that nation, driven with her people from the mainland by the tyranny of the Hovas, took refuge, in 1839, on the small island of Nossi-bé, and, in consideration of protection from the French, made over to them her territory on the west coast of Madagascar, from Cape St. Vincent to the Bay of Passandana. They have since then been in occupation of the islands of Nossi-Bé and Mayotte, but their claims to dominion on the mainland have remained dormant for over forty years, while they have recognized that of the Hova Government by the payment of dues, and by the acceptance of an indemnity for the act of one of the chiefs in the ceded territory.

The amenities of Ranavàlona's rule over conquered peoples may be gathered from a single fact—the massacre, in 1831, of the whole manhood of one of the coast tribes, summoned to appear in a given place, and there butchered to the number of 25,000. Her hereditary subjects fared little better, and the announcement of a *kabary*, or public assembly, invariably struck terror to their hearts as the preliminary to fresh atrocities. Thus, in 1837, she made proclamation at one of these meetings that all criminals confessing their misdeeds should be spared, while those accused by others should suffer death. Ninety-six of the latter category accordingly underwent various cruel modes of execution, while fifteen hundred self-accused malefactors were spared, indeed, but only for a living death. Fastened together in gangs of four or five by iron bars soldered round their necks, they were set free in indissolubly associated misery, liable to aggravation as the death of one of the group left the survivors to bear the added weight of his chains.

If such was the justice of Ranavàlona, her sports were scarcely less fatal, and one buffalo hunt was said to have cost the lives of 20,000 wretches, impressed as carriers and messengers without any provision for their sustenance. Her wars were on a corresponding scale of destructiveness, and those waged by her up to 1840 are believed to have caused the slaughter of 100,000 men, and the slavery of double that number, sold as prisoners by her victorious troops. These campaigns drained the province of Ankova of 20,000 or 30,000 soldiers, attended by a like number of camp-followers, of whom not more than one half returned to their homes.

Nor were the royal caprices less terrible to individuals than to the community at large; witness the case of a hapless silversmith, sold into life-long slavery for having failed in his first attempt to execute an order which he successfully carried out on a second trial.

It was under the reign of this ogress that there began, in 1849, that persecution of the native Christians spoken of amongst them still as "the dark days." Hunted from their homes, compelled to take refuge in caves and holes in the ground, condemned to agonizing forms of :h, or to the scarcely less agonizing doom of life-long fetters, recently-converted and half-instructed savages displayed tancy worthy of the early martyrs. Nor could their imperfect faith deprive them of any of the merit of their sufferings, since, having accepted Scripture truth in the only form presented to them, they could not, in any proper sense, be classed as heretics. Two thousand are believed to have suffered various degrees of punishment, and many hundreds to have perished utterly. In Antananarivo eighteen executions took place in one day, the victims being precipitated from a rock 150 feet high, in the heart of the city, called, from its use as a place of punishment, Arapimarinana, " the place of hurling down." Suspended by a rope over the abyss, each sufferer in turn was asked, " Will you cease to pray?" and on answering in the negative, was launched into eternity. One young and beautiful girl, for whom the queen had a personal regard, was reserved to the last in the hope that her fortitude would not be proof against the horrors of the scene; but as she still refused to recant, the executioner, doubtless having orders to spare her, declared her insane, and on that pretext restored her to her friends. Four Christians of noble birth were, about the same time, burned at the stake, the mode of execution prescribed for the aristocracy. They died singing a hymn, and, as far as could be perceived by any visible sign, without feeling pain.

The first Christian martyrdom in Madagascar was that of a young woman named Rasolama, put to death in 1836, and the bystanders maintained that her spirit passed away in the act of prayer before the spears of the executioners had actually touched her body. The impotence of persecution against even partial truth was shown in Madagascar, as elsewhere, by the extensive spread of Christianity during this time of trial.

The heart of the fierce Queen was accessible to but one softer feeling—love for her only son, Prince Rakoto, the late blossom and unexpected joy of her maturer years. By a strange legal fiction prevailing in Madagascar, as among the Bechuanas of South Africa, a woman's first husband is the reputed father of all her children, though the offspring of subsequent marriages; and Rakoto, born more than a year after the late King's death, was his heir and representative.

Never a convert to Christianity, yet the protector of its votaries, and imbued with its divinest spirit of compassion, this young man, strange offshoot from such a parent stock, stood like an angel of mercy beside the blood-stained throne of Ranavàlona. No cry for pity reached him unregarded, and he never failed, when informed of an impending execution, to fly to the prison or scaffold and snatch the victim from his mother's ministers of death. Nor did the Queen resent his interference, but only contrived by the speed and secrecy with which her sanguinary deeds were executed to render it unavailing.

Many of his acts of charity were of so striking and dramatic a character as to deserve the term "heroic." On one occasion, meeting a captive limping along with lacerated feet, he snatched off his own shoes to bestow them on him; on another, descended from his litter to give his place to an unfortunate undergoing similar maltreatment; again, meeting a gang of slaves harshly driven towards the capital, he flung aside his shoes and head-gear, placed himself with disordered garments and dishevelled hair in the front rank of the sad procession, and took his seat among the wretches composing it, in the courtyard of the palace, to await his royal mother. The mute eloquence of the appeal was not lost even on Ranavàlona: she embraced her son with tears, and released the prisoners for his sake. Ingenious in his devices of benevolence, the amiable Prince made even his amusements serve the same end, and, directing his hunting parties to a district where he knew that the Queen had assigned the unpaid labour of her subjects to some local magnate, would desire a distribution of food to be made in his presence to the unfed and oppressed workmen. He saved the lives of five Jesuit missionaries, settled among the Sakalavas at Ibaly, on the west coast, by giving them notice that the Queen had sent an army of 1,500 men to demand their extradition from the natives. Warned in time, they were able to escape, and Ranavàlona was baulked of her prey.

There was one exception to the Queen's hatred of foreigners, and a Frenchman, cast away on her shores, became one of her most trusted counsellers. Jean Baptiste Laborde, the son of a merchant in the south of France, having embarked early in Eastern commerce, was shipwrecked in 1831 on the coast of Madagascar, and conducted to Ranavàlona as one capable of instructing her subjects in the arts of Europe.

This his mechanical genius singularly fitted him for doing, and he speedily rose to great eminence. At Mantassoa, on the edge of the great forest, forty kilometres from Antananarivo, he created an industrial town, where 5,000 people were employed in different branches of industry. Cannon foundries, match factories, glass and paper works, a mulberry plantation and nursery of silk-worms, sprang up as if by magic in the wilderness, and the deserted streets of the once busy settlement still attest the energy of the mind that had called it into existence for a time.

M. I   le, who was for many years French Consul in
Madag: was, up to his death in 1878, the most influential
protect   Catholicity in the island, and even during the reign
of the   e Ranavàlona sheltered two Jesuit missionaries in
the c   of tutor and doctor to his household. One of them,
Père   elebrated Mass for the first time in Antananarivo,

on July 8, 1855, in the presence of the Crown Prince Rakoto, but with great precautions for secresy.

In the same year there came to Antananarivo another Frenchman, destined to exercise a considerable influence over the course of public affairs in Madagascar, and to play the part of evil genius to the young Prince This Lambert, originally a planter from the Mauritius, was so struck by the sufferings he witnessed under the tyranny of Ranavàlona, that he devoted his energies to intriguing for her deposition. With this view he visited France and England, and in interviews with Lord Clarendon and the Emperor Louis Napoleon, sought to procure the armed intervention of those two Powers. Having failed in this attempt, he returned to Madagascar in 1857, to try and carry out his design by other means. A plot was organized, with the privity of the Prince, to substitute him for his mother on the throne; but the intrigue coming to the knowledge of Ranavàlona, led only to the expulsion of all Europeans from her capital, and to a fresh persecution of native Christians.

Among the foreigners banished under this decree was the celebrated Madame Ida Pfeiffer, who had availed herself of M. Lambert's escort to travel in Madagascar. The visit ended fatally for her, since, from the hardships undergone in the return journey to the coast, protracted by the native guards who accompanied the party for fifty-three days, during which she never took off her clothes, she contracted the germ of the disease from which she died a few months later.

Her lively pen gives a graphic view of the social life of Antananarivo, describing the royal costume-ball, when the guests danced by daylight in the courtyard of the palace in fancy dresses copied from European prints, the Queen looking on from a balcony; the State banquets lasting twenty-four hours, at which beetles, locusts, and silkworms in the pupa stage figured among the delicacies; and the fierce Queen's thraldom to her twelve attendant diviners, who, by means of *sikidy*, or combinations of beans on a ruled board, prescribed the time and manner of all her actions, indicating even the well from which her drinking water must be drawn.

During the remaining four years of this female tyrant's reign of terror, her doings remained a sealed book to the rest of the world, but her death on August 16, 1861, once more threw Madagascar open to European intercourse. Despite a formidable conspiracy in favour of his cousin Ramoosaluma, Rakoto succeeded to his mother's throne under the title of Radama II., and inaugurated a reign which he hoped, as he himself said, should be remembered as the happiest era of his country. His first acts were in harmony with these utterances and with his previous character. He showed a magnanimity probably unparalleled in the annals of his house by pardoning his rival for the throne, whom he left in full enjoyment of all his possessions, and sentenced only to banishment from the capital.

His next act of mercy was to set at liberty a number of Sakalava chiefs, detained in long and cruel durance by his mother, and now sent home by him with valuable presents, and, what they prized still more, the mortal remains of their comrades who had died in exile, restored to their people for honourable sepulture. When the liberated captives appeared in their homes, like ghosts risen from the tomb, to tell their friends of the unheard of clemency of the Hova King, the effect produced on these rude savages was electrifying. They instantly showed their gratitude by the restoration of all the prisoners and booty taken in a recent successful raid on the Hova border, and sent ambassadors to offer allegiance and voluntary submission to Radama. Their envoys were received by him with royal hospitality, and on their offering to surrender their arms he bade them, instead, take them home and have them in readiness to come to his assistance when he should call on them. Such magnanimity was not lost on the Sakalavas; they became the most loyal of Radama's subjects, the war-wasted border-land dividing them from his people was brought under cultivation, and peaceful intercourse took the place of mutual aggression between the villages on either side its neutral zone.

The following letter, written by Radama to the Pope on November 9, 1861, and published in *Les Missions Catholiques*, November 7, 1879, shows by what exalted sentiments he was at this time actuated:—

MOST HOLY FATHER,—I desire to announce to you the death of my mother, which occurred on August 16, 1861, and my accession to the throne under the title of Radama II. A great conspiracy was formed against me to prevent my succeeding my mother, but Providence watched over me, and frustrated the designs of the wicked.

I have pardoned them all in imitation of the example of Christ, and not a single drop of blood has been shed. I have set at liberty all the unhappy wretches who groaned in prison and in chains.

I have but one desire, Most Holy Father: it is to see my people happy and civilized. I have thought that the surest means to this end was to have them instructed in the Christian religion.

I have. therefore, summoned missionaries and authorized them to teach th   out my dominions. Père Jouen, with his companions, has alre   :ived in my capital to open schools and charitable institutions.   will be directed by the Sisters he has procured for me.

Mos'   Father, I am but a very young King, without much experi   d have great need of help in order to accomplish worthily the high mission God has confided to me. I venture to count on the prayers and blessings of your Holiness, and entreat them with all the respect and affection of a son for his father.

It is sad to have to relate that so many lofty aspirations, and virtue of such a heroic type could not permanently struggle against an inheritance of evil tendencies entailed from generations, and that the deterioration in the King's character under the influence of a body of young companions and officers known as the mena-maso, soon began to grieve his European counsellors. His policy, however, was still guided by a wise and enlightened liberality; he restricted to the utmost of his power the oppressive system of forced labour, setting the example of paying his own workmen, and abolished the duties on imports, establishing free trade throughout his dominions.

Thus the opening of the new reign seemed to promise a golden era for Madagascar, and the festivities in honour of Radama's coronation, to which both England and France sent representatives, were an occasion of real national rejoicing. A motley gathering flocked to Antananarivo, as all the various tribes of the island sent deputations to attend, and wild, uncouth figures from outlying provinces were met in the steep ways of the town of a thousand villages. Rough Buras and Betsileos from the southern plateaus; Tanalas from the shades of their great forest-fringe; Sibànikas or lake-dwellers inhabiting the marshlands around the spreading island mere of Aloatra; Tankay, natives of the long valley-trough which breaks the eastern declivity; Betsimsarakas, cotton-clad in European fabrics, from the shores of the Indian Ocean, and long-limbed, swarthy Sakalavas from those of the Mozambique Channel, crowned like Tritons with fillets of shells—all came to offer the hásina, or coin of tribute, to the new Sovereign.

The illumination of the whole plain of Imèrina was a striking feature in the celebration, as all the villages in that populous basin and on the surrounding heights blazed out simultaneously in the darkness. The coronation itself took place on September 23, 1862, and was rendered impressive from the vast and orderly concourse of people assembled to assist at it in the great natural amphitheatre consecrated by usage to such ceremonies. It might have appeared, by the light of subsequent events, an incident of sinister augury that the King's charger reared and threw him as the royal cortège was on its return to the city.

Indeed, the ill-fated monarch had already signed the instrument of his own downfall, duped by the arts of a designing adventurer. Among the foreigners who flocked to Antananarivo on his accession was the speculative Frenchman Lambert, anxious to make the most of his influence over the young King. The latter had, on

June 28, 1855, while still heir apparent to the throne, signed a document conferring on this man extensive proprietary rights over the whole of Madagascar, under the form of a concession for developing the natural resources of the island. The cultivation of unoccupied lands, the extraction of minerals, the construction of roads, bridges, and canals were among the privileges contained in the charter, which reserved to the Hova Government only the right of receiving ten per cent. of the profits, in exchange for such extraordinary powers. This concession, Radama, on September 12, 1862, was induced to confirm by a fresh signature, obtained while he was under the influence of intoxication, to which his generally temperate habits rendered him on convivial occasions peculiarly liable.

All representations of the disastrous character of the act were vain; he considered his honour pledged, and refused to retract the fatal document. Jealousy of foreign intervention, a powerful sentiment among semi-civilized people, was thus aroused among his subjects at the very outset of the new reign, whose social reforms had already evoked the hostility of a combination of powerful classes. The restriction of the oppressive labour conscription deprived the great nobles of the unpaid service liberally placed at their disposal by the Crown in former reigns; the idol keepers and hereditary sacerdotal caste saw their influence undermined by the encouragement given to Christianity, and the Prime Minister and Commander-in-chief, the King-makers of Madagascar, and chiefs of the powerful faction which had placed Radama on the throne, found their hopes of ruling through him thwarted by the influence of his personal followers, the menamaso, who formed a ministry of the palace.

But the immediate pretext for the King's overthrow was furnished by an act of his own, so unaccountable as to give the idea that his reason had given way under the pressure of superstitious terrors artfully brought to bear upon him.

During the spring of 1863 strange reports began to reach the capital from the neighbouring villages of a mysterious sickness prevailing there, affecting the patients with paroxysms of dancing madness about the period of the full moon. This epidemic, called "ramenjana," was accompanied by other supernatural manifestations, and by visions and apparitions in the heavens, where the spirits of the King's ancestors were seen, as though in prognostication of startling events. As time went on, groups of these maniacs began to appear in the streets of the capital, dancing along to the sound of singing, or the music of rude instruments, and even invaded the precincts of the palace, creating scenes of tumult and excitement. The King's mind was much disturbed, and in recognition of the sacred character of the malady was conveyed in a decree, desiring all who came in the way of those affected by it to stand aside and uncover as they passed. A still more extraordinary edict, promulgated on the 3rd of May, licensed an appeal to arms after a declaration before witnesses, as the lawful mode of settling all causes of dispute between individuals, groups of people, or even entire villages, and abrogated the enforcement of any penalty for the blood shed in these combats. Such a proclamation amounted to a legalisation of civil war, and was believed to be designed to cover a general massacre of Christians, against whom the supernatural machinery just described had been doubtless set in motion by the priests.

The effect of the decree was, however, never tested, as the Prime Minister and his party, after remonstrating in vain with the infatuated prince, took the remedy into their own hands, and organised a revolution for his overthrow. During the next few days the capital was filled with troops, the palace surrounded, and the mena-maso, the detested Ministers of the King's policy, hunted out and summarily executed to the number of about thirty.

The closing scene of the tragedy soon followed. At daybreak on May 12 a party of soldiers and conspirators broke into the royal apartments, and, after forcibly removing the Queen, who vainly tried to shield her husband's person, flung a mantle over his head and strangled him with a girdle. "I have never shed blood," was the unfortunate monarch's last utterance—a plea for mercy which availed, one may well hope, in heaven, though not on earth. The first reforming sovereign of a despotic dynasty, Radama died, like Louis XVI. of France and Alexander II. of Russia, a victim to the violent reaction of forces crushed into impotence by the iron rule of his predecessors.

His Queen and cousin, Rabodo, was forthwith proclaimed by the title of Rasohèrina, and her consent to the new constitution promulgated was demanded by the nobles with the significant intimation that, if they violated it they were to be held guilty of treason, and if she violated it they would do as they had just done at that moment. The first article of this instrument provides "that the sovereign shall not drink spirituous liquors," in obvious allusion to the circumstances under which M. Lambert's concession had been obtained, and another clause enacts that the concurrence of the sovereign, the nobles, and the heads of the people shall be required for legislation as well as for capital sentences.

Radama's assassination was not effected without giving rise to considerable indignation among his subjects, and their attachment to his memory was shown in the persistency with which rumours of his escape and survival in concealment were circulated, despite severe penalties and even eighteen executions in one day. The Sakalavas, too, rose in revolt to avenge his death, and though conquered, never resumed the peaceful intercourse with their neighbours which had subsisted during his reign of twenty months.

Foreign relations were complicated by the claims of M. Lambert, as France threatened to enforce them at the cannon's mouth. The raising of the indemnity of 240,000 dollars by which he was eventually bought off, proved a severe strain upon the resources of the country, and nearly provoked a rebellion, although the Queen provided the greater part of the sum from her private funds.

Dissensions among the ruling faction shortly after Radama's death led to the degradation and banishment of the all-powerful Prime Minister, Rainivoninahitraniany, an event equivalent to a fresh *coup d'état*, as the office, for which, together with that of Commander-in-Chief, plebeians alone are eligible, is constitutionally held for life. The deposed Minister was succeeded by his brother Rainilaiarivony, who, in accordance with the law or custom prescribing the marriage of the head of the Executive with that of the State, if a female, has now been the husband of three royal consorts successively.

The reigns of Radama I., of Ranavàlona and her son form the transition stage of Malagasy history, which entered on its present phase with the crisis of the last monarch's assassination.

Rasohèrina's reign was beneficent and uneventful; she encouraged the teaching of Christianity, and herself received baptism at the hands of M. Laborde within four days of her death, which occurred on March 29, 1868. Her cousin and successor, Ramoma, who reigned as Ranavàlona II., was baptized, together with the Prime Minister, on February 21, in the year after her accession; and her conversion was further emphasized by the public ceremony of burning the national idols on September 19 following. The royal example was widely followed; private fetishes and household gods were universally consigned to the flames, and the crowds of uninstructed converts who thronged into the churches, from imitation rather than conviction, became a source of embarrassment to the Protestant missionaries.

Catholicity, though only tolerated, not encouraged, by the ruling powers, began to make progress, owing to the labours of devoted ˮ ich missionaries, and their success aroused a hostile spirit o   ; the Protestant sectaries, which found vent in outbreaks   :al persecution. Pupils of the Catholic schools, and even t   :sts themselves, were sometimes waylaid and beaten, while   thorities were slow to afford redress for these outrages

Various useful reforms distinguished the reign of this Queen, and the edict passed in 1877 for the emancipation of all the Mozambique or African slaves throughout her dominions is especially worthy of mention. On her death, July 13, 1883, her niece, Razafindahety, a young widow, and also a Christian, succeeded to the throne, and assumed the title of Ranavàlona III. But as the Prime Minister, the virtual ruler of the country, retained his office and became her consort, the inauguration of a new reign has effected little actual change.

The nice constitutional balance which establishes an all-powerful plebeian Minister beside a despotic hereditary throne, corresponds to a similarly complex social organization among the Hovas. The highest class is formed by the *andriana*, or nobles, descended from royal clans, tracing their origin to former princes or chieftains. Whole villages are inhabited by these patricians, whose aristocratic lineage is, however, no bar to their earning their bread as artisans or tradesmen.

The middle-class consists of the Hova freemen, divided into numerous tribes and families, each intermarrying only within its own circle. Another line of demarkation is that between "borozana" and "màramila"—civilians and soldiers—so classified according to the form of service rendered to the State. Military grades, called "honours," represented by numbers from one to seventeen, confer social and political distinction, and are esteemed accordingly.

The slaves, since the enfranchisement in 1877 of those of African orgin, are divided into two categories—the "Andevo," descended from conquered tribes, and the "zaza Hovas"—"offspring of the Hovas"—enslaved for debt, crime, or political offences. The absence of public prisons renders slavery for life a frequent penal sentence, not only relieving the State of the charge of its criminals, but enriching it by their sale. Domestic slavery, although the law invests the owner with the power of life and death, is not in general a harsh form of service, and masters and slaves frequently share the same household tasks.

Far more burdensome is the "fànampoàna," or labour conscription, to which the free population is liable, and in virtue of which the Crown requisitions the unpaid service of its subjects for all public works. Removed from their homes, and deprived of their ordinary means of subsistence, the wretched labourers are sometimes left to starve, and as military service is exacted under similar conditions, the soldiers during a campaign are in equally miserable plight. The duties of the latter in time of peace consist only of appearing at reviews or other public spectacles, equipped for the day with arms and accoutrements, duly restored to the magazines at its close. Under the more enlightened *régime* of recent years the abuse of the "corvée" has been much restricted, but on a journey of some weeks' duration, undertaken by the late Queen to visit Fianarantsoa, the Betsileo capital, her *cortége* consisted of 50,000 people.

Statistics as to the population of Madagascar are totally wanting, but it probably does not exceed four millions, the Hovas forming about a fifth of the entire. The latter, like most conquering races, are of a lighter complexion than their subjects. Many whose features approach the Caucasian type might pass for natives of South-Eastern Europe, while the admixture of African blood, due to the importation of Mozambique slaves, is apparent in the features of others. They are distinguished from Europeans by a curious physical peculiarity—a lower temperature of the blood, appreciable by the thermometer.

Rice is their staple food, and time and distance alike are calculated by the term of about twenty minutes required for its cooking : thus a place is described as so many boilings of rice away, according to the length of the journey thither. Eleven varieties are grown, and great labour is bestowed on its culture. In Imèrina the hills are terraced in ledges, forming so many separate irrigation levels, and at a certain stage of their growth the young plants are carefully transplanted by women, at a cost of incalculable toil. In the rich forest country of the Tanalas, east of the plateaus, a simpler mode of culture is practised, the ground being merely cleared by burning the brushwood, and then trampled by oxen, preparatory to sowing the grain at the close of the rainy season. This mode of husbandry, however, necessitates perpetual migration, as the villages have to be shifted in search of fresh rice-grounds every year.

Edible roots, manioc, yams, and sweet potatoes abound, and oxen are reared on a very large scale. Fattened on sugar-cane and other succulent food, in a deep pit called "fahitra," those killed on festive occasions often attain the obesity of an English prize beast. The flesh, cooked with the hide on, is the great luxury of the natives, four of whom are said to be capable of consuming an ox in twenty-four hours.

A favourite beverage is supplied by water boiled in a vessel, to which rice in cooking has been allowed to adhere; but a more potent drink, called toak, is manufactured from the fermentation of honey or sugar-cane. The sale of spirituous drinks is forbidden throughout Imerina, where drunkenness was at one time a capital offence, but the other islanders are under no such restrictions, and are much addicted to stimulants. The Hova Government, compelled by treaty with foreign Powers to permit the importation of spirit   ly declines to make a profit on their consumption, and   ntitled to charge a duty of 10 per cent. on their entry, levies it in kind, and has every tenth barrel of rum broken on the beach at Tamatave.

The export trade of Madagascar consists almost entirely of cattle, shipped to the neighbouring islands of Mauritius and Réunion. As in other parts of the globe, the Manchester fabrics, once extensively imported, are losing the market owing to deterioration of quality, and are gradually being supplanted by American goods, despite the greater length of the voyage. Mr. Hall, the English Acting Consul, says in his report on the trade of Madagascar for 1882 : " The imports of grey shirtings show a falling off of about 30 per cent., and it is to be feared that the trade in this once flourishing staple will continue to decrease, for the worthlessness of Manchester clayed cottons is now being found out by the customer."

One cannot regret that fraud, tolerated at home, should be detected and exposed abroad, and that commercial dishonesty should draw down the penalty of commercial failure.

The currency of Madagascar consists of silver dollars, or piastres, chopped up into minute fragments to the number sometimes of 600, and a small pair of scales for weighing this microscopic coinage is a common article of personal equipment. The commercial shrewdness, as well as the oratorical fluency of the Hovas, finds full scope in the protracted chaffering with which they transact all their bargains.

The Malagasy dwellings, constructed of wood, bamboo, or a composition of earth, kneaded with water, generally consist of a single room and a sleeping loft, under a high-pitched roof, thatched with grass, reeds, or the fronds of the traveller's tree, arranged so as to overlap like tiles and be impermeable to weather. Carefully oriented, with its gables facing north and south, the house forms at once a sun-dial, compass, and calendar; its interior geography is referred to the points of the heavens, and the hours of the day are named according to the position of the sun in regard to it. Noon is "the coming above the ridge;" one o'clock when the first rays penetrate the open door; "the peeping in of the day," three in the afternoon when they reach the central post to which domestic animals are attached at night, is called " at the place of fastening the calf;" and half-past four, when the sunlight gains the eastern wall, "touched."

A stand for the capacious water-jars, a rude hearth, a frame for drying grain and fuel, a wooden mortar and long pole for husking rice, mats and baskets of woven reeds, a few pots and primitive agricultural implements constitute the ordinary domestic furniture. There are neither chairs nor tables, and plates and dishes are supplied by the leaves of the banana or of the traveller's tree, thrown away after each meal. The women are wonderfully skilful in spinning and weaving with the simplest appliances; a piece of bark of anivona palm, fitted with a splinter of bone, serves as a spindle, and four pegs driven into the earthen floor, with a shuttle and piece of wood to stretch the woof, form the loom, on which hemp, cotton, silk, as well as rofia-palm, aloe, or banana fibre, are woven into serviceable, and even beautiful, stuffs.

The lamba, the characteristic article of national costume, is generally homespun. It is a piece of drapery, most frequently white, but often striped or fringed at the edge, reaching from the neck to below the knees, and worn as an outer covering by both sexes alike. Made without sleeves or openings for the arms, it is an inconvenient though picturesque garment, and has to be laid aside, or fastened around the waist, when really active work is undertaken.

The Malagasy language belongs to the Malay family, but has assimilated a certain number of Arabic terms, of which the names of the days and months are the most conspicuous—a soft and liquid speech abounding in vowels, it is spoken by orators with a sonorous and rhythmical cadence. Great richness of expression for certain ideas—its vocabulary containing, for instance, a series of adverbs to describe minute gradations of distance from the speaker—is counter-balanced by curious blanks in other directions, the absence of a plural form for either nouns or verbs being one of the most striking. It is largely inflected by prefixes, and change of tense is marked by variations in the initial letter. Metaphorical names are frequent, such as *maso andro*, "the eye of day," for the sun; *ny anivon ny riaka*, "the land in the midst of the moving waters," for Madagascar itself; and *tsi afa javona*, "that which the mists cannot climb," for its highest peak. Some of these descriptive epithets, generally compounded with the negative prefix *tsi*, are full of quaint suggestiveness. Thus the thorny acacia Indica is called *tsi-afaka-ombe*, "not penetrable by oxen;" the turkey *voron-tsi-loza*, "the *not* terrible bird," with an evident correction of the first impression produced by its aspect; and a small grey fly of mosquito-like pertinacity, *tsi-mati-tehaka*, "not killed by a slap," a phrase comprising a whole elegy on a wakeful night. As in Greek, the soul and the butterfly, that living parable of the resurrection, are described by the same word, *lolo*. Frequent changes of nomenclature are introduced by the *tabù*, here called *fady*, of all words entering into the composition of royal or princely names. When Rabodo, on her accession, assumed the title of Rasohèrina, the word Sohèrina, previously applied to the silkworm moth, had to be dropped from ordinary parlance, and the insect rechristened *zaza dandy*, "offspring of the silk." In similar fashion, the word *mamba*, a crocodile, was interdicted because it entered into the name of Andriamamba, a chief in western Imèrina, the alternative word *voay* being exclusively sed thenceforward. There are private as well as public forms of *tabù* and for the members of a tribe it may be *fady* to utter their own names, or for an individual to mention or touch some common article of household use.

The great Malagasy festival is that of the New Year, when, as at Christmastide in England, numbers of oxen fatted for the occasion are slaughtered for consumption during three days of universal rejoicing, and the villages reek with the odours of the shambles. The central incident of the celebration is the bathing of the sovereign, who, during the public reception in the palace on New Year's Eve, retires behind a screen held up by her attendants, and re-appears with hair and face still dripping from recent immersion. Rice is then boiled on the spot, and handed round, mixed with honey, as were the cakes eaten by the Romans on their New Year's feast in honour of Janus. A little dried beef, preserved from the previous year, also forms part of this symbolical meal, served in all households under the name of *jaka*, while the moment of the Sovereign's entering the bath is signalized by the simultaneous kindling of bonfires, like those lit in Europe at the summer solstice.

Another national celebration, in honour of the circumcision of the boys of suitable age, was formerly observed during several days' solemnity; but though the rite, derived doubtless from the Arabs, is still adhered to, it is now performed more privately.

The description of manners contained in the interesting narrative of Robert Drury,[*] an English lad, shipwrecked on the coast of Madagascar in 1702, and rescued after fifteen years' slavery, still holds good for great part of the island, where the same intertribal warfare continues to prevail with the results so vividly portrayed by him. In the wild country west of Imèrina, hostile tribes are separated by a belt of unoccupied land, resembling the marches of feudal Europe; and the same defensive precaution described by Tacitus as forming part of the system of the early Germans is also observed through a great part of Africa. The fortifications of the mountain villages in Madagascar consist of fences of thorny shrubs, mimosa or prickly pear, sometimes forming a double or triple *enceinte*, and alternating with ditches serving as orchards, and planted with bananas, mangoes, peaches, and edible arums. In some of these hamlets is an amphitheatre for bull-fights, an amusement once held in such esteem, that the favourite bull of Ranavalona]

---

[*] "Madagascar." Robert Drury. London, 1729.

buried with almost royal honours. The residence of the chief, standing in a separate enclosure, generally occupies the centre of the village, and commands the other habitations. A structure for storing rice is an indispensable adjunct of each of these, sometimes excavated as a subterranean chamber, sometimes raised above the ground on wooden poles or stages.

Throughout the whole of Madagascar the same superstitious beliefs prevail, forming an elaborate and degrading system of fetichism.* A singular identity with Greek tradition may be detected in the character of one of the most venerated idols, who, in his healing powers, in his association with the serpent as a symbol, and in the sacrifice of a cock required to propitiate him, corresponds closely with Esculapius. To Arab influence is probably due the complicated fabric of astrology, according to which an inexorable destiny, varying with each month, day, and hour, attaches to every individual on his entrance into the world. Infants born at inauspicious times are summarily made away with, as are those whose mothers have died at their birth, or suffered prolonged illness consequent on it. Wednesday and Friday are the days of evil omen, while Sunday, though especially propitious, is sometimes equally fatal to those born on it, as their over prosperous destiny may eclipse that of their relatives. An ordeal is often resorted to in such cases to decide the fate of the new-born favourites of fortune, who are laid in the path of the returning oxen, and, if untouched by their hoofs, are allowed to live. Others are mutilated as a sort of compromise with destiny, as was the present Prime Minister, deprived at birth of the first joint of the index and middle finger in conformity with this superstition. Even this sacrifice did not, however, in his case avert the decree of fate, and he fulfilled his horoscope by supplanting his elder brother. Twins, though of royal lineage, are also condemned, and the daughter of the late Queen having given birth to two fine boys, they were both remorselessly destroyed. No native woman could be induced to rear these victims of credulity, and the missionaries find it impossible to rescue them from destruction.

The most terrible of all fates overhangs those born at midnight, for they are predestined sorcerers, the living personifications of evil. Vain are all attempts to elude the decree, like that of a woman who concealed the fact that her son had come into the world at that dread hour, only to find him self-betrayed a few months

* Many
Abinal in
(*Astrologi
fabuleuses*
VOl

later, playing on a tombstone with the wizard's gossips, the owl and cat. Nor in the remote country whither she then fled with him for refuge could she shield him from fulfilling his doom; he grew up a noted sorcerer, and was guilty of dreadful crimes before his death.

Various forms of exorcism are, however, resorted to, and the baneful influence is sometimes believed to be averted by a childish mimicry of its effects. Thus a man menaced with the lurid horoscope of fire, solemnly burns a miniature straw hut, thereby ransoming his dwelling from destruction; or a girl doomed to see her offspring perish, performs the funeral obsequies of a dead grass-hopper with all the pomp of woe, and by the fiction of maternal sorrow averts its reality.

The Malagasy beliefs as to the animal kinship and descent of man would do credit to a modern evolutionist. Each tribe has a brute ancestor which its members hold sacred, and more than one traveller, after shooting a lemur or babacoot as a zoological specimen, has had to surrender its remains to his attendants for honourable burial. A boy having been tricked by his companions into making a meal on the flesh of his supposed ancestor the sheep, in the belief that he was eating goat, is described by one of the missionaries as having become violently ill when he learned the truth.

The crocodile is venerated in many places, and is safe from persecution under the ægis of an imaginary compact between its ancestors and man, binding both parties to peace and amity. When a saurian violates this truce by devouring a human victim, one of the brutes is captured and slain, after sentence has been passed on it in regular judicial form, and then receives the posthumous honours of a public funeral, amid the mourning of the population.

Transmigration of souls is a cardinal article of faith, and among the Betsileos is supposed to be regulated by the same rules of precedence that govern the social hierarchy. Thus the soul of the noble, after a ghastly three months' watch beside the unburied corpse, is believed to pass into a seven-headed worm, which developes later into a great serpent, the fanano, and no Betsileo will pass these creatures save with bended knee and face reverently bowed between his hands. When one supposed to harbour the soul of a recently-departed chief approaches a village, it is escorted by the whole population, who trace in its movements a resemblance to the stately bearing of the deceased, and in the markings of its skin a reproduction of the bead embroidery of his winding sheet. Middle-class souls meantime can aspire to no higher avatar than that of a crocodile, and those of the lower orders are mud-born once more as vulgar eels. Some souls fail to achieve complete metamorphosis, and obtain only an uncomfortable lodging in a hobgoblin body, transparent or riddled with holes, while the spirits of the wicked survive as the principle of pains and aches, to inflict suffering on others.

Among Malagasy superstitions must be ranked the strange, but widely diffused, belief in ordeal by poison—a form of jurisprudence, common also to great part of Africa. The kernel of the tanghena nut, scraped in water, is the test of guilt and innocence, the accused being acquitted if his system reject the poison, together with three pieces of chicken-skin swallowed with it, but convicted if these *pièces justificatives* be not forthcoming. The ordeal, whose abolition was one of the reforms of Radama II., was, before his reign, resorted to on such a scale as to have an appreciable effect in diminishing the population, whole communities voluntarily subjecting themselves to it as a means of rebutting accusations. The administration of the poison in large quantities was also a common mode of execution.

Debased by generations of corruption, the Malagasy are devoid of the most rudimentary conceptions of morality, and the whole system of Christian ethics has to be built up amongst them from its foundations. They are nevertheless occasionally capable of exalted virtues, and the brief memoir of Victoire Ratsaraibe, a noble Malagasy widow, in *Les Missions Catholiques*, November 10, 1882, reads like a chapter of early Christian biography.

The early Catholic missionaries who accompanied the French and Portuguese shared the fate of their countrymen, falling victims either to the unhealthiness of the climate or the hostility of the natives. The coast populations have, moreover, hitherto proved obdurate to Christian teaching, and it is only since the reign of Radama II. that the Jesuit missionaries have been able to gain a footing in the interior. There they had, down to July, 1882, established 316 Catholic stations, with 224 churches completed or in course of construction, and an ecclesiastical staff of 48 missionary priests (one a native), 21 lay brothers, 8 Christian brothers, and 20 sisters of St. Joseph Cluny, who had admitted six native novices. The Catholic population is estimated at 80,905; the pupils at male and female schools at 19,103; and the annual baptisms at 1,611 of adults, and 2,882 of infants. Among the most interesting of the Catholic charities is the leper hospital, established in great part by the beneficence of the late Comte de Chambord, and affording an asylum to ninety-eight unfortunate patients, maintained at the expense of the Missio   'hus Catholicity has hitherto prospered and extended, despit·   ional outbursts of local persecution on the part of Prote   ectaries in remote places.

N,   changed by the recent French aggression, in itself

unjust, and in its immediate effects most disastrous to the
Catholic Missions in Madagascar. The claims of France to a
protectorate over the north-west coast, founded on its cession by
the fugitive Sakalava princess in 1839, might have seemed abrogated by over forty years' tacit acquiescence in the *status quo*,
as well as by the treaty negotiated in 1868 with the Queen of
Madagascar, whose sovereignty over the whole island is implied
in the unrestricted recognition of her title. The action of France
is, moreover, a violation of the agreement concluded in 1854
between Lord Clarendon and Count Walewski, in which it was
stipulated that neither Government was to seek any advantage
to the detriment of the other, and that they were for the future
to act in concert, fully recognizing the entire independence of
Madagascar. But the rights of England have ceased to count
as an obstacle to the designs of other Powers in any quarter of
the globe.

On May 5, 1882, the French Commandant formulated a
demand for the withdrawal of the Hova flag from the northwestern districts, and the embassy subsequently sent to Europe
by the Queen of Madagascar, having failed to arrive at a pacific
solution, hostilities were commenced by Admiral Pierre on May
8, 1883. The bombardment of the Hova ports on the west
coast was followed on June 10 by that of Tamatave, and by
the occupation of that town on the ensuing day. The expulsion
of all French residents in the interior was the immediate consequence, nuns and missionaries being included in the decree. Two
of those serving at the remote station of Ambositra, Père de Batz
and Frère Bratail, died of the hardships they were subjected to,
but all the others reached the coast in safety, and the Hova
Government had, up to the last accounts, exercised a strict
guardianship over the churches and property of the Missions.

The French forces on the coast, blockaded by the Hovas and
with the unhealthy rainy season (November to May) before
them, are in a difficult position, but of the ultimate success of
France, should she persevere in the enterprize, there can scarcely
be a doubt. The Hovas have, in the European sense, no army,
and natural obstacles cannot prevent the conquest of a practically
undefended country. As an alternative to the difficult route
from Tamatave to Antananarivo, the invading force might
advance from Majunga on the west coast, by a line which, though
longer, offers greater facilities. A road hence to the capital once
existed, and the rivers Betsibouka and Ikoupa admit of canoe
navigation for part of the way. On this side, too, the co-operation of the Sakalavas, ever ready to rebel against Hova
might be looked for, but the Commissariat would offer cons

able difficulties, as part of the line of march would lie through uninhabited desert.

Meanwhile, it is difficult to see what advantage France seeks to gain from a distant and costly enterprise which promises little glory, and no substantial benefit. It may, however, be that a conquest, barren of profit to herself, will ultimately prove fruitful to the religion which, persecuted at home, her Colonial Council has recently decided on associating officially with her efforts at colonization abroad. For, beside the aggressive and rapacious France of the Sword, stands the meek and self-denying France of the Cross, ready to sow the seed of truth on the soil furrowed by the iron plough of war, and preach the Gospel of peace where the cannon's wrath has thundered. Nor is it in the insolent triumphs of her military history that her true glory is to be found, but rather in the pacific records of that missionary enterprise in which she still leads the van of civilization.

E. M. CLERKE.

ART. VII.—THE CITY OF OUR MARTYRS.

1. *Souvenirs à l'usage des Habitants de Douai.* Par M. PLOUVAIN. Douai: Derignaucourt. 1822.
2. *Chroniques de Douai recueillies et mises en ordre.* Par M. le Président TAILLIAR. Three vols. Douai: Decbristé. 1875.
3. *Histoire ecclésiastique et monastique de Douai et de sa contrée.* Par H. R. DUTHILLŒUL. Douai: Vᵉ. Adam. 1861.
4. *Les rues de Douai d'après les titres de la ville.* Par JULES LEPREUX, archiviste municipal. Douai: L. Crépin. 1882.
5. *Douai et Lille au XIIIᵉ siècle, d'après les manuscrits originaux, &c.* Par H. R. DUTHILLŒUL. Douai: Vᵉ. Adam. 1861.
6. *Essai sur les rélations commerciales de la ville de Douai avec l'Angleterre au moyen âge.* Par l'Abbé C. DEHAISNES. Imprimerie Impériale. 1866.
7. *Mé͏͏ ͏ ͏sur les séminaires et collèges Anglais fondés à la fi͏ ͏ ͏ ͏XVIᵉ siècle dans le Nord de la France, &c. &c.* ͏͏ ͏bé C. J. DESTOMBES. Cambrai: Adolphe Hattie.

8. *Histoire des établissements religieux brittaniques, fondés à Douai avant la révolution française.* Par M. l'Abbé DANCOISNE. Douai: Lucien Crépin. 1880.

9. *Les frontières de France et des Païs Bas où se trouvent le comté de Flandre, &c., &c.* Par N. DE FER. Paris: 1522.

10. *Plan de la ville de Duai au XVIIe siècle.* Douai: Alf. Robaut.

THE Low Countries or Netherlands of the north-west corner of Europe, before the name was confined to the *Pays-bas Hollandais*, contained no province more famous in history than Flanders. It comprised the wide and fertile plain stretching from the ridge of higher ground which marks off Flanders from Artois, to the North Sea. From the slope forming its southern boundary numerous streams, great and small, spread over the plain, and then, converging and uniting, fall into the ocean. This province of Flanders, at the present day, is divided into three parts. West Flanders and East Flanders both belong to Belgium. French Flanders, more commonly known since 1816 as the *Département du Nord*, forms the third part; and in this northern frontier department of France, and about the middle of it, on the borders of the department *Pas de Calais*, stands the ancient and fortified town of Douai.* It rises up in the midst of a broad corn plain watered by the Scarpe, a river which has much to do with the natural and social features of the district. The Scarpe has its source near Aubigny, a village west of Arras, and flows in a north-easterly direction under the pebbly ridges of Bapaume. The streams running down the slopes of Bapaume, and the lakes of Arleux and Lécluse lying at their foot, swell the stream considerably, so that by when it reaches Douai, six leagues further on, it has grown into a river of some volume. Entering the town on the south, it divides it into two almost equal parts, and then, flowing out under the northern walls, it scatters its waters on the lower grounds to the north-east, forming the marshes between Douai and St. Amand. A few miles beyond St. Amand, the river joins the Scheldt. The Scarpe has been navigable as far up as Douai for more than a thousand years, and the still extensive water-traffic, with the network of railroads which modern enterprise has knit around the town, doubly connecting it with the principal coast and inland cities of Bel-

---

* The late Fr. Knox, in his Historical Introduction to the first volume of "Records of English Catholics," p. 27, places Douai in the province of Artois. It will be seen in the course of this article that Douai has ever been considered as situated in Walloon Flanders.

gium and France, account to some extent for Douai's present prosperity and thriving trade.

With the Douai of the present, however, we are not so much concerned as with that Douai of the past which sheltered our forefathers in days of persecution, in which for two hundred years most of our clergy were educated, where our religious orders rallied again, whence came our English translation of the Bible, our old catechism, and all but every English Catholic book which saw the light during the seventeenth and eighteenth centuries.* Douai has with reason become a household word with English Catholics. Alban Butler, in 1745, calculated that it had sent to England 1,600 missionaries, besides those who had gone forth from St. Gregory's, Paris, and from the English colleges of Lisbon and Rome, all started by colonies of students from Douai.† A French writer, the Abbé Dancoisne of Lille, in his work at the head of this article, gives the following statistics of one only of the five British Foundations of which he is treating :—

To form some idea of the importance of the English College at Douai, suffice it to know that during the two centuries of its existence there set out from its walls one cardinal, 33 archbishops and bishops, 100 doctors of theology, 169 writers, and many eminent religious, who filled in different orders the highest positions; but what has rendered this house still more dear to Catholics is, that from it issued forth 160 generous martyrs."‡ (" Histoire des établissements religieux brittaniques fondés à Douai," &c. p. 13.)

The process of the beatification of these and others of our martyrs is proceeding apace, and Douai, though not their birthplace, nor the spot which witnessed their martyrdom, interests us as being the place in which they sojourned, some of them for many years. In the Douai schools they studied. At its shrines they knelt. They trod its streets: they visited its churches. They took part in its religious processions. They made its pilgrimages. Here their hands were consecrated and they made their vows, and here their piety and fortitude bore their first fruits. And after being trained amidst the associations of so ancient and orthodox a city, the *Flores Martyrum* of England

---

* See " Bibliographie Douaisienne." 2 vols. Douai : Adam d'Aubers. 1842. *Passim.*

† "Travels through France and Italy, &c. during the years 1745 and 1746." By the late Rev. Alban Butler. Edinburgh and London : Keating, Brown   ing. 1803. P. 46. Historical Introduction to " Records of Engl   holics," (i.) p. 57.

‡ Fo   if our martyrs refer to the authorities quoted by Fr. Law in the   (p. 27 *et seq.*) of his edition of Challoner's "Memoirs of Missic   iests."

went forth to their own land. No town in Europe, save the Eternal City, can be so interesting to an English Catholic. And yet no formal history of it has been written. But notwithstanding the absence of any complete historical account of the town, information gathered from the most original sources and treating of every phase and epoch in its long career has been embodied into book and pamphlet. The works of M. Plouvain, M. Duthillœul, of M. Tailliar, and others, are the result of researches in the library of the town. M. Duthillœul's work on Douai and Lille in the 13th century is a publication of original manuscripts preserved in the archives of East Flanders at Ghent. Abbé Dehaisne's short but clever essays contain, on the subjects of which they treat, the substance of cartularies kept in the archives of Douai and in those of the *Préfecture du Nord,* of which he is archivist. From these, and works of like character, to a great extent known only locally, and too numerous to be generally read, may be obtained a very clear and accurate view of this old Flemish city.

Going back to the earliest times, M. Tailliar, in the first volume of his "Chroniques de Douai," in the absence of any authentic records of the spot itself, gives an interesting and learned sketch of the neighbourhood, as far as ancient remains and ancient authors allow him. The whole tract of country on the banks of the Scarpe, from Nemetocenna or Arras to the Scheldt, was peopled by the Atrebates,* a Celto-Belgic tribe; and it is interesting to call to mind that a colony of these same Atrebates occupied, previous to the English conquest, the district south of the Thames now comprising Berkshire and Surrey. Many of the villages around Douai still retain their Celtic names. On the north is Flers, the village on the damp land; Roost, the sunken mossland; Rache, *Raskia,* the muddy land; on the south is Fressain, the village in the wood, Féchain, the rock-bound; Cantin, the village on the eminence; and to the east is Equerchin, *Skelcinium,* the stone-enclosed; and Cuincy, the coin-shaped hamlet. The Gohelle, the land of the Goh or dark forest, on the right and left banks of the Lower Scarpe, of which the Bois de Lallaing, Bois de Bruille, Bois de Rieulay, and the forest of Marchiennes, are remnants, favoured the mysterious rites of the Druids, while in the more open country to the south plainer evidences of the Celtic race and its worship are visible in the dolmen of six colossal stones at Hamel, near Tortequesne, in the simple menhir, twenty feet high, at Lécluse, and in similar remains nearer to Arras and Cambrai.

Mingling with these vestiges of the Celt and his worship are

---

* Comment. de Bel. Gal. B. ii. c. 4, iv. 21, vii. 75.

others, giving us a glimpse of the Roman civilization which spread even farther north than Douai. But the Roman remains unearthed in modern times in this part of France throw no more light on the history of the town itself than the Celtic remains; and yet it was the last supreme effort of Roman civilization to stem the flood of barbarian invasion which was breaking it to pieces that planted the first Douai on the river Scarpe. The rivers were the natural inlets by which the northern pirates in the 5th century everywhere made their way in their narrow boats into the heart of Europe, and it was on the rivers that the Romans raised those fortified camps which were destined to grow into many a modern city. Such was the origin of Ariacum, *Aire;* Viroviacum, *Verivick;* and Cortoriacum, *Courtrai*, on the Lys; of Cameracum, *Cambrai;* and Tournacum, *Tournai*, on the Escaut; and of Nobiliacum, for the protection of Arras; of Victoriacum, *Vitry-en-Artois;* and lastly of Duacum, *Douai*, on the Scarpe. On a slight eminence, embraced by two arms of the river, now hidden by the buildings, sprang up the early fortress. It received its name, like other towns of similar origin, from the waters near, and was called Duacum, on account of the double stream, *duæ aquæ*, which washed its base.*

The fort at Douai stands almost unnoticed in the events which followed the invasion of the Franks. Clovis, indeed, sent St. Vaast, who, with St. Remigius, had instructed him in the faith, to preach the gospel† in these parts, and Arcanald, a courtier, and one of the great officers of Clovis, is said by Guicciardini ‡ to have built a rude chapel to our Lady actually within the Douai enclosure, but of all else the annals of the time are silent. At a later time, however, within two leagues of its walls, the armies of Neustria and Austrasia, under their kings, Chilperic and Sigebert, engaged in deadly conflict on the field of Vitry, and there the victorious Sigebert was stabbed to death in his tent at eventide by the scramasaxes of two pseudo-deserters from the slain Chilperic's camp. Sigebert was buried at Lambres, then a royal fisc, and almost within a stone's throw

---

* Some have thought it to be the ancient Aduatuca, a fort mentioned by Cæsar (De Bello. Gal. B. vi. c. 32, 35). Others trace its name to the Celtic *Don* or *Dour* water, referring to the fountain dedicated to St. Maurand in Christian times, but an object of worship among the Druids. This is borne   r the fact that there exists in the village of Mouthier in Franche-C   copious fountain supplying all the neighbourhood with water, a   ig by the name of *la fontaine de la Douai*.

† See "B   im Monasticum" (Dessain) supplement, Oct. 1ᵐᵃ. Lect. 2 Noct   ːmigii, and "Histoire ecclésiastique," par M. Duthilœul.

‡ Guiccir   . 315, C.D.E. Duay, Flandre.

of the fort on the *duae aquae*.* To his queen, Brunehaut, is attributed the road leading from Tournai, then the Frankish capital, and running by Orchies to Douai and Arras. Though not one of the famous *Chaussées-Brunehaut*, this road did much to bring Douai into notice. For the first time we approach true historic ground, and are prepared to hear without surprise, in the reign of Clotaire II. (A.D. 575–628), of Theodebald, Duke of Douai.

Among all the Frankish families of this period, none perhaps is more justly remarkable than Theodebald's. By his daughter St. Gertrude's marriage with Duke Rikomer, a blood relation of Bertrade, King Dagobert's mother, was born Gerherte, the mother of Erkhinvald and St. Adalbald.† These in their mother's right inherited among other domains the lands and castle of Douai. The castle had long fallen into disuse, but the young lords repaired it, rebuilt the chapel called the *chapelle rouge* in honour of our Lady, and erected the massive *Tour de Creux*, whose grey-stone foundations have survived the wear and tear of time and lasted to our own day. Erkhinvald afterwards embraced a public life, and rose to the highest rank in Neustria. He succeeded Æga as mayor of the palace under Clovis II., and on the annexation of Austrasia ruled over the whole of France. "He was," says Fredegarius, "a man full of sweetness and amiability, forbearing and discreet, unpretending and charitable, with bishops ever affable, towards all men kindly, without pride or greed, and beloved by all the world."‡

The story of St. Adalbald§ and of his saintly spouse and her children, as touching and simple as any legend of our Saxon saints, eclipses by its very simplicity the more worldly glory of Erkhinvald. Despatched by his early playmate King Dagobert to quell an insurrection of the Gascons, Adalbald met in the course of his campaign Rictrude, the daughter of Ernold, a Gascon chief. Won by her modesty as much as by her great beauty, the young duke sought her hand in marriage. Probably his suit was furthered by St. Amand, then an exile in Gascony, and the instructor of Rictrude. However this may be, Adalbald was

---

* His bones were afterwards removed to the Cathedral of Soissons and laid beside those of his father Clotaire I.

† Abbé Destombes, in his "Vies des Saints des Diocèses de Cambrai

espoused to the Gascon maiden in spite of the opposition of her brothers, and he returned with her to his northern home on the banks of the Scarpe. There they edified all by their frequent alms and holy lives. The most saintly persons of the time were guests at their table. St. Ricquier became their chaplain ; St. Amand was their personal friend. Their union was blessed with four children, St. Maurand, the spiritual son of St. Ricquier, St. Eusebie, whose godmother Nauthold was the mother of Clovis II., B. Clotsende, the god-daughter of St. Amand, and B. Adalsende, who died in the flower of childhood.* St. Adalbald's life, so heroically virtuous in an age so barbarous and rough, was cut short by a death most cruel. Sent by his brother in 645 to treat with the Gascons for peace, he was waylaid as he rode over the wild wastes of Perigord, and stabbed to death by his own wife's brothers. He was at once raised to the altar by the public voice, and, according to the custom of the time, styled a martyr. His relics were laid in Elnon Abbey, though his head was afterwards taken to Douai, as is seen from an old manuscript of the church of St. Amé,† and the feast, both of his martyrdom and the translation of his relics, was celebrated on the 4th of February.

Rictrude, after the martyrdom of her husband, led a most retired life in her château at Douai. In spite of the persuasions of both King Clovis and of Erkhinvald, she refused the most powerful lords of the kingdom who became her suitors, and at last, taking the king by surprise at a festival held in his honour at Boiry, a spot midway between Douai and Arras, in the midst of a splendid banquet, she begged him to grant her a sole request. On his assenting, she drew from her breast a blessed veil, and, by the counsel of St. Amand, put it over her head, thus publicly consecrating herself to God. The king, seeing his wishes in her regard thwarted, is said to have at once left the place, called to this day *Boiry-Ste-Rictrude*. The pious widow betook herself to her abbey of Marchiennes, where she

---

* See Boll. 30 Junii. Acta SS. Belgii, tom. iv. p. 570. M. Plouvain, in his "Souvenirs," p. 795, has added a fifth, St. Ursin, who was, he says, brother of St. Maurand.

† See Abbé Destombe's "Vies des Saints," vol. i. p. 176. According to Raissius (Auctarium ii. Feb.) only the arm of St. Adalbald was kept in the treasury of St. Amé—"Brachium Sancti Adalbaldi ducis et martyris Mauronti patris." St. Adalbald's relics were kept in a rich chapel  lly erected in honour of him and his family. The statues of St. Ad   St. Rictrude, and St. Maurand stood from time immemorial in the   ı of St. Amé at Douai. St. Maurand, clothed in a prince's robe,   ceptre in his right hand and a church in his left, had on his right   ılbald in a flowing robe sprinkled with fleur-de-lis, and on his l   ictrude in a Benedictine habit.

also built a church under the invocation of SS. Peter and Paul. Into the vicinity of Marchiennes others of the family had retired before her to lead a life of prayer and penance. St. Gertrude was governing the abbey of Hamaige, on the opposite bank of the river, and under her care Rictrude's daughters, St. Eusébie and B. Clotsende, both destined to be the abbesses there, were being trained in the religious life. St. Rictrude died at the age of seventy-four, and her feast is still kept throughout Flanders on the 12th of May. The memory indeed of all these saints in many ways lingers round the spot where they dwelt, in the relics of them which are preserved, in the statues which perpetuate their memory, and in the churches erected in their honour.

Of the eldest of St. Rictrude's children we have still to speak. This is Maurand, the young soldier, *Seigneur* of Douai, the brilliant man of the world. On the eve of his espousals, the death of his uncle Erkhinvald made him so enter into himself that he resolved to die to the world ere the pangs of a more terrible death came upon him. In these dispositions he sought his mother, the abbess Rictrude. She wisely bade him tarry and pray. And he did so, till one day, kneeling at the foot of the altar at which St. Amand was saying Mass, he noticed a look of concern clouding the venerable bishop's face. Thrice the father's eyes were turned towards his son. They seemed reproachfully to chide him for tarrying so long, and sweetly to invite him at once to make the sacrifice. When the solemn rite was over, the young soldier unbuckled his sword, laid aside his armour, and falling at the pontiff's feet, prayed to have his long fair hair cut off, and to be received among the number of the clerics. Ordained priest, Maurand longed still further to fly the world; so erecting the Abbey of Merville, in a secluded wood on the river Lys,* between Bethune and St. Omer, he retired thither with some companions to serve God under the rule of St. Benedict. Such is the simple story of Maurand's conversion.†

By the side of St. Maurand in the history of Douai stands another saint, St. Amé, around whose shrine and under the shadow of whose church clustered the early town. St. Amé, bishop of Lens,‡ in 670 was confined by order of Elroin, mayor of the palace, in the abbey of Peronne. On the death of St. Ultan, the abbot of Peronne, and brother of St. Fursey and St. Foilan, the

---

* "Pater monasterii a se conditi sub annum 686 apud Lysam in suo fundo, tunc a situ paludoso Broylo, postea a fundatoris nomine Maurontivilla nuncupato."—*Cameracum Christianum*, p. 106.

† Abbé Destombes' "Vies des Saints," vol. ii. p. 230. Boll. and Molanus, v. Maii. Acta SS. Belgii, tom. v. p. 738. Buzelin. *passim.*

‡ *Ibid.* vol. ii. p. 170. Boll. and Molanus, 13 Sept. Acta SS. Belgii, tom. iv. p. 573. Off. Prop. Eccl. Colleg. Sti Amati.

saint was placed under the charge of St. Maurand, abbot of Merville, who hastened at once to conduct the disgraced prelate to his abbey on the banks of the Lys. The two on their journey stayed to pray in the metropolitan church of our Lady of Cambrai. St. Amé, wearied by his journey, took off his mantle and gloves, to rest awhile, and his eyes having failed with weeping,* and his eyelids being dim,† he laid them on a beam of the setting sun that broke through one of the long deep windows, and lay across the dusky choir. They remained suspended in the air. St. Maurand, astonished at the miracle, recognized in his venerable prisoner no longer a traitor to his earthly king, but a favoured servant of God. He led him to Hamaige, where his sister St. Eusébie was then abbess, and to Marchiennes, where his mother still governed, and thence to Merville, where, laying down his crozier, he bade the monks receive in his place the saint he had brought them. When St. Amé died, St. Maurand, who had sat at his feet as a humble disciple, buried him in the new church he had built in honour of our Lady.

St. Maurand was not long in following St. Amé. In one of his visits to Marchiennes, which he had promised his mother on her death-bed to watch over, he fell sick and died (May 5th, 701). He was buried at the east of the church by the side of St. Rictrude; but in the year 900 his body was translated to Douai. In the old office for his feast he is called "Fundator et Patronus oppidi Duacensis;" and to his special intervention was attributed the safety of the town on more than one occasion, and particularly its deliverance from the French in 1479 and again in 1556. His feast is still kept solemnly every year on the 5th of May in all the churches of Douai, which still regards him as its patron.

In life so also in death St. Maurand and St. Amé were destined not to be separated. They were to rest side by side in the same church and in the same town. The same troubles which led the monks to bring St. Maurand's body into the town led them to bring St. Amé's also. It was when "the Norsemen rushed from their barques on to the land with cries and shouts, and spread over the country, setting in flames villages and towns, leading captive men and women, scaling fortresses and castles," that the monks of Merville, like those of our own land with St. Cuthbert's, ⸺⸺ered from place to place with the body of St. Amé, till at took refuge in the fortress of Douai. It was well en. Charlemagne had stopped there in his journey is to Valenciennes to try the murderers of St. Saulve.

Lamentations ii. 11.   † Job xvi. 17.

Its saints had made it famous in the church. It was in the territory of Baldwin, the last of the grand foresters so famous in French legend, and the first Count of Flanders, a man who had dared to espouse Judith, the daughter of Charles the Bold, and mother of our Alfred the Great, in spite of king and Church. But in defiance of Baldwin the Iron-armed, the Norsemen, like the Franks four centuries before, swarmed up the river courses in their light boats sacked Terouane, Cambrai, Arras, Tournai. The monks fled with their sacred charge to Soissons before the Norsemen reached Douai. When this happened, the massive towers erected by Erkhinvald and St. Adalbald, their base protected by the swift torrent, withstood the invaders. They gave up the attempt to scale the walls and turned aside into other fields. So the monks brought back the bones of St. Amé and laid them to rest securely in the old castle chapel.

The invasion of the Norsemen and the translation of St. Amé's relics opens a new page in the history of Douai. Among all the castles rebuilt or strengthened after the treaty of St. Clair-sur-Epte (A.D. 912) in Flanders or elsewhere for the protection of the inhabitants around, Douai holds a foremost place. It was made the centre of a castellany. Thoroughly enclosed and placed in a state of defence, within its strong and spacious enclosure extensive buildings were raised for the castellan and his household, for his serving-men and men-at-arms. Under its walls, principally towards the west, sprang up numerous dependencies. The domains around formed fiefs, to which were attached privileges and obligations.* The feudatories were immediately subject to the castellan. They owed him a subordinate allegiance. Under his presidentship they assembled in council. They aided him in the administration of justice. At his call they rallied their forces at the approach of danger. Such organizations brought back peace and security to the whole country. Monks and nuns returned to their abbeys, and at this time Marchiennes was restored and the Abbey of Denain founded. Towns and villages, the seedlings of Flanders's future prosperity, were planted, but amidst all the restorations of the period Douai holds a recognized position which it had never held before.

From the middle of the ninth century till the latter end of the fourteenth, Douai remained almost without interruption under the rule of the famous Counts of Flanders. These counts, like other great vassals of the period, rose to all but absolute power amid the disorder consequent on the Norman invasion and

---

* The fiefs of Douai were Montigny, Cantin, Wattines, la prévôté of Douai, the Seigniories of Estrées, Nomain-Roupy, Landas, Waziers, and Lécluse ("Chroniques de Douai," vol. i. p. 51).

the dissolution of the Carlovingian dynasty. The king was, it is true, liege lord and suzerain, from whom town and abbey sought the confirmation of their charters; but he had a mere pre-eminence, no direct power such as the Conqueror introduced into England in his feudal system. Lothaire indeed tried to assert a more practical sovereignty, and, unsuccessful in his contest with duke Richard of Normandy, he took advantage of the extreme youth of Arnold-le-Jeune to attack Flanders. After taking Arras, one of the conquests of the fierce and savage Arnoul the Old, he laid seige to Douai, which he took and held till at least as late as 976, the date of a deed signed by him in its very walls, granting Judith Abbess of Marchiennes the village of Aisnes near Bassée, which Arnold the Old had taken from her. Restored to the Flemish counts on Arnold the Young taking the oath of allegiance to Hugh Capet, it ran still greater risk of being separated from the rest of Flanders when Count Robert the Frison, in 1070, usurped the county to the injury of his nephews Arnold and Baldwin, successively counts of Hainault. Philip I., Eustace of Boulogne, and their mother the Countess Ricthilde, supported the young counts, and for fifteen years Flanders was a scene of lawlessness and strife. At last, by the mediation of Arnold de Christophere, bishop of Soissons, peace was made. Baldwin was to give up his claim to Flanders, and Robert was to make suitable compensation. The young Baldwin was to marry the daughter of Robert, and with her receive Douai.

But [says Gislebert, as well as Jacques de Guise] when Baldwin saw the daughter of Robert, her ugliness so filled him with disgust, that he rejected that part of the treaty and espoused Ida, daughter of Lambert, Count of Louvain, a lady of great piety and of most refined manners. So the castle of Douai remained in the hands of Robert the Frison and his successors the Counts of Flanders, and up to our own days the men of Haynault have never been able to get it back, either by bribes or by arbitration.*

They tried to do so, however.† When Robert of Jerusalem took up the cause of the Church against the Emperor Henry IV., the Count of Haynault thought to get possession of Douai by supporting the Emperor. But at the assembly held in it to settle the terms of peace, Douai was formally given up by the counts of Haynault. The Peace of Douai was broken by the Emperor Henry V., who laid siege to the town at the very commencement of the war. Robert, with the aid of the burgesses

* "Chroniques de Douai," vol. i. p. 95.
† ⁒ ' n was the dower of the Countess Ricthilde, and hence the ₁ault.

and even of the women and children, repulsed the imperial forces, (1107); and when the war was over, Douai by the treaty of Mayence was left in the hands of the counts of Flanders. The contest between the two counties for the possession of the town was brought to an end only by the marriage of Marguerite, daughter of Thierry of Alsace, the fifteenth count of Flanders, with the young Count of Haynault. After the death of her brother Philip, Marguerite succeeded him, and reigned conjointly with her husband Baldwin VIII. over both Flanders and Haynault.

The contests of the counts of Flanders with their liege lords brought Douai on two occasions into the hands of the kings of France. Like many a Flemish town, Douai had become a rich and flourishing republic in the 13th century. The châtelain's rights had mostly become obsolete—been sold or made over by charter to the burgesses. Douai ranked with Bruges, Ghent, Ypres, and Lille as one of the *bonnes-villes* of Flanders. Hence we find it taking part with these in the strife and politics of the age, and suffering more perhaps than the others, on account of its border position. The burghers of Flanders are famous in history for their spirit of independence. Such a spirit was fostered by the long absence of count after count in the Holy Wars,* so that at last the burly townsmen claimed, even by force of arms, a voice in the marriage of their counts, in their alliances, in their succession to their county, in the sacred question of their taking the oath of submission to their liege lords. Commercial interests in most cases decided the policy of the towns, and account for the general leaning of Flanders towards the English alliance. Thus Baldwin IX. sided with Richard the Lion-hearted against Philip Augustus, who at once marched towards the north, and arrived before Douai on the eve of the Assumption, 1197. A procession of priests issuing from the gates interceded with the king, and saved the city from a siege; and peace being made for the time being, the king withdrew. But when Count Ferrand, backed by the *bonnes-villes*, refused to take the oath of fealty and joined John Lackland, Philip again set march for the north, from Peronne, where he had assembled his forces. Ferrand, supported by his sturdy burghers, by the Emperor Otho, Count Reynault of Boulogne, and William Longsword, Count of Salisbury, met the king at the Pont-à-Bouvines, between Lille and Tournai, A.D. 1214. The "Grandes Chroniques

---

* With one of the counts, Robert of Jerusalem, who took the cross at Clermont and scaled the walls of Antioch and Jerusalem with Godfrey of Bouillon, is mentioned Walter II. castellan of Douai. ("Chroniques de Douai," vol. i., p. 146.)

de St. Denis,"* published by M. Paulin, Paris, give twelve
chapters to the relation of this battle, in which the feudalism of
the north received its death-blow. The battle raged three hours.
In the thick of the fight Count Ferrand was struck to the ground
and taken prisoner. The Emperor Otho fled on seeing the battle
lost. Royalty was triumphant. Ferrand was kept a close
prisoner in the Louvre during the remainder of the reign of
Philip Augustus, and Douai, as well as several other towns,
were held by the king.† And though by the treaty of Melun
with Louis VIII., Douai was to be given up on the payment of
a ransom for Count Ferrand of 50,000 Flemish livres, it was
held by Queen Blanche and St. Louis till 1239.

The longest French possession of the town, however, was from
1299 to 1369. Count Guy, urged on by his son, and supported
by Edward I. of England, met his vassals and his burgesses at
Grammont in 1296, and proclaimed himself independent lord of
Flanders. The year following Philip-le-Bel, whose life policy
was the subjection of his great vassals, assembled a great army
at Compiegne, and at once commenced the conquest of the north.
His son, Charles of Valois, took Douai in January, 1299, and in
the course of the next year the King, being on his triumphal
progress through Flanders as its supreme liege lord, made his
solemn entry into it. Four times the Flemings, fighting for
their counts, rose against the King. The Douaisians invariably
joined them. The fullers and clothweavers from Douai were in the
heat of the battle on the field of Courtray, and their victorious cry,
" Gloire aux vainqueurs !" has since been the motto of the town.
The war continued till 1304. In the August of that year the
French and Flemings met near the wooded eminence of Mons-en-
Peulle, a few miles west of Douai. "The Flemings," says the
"Chroniques de St. Denis," "were utterly overthrown, crushed,
and broken to pieces ; and at last they fled in unseemly flight."
The spot where this happened became as memorable in the
annals of French Flanders, writes a modern traveller, as Agin-
court, in Picardy, in the estimation of the English.‡ In that
fatal fight Douai lost her bravest warriors ; and from that date
the shield of the city arms has displayed an arrow striking it, with
six drops of blood falling from the pierced centre.

During the more than half a century that followed the terrible

* "Chroniques de Douai," p. 217, vol. i. note 1.
† Besides the "Chroniques de St. Denis," see for the battle of Bouvines the "Annales de Hainaut," by Jacques de Guise, livre xx. On the
importance of it to Philip Augustus, see Guizot's "Hist. de France,"
tom. i. pp. 494, 495. See also "Mémoire sur la Bataille de Bouvines en
1214," par M. Lebon. Paris et Lille, 1837.
‡ "A Ramble into Brittany." By the Rev. George Musgrave, M.A.
Vol. i. p. 15. In this work 80 pages are given to an account of Douai.

defeat of Mons-en-Peulle, Douai figures more than once in the annals of France. By the "Transport de Flandre", it was made over with Lille and Bethune to Philip-le-Bel, and he confirmed its charters, gave its merchants free market to Paris and a hall there, enlarged its boundaries, and strengthened its fortifications. King Louis X. visited it in 1315, and in 1355 King John II. paid his devotions at the shrine of its patron, St. Maurand. The fortunes of Douai became so bound up with those of France that the Douaisians actually took part in the war of defence waged against Edward III. of England. A Douai contingent fought in the army which was so totally routed in the hedgerows and vineyards around Poitiers; and in the Treaty of Bretiguy among the hostages given to England by the *bonnes villes* of the north, are mentioned four from Douai—Bauduin, Bonnebroque, and Jean de Douaieul, who were afterwards replaced by Amand de Landas and Engrand Pilate. The town, however, was destined to return again to the counts of Flanders, but this did not take place till Charles V.'s time. Then the alliance between Edward III. of England and Louis-de-Mâle, Count of Flanders, which had guaranteed the restoration of Douai, ceased, and the match between the young Countess Marguerite and the Prince of Wales was broken off, in spite of the opposition of the French communes. The young countess was given in marriage to Philip, Duke of Burgundy, brother of the King of France, and by the marriage articles, Douai was given up to Louis-de-Mâle, the twenty-sixth and last of the illustrious counts of Flanders. On May 13, 1369, a proclamation, signed by Charles V., announced to the burgesses of Douai that they had returned to their ancient rulers.

With the exception of its short occupation by Lothaire in 976, and of the two French occupations which we have just glanced at, Douai was for 500 years under the rule of the counts of Flanders. During those 500 years of a rule generally wise and firm, it grew into one of those flourishing and independent Flemish towns of which the Middle Ages contained so many examples.* A sketch of its development will not be out of place here. It must, however, be but a faint outline. Those minor events which give light and shade and colour to a formal history must necessarily be omitted. Neither can every line in the general picture be even slightly traced. The gradual expanding of its liberties in charter after charter, the dying out of the *châtelain's* rights and the proportionate growth of the burgesses' power, the total absence as time went on of the count's bailiff or representative, and the natural assumption of his authority by

---

* "Délices des Païs-Bas," *passim*.

the *skepens* or freely-elected magistrates, all these in their various stages cannot be dwelt upon at any length here. Passing over, then, the development of the arts of social intercourse, of local government, and of local institutions, and even the interesting subjects of the limits of sacerdotal and magisterial jurisdiction in this Flemish mediæval city, we shall confine ourselves chiefly to describing the material growth of the five *escrowetes** or quarters of the town, and their actual state at different periods.

In carrying out this plan, we notice that the material development of Douai went on hand in hand with its ecclesiastical. The first beginnings of a real town sprang up, like a Durham or a St. Edmund's Bury, under the shadow of a saint's shrine. St. Amé's relics rested in the old castle chapel till the middle of the tenth century. About that time Count Arnoul-the-Old, full of gratitude for a cure almost miraculously brought about by St. Gerard, Abbot of Brogne, commissioned the pious abbot to found certain religious houses and to re-establish others. The clerics who guarded St. Amé's relics had a large share in Count Arnoul's abundant alms.† A church was raised over the saint's tomb and given in charge of a chapter of 20 canons,‡ under a provost. The collegiate church of St. Amé thus constituted became, after the reorganization of the only two others then existing in Flanders—Saint Donat's, at Bruges, and Saint Bavon's, at Ghent—the most ancient in the north of Europe. Robert the Frison, in 1076, confirmed its former rights and possessions, at the same time bestowing new ones. The charter in which he does this is of extreme interest. It begins by calling to mind with the minutest details, and in words surprisingly beautiful, the whole history of the foundation from the time of St. Maurand. Then, in terms which give us a full and picturesque view of the feudal system of that age, we are told that Philip I., the sovereign lord of France, and his great vassal Robert, take under their protection the collegiate church of St. Amé, at Douai, its dean, canons and prebends—in a word, the whole corporate body, with its twofold organization, spiritual and temporal, and its wealth and wide domains. The four great dignitaries of the college are to be freely elected by the chapter, and the provost is to be a

---

* Literally the word *escroa* or *scroweta* signifies a *list*, and hence the present word *écrou*, a register containing a list of those detained in prison, and the verb *écrouer*. The five lists of the burgesses of the town were used to i ⸺ ⸺ the five quarters in which they lived.

† The ⸺ ans of St. Amé's shrine ceased to be Benedictines in 870. See But ⸺ ravels through France and Italy," &c., p. 43. Plouvain in his " ⸺ irs" (p. 15) says this change took place in 1170.

‡ Af ⸺ increased to 35.

spiritual and feudal lord. His jurisdiction is to extend over the precincts of the church, over the cloisters, the houses of the canons, and the buildings inhabited by their serving-men. Then are enumerated its properties and possessions, its mills, its breweries, and its taverns within the town; its villages, manors, and lands beyond; its tolls, tithes, and other revenues; its serfs and freemen.* Besides these temporalities, spiritual favours equally great were given it. Gerard II., Bishop of Cambrai, granted it many exemptions, till at last it was made immediately subject to the Apostolic See. Pope Paschal II. in 1104, Pope Lucius II. in 1144, Pope Alexander III. in 1163, and Pope Lucius III. in 1811, all confirmed the privileges previously granted, "provided no layman govern your church," ran the bull of Alexander III. One of the last great names that figure in its charters is that of the Emperor Charles V. In 1191, the age of some of our finest cathedrals, a new church was commenced on a magnificent scale, and in 1206 a great concourse of people, of bishops and nobles, of abbots, priests, and monks, thronged the town to assist at the ceremony of its consecration. It was on this occasion that, after a three days' fast, the clergy and monks barefoot, carried in procession through the town the bodies of SS. Amé and Maurand, which were then translated to new and gorgeous shrines, the offering to the church of Walter the castellan. During its thousand years of existence, St. Amé's accumulated into its innumerable chapels many other treasures besides the relics of its patrons. It possessed the body of Blessed Raymar, one of its earliest provosts; and year by year were venerated within its sanctuary the right foot of St. Anne, the mother of the Blessed Virgin; a good part of the head of St. Clement, pope and martyr; one of the arms of St. Gertrude of Marchiennes; the right arm of St. Stephen, and the head of St. Monica. But what, perhaps, makes the church of St. Amé most known to the world at large is the miracle of the Blessed Sacrament, which took place here in 1254. Father Faber, in his work on the Blessed Sacrament, has given an account of this miracle taken from the works of an eye-witness, the Ven. Thomas de Cantimpré, a fellow-disciple of St. Thomas of Aquin.† The venerable friar, after mentioning that Douai is a large and spacious town situated on the right hand side of the road connecting the noble cities of Arras and Cambrai, thus proceeds:‡—

---

* See "Histoire de la Collégiale de St. Amé de Douai," par M. Brassart. Douai, 1872.

† See ". Vies des Saints de l'Ordre," par Hyacinthe Choquet, p. 89. Raissius xv. Maii. Foppens. Art. Thomas Cantipratensis. Abbé Destombe's "Vie des Saints," p. 230, vol. iv.

‡ "V. Thomas Cantimpré de Apibus." Douai: Bellère, 1597.

In the church of the canons of St. Amé, a priest, after having given Communion to the faithful, perceived a Host on the ground. Whilst trembling he went on his knees to take It up; It lifted Itself from the ground and laid Itself on the purificatory. Crying out in astonishment the priest called the canons, who beheld lying on the cloth a beautiful infant. The people pressed round to see the miracle and were all witnesses of it. The rumour of this wonder spreading far and wide, I came to Douai, and knowing intimately the dean of the church, I prayed him to let me see the miracle. The dean consented, and no sooner had he opened the tabernacle than the people ran forward crying out, "Ah! look! look at Our Lord! I see him!" I saw nothing but the pure white bread, and yet I was not conscious of any secret sin which could hinder me from seeing the sacred person whom others saw. But while pondering on this, all at once my eyes were opened, and I beheld the countenance of Jesus Christ of mature age, and the size of life. Upon His head was a crown of thorns, and two drops of blood trickled down His brow upon His face. Immediately I prostrated myself, and bursting into tears, adored my Lord. When I rose again I saw neither crown nor blood, but His face was turned to the right so that the right eye was hardly visible. He was beautiful and radiant; His nose long and straight, His brows arched, His calm sweet eyes downcast, His hair floated over His shoulders, His beard untouched by razor flowed under His chin, and near His mouth it more thinly grew, gracefully revealing on each side of the chin two spaces without hair, as we see on those whose beard has been let to grow uncut from infancy; His forehead was high, His cheeks thin, and His head as well as His long neck slightly bent forward. Thus did He look, the beautiful and most sweet Saviour. During the space of an hour people saw Him under different forms; some, fastened to the cross; others, as coming to judge mankind; but most beheld Him as an infant." ("Chroniques de Douai," vol. i. p. 241; Father Faber's "Blessed Sacrament," p. 539-40.)*

This is but a brief account of the famous sanctuary of St. Amé, visited and enriched by the most renowned counts of Flanders

---

* The miraculous Host is still preserved, and though it is prohibited to show or venerate it publicly, the writer had the happiness of handling it in September last, thanks to the kindness of the Dean of St. Peter's at Douai, in whose church it is kept in the tabernacle of the altar of the Sacred Heart. For a complete history of the *Saint Sacrement, ou Miracle de Douai*, up to the present day, see—1st. "Souvenir du Jubilé séculaire du Saint Sacrement de Miracle célébré à Douai en 1855," par l'Abbé Capelle. Douai: Adam d'Aubers; 2nd. "Pélérinage national au très-saint Sacrement de Miracle à Douai, 17 mai, 1875," par l'Abbé Marchant. Douai: Déchristé; 3rd. "Programme du Pélérinage national en l'honneur de t.-s. S nt de Miracle à Douai, le lundi de la Pentecôte, 17 mai, 1875;" 4t ınoncement du 629e Anniversaire de la Manifestation miraculeu la Place St. Amé de la Présence réelle de n. s. J. C." See also ' ue de Dévotion au St. Sacrement de Miracle établie dans l'Eglise   e de St. Amé." Douai: Willerval, 1672.

and dukes of Burgundy, and by the greatest kings of France, including St. Louis. But, cursory glance though it is, it serves to introduce us into the early town which gathered around it.

Outside the immediate precincts of St. Amé's, then clustered on the east Duayleul (Duaciolum or Duiellum, *Little Douai*), the *petite-place* of to-day. But the fief over which the Provost of St. Amé had jurisdiction, and even power of life and death, extended towards the north beyond Duayleul, along the left bank of the river, "from the tavern of St. Christian as much as it will take three muids of corn to sow," so the earliest charters had it. To supply the spiritual needs of this portion of their fief, the canons of St. Amé, before the year 1097, had built a church to St. Albin, under the shadow of whose graceful spire arose in after days the English Benedictine monastery of St. Gregory the Great. In St. Albin's church, resting on four marble pillars, was the shrine of St. Christian, one of the priests of the church in the twelfth century,* and who was born in a house that stood at the corner of the Rue des Potiers and Rue St. Benoît, near the spot where is still *la fontaine de St. Chrétien*, and whither yearly, on his feast, his relics are carried in procession.

The principal quarter, however, of the five quarters mentioned in the charter of 1228, which constituted the Douai eschevinage, was on the right bank of the river, more to the south, and opposite the group of buildings which comprised the old castle, the strong *tour de creux*, and the château of the counts. It was called the castle of the burgesses—*castel as bourgois*. This was the free landholders' town. It had its enclosure and its four gates, through which, if a stranger entered, he fell under the surveillance of the burghers. Outside the gates of the *castel as bourgois* other buildings soon spread alongside the river towards the north and formed the *Villa sancti Petri*—St. Peter's borough—so named after the Church of St. Peter built by Count Baldwin IV. Bellebarbe in 1012, and made a collegiate church by Count Robert the Frison about 1076. St. Peter's became the rival of St. Amé's. Its charters were confirmed by Popes Alexander III., Clement III., and Innocent III. It possessed a not inconsiderable temporal jurisdiction, not only over the church itself and its precincts, but also over the space descending in front of the church tower towards the river, by the street of the Puits-Pilori, *Puich-Philory*, which formed its boundary. Its spiritual jurisdiction as a parish embraced all the inhabitants on the right bank of the river, and reached as far out as the extreme limits ⸴he Grande Place. But by the beginning of the thirteenth ⸴ry the town had

---

* Boll. vii. April, p. 723. Rai⸴   l.

extended beyond the Villa Sti. Petri, and had formed the *Neuve Ville*. This part of the city became the parish of St. Jacques in 1225, the date of the building of the fine old Gothic church of St. Jacques,* that in the pre-Revolution times graced the square now named after it. In the title of the erection of the parish of St. Jacques, the provost and chapter of St. Peter's allege, as the reason for the new parish, the unchecked increase of population—" *effrenatum populi multitudinem*." In 1228 another parish and church, under the patronage of St. Nicholas, were established in the quarter to the south, and thirty years later was created the parish of Notre Dame, its church being raised on a spot where had stood a chapel of Our Lady from time immemorial. These three parishes, placed under the patronage of the collegiate church of St. Peter, show how widely the city had extended itself by the middle of the thirteenth century.

The religious orders of the day were not slow in coming to a town which by its populousness and wealth presented such a suitable field for the exercise of their charity and zeal. On the marshy ground outside the north-east gate, called the Porte de Wetz or *Gués*, because of the *gués*, or fords, of the Scarpe at this spot, was founded by Count Thierri, of Alsace, a house of the Templars, an establishment which proved of the utmost importance to the commerce of the town. In 1218 a Bull of Pope Innocent III. founded the Abbey des Prés, in the quarter of St. Albin. The Friars Minors built their convent in 1232. Twenty years later the Dominicans came to the town, and, by the generosity of the Countess Marguerite, raised their immense convent and church of the Holy Cross. The Dominican convent, soon after its foundation, had the honour of receiving two saints within its cloisters—St. Thomas of Aquin, who rested there on his way from Paris to Cologne to attend the lectures of B. Albert the Great,† and St. Louis, one of its greatest benefactors.‡ The Trinitarians were established at the east of the town in 1252. Besides these large religious houses, there were eight hospices, or pious foundations, and numerous chapels, such as the chapel of St. Mary Magdalen, built by Peter Honoric, Almoner of St. Louis, and that of our Lady *de la Treille*, afterwards called *Notre Dame des Miracles*, by reason of the

---

* The old church of St. Jacques stood on the present Place St. Jacques. The present church of St. Jacques is on the opposite side of the town, and, previous to the Revolution, was the English Recollects' Church of St. Bonaventure.
† The convent afterwards received an arm of St. Thomas.
‡ *Vi*   ondation du Convent de la Saincte Croix," etc. Par Philippe Petit.   : 1653.

wonderful cures wrought there. When St. Peter's Church was rebuilt in 1734 the miraculous statue of our Lady was placed under the present lofty dome, in the chapel prepared to receive it.

Of the abbeys in the environs of the town a word should be said. Hénin Abbey, belonging to the Augustinians, was never of much importance; but the Abbey of Flines, belonging to the Bernardines, became one of the richest in Flanders. It was endowed by Marguerite of Constantinople in 1234. So many counts and persons of royal blood were buried in its church that it was named the St. Denis of Flanders. But the large and magnificent Benedictine abbeys of Anchin and Marchiennes are far more famous than the Abbey of Flines.

The legend of Anchin, Aquacegnum, or Aquicenclum, as it is written in the old records, on account of its island situation, is as pretty as the legend of an Evesham or a Croyland.[*] Sohier, lord of Courcelles, lost in the forest depths as night closed in, all at once, through the dark woodlands, saw the light streaming from the casements of a castle near. He made for it and struck at the castle gate, as its lord and his men were sitting down to their evening repast, and was ushered into the halls of the château of Montigny to find himself face to face with its master, who was his most deadly enemy. But the rules of hospitality were kept in spite of private feud, and the benighted noble was conducted to his chamber. That night the same dream visited both the barons—a white stag marking the site of an abbey and church. From the castle terrace, next morning, they both beheld, through the northern woodlands, the wild isle hallowed by the holy life of the solitary St. Gordaine, and recognized it as the spot seen in their vision, and that very day, on entering one of its silent glades, they came upon a snow-white stag of supernatural beauty, running its mystic course. The silent glade became the site of an abbey dedicated to the Holy Saviour, which was the bond of reconciliation between the two nobles. In after times St. Gossium, a native of Douai, and a rival of Abelard, filled its abbatial throne,[†] and St. Thomas à Becket left a memento of his visit there in the chasuble, dalmatic, and tunic he had worn. The last abbot in commendam of Anchin was none other than Cardinal Henry of York. Of Marchiennes Abbey we have already said something. Its great library, says Martène, numbered 70,000 volumes. St. Thomas also rested at Marchiennes on his way through Douai to Pon-

---

[*] For the history of Anchin see "L'Abbaye d'Anchin, 1079-1792." Par E. A. Escallier.

[†] "Vies des Saints," &c., vol. iv. p. 152. Boll. IX. Oct.

tiguy, and the two Benedictines in their "Voyage Littéraire,"*
were shown the cross set with pearls and relics, the chasuble and
the monstrance, by which the saint had amply repaid the
hospitality of the abbey, as well as the old pontifical in Anglo-
Saxon type, now among the manuscripts of the Douai library, with
this inscription upon it by the monk Godin : " Pontificale hoc ad
usum ecclesiarum Anglicarum recepisse nos à S. Thomâ Can-
tuariensi traditione constantí habemus."†

Intimately connected with this ecclesiastical and material
growth of the town, was the commercial activity which formed
its life and soul. The Abbé Dehaisnes has so concisely and
vividly described the commercial glory of Douai in the 13th
century, that we quote his words, even at the risk of repeating
ourselves, as the text of any further remarks we may have to
make.

Douai was among the number of the *bonnes villes* of Flanders. Its
position on one of the navigable highways of the country, its municipal freedom, granted as early as 1174, its privilege of a staple of corn
and of a free annual fair, the spirit of association which united the
burgesses amongst themselves and with the inhabitants of all the
great neighbouring cities, made it at the beginning of the 13th century a very wealthy trading centre. The manufacture and dyeing of
woollen stuffs gave occupation to a great number of hands. Halls,
both large and small, were constructed for the sale of cloth, and Douai
enjoyed reserved places in the markets of Arras and Paris; in the
fairs of S. Denis, Provins, Bar-sur-Aube, and Troyes; in those of
Bruges, Ghent, Thouroutte, and Aix-la-Chapelle; and in those of
Stamford, Boston, St. Ives, Winchester, and Northampton in England.‡
Organised into guilds, its craftsmen were not less powerful than those
of other great cities in Flanders, and not less terrible in any popular
disturbance. In 1280, irritated by restrictions put on their handi-
craft, the weavers rose and put to death several of the wealthier
merchants and eleven of the twelve eschevins who formed the governing body of the town. The Count of Flanders put an end to the
struggle by beheading some of the most guilty, hanging others to the
spouts and roofs of their houses, and condemning others to perpetual

* " Voyage Littéraire de Deux Bénédictins," t. ii. pp. 92 and 97.
† *Vide* " Catalogue des Manuscrits de la Bibliothéque de Douai."
Par M. Abbé Dehaisnes. No. 61, pp. 44, 45. Paris : Imprimérie Na-
tionale. 1878. Also " De Antiquis Ecclesiæ Ritibus," pp. 250, 334, 378,
and tom. iii. pp. 476 and 199. For the history of St. Thomas's visit to
March' ı, see Buzelin, " Annales Gallo-Flandriæ," p. 244 d. For an
accoui ue many relics and traditions which remain of St. Thomas's
passa ugh Flanders, see the Abbé Destombe's " Vies des Saints,"
vol. iv 56, *et seq.*
‡ ı of the Town of Douai, cartulary OO. and cartulary L.
See ' " Mémoire sur les Manufactures anciennes de la Ville de
Dov ie learned archivist, M. Guilmot.

banishment.* Besides the craftsmen, or "commune," the commerce of the town created a *bourgeoisie*, or merchant-class, several members of which were wealthy enough to lend large sums of money to the Counts of Flanders as many as four times in the course of twenty-five years.† Some wore the armorial bearings and assumed the title of chevalier, and did not deem it inconsistent with their commercial enterprises to do so. Armed at all points, mounted like the nobility upon handsome chargers caparisoned with steel armour, they were ready at a day's notice to march to battle, on receiving the orders of the eschevins, under the leadership of the high constable who commanded each company. They formed the merchant aristocracy, the *milites burgenses*, so renowned in Flanders during the Middle Ages. Philippe-le-Breton, the historian of the conqueror of Bouvines, has said happily that Douai was, from 1184, a well-to-do city, strong in the battle-field and fecund of illustrious citizens—"Duacum Dives et armipotens et claro cive refertum, indignata capi numero."‡— "Les Relations Commerciales de la Ville de Douai avec Angleterre au Moyen-Age," pp. 2, 3.

Many circumstances combined to render Douai so flourishing. A navigable river connected it with all the towns on the Scheldt, and at the same time with Arras, a centre of French trade, whose tapestry was famous even in the time of the Antonines. The small channels into which the Scarpe branches out at this point of its course, dividing the town into a group of islets, greatly favoured the cloth industry, while at the same time Douai had an immense advantage over many another town in having two houses of the Templars in its midst. The Knights Templars were the money-changers of the time. It is little known, says M. de Noiron in his "Banques de France,"§ what an important part the Knights of the Temple played in the financial history of Europe. They propagated the letters of exchange invented by the persecuted Jews. They originated the circulation of paper money when the specie of metallic currency was debased, cut up, or worn out. Moreover, the *cahoursins*, or Italian bankers, also set up their counters in the town, as is seen from a ban respecting them in the year 1247. Possessing such advantages as these, the Douai merchants had the other towns at their mercy. When its magazines were well stocked, its

---

* For a full account of these strikes (*mouvements*), popularly called *takehans*, so common in the thirteenth century among the craftsmen in the Flemish towns, see Ducange, "Glossaire," t. vi. p. 504.

† "Archives Départem[entales] s de Lille," Chambre de Comptes, Août, 1268; Septembre, 1269; [Févr.], 1270; Mars, 1271, &c.

‡ "Guhelmi Britonis P[hilippi]dos," lx. v. 122.

§ "Banques de France [leur] Mission, leur Isolement actuel: moyen de les co-ordonner," &c. &c. [par] Louis de Noiron. Paris: Marc Aurel. 1847.

merchants closed their purses, and the eschevins the counting houses. Without capital the industry of the neighbouring towns was at a standstill, till the merchants of Douai had found a market for their goods. It was by their money also that they obtained a monopoly of trade with the Italians who had settled at St. Omer, to the exclusion of the Lillois. The tyrannical exercise of these commercial advantages raised the terrible feud between the men of Douai and the men of Lille, unfolded to us at such length in the manuscripts published by M. Duthillœul.

The risings of the lower craftsmen and their associations or guilds for the protection of their rights, brought forth regulation after regulation from the authorities which reveal to us many of the trades thriving in the old town. Besides those tradesmen necessary to every community—the millers, the bakers, the butchers, the fishmongers—we have those connected more immediately with the staple trade, the wool-combers, the spinners, weavers, fullers, dyers and those who prepared the woad and the madder root; then come the tanners and shoemakers, the masons, tilers, carpenters and joiners; and lastly such important artisans as the armourers, the cutlers and ironmongers, the locksmiths, the shoesmiths and the jewellers. Each had its special quarter or street. There was the boucherie, the Rue des Ferronniers, the Rue des Potiers, the Rue des Fripiers, the Rue des Foulons, the Rue des Lombards, and others. One street, now named from the monastery of the English Benedictines, by a singular coincidence was called in the thirteenth century the Rue des Englais according to two registers, one of the year 1273, and another of 1292. In a memorandum dated 1374 the same street is termed the Rue Englemer, a name which it retained till the seventeenth century. Such a name naturally leads us to enquire into its origin, and brings us to the interesting subject of Douai's relations with England in the Middle Ages. That there were Englishmen at Douai in the Middle Ages may be gathered from an occasional fact like that in which "Colars from London" gives evidence, in a quarrel between the Lillois and Douaisians, " that he was set upon in Douai by Lille people armed with hatchets, clubs, pikes, and crossbows, but on his saying that he was from England, they let him pass unmolested.* The commercial relations of Douai with England incline us to think that English merchants frequently visited the town for purposes of trade or friendship, and in many instances perhaps became pern   ; residents. That Douai merchants traded with England we   from abundant sources. Of the twenty-four towns of Fr   nd Flanders which formed the association for

)ouai et Lille au XIIIe Siècle," p. 71.

trade purposes known as the Hanse de Londres, Douai is the seventeenth on the list. Besides this general alliance, Douai made private alliances. In March 1239 the Douai merchants joined those of Ypres in publishing "bans sour ciaus ki mainnent draperie en Engleterre, et en tels pais de la outre."* Some years later, in 1261, the merchants of Ghent, Ypres, Douai, Cambrai, and Dixmude, being at the fair of Northampton, formed a company for the buying of wool with "li compagnie Jehan Delbos et li neveut Renaut Wiltonne."† The archives of Douai tell us of the permission granted to its merchants by Henry III. to sell their cloths and stuffs in London, and in the great fairs in the country; of their losing in different wars, especially in that of 1290, their merchandise and their liberty, and of their receiving fresh privileges from Edward II. in 1317. The river tariffs and the frequent enactments for the ordering of navigation from Douai to Rupelmonde, of which the cartularies of the time are full, reveal to us the busy traffic in wool and stuffs between the town and England.

In their relations with England the Douai merchants had a double object—the buying of wool and the selling of cloth. Neither the flocks of the country, nor the Normandy sheep of the Ostrevent and Artois, nor those which grazed in the vast abbey enclosures, nor even the wool which supplied the markets of Champagne, could satisfy the demands of the industrial towns of Flanders. The mountains of Scotland, the green sides of England and Ireland, and the meadows and commons of their many abbeys, grazed such immense flocks of sheep that wool in England became so common as to be used instead of money to pay tolls and imposts. The king himself traded in it with foreign countries, and had his "captores, provisores, et receptores lanarum regiarum." English wools were not indeed so fine as those of France or Spain, but they were equal to those of Holland or Flanders itself, and even superior to them for certain kinds of stuff. Hence Legrand d'Aussy tells us in his "Fabliaux" that "En la terre de Flandres viennent d'Engleterre laines, charbons de roche, etc. ; d'Escoche, laines et cuir d'Irlande, cuir et laines."

Necessary as was the produce of the English flocks to all the towns of Flanders, it was more particularly so to the manufacturers of Douai. Their trade principally consisted in stuffs called *brunettes*, which owed their special gloss and perfection to their being woven with English wools, and English wools are mentioned in ordinances of the eschevins and in the testa-

---

* "Archives de Douai," cartulaire L., fol. 47.
† "Archives de Douai," cartulaire L., fol. 29.

ments and contracts of the burghers as having a special value for this purpose. The most curious document, however, on the purchase of English wools which the archives of Douai have preserved is a memorandum in a cartulary of the 13th century, headed thus: "Che sunt chi les abeies d'Engleterre et ke (ce que) leurs laines valent au moins."* Then follow the names of 102 monasteries, from Fontaine and Furness in the north to Tintern, Bodenham, St. Alban's, and Waverley in the south, with the prices they charge for their wools.

What reached Douai as raw material was destined to cross the Channel again in the form of cloth. The Douai merchants exported into England cloths of three qualities—the *draps mollets*, a mixture of silk and wool; the *burels* or *tiretaines*, stuffs half wool and half thread; and the *brunettes* or dark woollen broad cloths. An immense quantity of stuffs found their way from the Douai looms to England, and entries in cartularies of the town again and again tell us how the Douai merchants themselves, or through their brokers, sold their merchandise in London and in the fairs of Stamford, St. Ives, Boston, Winchester, and Northampton. A curious letter of G. de Clare, Count of Gloucester, preserved in the Douai archives,† gives us the names of nineteen cloth merchants of Douai from whom this noble and powerful count had bought cloth at London, and some *brunettes* and other stuffs at the fair at Stamford for " onze vins cinq livres et duze deniers de bons et léaux esterlens."† In this letter, sealed with his own seal, the noble lord promises to pay this sum in three instalments before the Sept. 29 1278. A note in the margin informs us that he had not done so on Oct. 28, 1283. We are not told whether at a later date this powerful Count of Gloucester acknowledged the signature he had given to the burghers of Douai.

Details like these prepare us to find the old town in the 14th century with all the constituents of one of the free towns of Flanders. It had its charters of franchise confirmed by each successive ruler, and which king and count, in the ceremony of their reception into the town, took an oath not to infringe. By their charters the townsmen had the right of electing as magistrates their fellow-burgesses men devoted to the interests of their native city and jealous of its liberties. Within the jurisdiction of the magistrates thus freely elected, and commonly known by the German name of *skepens* or eschevins,‡ came the

---
* Cartulaire L., fol. 44. † Cartulaire N., fol. 57.
‡ The eschevins were first of all seven in number, including the mayor. They were increased to twelve in the charter of 1228, and afterwards to nineteen. In 1373 the military defences were put into the hands of a committee, known as the " six hommes."

regulation of the police of the town, as well as the providing for its security in time of danger by organising the *milice bourgeoise* and repairing and strengthening the walls which encircled the burg. The belfry, or watch tower—in a Flemish town the special sign of freedom—in Douai, as in Ghent or Antwerp, served as a look-out in time of war, and its great bell summoned the burghers together when their active co-operation was needed for some important act in communal life, or for the defence of the city against neighbouring attacks. Having, then, within itself the source of its own government, the town had its own distinctive seal, whose stamp marked the authenticity and authority of its magisterial enactments. Last of all, Douai had the supreme privilege of a free town—the right of coining its own money.* Thus the town had reached the acmé of its prosperity when, in 1384, on the death of Count Louis-de-Mâle, it passed with the rest of Flanders to his daughter Marguerite, duchess of Burgundy.

The period of the Burgundian rule, a period of 145 years, was for Douai one of decadence. It brought Douai, with the rest of Flanders, into French hands, and union with France meant separation from England, the source of Flemish wealth and industry. Flanders, Knighton the chronicler tells us, was lifeless during a war when her merchants could no longer buy in England the wool which supplied the looms of her myriad weavers.† "It is true that from France comes our wheat," answered the Flemings to the envoys of Philip of Valois, "but to buy wheat we must have money, and it is from England that the wool comes which is the source of our wealth, and which enables us to enjoy life."‡ Later on, Jacques Van Arteveld urged no stronger argument to win the Flemish towns to the alliance with Edward III. than that "all Flanders depended on the cloth industry, and without wool from England no cloth could be made." Realizing the importance of their connection with England, the English alliance was always popular with the Flemings,§ till finally, under Count Guy de Dampierre, with the aid of Edward I., they attempted a total separation. But their *milice urbaine*, with the few Welsh archers despatched from England under Bohun of Hereford, were no match for the French knights. The im-

---

* "La monnaie Douaisieme," the copper denier and the silver livre, Ducange has fully described in his Glossary under the word "*moneta*," t. iv. p. 523.

† "Terram quasi exinanimatam eo quod cives sui lanas ang[...] et coria non haberent, ut solito mercando habere consueverant ad op[...]m, cum sint multi operarii."--Knighton, t. iii. cap. v.

‡ Edward Leglay's "Histoire des Comtes de Flandre," t. ii.
§ "Archives of Douai," cartulaire L., fol. 30 ; and cartul. OO

prisonment of their count, the destruction of their flocks, and their total subjection to France, were the only results of their rebellion. Again and again they rose, and, with the old cries of "Flandre au léon," and "Gloire aux vainqueurs," threw themselves on the French horsemen, as at Courtrai and Mons-en-Puelle; but they were invariably crushed, and, exhausted, they settled down in the silence of despair. Their hopes revived on the declaration of war by Edward III., but they were destined to be for ever blighted by the casting off of the English alliance by Louis-de-Mâle, and the union of their countess with the house of Burgundy. Douai especially suffered in these troublous times. In the very midst of the contest, it was twice taken by the French, and held by them once for a space of seventy years. During that time its merchants were imprisoned and their merchandise seized by the English and Flemings in turn, and their commercial relations with both were utterly ruined. The accession of the house of Burgundy, while it united Douai to the rest of Flanders, took away from both all chance of satisfactorily reviving the trade with England, and the extravagance and consequent penury of the Dukes of Burgundy, their alliances and political intrigues, brought on the final ruin of Flemish and Douaisian prosperity.

King Henry VI. could speak of Douai, in his decree of April 23, 1423, as being "deserted, laid waste, and depopulated by reason of excessive taxes and debts with which it is burdened, and by reason of the diminution of its revenues because of the wars afflicting the kingdom.*" For the first time the townsmen rise against the excessive burdens put on them; the water communication gets blocked up for want of traffic; even the alliance of Burgundy with England, after the murder of Duke Jean-sans-Peur at Montereau, did nothing to revive an industry which had lost its life. The English, indeed, while in possession of the country, by the proclamations of March 15, 1425, and of Aug. 9, Aug. 14, and Sept. 20, 1429, made every effort to bring back the Douaisian trade; but, after the Congress of Arras, Duke Philip broke off from the English alliance, and, after that, every attempt of the eschevins, unsupported by their rulers, to revive the cloth industry failed. Even the few merchants that were left dared hardly venture beyond the walls, for fear of their merchandize being seized by the creditors of the town. However bright the glories of the twelfth and thirteenth and fourteenth centuries of Douai's history may have been, they were all but extinguished   e end of the fifteenth. The future renown of the town w፡   in indeed to be due in great part to England,

---

Chroniques de Douai," p. 27, vol. ii.

but it was to be gained in the new sphere, quieter but not less brilliant, of learning and sanctity.

In the year 1477, on the death of Charles-the-Rash, Burgundy, being a male fief, reverted to France, while Flanders remained to his daughter, the Duchess Mary. By her marriage with the Archduke Maximilian, son of the Emperor Frederick, and afterwards himself Emperor, Mary of Burgundy had one son, Philip-le-Beau. It was through Duke Philip, by a curious and exceptional instance of hereditary right and matrimonial connection, that Douai came into Spanish hands—a fact which had as much to do with the English Catholics seeking refuge in its walls as its nearness to England and its scholastic advantages. In 1496 Duke Philip espoused Joan, Infanta of Spain, daughter of Ferdinand and Isabella, whose heir he was acknowledged to be on his visiting Spain in 1501.* On the death of Isabella he changed the ducal coronet for the crown of Castille, and died in 1505, leaving one son, Charles, then only a boy of five years. Besides the vast domains to which he succeeded on the death of his father, Charles succeeded Ferdinand as king of Arragon, Naples, and Sicily in 1516, and three years later, on the death of his grandsire, the Emperor Maximilian, in spite of the candidature of the King of France, was chosen emperor. Charles V., to the day of his abdication, treated Douai with special favour. He visited it on three several occasions. The burgesses, on their side, showed themselves his most loyal subjects. On the news of his election to the empire, they named the present Place Jemmappes, which they were planting, the *Boulevard des Bonnes Nouvelles*. In the Traité des Dames, better known as the Treaty of Cambrai, Douay was formally made over to France with the rest of Flanders.

From the period of the Spanish possession dates the University of Douai, the renown of whose schools and professors gained for the town the title of the Athens of the North.† The friendship ever shown by Charles for their town induced the chief burghers in their loyalty, as well as from a desire to restore in some way the ancient glory and splendour of their city, to petition the Emperor

---

* *Apropos* of this marriage was composed the following distich:—

"Bella gerant alii, tu felix Austria nube
Nam quæ Mars aliis, dat tibi regna Venus."

† From the eleventh and twelfth centuries there flourished at Douai a famous school within the cloisters of S. Amé's, and in the middle c⋯ thirteenth century Douai possessed, in the University of Paris, a cc which might justly be called its own, the renowned Sorbonne. I: Robert of Douai who, in 1250, bequeathed for its foundation the s⋯ 1,050 livres. "Robertus Duacensis . . . . mille et quinquaginta ' parisienses reliquit ad opus quorumdam scholarium quos intendebat !

to establish in their midst a university, in order that those of his subjects speaking the "Flemish tongue might no longer be under the necessity of going into France to learn French, and that students might not spend money out of the county." This was in 1530.

In the February of 1531 Charles himself visited the town and found it, "bien bonne, belle et forte, de bon air, nette, garnie d'artillerie et d'autres munitions." Notwithstanding the opposition on the part of the University of Louvain, the emperor appointed a special commission to examine the petition of eschevins. On visiting the town, the imperial commissioners were conducted by some of the leading burghers to the top of the belfry, and thence was pointed out to them the town clustering below and the country around. It was a large city, the report drawn up at the time tells us, possessing all the requirements of a university city, being situated in the midst of a salubrious and fertile plain, having in its suburbs extensive gardens, and within it numerous and copious fountains of freshest water. Poor scholars would find to assist them many rich people within the walls themselves, and prosperous farmers cultivating the fields around. Within easy distance of the town were many flourishing cities like Valenciennes, Cambrai, Arras, Lille, Tournay, Orchies, St. Amand, while the richest abbeys of Flanders lay almost at its very gates. Its watch-tower would give the alarm in time of war; its fortifications defend it from depredators, and secure for it peace and freedom from disturbance. Lastly, it was renowned for its othodoxy, its exemption from heresy, and its numerous religious foundations. Political difficulties, however, hindered Charles from completing a work in which he seems to have taken a special interest. It was reserved for his son Philip II. to finally accomplish it. At his request Pope Paul IV. prepared a Bull, July 31st, 1559, erecting a university at Douai on the plan of that at Louvain, with the object of "checking somewhat the spread of the poisonous teaching of heretics and schismatics against the Catholic faith."† Paul IV.

---

studentium in theologia ex consilio magistri Roberti de Sorbona." (Du Boulay, "Historia Universitatis Parisiensis," t. iii. p. 223.) Robert de Sorbon, who gave his name to the school, was a Canon of Cambrai and executor of Robert of Douai's testament. Among the first three professors of the Sorbonne, two were from Douai, Dom Félibien and Dom Lobineau (" Description de Paris," t. i. p. 329) and seven of the first sixteen students were ir compatriots.—" Les Origines de l'Université de Douai d'après d⋅ iments inédits." Par M. l'Abbé Dehaisnes, p. 1.

* "Archives tai." Mandement de l'Empéreur Charles-Quint à M. de Gavre d⋅ embre, 1530.
† "Chroniq⋅ Douai," vol. ii. p. 112. See the Bull given in the Appendix of " of English Catholics," i. p. 267.

died before this Bull was promulgated, but his successor, Pius IV., confirmed and published it January 6th, 1560. The other necessary stages were quickly passed through, and the university was installed October 5th, 1562, its first chancellor being M. Wallerand Hangouart, provost of St. Amé's.* The University of Douai being thus established was remarkable during its two hundred years' existence for two qualifications—its teaching of St. Thomas and its orthodoxy. The three Dominican foundations in the town account somewhat for the former. Its orthodoxy had ever been one of the glories of the town, and the university subscribed to the decrees of Trent the very year the council was closed. The Sovereign Pontiffs, Innocent X. and Alexander VII., both addressed briefs to the University of Douai in praise and approbation of the stand it had taken against Jansenism.

Colleges and seminaries soon sprang up under the shelter of the university. Dom Lentailleur, Abbot of Anchin, founded the college of Anchin, and intrusted it to the Jesuits. The Abbot of Marchiennes built the college of Marchiennes. King's College was founded by Philip II. at the same time as the university. Abbot Caverel was the founder of the college of St. Vaast, while the Dominicans still continued their college of St. Thomas. Of the nineteen seminaries affiliated to the university, two were royal foundations, four were the diocesan seminaries of Cambrai, Arras, Tournai, and Ypres. Several owed their origin to the generosity of one or other of the canons of St. Amé's or St. Peter's, or to rich burgesses. The Hôtel des Nobles was erected and endowed by a noble of Antwerp, the Seminary de la Torre by Gaspard de la Torre, Dean of the Cathedral of the Bruges, and the Seminary de la Motte by the the Chevalier Seigneur de la Motte, a governor of Gravelines. Besides colleges and seminaries, new monasteries, convents, and churches rose in every street and square. The Benedictine Abbey de Paix was founded in 1604. The Augustinian Abbey de Sin in 1616. The Benedictine Priory of St. Sulpice was built as a dependency of Anchin Abbey. The Capuchins entered the town in 1591, and were followed by the Carmelites of both observances, by the Augustinians, and the Minims. The Jesuits

---

* Fr. Knock, in his Preface to the "Douai Diaries," p. xxviii., says: "Dr. Richard Smith, formerly Fellow of Merton College and Regius Professor of Divinity at Oxford, was appointed Chancellor, and actually filled the office." No record at Douai itself makes mention of him save as one of the earlier professors. Local writers, treating of the university and its commencement, all speak of M. Wallerand Hangouart as its first Chancellor. The statement in the Appendix to the "Douai Diaries," p. 270, implying that the provostship of St. Peter's and the chancellorship of the university went together is misleading and incorrect.

had four residences. The Fathers of the Oratory received from the chapter of St. Peter's the administration of the parish of St. Jacques. The Fathers of St. Bridget took up their residence in the old Irish seminary. A rich heiress, daughter of a Douai notary of noble extraction, left her fortune for the foundation of the Carthusian priory and church.

Convents of religious women increased in like proportion. A Beguinage was instituted in 1607. The Poor Clares received a home in the town through the kindness of the Baroness de Mérode and the abbots of Anchin and Marchiennes. The Annunciads, the nuns of St. Catherine of Sienna, the Teresians, the Brigettines, the sisters of St. Agnes, the sisters of St. Julian, the hospital sisters, a local congregation, and the Capuchin nuns were established in the town in quick succession within the course of twenty years. The wealth accumulated by past trade and commerce was now spent in furthering education and religion. The fervour of this new life found vent in works of charity also. As early as the twelfth century Popes Alexander, Honorius, and Celestine had approved of the *Hôpital des Chartriers*. Celestine II. issued a bull, dated December 21st, 1197, in favour of the lazar-houses of Douai, three of which the burgesses founded in the next century. The hospice of St. Samson owed its origin to Garin, a former canon of St. Amé's, and afterwards archbishop of Thessalonica. It was not the only hospice for pilgrims. That of St. James-the-Less was the offering of a party of burghers who made the pilgrimage of Compostello in 1452. A hundred years before that John Deroqueguies had endowed the hospice of our Lady of Loretto for thirteen poor travellers. There were a dozen such pious institutions before the end of the fifteenth century. They increased to upwards of forty before the end of the eighteenth, and were for the relief of every description of human wretchedness and misfortune; there were homes for the old and infirm, for aged priests, for orphans and widows, for foundlings and poor women, for the sick and plague-stricken, for beggars, and for artisans without work.

But what most concerns English Catholics in the history of this period, is the foundation of the British colleges and convents. We have to thank the Abbé Dancoisne of Lille for having brought together in one book original and detailed accounts of each of the English foundations at Douai, and for the researches he has made to throw new light on their history. The late Fr. Knox, of the London Oratory, has given us a fair " narrative of the foundation and early years" of the chief English foundation at Douai in his Historical Introduction to the first series of " Records of the English Catholics," and in the second series we have a compl   ography of Cardinal Allen, its founder. It is sometimes called the College des Grands-Anglais on account of the nobility of many of its scholars, and sometimes the College du Pape on account of its having been endowed by Gregory XIII. It had in connection with it two other houses, a country seat at Coutiches, on the north of the town, and a school for younger students at Equerchin, established in 1750 by Dr. James Talbot, Vicar Apostolic of the London district. In the middle of the eighteenth century, by the generosity of the English Catholics, the imposing college, now standing and used as a barrack, was erected, on plans submitted to the then superiors of the college by M. Boulé, a local architect. In 1744 its community numbered fourteen priests, 104 students, and twenty-four servants.

What Fr. Knox has done for the English Secular College, a monk of Downside has done for the Benedictine monastery of Douai, in publishing the abridgment of Br. B. Weldon's Notes.* The first English Benedictine who came to Douai was Fr. Augustine Bradshaw, who had been professed in Spain. Fleeing from England after the Gunpowder Plot, he determined to establish a refuge and noviciate at Douai. With some others who joined him, he took rooms in the college of Anchin. The struggling community, afterwards removed to a house lent them by the Trinitarians, till Philip Caverel, abbot of St. Vaast's at Arras, built for them the church and monastery dedicated to St. Gregory the Great, and which they took possession of on Oct. 15th, 1611. Yearly at the offertory of the high mass on October 1st, the feast of the Translation of St. Vaast, the English monks did homage to the abbot of St. Vaast, or his representatives, for his noble gift.† "Collegium Benedictinorum Anglorem Duacensium" exclaims the author of the "Certamen Seraphicum," "ubi quot sunt monachi, tot coelestis ac humanae sapientiae antistes jure dixeris."‡ Abbot Caverel also gave the English monks a country-house at Equerchin. In 1770 the Benedictines built the magnificent college now owned by the community of St. Edmund's. The inscription still to be read on the foundation-stone runs thus:

PRAE NOBILIS ÆDRED DOMNA
STOURTON MAG : BRIT : BARONISSA
HUJUS ÆDIFICII LAPIDEM
DIE APRIL : ANNO. DNO : 1770.

---

* The original from which this abridgment has been made is still kept in the library of S. Edmund's, Douai. We hope it may soon be published in full. It would probably throw more light on English history during the past three hundred years than any work yet the public.

† "Cæremon : seu Ordinar : Vedastin : 1726," p. 184. See ' Littéraire de Deux Bénédictins," t. ii. pp. 75 and 76.

‡ "Certamen Seraphicum," p. 17.

From the English Benedictines we turn to the English Franciscans, whose history in many respects resembles that of their Benedictine brethren. The English Franciscan province was restored by Fr. John Gennings, who, on the martyrdom of his brother, sought the habit of St. Francis from one of the old surviving Franciscans, Fr. William Stanley, who later on gave him the ancient seal of the province, which he had received from the martyr Fr. Godfrey Jones. Fr. Gennings, with the help given him by the abbots of St. Vaast's and of Marchiennes, took a house near the church of St. Albin's and there received the first novices. Afterwards, in 1706, Henry Fletcher, Baron of Button, built for them the spacious church and convent of St. Bonaventure. In 1730, Father Mason tells us, the English Franciscans were 130 in number, and fifty of these were in the convent at Douai. The Scotch Recollects, reorganized by Father Arthur Bell, who was for some time their provincial, were not so successful in establishing themselves in the town. In 1626 they occupied a house given them by M. Antoine Chemyn, curé of Masuy, but they left the town after a short time, under what circumstances is not known.

The Scotch secular clergy were more fortunate. Their college of St. Andrew was an amalgamation of three others, that founded at Antwerp, by John Lesley, Bishop of Ross and the Allen of Scotland, the college formerly at Pont-à-Mousson endowed by Queen Mary, and the Scotch college at Madrid founded by Philip III. The great benefactor of the Scots' College, however, was Hippolytus Curle, son of Mary Stuart's secretary. On becoming a Jesuit, Fr. Curle rebuilt and endowed the college with a fortune of 60,000 florins, which had been left him by his aunt, a maid-of-honour to Queen Mary. The Scotch college was conducted by the Jesuits till their suppression, and hence is generally known as the *Séminaire Jésuites Écossais*.

The Irish seminary of St. Patrick was founded by Philip II. in 1596 or 1598.* A certain Jean Parisis is said to have founded the Séminaire du Soleil for six Irish priests in 1600. Fr. Cussack in 1604 seems to have united the two and thoroughly reorganized the college, which during the century and a half of its existence gave twelve bishops and eight archbishops to the Irish Church. The Irish Bernardines obtained permission from the authorities in 1600 to establish a community at Douai, but they do not seem to have used their permission.

From the new life and progress which we have been describing, from the peace and fervour of cloistral and scholastic life, we turn with reluctance to the war and bloodshed which brought Douai

---

* "Canquelain," p. 1067.

into the hands of its present owners. The war started in the determination of Louis XIV. to dispute the thirty-third article of the Peace of the Pyrenees, by which Marie Thérèse, on her marriage with him, had made a formal renunciation of all claim " pour cause des héritages et plus grandes successions de leurs majestés catholiques ses père et mère." On the death of Philip IV. and the accession of Charles II., a child of four years of age, the *Grand Monarque* found an opportunity of asserting a claim which all Europe looked upon as long since settled. In his *Traité des droits de la Reine sur divers Etats de la Monarchie d'Espagne*," Louis refused to regard as binding his queen's renunciation of her rights, principally with respect to Flanders, first of all because she was a minor at the time she made it, and secondly because its conditions had not been fulfilled. Falling back on the *droit de dévolution*, a Flemish custom by which females by a first marriage inherited in preference to males by a second, he laid claim to at least Walloon Flanders. The Flemish lawyers answered, with crushing force, that a minor who could contract marriage could also ratify matrimonial settlements, that mere delay in payment of a dowry was of no force, and lastly that the *droit de dévolution* was not of general application in the Low Countries. But arguments and negotiations alike failed, and in the spring of 1667 the King of France invaded the Flanders with two armies of 35,000 men each.

It was not the first time during the Spanish rule that the French had ravaged the North. Flanders was already beginning to be called the battle-field of Europe. Douai being a border town, was more liable to be attacked than many other towns. In 1521, during the protracted war between Francis I. and the Emperor Charles V., the French came to the very gates of the town, and, in spite of the truce existing, they made another attempt to surprise it in 1556, under Admiral Coligny. The alarm given by three villagers, who noticed armed men lurking about the outskirts of the town, and the special protection of St. Maurand, saved it.* French intrigue afterwards created a party in favour of French rule, within the town itself. Its members went by the name of patriots, and played a very important part in the expulsion of the English students in 1578. It was with great

---

* An old chronicle thus gives us an account of St. Maurand's intervention:—" On the Eve of the Epiphany of 1556 the men of Douai, after a day of great rejoicing, slumbered heavily. The French hoped to surprise

difficulty that the eschevins and the more respectable citizens kept down the risings of the patriots when the French were ravaging the neighbourhood in 1574 and 1578. Douai was actually provisioned for a siege in 1640, when the French, having taken Arras, marched towards the town. But they retired after laying waste a part of the country, and destroying amongst other property the English Benedictine country-house.

The strength of the town and the traditional protection of its saints won for it a reputation for security which gave rise to a new class of foundations within its walls. These were the houses of refuge, buildings large and with some pretensions to architectural beauty, which served as asylums in which the religious of the country abbeys might seek security in time of war. The abbey of Anchin had two such houses as early as the middle of the fifteenth century. Its example was quickly imitated by the neighbouring abbeys of Marchiennes, Hiénin-Liétard, Flines and Oisy. Its long freedom from actual invasion, and the favour, almost reverence, shown to the town on account of its religious character, caused even the abbeys at a distance to establish their refuge within its fortifications. The abbeys of St. Callixtus, near Lille, of St. Bertin at St. Omer, of St. Vaast and St. Eloi at Arras, of St. Andrew and of the Cistercians of Vaucelle, near Cambrai, all had sought a place of shelter at Douai, so that the houses of refuge were as many as thirteen in the seventeenth century.

It was with reason, then, that the Douai burghers, on hearing of Louis' approach, prepared to defend the town, which had long been regarded by the French as the key of Walloon Flanders. After forcing Tournai to capitulate, Louis, with the object of deceiving the Spaniards, commenced a feigned march on Courtrai, but in reality he was dispatching his troops to Douai, where he arrived himself with the main body of his army on July 2nd, 1667. He found the town defended by 400 trained infantry, three bodies of cavalry, and 16 companies of armed citizens. These last were made up, not only of the lay townsmen, but also of the canons of the collegiate churches, of the parish priests and religious, of the monks from the houses of refuge, the students from the seminaries and the professors of the University. The

---

deep silence of the night just as the enemy prepared to scale the walls. The townsmen, wakened from their slumbers, ran to the walls, and there beheld St. Ma????? making the round of the town, clothed in his religious habit, all glit'   ; with golden fleur-de-lis, and with a royal sceptre in his hand. T   were quick to recognize their patron saint, who had guarded thei   while they slept, and they instituted a yearly procession to his honor   e successful resistance of the French in 1478 was also attributed t   aurand, and a procession of thanksgiving instituted in his honour

document from which these details are taken enumerates the companies and the posts assigned them. We quote the following as being particularly interesting to the English reader:—

3rd. Andrew Becquet's company was placed at the Arras Gate, with the canons, habitués, and officials of St. Amé's, the students of King's College and the English Recollects.

5th. William Caudron's company was stationed to defend the Porte d'Ocre, with the Dominicans, the professors and students of St. Vaast's College, the English Benedictines, and the religious of Furnes.

8th. Peter Lemaire, with his company, was ordered to guard the gate of Notre Dame, with the English, the Irish, and the students from the Seminaries de la Motte and du Soleil.—*Chroniques de Douai*, vol. ii., Appendice, p. 355.

Resistance, however, was useless against the disciplined troops and complete siege-artillery of Louis. The burghers capitulated, and on the 6th of July the Spanish garrison marched from the gates with all the honours of war, with their arms and baggage, but no cannon. The same day Louis, who had conducted the siege in person, made his triumphal entry into the town, and going in procession to the "rich and majestic church of St. Amé," chanted a solemn Te Deum in thanksgiving for his victory. A medal impressed with a figure of the king in the trenches and the legend "Rex dux et miles," was struck to commemorate the taking of the town, and on the 23rd of the month, the king and his queen visited the town, which the Treaty of Aix-la-Chapelle in the following year confirmed to them for ever.

During the long and terrible war of the Spanish succession, Douai was destined to go through other sieges far more disastrous than the one of 1667. The rough refusal of England of terms which granted all that the allies had fought for, with a further demand that Louis should compel his grandson, even by force of arms, to give up the crown of Spain, wrung from the king, exhausted though he was, the resolve to continue the contest. "If I must wage war," he exclaimed, "I had rather wage it against my enemies than against my children." Thus the war was re-opened in 1709. On the 22nd of April, 1710, the allied forces began to close round Douai. By the first of May the plan of attack was agreed upon, and in the early morning of the 14th the bombardment commenced. A hundred thousand shells are said to have been thrown into the town. The English Recollects gathered up as many as 150 that had been shot on to their single property. The spire of St. Albin's was the first to be battered down, then followed the destruction of many another noble building. After holding out, in spite of hunger and fire, for sixty-five days, the townsmen capitulated, and on July 2nd, the Duke of Marlborough and Prince Eugene, at the head of the allied forces, entered the town and were presented with the keys of the city.* The town remaiued in the hands of the allies only till 1712, when it was retaken by General Villars, and in the Treaty of Utrecht it was finally made over to France.

The French possession developed a new feature of the town— its military character. Douai had ever been a strong place, from the time it had held at bay the Norsemen, and the state of its fortifications, their strength and improvement, fill many a page of its annals. The inundation of the country for two or three leagues around, one of its great means of defence, is mentioned as far back as the twelfth century. Its fortifications were irregular, but the great ditches and the outworks of every description which formed them made the town one of the strongest of French fortresses even before Vauban, "the first of engineers," designed and executed the works which have made it impregnable, if any town can be called so in this age. Louis XIV. made it a military depôt, establishing in it an arsenal to contain arms and ammunition, always in readiness to supply 30,000 men. On the spot where the first castle was raised, more than a thousand years before, a foundry was built, once the largest and most important in France, and at the same time a school of artillery was instituted. These were the latest developments of the town previous to 1789.

At the end of Louis XIV.'s reign Douai was described "as being as large as Orleans, with streets straight and wide, and public buildings magnificent and numerous, a town of much importance, though fallen from its ancient splendour." But though "larger than Lille," says a memoir of 1698, "it has not a third of its inhabitants, nor a tenth of its wealth." Its inhabitants were in fact too indolent to have recourse to trade or industry as long as they could live by boarding scholars. Hence the town continued to be a city of schools and monasteries. It counted at times as many as 4,000 students in its university. A thousand of its residents wore the religious habit. Two-thirds of the town, Villars was told, when asked to spare it, was made up of churches, hospitals, colleges, seminaries, and religious houses. There were indeed in the town three abbeys, fifty charitable endowments, ten colleges, nineteen seminaries, thirteen houses of refuge, sixteen communities of religious women and fifteen of men, at the close of the eighteenth century, and the steeples of thirty churches

---

* See "Histoire de Louis XIV," par M. le Baron de Quincy. Also "Rélations des Siéges de Douai" in the "Etrennes aux Habitants de Douai."

were visible from the plain around pointing to the sky. Suddenly the Revolution broke over the land and swept away in its mad career cathedral and abbey, shrine and chapel, with every tradition and custom of the ages gone by. It laid Douai waste. But what havoc it worked in the old town, what few traces of the sacred past it left behind, what desolation profaned the hallowed homes of our martyrs, and what the modern town has recovered of its ancient glory and importance, these we hope to dwell upon at a future time.

JAMES BONIFACE MACKINLAY, O.S.B.

ART. VIII.—NEW TESTAMENT VATICANISM.

1. *Novum Testamentum Vaticanum.* Post Angeli Maii aliorumque imperfectos labores ex ipso codice edidit A. F. C. TISCHENDORF. Lipsiæ. 1867.

2. *The New Testament in the Original Greek.* The text revised by B. F. WESTCOTT, D.D., and F. J. A. HORT, D.D. Cambridge. 1881.

3. *The Revision Revised:* three Essays, reprinted and enlarged from the *Quarterly Review.* By J. W. BURGON, B.D., Dean of Chichester. London: J. Murray.

4. *The Revisers and the Greek Text of the New Testament.* By Two Members of the New Testament Company. London: Macmillan. 1882.

5. *The Revised Version of the First Three Gospels,* considered in its Bearings upon the Record of Our Lord's Words and of Incidents in His Life. By F. C. COOK, M.A., Editor of "The Speaker's Commentary." London: Murray. 1882.

ABOUT eight years ago Mr. Gladstone wrote a pamphlet against what he was pleased to call "Vaticanism." Since that time a new form of Vaticanism has arisen, claiming to settle, with infallible voice, the very text of Holy Writ. Not Rome, but England, is the birthplace of this new religion; not the successors of St. Peter, but certain Cambridge professors, are its high priests. From the Jerusalem Chamber at Westminster has this new Law been proclaimed, and the new Gospel is preached alike in Established Church and Dissenting chapel. Against Vaticanism in this new form Mr. Gladstone makes no protest and writes no pamphlet. And yet the danger is more urgent than before. The old form, he complained, was an ad-

dition to the Gospel, but the new, he must admit, is a taking
away of essential parts. If the old was, in his opinion, a human
edifice erected on a divine foundation, the new is a mine sapping
the divine foundation itself.

"Vaticanism," in the sense in which we here use the term, is a
word borrowed from Dr. Scrivener to express the opinion of
those who think the Vatican Codex to be the truest and best
text of the Greek Testament; who adopt its peculiar readings
as the purest Gospel, accounting even its blemishes as perfections, and its omissions as unauthorized additions. According
to them, the Vatican is the *one* infallible manuscript, relating
with unerring voice what the Lord said and what He did. It is
the King of codices, the Uncial of uncials, lording it over the
oldest Fathers, and supreme over the most ancient versions.

An opinion so extravagant would hardly call for serious consideration were it not that it has been adopted by certain writers
of distinction, and thus obtained a hold on the public mind.
Two years ago, Drs. Westcott and Hort published a Greek
text of the New Testament, with an elaborate treatise explaining
their new system of textual criticism. The learned Editors
claimed that their text was " a true approximate reproduction "
of the Apostolic autographs. Their admirers pronounced it to be
an " epoch-making book." But it soon became clear that their
new text was but little else than a corrected reprint of the
Vatican manuscript; and the fundamental principle of their
new theory was the general infallibility of that manuscript.
According to Dean Burgon, "All is summed up in the curt
formula—the Vatican Codex!" Now, it must be borne in mind
that the making of the new text was coincident with the Revision of King James's Version ordered by Convocation, and
that Drs. Westcott and Hort were chosen as Revisers. We
learn that privately-printed copies of their new text were placed
in the hands of each member of the Committee, and that in
textual questions their influence was paramount. Dr. Scrivener,
" the solitary representative of conservative criticism," as Canon
Cook calls him, was systematically outvoted, and six thousand
textual amendments were carried. It is not surprising, then,
that the Revised Translation is merely Westcott and Hort's
Greek text done into indifferent English. Their pet readings
were adopted, passages which they thought doubtful were voted
off to the margin, and what they accounted spurious was cast
aside. Hence it follows that the Revised Version is a virtual
reproduction in English   e Vatican Codex, an embodiment
of the new Gospel of ˜   ism.

The natural consequ   ˙ this rash tampering with the text
has been the raising   most difficult questions of textual

criticism. The Bible-reading public, which hardly suspected the existence of differences of reading, is now informed by marginal notes running through the length and breadth of the new Testament, that "*some ancient manuscripts*" add this verse, "*the two oldest manuscripts*" omit the other. The question at once arises; when ancient manuscripts differ, when even the oldest cannot agree, who is to decide? We blame the Revisers for raising a question which they themselves cannot answer satisfactorily. We blame them the more for leading unskilled readers to form for themselves the mistaken notion that the oldest manuscripts are for that very reason the truest. Now Dean Burgon gives two very striking instances to show that the oldest manuscripts are not always the purest. The first is a passage from the Medea of Euripides, as it is found in a papyrus uncial manuscript of B.C. 200. Of this papyrus, M. Weil, its learned editor, says:—

We see that its text bristles with the gravest blunders. The latest and worst of our manuscripts of Euripides are worth infinitely more than this copy which was made two thousand years ago in the city (Alexandria) where Greek learning and textual criticism flourished.

The second instance is from St. Clement of Alexandria, A.D. 182, and consists of 15 verses of St. Mark (x. 17—31):—

There are but 297 words in these fifteen verses, according to the traditional text, of which, in the copy which belonged to Clemens Alexandrinus, thirty-nine prove to have been left out; eleven words are added; twenty-two substituted; twenty-seven transposed; thirteen varied; and the phrase has been altered at least eight times.

This bears out Dr. Scrivener's well-known opinion :—

It is no less true to fact than paradoxical in sound that the worst corruptions to which the New Testament has ever been subjected originated within one hundred years after it was composed: that Irenæus (A.D. 150) and the African Fathers, and the whole Western, with a portion of the Syrian, Church used far inferior manuscripts to those employed by Stunica, or Erasmus, or Stephens, thirteen centuries later, when moulding the Textus Receptus. (Introdn. to "Textual Criticism," p. 453).

Age, then, by itself, and apart from other considerations, does not necessarily give authority to manuscripts. A tenth century cursive may give a purer text than a fourth century uncial. Manuscripts do not grow wiser as they get older. If corrupt in their youth, they are corrupt in their old age. Why, then, do the Revisers, who ought to be perfectly aware of this fact, keep on printing in their margin "*The two oldest manuscripts,*" and thus terrorizing simple-minded readers who are not aware of i ? The Revisers were commissioned by Convocation to correct ı faulty translation, and they have unsettled the original text. Like officious workmen, asked to repair the walls, they have meddled with the very foundations. But for one thing, we might compare them to the fisherman in the "Arabian Nights," who could not resist the temptation to open the sealed vase, whence there came forth smoke, spreading itself over land and sea like a thick fog, and finally taking the form of a frightful spectre. The Revisers, too, have broken the seal of the precious vase intrusted to their care, and there comes forth the smoke of controversy, resulting in a thick fog of uncertainty, which must ultimately develop itself into the gaunt spectre of unbelief. In one respect we admit our comparison is faulty: the fisherman got his spectre back again into the vase; but we fear the Revisers will not be so clever. Through the unwisdom of the Revisers, the public are forced to be spectators of a real battle of texts. Whichever side wins, the Gospel of Peace must lose by the conflict, and the faith of the weak will be endangered. Nor can the issue be narrowed, as "the two Revisers" strive to narrow it, with a contest between the Textus Receptus and the Vatican Text. No one in these days cares much for the Textus Receptus, except inasmuch as it is substantially the traditional Greek text, handed down from the fourth century. It were an easy matter to reckon with Erasmus and Stephens, Beza and the Elzevirs, but behind them there stands the serried phalanx of the Greek Fathers, with St. Chrysostom at their head. For it is, of course, well known that the Received Text was based upon cursive manuscripts of the tenth century, and even Dr. Hort admits that "it is virtually identical with that used by Chrysostom and other Antiochean Fathers in the latter part of the fourth century," so that the conflict really lies between the traditional Greek Text, supported by the vast body of uncial and cursive manuscripts, witnessed to by Greek Fathers and Lectionaries, and a text based upon two anonymous manuscripts of the fourth century. Dean Burgon and Canon Cook are the champions on the one side, and on the other Dr. Westcott and the "fearless" Dr. Hort, supported by "the two Revisers" (Dr. Ellicott and Archdeacon Parker), and Drs. Farrar and Sanday. Considerable heat, if not light, has been evolved by the clash of these critics. Dean Burgon calls the new text "a vile fabrication," "a corrupt text, based on false witnesses," and "demonstrably more remote from evangelic verity than any which has ever yet seen the light." The other side retaliate by saying that their assailant has "no grasp upon the central conditions of the problem," that "he is innocently ignorant of the now established principles of textual criticism," and, unkindest cut of all, that his erudite articles in the *Quarterly* "must have been written by a lady."

Lest our readers should be tempted to think that these learned scholars are fighting about a matter of no concern to anybody but themselves, we will try to show how great are the issues at stake. It is a question which affects the very integrity of the Gospel, and the most touching incidents of our Lord's Divine life. On account of the number and gravity of its omissions, the Vatican has been called "an abbreviated Gospel." In this Gospel, our Lord's agony in the garden is left out (Luke xxii. 43, 44), also His first word upon the Cross (Luke xxiii. 34), and His last cry (Mark xv. 39). The Ascension and Session at the right hand is struck out of both Gospels (Luke xxiv. 51; Mark xvi. 19). The last twelve verses of St. Mark are omitted; also the first twelve verses of St. John's eighth chapter, and two verses from the fifth (4 and 5). Our Lord makes no reference to fasting (Mat. xvii. 21; Mark ix. 29), says nothing about the "one thing needful" (Luke x. 42). On the other hand it contains some startling statements—*e.g.*, that our Lord's side was pierced before his death! (Matt. xxvii. 42), and that the darkening of the sun was caused by an eclipse, though the moon was at its full! (Luke xxiii. 45). Many other variations from the current narrative might be quoted, but this will suffice to show how serious is the divergence between the two texts, and how grave the interests at stake. So much so, that it is scarcely an exaggeration to say that, if the Vatican is the genuine text, the whole Christian world has not known the true Gospel till now, or rather that it has been largely imposed upon by an interpolated text. Now, it is clear that two manuscripts, twin sisters in mischief, the Vatican and Sinaitic, have brought about this revolution in the biblical world. And we are at once led to inquire into their antecedents. Where did they come from? What Father or Doctor of the Church will vouch for their respectability? Unless we can get a satisfactory answer on these points, we cannot have much confidence in their testimony.

The first mention of the Vatican manuscript occurs in a Catalogue of the Vatican Library, made in 1475, about twenty years after the taking of Constantinople by the Turks. As Cardinal Bessarion's name is found in connection with the manuscript, it may be inferred, with some probability, that the library was indebted for this precious jewel to him who was the light of the Eastern Church, and that through him it was saved from ruthless Turks. Half a century later the manuscript figures in the controversy between Erasmus and the editors of the Complutum Polyglot. In 1587 the Old Testament part of the manuscript formed the basis of the grand Sixtine edition of the Septuagint. In the following century, Bentley commissioned certain Roman priests to collate the New Testament for him. In the beginning of this century the precious manuscript was carried off to Paris with other spoils from Rome. There the great Catholic scholar, Hug, studied it, and first made the world aware of its true age and importance. With his estimate Tischendorf agrees "non propter Hugonem sed cum Hugone." After the restitution of the manuscript to the Vatican library, Cardinal Mai, the Papal librarian, undertook the labour of editing it as a whole. But it was not till after his death that the result of his labours was published to the world by Padre Vercellone. On account of defects of method and accuracy this edition failed to satisfy critics. Then Tischendorf, the Adamantius of textual criticism, obtained permission from Pope Pius IX. to remedy the defects of Cardinal Mai's editions. In justice to the learned Cardinal, to whom the world of letters owes so much, it must be remembered that it was no easy thing to edit a fourth century manuscript, written over and corrected by many hands besides that of the original scribe. Yet Tischendorf admits that Cardinal Mai far surpassed others who had attempted the task before him. Not content with bringing out his amended edition of 1867, Tischendorf asked the Holy Father's leave to bring out a large facsimile edition of the Vatican, like that which he had lately published of the Sinaitic. But Pope Pius IX. signified his intention to do this himself and at once committed the work to Fathers Vercellone and Cozza, Tischendorf contributing his Sinaitic type. Five "superb volumes" have appeared, and now the sixth and last has just been published, containing the apparatus criticus. "The learned, genial, modest Vercellone," as Dr. Scrivener calls him, died in the course of the work, and his place was taken by Fr. Cajetan Sergio, a Barnabite, like himself. The gem of the Vatican Library has at length found a setting worthy of it. Enshrined in an édition de luxe, it now lies open to the admiring gaze of the world. It is, perhaps, too soon to anticipate the verdict of scholars on the critical value of this grand edition. Dr. Roberts, no mean judge, has said that it "leaves nothing more to be desired." We congratulate the learned editors on the completion of a work which sheds fresh literary glory on the reigns of Pope Pius IX and Pope Leo XIII. We may hope, too, that an end has been put to Protestant murmuring about the "jealousy of the Vatican," and the excessive strictness of the library officials. Tregelles complained of being searched, Alford that the librarian would ˈ ˈy let him look at the manuscript, and Tischendorf was indig with the Prussian Jesuit who reported him for doing whᵣ n Dr. Scrivener admits to have been a breach of contrᵣ Unless the collectors of various readings are more scruᵢ than other collectors, experience shows that the Library officials were right to keep a watchful eye upon them. The authorities of the British Museum Library would be quite as particular with any one who asked to collate the Alexandrian Codex. But the last and drollest example of this sort of conventional grumbling is afforded by an Irish Protestant Bishop—Dr. Alexander. In a note in the "Speaker's Commentary" on the disputed reading of 1 Tim.iii.16, he deplores "that the Vatican manuscript cannot be appealed to because *the jealousy of Rome has prevented accurate collation*"! Would it surprise the learned commentator to hear that the passage in question is not in the Vatican manuscript at all? The Codex is imperfect and breaks off at Hebrews ix. 13, and it is strange that Dr. Alexander should not have known that in the oldest manuscripts the order of St. Paul's Epistles is somewhat different: Hebrews follow Thessalonians, and then the Pastoral Epistles—a proof, by the way, that no doubt was entertained as to St. Paul being the writer of the Epistle to the Hebrews. Hence the world has suffered a double loss: the Vatican text of the Pastoral Epistles, and their "accurate collation" by Dr. Alexander. If some distinguished foreign scholar wished to collate "accurately" the early chapter of St. Matthew in the Alexandrian manuscript, would it be the jealousy of "perfidious Albion" which would prevent him, or the unhappy fact that the Codex does not contain these chapters? We hope Dr. Alexander will condescend to explain this little difficulty in the next edition of the "Speaker's Commentary."

Of the Sinaitic Codex we know very little beyond the curious story of its discovery by the indefatigable Tischendorf. In 1844, when on a visit to the Convent of St. Catherine on Mount Sinai, he saw some old vellum leaves in a basketful of paper meant for the convent oven. He picked them out and obtained them for the asking. These forty-three leaves contained Esther and Nehemias and were evidently part of a very ancient manuscript. Having in 1846 published them as the Codex Fredericus Augustanus, his whole endeavour was to find the remainder of the precious manuscript. A second visit to the convent in 1853 brought no success; but a third visit, in 1859, and the name of the Emperor of Russia, obtained for him the coveted treasure, comprising the rest of the Old Testament and the whole of the New, the Epistle of Barnabas, and part of the Shepherd of Hermas. At Tischendorf's suggestion, the community gave it as a present to the Emperor of Russia, the patron of the convent and of the Greek Church. So, after a narrow escape from the oven, the Sinaitic Codex has passed from the sands of the Desert to the snows of St. Petersburg. Of its previous history nothing is known. It may have been presented to the monastery by its imperial founder Justinian about the year 540, or possibly it may have belonged to the old hospice which the Empress Helena founded for the benefit of pilgrims to Mount Sinai. No sooner had Tischendorf completed his Imperial fac-simile edition of the newly-found manuscript than Constantine Simonides, a Greek from Syme, shocked the world by asserting that he had written the whole of this so-called fourth century manuscript himself, and that the learned German scholar had been sadly taken in. Simonides said that he had copied it out of a printed Moscow Bible in about eight or nine months, and meant it as a present for the Emperor of Russia, but for want of money he sold it to the Patriarch of Constantinople for £250, and the Patriarch had given it to the Convent at Sinai. Many people in England believed this absurd story, and a certain religious newspaper, which Dr. Scrivener nicknames "The Illiterate Churchman," advocated his cause. Suffice it to say that the fate of most impostors befell Simonides: he was found out.

This is all that we can gather from external sources concerning the history of these two manuscripts. On intrinsic grounds critics are generally agreed that both manuscripts must have been written about the same time—the early part of the fourth century; that, though there is a marked similarity of type, yet they were not copied from the same exemplar, and that they agree together, especially in omissions. Tischendorf, whose opinion is entitled to the greatest weight because of his general experience of manuscripts and his special study of these in particular, thinks that the Vatican was the work of one and the same scribe from beginning to end, that the scribe corrected his own work in great part, but that a professional corrector (διορθωτής) added readings from some other source; that a third hand, when the original writing had faded from age, inked over the whole afresh, adding accents, breathings, and fresh corrections. In the Sinaitic he found the work of four different scribes and a dozen correctors at different times. But what most interests us is that, from certain peculiar tricks of penmanship, he is positive that the writer of the Vatican was one of the four scribes of the Sinaitic. The scribe of the Vatican, he says, wrote Tobias, Judith, and part of the first book of Maccabees in the Old Testament, and six sheets of the New Testament, besides acting as general corrector of the Sinaitic. This strange discovery of the great critic was at first received with some incredulity. But Canon Cook and Dr. Hort both agree in v   ing it as an established truth. As this is a matter of great   tance for our future argument, it will be well to quote D   's own words:—

The fact appea·   ıfficiently established by the concurrent culiarities in ↑   ˙ one letter, punctuation, avoidance of contractions, and some points of orthography. As the six leaves are found on computation to form three pairs of conjugate leaves, holding different places in three distant quires, it seems probable that they are new or clean copies of corresponding leaves executed by the scribe who wrote the rest of the New Testament, but so disfigured, either by an unusual number of corrections of clerical errors, or from some unknown cause, that they appeared unworthy to be retained, and were therefore cancelled and transcribed by the corrector (Introduction, p. 213).

Dr. Hort's testimony to this point is all the more valuable because it is part of his theory to claim the two manuscripts as wholly independent witnesses, and this they cannot be if the writer of one was the corrector and part writer of the other.

We will leave the manuscripts for a moment in order to transcribe out of Eusebius of Cæsarea's life of Constantine a letter which was written fifteen hundred years ago by the Emperor to Eusebius:—

Through the Providence of our Divine Saviour a very great multitude of persons in the city, which has taken its name from ourselves, has joined Holy Church (ἁγιωτάτῃ ἐκκλησίᾳ). Wherefore, to make provision for so great an increase, it is in the first place necessary to build several new churches. Give, then, a ready obedience to what I have determined upon. For it has seemed good to require of your wisdom to get fifty copies of the sacred Scriptures, which you know are so needful for the Church's teaching, transcribed, *on vellum, specially prepared, and by skilled copyists who thoroughly understand their work*. Let them be easily legible and adapted to common use. Further, that we have sent letters to the procurator of the province to provide whatever is needful for their preparation. You will use all diligence to have these codices got ready *as soon as possible*. This letter hereby empowers you to employ two public vehicles. When these beautifully-written codices are finished, let them be brought for our inspection by one of the deacons of your church, who shall have experience of our generosity. May God preserve you, dearest brother.

Eusebius then records the *prompt* fulfilment of the Emperor's commands and the sending of these costly volumes ("Vita Const.," l. iv. c. 36).

The question at once suggests itself, can it be that the Vatican and Sinaitic Codices were among the fifty copies which Eusebius of Cæsarea procured for the Emperor of Constantine the Great? Canon Cook has made a strong case for thinking that they were. We proceed, then, to lay before our readers some of his reasons. In the first place, there is no question but that the age of our manuscript corresponds with the time of Co⟨nstan⟩tine. Secondly, his letter leads to the expectation that his co⟨pies⟩ would combine three qualities—precious material, splendi⟨d work⟩manship, and extreme haste. Both the Vatican and the Sin⟨aitic⟩ are this threefold characteristic. They are formed of the finest vellum, each sheet being the skin of an antelope. The beauty and regularity of their uncial letters betoken the work of professional scribes. They are considered to be " by far the best extant specimens of early calligraphy." And yet the immense number of mistakes shows that they were written most hastily and carelessly. Tischendorf blames both manuscripts for what he calls "magna scripturæ vitiositas." Dr. Dobbin has calculated that the Vatican leaves out words or whole clauses no less than 330 times in St. Matthew, 365 in St. Mark, 439 in St. Luke, 357 in St. John, 384 in the Acts, 681 in the Epistles—in all, 2556 times. Dr. Scrivener says:—

That the Sinaitic abounds with errors of the eye and pen to an extent not unparalleled, but happily rather unusual in documents of first-rate importance ; so that Tregelles has freely pronounced that the state of the text as proceeding from the first scribe may be regarded as very rough.

The calculation of another critic, quoted by the Quarterly Reviewer, is that in St. Matthew the Vatican leaves out 648 words, the Sinaitic, 808; in St. Mark, the Vatican omits 762, the Sinaitic, 870; in St. Luke, the Vatican 757, the Sinaitic, 816; in St. John, the Vatican 710, the Sinaitic, 961. The correctors seem to have been as careless as the copyists—

It appears (says Tischendorf) to have been generally the custom of these correctors, as mere hirelings, in order to get through their work rapidly, to be satisfied with such corrections and remarks as might be made with ease in a hasty perusal and collation of the manuscripts.

Clearly, then, we may infer that these manuscripts were transcribed by hired scribes, pressed for time and regardless of accuracy.

In monasteries (Canon Cook says) the transcriptions were always made by members of the conventual body; haste and carelessness were of all faults least to be looked for in the leisure of the convent, in the work of men who, whatever may be thought of their discretion, were beyond all doubt heartily devoted to the Master, whose Word was intrusted to their diligence (p. 175).

A third reason for identifying these manuscripts with those which Eusebius prepared for Constantine lies in the general character of their readings. We know perfectly well where Eusebius would have gone for his text. He was the disciple and earnest defender of Origen. The library at Cæsarea was possessed of Origen's choicest manuscripts. We may expect that the readings adopted by Eusebius would be those which had the authority of Origen. And we find that the text of our two manuscripts bears out the expectation. Canon Cook, who has carefully verified the fact, tells us that "as Eusebius is substantially one with Origen in his views touching the criticism of the New Testament, so are the readings in the two codices for the most part identical with those in the citations in Origen" (p. 180). For instance, Origen "*alone among the early Fathers*" leaves out certain clauses in St. Luke's "Our Father," the Vatican and Sinaitic "*alone among ancient manuscripts*" do the same. But the strongest reason for the identification is furnished by the last twelve verses of St. Mark's Gospel, which, as we before stated, are left out by both manuscripts. This points without doubt to Eusebius, who is known to be the only writer up to the end of the fourth century who rejected these verses. His letter to Marinus explains why he did so—viz., to escape the difficulty of harmonizing St. Mark with St. Matthew in regard to the Resurrection. If Eusebius, then, had to prepare copies of the New Testament we may be sure that he would have left out the verses, and that he is the only man who could have done so. The Vatican and the Sinaitic *alone among ancient manuscripts* have omitted the verses. The Vatican has a blank space at the end of St. Mark's Gospel, a proof that the scribe knew of the missing verses, and perhaps saw them in the exemplar from which he copied. In the Sinaitic there is no blank, for the writing has been purposely spaced out to prevent it. It is very remarkable that this is one of the six sheets which the Vatican scribe who corrected the Sinaitic rewrote himself, having, as is supposed, cancelled what the Sinaitic scribe had written. For an explanation of this curious fact we must quote Canon Cook's own words:—

What more natural, what more probable, than the conjecture—may I venture to ask what more cogent than the evidence thus supplied—that Eusebius superintending the scribe of the Vatican when he was copying a part of Scripture in which Eusebius felt a very special interest, should interfere and order the omission of the verses to which he has recorded his antagonism ; or again that the scribe, when he was called upon to transcribe the same portion in the Sinaitic manuscript, written, as we know, on even more costly and rare materials, in much larger characters—both points of importance taken in connection with the demand for extreme haste—should save the extra column, and thus, whether consciously or unconsciously, obliterate, as far as the authority of that manuscript extends, all indications of the change (p. 179).

We now come to the crucial difficulty in the way of the identification of one at least of these manuscripts with those sent by Eusebius to the Emperor. Eusebius expressly says that they were τρισσά καί τετρασσά, that is "terniones" and "quaterniones," as Valesius renders the phrase. This is commonly explained to

refer to the way the sheets were folded in quires of three or four.
In the Vatican Codex the sheets are arranged in quires of fives;
the Sinaitic in fours. But Canon Cook maintains that these
terms have not been rightly understood; that they mean literally
"three by three," "four by four," and Eusebius wished to denote
the arrangement of columns on each page. A triple or quadruple
arrangement of vertical columns prevails in manuscripts written on
papyrus. These vellum manuscripts were evidently copied from
papyri and this is what Eusebius meant to convey. Had he
wished to describe the manner of folding the sheets, Canon Cook
says, "he would naturally have used words compounded of a
cardinal number and a termination implying folds, such as
τετραπλόα; such words were in common use and specially
applicable to the case" (notes, p. 163). The Vatican has three
columns to the page, the Sinaitic four: so that the description
fits both exactly. We think, then, that a strong case has been made
for supposing that these two manuscripts are the sole survivors
of the fifty Imperial codices ordered by Constantine for his new
capital city. At length we have got to the end of a long
inquiry and we find that textual Vaticanism rests mainly upon
the authority of Eusebius of Cæsarea. The Gospel of Vaticanism
was revised, corrected and abbreviated by him.

Another question remains, and a most important one—What is
the value of Eusebius's authority? Was he an orthodox Catholic
bishop or an Arian heretic? We behold him defending the
truth at Nicæa and presiding over Arians at Tyre; he was the
friend of "one-eyed" Acacius, but the enemy of St. Athanasius;
Socrates and Gelasius defend him, Nicephorus and Photius
condemn him. His name is found in martyrologies, yet a General
Council pronounces him "Anathema." He is styled the Father of
Ecclesiastical History, yet St. Jerome calls him "the standard-
bearer of the Arian faction." Justly, then, may Rohrbacher call
him

A man of equivocal reputation, more erudite than profound, more a
rhetorician than a theologian, more courtier than bishop, more Arian
than orthodox.

Cardinal Newman's judgment of Eusebius is yet more severe:—

His acts are his confession. He openly sides with those whose
blasphemies a true Christian would have abhorred, and he sanctioned
and shared their deeds of violence and injustice perpetrated on the
Catholics.

Apart the general question of Eusebius's Arianism, we ask
ourse   ow far his heretical opinions would tend to vitiate and
affec   cripture codices he sent to Constantine? Canon Cook
doer   hink that Eusebius would have dared knowingly to

interpolate or corrupt the sacred text. But he wisely remarks that:—

> In cases of disputed or doubtful readings, which could not but occur frequently in the actual state of recensions or written authorities at that time, it would be too great a strain upon our candour or credulity to assume that a preference would not be shown for that reading which favoured the views of the party of which Eusebius was an avowed partizan and, with all his discretion, an earnest defender. Consciously or unconsciously, as is unquestionably the case with translators, critics and even transcribers are influenced by their dominant tendencies and prepossessions (p. 166).

A circumstance which strengthens our suspicions is that these codices were written at the very time when Arianism was in the ascendant and thought to keep there. What are we to think of the literary sincerity of the man who was a party to suborning false witness against St. Eustathius at Antioch, and against St. Athanasius at Tyre? If Eusebius acted thus dishonestly with God's Saints, he may well be suspected of dealing deceitfully with the Word of God. If he could leave the Council of Nicæa out of Church History because it displeased him, he may rightly be suspected of omitting from the New Testament verses of which he did not approve. That in his Life of Constantine he should flatter the Emperor need not surprise us. But "what are we to think," Moehler asks, "when we see Eusebius, so great a flatterer himself, accusing another of flattery?" for this was one of the many accusations Eusebius brought against Marcellus of Ancyra. Eusebius lies under grave suspicion of having tampered with the text of Josephus. The owl, which Josephus says that Herod Agrippa saw before his death, Eusebius by dexterous textual manipulation turns into an angel—the one case in which is a defender of Eusebius forced to admit "a sinceritatis viâ deflexit noster." The treatment of St. Mark's last twelve verses in the Sinaitic Codex is another, and we think a stronger, case. Here Eusebius seems to be caught in the very act of making away with the verses he objected to. Thanks to Tischendorf's keen vision we see him tearing out the page and substituting for it another page written large, so that the fraud might not be found out. As far as it lay in his power Eusebius is convicted of an attempt to suppress a vital part of the Gospel message. Supposing that other manuscripts had perished and only *the two oldest manuscripts* and their transcripts had been handed down, who would have suspected the robbery? Surely this fact alone should make scholars cautious about attributing too much importance to the omission of 1 John v. 7-8 by these same manuscripts. Archdeacon Farrar in his last work on "The Early Days of Christianity" makes an offensive remark about "the gross immorality of defending a passage, manifestly spurious, because of its doctrinal usefulness." We do not know of any one who has defended the verse on such a ground, but we have good reason for saying that Eusebius was quite equal to omitting the verse if it was "doctrinally useful" to him to do so.* We are tempted to retort that certain latitudinarian clergymen of the Church of England seem ready to give up to biblical rationalism everything, except their livings. Dr. Farrar says that the last verses of St. Mark are *canonical but almost certainly* unauthentic ("Life of Christ," p. 721).

That for some reason or another Eusebius and his revised text had no great weight with the age in which he lived, is clear from undoubted facts. We should surely expect that at least in Constantinople the fifty Imperial codices would have sufficed to give a long pre-eminence to the Eusebian version of the New Testament. But St. Chrysostom's homilies delivered in that city prove that in fifty years their influence was extinct. So, too, the other Greek Fathers at the close of the fourth century give no sanction to his peculiar readings and omissions. They all agree in using a text which closely resembles that found in the Alexandrian Codex and accords with the traditional Greek text. St. Jerome is invited by Pope St. Damasus to revise the old Latin versions "ad fidem Græcorum codicum, sed veterum." What class of manuscript did this great doctor choose out as being *vera exemplaria*—those like what Eusebius edited, or those which harmonized with the traditional text? We have to thank Dr. Hort for supplying an answer to this decisive question :—

By a curious and apparently unnoticed coincidence, the text of the Alexandrian Codex, in several books, agrees with the Latin Vulgate in so many peculiar readings devoid of old Latin attestation as to leave little doubt that a Greek manuscript, largely employed by Jerome in his revision of the Latin version, must have had, to a great extent, a common original with the Alexandrian manuscript (Introduction, p. 152).

From the Apologia of St. Athanasius we learn that Constans, the Catholic Emperor of the West, gave him a commission very similar to that which Eusebius received from Constantine, and that he fulfilled the commission at Alexandria. If one of these Athanasian codices could be produced and confronted with the Vatican text, we are convinced that it would exhibit what Dr. Hort calls "a broad contrast." But unhappily the Darwinian law of the survival of the fittest does not hold good in the

---

* We are glad to call attention to the Rev. H. T. Armfield's new book in defence of "The Three Wit s" (London : Bagster & Son). We congratulate the learned auth his courage in joining what he justly calls the "forlorn hope" of g the verse.

world of manuscripts, and the Athanasian codices have perished. Were it not for a slight discrepancy of date, one would be tempted to think that the Alexandrian Codex might be one. But we must content ourselves with the fact that the Scripture citations in St. Athanasius agree in the main with the Alexandrian readings, and this fact alone serves to discredit the authority of Eusebius and his recension. Why, then, should the nineteenth century think so much of what the fourth thought so little?

Immediately the Revised Version of the New Testament was published we raised an indignant protest against its omissions. Instead of defending each passage in detail, we have sought out the fundamental error underlying all its sins of omission, and we find it to be textual Vaticanism—that is, implicit confidence in the Vatican Codex. We have striven to show that the Revision Company have done wrong to abandon the old traditional text to pin their faith to a carelessly written manuscript of most doubtful antecedents. One question the editor of the " Speaker's Commentary" asks more than once—What will Convocation do? "*Will it dare*" to approve a Version which mutilates St. Luke and abbreviates St. Mark? "*Will it dare*" to sanction the omission of the Heavenly Witnesses and the insertion of Arianizing notes like that on Rom. ix. 5?* It is evident that the Revisers have brought upon their State Church a grave difficulty by unsettling the traditional text of the New Testament. They have raised a question which neither Parliament, nor Privy Council, nor Mr. Gladstone himself can answer. Their Bishops and their Deans and wise men cannot say with certainty what were the actual words, the *ipsissima verba*, which Apostles and Evangelists wrote in certain vital passages where manuscripts differ. Their

---

* The note referred to is a marginal appendix to one of the strongest texts for proving the Divinity of Christ. " Of whom (*i.e.* the Israelites) is Christ according to the flesh, who is over all, God blessed for ever. Amen." The note is—" Some modern interpreters place a full stop after *flesh*, and translate, *He who is over all be* (*is*) *blessed for ever;* or, *He who is over all is God, blessed* for ever. Others punctuate, *flesh, who is over all. God be* (*is*) *blessed for ever.*" The American Committee apparently could not be satisfied with any of these renderings, and so have recorded one of their own, which is " *flesh : he, who is over all, God, be blessed for ever.*" Canon Cook is right in calling this " a very painful and offensive" note. He evidently thinks that Dr. Vance Smith, the Unitarian, led his brother Revisers to offer this gratuitous insult to believers in the Incarnation. Nor had they here their common excuse ab---' " the two oldest manuscripts," for it is well known that the oldest ma scripts have here no punctuation at first hand, though Dr. Vance Sm looking through Unitarian spectacles, thinks he can detect such m· in the Alexandrian Codex.

textual critics may theorize about Western and Syrian and neutral texts, but in the end they must own, with Dr. Hort—" We are obliged to come to the individual mind at last." Their Church established itself on an appeal to the Scriptures only. For three centuries it has been disputing as to what the Scriptures really *meant*. And now at length stern logic moves the previous question—What does the Scripture really *say?* On Protestant principles there is no adequate answer to this short of the production of the sacred autographs of the inspired writers, and these have perished. If "the Bible, and the Bible only" were the true rule of faith, Divine Providence would not have suffered those autographs to have been lost at the very dawn of the Church's history. Surely then New Testament Vaticanism, the vain appeal to the dead letter of a suspected manuscript, is the *reductio ad absurdum* of expiring Protestantism.

Science Notices.

Prof. Henrici on Mathematical Teaching.—Prof. Henrici's fondness for modern geometrical methods is well known. He never had a better platform for enunciating his views than in the Mathematical Section of the British Association. As president of the Section his remarks were received with great attention, and he used his position to deliver a most decided attack upon the results of geometrical teaching in England. The words of so experienced a teacher are well entitled to a respectful hearing. He considers the use of Euclid as a text-book most unsatisfactory for imparting the elements of geometry. In advancing this he knows that he will have the masters of our schools and colleges as a body opposed to his views. The reason is not far to seek. There are two results that may be fairly expected from a study of geometry: the strengthening of the reasoning faculty, and the advancement of geometrical science. Now, our teachers naturally are more concerned with the improvement of the students under their immediate charge than with the geometrical reputation of the nation before the savants of Europe. They have under their own eyes proofs of the educational value of Euclid, and they sturdily decline to yield to the modern demands. Yet there is much to be said for Prof. Henrici's view, that the country, as a whole, is a distinct loser by this slavish adherence to Euclid. The spirit of Euclid has departed from our midst and it is with his dry bones that we are consoling ourselves. England is singularly behind other continental nations in geometrical science. The schools that produced a Newton have found themselves reduced to utter barrenness. France has since produced Lagrange and Laplace, while a host of mathematicians, among whom is the far-famed Steiner, have testified to the keen pursuit of geometry in Germany. All these years England has scarcely added a name to the muster-roll of original workers in mathematics. For this decadence the Professor holds that there is only one cause—our worship of the golden calf Euclid. But there is a graver charge still—of the unproductiveness of our schools. Our engineers in their practical work have received little or no help from the mathematician. The formulas on which their calculations are based have all been invented by themselves, and have often entailed costly and elaborate experiments. It may be objected that pure science is not bound to connect itself with practical results, that its highest efforts can be achieved only by the rigid exclusion of all mercenary considerations. This is perfectly true. But pure science should, to justify its pretensions, make some progress in theory at least. A school that can record no extension into the realms either of the practical or the absolute must be barren indeed. Such we fear is the condition of our English Universities.

The Imperfections of Euclid. — Curiously enough Prof. Henrici's words are supported by a very striking article in the October number of the *Revue des Questions scientifiques*. It is F. Carbonelle, S.J., who undertakes to point out that those very parts of Euclid, the definitions and axioms, which seem even to compel assent, are after all far from possessing the universal application with which they are credited. Euclid, he contends, is sailing under false colours. His work is put forward as a practice of pure reason, but properly understood it is only founded on experience. Geometry blends in inextricable confusion two ideas of the term "space" which should be kept quite apart. In metaphysics we distinguish between a real and imaginary space. Real space is that region within which the material universe is wholly contained, a thing essentially finite. But beyond this there is an exterior space which is termed imaginary. Now, it is laid down by Euclid as an axiomatic truth, that a straight line may be prolonged indefinitely. Is this correct? It is certainly untrue of real space, for there can be no indefinite prolongations in a finite system. Then perhaps it is true of imaginary space? We have no right to assume that it is; a self-evident truth cannot lay claim to be such as long as the contrary is conceivable. Now, it is barely conceivable that in imaginary space straight lines may be allowed to reach a maximum distance and no more, just as in a circle there is a maximum distance between two of its points. We do not intend to assert that such is the case. It is enough for our purpose to point out the confusion in the use of the term "space" in Euclidean geometry, and that from this confusion of thought an axiom is deprived of its very essence—viz., self-evidence.

Electrical Progress.—It is not necessary that electro-motion should be confined to the narrow field of propelling the huge coaches that are necessary for the comfort of human travelling. A most useful function might be filled by an electric railway devoted exclusively to the conveyance of letters and parcels. The necessary features in the construction are a very high speed and very light material. Such an idea has been worked out by Mr. F. H. Danchell, C.E., who is exhibiting in London a working model of his machine. The engine runs on a single rail balanced by a rail overhead; this latter also serves to convey the current from the central works. Friction is reduced to a minimum, and the most extraordinary speed of 200 miles an hour has been achieved. Such an invention applied to the Parcels Post would soon remove the stigma of failure now attached to it.

It is with great pleasure that we have to record from the Sister Isle a discovery that promises important results in dynamo-machines. Dr. Meldon, of Dublin, is the patient investigator who has come across a new property in electric magnets hitherto unknown or unappreciated. Let us take a magnet capable, say, of supporting a pound weight. If we join to this twelve other magnets of equal power we might reasonably expect them to hold a weight of 12 lbs. But such is not the case. The twelve are no better than one. They can support no more than a weight of one pound. This anomaly it was that Dr. Meldon set himself to study, and his researches have enabled him not only to explain but to master the difficulty. It is a mere question of insulation. By placing layers of gutta-percha between the magnets, he had the satisfaction of seeing the energy of each magnet preserved and equal to the theoretical demands. It is easy to see what an important bearing this will have on the development of electric propulsion. The great drawbacks hitherto experienced in this matter have arisen from the bulky and cumbersome machinery that was necessary. Here we have a light, powerful combination that will require only one-tenth of the battery-power that the systems actually in work demand. The practical value of the new principle was put to the test by fixing one of Dr. Meldon's motors in a small launch. The results seem to have been satisfactory. The battery-power was derived from bichromate cells—a method, of course, too costly for general use. It will be interesting to hear further results of Dr. Meldon's motor, and to learn what *weight* of accumulators he will use to produce results equal to those achieved by the actual electric launches.

Prehistoric Footprints.—A find of a somewhat curious nature has been stumbled across in Nevada. Within the precincts of the prison at Caiston there is an extensive quarry; and the workmen in their progress have uncovered some blocks of sandstone on which are imprinted unmistakable tracks and trails. Among these the footprints of the mammoth, the hyena, the horse, and other animals have been recognized. There are, however, other impressions which, were it not for their size, would certainly be declared human footprints. They vary from eighteen to twenty inches in length. The longest human foot on record was that of a Chinese of Shang-hai, and measured $13\frac{1}{2}$ inches. These prints, if human footprints they be, must have belonged to a race of giants surpassing in height the tallest individual of which we have any record.

Some will no doubt welcome these discoveries as calculated to throw light on the great mound builders of Ohio, the constructors of dolmens, cromlechs, and other enormous works of prehistoric times. If we have here human footprints we shall have additional reason for attributing these mighty fabrics to a race of giants. Judging from the size of the prints we should say that such men must have been over ten feet in height. Others maintain that these tracks are caused by an ordinary-sized human foot covered with moccasins. It may reasonably be urged that until we are sure that they are not the traces of some animal not yet determined, we should hesitate to ascribe them to man. In the meantime, the safest course is to suspend judgment. Scientists have so often been deluded by similar startling announcements that they can hardly be blamed if they remand the case until further evidence is forthcoming.

The Persistency of Animalcules.—Mr. Jabez Hogg has been pursuing some researches into the life-history of that interesting little animalcule, the *rotifer vulgaris*, which promise some curious results. The dry dust of a garden in Devonshire was found by Mr. Hogg to be teeming with insect-life. A few drops of water on this dust soon set in wheel-like motion the cilia of the rotifers, and sent them darting hither and thither in wild excitement across the microscopic cell.

How long these little animals had lain dormant in that garden dust it was impossible to say; Mr. Hogg therefore resolved to put their tenacity of life to some pretty severe tests. The first few grains of dust revealed about twenty rotifers, they were regularly supplied with water for about a month until their number had increased to thirty. The water in the cell was then allowed to dry up, and nothing remained but a thin film of dust. But this, when submitted to the highest powers of the microscope, failed to show any trace of the little inmates. This alternate moistening and drying was repeated for twelve months and the same phenomena were exactly repeated. The animals seemed to take up life and sensation at the point where it had been so rudely cut short by the drought. At the end of the fourth experiment their number had swollen to sixty, of different sizes and growths. It is instructive to note that no other species of rotifer made its appearance in the cell. When we consider the large variety of the species, and their ubiquity in common water, this fact is almost conclusive that no increase came from without. This other pole of creation seems to show a superiority to the ordinary conditions of decay and death which is denied to the nobler part. If man in his evolution had to pass through this germ-like state of existence he has sadly forgotten "the glories he hath known, and the imperial palace whence he came."

Science and Religion.—Mr. Leslie Stephens is a bold and original thinker, and his remarks are always interesting and stimulating. At a late meeting in University College, London, he was called upon for his views on the supposed conflict between Religion and Science. He did not conceal from his hearers that he felt great interest in the progress of science and very little concern at the wholesale destruction of Christian belief. But when he proceeded to state his views we hardly know what to think; for if he came to curse, his words certainly convey no other meaning than a blessing. There is no earnest believer who will not hail his definition of "science," and heartily join in a wish that it were more widely accepted. "Science," he says, "is that body of truths that may be held to be definitely established, so that no reasonable person doubts them." The acceptance of such a definition would go far to silence much vague language as to the supposed antagonism of the Church to Science. Of the facts of Science, properly so-called, not many are so definitely established as to receive the assent of all reasonable men. The law of gravitation and the laws of astronomy generally certainly fulfil the conditions that entitle them to universal acceptance. Such well-established laws as these the Church shows no unwillingness to accept. The case is different with that other class of assertions that claim the name of science—theories, hypotheses resting on feeble arguments, views that are very far from commanding universal consent. Of such a nature is the theory of the existence of man in miocene times, the theory of the multiplicity of the human species, the attempt to explain all spiritual phenomena by material laws. Judged by the light of Mr. Stephens's definition these crude assertions are not yet able to claim the title "scientific." That the Church is opposed to such assertions is quite true, but it is a little presumptuous on these grounds to accuse the Church of general antagonism to Science. Few reasonable persons will be surprised at our reprobation of this latter class of doctrines. Their propagation as matters of certainty is singularly pernicious in its effects. The faith of thousands is destroyed by putting trust in men who put forward startling, ill-digested views as if they were enunciating matters of universal acceptance. As we condemn the action of those colonists who introduce the resources of civilization among the poor Indians only to effect their more speedy extermination, so we cannot but reprobate those reckless scientists who are deliberately ruining the faith and the morality of many. Evils of this kind Mr. Stephens is ready to admit. "Modern Science," he says, "is inevitably destroying many beliefs under which people have lived well and happily. It is undeniable that this causes pain; and that it may be injurious to their morality, I shall not attempt to deny. But when I am asked to say that therefore Science is injurious I have to come back to my original proposition—the remedy is more Science."

Such words, coming as they do from a leader of modern thought, more than justify the attitude taken by all earnest believers to the crude theories of modern Science. It is curious, too, to find the advice of our Holy Father in his Encyclical to the Bishops of Northern Italy receiving confirmation from so unexpected a quarter: "Revera fidei nostræ defensio, in qua laborare maxime debet Sacerdotum industria, et quæ est tantopere his temporibus necessaria, doctrinam desiderat non vulgarem neque mediocrem, sed exquisitam et variam ; quæ non modo sacras sed etiam philosophicas disciplinas complectatur, et *physicorum* sit et historicorum tractatione locuples" (Encyclical "Etsi Nos").

Notices of Catholic Continental Periodicals.

GERMAN PERIODICALS.
By Dr. Bellesheim, of Cologne.

1. *Katholik.*

THE "Katholik" for September and October contains a series of curious documents collected by Dr. Schill, of Freiburg University, from the Roman Archives. As far back as 1875 Professor Schill, a gifted disciple of Cardinal Hergenröther, brought out an exhaustive history of the celebrated Bull, "Unigenitus" (Freiburg: Herder). At present he is engaged writing the general history of Jansenism—a work which he expects to publish in the course of 1884—and has

No heresy of the last three centuries has more sorely vexed France, or under the species of piety, laid waste so wide districts of its church, or elicited more important decisions from the Holy See, than the heresy of Jansenius. From the first prohibition, August 1, 1641, of the Bishop of Ypres' works by the Roman Inquisition, to August 28, 1794, when Pius VI. condemned the decisions of the synod of Pistoja, Jansenism, like another Proteus, has been continually re-appearing under new forms. And any documents throwing new light on the development of that momentous religious movement must be warmly welcomed. It was in the Bibliotheca Angelica that Dr. Schill discovered two bulky volumes containing manuscripts of Cardinal Tamburini, first Abbot of St. Paolo fuori le Mura, afterwards member of the Inquisition, whom Benedict XIV., in 1743, raised to the purple. These manuscripts furnish narrations prepared with a view to the discussions which took place in the Inquisition, having been, for the most part, collected to afford due information to the members of the Holy Office when they should be called upon to expatiate on and investigate their subject-matters. The narrative gathered by Dr. Schill refers to one of the most prominent epochs of Jansenism; for it embraces the grave transactions of the congregation convened by Innocent X., April 12, 1651, which lasted for two years, and resulted in the well-known Bull, "Cum occasione," and was the first condemnation of the pernicious Jansenistical error. The very man who took the most prominent part in these transactions is likewise author of the narration in Cardinal Tamburini's volumes—Francesco Albizzi. Acting as Assessor of the Holy Office, he was one of the most influential and dextrous opponents of the error; indeed, no Roman prelate of that time was more deeply hated by the Jansenists than Mgr. Albizzi. To him we are indebted for the celebrated Bulls "In eminenti" and "Cum occasione." The purple given to him by Innocent X. was but the becoming reward of his singular merits. The space at my disposal does not allow me to give any details of Albizzi's narrative. But the general impression which it leaves on the mind may be mentioned. First, then, the five propositions were most accurately and conscientiously examined and discussed before the Pope passed formal judgment upon them. Secondly, any abettors, either direct or indirect, of Jansenius, were allowed ample opportunities of explaining and defending their doctrine: opportunities which they largely used. Lastly, the Pope, in rejecting the five propositions, did not in the least condemn any abstract topics; it was the very doctrine of Jansenius, as implied in his well-known works, on which judgment was passed. In concluding his narrative Mgr. Albizzi mentions a curious fact which occurred after the publication of the Bull, May 31, 1653. The French doctors who had come to Rome to second the cause of their master, before setting out on the return to France had an audience of Innocent X. The Pope paternally received them, whilst they spontaneously promised the Holy

able to him: "Quantum vero in hoc tam gravi negotio ego laboraverim, Deus scit. Utinam reposita mihi sit merces in Paradiso."

Professor Pohle, of Leeds Seminary, who shows himself to be as able a theologian as he is well versed in natural science, continues his study on the system of P. Secchi. He here deals mainly with Secchi's opinions about God and the world, Christianity and Catholicism. Professor Pohle would deserve well of English Catholic literature if he would bring out in English a biography of P. Secchi. His able German work on the great astronomer could easily be completed, and its value enhanced by combining with it the articles contributed to the *Katholik*.

Historisch-politische Blätter.—The October number of this Review relates to a collection of documents gathered from the Vatican and Vienna Archives by Rev. Sauer, priest of the German Campo Santo, opposite St. Peter's, Rome. They are headed " Rom und Wien im Jahre 1683" (Wien, 1883). The main result of these documents may be briefly expressed in the words of John Newald: "From his extreme embarrassment the Emperor Leopold I. has been rescued by the large subsidies contributed by Innocent XI." Indeed, this Pope exerted every nerve to help the Emperor's cause, which undoubtedly was the common cause of all Christian peoples. But a full, just appreciation of what this holy Pope did towards opposing the Turk is to be measured less by his material contributions than by his political exertions. The story of these latter is also traced by the author of this rare collection. Besides letters of the Pope and the Emperor, we have a large quantity of despatches sent by the Venetian Ambassador Contarini, and the Nuncios of Vienna and Warsaw, Monsignori Buonvisi and Pallavicini. The international position of the Holy See is brought into prominence in these events ; more so, indeed, than by any events of late centuries. A contemporary clever Dutch statesman, Leo van Aitzema, could not help uttering those memorable words: " Politically speaking, the Papacy or the Papal Government is one of the most illustrious and durable republics that has ever existed." Canon Morgott, of Eichstädt (Bavaria) contributes several articles under the heading "Monumenta Franciscana," giving a wonderful account of the marvellous literary activity being shown at the present time by the order of St. Francis. The accomplishments of its best champions in our century recall the period of the Middle Ages in which the Order poured out its first enthusiasm. In Morgott's review we meet with a host of learned Italian Franciscans who, supported by St. Bonaventure, are treating the highest topics of metaphysics and dogmatic theology. It would be tedious to enumerate a long list of mere names. Only two seem to demand special mention: P. John of La Rochelle (Joannes a Rupella), and P. Gerhard a Prato. To the former we are indebted for a "Summa de Anima," published by P. Domenichelli: Prato, 1882, whilst the latter left behind him "Breviloquium super Libros Sententiarum," edited by P. Marcellino da Civezza: Prato, 1882. Domenichelli accompanies his edition of John of La Rochelle by a learned dissertation " La Filosofia e la Scuola francisiana" the gist of which may be said to lie in the small, but suggestive phrase :

"Outside of Christianity there is not to be found a true and exact philosophy." Whatever progress psychology may boast in modern times, the principles of this noble science, as established by Catholic Schoolmen, can never be forsaken without wrecking the whole system. To the November number I contributed a notice on F. Stevenson's book, "Nau's Narrative" concerning Mary Queen of Scots. I may here mention the curious fact which Dr. Cardauns in his recent able pamphlet on Queen Mary has conclusively established—that Nau's narrative was, in great part, published in the chronicles of Holinshed.

3. *Historisches Jahrbuch der Görres-Gesellschaft.*—Three learned articles on "The False Donation of Constantine" contributed to this Jahrbuch have been exciting the deepest interest throughout Catholic and Protestant Germany. The author is Dr. Grauert of the Bavarian Public Record Office, Munich. Critical sagacity, wide historical reading, diligent study of manuscripts in both German and foreign archives, and more especially a clear "sensus Catholicus" concur to give high value to these articles. Dr. Grauert establishes the fact that the oldest code of the donation belongs to the National Library, Paris (Cod. 2777), and beyond any doubt originated in the celebrated convent of St. Denis, where it was written in the ninth century. The origin of the donation is not at all to be traced to Italy, still less to Rome, the Popes alluding to it only as late as Leo IX. It can only have originated in a country where the veneration of images was permitted but not approved of—that is France, the home of the Pseudo Isidore.

4. *Stimmen aus Maria Laach.*—F. Lehmkuhl, who, by the way, has just published the first part of a "Theologia Moralis," contributes an article on the much agitated question of the German labourer, and vindicates the Catholic idea of the labourer's position towards the capitalist-employer against several modern theories launched in Germany during last summer. F. Spillman has finished his interesting series of articles on the "justice murders" of Titus Oates' persecution, which have been read in Germany with general interest. Two articles are devoted to the life of the late F. Kleutgen. The more this great man has done for Catholic higher studies the more does he deserve an exhaustive biography. What we here learn concerning his youth deeply impresses one with the dangers to which Catholic youth are exposed in our century, and not less with the wonderful providence which watched over young Kleutgen's career. F. Kreiten continues his biographical notice of our great German Catholic poetess, Annette von Droste Hulshoff.

ITALIAN PERIODICALS.

La Civiltà Cattolica. 6 Ottobre.

Letter of Leo XIII. on Historical Studies.

THE number of the *Civiltà Cattolica* for October 6 contains a good article on the Letter of XIII., "Sæpenumero considerantes," upon the subject of historical studies. The wisdom of this letter is considered both in its religious and political aspects, for the Pope, as the writer observes, is the first personage in the world, and his dignity is supreme in both orders. In the religious, he is the Vicar of Jesus Christ and Head of the whole Catholic Church—that is, by right, of the whole human race. In the political order his sovereignty is the most ancient, the most legitimate, the most sacred and inviolable, and, by its union with the Pontifical authority, it is the centre and ought to be also the safeguard of all other authority. From hence is derived the double influence which he ought to exercise on earth, religious and political, with subordination of the latter to the former. This influence all the Popes more or less have exercised, and we have seen our present supreme Pontiff, Leo XIII., ever intent on using it, directly or indirectly, for the prosperity of the Church and the welfare of the State. Aided by supernal light, he discerns the special character of modern warfare against the Church of God, the aim of which is to destroy it, if possible, by rendering it despicable and hateful. For this end, its enemies strive to prove its doctrines to be false and thus bring it into contempt, and show that it has never caused anything but evil to mankind, thereby exciting hatred against it. To attain the former end, they oppose science to the Church; to accomplish the latter, they falsify and pervert history. Pope Leo, certain of the truth of the Church's teaching, and that any science setting itself in opposition thereto must be false and deceitful, desired nevertheless that the doctrine of the Church should be defended by true and solid science. He accordingly published the Encyclical "Æterni Patris," the effect of which has been most beneficial in the Catholic schools. And now, before five years had elapsed, he proceeds to snatch their weapons from the hands of those who, by falsifying history, would make the Church appear the cause of all social evils, and thus incite the ignorant multitudes to detest and abhor it. Waiving the à priori certainty of the Church's innocence and the falsehood of the calumnies of its adversaries, he desires that the truth should be demonstrated by rigorous proofs drawn from authentic documents, and with this view has thrown open for inspection the historic treasures of the Vatican archives.

The writer, after noticing some of the sneers with which the extreme Liberal journals have met this generous offer, alludes to the comments of the so-called moderate Liberals, which, however disguised, do not differ in substance from those of the more advanced party. While confessing that the Pope is right in maintaining that history has been falsified to a considerable extent, and specially in regard to the relations between the Popes and Italy, and that in consequence an erroneous public opinion has been formed concerning the Church, the Popes, and the clergy, they themselves, in point of fact, repeat the same calumnies, and adopt the same sophisms and the same equivocations wherewith to delude the masses. They have found a mouthpiece in Bonghi, who has published an article entitled "Leo XIII. and History" in the *Nuova Antologia*. "It is a marvel to us," says the writer, "that passion can so far blind Bonghi, who is a man of no mean intellect, as to induce him to indulge in sophistry worthy of the meanest Liberal scribbler of our days; but he must serve his party." This letter is reviewed in three articles in the *Civiltà Cattolica*, which have appeared successively on October 20 and November 3 and 17, and are devoted to meeting the aspersions cast by Bonghi on the Holy Father—aspersions in direct contradiction to his exordium, which contains a laudatory recognition both of the end the Pontiff has in view and the means he has adopted in order to attain it; for, after the more or less sincere panegyric bestowed on Pope Leo in his first six paragraphs, Bonghi proceeds to string together a series of impertinent accusations, imputations, and baseless assertions, calculated to demolish all that he had previously conceded. The writer follows him in the weary task of exposing the futility, inconsistency, and sophistry contained in this abusive tirade.

The Modern Idea of Liberty.

THE article entitled "Modernismo a rispetto della Libertà" demonstrates the false notion of liberty held by modern Liberals, contrasting it with the true definition. The conception of liberty, or the freedom of the will, in a created being, involves that of authority. To separate the one from the other is to confound the creature with the Creator; in other words, it is to deny God. The Divine will alone, in its free action, has no need of a directing authority, and this because the will of the First Cause, independent and absolute, is identified with wisdom itself, and is in itself the supreme rule of the good and the just. But the created will needs guidance in its free action. It is not essential good but only a tendency to good, hence it must be regulated; and it is not a rule to itself. But according to modern Liberalism man is a law to himself. Such a proposition is sheer folly. Liberty is the gift of a faculty to the human soul which has essentially for its end the perfecting of that soul and its consequent felicity. The soul necessarily loves and desires its own felicity. In this respect the will cannot have a free choice, for no one can wish for unhappiness, known to be such. But as regards the ascertaining that in which true felicity consists, and the means for attaining to it, the will is not necessarily attracted, but has the free exercise of choice; accordingly it needs light and guidance that it may not err in that choice. The proper sphere, therefore, of the exercise of liberty is within the circle of what is good, for it is thus alone that liberty can answer the end for which it was bestowed.

Even Montesquieu, in a moment of distraction, when common sense prevailed over his false principles, said, "Liberty can only consist in being able to do what we ought to wish to do and in not being constrained to do that which we ought not to wish to do." To be able to do what is good and right without obstacle, this is true freedom, as respects man, both individually and socially. But those societies which are infected by Modernism do the precise opposite. They grant full licence to evil, and place a thousand obstacles in the way of good. Thus is the very idea of society perverted, which is designed to be an aid to individuals for the more easy attainment of their proper end. From a help thereto, society is converted into a hindrance. It is a society opposed to both nature and reason. It is the worst kind of tyranny—a tyranny over souls. If such a society cannot be otherwise freed from the clutches of Modernism, it would perhaps be a lesser evil that it should be dissolved, since the disconnected elements might, from the social nature of man, reunite to form a better order. And not a few in the present day use this language, and it is difficult to prove them altogether wrong. Liberty, as understood and favoured by modern Liberals, tends to the worst of servitudes. Having shaken off dependence on God, society falls into dependance on man. Force is substituted for right, arbitrary will for reason. The ultimate goal of Modernism is Cæsarism—that is, the absorption of society, and hence of the individuals composing it, in the omnipotent power of the ruler. And it is not necessary that Cæsarism, as such, should be embodied in one person with the title of emperor or king; it can easily take form in a more or less restricted oligarchy or in a republic of an extremely popular character. We see this exemplified in France at this very moment, where, under the garb of the most radical democracy, the vilest Cæsarism reigns. Where the principle of Cæsarism is dominant it matters not what shape or name it assumes. That principle always implies the substitution of force for right. Now, it is plain that to this rule of force of Modernism, which casts off Divine authority, the regulator of liberty, whether in itself or through its appointed representatives, is necessarily leading. For since the independent, unchecked liberty of each individual must result in utter discord, no resource remains in order to create a preponderant principle of unity but to ground it on a self-devised, arbitrary consent. In the prevalence of number, the numerical majority, this arbitrary consent is embodied: such is the principle of sovereignty according to Modernism. Now, number, as such, only gives force, which thus becomes the arbiter in the place of right and reason. From such an evil there is no escape but through the Church of Jesus Christ. The adherents and promoters of Modernism know this well, and accordingly strain every effort to combat the Church, to suffocate its voice, and to remove its influence from society and from every department of civil organization. Society, therefore, is now called upon to choose between Catholicism and Cæsarism. The former, by submitting human liberty to God, will save it; the second, by emancipating it from God, will destroy it and subject it to man—that is, to the vilest slavery. On its choice depends the salvation or ruin of this world of ours.

Martin Luther. 3 e 17 Novembre.

AMONGST several other articles of interest during the last quarter, the two upon Martin Luther, as being th subject of the day, claim special notice. The first, that of entitled "Chi fosse Martin Lutero," treats of the man himsel ·cond, that of Nov. 17, entitled "Dell' Opera di Martin Luter vs his work.

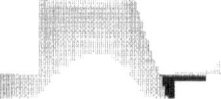

We do not think we have seen the subject better treated within the compass of a few pages than it is in these articles. What were the immediate effects of that apostasy from the Church, from faith, and from morals which has been masked, ironically, we should say, under the name of "reformation," Luther, as the writer observes, has himself declared, as well as his great disciple, Melanchthon, and, after them, Calvin. "The world," says Luther, "is getting worse every day, and is increasing in wickedness. Men are now more prone to vengeance, more avaricious, more inhuman, less moral, more rebellious, in short, greater scoundrels than they were under the Papacy. It is both a scandal and a marvel to see how, since the pure doctrine of the Gospel has been placed in its natural light, the world has been continually sinking into a worse state. The nobles and the peasantry refuse to listen to sermons, the Word of God is thrown away upon them; in their eyes all our discourse is not worth a farthing. Neither do they believe in a future life. They live as they believe; they are hogs, they believe like hogs and die like hogs. Most of my disciples live like Epicureans, amusements and diversions their whole occupation. Truly amongst the Papists you cannot meet such vicious men, pigs and monsters of this fashion. They call themselves *reformed*, but one might rather call them incarnate demons. The disorder is arrived at such a pitch that, if any one had a fancy to see a mass of rogues, usurers, scapegraces, and rebels, he need only enter one of those cities which style themselves *evangelical* and he would find shoals of the men he is in search of;" and much more to the same purpose may be quoted from the pen of the Patriarch of the Reform. Of Melanchthon we need only record this telling lamentation: after describing the wretched results of change of religion, he says he has been mourning over them for the last thirty years, adding, "The Elbe itself with all its abundant streams could not furnish sufficient water to weep for the miseries and woes of the Reform." We find Calvin afterwards writing, "Out of a hundred evangelicals you will with difficulty find one who became such for any other motive than to be able to give himself up with more unbridled licence to pleasures and incontinence." Numbers of the chief proselytes to Protestantism join in the same chorus of lamentation over the vices of their co-religionists, which would have been, they say, a disgrace to Turks. How could it be otherwise since the great means used by Luther to advance the "Reform" and to get rid of the Church was his doctrine that works were of no use to salvation, as faith alone saved?

For those who would give credit to Luther for, at least, a rough kind of honest sincerity, it might be sufficient to point to his perpetual self-contradictions, but his want of inward conviction is more clearly manifested in such despairing words as the following: " I hate the whole world. Still, as I have entered on this path, I am obliged to say I have done right. But I cannot believe what I teach, although others believe me to be profoundly convinced of its truth. How many men, I say to myself, have seduced with your doctrine! You are the cause of all their dis This thought leaves me not a moment's peace." Again, he   was by chance, not choice, that he had thrown himself into these religious conflicts, that he had abolished the elevation of the Host *to spite the Pope*, and, if he had retained it for some time, it was *to enrage Carlostadt;* that he had upheld communion under two species solely to insult the Pope, but that, if a council were to enjoin communion under the two, his followers should receive it under one or not at all, and he would curse all who obeyed the Council.

The reviewer draws out well in a few pages the fruits, social and political, which Lutheranism produced. The two numbers together would make an admirable little pamphlet to add to those already in circulation.

We would just observe, in conclusion, that it is the common belief that Luther was moved first to prevaricate by the promulgation of the Indulgences in 1517, but the writer shews this opinion to be quite a mistake. The incident did but furnish him with a pretext for public declamation against the imputed abuses; but ever since the beginning of 1516 he had been bitterly assailing the teaching of the schools, which he called *mud and filth*, and throwing discredit on all those weapons by which they defended Catholic truth. He had circulated ninety-nine propositions against the theology of the Scholastics and the "*dreams* of Aristotle," which gave great scandal, and this will hardly surprise when we notice that in the 39th he denied free will, and asserted that we are slaves from first to last, and in twenty others taught that man can do only evil, to which by his nature he is necessitated, and that God is therefore the author of sin: blasphemies which, as Bossuet observes, will perhaps not be uttered even in hell. So untrue is it that Luther's indignant soul was first stirred to opposition by the so-called "sale of Indulgences."

FRENCH PERIODICALS.

Œuvre des Écoles d'Orient. Paris, Novembre, 1883.

"RELATION of M. Bedjan, Priest of the Mission,* Missionary in Persia, concerning the publication of a Chaldæan Breviary." This report in the pages of a small but always interesting magazine deserves, we think, to be referred to here. The complaint is not of to-day nor of yesterday that the Levant is being inundated with Protestant Bibles and books, and that the confusion of the old heretical Christianities is being worse confounded by the presence of Protestant missionaries of various sects and jarring doctrines. And the complaint continues. The same number of this magazine contains a letter from Mgr. Kouyoumji, the Greek-Catholic Bishop of Saïda and Daïr-el-Kamar, to the Cardinal-Prefect of Propaganda, lamenting the potency of European wealth on the grinding poverty of his people. The Relation of M. Bedjan, with which we are here concerned, is addressed to the Director of the "Œuvre" of the schools of the East, to ask his

---

* That is, of the Congregation of the Mission, Vincentians as they are termed in England.

help and patronage in the efforts which the writer is making to begin the publication of a Chaldæan Breviary.*

"The Chaldæan Breviary is one of the most precious monuments of Christian antiquity, and has never been printed, except the psalter and diurnal; its publication would have a historical and philological as well as religious import. Having fallen centuries ago into the hands of the Nestorians, it has been much altered in parts, so far that, sadly enough, we find the feast of the heresiarch Nestorius figuring side by side with one of Our Lady. The text has to be brought back to its primitive purity." Fast fading old manuscripts are the only available copies of it; these have become so very rare that Catholics are driven in some parts to use copies full of heresy. "The Chaldæan priests can only recite the office when they are fortunately near one of the churches which possess a breviary." M. Bedjan, born in Persia, knows the sacred language—the language of the liturgies of his country. He has, after many efforts and sacrifices, obtained a complete copy of all the parts of the Breviary; no easy task; neither the National Library of Paris, nor the British Museum, nor the Vatican, "possess this treasure, in its entirety, such as I now have it." The books which make up this collection are: 1. The *Khoudra*, 1,100 pages quarto, which comprises the offices of Sundays, Rogation-days and Lent; 2. The *Keschkoul*, of 400 pages quarto, contains final offices; 3. The Catholic *Guezza*, 400 pages in folio, contains the feasts; 4. The *Mimra*, of 200 pages in octavo, contains the lessons and prayers for Rogations; 5. The *Dikdèm-Vedvatar* or Diurnal, and 6. The *Mesmouris* or Psalms. The writer purposes to combine these elements, retaining at the same time untouched their venerable text and even titles of the books, making of them two or four volumes, each containing the "Commune," the "Propria temporum," and the "Propria Sanctorum."

The cost of this publication M. Bedjan reckons at thirty thousand francs (£1,200), and as he believes that immense good will be done for the Catholic religion by it, he looks to Providence to send him the means. There are two thousand pages, hitherto unpublished, to be brought out—pages which go back to an early period of Christianity. It is, he says, a *chef d'œuvre* of Chaldæan literature, abounding in sublime thoughts, poetic in tone, pure in style. It will serve not only Persia, but all the Chaldæans of Kurdistan and Mesopotamia. He is persuaded, furthermore, that it will even work as an apostle among the Nestorians, who will regard it with favour, being their own, and "once accustomed to their liturgy purged of heresy, these simple souls will become Catholic without doubt." It will also be a tribute to science, and enrich the libraries of Europe. "Once printed, it can be put into the hands of our seminarists as a book of study, and will thus free them from the necessity of learning their own language in

---

* It may prevent confusion with some to say that the Catholics of

Protestant books." If subscription come in to help him, the printing will be begun this year—1884. Donations, or subscriptions for copies, through the director of the "Œuvre" aforesaid (at Paris) will much encourage him.

One more sentence of this interesting appeal we will give in the writer's own words: "Protestants of America, Prussia, and England invade the Levant in a frightful manner, and do immense harm by their books. The schismatics become Protestants, even while they are anathematizing Protestantism, and the Catholics equally feel the evil influence of this untiring Press. Every Chaldæan and Armenian house is, so to say, inundated with Protestant books, whilst the Catholic priest has neither a theology, sermon-book, nor a spiritual work, not even a 'Breviary.' Will it be believed—our scholars, even our seminarists, study their language in Protestant Bibles? One feels profoundly humbled before such sad facts."

La Controverse. Novembre, Décembre. Lyon: 1883.

THE November number contains three articles *apropos* of the Luther celebration—one from the pen of Père Delplace, S.J.; another on Luther and the Bible, by the Abbé Vigouroux, and a third, on the moral character of Luther, by Professor Jungmann. Each of them is excellent in its special way, but we refrain from doing more than point them out should any one wish to consult them. We fear our readers will have, on all sides, heard enough for the present about Luther before this January number reaches them.

"L'Infanticide en Chine et l'Œuvre de la Sainte-Enfance" is the title of a very interesting article in the December number from the pen of Professor de Harlez of Louvain. No doubt it is well in every one's remembrance that the "Œuvre" of the Holy Infancy for the rescue of castaway infants in China was one of the three meritorious works which the Pope recommended to the charity of the Catholic world in proclaiming the last jubilee. And most of our readers will know that the "Œuvre" is the special work of the Sisters of Charity and the Fathers of the mission, the sons and daughters of St. Vincent de Paul, in China. Whether or not the Holy Father's marked approval has roused those who hate him, we do not know; but of late the much miscalled "Liberal" papers of the Continent have been writing the work down; and doing this, strange to say, by blankly denying that there are children in China to be so rescued: saying that infanticide is not practised in China, except so far and in such manner as it is in Europe; that the Chinese father and mother, especially the mother, are model parents; that all that the Catholic missionaries, with their bishops at their head, have written about the frequent murder of the Chinese babies is fancy or falsehood.

Truly this is a grave charge, even for the XIXe *Siècle* and the free-thinking press, and the least objectionable consequence which their contention would necessitate, is that so much money is deliberately collected under false pretences. Men who could so lie, and women who could help on the imposture, would be a disgrace, instead of being, as the world believes them to be, an honour to the Christian name. This denial of Chinese infanticide is based on three arguments: firstly, that the Chinese code contains no penal provisions against this dereliction and murder of the newly born; secondly, that the Chinese cannot expose their babes in the streets of towns, as it is said they do, from which they are gathered in carts, because the streets are so narrow that no cart could pass. By this falsehood, cries the "liberal," judge of the others. But, thirdly, numerous travellers who have travelled in and lived in China, Anglican missionaries, merchants, tourists, soldiers, all attest that they have never seen children exposed or killed. M. de Harlez examines and refutes these arguments in detail:—1. It is a bold thing for an European journalist to pretend that he knows all the penal provisions of the Chinese criminal code! M. de Harlez appears to have found it difficult to get possession of it; but when he succeeds, as he hopes shortly to do, he will be ready to make known the truth. Meanwhile he shows at length that numerous Imperial and Prefectoral decrees condemn the murder of newborn children and prescribe punishment against offenders: the Chinese authorities are frequently occupied with infanticides. 2. This is mere folly. The Chinese streets were wide enough in the sixteenth century for sixteen horsemen to ride abreast along them. 3. This argument is no better: it is a *non sequitur*. Many *have* seen the exposed children, many *have not*: it is a question of credibility of witnesses whether for or against. One curious witness adduced by the XIXe *Siècle* was a captain who had never left his vessel whilst it was anchored by Canton: *he* had seen no deserted children—nor even the Catholic Orphanage! There are good reasons, the writer explains, why many tourists and even Anglican missionaries whose honesty is quite above suspicion should not see the deserted or murdered children. But, fortunately, if the testimony of Catholic missionaries, otherwise, also, above suspicion, has been hitherto the only witnesses for us of the existence of this crime in China, a very large collection of Chinese documents of various kinds has now been collected and published at Shanghai. In these the Chinese themselves speak to the truth of what the Catholic priests have all along asserted. Using this abundant material the writer abundantly proves from Chinese evidence that the practice of infanticide is an *old* and *universal* one. Daughters are the chief victims of the hideous custom, but boys are also sometimes *mis de côté*; want is the chief impelling cause of the crime, but idleness, dread of inability to endow daughters also operate. The doomed children are sometimes exposed in the streets or thrown into a river, but most f   ently are smothered or drowned at birth; the rich are sometimer   ders, but chiefly the poor. But the legitimacy of infanticide i   among the recognized moral principles of the Celestial Empi   r from it; their moralists combat it with zeal, and legislators many a time have striven to outroot the practice, but custom has hitherto been stronger than the civil authority. There are special reasons why the mandarins dare not carry out with over zeal ordinances directly opposed and bitterly resented by the people over whom they administer. M. de Harlez concludes a most interesting article thus: " Infanticide on a vast scale in China is beyond doubt or cavil; the work of the Holy Infancy is eminently useful and worthy of universal sympathy; lastly, in the whole affair, only the Catholic missionaries have been calumniated."

Notices of Books.

The Eternal Priesthood. By HENRY EDWARD, Cardinal Archbishop of Westminster. London: Burns & Oates. 1883.

THIS book is probably already in the hands of most of our readers who are Priests. In the short compass of less than 300 pages the Cardinal Archbishop offers to his clergy, and to all English-speaking Priests, a body of instructions and exhortations in their sacred vocation which displays all his well-known power of brightening and vivifying every subject on which he touches. Books on the Priesthood, from that of St. John Chrysostom downwards, are not rare. But it is rare, or rather unique, to have the ancient patristic sayings, the well-worn scholastic definitions and the commonplaces of clergy retreats presented to English readers by a master of the English language. The work contains twenty chapters, of which some few are dogmatic, but the greater part are in that strain of mingled exposition and exhortation in which Cardinal Manning excels. After considering in the first four or five chapters the Nature of the Priesthood and its Powers, the relation of the Priest to our Lord, to His sacramental Presence and to the flock, and also the Priest's obligations to Sanctity, he passes on to treat of every duty and office of a Priest in the most practical and effective way; of his dangers, his helps, his time, his sorrows; of his preaching; of his home; of his life and of his death. It is obvious that even if we were so inclined it would not be proper to criticize, even in a favourable sense, a work of this kind, and we therefore content ourselves with giving a few extracts.

THE PRIEST'S TITLE OF FATHER.

from the schools of learning many degrees, from the ecclesiastical law many dignities; but none has so deep and so high a sense as father, and none but the spiritual fatherhood will pass into eternity. The world has overlaid the title of father with its own profuse adulation, and priests have consented to their deprival in accepting the world's addresses. With the title, the consciousness of paternal or filial relation has been first obscured, then forgotten, and in the end lost. The closest bond of mutual confidence and charity between the priesthood and the faithful has been thereby relaxed, and a distance and diffidence has often grown up instead (p. 22).

THE PRIEST EVER NEAR TO CHRIST.

It is no mere imagination in our work, early and late, to believe that He is near us, in the ship or on the shore; nor when we are in the hospital, or in the poor man's home, or by the bed of the dying, or walking through the fields, or in the crowded streets, or in the mountains seeking His scattered sheep, that He is with us at every step and in every moment. It is no illusion to believe that the words He spoke are spoken still to us, or that every word we speak is spoken in His hearing. When He was on earth, and His disciples round Him, their eyes were not always fixed upon Him; still less were their words and thoughts always directed to Him. They saw all that was around them in the streets, or the fields, or upon the sea, and their thoughts multiplied and, as we say, wandered, and they spoke with one another with the freedom of daily fellowship; but they were always conscious that He was in the midst of them, and that He not only heard their words, but read their thoughts, and answered them before they spoke. In what, except in sense, does our relation differ from theirs? And are not Nazareth and Bethlehem and Jerusalem and Capharnaum and Bethania as real to us as if we had seen them? (p. 29).

THE DIVINE OFFICE.

The divine office is a part of the divine tradition. It is a perpetual witness for God and for the faith. It has been wrought together by the hands of men; but those men were Saints, and their work was wrought under the guidance of the Holy Ghost. The framing of the Ritual may have been the work of human hands; but the materials of which it is composed are the words of the Spirit of God. The Psalms and the Scriptures of inspired men under the Old Law and the New, with the writings of the Saints, are all interwoven into a wonderful texture of prayer and praise, of worship and witness of the kingdom of God, and of the Communion of Saints. The perpetual revolution of yearly solemnities and festivals—winter and spring, summer and autumn—brings round continually the whole revelation of faith. Prophets and Apostles, Evangelists and Saints, speak to us with voices that never die. The whole history of the kingdom of God is always returning upon our sight (p. 94).

THE PRIEST'S SOURCE OF CONFIDENCE.

Among us the Church is both old and new. We are a handful, but separate from the world, and from courts, and from the corrupt atmosphere of secular patronage and secular protection. The true protection of the Church is its own independence, and its true power is its own liberty. We are pastors of a flock descended from martyrs and confessors, and their fervour is not extinct in their posterity. We are in a special sense pastors of the poor, for the rich have gone away, and the vast prosperity of England is in hands that know us not. But to live among the poor was the lot of our Divine Master, and to share His lot is a pledge of His care. We are not only the pastors of the poor, but poor ourselves. Poverty is the state of the priesthood in this the richest of all the kingdoms of the world. We are here bound together in mutual charity and service. Our people are united to us in a generous love and mutual trust; and our priests are united to each other and to their bishops. They are united to each other with bonds of fraternal love as close as, if not closer than, can be found in any region of the Catholic unity. If all these things be for us, what shall be against us ? (p. 118).

THE PRIEST'S SORROWS.

But besides the sins of bad men, a priest has to suffer by the lukewarmness of good men. That people should be so good, and yet not better; that they should be so full of light, and yet fall so short of it; that they should do so many good acts, and yet not do more; that they should have so few faults, but so few excellences; that they should be so blameless, but deserve so little praise; so full of good feeling, but so spare in good works; so ready to give, but so narrow in their gifts; so regular in devotions, yet so little devout; so pious, yet so worldly; so ready to praise the good works of others, and yet so hard to move to do the like; so full of censures of the inertness and inconsistency, omissions, faults, and lukewarmness of other men, and yet so unhelpful and soft and unenergetic and lukewarm themselves—all these are spiritual paradoxes and contradictions which vex and harass a priest with perpetual disappointment. Where he looked for help he finds none; where he thought he could trust he finds his confidence betrayed; where he thought to lean for support he finds the earth give way (p. 140).

THE PRIEST'S TENDERNESS OF HEART.

Do not let anyone think that a priest who has one Divine Friend will be cold or heartless, or careless of flock and friends, of the lonely and the forsaken. The more united to His Master, the more like Him he becomes. None are so warm of heart, so tender, so pitiful, so unselfish, so compassionate, as the priest whose heart is sustained in its poise and balance of supreme friendship with Jesus, and in absolute independence of all human attachments. His soul is more open and more enlarged for the influx of the charity of God. We are straitened not in Him, but in ourselves (p. 172).

THE PRIEST AND LITTLE CHILDREN.

Among the many rewards of a faithful priest come the love and the joy of children. By the faith infused in Baptism, they recognise in the priest a spiritual fatherhood. Children come round a priest not only by a natural instinct, drawn by kindness, but by a supernatural instinct as to one who belongs to them by right. The love of children for a priest is the most unselfish love on earth, and so long as they are innocent it binds them to him by a confidence which casts out fear. The most timid

THE GOOD PRIEST'S DEATH.

The world never knew him, or passed him over as a dim light outshone by the priests who court it. But in the sight of God what a contrast. Ever since his ordination, or earlier, ever since his second conversion to God, he has examined his conscience day by day, and made up his account year by year; he has never failed in his confession week by week, or in his Mass morning by morning, or in his office punctually and in due season. He has lived as if by the side of his Divine Master, and, beginning and ending the day with Him, he has ordered all the hours and works of the day for His service. He has lived among his people, and their feet have worn the threshold of his door. His day comes at last, and a great sorrow is upon all homes when it is heard that the father of the flock is dying, and the last Sacraments have been given to him. And yet in that dying-room what peace and calm. He has long cast up his reckoning for himself and for his flock. He has long talked familiarly of death, as of a friend who is soon coming. .... He fears, but his fear is a pledge that the Holy Ghost, the Lord and Life-giver, is in the centre of his soul, casting light upon all that is to be confessed and sorrowed for, and absolving the contrite soul from all bonds of sin and death. None die so happily as priests surrounded by their flocks. As they have laboured, so are they loved; as they are loved, so are they sustained by the prayers of all whom they have brought to God (p. 283).

Geschichte der Katholischen Kirche in Schottland, von der Einführung des Christenthums bis auf die Gegenwart. Von Dr. ALPHONS BELLESHEIM. Mainz: Franz Kirchheim, 1883. (History of the Catholic Church in Scotland from the Introduction of Christianity to the present time. By Dr. A. Bellesheim. 2 vols.).

THIS history of the Church in Scotland forms two large volumes in 8vo of 488 and 446 pages respectively. The first is divided into two parts, the former of which terminates in 1057 with the accession of Malcolm II., and treats chiefly of the work of St. Columba, of Iona, and of the Culdees; the latter concerns the centuries from 1057 till the Reformation, when the Church in Scotland was allied to the State. The second volume is in one part, from 1560 to our own times.

The race of writers amongst whom Dr. Bellesheim takes rank by the production of so stupendous a work of learning and industry as that which we now have before us is an encouraging testimony to the divine force of truth. At a time when the spirit of rationalism is denying the very existence of the great Christian family of the Church, the Spirit of God is fruitful in proving her title-deeds, and her pedigree, that is, the inheritance of the One Faith handed down from the remotest times, not as mere human utterances which have their day and pass away like a voice in the night, but as a divine heirloom for the possession of every man of good will coming into this world. To deal with the history of the Church, moreover, is not to draw up a paper pedigree for which few have any interest. The Catholic family is numerous on earth, and its great men live on in mortal minds because they have taken deep root in human hearts. We say, then, that the study of Church history has a peculiar pertinence for our own day, because testimony in favour of the existence of this divine Institution leads men up to the knowledge and love of its personal Founder, the Son of God.

Dr. Bellesheim begins his work from the introduction of Christianity into Scotland in A.D. 400, and brings it down to the present time, since his closing chapter speaks of the recent establishment of the Hierarchy by our present Holy Father (1878). Besides the learning and thoroughness of the history itself, which mark the true German, we may note two very important features in the treatment: there is a simple exposition of facts, without any of those comments of the author which often degenerate into the pure small talk of writing, and an entire absence of invective. It is, indeed, the highest privilege of the Catholic historian not to require other arms than the unvarnished truth. The history of our Catholic forefathers in Scotland is divided into distinct periods, and if we are not mistaken, the reader will linger over what may be called the first, which is full of the ardour and vigour of St. Columba's master-spirit, and fragrant with the holy traditions of Iona. Following upon the monastic era, from 700 till the accession of David I. (1124), who gave shape and structure to the outward form of the Scottish Church, comes the period of the rise and growth of the secular clergy. The Catholic historian need not fear the exposition of abuses. Dr. Bellesheim notes two which in those early days he describes as the "gangrenous tendency"* of the spiritual power. The handing down of Church property as a provision for the illegitimate children of priests established a cancerous fibre which tainted and threatened the whole body. As long as the disorder met with Catholic treatment—the restraint of moral discipline and examples of holy living—the disease was kept under. Had there been more great men, by which we mean saints, that fearful defection of the Reformation would never have taken place; but a latent cause for the future falling away is revealed to us by the early appearance of this double evil. Amongst other things it is recorded of St. Margaret, Queen of Scotland in 1057, that she displayed an ardent zeal for the sanctification of Sunday. "Let us observe the Lord's Day with all respect," she used to say, "because Our Lord rose on this day from the dead; let us do no servile work, He having delivered us from the slavery of Satan on this day."† The fifteenth century opens a new epoch, in which intellectual culture is the predominant feature as connected with the founding of the first university in Scotland at St. Andrews. Besides the causes from within, which were silently preparing the Reformation, there were evils from without. The doctrines of Wicliffe and John Huss, forerunners of Luther, Calvin, and Knox, found an echo in Scotland, and began by undermining the basis of men's faith; and what those first Protestants were doing with regard to the principle of authority, human passions were threatening to do with the Chair of St. Peter. Only in 1417 had the accession of Martin V. put an end to the most fearful trial which the Church has ever sustained, a disputed Papacy. Its effect had been, as our author observes, to loosen the relations between Church and State in consequence of the temporary weakening of Catholic unity. Scotland was a singularly good instance to choose in proof of the divine power of

---

* Vol. i. p. 156. † P. 166.

the Church, for apart from the question of the Reformation, we read through the history of centuries without encountering a single great name or a man capable of shaping any given period after the mind of the Holy Spirit. If Cardinal Beaton, for instance, had been a St. Anselm, or even a Lanfranc, there is no saying whether the progress of ecclesiastical innovations might not have been arrested. The closing chapter of the first volume contains an interesting survey of art and science under the old religion, which will compare most favourably with the account rendered by pens hostile to Catholicism* after the blight of Protestantism had passed over fair Scotland.

The second volume of Dr. Bellesheim's work is naturally the most interesting. The oft-repeated story of Queen Mary has ever a new charm, and in Scotch ecclesiastical history it has a very prominent place. From the very beginning, the party of the Reformation, the men who stirred up the people against their sovereign, and she a helpless woman, is clearly defined as that of sedition and disorder. Knox, the apostate priest, general-in-chief of the Scotch defection, is admirably drawn in the first pages of the second volume. His words and deeds are calmly noted down, and the reader is wisely left to draw his own conclusions. Widely removed from the true apostle, Knox is chiefly distinguished by a bitter hatred of the powers that be, and an overweening confidence in himself. In many instances the author has allowed Protestant authorities to speak for themselves so here he quotes Tytler and Hume. Tytler says of Knox: "It appears to me that on many occasions he acted upon the principle so manifestly erroneous and antichristian that the *end justifies the means.*" " It makes us shudder," writes Hume " to see what satisfaction and delight Knox shows in his description of the murder of Cardinal Beaton. He had taken upon himself in its most superlative degree the fanaticism of sect, which his natural bitterness strengthened."† As to his teaching it would appear that he has been over-rated; his standing-ground was a sour Calvinism, for theological system of his own he had none.‡ We may pass over the tragical pages treating of Queen Mary and the sorrows heaped upon her as a sovereign and a Catholic. About 1574, whilst the Scotch Queen was wearing away her life in captivity, the Jesuits began their labours in Scotland. Like the faint twinkling of a star in blackest night, they kept alive through two centuries the light of the faith. Confessors and martyrs watered the soil with their suffering and their blood till the times which we have all seen when Scotland was ripe for the king's second advent (1878). How close a struggle it was, is revealed by one fact amongst many. In the year 1653 there were only five secular priests in the length and breadth of Scotland. Great as was the penalty for professing the Catholic religion after the promulgation in Scotland of the laws against recusants, where is the man whose secret sympathies,

body. In 1596 the General Assembly thus describes the spiritual state of the Scotch people:—

Universal coldness, want of earnestness, ignorance, despising of the Word. Prayer, psalm-singing, and God's word are dishonoured and abused; superstition, idolatry, oaths, blasphemies and execrations are predominating; the Sabbath is profaned by servile work, travelling, gambling, dancing, drinking, and murder. Children no longer obey their parents, but go into court against them, and marry without their consent. There is fighting for life and death; immorality, forbidden marriages and divorces are spreading; intemperance in eating and drinking, obscene talk and songs, sacrileges of all kinds are noted, to the intense grief of the kirk; the poor are oppressed, and serving-people looked down upon. Except the churches in Argyll and the Isles, four hundred churches lack teachers of the Word, by which the people is being completely ruined in ignorance, godlessness, and worldliness.*

These are negative facts which Dr. Bellesheim exposes, but the worth of his book lies essentially in his positive ones. By the side of the impotent kirk he places the labours of the outlawed Catholics, and, as we have already remarked, the divine power of the Church is more successfully proved in the throes of persecution than in the splendour of dominion. "The Puritans wish to extinguish every trace and even the name of Catholic," wrote a Jesuit Father in 1641, when the night was blackest.

These volumes possess only one drawback, that of being written in a language which the majority of Scotchmen do not read. As to style, impartiality, and the dramatic writing of history, they leave nothing to be desired. In the concluding chapter, in which the author speaks of the present condition of Catholic Scotland, we feel that day has dawned after the long darkness, and Our Lord's words rise to our minds, as they are the stay of our hearts in all the trials of our faith, "veritas liberabit vos."

Principles of Religious Life. By the Very Rev. FRANCIS CUTHBERT DOYLE, O.S.B. London: Washbourne. 1883.

THE publication of this ample book seems to mark the existence of a want and a demand. Religious communities, especially those of women, are multiplying in the country, and persons in the world with aspirations after the spiritual life are becoming more numerous, we may presume, year by year. The literature of the Spiritual Life is enormous. It has been accumulated on the banks of the Nile, in the Mediterranean islands, in the monasteries of the Middle Age, in the great Jesuit houses of the seventeenth and eighteenth centuries, and in France and Italy during a more recent period of devout souls and industrious literary priests. Not one book, nor a score of books, will suffice to give English-speaking races an adequate share of the treasures which lie sealed up in foreign tongues. Therefore we may well be gratified when an earnest religious like Canon Doyle devotes several years of his cloistral Benedictine life to the exposition in an English form of those principles and practices of spiritual perfection which he has gathered from many teachers and masters, and which he and those with him have tested in

---

* Vol. ii. p. 211.

the actual working of a monastery. That it is an exhaustive book, or an original one, we shall not be expected to say; first, because no single book can contain as much as two or three conferences of Cassian, or a treatise of St. Bernard, or a tenth part of one of the thick tomes of Father Alvarez de Paz; and secondly, because originality is not usually considered a decided merit in matters spiritual. But it is fairly complete, and it may justly be called new. Perfection, Prayer, the Divine Office, Divine Grace, Imitation of Christ, Mortification, the Vows—such is a slight sketch of its contents, and the list covers with sufficient completeness the whole of the spiritual life. Perhaps, if we might note any omission, it is that of any distinct treatment of the Sacraments—that is, of the Holy Eucharist and of Penance. The novelty of the work consists, we think, partly in a certain painstaking simplicity of style, and partly in a very free and solid exposition of certain fundamental spiritual views. As to style, it is refreshing to find that the author does not consider himself to be a master of "fine writing," and does not, therefore, distract us by any obtrusive patches of literary purple. The highest style, combining perfect directness with exquisite picturesque reinforcement, such as one knows where to find in Demosthenes or in Newman, is not to be attained by every one. In the absence of this, the efforts of second-rate artists in language to illuminate or intensify their conceptions have frequently no other result than what we have called distraction—the diversion of the attention from the substance to the mode. The style of this book is that of a man who merely pretends to say what he has to say without calling anyone's attention to his way of saying it. The other point to which we have referred is the writer's view that "Perfection" is a three-sided term, which includes Charity, Purity of Heart, and Humility; includes them not as component parts, but as equivalent expressions. Thus Charity means, " God before all things ;" Purity of Heart or Detachment means "Nothing created before God ;" and Humility signifies "God before self." The two former expressions are evidently equivalent; the latter is that peculiar form of detachment rendered necessary by the fact that we are conscious, reflective beings, and related both to God on the one side and creatures on the other by our consciousness. If we mistake not, many chapters in the older spiritual writers who lived before days of scholastic theology will be explained by this view. The scholastics, following St. Thomas, place the essence of the "perfect life" in Charity; the earlier ascetics, with Cass'an, take it to be Purity of Heart; and the mystics, following, perhaps, St. Augustine, are fond of making it out to be Humility. Bishop Ullathorne's "Ground work of the Christian's Virtues" supplies a large amount of illustrations of the last view. Canon Doyle excellently reconciles and enforces these converging theories. We have very great pleasure in welcoming this book. It will be useful for religious, and more especially in the noviciates of many of our convents, where almost the only available sources of necessary instruction are at present either in a foreign language or in very imperfect English. It will be a boon to priests, who will find in it a store of spiritual thought, for their own spiritual profit and for the instruction of others. And there is no Christian, aspiring ever so faintly after perfection, to whom its pages will not prove attractive, intelligible and helpful to spiritual progress. There is a very full analysis of every chapter, and a good index.

La Vie de N.S. Jésus-Christ. Par L'ABBÉ E. LE CAMUS, Directeur du Collège Catholique de Castelnaudary. 2 tomes. Paris: Poussièlgue Frères. 1883.

AS the errors of Cerinthus and the Ebionites gave the Church the great treasure of the fourth gospel, in a similar manner has the destructive rationalism of Strauss, Baur and Renan been the occasion within the fold of a new departure in Christology that is destined to be a lasting and precious boon. Lives of Christ are daily multiplying, of a character eminently suited to present intellectual needs; critical and scholarly, yet reverent and credulous; shirking no difficulty that has been thrown by the critics in the path of the old faith, but even triumphantly defending that faith with new arms wrested from the enemy, and marked, lastly, by a ready adaptation of all that modern research has brought to light of the past, to give reality and life to their presentment of the Divine Saviour, giving the picture freshness and a new attractiveness. In England it is true that thus far such works are only partially satisfactory, being in part weighted with the errors inseparable from their non-Catholic authorship. In France and Germany it is otherwise. The work under notice, in two octavo volumes of nearly six hundred pages each, is the second of the class that we have noticed which have appeared quite lately, the other being the favourably-received " Vie de N.S. Jésus-Christ," by the Abbé Fouard, which has already gone to a second edition. On not a few points, had we space, the two works might repay comparison. We will only remark in passing that both authors are not unworthy disciples of a great master. For it is not a little remarkable that both authors, together with M. Renan, were alike pupils at St. Sulpice of the learned Professor le Hir. It is very appropriate that two of them should give to their countrymen an antidote for the poison of the third.

Of the two Catholic writers, the Abbé Le Camus is to our judging less direct and nervous in style, less abundant and solid as to matter, but not less orthodox and more attractive than his confrère. The Abbé Fouard would respond more satisfactorily and fully to the needs of a student of the Scriptures, searching for matter, not to be delayed by any charms of manner. The Abbé Le Camus, on the other hand, is elegant and rhetorical, has put on some of the graces of M. Renan's pen, is full of colour and warmth, has filled in the background of his tableau with finely finished descriptions of the scenery and the social surroundings of the life of Our Lord; his text everywhere marches with stately step; his method of stating hard-studied results and amplifying on their dogmatic and moral import, makes not a few chapters read like so many eloquent *conférences;* there is never a suspicion of dryness of manner, nor of looseness of structure, and the even flow of a pleasant text rarely meets obstruction—for the most part technicalities and crude erudition are relegated to the numerous foot-notes. Truly a work this, on the noblest of themes, wherein orthodoxy is wedded to beauty in one harmonious narrative! The bishop of Carcassonne, in a prefatory letter, speaks of the charm with which readers will taste "le parfum d'onctueuse piété" which its pages exhale. We must not forget the force of this with the public of that France where M. Renan has exercised so baneful an influence, not from any solid learning (even the German rationalists called his " Vie de Jésus," " un livre parisien," " un produit superficiel," " nul pour le savant"), but from the abundant display of meretricious sophistry, a morbid sentimentality, and the fascination of style. Let us add, as to the volumes before us, that both intelligent criticism and sound theology are their deeper and more lasting claim to a place in Catholic literature. So that whilst we acknowlege with the same Bishop of Carcassonne that " all will admire the rich painting of Jewish manners and life, and the delightful topographical descriptions which frame and throw into relief the living figure of Our Lord," we venture to join him in assuring the Abbé Le Camus that his work "will strengthen the faith in many souls which guard that faith intact, will awaken it in those wherein it sleeps, and will perhaps also bring it back to some of those which have lost it."

Passing by the Introduction, a somewhat long one, in which in three chapters the author first traces the philosophy of the Incarnation, next the value of the original sources for the Life of Christ, and lastly describes the state of Palestine and its people in the time of Our Lord —we find the body of the work divided into three parts, " The Beginning," "The Public Life," and "The End"—three headings which sufficiently explain themselves. Of the first part, the first book relates to the precursor, St. John. There is little in it which need be specially noted save the finely executed picture of the precursor himself in his desert home; but we may express slight disappointment that in chap. iv., in narrating the baptism of Our Lord by St. John, more direct notice is not taken of that frequent assertion of non-Catholic writers, that in some true way the voice from the heavens made known to Our Lord Himself the divinity there conferred or reconferred on Him. In book the second the author treats very fully the birth, infancy and boyhood of Jesus. In this portion he makes large use of most modern information regarding the laws and manners of the Jews, with good effect, whilst several descriptions of the actual scenery give picturesque vividness. We note that he holds with the modern against the more ancient interpreters that at the time of the Incarnation the Blessed Virgin was affianced only and not yet married to St. Joseph—a view which is not without its difficulties. If the following extract is found to be somewhat commonplace, it is the fault of our English dress, and there is something in the author's art of composition which produces its telling effects by accumulation of detail. It is difficult to find a short paragraph that does not lose its significance and brilliancy by extraction.

Nazareth, the home of the Saviour, is, after Jerusalem, the spot of solemn memories for the Christian. Lying outside the more frequented routes of Palestine, and distant from its busiest centres, this old-world, straggling, Galilean village is to-day very much what it was centuries ago. A bend of ground, spacious and open amidst the hills which close in the north of the plain of Esdrelon, still holds it in the picturesque site which it occupied in the days of Jesus. When one looks at those groups of square cottages coarsely built of white stone, with their flat roofs, and a window here and there lighting up the poor interiors, and scattered without order along the narrow, badly-kept streets; at those clusters of trees, joyous like the sycamore, or sad like the cypress, but all of them centuries old, one forgets that eighteen hundred years have gone by, and fancies that it is still in the day of Joseph the Carpenter. When at eventide the family goes up to the terraced roof to be alone together, or to join in prayer, we think—thus did Mary and Joseph. When the children run to the hill-sides in their showy dress of linen or wool to play their noisy and simple games, the thought arises—may not Jesus have played once like them and on the same rocks? and when the fair Nazarene women, of Syrian style of splendid beauty, full of candour in aspect and of gentleness in speech, start for the fountain to fill their jar, holding a child by the hand, one almost waits to see if among them will not come, as once came, the young virgin of Juda taking her place amid the good wishes of the kindly daughters of the soil.

The traveller finds along one of the winding streets the shop of a carpenter; and imagination easily calls up within its outlines the lowly and quiet scene of thirty years of Jesus's life. At one end the old building overlooks the streets at the other it is hidden, arched into the rock. At the door a few rough tools hang on the wall, or are ranged in spacious boxes; planks of sycamore or cedar, and some furniture yet rough and unfinished, tell of the joiner's workshop. The shop runs deep into the rock, and serves also for bedroom and kitchen; three stones laid together make the fireplace, the smoke from which escapes by creeping along the rock up the mountain side; a few cupboards arranged in the wall hold the mats and cushions brought out at meals or at bedtime. Everything breathes of poverty, but not of sadness. A man, still young, whose expression tells of a soul peaceful and devout, sings to the time-beat of his hammer-strokes; a wife looks on at him from her distant place where she is nursing on her knee a sleeping child.

Thus lived the Holy Family! Mary, according to the Eastern manner, would suckle her child for two years. Relatives and friends, observant of Jewish custom, would come to congratulate her and keep feast together at the weaning. The rule also was that the child would continue under his mother's care and direction until he was five years old; and then the father would take him in hand, teaching him the law of God and the trade by which he himself lived (vol. i., 183).

We must be content to leave the rest of the volume, with briefest mention. The chapters in the second part, on the public life, are more full of incident, and give rise to more frequent notes for resolution of chronological or other difficulties. The miracle at Cana is very well told with reference to Our Lady, without any intricacies of argument or criticism, but ingeniously and with a sufficiency of erudition to satisfy the reader. The student will find one whole chapter, the second of the third part, devoted to a discussion of the well-known difficulty about the date of the paschal supper and the consequent date of the crucifixion, arising from the apparently discrepant details of the synoptics and of the fourth gospel.

We cannot too warmly recommend these volumes to English Catholic readers. The theme of which they treat is of perennial and transcendent interest; and the treatment is able and devout, whilst the learned author's graceful pen makes reading a pleasure, and his knowledge of the land he describes gives to his pages a charm of local colouring which we have hitherto been obliged to consider as a sort of attraction of which non-Catholic volumes of this class held the monopoly.

The Principles of English Canon Law. By J. BROWNBILL, M.A. Part I. General Introduction. London: Kegan Paul, Trench & Co. 1883.

A CATHOLIC must fairly rub his eyes to be quite sure that he is not the victim of some delusion as he turns over the pages of this work. The title, the author's description as "Naden Divinity Student of St. John's College, Cambridge," would seem to indicate pretty clearly its source. But Mr. Paul Bultitude in the toils was hardly more puzzled than we were as we read in this Anglican work "of the great and undefined powers of the Pope as the successor of St. Peter. These powers at least imply that no bishop can act in opposition to the Pope without incurring the charge of schism." It is still more startling to read further on (page 66) "that the doctrine of Papal infallibility appears to be founded on the consideration that such an infallibility is necessary for the good of the Church, and that God provides all things necessary for the good of the Church." And in a note he adds: "Many breakdowns of infallibility have been alleged from the history of the Church, but none of them seem worth much." We have heard of the "advance" of Ritualists at the present day, but surely Mr. Brownbill is the very apex of the advancing *cuneus*. Simply, then, the book is laid down on the lines of Craisson's *"Manuale Totius Juris Canonici,"* and is a very creditable summary of the celebrated canonist's first two volumes. Under the head of "Persons" are treated the Pope, the Roman Congregations, Bishops, Religious Orders, &c. The second section is headed "Things," in which are discussed the Sacraments, the Divine Office, Vows, &c. The dependence of the Church of England on the Parliament is carefully ignored, and the ecclesiastical lawsuits of the last few years are simply referred to as "painful events." The work is interesting to Catholics as indicating the high water mark of the advancing wave of Ritualism. Surely it is not without a touch of humour that the author trusts "When the book is completed by the publication of the second part, the English bishops may perhaps be able to recommend it as a manual for candidates for ordination."

A Narrative of Events Connected with the Publication of the Tracts for the Times. By W. PALMER. Rivingtons. 1883.

IT is now forty years since Mr. Palmer published his "Narrative," of which the present volume is a reprint. The former narrative has been considerably added to by the addition of a head and a tail. If the earlier work induced C   Newman to characterize the author as "deficient in breadth," what would he say of the new head and tail piece. We can see nothing more in them than creditable specimens of Exeter Hall eloquence. No epithet is too spiteful for the Catholic Church. "Romish," "Romanist," "Jesuitical," are terms with which every page bristles. "Romanism is allied with infidelity," "it naturally sympathises with infidelity," "it steadily seeks the destruction of the Church of England," such are the wild assertions scattered broadly over the book. Is this the Palmer whom Cardinal Newman describes as "cautious and even subtle in the expression of his religious views, and gentle in their enforcement?" "Quantum mutatus ab illo Hectore." It must needs be that long years passed in the cold shade of neglect has soured the disposition of the veteran controversialist. With a vanity pardonable perhaps in an old man, he fondly dreams that his works have silenced all Catholic apologists. He refers on p. 70 to his answer to Cardinal Wiseman, and naively adds "It effectually disposed of the Roman Catholic argument against the validity of our orders. I had reason to believe that it completely answered its purpose, and I heard no more of the objections which had been raised against the English Orders." The days are passed when the bitter, biting, taunt could influence the current of religious thought. Catholics can now afford to smile and pass on. "Non ragionam di lui ma guarda et passa." But one cannot refuse a tribute of pity to a man whose closing years are embittered by the triumphant progress of his foe, while his weapons are falling from his hands. "Alas! for this grey shadow, once a man!"

Reformatorenbilder; Historische Vorträge über katholische Reformatoren und M. Luther. Von Dr. CONSTANTIN GERMANUS. Freiburg: Herder. 1883. (Reformers; Historical Lectures on Catholic Reformers and Martin Luther).

THE Luther centenary has been the occasion of numerous books and pamphlets on the so-called Reformer and the Reformation, a large part of which will not more than outlive the festivities of the occasion; but a few of them will secure a deserved place in the ranks of controversial literature. One of these last is the above-named volume, which we are glad to recommend to English readers. Constantin Germanus is an assumed name, but we believe we are not mistaken in believing him to be one of the most prominent historians of Germany.

As the title of the book tells at once, the author compares the true reformers of the Church with Luther. Having placed before his readers the picture of a true reformer of the old times, of Gregory the Great, he describes and characterizes in the second and third lectures the Reformer of Wittenburg, or rather, by quoting Luther's own words, he makes the Reformer characterize both himself and his work. The five remaining lectures include one each on Blessed Peter Canisius, St. Charles Borromeo, St. Vincent de Paul, and two on other great saints of the epoch of the Reformation (1540-1640). The contrast between the true and the pseudo-Reformers is brought out in a striking and ingenious manner. The style is easy and attractive—the popular style of lectures; whilst a great many references at the end of the volume show that the doctrine contained in its pages is based on a very solid foundation. The volume is not bulky, only 320 pages, and the price is low, four shillings.

Les Espérances Chrétiennes. Par AUGUSTIN COCHIN. Publié avec une Préface et des Notes par Henry Cochin. Paris: E. Plon, Nourrit & Cie. 1883.

THIS work has been closely shaped on the plan of the "Pensées" of the great Pascal. Under the above title M. Cochin has given to the world a number of detached reflections and criticisms on the different phases of modern thought. God, Life, Our Redeemer, and the Present Times are the topics which he discusses from the most fundamental point of view. It must at least be conceded to him that he is never dull; his writing has all the merit of French prose, an entire absence of "*des longueurs.*" Almost every sentence sparkles with points, often of genuine worth, sometimes, it must be allowed, of tinsel. His readers are treated with the most delicate consideration. The very form in which the book is cast is probably kindly intended as a condescension to the feeble attention of the present race of readers.

The work is undoubtedly that of an able man. The play of fancy throughout is almost exuberant—the conceits, ingenious parallels of imagery and antithesis enliven every page. But of imagination in the proper sense of the word there is none. His arguments open brilliantly to fall flatly; the nail is delicately inserted, but the blow that is to drive it home is strangely withheld. The work of the rhetorician is more apparent than that of the philosopher. The absence of hard-headed proofs must seriously detract from the value of the work as a contribution to modern Christian polemics. Take the following arguments, on the existence of God, submitted to the unbeliever:—

There is a cause, and it is not me. There is a perfection, and it is not me. There is a truth, and it is not me. But I see them in myself, always, from the moment I look there. It is God. He dwells in me (p. 29).¶ There is a certain thing called duty. Who imposes it? God. Who would have the right to impose it but God? And if duty was not imposed this earth would be nothing but a field of slaughter, an abode of thieves great and small (p. 30).¶ A stone is found in the form of a hatchet; there was then a worker; but this stone lies in a deposit to which I assign a date, therefore man has lived at this date. Lived on what? On certain species now found in Greenland. And this is enough to make away with the Bible; one iota passes away, and the whole is shaken (p. 143).

Such arguments, we fear, are hardly of a nature to bring our men of science to their knees.

Turning now to another feature of the work, the reader will hardly refrain from a smile at certain little traits, so characteristic of the nation, curious turns of expression which we can only regard as a sort of *attitudinizing* in language. "God speaks. I hear Him; that is conscience. I speak; God hears me: that is prayer. This dialogue is religion" (p. 66). "To have created laws is sublime; to have created beings is more than sublime; and free beings, that is beyond all conception and certainly divine" (p. 148).

Passages of beauty, not perhaps of the highest order, but pleasing and instructing, abound throughout the book. The following is almost taken at random:—

I have a child, I love him, let him be covered with rags or silks I care not; my look and my heart turn to him, his destiny weighs upon me, I suffer and rejoice in him. Poor little one! he will be tempted, be exposed to the floods like the others. Empress or shepherdess, tears will flow from thy eyes. The ball of the Prussian is being melted for the village boy, and the wind that sweeps over the marsh is going to blanch the cheeks of that beautiful girl, and death will take her. Profound realities under deceitful forms! It is in the depth of thy soul, in thy troubled blood, that thou art a man, and that thou hast a necessity for religion (p. 210).

It is a pity that the author has chosen to be so combative; his attack is weak, his proofs unconvincing. It is his poetry wherein lies the charm of his work, dreamy and pleasant are his meditations, like "the winds that blow to us from the fields of sleep." We could have enjoyed many more passages like the following, but their scarcity through the work is much to be regretted:—"But to nature I say without ceasing: O Nature! why are you so harsh to me, you who are so fair? Why do you bring me suffering with ecstasy? Through you I touch God, but He escapes me, your life radiant with order preserves His traces; but mine is disorder and He escapes me. I explain your life; explain mine, O Nature, and why you make it at once so harsh and so fair" (p. 155).

La bienheureuse Delphine de Sabran et les Saints de Provence au XIVe Siècle. Par LA MARQUISE DE FORBIN L'OPPÈDE. Paris: Plon, Nourrit et Cie. 1883.

IT is always a pleasure to be taken back to the Middle Ages, the childhood of modern nations, when faith was something more than a profession, and the simplicity of manners gave to the times a charm which "has now passed away from the earth." The volume before us gives us a charming glimpse of that period—the lives of two favoured souls, whose virtues indeed are the common inheritance of the saints of God, but whose actions are a singular reflection of the simple days of the Ages of Faith. Elzear and Delphine were born about the close of the thirteenth century in fair Provence, where the sun is always warm and the fields are always green. The harsh customs of the times allowed the king to give in marriage the hand of his noble

the little maid had plucked from her breast the fairest flower she could offer to God, a secret but firm vow of perpetual virginity. And on the wedding-day, when Delphine's secret was whispered to her spouse, Elzear, in child-like faith, looked upon the vow as an inspiration from on high. It must have been a beautiful sight for the angels of God to see the two children pass the first night by the side of the bed in prayer, imploring God to give them grace to guard and cherish the holy virtue. And thus these two lilies grew up like brother and sister, and for twenty-five years hid from all the world the secret of their lives. How they lived and died these pages under review best can tell. The author has entered with genuine literary appreciation into her subject, and writes with an unction that she has caught from the spirit of the Ages of Faith. We have, however, one very serious fault to find. The story of these holy souls is constantly broken upon by episodes of contemporary history. Kings and their quarrels, the great men of the times, are thrust upon us and painfully jar with the recital of the sacred idyll. Had the authoress relegated Charles and Robert, and Joan of Naples to the obscurity they deserve, she would have produced a charming bit of hagiography which we would class in that group of which Montalembert's life of St. Elizabeth is the model and *chef-d'œuvre*.

Four Essays on the Life and Writings of St. Francis de Sales, Doctor of the Church. By the REV. H. B. MACKEY, O.S.B. Reprinted from the DUBLIN REVIEW. London: Burns & Oates. 1883.

WE are glad that Father Mackey has gathered into one cover the four articles on St. Francis which appeared in our pages during the past two years. We think that he is doing a good work in translating the holy Doctor's writings—a work in which we have heartily wished him success. There will, doubtless, be some, we trust there will be many, who from the perusal of those writings will be desirous of seeing an able, critical conspectus of the doctrinal method and moral teaching of the Saint set forth lucidly and in connected form. Such persons will be pleased to have it in a separate form. We will only add that we trust their separate publication may in yet other ways help the great object which Father Mackey has at heart of making St. Francis de Sales better known and more widely loved.

The Parochial Hymn Book. Words and Melodies. London: Burns & Oates. 1883.

FATHER POLICE has the merit of making the first serious attempt amongst us to bring out a collection of hymn-tunes to rival the well-known Anglican "Hymns Ancient and Modern." We cannot sufficiently n the labour and devotion that must have been spent by the autl on the arrangement and composition of so vast a number of s—some 700 in all. Each hymn is printed in clear, distinct ty] in almost every case the melody is enriched by the addition of a second or alto part. These little additions to the melody are often very happily conceived, in spite of some very awkward fourths that are unavoidable from the limitation to two-voice parts. The style of the melody is that which at present is in vogue amongst us—light, catching tunes. The more ambitious attempts follow in the direction of the gossamer style of French *cantiques* rather than in that of Webbe and the old English school. A very useful feature is the insertion of a very large number of liturgical hymns and canticles arranged for different seasons of the year. We fear, however, that choirs will find a practical difficulty in singing through a Latin hymn when the music is given for the first verse alone. The "Te Deum" as given on page 298 would tax the best choir to render it with anything like unison and precision. We fancy the value of the work would have been increased by the addition of a simple bass, as in "Hymns Ancient and Modern." There are so very few of our organists acquainted with even the elements of harmony, that they will be dismayed when asked to accompany the tunes of this collection. No doubt the melodies are intended for unaccompanied singing, but there are many congregations who consider the service very heavy where the voices are unsupported by an instrument. These, however, are mere spots in a most meritorious and excellent work. In addition to the hymn-tunes a large number of prayers, instructions, &c., have been given, so that nothing is wanting to make it a most serviceable collection. We must therefore congratulate Father Police on the production of a work quite unique amongst us, and we hope that its publication will lead to its general adoption in our churches and schools.

Reminiscences of Rome. By the Rev. EUGENE MACCARTAN. London: Burns & Oates. 1883.

IN this age of multitudinous books it is becoming more and more natural to ask why an author claims our attention for his production. It is quite certain that Rome is a perennial source of interest to the civilized world. But we have had many books on the subject, written from all points of view; we have had "Walks in Rome," and "Pictures of Rome," and "Winters in Rome," and "Memories of Rome," and, in short, countless effusions of one sort or another. The Rev. Eugene MacCartan gives us his "Reminiscences of Rome." He made, it appears, a four months' stay in Rome during the year 1870, whilst the Vatican Council was sitting.

The Eternal City was at the time in the height of its splendour. The proceedings then taking place in it were of great and absorbing interest, especially to Catholics throughout the world.

An account, therefore, however imperfect, of these proceedings, by an eye-witness, will, I think, interest the public, the more so that the beauty and grandeur of the ceremonies which then were gone through, and the concourse of so many bishops from all parts of the world, may not be seen or witnessed again, perhaps for generations; and, particularly, the different rites in use in the Church, which were celebrated with every splendour and magnificence by the Eastern bishops and the others who were present on the occasion.

It is an undeniable recommendation to the book that the writer has seen everything and visited even many times every place described by him. But it is an obvious drawback, on the other hand, that the book comes thirteen years after the last events and functions described. Still, to many the book will not fail to be acceptable. It is pleasant and refreshing to read over again of those memorable days when Rome saw gathered within her precincts once more the intellect, the heroism, and the external splendour of the Catholic world; and one feels the heart catch fire from the warm piety and enthusiasm of the reverend author. He does not trouble himself with the historical or classical aspect of Rome, but is completely absorbed with the religious side of things, and hence he enters into the great functions which he witnessed with a thorough intensity of interest and describes them with a glowing pen.

Whilst, however, readily admitting the good qualities of this book, we are sorry to have to point out one or two serious defects which go a good way to mar its excellence. In the first place, parts of it are written with evident carelessness, the sentences, in some cases, being ill-formed and sometimes quite ungrammatical. For instance, the following:—

As we stood round, silently contemplating and reverencing this sacred relic (St. Lawrence's head) of one of the most glorious martyrs and witnesses of the early Church, we profoundly felt the force of the testimony that, sufferings such as those of St. Lawrence bore, to the truth and divinity of the Christian religion, for it was a testimony more than human—it was divine (p. 79).

Besides this carelessness in writing, the book is very much disfigured by a large number of mis-spells. The eye easily catches such deformities as "catachumen," "Propoganda," "Isodore" (which occurs five times in one chapter), "patriarchíal," "entablíture," "cresent," "ninty," "collonades," "scortched," "Coloseum," &c. We hope that if this volume of "Reminiscences" should reach a second edition it will first be subjected to previous careful revision.

Das Privilegium Otto I. für die römische Kirche vom Jahre 962. Erläutert von TH. SICKEL. Mit einem Facsimile. Innsbruck: Wagner. 1883. (The Diploma of Otto I. in favour of the Roman Church, in the year 962. Explained by Th. Sickel.)

THIS publication of the Diploma given by the Emperor Otto I. to Pope John XII. in favour of the Roman Church is worthy of special record, since it means a new departure in treating the ecclesiastical history of the Middle Ages, and it throws new light on the beginning of the Temporal Power. The Diploma we may say is the most important of the Imperial donations to the Popes, because we now have it in the original. Previously copies of it existed, but as they contained a corrupted and uncertain text, they were eagerly attacked and denounced as spurious by modern Protestant historians in Germany.

Pope Leo XIII., graciously complying with the desire expressed by Professor Sickel, of the Vienna University, allowed him to examine the original document preserved in the Vatican archives, and to reproduce it by photography. Catholics are greatly indebted to Professor Sickel for now publishing the Diploma, the authenticity of which he here establishes so cleverly and peremptorily, that we may say: *causa finita*. The most curious portions of his work refer to the paleographical and diplomatical peculiarities of the document. These are, however, only introductory to more serious inquiries into other donations either preceding or following Otto's diploma. Externally this diploma is written in italics of tenth century character, with ornaments in harmony; and it is written with gold ink on purple vellum. Such passages in it as refer to circumstances of Pope and Emperor synchronize with the date of the writing. Professor Sickel would not, however, declare this document to be strictly the original, but a copy executed in the Imperial Chancery; but its lavishly splendid get-up suggests that it was made for a special purpose. Hence he holds the Vatican document to be an official copy, intended to be laid on the confession of St. Peter. This opinion is the more probable, as we know that documents of undisputed authority witness the deposition on the tomb of St. Peter of the donations of Charlmagne and Pippin. The contents of our document we may divide into two sections: in the first, the Emperor Otto solemnly pledges himself to bring back to the Holy See all those territories which were assigned to him in former Imperial donations; and promises, further, to add to these gifts several towns still subjected to his own dominion. A large part of the Otto diploma is made up from the privileges and donations given in 817 to the Roman Church by the Emperor Louis the Pious. It is precisely to these quotations that Protestant criticism pointed in order to denounce it as a forgery. On the contrary, Professor Sickel successfully vindicates its authencity, and meanwhile destroys the foundation on which those critics stood—viz., the too high esteem in which the magistrates of the Imperial Chancery of the tenth century are held by modern authors. Professor Sickel felt under a kind of necessity to bring within the scope of his treatise the privileges and donations made to the Holy See in 1020 by Henry II., in 815 by Louis the Pious, and the diplomas of Charlemagne and Pippin. Unfortunately, we have to lament the loss of the original documents; but indirectly they are confirmed by the previous document, now for the first time published. It affords, too, the means for destroying the calumny against the author of Hadrian's life in the " Liber Pontificalis," who in describing the territories of the Roman Church is asserted to have used equivocal terms in order to mislead public opinion in favour of the Holy See. Professor Sickel clearly shows the language in the "Liber Pontificalis" to be in full keeping with the customs of that age.

XIII. in the service of history could not have been inaugurated by a more happy and far-reaching result than is afforded by the discovery of the Ottonian MS. and its publication in this treatise. I may add that a well-executed photograph of the remarkable document enhances the value of the treatise.

BELLESHEIM.

Groundwork of Economics. By C. S. DEVAS. London : Longmans. 1883.

THIS elaborate and serious attempt, by a most able Catholic writer, to infuse Christianity into Political Economy should be warmly welcomed. There is no science or subject which has been more ruthlessly paganized by the utilitarian school than Economics. The reason is that you cannot treat of land and labour, of values, of food and of pleasures, without holding some theory or other as to man's purpose and end here below; and therefore economics must be either Christian or pagan; there is no medium; and, as the eminent writers of the school referred to have not been Christians in any definite sense, they have written like pagans. Mr. Devas begins his book with the statement that economical science is a portion of ethics or moral science. His book, however, does not concern itself exclusively, or even chiefly, with the fundamental ideas on which true economical science rests. For our own part, we confess that we should have been better pleased if he had devoted more space to the destructive heresies of modern writers on such matters as wealth, utility, pleasure, land and labour. The errors which lie at the root of the greater part of the pernicious teachings of Protestant writers are mainly five in number : First, the dogma that all men are equal ; secondly, an erroneous idea of liberty ; thirdly, the self-contradictory view that " utility " is the last end of human action ; fourthly, a misconception of the nature of Christian charity ; and fifthly, a denial of the existence of any law of asceticism. No economic treatise can have any pretension to be called scientific, unless it plainly expounds, and firmly establishes, the truth on these five points. Not that we are so unpractical as to expect, in every economic manual, a detailed exposition of applied ethics. Still there is no doubt that these fundamental questions are most important and interesting, and were never more so than at this moment. Mr. Devas, in the most able manner, recapitulates the fallacies, whilst admitting the merits, of every economical writer of repute, from Adam Smith to Mr. Jevons and Mr. Cliffe Leslie. He has a unique acquaintance with foreign and especially with German writers on his subject. His chapters on literature and on the method of economics are extremely useful, and afford a valuable guidance to any student or general reader who may wish to take up any of our modern authors. But most persons will feel that a chapter or two dedicated to downright exposition. proof and illustration, of fundamental Catholic views such as th͏ ͏o which we have referred would have been most welcome. Mea͏ ͏: the book is full to repletion of the most valuable and recent infc͏ ͏n. On Labour, on Production, on Industry, on Enjoyment, on Food and Drink, on Houses, Furniture and Clothes, on Recreation, and on a score of other matters he affords us not only true and sound views, but the most authentic facts and figures. He is no dogmatist; he presents with the most perfect fairness both sides of every question which is capable of having two. As an example, we may point to his exposition of the arguments for and against Free Trade. The fourteen or fifteen pages (pp. 256–70) which he devotes to this discussion are written in a close, clear and interesting style, like the rest of the book, are full of matter and rich in references to other writers, and any one who took the trouble to master them would be equal to any ordinary discussion, and able to correct most newspaper articles on the subject; and—best result of all—would be utterly incapable of that blind and noisy partisanship which usually does duty for argument in the Free Trade controversy, whether among country gentlemen or Liberal stump-orators. Mr. Devas's book is one which we desire most cordially to welcome, and for which we predict a wide popularity. The reading he displays in its pages is immense, his style is happy, and his principles are (we need not say) Christian, Catholic, and thoroughly sound. Such an essentially serious book is one to which frequent reference must be made. In the meantime, may we advise every Catholic with leisure, and any claim to literary cultivation, to get it and read it.

Attempts at Truth. By St. George Stock. London: Trübner. 1882.

A VIGOROUS French critic has left us a description, which Mr. Stock's book admirably illustrates, of the "philosophic" method very commonly used by writers at the present. Our nineteenth century philosopher, he tells us, sets out with the modest assumption that up to his time people have not known how to think, and that it is his business to teach them: that hitherto the world has not been in possession of truth, and that it is his mission to discover or to create it, and to enrich the human race with this treasure. And so he shuts himself up in himself, gags, bolts, and padlocks his conscience, and proposes to himself a few problems, such as these: Do I exist? Is there a world? Is there a God? And on these high themes he will construct volume upon volume, weighing the reasons, or what he calls reasons, for and against, and arriving probably nowhither. Now, in the volume before us, Mr. Stock discusses, among others, the following questions: Why must I do what is right? What is right? What is reality? Where is heaven? and in deprecation of criticism, which, as he apprehends, might be founded upon "discrepancies of thought or expression," urges that his "pages are, as their name imports, Attempts at Truth, thrown out at various times and in various modes, and never intended as a formal exposition of a system." Well and good; but who is right, and why he must do right, and where Heaven is, and the rest, are—we hope he will forgive our frankness—utterly valueless. These, and the other topics with which he deals, have all been investigated by thinkers whose claims upon the attention of mankind it would be ridiculous to compare with his, and whose high thoughts and noble words will dwell in the minds and guide the lives of men "long after the grave has heaped its mould upon his presumption, and the silent tomb shall have imposed its law upon his pert loquacity."

We decline, then, altogether to enter upon a detailed examination of Mr. Stock's book. Still, that we may not be unjust to him, let us indicate one element of positive value in it. He has set himself, as it would seem, to investigate the subject of spiritualism, and he has arrived at the conclusion, which seems to us indisputable, that it is by no means all delusion and imposture. It will be worth while to hear him on this subject:—

What are the facts of Spiritualism? There is no room here to answer this question in detail. But let the reader recall some of the stories of the supernatural that have sounded to his ears most grotesquely incredible, fit only to raise a passing smile, or tickle the fancy by the quaintness of their conception—these are the kind of facts that have to be admitted. This may sound uncompromising, a pill without gilding; but plain dealing prospers best in the long run. Spiritualists, as a rule, believe over-much; they multiply the real marvels; but they cannot out-miracle them. The facts of Spiritualism are obstinately objective; they refuse to be quenched either by laughter or scorn; they force themselves with increasing persistency upon the attention of thoughtful minds (p. 140).

True; and equally true is what we read a little further on:—

It is the office of reason to teach us that since even the limits of our conceptive faculties are no measure of the possibilities of nature, much less should our beliefs be accepted as such. But it is rare indeed to find a mind that has learnt this lesson in its full application, and to which "secondary evidence" is more than a grain of dust in the balance, when weighed against a prior belief. Students of physical science exhibit, in an eminent degree, this incapacity of escaping from a groove of thought. They have grown so accustomed to one uniform flow of natural phenomena, that they cannot comprehend any perturbation by unusual causes, and avenge the mental disquietude that testimony causes them by angry denunciations of the witness. It is a curious and instructive sight to watch the sanguine condescension with which each new observer extends his patronage to the facts of Spiritualism—he knows that he is unprejudiced, and thinks he surely will be believed—only to find himself consigned by the world at large, and scientific men in particular, to the same limbo of folly as his predecessors (p. 142).

Then, as to the psychological importance of the facts of spiritualism:—

The facts of Mesmerism, Clairvoyance, Spiritualism, reveal a universe of unsuspected laws, regulating the interaction of mind on mind. They reveal the indelibility and recoverability of impressions on the memory. Every thought, word, and deed of our lives is there; the Books of Judgment are there. They show there is a self within, latent to consciousness, of an apt apprehens t needs no repetition to fortify its remembrance. There is a vr of evidence tending to show that what are mistaken for the utterances of spirits, because no author is forthcoming to claim them, are but the hidden contents of our own minds; but there is another mass, equally vast, equally irrefragable, which seems to force us to the inference of external intelligence, of what kind soever, but acting through the human mind, and modified by the nature of its medium (p. 145).

Lastly, as to the importance of the facts of spiritualism in the "Science of Religion":—

Every religion is founded upon spirit-manifestation; and without such displays of a power to command matter, none would ever take root among the vulgar. The long mooted question of miracles is at length decisively settled by Spiritualism. Miracles do actually occur. Of that, keen and sceptical minds have been amply satisfied by observation; and any reader of this paper may satisfy himself too, if he take the proper pains. It is not true that scepticism interferes with spiritual manifestations, though, as they depend upon psychical conditions, it is quite feasible for a strong antagonistic will to hinder them, just as a mesmerist on the platform may find himself defeated by a person in the crowd resolutely setting his will in opposition. And since it is certain that miracles occur in the present, what more reasonable than to believe well-authenticated accounts of them in the past? The controversy on miracles is now obsolete; and for this boon we are indebted to the facts of Spiritualism. But mark the consequence. Miracles are the monopoly of no religion; neither do they invariably accompany moral superiority. If St. Paul cured deseases by handkerchiefs taken from his body, so does Mr. Ashman—a worthy man, but no saint; if Philip was levitated, so was Mrs. Guppy; if Christ healed the blind by the touch of His spittle, so did Vespasian. No claim to authority can be grounded on miracles. If we were to pin our faith to the greatest miracle-monger, we would have some queer prophets. There is, however, a natural connection between miracles and religion. Religions are the products of spiritual forces; their origin is behind the veil of our world; and these spiritual forces at the outset of every new religion over-ride and master the laws of matter. There is no interruption in this of the course of nature; only we must learn to extend that term (p. 146).

Of course, we should not express ourselves in this way. But it is quite true, in the first place, that supernatural manifestations are as well attested as any facts of contemporary or past history; and, in the second place they are not confined to the true religion. As St. Augustine somewhere says, "Miracula alia fine aliaque potestate et jure fiunt per magos et per sanctos."

The World as Will and Idea. By ARTHUR SHOPENHAUER. Translated from the German by A. B. Haldane, M.A., and J. Kemp, M.A. Vol. I., containing Four Books. London: Trübner & Co.

MR. TRÜBNER has determined to add to his Philosophical Library a translation of Schopenhauer's principal work, and we suppose he has been well advised. The chief doctor of modern Pessimism has become something more than a name to educated people in this country, as throughout Europe; but knowledge of German is by no means a common accomplishment and Schopenhauer is not easy reading in the original, even to students well acquainted with German; hence there is a certain demand for versions of him in the various other European languages. Messrs. Haldane and Kemp have done their work faithfully; almost too faithfully, indeed. Their account of their chief canon in executing it is " the alternative of a somewhat slavish adherence to Schopenhauer's *ipsissima verba* has been preferred to inaccuracy." Well, unquestionably that is the less error of the two. But surely it would have been possible for them to present the vigorous idiomatic German of Schopenhauer in vigorous idiomatic English. In their anxiety to be scrupulously exact, they have often been inelegant and sometimes obscure. Almost any page would furnish an example of the fault we censure. We open the volume at random, and light upon the following sentence:—" But most readers have already grown angry with impatience, and burst into reproaches with difficulty kept back so long." It is not particularly bad; but it is not good. Messrs. Kemp and Haldane might, we feel sure, have done better without any sacrifice of accuracy. And why we are sure of this is because their version is upon the whole excellent. So much must suffice for the present about this translation of Schopenhauer. When the remaining two volumes of it reach us, we shall probably have more to say about it and him.

Fifty Years of Concessions to Ireland, 1831—1881. By R. BARRY O'BRIEN. In two vols. Vol. I. London: Sampson Low, Marston, Searle & Rivington.

SCANTY justice can be done to a work of such excellence within the short limits of a book notice. Mr. O'Brien's masterly sketch of the "Land Question," which was received with so much favour three years ago, led us to expect great things from the present volume. Nor have we been disappointed. It is the "old, old tale thrice repeated," that is, put forward again. The object of the work, however, is not merely fine writing calculated to make the blood boil, but a scientific historical sketch—a real handbook for students and politicians of the future. The author has not been afraid to burrow in the dustiest and driest corners of our libraries to obtain historic truth at first hand. The result in this volume is a masterly treatise of the different schemes for National Education and for Parliamentary and Municipal Reform in Ireland. No important statement is put forward which is not supported by either Parliamentary paper or the authority of some well-known name. It may be inferred that a work of this sort is the production of a Dryasdust. This is far from being the case. The author expressly disclaims any intention to rouse party spirit, and he writes with singular ease and grace. There are passages in the work of an eloquence at once noble and masculine, befitting the calm dignity of the Muse of History. We hope, however, to be able to return to the subject at no distant date, as the work is still incomplete, and the second volume is on the eve of publication.

The Law of Compensation under the Agricultural Holdings (England) Act, 1883. By CHARLES D. FORSTER. London: Walter Scott. 1883.

THE Agricultural Holdings Act, which was passed last session for the relief of English farmers, comes into operation on the first day of the present year. It is practically, as the compiler of this clear and useful manual explains, a law for determining the compensation due from a landlord to a tenant for improvements made during tenancy. This has always been a fertile subject for disagreement and complaint, and it is only right that some kind of legal protection should be given to tenants. An eminent agricultural authority said, a few years ago, "In some degree none of us carry out all that is in our power; but want of capital and want of confidence in the tenure of farms are, I suppose, the two principal causes of this omission." The question of tenant-right in England, and even more in Wales, must come within the range of practical discussion before long. The risks and costs which at present attend the transference of land are an obstruction to agricultural progress which will have to be removed. The law of settlement and the burdens on copyhold lands should also be largely modified if farming is to be free. Meanwhile, the present Act does something for the farmer. The work before us presents landlords and tenants with a practical handbook of the provisions and working of this important measure, together with the text itself and several interesting appendices. Mr. Forster has noted some of the obscurities of the Act. There is a phrase, for instance, which will probably become a fruitful text for that denunciatory style of discussion which the British farmer affects—What is the "inherent capability of the soil?" A farmer, by dint of expenditure or diplomacy, might get a chemical works removed from his neighbourhood; would the increased productive value of his land be entitled to compensation, or would it be set down to the "inherent capability of the soil?" The machinery of referees and umpire will not, perhaps, prove an unmixed boon to a race so fond of "law" as farmers are. There will be a great temptation to reject the decisions of these gentlemen, and to carry the matter to the county-court, and further. But the amendment of the law of distraint cannot fail to act beneficially. Formerly the power of distraint for rent was available for six years; now it must be exercised within twelve months. Cattle which do not belong to the tenant cannot be touched, or at least cannot be disposed of; neither can machinery which belongs to another person. And the Act makes useful changes in regard to legal processes and the employment of bailiffs. A most useful, and, as far as we know, completely novel feature in Mr. Forster's manual is a table showing the estimated duration of artificial and other manures; or, in other words, the proportion of the fertilizing material which is exhausted each successive year, until it entirely disappears; and this on lands of every kind, whether arable or pasture, clay or light. From this we gather the fact that whereas nitr‍ soda, applied to arable land, is wholly exhausted in the first yea‍ ρ, lime will last for twelve years. We are not aware on what ‍ ty Mr. Forster bases his figures in this very remarkable table; what, for example, is his warrant for saying that lime as a manure exhausts itself in twelve years precisely at the yearly rate of one-twelfth of its initial virtue. Perhaps he would be the last to claim exact precision for these calculations. But at any rate they cannot fail to prove of great service to occupiers and to referees under the Act, who will now have to calculate what a tenant ought to receive for this class of improvements, which it is so peculiarly difficult to value. This opportune book is sure to recommend itself by its clearness, its completeness, and its practical character, to the large class who are interested in the land.

Merry England. An Illustrated Magazine. Vol. I., May—October, 1883. Office : 44, Essex Street, London.

IT does not need any words of ours to ensure the success of this clever and popular Magazine, the first volume of which has been sent to us as we go to press. It is not our custom to review current English periodical literature, but the volume before us is a collection of essays and sketches which will perhaps have a more enduring interest than the contents of most of our monthly contemporaries. There is an earnestness in some of the papers, an originality in others, and a brightness and literary " distinction" in all of them which indicate them to be the contributions at once of practised and of eminent writers. The ordinary Magazine consists of one or more novels and of " padding ;" the " extraordinary" one (if we may use the phrase) is made up of " serious" papers, of which it is really wonderful that so many can be provided for the price. When, on the first day of the month, we wish to escape from novels, from party politics, from the dreary hack-work of the pot-boiling professional, and from the ponderous dissertations of the eminent doctrinaire, it is somewhat difficult to know where to turn. *Merry England* has solved the question. Its distinctive character we take to be its combination of freshness and of finish. Its contributors might all be very young people if one judged by the spontaneity and vigour of their work. Many of them are certainly nothing of the sort ; and the excellence of the literary workmanship of every one of them proves they are not novices in their trade. In fact, when we look at the list of names, we see that very many of them are men and women who are doing solid and lasting work in other spheres of literature, and that *Merry England* is to a great extent made up of a kind of literary production which, in many respects, is more attractive than any other—the occasional unforced thought and fancy of first-class literary craftsmen. Many of the papers in this first volume have attracted wide ; we need only mention " The Light of the West," by Col. ⊤   "The Story of a Picture," by Mrs. Meynell ; " The Young   nd Party," by Mr. G. Saintsbury ; and " Horny-handed B   and "The Law of the Mother and Child," by Mr. J. G. Cox   ort tales are admirable ; the articles on

Art are brilliant and instructive; and the verse is such as one might expect from Mr. Aubrey de Vere and Mr. Blackmore.

LIST OF BOOKS RECEIVED TOO LATE FOR REVIEW IN THE PRESENT NUMBER.

"La Terre Sainte." Par Victor Guérin. 2°. Partie. Paris: Plon, Nourrit et Cie. 1884.

"Kant's Critique of Practical Reason." By T. K. Abbott, B.D., London: Longmans. 1883.

"Life of Christ." By Dr. B. Weiss. Translated by M. G. Hope. Vol. II. Edinburgh: T. & T. Clark. 1883.

"The Parables of Jesus." By S. Goebel. Translated by Professor Banks. Edinburgh: T. & T. Clark. 1883.

"Popular Life of Buddha." By A. Lillie. London: K. Paul. 1883.

"Sacred Eloquence." By Rev. T. J. Potter. Dublin: M. H. Gill & Son. 1883.

"Short Sermons for Low Masses." By Fr. Schouppe. Translated by Rev. E. T. McGinley. New York: Benziger Bros. 1883.

"Handbook of the Irish Tramway Acts." By G. and H. G. Fottrell. Dublin: M. H. Gill & Son. 1883.

"Pilgrim Sorrow: a Cycle of Tales." By Queen Elizabeth of Roumania. Translated by Helen Zimmern. London: T. Fisher Unwin. 1884.

"Alice Riordan." By Mrs. J. Sadlier. Dublin: M. H. Gill & Son. 1884.

"The Life and Teaching of Jesus Christ." By N. Avancino, S.J. Two vols. London: Burns & Oates. 1883.

"Parish Priest's Manual." By J. Frassinitti. Translated by Rev. W. Hutch, D.D. London: Burns & Oates. 1883.

"Hints in Sickness." By Henry C. Burdett. London: K. Paul and Co. 1883.

"Young Ireland." By Sir C. Gavan Duffy. The Irish People's Edition. Dublin: M. H. Gill. 1884.

"The Christian Brothers." By Mrs. R. F. Wilson. London: Kegan Paul & Co. 1883.

"Continental Law of Landlord and Tenant, Past and Present." By Rev. T. Meagher, P.P. Dublin: M. H. Gill. 1883.

"History of the Church." By J. Chantrel. Translated by E. F. Vibart. Dublin: J. Duffy. 1883.

"The Knout: a Tale of Poland." Translated by Mrs. J. Sadlier. Dublin: M. H. Gill & Son. 1884.

Several Book Notices are unavoidably held over till April.

The "TABLET" Office,

27, WELLINGTON STREET, STRAND, W.C.

London, January, 1884.

Important Notice to all interested in the Work of Education.

The Permanent Enlargement of the TABLET, rendered necessary by the introduction of fresh features of Catholic interest, enabled its conductors to open a special department dealing with all such scholastic intelligence as may be useful or interesting to persons engaged in Education. Whether it be parents whose children are in the schoolroom or college, or managers and teachers busily occupied in elementary, secondary, or higher Education—all interested in the great work upon which the future of society must depend, will find that "**News from the Schools**" contains a most valuable, varied, and indispensable amount of information. Without some such record as is here aimed at, it is impossible to be abreast of the educational progress of the day.

The great favour and success which have hitherto attended the publication of this Department in the TABLET justify still greater pains being bestowed upon it.

One of the main objects of this Department will now be to bring home to the Catholic public all the latest and best Educational works and appliances. The Manager is therefore instructed to obtain the earliest information on all such matters from publishers and inventors.

Respecting the Advertisements of Schools and Colleges, experience has abundantly proved that it is only by thoroughly familiarizing the public through a high class medium, with the name, scope, and work of particular Institutions, that a school or college insensibly takes its place in the public mind, and definite results are obtained.

The terms for such Serial Advertisements which have been calculated on a reasonable basis, may be known on application to

JAMES DONOVAN, PUBLISHER.

PYRETIC SALINE,

EFFERVESCING AND TASTELESS;

Forming a most Invigorating, Vitalising and Refreshing Beverage. Gives instant relief in Headache, Sea or Bilious Sickness, Constipation, Indigestion, Lassitude, Low Spirits, Heartburn, Feverish Colds: prevents and quickly relieves or cures the worst form of Typhus, Scarlet, Jungle, and other Fevers; Prickly Heat, Smallpox, Measles, Eruptive or Skin Complaints, and various other altered conditions of the Blood.

The Testimony of Medical Gentlemen has been unqualified in praise of LAMPLOUGH'S PYRETIC SALINE, as possessing most important elements calculated to restore and maintain health with perfect vigour of body and mind.

Dr. Turley.—'I found it act as a specific, in my experience and family, in the worst form of Scarlet Fever, no other medicine being required.'

Dr. S. Gibbon (formerly Physician to the London Hospital).—'Its usefulness in the treatment of disease has long been confirmed by medical experience.'

Her Majesty's Representative, the Governor of Sierra Leone, in a letter of request for an additional supply of the Pyretic Saline, states:—'It is of great value, and I shall rejoice to hear it is in the hands of all Europeans visiting the tropics.'

Dr. Morgan.—'It furnishes the blood with its lost Saline constituents.

Dr. J. W. Dowsing.—'I used it in the treatment of Forty-two Cases of Yellow Fever, and I am happy to state I never lost a single case.'

Rawul Pindee, Punjaub, India, 28th March, 1871.—'Solely from the ascertained merits of your preparation in the Fever-stricken Districts by which we are surrounded, we firmly believe that the use of your Pyretic Saline will do more to prevent Fever than all the Quinine ever imported can cure.'

In Patent Glass-Stoppered Bottles, 2s. 6d., 4s. 6d., 11s., and 21s. each.

LAMPLOUGH'S CONCENTRATED LIME JUICE SYRUP,

A perfect luxury—forms, with the addition of Pyretic Saline, a most delicious and invigorating Beverage. In Patent Glass-Stoppered Bottles, at 2s. and 4s. 6d. each.

H. LAMPLOUGH, 113, HOLBORN HILL, LONDON, E.C.

OLDRIDGE'S

SIXTY YEARS' SUCCESS.—The best and only certain remedy ever discovered for preserving, strengthening, beautifying, or restoring the Hair, Whiskers, or Moustaches, and preventing them turning Grey. Sold in bottles, 3s. 6d., 6s., and 11s., by all chemists and perfumers, and at 22, Wellington Street, Strand, London, W.C. For Children's and Ladies' Hair it is most efficacious and unrivalled.

BALM OF COLUMBIA.

"Crescat et proficiat tam singulorum quam omnium, tam unius hominis quam totius Ecclesiae Intelligentia, Scientia, Sapientia."
Concil: Oecum: Vatican.

THE
DUBLIN REVIEW

THIRD SERIES.—No. XXII.

APRIL, 1884.

CONTENTS.

I. Dreizehnlinden. By Rev. W. Barry, D.D.
II. From Logic to God. By Rev. Thomas Harper, S.J.
III. The Life of St. Olaf. By Very Rev. T. E. Bridgett, C.SS.R.
IV. Adrian IV. and Ireland. By Rev. Sylvester Malone, M.R.I.A.
V. The Experiment of France. By W. S. Lilly.
VI. Christendom in Ideal and in Fact.
VII. The Revolution in the Soudan. By Miss E. M. Clerke.
VIII. The Dwellings of the Poor. By H. D. Harrod.
Encyclical of Pope Leo XIII. to the Bishops of France.
Science Notices.
Notices of Catholic Continental Periodicals.
Notices of Books.
Books of Devotion and Spiritual Reading.

LONDON: BURNS & OATES.
DUBLIN: M. H. GILL & SON.
NEW YORK: CATHOLIC PUBLICATION SOCIETY CO.
9, BARCLAY STREET.

Price Six Shillings.

All Advertisements for this Review should be sent to JAMES DONOVAN, Tablet Office, 27, Wellington Street, Strand, W.C.

JUST PUBLISHED.

Two Vols., demy 8vo, cloth, 21s.

ESSAYS ON THE PHILOSOPHY OF THEISM.
By the Late WILLIAM GEORGE WARD, Ph.D.
Edited, with an Introduction, by WILFRID WARD.

Demy 8vo, cloth, 21s.

A CATHOLIC DICTIONARY.
Containing some account of the Doctrine, Discipline, Rites, Ceremonies, Councils, and Religious Orders of the Catholic Church.
By WILLIAM E. ADDIS, AND THOMAS ARNOLD, M.A.

"This handsome volume fills a very real and obvious gap in ecclesiastical literature. . . . Making full allowance for the fact that it is not only avowedly denominational, but even controversial, it is written with commendable moderation."—Dr. LITTLEDALE in the *Academy*.

Second Edition, Enlarged, square 8vo, cloth, 5s.

FASTI APOSTOLICI.
A Chronological Survey of the Years between the Ascension of our Lord and the Martyrdom of SS. Peter and Paul.
By W. H. ANDERDON, S.J.

BY THE SAME AUTHOR.

EVENINGS WITH THE SAINTS.
Crown 8vo, cloth, 5s.

"The charm that renders these little narratives most delightful reading is, undoubtedly, the vivid colouring Father Anderdon has everywhere given to his subject. The subject itself was in no instance unfamiliar to us, and yet we have read the volume with all the interest we should have felt in listening to these thrilling tales for the first time."—*Tablet*.

London: KEGAN PAUL, TRENCH & CO.

ROWLANDS' ODONTO
Is the purest and most fragrant dentifrice ever made; it whitens the teeth, prevents decay, and gives a pleasing fragrance to the breath. All dentists will allow that neither washes nor pastes can possibly be as efficacious for polishing the teeth and keeping them sound and white as a pure and non-gritty tooth powder; such Rowlands' Odonto has always proved itself to be.

ROWLANDS' MACASSAR OIL
Has been known for the last 80 years as the best and safest preserver and beautifier of the hair; it contains no lead or mineral ingredients, and is especially adapted for the hair of children. It can now also be had in a golden colour as well as in the ordinary tint. Sold in usual four sizes. Ask any chemist, perfumer, or hairdresser for Rowlands' articles.

ERRY & CO.'S PATENT AUTOMATON PENCIL.

In bringing this ingenious novelty before the Public, the atentees desire to state their lief that it creates a new era in ncil-making, being the most portant improvement in pocket ncils since the introduction of e famous Perryian propelling d withdrawing motion, more an a quarter of a century ago.

The action is simple and ective; when not in use the int is concealed in the tube, us protecting the lead and ortening the pencil to a conmient size for the pocket. If quired for use, press on the d or seal, holding the pencil wnwards; to close, reverse e pencil, press against the seal th the forefinger.

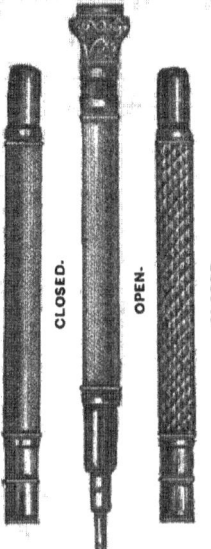

PRICES.

	EACH. £ s. d.
Aluminium Gold plain, or engine turned............	0 2 6
Aluminium Gold with seal or ball top............	0 4 0
Aluminium Gold, richly engraved............	0 5 0
Aluminium Gold, with mother-o'-pearl tube...	0 7 6
Hall-marked Silver, plain	0 6 0
Hall-marked Silver, richly engraved............	0 7 6
Hall-marked Silver, barleycorn pattern........	0 10 6
15ct. GOLD SERIES.	
Engine cut............	3 0 6
Barleycorn pattern........	4 10 0
18ct. GOLD SERIES.	
Engine cut............	3 15 0
Barleycorn pattern........	5 5 0
Pearl tube, mounted in 18ct. gold............	3 10 0

SOLD BY ALL STATIONERS & DEALERS IN FANCY GOODS.

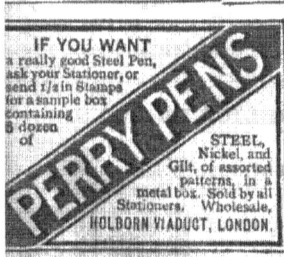

IF YOU WANT a really good Steel Pen, ask your Stationer, or send 1/3 in Stamps for a sample box containing 6 dozen of STEEL, Nickel, and Gilt, of assorted patterns, in a metal box. Sold by all Stationers. Wholesale, HOLBORN VIADUCT, LONDON.

PERRY & CO.'S Patent Nickel Silver Pens.

The great success and favour these Pens e finding with the public have induced the atentees to publish the following patterns; the l, of soft and quill-like action, the Nickel, J.

bold and fashionable writing; and the Cleotra, 1448, a hard Pen, suitable for Bookkeepers. per Box, or 3s. per gross. Sold by all Stationers.

PERRY & CO.'S Royal Aromatic Elastic Bands

The universal favour that these assorted boxes of Bands have met with from the public fully justifies us in stating that they are one of the most useful requisites for the counting-house or library. For domestic use they are invaluable to supersede string for jams, preserves, pickles, &c., being much more economical and convenient. Price 6d., 1s., 1s. 6d., and upwards, per Box.

Two good Blades highly finished, 5 inches long when open, 9d. each. Two good Blades, 4½ inches long when open, 1s. each. Two good Blades, Ivory Handle, 4½ inches long when open, 1s. 6d. each.

Wholesale:—18, 19 & 20, HOLBORN VIADUCT, LONDON, E.C.

COLLEGE OF BEAUCAMPS, PRÈS LILLE, FRANCE. Conducted by the Marist Brothers. Under the Patronage of his Eminence the Cardinal Archbishop of Cambrai. Established 1843. Pension, £26. No extras. For Prospectus, &c., apply to the Superior as above, or 9, Polygon, Clarendon Square, London, N.W.

ST. JOSEPH'S COLLEGE, WESTON HALL, near RUGBY.

This School is intended to afford to Catholic youth the advantages of a good education at a moderate pension (£7 per quarter, no extras). Since June, 1879, 22 Certificates have been gained at the Public Examinations. For particulars address the Principal.

CONVENT SCHOOL, MARK CROSS, TUNBRIDGE WELLS.

Conducted by the SISTERS of the HOLY CHILD JESUS from St. Leonards-on-Sea.

The pension is £18 per annum, inclusive terms.

Music, 15s. per quarter. Entrance Fee, £1 1s.

W. GARSTIN & SONS,

Catholic Undertakers,

5, WELBECK STREET, CAVENDISH SQUARE.

Funerals furnished agreeably to modern taste and requirements. Terms extremely moderate. Choice equipages and appointments. Monumental Works at Kensal Green, opposite All Souls' Cemetery. A Private Mortuary, also Reception Rooms can be engaged where removals from hotels, &c., are necessary.

INSTITUTION OF STE. CATHERINE.

Près Arras (Pas de Calais), France, at three hours express from Calais.

Under the Patronage of His Grandeur the Bishop of Arras.

The Course of Instruction is particularly calculated for boys destined to teaching, business, agriculture, finance, and different branches of administration.

Terms per annum. For boarders from 6 to 10, £35; 10 to 15, £40; 15 to 18, £50; Parlour Boarders £80.

ST. MARY'S LODGE, PEVENSEY ROAD, ST. LEONARD'S-ON-SEA.

PREPARATORY SCHOOL for the Sons of Gentlemen. Under the Patronage of the Right Rev. the Lord Bishop of Southwark. The educational course is specially designed to prepare the pupils for College. The healthy climate of St. Leonard's renders this school very desirable.

For Prospectus and further particulars apply to Miss Stevens, as above.

LIFE OF
ST. JOHN BAPTIST DE ROSSI.

Translated by LADY HERBERT.

INTRODUCTION

ON ECCLESIASTICAL TRAINING
AND
THE SACERDOTAL LIFE.
BY THE
BISHOP OF SALFORD.

Price Six Shillings.

THOS. RICHARDSON & SON, 23, KING EDWARD STREET, LONDON, E.C., and DERBY.

DELICATE BOYS.

ST. ALOYSIUS. Bournemouth. Established 1872. School Home and Sanitorium for Delicate boys requiring a mild dry climate, with liberal diet and attention. Apply to the Principal.

In two Vols., with Portrait, demy 8vo, price 30s.

Thomas à Kempis and the Brothers of Common Life. By Rev. S. KETTLEWELL, M.A.

"These volumes abound in suggestions so valuable, that they might be made the basis of lengthened articles. .... Mr. Kettlewell will, no doubt, feel that he has been fully rewarded, should impulses to fuller and more healthful and expansive Christian work be derived from it. With this hope in our hearts we close these valuable volumes, which are from first to last pervaded by the fine atmosphere of reverence and charity. As such we cordially recommend them to those who are desirous to draw water from such wells of refreshment and strength."—*The British Quarterly Review.*

Nine Hundred Millions of Heathens to be brought into the Church.

ST. JOSEPH'S
FOREIGN MISSIONARY COLLEGE
OF
THE SACRED HEART.
MILL HILL, N.W.

PLEASE help us to educate Priests for the Foreign Missions. No work lies nearer to the Heart of Our Lord.

NEW ILLUSTRATED CATHOLIC PERIODICAL.
PUBLISHED QUARTERLY.
ST. JOSEPH'S
FOREIGN MISSIONARY ADVOCATE.

It contains five beautiful and striking illustrations—16 pages. Price 1½d., by post 2d.
Order copies at once direct from the EDITOR, ST. JOSEPH'S COLLEGE, MILL HILL, LONDON, or through your bookseller.
Order as many copies as you can for distribution in Workhouses, Schools, Colleges, Convents, Households and Congregations.

ANNUAL SUBSCRIPTION FOR THE FOUR QUARTERS.

1 copy	6d.,	if post paid	8d.	per annum.
4 copies	2s.,	,,	2s. 4d.	,,
12 copies	6s.,	,,	7s.	,,
24 copies	12s.,	,,	14s.	,,

TERMS CASH. Enclose stamps or P.O.O. to the Rev. J. R. MADAN, ST. JOSEPH'S COLLEGE, MILL HILL, LONDON.

DR. J. COLLIS BROWNE'S CHLORODYNE.

ORIGINAL AND ONLY GENUINE.

COUGHS,
COLDS,
ASTHMA,
BRONCHITIS.

DR. J. COLLIS BROWNE'S CHLORODYNE.—This wonderful remedy was discovered by Dr. J. COLLIS BROWNE, and the word CHLORODYNE coined by him expressly to designate it. There never has been a remedy so vastly beneficial to suffering humanity, and it is a subject of deep concern to the public that they should not be imposed upon by having imitations pressed upon them on account of cheapness, and, as being the same thing. Dr. J. COLLIS BROWNE'S CHLORODYNE is a totally distinct thing from the spurious compounds called Chlorodyne, the use of which only ends in disappointment and failure.

DR. J. COLLIS BROWNE'S CHLORODYNE.—Vice Chancellor Sir W. PAGE WOOD, STATED PUBLICLY in Court that Dr. J. COLLIS BROWNE was UNDOUBTEDLY the INVENTOR of CHLORODYNE, that the whole story of the defendant was deliberately untrue, and he regretted to say it had been sworn to.—See *The Times*, July 13th, 1864.

DR. J. COLLIS BROWNE'S CHLORODYNE is a LIQUID MEDICINE which ASSUAGES PAIN of EVERY KIND, affords a calm, refreshing sleep WITHOUT HEADACHE, and INVIGORATES the NERVOUS SYSTEM when exhausted.

DR. J. COLLIS BROWNE'S CHLORODYNE is the GREAT SPECIFIC FOR CHOLERA, DYSENTERY, DIARRHŒA.

The GENERAL BOARD of HEALTH, London, REPORT that it ACTS as a CHARM, one dose generally sufficient.

Dr. GIBBON, Army Medical Staff, Calcutta, states: "TWO DOSES COMPLETELY CURED ME of DIARRHŒA."

DR. J. COLLIS BROWNE'S CHLORODYNE rapidly cuts short all attacks of EPILEPSY, SPASMS, COLIC, PALPITATION, HYSTERIA.

COUGHS, COLDS, &c.

From W. VESALIUS PETTIGREW, M.D., formerly Lecturer at St. George's Hospital, LONDON.

"I have no hesitation in stating that I have never met with any medicine so efficacious as an Anti-Spasmodic and Sedative. I have used it in Consumption, Asthma, Diarrhœa, and other diseases, and am perfectly satisfied with the results."

From W. C. WILKINSON, Esq. F.R.C.S., Spalding.

"I consider it invaluable in Phthisis and Spasmodic Cough; the benefit is very marked indeed."

DR. J. COLLIS BROWNE'S CHLORODYNE is the TRUE PALLIATIVE in NEURALGIA, GOUT, CANCER, TOOTHACHE, RHEUMATISM.

From Dr. B. J. BOULTON and Co., Horncastle.

"We have made pretty extensive use of Chlorodyne in our practice lately, and look upon it as an excellent direct Sedative and Anti-Spasmodic. It seems to allay pain and irritation in whatever organ, and from whatever cause. It induces a feeling of comfort and quietude not obtainable by any other remedy, and it seems to possess this great advantage over all other Sedatives, that it leaves no unpleasant aftereffects."

IMPORTANT CAUTION.
The IMMENSE SALE of this REMEDY has given rise to many UNSCRUPULOUS IMITATIONS.

N.B.—EVERY BOTTLE OF GENUINE CHLORODYNE BEARS on the GOVERNMENT STAMP the NAME of the INVENTOR,

DR. J. COLLIS BROWNE.

SOLD IN BOTTLES, 1s. 1½d., 2s. 9d., 4s. 6d., by all Chemists.

SOLE MANUFACTURER,
J. T. DAVENPORT, 33 GREAT RUSSELL STREET, W.C.

LITTLE LENTEN BOOKS.

THE PEOPLE'S MANUALS.

By the BISHOP OF SALFORD.

1d. each.
Who is St. Joseph?
On Spiritual Reading.
The Sanctification of Lent.

2d. each.
Love and Passion of Jesus Christ.
Holy Sacrifice of the Mass.
St. Peter, and his Mouth and Work, &c.

BURNS & OATES, AND ALL BOOKSELLERS.

PAX.

ST. AUGUSTINE'S BENEDICTINE COLLEGE, RAMSGATE, KENT.
Complete Collegiate Course. ST. PLACID'S HOUSE for the younger boys under an experienced Lady Matron.

URSULINE CONVENT (from Hanover), Crooms Hill, Greenwich, S.E. (on Blackheath). Select Boarding School for Daughters of Gentlemen. Inclusive terms from £45 per annum. Pupils prepared for Oxford and Cambridge Local Examinations.—See Prospectus and Letter from the late King of Hanover.

CONVENT OF NOTRE DAME DE SION, WORTHING, SUSSEX.

Under the Patronage of his Lordship the BISHOP OF SOUTHWARK.

A superior School for Young Ladies is conducted at this healthy watering-place by the Religious of Notre Dame de Sion. Large house and gardens attached.

For particulars apply to the Rev. Mother Superior, or to the Rev. J. Purdon, St. Mary of the Angels,

ST. BEDE'S COLLEGE.

ALEXANDRA PARK, MANCHESTER.

UNDER THE DIRECTION OF THE BISHOP OF SALFORD.

RECTOR:

Very Rev. MONSIGNOR CANON WRENNALL.

PREFECT OF STUDIES:

Rev. L. C. CASARTELLI, M.A.

This College is designed to prepare the sons of gentlemen directly for business and for various professions.

Applications for prospectus, terms, and admission to be made to the Rector. They may also be made direct to his Lord-

The Works of S. Francis De Sales,

TRANSLATED INTO THE ENGLISH LANGUAGE BY THE

Rev. H. B. MACKEY, O.S.B.,

UNDER THE DIRECTION AND PATRONAGE OF

THE RIGHT REV. DR. HEDLEY, O.S.B.,

Bishop of Newport and Menevia.

We propose, under the title "Library of S. Francis de Sales," to publish an English translation of the chief works of this great Doctor. This will form, as nearly as is demanded in the present state of ascetical literature in this country, an English "Complete Works" of the Saint.

The Bull, *Dives in Misericordiâ*, by which S. Francis was declared *Doctor Ecclestiæ*, supersedes all need of praise. And, indeed, his writings are in veneration with all the faithful. They are, however, with the exception of the *Introduction*, more highly venerated than fully or exactly known. Persons are familiar with quotations from them, which occur abundantly in most of the spiritual writers of the last three centuries. But we wish to make accessible to English readers the whole works from which the extracts are taken, the treasures of which these are but samples. S. Francis is called, and he is, the *Doctor of Devotion*. "Other Doctors," as Bourdaloue says, "have excelled in their kind, but to form the moral character of the faithful, and to establish in souls a solid piety, none have had the same gift as the Bishop of Geneva."

His two great controversial works, *The Controversies* and the *Standard of the Cross*, with his sermons and many of his shorter works, have never been translated at all. We have fair translations only of the *Introduction* and the *Conferences*.

The great mine of his letters may be said to have no shaft from English soil. An Anglican lady has translated a sixth part of them, or rather extracts from a sixth part of them. She uses her own spiritual light and her own authority. The most important and distinctive Catholic truths are calmly omitted or slurred over; what is worse, the doctrine is sometimes most erroneously stated. Even from a literary point of view the work is not recommendable, for though we willingly concede it the praise of being good English, it fails, most importantly, in being a faithful rendering of the Saint's language or expression of his thoughts. The meaning is not exactly given, the difficulties are baulked, the delicate shading and the individuality of style are almost obliterated.

The current English edition of *The Love of God* does not deserve to be called a translation. While giving pretty correctly the essential points of the Saint's doctrine, it continually mis-states things which are less absolutely important. Omissions are made, just at the translator's fancy, though of course these are not made, as in the Anglican *Letters*, on false and uncatholic grounds. It may be said that *all* the beauties are carefully left out, and for the rich and exquisitely natural language of the Saint, a style alternating between baldness and tedious paraphrase is substituted.

The First Volume, namely, *Letters to Persons in the World*, with *Introduction* by Dr. Hedley,—is now ready, and we shall be glad to receive orders for it, and for the forthcoming volumes of the series. Price of Volume I., 6s.

BURNS & OATES,
28, ORCHARD STREET, LONDON, W.

TRÜBNER AND CO.'S LIST.

THE WORKS OF THE TWO GREAT PESSIMISTS.

THE WORLD AS WILL AND IDEA. By ARTHUR SCHOPENHAUER. Translated from the German by R. B. HALDANE, M.A., and J. KEMP, M.A. Vol. I. Post 8vo, cloth, 18s.

THE PHILOSOPHY OF THE UNCONSCIOUS. By EDWARD VON HARTMANN. Speculative Results according to the Inductive Methods of Physical Science. Authorized Translation by W. C. COUPLAND, M.A. 3 vols. post 8vo. cloth. *[In a few days.*

NEW WORK BY MR. SAMUEL BUTLER.

SELECTIONS FROM HIS PREVIOUS WORKS. With Remarks on G. J. Romanes's recent Work, "Mental Evolution in Animals." Crown 8vo. cloth, 7s. 6d.

ESSAYS ON THE SACRED LANGUAGE, WRITINGS, AND RELIGION OF THE PARSIS. By MARTIN HAUG, Ph.D. late Professor of Sanskrit and Comparative Philology at the University of Munich. Third Edition. Edited and Enlarged by E. W. WEST, Ph.D. To which is also added a Biographical Memoir of the late Dr. HAUG, by Professor EVANS. Post 8vo. cloth, 16s.
"We have, in a concise and readable form, a history of the researches into the sacred writings and religion of the Parsis from the earliest times down to the present—a dissertation on the languages of the Parsi Scriptures, a translation of the Zend-Avesta, or the Scripture of the Parsis, and a dissertation on the Zoroastrian religion, with especial reference to its origin and development."—*Times.*

OUTLINES OF THE HISTORY OF RELIGION, TO THE SPREAD OF THE UNIVERSAL RELIGIONS. By Professor C. P. TIELE. Translated from the Dutch by J. ESTLIN CARPENTER, M.A., with the Author's assistance. Third Edition, post 8vo. cloth, 7s. 6d.
"Few books of its size contain the result of so much wide thinking, able and laborious study, or enable the reader to gain a better bird's-eye view of the latest results of the investigations into the religious history of nations."—*Scotsman.*

RELIGION IN CHINA; containing a Brief Account of the Three Religions of the Chinese, with Observations on the Prospects of Christian Conversion amongst the people. By JOSEPH EDKINS, D.D. Third Edition, post 8vo. cloth, 7s. 6d.
"Dr. Edkins has been most careful in noting the varied and often complex phases of opinion, so as to give an account of considerable value of the subject."—*Scotsman.*

A COMPREHENSIVE COMMENTARY TO THE QURAN. To which is prefixed Sale's Preliminary Discourse, with additional Notes and Emendations; together with a complete Index to the text, Preliminary Discourse, and Notes. By Rev. E. M. WHERRY, M.A., Lodiana. Vol. II. Post 8vo. cloth, 12s. 6d.

LANGUAGE AND THE STUDY OF LANGUAGE; Twelve Lectures on the Principles of Linguistic Science. By W. D. WHITNEY. Fourth Edition, crown 8vo. cloth, 10s. 6d.

ANGLO-SAXON AND OLD-ENGLISH VOCABULARIES. By THOS. WRIGHT, M.A., F.S.A., Hon. M.R.S.L. Second Edition. Edited and Collated by RICHARD PAUL WULCKER. 2 vols. demy 8vo. cloth, 28s.

SPANISH AND PORTUGUESE SOUTH AMERICA DURING THE COLONIAL PERIOD. By R. G. WATSON, Editor of "Murray's Handbook of Greece." 2 vols. post 8vo. with a Map, cloth, 21s.
"That portion of his book relating to Brazil, in particular, seems to us to cover ground which is new, or at least has not been fully occupied by any previous English writer."—*St. James's Gazette.*

CREEDS OF THE DAY; or, Collated Opinions of Reputable Thinkers. By HENRY COKE. In Three Series. 2 vols. demy 8vo. cloth, 21s.
(An Index and List of Contents of Vol. II. is now added, copies of which can be had by previous purchasers, gratis, on application.)
"It is not a light task which Mr. Coke has set before him—to present the theological outcome of Biblical study, modern science, and speculation in intelligible, clear, and simple form—yet it must be owned that he has carried out his purpose with no little intelligence and skill.........An accurate view of the opinions on the most important questions of the day can be got from these pages, which are full of information."—*Scotsman.*

MICROSCOPICAL MORPHOLOGY OF THE ANIMAL BODY IN HEALTH AND DISEASE. By C. HEITZMANN, M.D. Royal 8vo. cloth, 31s. 6d.

THE WAVE OF TRANSLATION, in relation to the Oceans of Water, Air, and Ether. By the late J. SCOTT RUSSELL, M.A., F.R.S., London and Edinburgh. 8vo. *[Nearly ready.*

MISCELLANEOUS ESSAYS. By the late W. R. GREG. Second Series. Crown 8vo. *[Nearly ready.*

ESOTERIC BUDDHISM. By A. P. SINNETT, Author of "The Occult World." Third Edition, crown 8vo. cloth, 7s. 6d.
"Mr. Sinnett delivers his gospel with much clearness and obvious good faith."—*Saturday Review.*

A SIMPLIFIED GRAMMAR OF THE OTTOMAN-TURKISH LANGUAGE. By J. W. REDHOUSE, M.R.A.S. Crown 8vo. cloth, 10s. 6d.

LONDON: TRÜBNER & CO., LUDGATE HILL.

DARLOW & CO.'S
IMPROVED PATENT MAGNETINE CURATIVE APPLIANCES

These Appliances are recommended and used by the Profession for the Cure of

Gout	Asthma	Chest Weakness	Sore Throat
Sciatica	Rheumatism	Spinal Affection	Heart Affections
Lumbago	Rheumatic Gout	Bronchitis	Liver Complaint
Neuralgia	Lung Affections	Winter Cough	General Debility

And every other form of Nervous and Rheumatic Affection.

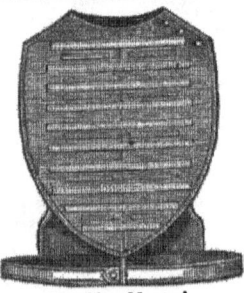

LUNG INVIGORATOR.

This is recommended in cases of incipient consumption, obstinate cough, weakness of the lungs, asthma, and bronchitis. It covers the entire surface of the lungs, back and front, and forms an excellent appliance as a Lung Protector, especially for winter use and night travelling.

The magnetic influence of this appliance, which penetrates the tubes and tissues of the Lungs, has in many cases given almost immediate relief, and effected rapid cures.

On the 3rd October, 1888, the Rev. J. CHARLESWORTH writes:—"Will you be good enough to forward one of your Chest Protectors? I have worn one during several winters with great benefit."

25s., 30s., 35s. each.

PAMPHLET] **DARLOW & CO.** [POST FREE
443, WEST STRAND, LONDON, W.C., 443.

B. HERDER, Publisher. Freiburg in Baden.

Just published, and to be had of

Messrs. BURNS & OATES, Publishers, 28, Orchard Street, London, W.

Manna quotidianum sacerdotum sive preces ante et post missae celebrationem cum brevibus meditationum punctis pro singulis anni diebus. Preces edidit, meditationum puncta composuit, appendicem adjecit *J. Schmitt.* Editio altera. Cum approb. revmi archiep. Friburg. 3 tomi in-12°:

Tomus *I.* Ab adventu usque ad Dominicam I. quadragesimae. (XII. 470 et LV. p.)
Tomus *II.* A Dom. I. quadrag. usque ad Dom. VIII. post Pentecosten. (XII. 574 et LV. p.)
Tomus *III.* A Dom. VIII. post Pentecosten usque ad Dom. I. adventus. (Sub prelo.)

Pretium uniuscuiusque tomi: in albis fcs. 3.75, religati fcs. 5.

THEOLOGY IN ALL ITS BRANCHES.

Biblical—Critical—Patristic—Dogmatic—Practical and Controversial—Church History and Miscellaneous Divinity of every description.

CATALOGUES FREE ON APPLICATION.

THOMAS BAKER, 20, GOSWELL ROAD, LONDON, E.C.

CONTENTS.

ART. I.—DREIZEHNLINDEN 245
    Frederick William Weber's youth in Saxony—He practises as a physician at Driburg and Lippspringe; writes occasional poems—The publication of "Dreizehnlinden" late in life makes him famous—Theme and outline of the poem: its epic character and general interest—The poet's contrast of the modern spirit with that of Catholic and monastic life in the past.

ART. II.—FROM LOGIC TO GOD 273
    The two wholes,—the logical whole or that of extension, and the metaphysical whole, or that of comprehension,—considered first from a conceptual, then from a metaphysical, point of view—In five different respects a philosophical antithesis between the two—Sir William Hamilton's additions to Logic tested by this antithesis—The genesis and objective value of these two wholes—Is the synthesis of the two possible? Conceptually and philosophically impossible; yet *somehow* possible, because the human intellect yearns for unity of science—The synthesis is theologically possible, because it exists objectively in God—In pantheistic forms of theology, no true synthesis; because one or other of the two wholes is suppressed—In Christian theology, the synthesis is objectively complete.

ART. III.—LIFE OF ST. OLAF 307
    Antiquity and historical value of the "Passio" recently edited by Mr. Metcalfe—Great excellence of his editorial work: a reservation as regards his judgment

on the Saint's character—A perplexing event in the Saint's life: an explanation offered—Mr. Hallam reckons saints' lives tedious: counter-statement illustrated from the "Passio" of St. Olaf.

ART. IV.—ADRIAN IV. AND IRELAND 316

The writer dissents from the view put forth in the "Analecta Juris Pontificii" and maintained in a previous article in this Review—Inherent probabilities of the long-accepted story of a Papal grant to Henry—Real state of Ireland in the twelfth century—The "Analecta's" objections to the grant of Adrian answered: interpolation in John of Salisbury's treatise: supposed Papal letter of refusal—Detailed reply to the seven reasons brought forward for denying that the letter of refusal applies to Spain.

ART. V.—THE EXPERIMENT OF FRANCE 344

Purpose of this article is to survey the condition and apparent prospects of public affairs in France and to consider the lesson thence derivable—Radical character of the Republic: growing deterioration of artisan and rural voters—Character of the Chamber of Deputies—Nothing left anywhere, even in the Army, to prevent the social dissolution desired by the Irreconcilables—Present state of affairs is the outcome and continuation of "The Revolution"—The social basis before the Revolution; attempted substitution of new foundation; social-geometric method adopted by the Revolutionists: their principle the sovereignty of the individual—Position of English people towards the democratic movement.

ART. VI.—CHRISTENDOM IN IDEAL AND IN FACT . ; . 366

Similar aim of St. Augustine's "De Civitate Dei" and Mr. Allies's "Formation of Christendom:" application of Christian philosophy to history—A glance at the work done by Mr. Allies's book: his study of heathen

man and the Christian method of regenerating him—
The task of regeneration too great for any but the
Church of God—The new method of education introduced by the Church: assaults of heresy and false
philosophy—Failure of Pagan philosophy—Mr. Allies's
work one of positive controversy, setting forth the truth
and results produced in the world by the kingdom of
truth—His study of "Church and State" shows divine
origin of power—Hope that he may be enabled to
complete his great undertaking.

ART. VII.—THE REVOLUTION IN THE SOUDAN . . . 392

Former and present Mahdis—Question of Soudan mainly
one of communications: difficulties of routes—Climate
and obstacle to foreign occupation of the Soudan—
Character of its soil and inhabitants—General Gordon's
popularity in the Soudan, his past work there—Zebehr
Rahama and the slave trade crushed by General
Gordon—The Catholic Missionaries of Kordofan: their
detention and treatment by the Mahdi—The future of
the Soudan.

ART. VIII.—THE DWELLINGS OF THE POOR 414

Difference between the Christian and the social estimate of the poor—Grotesqueness of recent awakening
in London: a passing excitement—Brief review of the
discussion of past few months—Difficulties in the way
of any proposed cure of the evil—Results of past efforts
to remedy the miseries of the Poor—Miss Octavia
Hill's system—Lord Salisbury's, Mr. Chamberlain's
and Sir Richard Cross's suggestions considered—
Writer's views as to immediate and temporary relief
and more lasting remedies.

ENCYCLICAL OF POPE LEO XIII. TO THE BISHOPS OF FRANCE . 438

SCIENCE NOTICES 444
Cometary Collisions—Recent Extraordinary Sunsets—
The Cholera Commission—Arctic Exploration—Three
Generations Contrasted.

Contents.

	PAGE
NOTICES OF CATHOLIC CONTINENTAL PERIODICALS	449

Katholik—Historisch-politische Blätter—Stimmen aus Maria Laach—Historisches Jahrbuch der Görres-Gesellschaft—La Civiltà Cattolica—Revue des Questions Historiques.

NOTICES OF BOOKS	458

Addis & Arnold's Catholic Dictionary—Ornsby's Memoirs of J. R. Hope-Scott—C. Rouhault de Fleury's La Messe—Allnatt's Cathedra Petri—Father Raymund Palmer's Obituary of Friars Preachers—The Bollandists for October—Mgr. Balan's Commenta Reformationis Lutheranæ—Lady Herbert's Life of Ven. Clement M. Hofbauer—Guerin's La Terre Sainte, second vol.—Macwalter's Life of Rosmini—Father Costa-Rosetti's Moral Philosophy—Father Formby's Familiar Introduction to Scriptures—Mrs. R. F. Wilson's The Christian Brothers—Father B. O'Reilly's True Men as we Need them—Repertorium Oratoris Sacri—Lanage's Text-book of Philosophy—Burke's Historical Portraits of Tudor Dynasty, Vol. IV.—Lives of some Sons of St. Dominic—Translation of Goebel's Parables of Jesus—Dean Burgon's Revision Revised—New English Dictionary on Historical Principles—More Leaves from Her Majesty's Journal—Beet's Commentary on Corinthians—Alice Riordan—The Castle of Roussillon—The Knout—Mary Queen of Scots—Ethelreda—Twitterings at Twilight—Coke's Creed of the Day.

BOOKS OF DEVOTION AND SPIRITUAL READING	491

THE DUBLIN REVIEW.

APRIL, 1884.

Art. I.—DREIZEHNLINDEN.

Dreizehnlinden. Von F. W. Weber. Sechszehnte Auflage. Paderborn: F. Schöningh. 1883.

FREDERICK WILLIAM WEBER, who is destined perhaps to be as celebrated as his namesake Karl Maria, the author of "Der Freischütz," was born December 26, 1813, in the village of Alshausen, called in the *Codex Traditionum Corbeiensium* Aldingeshus, in Westphalia. The place is no long way from a great heathen sanctuary of the Saxons, Driburg. It is the land of red earth and of the White Horse, as we may see by the standard let into the decorated binding of the volume before me, a white horse in a field gules, to speak with the heralds. But it does not appear that Weber had any arms of his own except the white horse. He came of a lowly stock. His mother's maiden name was Maria Anna Gehlen. His father, Johannes Weber, I understand, was a woodsman or ranger about Alshausen. The boy learnt to read in the village school, and showed a quick aspiring genius and a thirst for knowledge, which it was hard to satisfy in his circumstances. By-and-by he went to the higher school, or, as the Germans ludicrously term it, the Gymnasium, at Paderborn, which was not far. He grew to be a young man ere he left it; his genius was manifest, but he was still poor. In 1833, at the age of twenty, he made up his mind to seek a university education, and was drawn, by what accident I do not know, to Breslau, as the place where he might study languages (for which he had a remarkable gift) and get his diploma as a physician. So far had he risen above the village school and its narrow horizon. He set out, I read, with much courage and a slender knapsack. But the motto of the Percies, which is that of every brave man, lay deep in his heart. His "plenteous lack" of means did but rouse him the more effectually to cry "Espérance, one can always hope." He became a travelling student of the genuine old type, hardy, bold, and observant. Journeying to Breslau and back on foot, he learned to know the wide land of Germany as he never might have known it carried along at his ease in a first-class railway compartment; and I dare say that out of his Lehr and Wanderjahre he would have many a pleasant, many a touching, droll, and curious story to tell us, were we taken into his confidence.

In the "Gedichte," published in 1881, he writes manfully about the time which, in a poet's memory, is often the dearest because the most romantic, *le bon vieux temps, quand j'étais malheureux.* He is fond of metaphors taken from the smithy, as are all northern poets; he recurs with affection to the forge and the anvil; and so he calls his bit of autobiography *Am Amboss.* It tells how he was laid on the anvil himself and beaten into shape; and, again, how he stood by the roaring fire, and with hammer and grimy smith's tools did his own work, not flinching, until he had wrought something of use if not entirely beautiful. What he wrought has proved a beautiful thing indeed, more like the fine work of a goldsmith than the sturdily-fashioned armour of a son of Thor. But his was no silken bringing up, no sauntering over velvet grass under a shower of roses. He sings with a cheery heart :—

> Life caught me by the curling hair,
>   While yet a child, with grasp unkindly,
> The boy had many a stripe to bear,
> Was haled and driven here and there,
>   Nor walked in showers of rose-leaves blindly.

But, curly-headed boy or earnest man, he was made of the right Westphalian metal. He was that kind of iron which, the more it glows in the fire, and the more it is smitten by the thundering hammers of destiny, only acquires the temper of a finer steel. He was not suffered to look idly upon life as from a gilded balcony, where he might recline at ease and sleep when it suited him. Weber was down in the throng, seeing, hearing, feeling, laying up good store of that experience for want of which our so-called poetry is too often "windy rhetoric" or conceited prettiness, neither manly nor simple, because it has never been plunged in the steel-bath of reality. How is a man to recognize the heavenly powers of which, in "Wilhelm Meister," the harper sings, if he has not felt the might of them in his own life, their stern wisdom in dealing with him, and their tenderness, disguised sometimes as a catastrophe of self-love? Poverty, which aims at making an end of the

man, calls out his genius when it cannot prevail against him.
To be poor but a poet is not an unenviable lot, and Weber rose
up to do battle with the ills that pressed on him, and gained the
upper hand. He made a profession for himself; took his degree
in 1838, passing his examination at Berlin, and found time and
means, the happy man, to travel not only through his native land,
but in France and Italy:—

> Where fancy led, I roamed afar,
> Of dwarfs and giants many a story
> I learnt; then staid my wandering car,
> Refreshed and strong, where like a star
> Home drew me 'mid the mountains' glory.

The green hills that he had always known about Driburg—a
country full of Saxon legends and memories of old time—offered
him a home, but on condition of hard work. He practised as a
physician at Driburg, and afterwards at Lippspringe; two of
the innumerable watering-places which, as it is said, Providence
has bestowed on afflicted Germans, in consideration of their
primeval cookery. Herr Weber won a distinguished position
for himself; but, like Lydgate in "Middlemarch," he felt that to
write a treatise on the medical properties of spring-water, though
it were the Arminiusquelle itself, was not the goal he had aimed
at. Weber was a poet; as he swung his hammer at the anvil,
it grieved him that he was banished from the golden world of
song into which he had so gladly wandered. Still, he took the
wise advice that I remember seeing in an unpublished letter of
Mr. Browning's, addressed to a young man of poetical genius:
he resolved on no account to make poetry a profession. One
cannot be always eating honey: plain bread is best for everyday;
and so Weber thought:—

> What though in spring the swallow sang,
> And rose and lily bloomed in beauty,
> Though from far heights the sheep-bells rang,
> I chose instead the hammer's clang,
> And by the roaring fire I did my duty.

He could not indeed forget that he was a poet by the grace
of God, and that some day he must sing to the world what was
sounding in his inward ear:—

> Yet in my heart, as lulled to sleep,
> Lay wondrous harmonies a-dreaming;
> The enchanted wood did silence keep,
> Nor sunlight broke the darkness deep
> To clothe it in the springtide's glorious seeming.

Now and then he composed a short poem, but delayed publishing; many such, we are informed, have been lost through sheer neglect of the author—a true token of genius, which "pipes but as the linnet sings," because it has something to express, and not for gain or fame.

I have just quoted Lord Tennyson. In 1869, Weber, who has studied the Laureate very closely, turned "Enoch Arden" and "Aylmer's Field" into German, a feat of graceful translation which met with applause, and encouraged him to deal in like manner with "Maud." The latter was translated in 1874. He also put forth "Swedish songs, rendered into German, with accompanying music," in 1869. But none of these efforts made him known to the world at large. He was a man advanced in years, and apparently at the close of a long, honourable, but not exceptionally marked career, when, in 1878, at the age of sixty-five, he published "Dreizehnlinden." In three months he was famous; in three years eleven editions of his work had seen the light, and that which I have before me is the sixteenth. It has been received with discriminating, but hearty and growing admiration, by the whole press of Germany, without distinction of creed or politics; it has already passed into the hands of the etcher and engraver, and will, without doubt, receive still more ample and fitting comment from the Catholic painters of the Fatherland. And it has been recently translated into French. The question now is not whether F. W. Weber is the greatest of living Catholic poets among his countrymen, nor whether he has achieved a literary success of the first magnitude. His success is so marked, and the power in his poem so evident, that the question is whether he may take his place among the undying few whose works are not for to-day, but for the everlasting to-morrow of humanity. When we begin to ask ourselves whether a man is to be reckoned with Schiller, Goethe, and Heine, he must clearly have achieved something remarkable, even should it prove *not* to be *ære perennius*. I will endeavour, without biassing the reader's judgment, to set before him the leading points in this pleasant matter. That "Dreizehnlinden" is a work of which Germans, and especially German Catholics, may be proud, I hope will appear; that it will repay reading and delight the reader I can affirm, after studying it more than once or twice; and if, beyond these things, it has any promise of immortality, as we human mortals speak, why we shall receive the assurance with gratitude. It would be a fine thing did the red earth of Westphalia bring forth a modern Minnesinger, as *naïf*, picturesque, and truthful, as bold and earnest, as quaintly rhythmical and melodious, as the old singers upon harp and violin, whose ballads charm us even now in their rug---

But I cannot talk about the story until I have, rough unvarnished prose, acquainted my reader wit

This may be done most briefly, perhaps, in the manner following:—

The people of the White Horse, it is well known, came into Britain, tribe after tribe, in the fifth and sixth centuries. But enough of them stayed about the Elbe, the Saal, the Weser, Ems, and Lippe to make that country of hill and dale a stronghold of Saxondom, with its consecrated woods and rude widely-lying villages dedicated to the immemorial northern gods. It was the land of Wodan, Frigga, Balder, and the golden Aser; and whatever strange beliefs we may still read in the prose Edda, concerning the beginning and end of things— beliefs grotesque and beautiful, wild, unkempt, but on a great scale of power, and with wisdom hidden in their uncouthness —were firmly rooted in the hearts of the Saxons. But whilst they were wandering to and fro, driving and being driven, along the low sandy shores of the North Sea and the Baltic, their neighbours, the Franks, a miscellaneous breed— German, Gaulish, and Latin in uncertain proportions, but, like every mixed race, quick to see their advantage and to make the most of it—had seized upon the remnants of Roman Gaul, and, after infinite fightings and horrors of every kind, had welded them into a new nation. They received baptism, with their long-haired King Chlodovig, at the hands of St. Rémy, and set up the first Christian kingdom. By A.D. 800, so greatly had they succeeded, that their king, Charles the Great, did not hesitate to call himself Roman Emperor, and, as a Christian Augustus, to begin that strangely chequered but heroic period called the Middle Ages. Charles was not a pattern Christian himself; he had the vices of the Franks as well as their virtues; he could be horribly heartless and cruel when occasion was given him. But he believed in Christianity with his whole soul; and, whilst bent upon conquering the world, desired to preach the Gospel also. As Cardinal Newman has remarked, he preached, like Mohammed, at the head of an army; which is not the best way, whether we take into account means or end. Unfortunately, the Saxons were his nearest borderers; but they were not promising subjects for conversion. One may say of them, as Carlyle says of his heathen Preussen, "they figure to us as an inarticulate, heavy-footed, rather iracund people. Their knowledge of Christianity was trifling, their aversion to knowing anything of it was great."[*] Neither did they love the Franks; their ways and thoughts were utterly abhorrent to them. A genuine Saxon is honest, but rough; silent, and given to hiding his feelings, as if ashamed of them; slow to understand, not capable of wit, and seldom

---

[*] "Frederick the Great," vol. i. c. ii. p. 55.

humourous. Describing himself, the kind of adjective he prefers is *stoltz, stumm, ernst*, and the like. And he is all that; proud, silent, serious, rather awkward and ungainly in mind as in body. But he is likewise tender, melancholy, good-natured, dreamy, and, putting these into one word, sentimental. He is *wehmütig-ernst*, in short; not brilliant, but not superficial; hardly to be liked at a first glance, yet worthy of the most loyal trust and life-long friendship when you know him at the core. There is no dulness like Saxon dulness; but is there a kinder-hearted people? Now the Franks, who are so brilliant, graceful, and witty, have, as they know themselves, *les défauts de leurs qualités*, flaws so serious and fundamental that all their genius for war and social refinement will never make up what they are wanting in. The Franks, then, were not well-equipped for the work they took in hand; nor was Charles the Great received by the Saxons as a messenger from Heaven. They had a leader, Witikind, whose splendid courage overthrew the Franks with almost as utter a defeat as his ancestor, Arminius, inflicted on the Romans. For in this country of Westphalia we are never long out of sight of the battle in the Teutobergian Forest. It was at Süntel, in 782, that the Franks suffered this mighty disaster; but the Saxons, who loved fighting, but understood little of the art of war, broke up when the enemy was put to flight, and went home again. The day of revenge was at hand. Charles came down upon the rebellious and still heathen Germans with an overpowering army; his host laid the country in ashes; and, at Verden on the Aller, this new Augustus held a court of justice, in which he was judge and jury. Emulating his great Roman namesake (one remembers the story, *siste, tandem, carnifex*), he condemned 4,500 men to death, and spent the day in beheading them. Witikind, as is matter of history, became a Christian, and many Saxons followed his example; but there is no counting the thousands that perished ere the work was done. One of Charles the Great's famous Capitularia is that entitled, "De Partibus Saxoniæ seu Paderbrunnense," of the year 785. It was called, with justice, *Lex Crudelissima*; for it punished with death where other laws inflicted a fine. Of course, it was intended to root out heathenism, even at the risk of rooting out the heathen too. "He that henceforth," says the seventh Capitulary, "shall persist among the Saxon nation in remaining unbaptized, and shall neglect to come to baptism, determined to abide an heathen, shall die the death." Easier laws were made later on; but in this way did the too zealous and by no means ove ᴖʰ ⁻istian Franks convert their ruder brethren. At the bid᷄   )f St. Rémy, Clovis had burnt what he formerly adored;   cendants were now doing their best to burn what their   ours adored. The sacred oaks were cut down and cast into the fire; heathen rites and sacrifices were forbidden; the great sacrifice of the horse could be done only in remote and secret places. To the wise men and women, the Walrunas and the soothsayers, it appeared that the long foreboded twilight of the gods, Ragnarök, as the Eddas call it, was indeed at hand. The "White Christ" appeared to them like the leader of the sons of Muspel, that are to come riding up from the burning south on steeds of fire and to set the world in flame. In these dim consciences the new religion, cruel, triumphant, and irresistible, inspired a pathetic melancholy, such as Montezuma and his Mexicans felt when the rough soldier, Hernando Cortez, delivered the message of the Gospel by the cannon's mouth. They loved their wild gods—their Wodan of the blue cloak and floating grey hair, their Thor of the conquering hammer, and Balder the shining sun-god. But either the old deities were wroth with them, or their day had come; and the Fenris-wolf and the spectral snake, Midgard, that encompassed the world in its folds, must now be looked for, according to the prophecies. The old order, rude and elementary as it had been, but still an order they loved and lived by, a religion infinitely sacred to them, was passing away from these poor heathen folk. But where was the rainbow in their cloudy sky?

Charles the Great died, and confusion worse confounded broke out among his descendants. The woes of the House of Atreus, of the family of Augustus, were renewed in the crimes, follies, and disasters of the Carlovingian dynasty. To that dynasty of imbeciles or madmen the world owes a century and more of retarded civilization, the most shameful in some respects, and, to those that lived in it, assuredly the most hopeless that Christian Europe has known. Well does our poet speak of it as the Wolves' Age, foretold in the Wöluspa:—

> Unerhörtes ereignet sich, grosser Ehbruch,
> Beilalter, Schwertalter, wo Schilde krachen,
> Windszeit, Wolfszeit, eh' die Welt zerstürt.

It was like that last weird day of battle in the Morte d'Arthur:—

> Shocks, and the splintering spear, the hard mail hewn,
> Shield-breakings, and the clash of brands, the crash
> Of battle-axes on shattered helms, and shrieks,
> Moans of the dying, and voices of the dead.

Louis le Debonnair, the pious Emperor, and all his progeny of Lothairs, Charleses, and Louises, made the time hideous and Christianity a thing to despair of. But there was a gleam of light. Where the kings failed, another, a wholly different order of men, wielding mightier and stranger weapons, succeeded. These were the men of the Beatitudes, concerning whom it is written from of old: "How beautiful upon the mountains are the feet of them that preach glad tidings, glad tidings of peace!" and that other saying was fulfilled in them, "The meek shall inherit the earth." They were children of the North and the South, sons of Benedict and Columbanus, companions of the Saxon Winfred, whose name Pope Gregory II. changed to Boniface; and they lifted up the cross in that German land instead of the sword. *Domuit orbem non ferro sed ligno*, cries the great Pope Leo, a chant that should rise for ever on the Church's lips. Charles the Great might baptize; but it was the monks that made Christians and a new world in the endless forests and by the waste Northern sea. They were the true legions of the sun, riding on from Muspelheim, from the land of light, prosperously, because of meekness, and truth, and righteousness; and therefore none could withstand them, and the Walas and the Skalds bowed down at their coming and fled away into the frozen seas, betaking themselves to furthest Iceland, and carrying thither a now vanquished religion and mythology fallen into disrepute. Not "Charlemagne and all his chivalry," as the idle romances feigned, but monks and bishops converted the heathen peoples; taught them the Gospel in the morning and the classics of polished Rome in the evening; making them like human creatures again, as well as sons of the Church. This is the true and lasting glory of Monasticism, which neither its later history nor its downfall three hundred years ago, nor modern indifference and unbelief, can take away. The cities and, in great measure, the nations of Europe were created by monastic genius; and as regards Germany, she must have been in the sixteenth century what Russia was down to the eighteenth, but for the pastoral crook of bishop and abbot, which became to her a creating and civilizing sceptre.

Now this great epic theme is that of "Dreizehnlinden," a noble and inspiriting but by no means light one to handle worthily. For good reasons, the literary public has grown shy, this long while, of poetry professing to be epic. The very sound of "Leonidas, an Epic Poem," scares away whoever is not condemned to earn his bread—a bitter crust indeed—by reviewing indifferent verse. In England there have been great poets since the French Revolution; but not one of them, neither Wordsworth, nor Shelley, nor Byron, nor Lord Tennyson, nor Mr. Robert Browning, has ventured to announce that he had written, or was going to write, an epic. Mr. Morris Lewis, indeed, has published the "Epic of Hades;" but, in good sooth, the name is all he has given us. The only genuine epics of the last hundred years are Walter Scott's novels,

Carlyle's "French Revolution," and certain of George Eliot's stories; but these are in prose. Not otherwise is it in Germany. Since Klopstock—but who can read Klopstock?—its world-renowned poets have bestowed on their countrymen lyric, idyllic, and dramatic verse in abundance. But they seem to have felt that the epic is an impossible kind of poetry for moderns. I hasten to add, lest my reader should at this point forsake me and "Dreizehnlinden" together, that Weber's beautiful poem is not strictly an epic. Its form is not the conventional heroic metre, but something quite different, as free from monotony as from stiffness and the pedantic and false sublime. Of this in its place. I may illustrate the point I am insisting on—viz., how difficult a thing Weber has taken in hand, from another side. Little as the world cares for unfledged epic poetry, it does not care more for the romanticism which was rife half a century ago, when Uhland, Fouqué, Novalis, Brentano, and many another spirit of the air was thought to have stolen the secret of Nature like a new Prometheus. The gorgeous monasticism, with the legends of Arthurian chivalry they sang, has had its day. The sound of it rings false and hollow, except when it is ever so lightly touched, as in the beautiful faded tapestries which Lord Tennyson has called Idylls of the King. And, to crown all, the ninth century is a gaunt uncertain horror, known in detail only to professed antiquarians and mediævalists. These considerations apply almost as forcibly to the German reading public as to our own, and Weber, in treating his great subject, has not overlooked them.

For the moderns, despising epics and monasticism and the mediæval religion, have a keen sense of Nature, an insatiate desire of accurate historical description, and, of course, an undying interest in "the tale of love." Only such an interest can explain why the latest species of romance, the novel, thrives so lustily. More than one novel in verse has commanded striking success. Upon this line Weber goes out. His epic is, in form, a long but skilfully divided ballad in the metre of "Hiawatha," with this distinction (which appears to me an improvement), that the lines fall into rhyming staves, four lines to a stave, and the second and fourth rhyming. Again, instead of the epic motive and treatment, in which a nation moves along audibly, so to speak, with the hero, we find a domestic idyllic motive. "Dreizehnlinden," in short, is a versified novel with an historical background, and a significance much deeper than the individual interests engaged. Though the hero does stand for his nation, this is felt rather than expressed: the poem, taken literally, is the story of his conversion to a new creed. But the Westphalians, for whom Weber sings, understand it, as more than one critic declares, as the *Hohelied von Sachsen-noth und Sachsen-treue*, as a noble presentment in epic colours of what is grandest in Saxon history, the people's submission to the person and teaching of Christ, though brought to their knowledge by victorious and unchristian enemies. Thus freshly moulded, a chapter of the world's chronicle, even recited upon the harp, may gain some listeners.

The poem consists of twenty-five cantos, unequal in length; narrative at the beginning, but, as the story goes on, developing a lyrical thoughtfulness and inward sense. The prologue, which will remind the English reader of Longfellow by its ease, and the odours it brings with it of the forest, is very charming.*

> Days of Spring, how sweet to wander
> Through the garden God has planted,
> Round the pilgrim's hat a garland,
> Staff in hand, his heart undaunted!
>
> Cloudlets white are sailing o'er him,
> Sapphire streams around him flowing;
> In the fresh array of springtide
> Wooded heights and vales are glowing.
>
> Half-forgotten antique ballads,
> Memories dim, the mind are haunting;
> Blackbird, could I steal thy music,
> Woods should echo to my chanting.
>
> All the limes have lightly whispered,
> All the oaks at even muttered,
> When amid their leaves I listened
> To the secret speech they uttered;—
>
> What the merry brooks were babbling,
> As they down the hills came leaping,
> Restless youngsters, silent never,
> Wild and noisy, seldom sleeping;—
>
> All I heard the elves discoursing
> In the moonlight on the meadow:
> All the moss-grown runes have taught me,
> Graved on rocks and sunk in shadow;—
>
> This, and all I read in dusty
> Leathern volumes, or in olden
> Faded parchments, I would fashion
> Into song with echoes golden.

---

* It is not without compunction that I have essayed to represent Weber's German by these rude translations, which, however, keep fairly close, except in a half line here and there, to the original.

> Phantoms peering as from cloudland,
>   Murmur sounds of scathe and sobbing,
> Joy or pain in hearts long mouldered,
>   That in darksome days were throbbing.
>
> Look we back a thousand summers
>   They were men by Nethe dwelling;
> Christian, heathen, how they struggled,
>   How they wrought I would be telling.

The triumph of mildness, charity, and simple faith is to be depicted as it came to pass in a wild and savagely beautiful region, full of the sounds and scents of the woodland, vocal with reedy streams and the song of ouzel and nightingale in the echoing solitudes. Under the name of Dreizehnlinden (the thirteen Lindens) is shown us the monastery of Corbey, or Corvei, founded, no doubt in a grove of sacred limes, on the Weser, about 822. For the people clung to their old sanctuaries, their oaks and limes and beeches under which the Walas, or wise women, sat to give judgment, like Deborah in Israel. The Benedictine missionaries, sent to change the hearts of this stubborn race, were not unwilling that they should worship in the consecrated spots, if they would take Christ for their God instead of Thor with the iron hammer. So the forests remained what they had ever been; only the rites and the doctrines were changed. Neither blackbird nor nightingale felt less secure; their song was innocent and the monks loved it. But now-a-days, says our poet, with a touch of Aristophanic quaintness, the favourite oracle of men is Minerva's owl, the bird of wisdom, to which, being purblind, light is not nearly so comforting as darkness, and the only good in the trees of the forest is that they make excellent fuel for the steam-kettle. The owl recommends him to "make money," if he can, but not by singing; to its democratic sense, conversant chiefly with mechanics and the multiplication table, singing is the idlest use to which articulate speech can be put; and these yellow parchments out of the ninth century are fit for nothing but to make an indifferent blaze:—

> But the owl between doth mutter,
>   Rude and wild is all thy singing;
> Who hath seen thy Nethe's waters
>   From Apollo's fountain springing?
>
> Quit thy lyre and harp-string thrumming,
>   Guerdon slight have poets singing;
> Best of music, only music,
>   Is the golden's guinea's ringing.

> Thrust the old moth-eaten papers
>   In the coals where hottest glowing;
> Need is ours of coals and coal-dust,
>   Engine-steam our noblest showing.
>
> Count and weigh is all our wisdom;
>   Heavenly powers are wheel and lever,
> Wedge and hammer;—in the furnace
>   Fling thy wares, thou rhyming weaver.

But, in spite of hard prose and the rule of mediocrity, our singer holds that the spring of divine poesy can never be sealed in the heart of man. Earth and sky are beautiful as with the freshness of creation; Nature is all around us; and when we look away from the misery of the time, unchanging life and loveliness are there to welcome us. The blackbird has not sung his last song, nor the nightingale :—

> Aged and worn, with envy yellow,
>   Owl, despite thy rage and scorning,
> Roses yet for man will blossom
>   In the gardens of the morning.
>
> Yet for him the lily's whiteness,
>   And, in sacred caves and hidden
> Dells o' the wood, the dark-blue flower,
>   Dreaming, still will bloom unchidden.
>
> In the twilight-haunted coverts
>   All the air is softly thrilling,
> Music-laden; and the blackbird's
>   Melody there is no stilling.
>
> And the nightingale within me
>   E'er must sing of joy and sorrow,
> While the Spring to hearts and roses
>   Bids a sweet or sad good-morrow.

In this bold spirit the story begins. It is spring-time round the monastery; snows are melting and sunshine lies upon the broad hills. Among limes and fir-trees the steeple of a modest belfry rises, for the age of soaring Gothic and its etherial symbolism is not yet come. These sharp roofs and gables are of the early time when monasteries held only what could be rescued from the waste moor and the forest. Monks were set at building and drove the plough; some understood a little gardening, like the friar in "Romeo and Juliet" :—

> Oh, mickle is the powerful force that lies
> In herbs, and roots, and their true qualities.

Others taught the flaxen-headed children around them—"young bears," to whom Latin seemed a kind of magic, and the old heathen stories and the new Christian were but variations on a theme, the white Christ being not distinguishable to them from the white Balder, and elves and angels having a cousinly resemblance. Again, in that most charming of mediæval reminiscences, the Scriptorium, we see the monks patiently at work on their snowy parchments—men that saved, as it were, out of the deluge, an island here and there to bear witness that the vanished world of Humanism in Rome and Athens was exceeding beautiful.

Then we turn to Habichtshof, or Hawkscourt, where the old Saxon stock of the Falken had dwelt time out of mind, and we see Lord Elmar, last of his name and race, returning from the boar-hunt. He is a fine young fellow, stately, handsome, silent; as melancholy at present as one of Byron's heroes, though innocent of their haughty self-esteem and interesting crimes. He is living by himself in the old oaken house, adorned with armour, trophies of the chase, and the other necessary scene-painting so familiar to us in Sir Walter Scott. The description of it all is fresh and picturesque. Elmar's father perished in the war with Charles the Great; and the boy, under his mother's care, was taught by the old Druidess, Swanahild, and by Thiatgrim, Wodan's priest, to fear his ancestral gods and hate the Franks. By-and-by, in search of an honourable profession, he joined the Norman sea-robbers under Thorkell the Viking, and did deeds of prowess. But all this lies behind him; he has come home, careless of the love of Thoralil (little Thora), the Viking's sister, and himself in love with a Christian, the daughter of the old Frankish count of Bodinkthorpe, his near neighbour. He rescued Hildegunde from drowning when they were boy and girl; and now he is home again, and his mother dead, it will not surprise us if his thoughts often take him to Bodinkthorpe. An old harper comes from Thorkell with an account of Ragnar Lodbrog's descent on "Bretland;" how he was flung into the serpents' tower, and, dying, sang the famous lament, in which Berserk rage and hardihood are so boldly uttered. Will Elmar go on the expedition to revenge him? Why should he not, this gentlemanly young pirate-hermit, as tired of things present and past as any Manfred or Lara? His trusty majordomo, Diethelm, reasons with him however. What has he to do with the chief of Leire or the snakes that made a meal of him? Though to Elmar his people are fallen beyond redemption, and, as the wise say, men's brains are woven of cloud and their hearts of wind, still, the old man argues, he must stay for the healing of his nation:—

> Elmar, must and would are often
> Quite asunder; to the pleading
> Of thy heart be deaf, and follow
> What thy conscience clear is reading.

A good saying, and Elmar hearkens to it; but he knows not why he is kept. The story tells us. In rapid alternation, we listen to the monks at their matins, and witness the great sacrifice of the horse at the Opferstein. We learn who are the brethren assembled in choir, and make acquaintance with the stiff-necked but not ill-natured heathen, to whom only the secret glade and the hour of midnight are left wherein to do their holy rites. This was no joyous feast. Whilst the monks, with grave clear voices, were singing their *Laudate Dominum*, the heathen sat round the Opferstein like wolves aware of the huntsmen. Among these wolves Elmar has a place—sad, thoughtful, and in love with the Frankish maiden. He is soon to meet her again. The swallows are gathering on the eaves at Bodinkthorpe, ready to fly south. It is harvest-home; the last load has been brought in from the corn-fields, and Count Bodo, the king's lieutenant in these parts, has called his neighbours to the old Teutonic festival. Near her father stands Hildegunde, "eine Ros' im wilden Walde," gentle and womanly, ruling the Count's household, and beloved of all. The harvest song, a pretty, antique composition, is recited, and one of the lady's attendants, the too forward Aiga, interweaves with its general good wishes a significant hope that Elmar and Hildegunde may shortly bring joy to all. Here, as was to be anticipated, the trouble begins. Elmar has a rival. I have read somewhere in Diogenes Laertius, of a cynical philosopher who had reckoned up the number of tragic or comic situations conceivable, and found that they amounted, I think, to 237. Of these, I should say, about 217 may be developed from the pair of rivals in a love-story. But no love story would run smoothly for the reader, who is naturally more to be considered than the *dramatis personæ*, without such a pair. Elmar's rival is not a taking specimen of the baptized Frank. It is Gero, the Königsbote, or royal delegate extraordinary, sent to raise fresh taxes in Saxonland, as also to harry the heathen all he can. That Elmar has attended the forbidden sacrifice has come to his ears. A quarrel on this delicate subject breaks out at Count Bodo's table, and Elmar, altogether in the right, contrives, as young men will do, to put himself in the wrong, and to draw down on his innocent head the wrath of Hildegunde's father. He quits the house vowing he will never return. He is wandering in the wood hard by, musing on his wrongs, when flames shooting up into the midnight heavens tell him that the hall is on fire. Hastening to the spot, he rescues the aged Count

Bodo, and, the house being now a ruin, offers him shelter at Habichtshof; but, to his horror, he is accused by the "yellow-face," Gero, of being the incendiary. He turns away indignant and heart-broken. To consult his revered teacher, Swanahild, is the thought that occurs to him, and he goes to seek her. Of this grand figure a picture is given, as she sits awaiting him in the forest, clad in white woollen raiment, and an otter's fleece about her shoulders:—

> Lonely with her loyal mastiff,
>   With the old gods ever lonely;
> For in stormy skies and voices
>   Of the air she heard them only.
>
> Near the spring that wets the cavern
>   Motionless her station keeping,
> Like a statue grey and olden
>   O'er a tomb in semblance weeping,
>
> Forehead high and sad and wrinkled
>   On her left hand resting, dreaming,
> Right hand on the loyal mastiff's
>   Brow, so sate she, in her seeming
>
> Like a sombre ancient Norné,
>   From the well of wisdom slaking
> Thirst of wisdom, to her bosom
>   Secrets of the ages taking.

She is a fearsome woman, this ancient Swanahild, to whom neither earth, nor air, nor water has any mysteries. But the feeling that exalts her makes her gentle; she sees clearly into the young man's heart, reproaches and pities him. All things are going the way she would not; she has outlived three generations, but her time is near, and ere long she must abandon her woods and altars to the new revelation. This our poet tells with an exquisite natural pathos, and for the moment is admirably epic. Swanahild announces to Elmar that his fate is coming towards him on the dim paths of the forest, a warning speedily fulfilled. He makes a pilgrimage to the grey Donnereiche, the thunder-oak, and, as his religion bade him, without arms or defence. He prays, almost like a Christian, that he may do the right, though he should fulfil no desire of his heart, not even the nearest and dearest. Who is it that he invokes?—

> Art Thou Wodan, art Thou Donar?
>   Idle names and echoes hollow!
> Thou art Thou, b   ' our searching,
>   All and One,   none can follow.

His last word is resignation; as he utters it, a sharp sound, and a hiss like the serpent's, is heard through the undergrowth. An arrow strikes him; but he turns quickly, and seizes Gero, the would-be murderer, ere he can escape. He will not, however, take the life of one so vile; but Elmar's scorn pierces Gero like a knife, and the king's herald plans his revenge. He brings the Lord of Habichtshof before a Saxon jury, empanelled in the old fashion, but cowed and bewildered since the loss of freedom. The trial is held, and the only evidence forthcoming is that of Gero, who charges him not merely with firing Bodinkthorpe, but with attempting Gero's own life. A stormy contest ensues; Elmar has no kindred to be his compurgators or oath-men, and he is condemned. He loses house and lands, is put to the ban, and declared, in the straightforward language of the time, to be Vogelfrei, free as a bird for any one to aim at, unless he quits the land and goes into exile. Gero takes a firm grip of Hawks-court; and the young man, sending his sword and a ring to Hildegunde, sets out, wounded with the poisoned arrow, "auf den Helaweg," to the cold north and the sea-robbers. A clear, quaint picture shows him standing at the smithy, whilst Fulk is shoeing his steed for the road, and singing over it Donar's Hammersegen, the blessing of the hammer of Thor:—

> Trusty steed of truest mettle,
>   Irons four I bind upon thee,
> Shoes of iron firm and holdfast;
>   Donar's hammer bind them on thee!
>
> Make for wood and make for homestead,
>   Straightest pathways take thou ever,
> Keep thee far from aught unholy,
>   Charm of Donar quit thee never.
>
> Bear thy master towards his fortune,
>   This the charge I lay upon thee,
> Bear him hence, then bring him hither;
>   Such the charm of Donar on thee.

The Frankish maiden sees him depart from a distance, and sings her half melancholy half loving prayer that he may come back to reclaim his sword, when he is no longer a dishonoured knight. And the birds, in a parable of which our author is very fond, see him as he rides along the woodland ways, and argue as to what his fate shall be, the owl thinking him a fool for his pains, whether in regard to love or religion. The golden rule is to think with the strongest:—

> Wise it is with eyes wide open,
>   Always on the useful musing,

> Like the strong to think and reason
> Humbly one's own way refusing.

The sun had gone down, but its purple and crimson light was still thrown up on the massy clouds in the west. Along the mountain-tracks, as they bent towards the valley, might be heard, when the voice of the streams ceased for an instant, the slow sound of a horse's hoofs bearing a tired and wounded rider. The waters of the Weser glimmered in the twilight, and out of grey mist arose the steeple and the roofs of Dreizehnlinden, whilst the everlasting lamp before the altar gleamed through the falling dusk. And as he came to the gate of the monastery, Elmar sank down from his horse in a deadly swoon. So it was that the last of the heathen came to seek healing and consolation from the Christian monks.

These kindly-hearted, wise, and guileless men have been already made known to us in an earlier canto, too long to transcribe, but a faithful picture of those to whom the monastery opened its arms. They were not, on the whole, deep in mysticism or wonder-working. The poet has striven to tell us the good and the bad in them; or, I should rather say, the good and the not so good:—

> Now, my Song, thou shame-faced maiden,
>   Finger laid on forehead, duly
> Call thy mem'ries up, and tell me
>   Names of monks and singers truly.
>
> Tell me all, nor shrink if any
>   Word or deed seem less than saintly;
> Men thou namest, not archangels,
>   True men, not to praise them faintly.

There was Abbot Warin, son of Ekburt the Saxon Duke, brought up among the wolves of Ardennes, a warrior in his day, who had fought at famous Roncesvalles and heard the dying song of Roland. And Father Prior, a true born Saxon, tall and commanding, skilled in speech, endlessly fond of fighting and "writing runes with his sword," in younger days, on the breasts of Romans, Welsh, and Wends, but now grown quiet, and not given to wrath unless a stranger unwittingly makes mention of the shameful day of Verden. And Heribert, the pale-eyed philosopher, sunk in the study of Aristotle, as our author remarks, with a pardonable glance towards times somewhat later. Father Luthardt was a different man: to him the office fell of catering for the monastery, and among his distractions at Lauds was the thought of to-morrow's hunting or bird-snaring. "Springes to catch woodcocks" came often in his prayers, good man as he was and meant to be. And Father Ivo, with his ugly face, had come into the cloister as much out of shame as piety; a good carpenter, whose adze and chisel might win pardon for his indifferent Latinity, which Raban the schoolmaster by no means admired. Father Bernhard was more like a saint, pining for the gleaming palaces of Heaven, chanting early and late, "Oh, that I had the wings of a dove; I would fly away and be at rest." And there were Sigeward the sweet singer, and Hatto the artist in words and colours, and Biso, the fine transcriber of Tacitus, and Beda from the Cheviots, the skilled physician—a world of characters and capacities inside those narrow walls. But there were others, too, among the lay-brethren, not all quiet and heavenly-minded: this one or that a little unruly, sharp in speech and stroke, fond of his jest and not too fond of the fasting-fare apportioned him, good at laughing, at asking riddles, and the rough horseplay of the time; honest Christians, but with a lining of heathen to their Benedictine habit. Natural, inevitable, but in the sequel dangerous, when the strong hand of men like Abbot Warin and Father Prior no longer ruled them! "Cosi è fatto l'uomo!" used an old Roman master of mine to say, sighingly. Too true, alas! But any seed of evil at Dreizehnlinden had as yet borne little fruit. And Elmar was now to learn how beautiful a thing is Christian charity. The monks tended him through his fever, and Father Prior told him the story of Bethlehem, Nazareth, and Calvary. This was the fate which Swanahild had seen advancing towards him through the forest—to learn the new lesson of humanity in Christ, and behold the Master and Friend in that inward vision which we call Faith.

This second part of the poem is, to my mind, of a more delicate and rare texture than the first. It is lyrical in motive, and, on the whole, may be compared, for manner and finished treatment, with Tennyson's "In Memoriam." Elmar's fever-dreams, Hildegunde's uncertain but loving thoughts, are expressed in brief stanzas, often clear and beautiful, though more tender than strong. I would not assert that Weber has such a depth of meditation in his "short swallow-flights of song" as our philosophic Laureate. But he has something of a like skill in painting thought; and his words are at once refined and genuine, natural and yet choice, as are the words of so many stanzas of "In Memoriam." The wild northern sea, as it appears in Elmar's dreams, is reflected with the distinctness of reality. For example, in the vision of the ship of ghosts, that oldest Märchen of the Norse sailors, known to us in later times as the Flying Dutchman:—

East south east! The seething billows
    England's cliffs of chalk discover.
Asbiörn, helm a-port, in darkness
    Else we sink and all is over.

Ship a-hoy! How strange a craft there,
    Stem and stern like midnight; dimly
On the deck, like wind-blown vapours,
    Phantom sailors hovering grimly.

Every shroud and every sailcloth
    On the masts o' the vessel, gleaming
Silver-grey like finest cobweb,—
    Through them starlight faintly streaming.

Ha, the ship of Ghosts, that melting
    Into air, is gone, yet chaseth
O'er the Sound till dreadful twilight
    Wodan and his gods effaceth.

Restless till the doom of twilight,
    From the Belt to Thames's river,
Night by night from Tweed to Skagen,
    It must race and chase for ever.

And the following, which I venture to add, seems to me one of the truest bits of sea-experience rendered in verse—the feeling of coming into port after a long storm. Elmar has just been dreaming of the river-fight in which his Norsemen, after going up stream, have beaten and cut to pieces the Frankish enemy. They have put to sea again, and are now coming in, laden with booty, Elmar lying on deck, wounded:—

Thou good ship! For winds and waters
    Round thy keel were ne'er dismaying;
Northern oak and rudest storm-wind
    Comrade-like their strength displaying.

Sigwald, gently steer; o'er ocean
    Fallen asleep the vessel riding,
'Neath a sky all flushed with sunset,
    Into harbour safe is gliding.

Gently steer, our good ship *Dragon*
    Knows the Sound; no word; for weary,
In the sea-rocked cradle sleeping,
    I would rest from journeys dreary.

Wake me not; I yield to slumber
    Now the hard day's done; and riding
'Neath a sky all flushed with sunset,
    Into port our ship is gliding.

Another exquisite page is the sea on fire, and the water-flowers blooming in the radiance, a confusion in the sleeper's brain, transferring the eventful fire at Bodinkthorpe to the realm of waters. The cloud-picture of Walhalla, and the apparition of Hildegunde in the sunset at sea, are equally distinct and powerful. But I might quote the whole of this book of dreams, if I were minded to dwell on its beauties. I must pass by many things on which it would be pleasant to linger: the cross in the forest, the visit of Father Beda to the Druidess, and her gentle answer to him, sending healing drugs to Elmar; the spinning and weaving in olden time; and the legend of the wild huntsman in the clouds, on which last a volume of curious lore might be expended. I come to "Des Prior's Lehrsprüche," or, as it may be called, the Prior's catechizing. Elmar is now strong enough to listen to the message of peace. Here again is a sort of Christian "In Memoriam," an earnest, faithful exposition of what is to be held concerning the beginning and the end of things, the need of humanity, the dimness of knowledge, the over-ruling Providence:—

> Denn unsterblich ist das Gute,
> Und der Sieg muss Gottes bleiben.

The Prior speaks of Charles the Great, and how his worldly aims proved almost fatal to the creed which this "Apostle in harness" desired to propagate. The broad mantle of the Church has been made to cover many an unhallowed thing. But Christianity remains, and the Carlovingians are passed away. The soul cannot find her questions answered in politics. We must turn to the Great King:—

> Of the Child of Peace, the Holy,
> To the garden of earth descending
> Out of Heaven, have I told thee,
> God and man in union blending,—
>
> From the sunny heights of Heaven,
> Son of God in flesh revealing
> All the promise, and his prophets'
> Message with fulfilment sealing.

And if Elmar will learn the good tidings of the Redeemer only from his own people, there is a sweet singer that has uttered them even in his native tongue, the framer of that great Epic, the Heliand:—

> This, whereof my speech is roughest
> Rind of prose to thee was token,
> Hath another, graced with ric
> Gift of poesy, outspoken.

Elmar, of thy kin the singer,
  Not in faint and foreign rhyming,
In our mother-speech hath uttered
  Music like melodious chiming.

Hark, thou seemest in the greenest
  Woods of thine own land to wander,
On the mighty boughs above thee,
  On the soaring stems to ponder.

Strange, at first, and unacquainted,
  Ringeth in thine ears the singing
Of the birds, yet homelike gladness
  To thy heart their song is bringing.

And amazed thou hear'st the whisp'ring
  And the singing softly blending
To the praise of God the Highest;
  Sacred anthem without ending.

But the Prior has done his part, and grace alone can do the rest:—

Shall the eye of man behold Him,
  Portals wide must ope in Heaven,
And a ray from out His brightness
  To the darkened heart be given.

Whilst Elmar is hesitating, Hildegunde is praying. Her tender poetical musings, her hopes and fears, are rendered with charming truthfulness. The stanzas on the wild swans, the root called Forgetfulness, the white water-rose, are not inferior in lightness of touch and subtle indication of feeling to Elmar's dreams. Here is Hildegunde's meditation as the swans move over the great waters:—

Sandy beach, and swans are bathing,
  White swan-maidens, southward flying
Ere the North is white with winter,
  Ere the yellow leaves are dying.

Snowy swans or milk-white maidens,
  Pleasant things to you are given,
Through the waters smoothly gliding,
  Soaring in the clouds of Heaven.

Could I don your snowy raiment,
  In the clouds I too would fling me;
Him to find that I am seeking,
  O'er the lands I too would wing me.

> Him to find that I am seeking,
>   I would roam your wide dominions
> Only once to greet him kindly,
>   Then, at home, fold my sad pinions.

The maiden, for all her shy affection, is proud of the untamed falcon, that would not submit to be bound or hooded. He has flown forth into the clouds, bleeding, perhaps to death. She likens herself to the midnight flower that blooms alone, forsaken, or not bold enough to court the sunshine :—

> Lost in moss and fern, the lakelet
>   Calm beneath the moon is sleeping :
> Midnight; and the rose o' the waters
>   Silently her watch is keeping.
>
> Not a voice and not a whisper,
>   Beech and birch in dreams are swaying
> Softly, lest the charmèd secret
>   Of the woods they be betraying.
>
> Nenuphar, the pale flower-maiden,
>   In the day herself concealing,
> Only to the stars above her
>   Will her sad thoughts be revealing,—
>
> Only to the stars so distant,
>   Cold and calm and dim discover
> All her love; thou pale flower-maiden,
>   Hast thou, too, a wandering lover?

She takes the five-petalled wild rose, and, in an artless lament of the true ballad kind, writes on each leaf words of love and pity, only not hope; the last petal must remain a blank :—

> Let the winds find out a meaning
>   In the runes, and blow them whither
> E'en they list; the silent kingdoms
>   Never sent a herald hither.

But, though she has no news of him, Elmar lives. In the cloister garden he wanders to and fro, considering the old religion he is unconsciously quitting, and the new that has taken more hold of him than he believes. He is struggling still with "the worm of heathenism," an unclean dragon, whose enchantments only an act of determined faith can overcome. The temptation assails him that there are no gods above, or only envious unfeeling gods; that the next world is but night, a darkness void of reality as of promise. The heroes were happy that believed and wrought great deeds; but he is not of them. He must go from the cloister; but whither can he go? And he thinks of that mysterious Wineland which the Norsemen, sailing over unexplored waters, have lighted upon, a fresh world where he might live forgetting and forgotten. But his doubts are dying all the while. Hildegunde, venturing to the cave of the Druidess, learns from Swanahild how things have fallen out, and how they are soon to end: a fine scene, in which the noble nature of the heathen woman, and her despairing belief in the fast-sinking gods of Asgard, touches our feeling nearly. The Northern stars are setting. She knows that Elmar will become a Christian; and, indeed, he has learnt the two great lessons, that not a sparrow falls without the Father in Heaven, and that we must forgive our enemies. The hour comes. He strives to leave Dreizehnlinden, but, conquered by the monks' charity and wisdom, consents to take up the new way, and we see him in the convent chapel, bowed, after the solemn scene of his baptism, in joy and thankfulness, the airs of spring breathing round him, sunshine upon his golden locks and in his heart. The storm-tossed Elmar has found peace at the feet of the white Christ. Swanahild disappears and is heard of no more. It remains to clear Elmar of the crimes imputed to him, to punish Gero, and to let the curtain fall upon bride and bridegroom united in faith as in affection. This, which I may call the "machinery" or "business" of the poem, is done indifferently well. For my part, I regret that it was needed; and though Hildegunde is a beautiful character, not without touches of individuality and life, I think the story would have gained in vividness and power had less been made of the purely romantic element. The modern Westphalian is no doubt sentimental; he dwells, as a friend once expressed it writing from Hagen, "in the land of Ach and Weh;" but, when I read those early ballads of the Völsungs and the Niblungs, I find a sort of noble lovemaking which is simplicity itself. Elmar is a modern young gentleman, very amiable and brave, but far removed from the rudeness of the ninth century. However, no one can be sorry to have read such a pretty piece of lover's musing as the lines beginning "Wind, du unsichtbarer Wandrer," or those others, "Wunderlich, ein altes Märchen," whilst one of the most striking reminiscences of Tennyson is that among Hildegunde's *Suspiria Amantis*, "Wenig sprach er stets, und einsam," a really perfect thing, so simple and sweet. And so all's well that ends well.

The poet modestly concludes that he has woven rhyme with rhyme, not for the multitude, nor as a singer on the great highway, but for one here and there that is willing to turn from the throng and listen to the far-off echoes, as a man may turn to some lonely little chapel in the wood, where he will find a rustic altar, and withered garlands waving in the breeze. But he takes leave in the good old fashion, as the monk did when he had written *Laus Deo* at the bottom of his manuscript, asking an *Ave* from the reader:—

> In your orisons remember
> Him that sang this antique story;
> Ends the Song of Dreizehnlinden,
> Grant us, Lord, thy heavenly glory.

And now the question arises, what has the poem done for us? One thing that it has done is straightway apparent; it has made us acquainted with a man of worth, "der mit sich und der Welt im Klapen ist," to use the admirable words of F. Kreiten. The spirit of its author speaks in every line of "Dreizehnlinden," clear, courageous, thoughtful, and modest, with a true feeling for everything that God has made. There is much pithy wisdom, much gentleness, and a kind of smiling humour in this poem; a knowledge of life that has not turned to cynicism, despair, or unbelief; a stedfast looking for truth which delivers the poet from that common vice—I mean the resolution to see nothing in history that is not to the credit of his own party. Herr Weber, without sacrificing one iota of his faith, has attained to an objective clearness which does really enable him to construe the mind of heathen and unbeliever in a credible shape. Swanahild is the most life-like of the characters he has drawn, the most powerful and distinct, but why? Because he has that profound confidence in truth which prompts him to let the facts alone; not to tamper with them, to let them speak for themselves. In like manner, Elmar's waverings between old and new are pictured with courageous fidelity; and thus we have, as I said, another "In Memoriam," not so clearly a work of genius as Tennyson's, but helpful because it is true. Such Christian faith betokens an enlarged and observant spirit, and has the power that comes of all just insight: it has grappled with a problem of life and solved it. This is a wise faith, from contact with which through so many pages we rise up strengthened. There is not a line of scepticism, nor a word of fanaticism in "Dreizehnlinden;" for Catholic poets it may, and will, in this respect, furnish the best of models.

As to the poem itself. It has been compared, for originality and power, with Scheffel's "Trompeter von Säckingen;" and in subject and beauty of colouring with Oscar von Redwitz's "Amaranth," whilst it contrasts strongly, according to the German critics, with the same writer's "Odilo." But these are poems of which the English reader has probably heard little or nothing. We must consider it rather on its own merits. Of these the most incontestable is undoubtedly its musical, flowing verse. In translation this can at the most be imitated, not really given to a foreign ear, and in a differently moulded speech. The ballad form, continued through hundreds of pages, is handled with astonishing ease, lightness, and variety. "Dreizehnlinden" is a kind of Nibelungenlied in twisted silk instead of coarse yarn; it is the ballad refined to the utmost, yet keeping an unaffected simplicity, a strength of sentiment and diction which might have seemed incompatible with so constant a use of the file. I am not going to compare it with Goethe's ballads; they, as Mr. Swinburne would say, are "in the strictest use of the term, divine." They are certainly fascinating, and the simple depth of feeling in them is like the very spirit of music. I will not say any such thing of Weber's stanzas. But these, too, have music and life in them. Not one of them but might be sung as it is written; and all true poetry, says Carlyle, has a kind of lilt in it that carries you along. The clearness, the natural yet not common words, the wealth and novelty of the rhymes, the characteristic alliteration, the absence of superfluous particles, the swift and finished utterance, all have had their meed of praise; and not a syllable more than they deserve. One knows that among the fine qualities of German such as these are seldom enumerated. But "Dreizehnlinden" has them in a rare degree.

Again, the truth of its natural descriptions—easy enough in a language that has lent itself so often to Pantheism—this I must count an excellent thing. Half the poem is a tale of stream and forest, of the change of seasons, the moods of the sky by day and night, the song of birds, the sea, and all the mystery of the painted veil of Nature. The effect is much increased by giving these things over again in the wondrous prismatic lens of the northern mythology; though here, I think, the poet's fine-spun dialect takes from the greatness, the rugged irregular vastness of the myths, which was, as we may see in the Eddas, a true reflection of the natural scenery wherein they grew. But an artist will find many landscapes in the poem, briefly and feelingly touched off. All this I gladly admit.

But I cannot altogether assent, as I should wish, to the view that "Dreizehnlinden" is the greatest achievement in German poetry since Goethe. It is, indeed, so far as I know, much the greatest thing that a *Catholic* poet has written of late years. But I am afraid the world will judge, and judge rightly, that there is enough genius in Heine's "Buch der Lieder," in his Hebrew melodies, and later ballads, to furnish forth many Dreizehnlindens. Herr Weber is an excellent craftsman in verse; he has an eye for Nature, and can render back something of the glamour in which a poet walks through this world; he does, in more than one stanza, lift up the reader's heart as well as charm his ear. But his genius, on the whole, is subdued and quiet, not of that supreme quality which "makes the undying music of the world." Perhaps he is best in pithy proverbial sayings, with a ring of the old world about them. These, however, make a wise, not a great poet. That he does not aim at dramatic effect shows right judgment in him, but indicates the limits of his genius, which, I repeat, seems to me real though not supreme. Again, he has been compared with Brentano, but contrasted also as less of a mystic and romancer. This seems true enough. The Romanticism which Brentano loved is not of the ninth century, nor Westphalian; and Weber has done well to keep clear of it as a thing outworn. His *naïveté*, wherever it appears, is very taking. One could wish there were even a closer resemblance to the fine unconsciousness of the old ballad, in which the rhapsodist came wandering again amongst mankind, and sang of gods and heroes by a divine thrusting on, because the song was in him and must come out. But I consider, and this is my chief criticism, that Herr Weber, in giving to the element of love in his poem the dimensions which it commonly takes in the prose novel, has done violence to the nature of epic poetry. I agree with a careful critic, Herr K. Leimbach, that the author did not propose to write an epic poem. So that we must judge his work according to its kind—namely, as a metrical romance. Nevertheless, the continuous ballad is essentially epic; and in an epic love has never the chief part; it must be there what it is in life taken as a whole, an undercurrent or an episode. Its minute analysis and exposition is too delicate, I had almost said, too flimsy for epic; the more so when such love brings with it no disaster. A tragedy of love may be infinitely moving; but the heart of an epic is life viewed on a national or universal scale; and for this the tale of love is, in a word, too subjective, too individual.

Now the "fable," as the critics say, of "Dreizehnlinden," is cast in this too narrow mould; Elmar loses rank and privilege as the consequence of a petty and not very passionate rivalry. If he represents his nation it is almost by accident, and never on a wide scene of action. Thus the interest is dwarfed almost to that of a domestic novel, and the Saxon Epic is shorn of its fair proportions.

From another point of view, we may look on it as a kind of "Past and Present," in which, like Mr. Carlyle, the author draws a comparison between the modern and the Christian spirit. For the interlude of "The Birds" is a running comment on industrialism, democracy, and the new kind   war against

Nature undertaken by our steam engine and board-school civilization. Mr. Ruskin would find an echo of his strong sayings in more than one verse of " Dreizehnlinden ;" although Herr Weber, less fired with apostolic zeal, or of a more restrained temper, is playful rather than fierce, and proposes no general abolition of machinery or of forces working by heat. Neither does he preach that a return to monasticism on the widest scale is expedient, even were it possible. His feelings are to be conjectured from the tenor of the story. It is a true and powerful description of what the monks accomplished in the ninth century. To the question, what could they accomplish in the nineteenth, it returns no direct answer.

It is well, indeed, to be reminded of that past which he sings. The monastery bells chiming to us over wide waters, and out of a distant age, cannot but stir, as with inherited memories, the heart of the modern world. All alike, Catholics and Protestants, we are children of the Middle Ages, whether we recognize our descent or disown it scornfully. And the most effective force in the Middle Ages was monasticism in its thousand shapes. But for Gregory and Benedict and Columbanus and Bernard there had been no mediæval Christendom. But for Francis and Dominic, Norbert and Vincent Ferrer, and the crowd that followed them into the wilderness, mediæval Christendom must have broken up in the thirteenth or the fourteenth century, or, at any rate, long before the trumpet of dissolution rang through Europe in the days of Luther. With the ruin of monasticism, whether in Germany, France, or Italy, the Christian creed has received a shock which its enemies judge to be fatal. For there is no living Christianity where the Beatitudes are not held as the foundation of it, the essence and sum of its teaching. But monasticism, in its idea, is nothing else than a life according to the Beatitudes, of outward humiliation, self-denial, and inward peace. *Beati pauperes, lugentes, mites, pacifici, mundo corde; beati qui persecutionem patiuntur*—who can meditate on these things, and consider a piety so tender-hearted, so contrite, bathed in tears of compunction, and set upon communion with God and the brethren in Christ, without perceiving that when multitudes have taken this way they will build them houses of penance and silent prayer, and retreat from the world which only by solitary thinking and heroic charitable living can, in any degree, be made better? Monasticism, formal and recognized, is no longer a European institution; its ruins cover all lands, beautiful in decay, strangely charming us as we gaze upon them and people their deserted cloisters with men who have bequeathed the past

partly because of its own excesses, more, perhaps, because new forces were growing up, and the world which had given it political dominion was now minded to take that dominion and bestow it elsewhere, it fell; and, truly we may say, great was the fall thereof. But, when we look round the Europe of to-day, can we help inquiring whether its fall was not a disaster to the world? What has taken its mediating place between rich and poor? Where is now the ideal of noble beneficent poverty? A feudal aristocracy struggling to maintain itself, a wealthy middle class, with no religion or some poor superstitious formalism to consecrate the worship of Mammon, an adventurous tribe of capitalists, Hebrew, Greek, or Anglo-Saxon, as the case may be, and below these the multitude whose labour is all their capital, who have needs and greeds not less imperious than those of the men set over them—such is modern society as organically built up. There was a time when the Church, like a reconciling spirit of life, bound these parts together; when monasticism raised up a standard which whoso looked upon was healed of his desire for riches and material gain. It is no comfort to say that Churchmen and monks abused their great power. I know they did, and that Christians have themselves to thank if the world has slipped from their guidance. But the need of guidance remains; without an ideal we cannot live. Whether they will or no, the multitude of men and women are called upon for many years of their lives, and not a few for all their lives, to practise poverty, obedience, and celibacy. The question is not whether these must be endured; there is no escape from enduring them. But in what spirit are men and women to accept this ordering of their lives? That is the question. Surely, whatever its faults and abuses, monasticism made the acceptance easier, more reasonable, more hopeful. It showed the good that such privations brought, and led even Christians in the world to perceive that the end of life is neither material gain nor a civilization abounding in physical comfort, but a higher spirit, a new character, the attainment of a level where self-control, zeal for an impersonal good, heavenly thought, and unselfish action may seem as natural as the struggle for existence which is now offered to us as the one great rule of conduct. If the poem I have reviewed does but serve to excite and strengthen the train of thought here indicated, its worth will not be small, and its fame may outlive more than one generation.

WILLIAM BARRY, D.D.

Art. II.—FROM LOGIC TO GOD.

FOR the sake of those readers who possibly may not have made a special study of logic, and in order to clear the way for an intelligent examination of the problem indicated by the title that heads the present article, I shall enter at once upon a careful examination of the received doctrine touching the nature of the two wholes of extension and comprehension, or (as they are commonly called) the logical and the metaphysical wholes.

The porphyrian tree exhibits the two from a purely logical point of view, and will help us onward to higher spheres of truth. It will prove to be the surest and easiest road. In it we find two terms, at which science is arrested. The one term is *substance*; the other *man*. The former is the "whole" of extension ; while the latter is the "whole" of comprehension. A word of explanation touching the meaning of these two terms: The whole of extension is that universal which, within the limits of a particular line of abstraction and of generalization, has the widest or most extended periphery—that is to say, contains under it the greatest number of subordinate universals. Thus *substance* includes under it *body, living thing, animal,* and *man*. The whole of comprehension is that universal which, within the limits of any particular line of abstraction and generalization, is the ultimate, or that which is proximately resolvable into its contained individuals ; and with these latter, it must be remembered, science as such has nothing in common. Thus, in the porphyrian tree, *man* is the last and lowest universal, and is proximately resoluble into *James, Henry, Jane, Susan,* &c. But a difficulty suggests itself touching each of these illustrations—a difficulty which I notice, only because it is indirectly connected with our destined problem. It may be said, then, that in the given instance *substance* is not the whole of extension, or the highest universal, since *being* transcends it. Hence, the whole of extension would be a transcendental. And yet not so. But why ? I answer: A logical whole is a universal capable of determination by a differentia that is logically or conceptually distinct from such whole, and that by its synthesis specifically limits the same. But no addition can be made to *being*, because if it is not being it is nothing. Neither can it be specifically limited, because being cannot limit itself. This is why being is called a transcendental. It runs through all the categories and transcends them. Being is everything ; beyond it, nothing or not-being. The other difficulty admits of being put in this wise : *Man* is not the last universal, capable of resolution only into individual men; because we can divide *man* into *black* man, *white* man into *man* and *woman*, into *European, Asian, African, American,* and so on. The answer is plain. All these are instances of other lines of abstraction; and it must be remembered that our example has been taken from the porphyrian tree. If we consider man physiologically or geographically, or in any other like manner; *man* would not be the ultimate species, but a subalternate, or even a *quasi*-genus. All these are very rudimentary truths; but we cannot afford to despise them on this account. They will do us good service presently.

Hitherto I have been setting forth these two wholes from a purely logical standpoint—that is to say, I have been considering them (so far as may be) in the light of pure forms of thought —the most contracted, or, on the other hand, the most extended universal in any given line of abstraction and generalization. But I now want to call special attention to the names which from of old have been given to these wholes. As I have said at the beginning, the whole of extension is called the logical whole; that of comprehension, the metaphysical whole. Is it possible, then, to regard these two antithetical wholes metaphysically? Not only is this possible, but I purpose henceforth to consider them exclusively as such, recurring to their logical being only as illustrative of their metaphysical truth. The problem set before us is not a psychological one, but has the highest objective value. It is supremely real; and metaphysic alone deals with these supreme, eternal, and immutable realities. Let us now, then, see what metaphysic has to tell us about these two wholes.

A metaphysical whole is a universal expressive of the essence of any class of entities. It exhibits the essential notes by which a given species is constituted. Hence, three things: It is not measured by its extension, because the measure is not logical; but it is measured by its comprehension—that is to say, by the completeness of the essential notes as representative of the object. For this reason *it concludes in;* it does not *include under.* Accordingly, a metaphysical whole is pre-eminently real. Its perfectness is not to be sought for in the form of thought, but in its representative power—not in the breadth of concept, but in its equation with the object or nature represented. Consequently, the more of essence (so to say) that it *concludes in* its representation, the nearer its approach to the perfectness of a metaphysical whole. This is the second point. The third is, that the metaphysical whole is an absolute not a relative universal.*

---

* See my article, "The Word," in the July Number of *Mind*, pp. 395, 396.

It is only potentially a universal, because it is *absolutely* expressive of essence; and it does not actually exhibit the relation of the essence or nature to the individuals *included under* it. This latter property attaches to the logical whole, and connotes the conceptual power of classification. Thus, then, the metaphysical whole is an absolute, the logical whole a relative, universal.

I now proceed to examine into the nature of the antithesis subsisting between these two wholes, as revealed to us by philosophical contemplation. It is to be remembered that every subalternate species is a metaphysical whole, just as every subalternate genus is a logical whole; and it suits with the course of the present inquiry, that the question of antithesis should not be limited exclusively to *the* two wholes, but should be extended to every metaphysical as contrasted with its corresponding logical whole.

(i.) The first antithesis is to be seen in their respective modes of determination—that is to say, in other words, in their respective processes for defining the representation of the object. From this, it may be observed in passing, that I am now treating the logical as a conceptual whole; since a logical whole is a pure form of thought, wholly irrespective of the content which may happen to constitute its matter. Now, every logical whole is determined by synthesis. You take a differential attribute, and in virtue of dichotomy divide the indeterminate concept, as it were, by accident; but, in reality, the synthesis of the differential attribute with the indeterminate concept constitutes the determination of this latter. Let *living thing* be the indeterminate concept, and *animated* (or *endued with a soul*) the differential attribute, it is evident that *living thing* + *animated* = animal, —in other words, *living thing* is determined, by the addition of the said attribute, to a more definite representation of the object. In purely logical phrase, difference divides genus and constitutes species. On the contrary, a metaphysical whole is determined by analysis. The essence is represented as a whole, its constituents *in confuso*; by analysis the mind discovers a formal and a material part, which together objectively constitute the entire essence. The concept of the material part is a logical ascent, because it is equivalent to the proximate genus; while the formal part is logically the specific difference. Thus we come across another phase of the antithesis at present under review—viz., that by determination the conceptual whole goes down the tree of abstraction and generalization, while the metaphysical whole goes up it. The first member of this assertion is sufficiently apparent from the instance just given. The following is an illustration of the second: *Man* is a metaphysical whole; logically, an ultimate Species. By analysis I discover in the idea, as truly representative of the object, two constituent ideas—one of which is *animal*, the other *rational*. The former I intuitively recognize to be common with other entities. Because it is thus indeterminate, I call it by analogy the material part of man. *Rational* I as intuitively recognize to be the property of man, to the exclusion of all other animals; and consequently regard it as the formal or determinant part in the said nature. It is further evident, that *animal* is the proximate genus to *man* in the porphyrian tree.

(ii.) There is another antithesis in the determination of the two wholes, discoverable in the determinant principle of each. In the logical or conceptual whole, the formal determinant depends upon the particular line of thought; so that the same concept may be limited now by one attribute, now by another, according to the exigencies of the thinker. To express the same fact in logical phrase : The difference that divides a genus may become a property ; and what may have been before a mere property, may become the genus in a different line of abstraction and generalization. Thus, for instance, if we are considering *man* according to the moral order, *free-will* would be the determinant attribute, and his *native place* would be a mere accident; whereas, if we turn to consider *man* geographically, the *native place* would be the formal determinant, and *free-will* (as it were) an accidental property. The determination is conceptual or subjective, rather than objective. Far otherwise is it with a metaphysical whole, which is representative of the essence of its object,—of those characteristic notes, of that material and of that formal part which justify its inclusion under a given species. As the species is one, unchangeable, eternal; so the formal part—and the same must be said of the material part—is one, unchangeable, eternal. Individuals may change and may perish, but not their nature; for this is not subject to time or space. For so long as *animal nature* was, is, will be, or is possible to be, for as long must it be *a living entity with a sensible soul*. Anything else would be a metaphysical contradiction. It follows that a metaphysical whole is representative of a reality, one, unchanging, eternal, which is not the individual *as* individual and existing, yet is notative of the individual as formed according to one specific type. In ultimate analysis this specific reality is the Exemplar Idea, after the model of which a definite portion of the universe has been modelled. Thus is vindicated the immunity of the concept and object from all conditions of time and space.

(iii.) Again : The logical, or conceptual, and the metaphysical wholes are antithetical in their respective unities of measure; for the conceptual whole is measured by unity extension, while the metaphysical whole is measured by unit omprehension, as is sufficiently plain from what has gone before. The former represents but two notes, at the outside, of *its* object (I am speaking now of *the* wholes); while the latter represents all the notes of *its* object. It follows as a consequence, that in proportion as you recede from the metaphysical whole you approach nearer to the logical whole, and that *vice versâ* in proportion as you recede from the logical whole, you approach nearer to the metaphysical whole. The more notes, the less extension; the greater the extension, the less the number of notes. Hence it is that, on reaching the metaphysical whole, anything like a logical whole disappears; while on reaching the logical whole, anything like a metaphysical whole is impossible. To translate it into logical phrase: The ultimate species can never be a genus, and the highest genus can never be a species. The reason of the former is, that the ultimate species is perfectly representative of the essence, so that nothing remains beyond it save individuals, with which science has nothing in common; since the material and formal part of one individual differs in nothing from those of another individual in the same species, save in its individuation. The reason of the latter is, that the logical or conceptual whole is not resolvable into its formal and material part, because it admits of neither one nor the other; otherwise, it could not be a highest genus. For a highest genus is a universal that has no subalternant genus above it; but, if it were capable of resolution into a material and formal part, the material part would necessarily constitute a higher genus. Let me illustrate the above observations from the porphyrian tree. First, as regards the metaphysical whole, or ultimate species: *Man* is resolvable into *animal* and *rational;* and *rational animal* is adequately expressive of the essence of that particular order of being in the universe. If you contract this your concept further, you must do so either by some accidental difference —moral, physiological, geographical, and the like—or by an individual difference made up of individual and accidental notes, such as the colour of the eyes, shape of the nose, &c., or the disposition, special talents, &c. But both these differences are outside the essence. Accordingly, *man* can never become a true genus—that is to say, a logical whole. Now let us turn to the logical or conceptual whole. I set aside the concept of *being*, for reasons partly suggested already, partly to be considered in detail later on. The highest genus, and consequently the logical whole, in the porphyrian tree is *substance*. There is no higher genus, unless we are to introduce being; and that is not per-

cludes the greatest number of actual and possible entities, of which univocal predication is admissible. Beyond it we pass into another category. Therefore, it is the conceptual whole in this particular order of being.

(iv.) Another remarkable antithesis between these two wholes, more notably in their strictest signification, is what I take leave to call numerical. The metaphysical whole is an adequate expression of the essence. Accordingly, an adequate representation of each specific nature is, in the strictest sense of the term, a metaphysical whole. It follows that the number of metaphysical wholes is measured by the number of specific natures, which is indefinitely large. If physical, botanical, and zoological classifications had only borrowed enough from philosophy to follow the typal forms of Nature, probably this number would have been appreciably augmented. Anyhow, as it is, the number can hardly be numbered. If, on the other hand, we submit the conceptual or logical whole to a similar proof, the contrast is very striking. Without intending to bind my readers to an act of faith in the Categories of Aristotle, I intend to use them, and this for two reasons: They have undoubtedly stood the sure test of time; and all efforts to supplant them by substitution of others have not been a distinguished success. I say, then, that the number of conceptual wholes is ten, corresponding with the aforesaid Categories. I dare not reduce them further. Some have thought they saw a higher universal in the division into *substance* and *accident*; but a little consideration will serve to show, that there is as little of the univocal between one class of accidents and another, as there is between *substance* and *accident*. The reduction of all concepts under that of *being* is still less admissible. In the first place, *being* is not a *summum genus*, but a transcendental. It is not capable of determination by division, because its divisor would, must, be being—that is to say, itself, though it is capable of determination by explicit contraction. In the next place, its predication is not universally univocal; for *accident* is not being simply, but—as Aristotle tells us most truly—being of being. Moreover, being, predicated of every entity, is not a univocal, but an analogous predication. Finally, itself is ambiguous, since it includes the being of existence as well as the being of essence; and these two in all finite entity have contradictory attributes. These continued efforts, however, after a higher universal and a nearer approach towards unicity of concept are an ideological fact, of which we shall have to take account in the sequel.

(v.) Another, and this the last, antithesis is discoverable in the respective representations exhibited by the two wholes of one and the same object. Exclusive of the accidental attributes of its object, the metaphysical whole gives an adequate representation of the same, including all that is necessary in order that *Hercules* (for instance) should be a man, and excluding all that is not necessary in order that the same individual should be a man. It must not be forgotten, however, that the accidents thus excluded are themselves represented under other lines of abstraction and generalization; for these too have their own proper essence. Thus, for instance, *the bodily form* of a man, stripped of its individual notes, is represented to the mind as a species of quality modally terminating quantity; since shape is the limit of extension. So again: *Will* is a property of man, and, in consequence, outside his essence; but, considered in its own essential nature, it is a spiritual faculty, and as such finds its place under another species of quality. A metaphysical whole, therefore, offers a plenary representation, including all the essential notes of its object. It is at once the clearest and the most distinct concept of the entity to be represented—the clearest, because it manifests the integral nature; the most distinct, because it completely discerns it from every other essence. Its perfectness in this regard is made explicit and patent by its proper definition. It is quite the reverse with a logical whole, as it is called. The nearer its approach to *the* conceptual whole, the less does it represent of the object. The idea may be more or less clear, but it becomes less and less distinct, till in *the* conceptual whole all distinction disappears; since the universal contains every actual and possible entity belonging to the given category. It is for this reason that a *summum genus* can never be, strictly speaking, defined. It has no formal part and no material part. It is one in unicity of representation, not compositely one—that is to say, not one by any conceptual composition. To illustrate: *Body* is but an imperfect and confused representation of *Hercules;* seeing that it is a concept which includes the whole visible universe, and does not distinguish Hercules from sodium, an oak, or an ox. Of *substance* there is no true definition, since it exhibits but one undiscriminating, irresoluble note.

From a careful consideration of these points of antithesis between the two wholes, much light will be thrown on Sir William Hamilton's system of logic. No one has been, in these later times, of more signal service to this propædeutic science than the above-named learned and illustrious writer; for the reason that he insisted on the necessity of separating the matter from the form of thought, and maintained most truly that this latter, and it alone, constitutes the adequate subject-matter of logic properly so called. This was one principal point which characterized his remarkable Article on Oxford Logic, originally published in the *Edinburgh Review*. Now, if we turn to his new syllogistic modes, as well as to his adopted principles of deductive reasonings, we shall find that he has been uniting matter in a new marriage with form, and coquetting with the former at the expense of the latter. He has, practically, at the least, confounded the metaphysical with the logical whole; and, in consequence, has permitted the entrance of the absolute universal into his syllogistic constructions, instead of reserving these deductive forms for the relative universal, as had been the practice hitherto. In fact, he has done more; for, in order to reduce the logical to the metaphysical universal in the syllogism, he has introduced the quantification of the predicate, and has thus exchanged the *contained under* for the *concluding in*. Thereby the whole Aristotelian teaching with regard to deductive reasoning has been annulled; and the so-called principle of identity has usurped the place of the *dictum de omni et nullo*. The result is, that we have been burdened with a series of clumsy, unnatural and defective forms; and the old time-honoured modes have been transformed into materialized nonentities. It may be urged, that in the demonstrative syllogism there is a real quantification of the predicate, and that the principle of equality (not, be it observed, the principle of identity) does in fact rule over this, the most perfect form of reasoning. But this enstasis is nerveless. For, in the first place, the form of the most perfect demonstration is logically included, like all other less perfect demonstrations, under the old modes; and is either *barbara* or *celarent*—the two most perfect modes in the first or direct figure. In the next place, the quantification of the predicate is not verified in virtue of the form but of the matter; and the applicability of the principle of equality owes its origin to the same cause. Further, the quantification of the predicate and the applicability of the principle of equality do not necessarily extend to all demonstrations, but only to the mother-syllogism in a chain of deductive reasoning. Finally, for reasons sufficiently indicated in the previous parts of this my answer, demonstration does not belong to pure, but to applied logic; where consideration of the matter—that is to say, of the representative element—in the concept is permissible, nay, necessary.

I am afraid that the reader will not perceive the drift of all these prolegomena till somewhat later on; so I must ask him provisionally to exercise an act of faith, while I proceed to examine the nature of the genesis, and the objective value (or the

From Logic to God.

that essence is the one native object of the intellect. Still, for all that, it is equally true, that many universals are acquired by a logical process not dissimilar from a cryptical induction. Now, it is just this process which I intend to analyze. In this process there are two powers of the human intellect, which are principally brought into play,—to wit, the power of *abstraction* and the power of *generalization*. By virtue of the former, the mind is enabled to resolve the composite concept into its constitutive notes or attributes, and thus mediately the object represented by the concept, and to *abstract* those notes which it wills to consider for the time being, while ignoring the rest. This abstraction has been instituted for purposes of comparison. Several individuals, we will say, are brought within the intellectual field of vision; and one after another they are subjected to the abstractive process. The particular note or particular notes are abstracted by the intellect, and are projected there to the exclusion of the rest. But, remark, the individuality of these notes remains. The note a is in A; a similar note a' in B; a similar note a'' in C; and so on for the rest. This will be best explained, or at least easiest understood, by an example. I have before my mind the ideas of the *sky*, of a certain *man's eyes*, of the *corn-flower*, of the *blue-bell*, of the *ampelis sialis* (blue bird), of the *ctenolabrus ceruleus* (blue perch), and the *blue cat*. I abstract from these the note, *blue;* but as yet I have seven notes of blueness present before my mind—blueness in the heavens, a similar blueness in the human eye, in the two flowers, in the bird, in the fish, and in the quadruped. An individual or numerical, and only a numerical, difference remains. Let us pursue the illustration one step further. I will suppose that, by a similar process of abstraction, we have acquired the concepts of *red, yellow, green, orange, violet,* &c. We compare these with that of *blue*, and abstract the note of *colour*—that is to say, of a property in bodies to pass on certain fasciculi of rays to the eye exclusively of the rest, by means of which definite impressions are made through the organs of sense in the sight-faculty of the soul. But colour is in the red, in the yellow, in the blue, &c. The numerical difference again remains. From the above exposition, no less than from the illustrations, it is easily seen that the process of abstraction is analytical. It simply resolves the object (I always assume that the concept is truly representative of its object) into its constitutive notes, selecting one or more *pro re nata*.

The process of generalization, on the other hand, is purely synthetical. By virtue of this faculty, the mind collects all these individually distinct notes into one concept expressive of a definite essence, entirely cutting them off (so to say) from the subjects to which they originally appertained, and *so* annihilating their individual distinction, and, as a consequence, all multiplicity of concept. To resume our former illustrations: Abstraction left us with *blue* in the sky, in man, in flower, in bird, fish and beast. Generalization gathers these *individual blues* into one general concept, applicable to each and all of the entities in which this attribute is or may be found, yet not actually applied to any; and the concept in outward speech is called either by the concrete name of *blue* or the abstract name of *blueness*—the former significative of its attribution, the latter of its essence. Precisely the same holds good in the second instance of *colour*. Such is the scientific genesis of a universal.

But I have already hinted, that this is not the only or the more common way by which the human intellect can acquire universals. The fact is, that absolute universals are *the* proper object of the mind; and this latter is only tied down to the individual in the present life, because of its intimate and necessary connection with the body. Purely spiritual natures cognize the individual in the universal; whereas we cognize the universal in the individual. Thus much is due to the imperfection of our nature, half animal and half spiritual. After all, however, the only proper object of intellect is essence, or an absolute universal, as far as the visible universe is concerned; whereas the individual and concrete determination is for us a sort of *conditio sine quâ non*, because there is nothing in the human intellect which has not previously passed through the senses, and is not actually conditioned by sensile phantasmata. Such concepts are not the result of a laborious process of abstraction and generalization; they are simple intuitions. But there are to be found, among these likewise, the same two wholes and the same antitheses between the two.

Before passing on, I would call the attention of the reader to a psychological fact which will stand us in good stead presently. If we consider the two wholes *genetically*—that is to say, in the natural order of their conception—the logical precedes the metaphysical whole. The reason of this is, that the logical law (which in subsequent act is logical form) is a directive element in our intellectual nature, and is independent of any object; whereas a concept of essence—more especially an intuitive concept—postulates two things—viz., a normal presentation of the object, and a robustness of intellect sufficient to emancipate this faculty from the tyranny of purely sensile perception. The one requires repeated and discriminating attention; the other habituation. Accordingly, the first universals of a child are logical or conceptual; adequate metaphysical wholes are the finished work of the philosopher.

But now comes the more important of the two questions originally proposed: Have these two classes of universals any objective value? if so, of what nature is the objective value that they have? These problems have been mooted and answered to a certain extent in a previous article; but I want to sift them again, in their connection with the proposed problem which we are nearing. It may be again said, as it has been often said by both ancient and modern, that the objective foundation of universal concepts is to be found in a certain similarity that exists among a definite number of things, which allures us to consider them in a group for convenience' sake. There is a certain element of truth in this answer; for similarity of notes is certainly the formal objective motive, or (if you will) foundation of these concepts. But the answer is scarcely philosophical: it only throws the question further back. One is at once tempted to ask: What is the nature and cause of the similarity? The similarity that is covered by a metaphysical whole, is it the same sort of similarity that suffices for the logical or conceptual whole? If so, how can we explain the antitheses that exist between them? Again: Let us suppose with the Angelic Doctor—and his opinions are never destitute of a sufficient reason—that each individual angel constitutes a distinct species among spiritual intelligences; how in this case could the metaphysical whole be based on notes of similarity? We must go deeper into the matter, if we desire to arrive at a satisfactory answer to these questions. The foregoing difficulties will have suggested the reasonableness, as well as the advantage, of considering these two classes of wholes separately.

I. First, then, as touching the metaphysical whole, I reply, that there is an objective value, and that it is founded in the essences of things. If you should contend that my answer is vague and obscure—an old scholastic phantom laid long ago by the priesthood of modern progress and civilization in the depths of the Atlantic or in the Desert of Sahara (out of sight or out of mind), a superstitious garment for the unknown—I appeal to the evidence of experience and of common sense. You have reared (we will say) a *dog*, from when first it was a pup. Its bulk or size has increased—shall we call this its quantity?—and with the accession of size the form has successively changed. It has upright ears, a thick woollen covering of white hair, lies on its belly with its hind legs extended, and the like. Are all these notes necessary, in order that the animal should be truly conceived as a dog? Is any one of them? Why, some change as the beast grows older. Has the greyhound or the bulldog similar notes or a similar bulk and form to the spitz, even though it has its own increase of bulk? It is evident to common sense, that such notes do not enter into the essential concept of a dog, but are mere individual or class additions to the essence. Well, these we call accidents—accessions happening to the essence. But it is equally plain that there are essential notes as well; otherwise, there would be no sufficient reason why we should conceive and name the said animal a *dog*, and distinguish it from a *wolf*, a *fox*, a *jackal*, or a *hyena*. It will be seen presently, that these essential notes comprise a material as well as a formal part; as I have already had occasion to remark. For the present I wish to confine the attention of the reader to the latter. By the formal part I understand that note or that collection of notes, by which one species is formally or characteristically marked off from every other species or essence. It may be difficult in many instances to lay one's hand upon it, especially in the case of material things; because, as the Angelic Doctor sagely remarks, the more an entity is immersed in matter, the less is its amount of intelligibility. In the above instance, the formal characteristic of canine essence is a point so difficult, that we leave it to the zoologist; and *he* is forced to content himself with a descriptive definition. Yet, somehow or other, there are few men who do not know a dog when they see it, or fail to distinguish between it and a wolf or a jackal. This shows that the *whole* is there in the mind, though difficult to analyze. But whence this specific nature? Some modern naturalists there are, who profess to have discovered in the principles of *heredity* (to adopt for once, under protest, a barbarous coinage of the day) and of evolution a sufficient reason for this similarity of type. But surely such a solution is no solution at all. There is nothing either in the structure or in the propagating faculties of vegetable and animal life, considered exclusively in themselves, which postulates of absolute necessity that each kind should propagate its like. What is there in the intrinsic nature of things to prevent each individual from being, like the angels, a species apart? No, even microscopic, difference, so far as I know, has as yet been discovered between the human sperm-cells and those of a rabbit; which would justify the conclusion, so far at all events as material structure goes, that the one could not be the instrumental cause of a rabbit and the other of a man. "True," it may be urged; "but the principle is discoverable in the orderly onward march of things; and the fact of hereditary descent is patent to universal experience." To this I reply, that an *orderly march* of things connotes *order*, and that *order* connotes an *orderer*. Is matter, then, its own orderer —self-ordered? Assuredly, this is not a fact of universal experience. Who would believe that a diamond or a piece of granite, if it has lived already for billions of years, or should live billions of

matter." This, however, is simply begging the question; because organized matter is equivalent to living structure. In the hypothesis, what is there to prevent a diamond from organizing itself? " Well, why might it not be so?" I thought we were dealing with facts, or, at the least, with theories based on facts. To the second part of the primitive answer I reply as follows: Certainly *the fact of hereditary descent is patent to universal experience*. But the mere knowledge of a fact is not science, properly so called, which consists in the knowledge of things by their causes. I am not contented with knowing *that* a thing is; I instinctively desire to know *why* it is. I am even going a little further. Since the learned professors of this new physical philosophy, with laudable prudence, declare that they limit themselves in these problems to the facts of experience, the field is open; and as they, however unwittingly, nevertheless do theorize in their way on purely material data, while confessing their inability to determine the *why* or *how* of specific differences, or the objective value of essential classifications, I may surely be permitted to offer a solution, not indeed based on experiment and observation (*à posteriori*), but on a rigid demonstration which in the Peripatetic School is called *regressive*. I require one only postulate—which Aristotle has demonstratively proved in his " Metaphysics"— viz., that one true God exists, Who is the Maker of all things visible and invisible. If we once admit the existence of a Divine Creator of the Universe, we are compelled to admit the existence of this Creator prior—at the very least, *in order of Nature*—to His creation. It is, therefore, evident that He cannot, like human artists do, borrow His exemplar ideas from anything whatsoever outside of Himself. By exemplar ideas I mean those concepts in the mind of the artist, under the direction of which he executes his work—for example the plan or conception of a building in the mind of the architect. On the other hand, the exemplar ideas, or patterns of the things that have been made in the universe, cannot represent an altogether new reality; otherwise, that reality being outside the nature of God, God would necessarily be limited by a reality which was not His—in other words, He would not be the infinite God at all. Consequently it follows, that the object of His exemplar idea must be something in Himself. But this can be nothing other than His own infinite and infinitely perfect Essence. Thus I have arrived at a rigid conclusion, which enables me now to offer a solution of the question mooted: What sufficient reason may there be for the specific natures in the various orders of creation? I reply: God, contemplating His own infinite Ocean of Essence, conceived it as imitable in an indefinite number of grades of limited perfection, beginning ͡   ͺ the lowest up to the highest grade which He *practically* conceives—that is to say, as determinable and determinated by His will to their ultimate production. I must explain the latter part of this sentence, which is necessarily somewhat obscure. There can be no doubt that, as the Divine Essence—in other words, God Himself—is infinite and infinitely perfect, so the same Essence is imitable in indefinitely numerous grades of finite being. It would, therefore, be impossible for the finite intellect to assume a highest or even a lowest. But out of these possible grades a definite number has been chosen by the Divine will to constitute the actual universe. Such may be denominated *practical* grades or types of finite being; because it has been the Divine intention to realize them outside His own nature. These are the models of the universe. It follows that upon every thing that has been created or made above, upon, or beneath the earth, the stamp has been impressed of the Divine prototypal idea. The impress of this idea in the constitution of the given entity constitutes its species—that essential nature, those constitutive notes, which are eternal in the midst of time, necessary in the contingent, immutable in the ever changeful. These, and these alone, with their unchanging attributes and laws, form the subject-matter of science according to its native signification. Let us here, however, be on our guard against an amphibology which is capable of seducing us into the errors of ontologism. It is not contended that the exemplar idea is the species itself or the formal object of thought, but the finite expression of this idea in finite being. It is not the seal, but the impression in the wax, which the human intellect intues. What I do maintain is, that in ultimate analysis the reality, necessity, immutability, eternity of each specific nature, are based on the reality, necessity, immutability, eternity of the Divine prototypal idea. Whence, then, the multiplication of individuals under the same specific nature? Without wishing to exclude other reasons, I offer two, which in my judgment, amply suffice to account for the fact. The visible universe is God's first Bible, whose pages He intended to be ever open to the children of men. "There is no speech or language where their voice is not heard. Their sound has gone forth to all the earth, and their words to the ends of the world." But if only one of each species had been produced, it could only have been perceived by the persons in the neighbourhood of its natal place, and by those who were living synchronously with its life; and this would have caused the knowledge of it to be geographical and momentary, in the place of being œcumenical and constant. The other reason is, if possible, still more cogent. The individual differences of entities included under one species can be constituted by accidents alone—that is to say, by notes independent of the essence; for instance, height, size, colour, form of features, &c.

But each of these accidental notes has an essence of its own, which itself becomes an object of science; so that in one entity, there is opened up to us a little world of essences, like the delineations received from the complex figure of the seal. Thus the charity of God has provided for the universality at once, and for the comparative fulness of human knowledge. The first Bible has been made a big book, rendered plain in every language and every dialect.

Now, I am specially anxious to set forth an evident corollary from the doctrine just explained. God is entitatively distinct from the finite beings which He has made; nevertheless, there is no reality outside of God, which is not precontained either formally or virtually, and always eminently, in Him. It is an old adage of philosophy, that the effect must be precontained in the cause; and the reason is plain. Nothing can give that which it has not the capacity of giving. But a capacity of giving connotes a possession either derivative or absolute—in other words, by delegation or in its own right. Let me illustrate the whole doctrine I am here developing, by a familiar instance taken from human art. It is of all necessity that the essential nature of a watch should be *somehow* in the possession of the watch-maker previously to its production; otherwise, he could never produce it. Further, the more complete and scientific the exemplar idea in his mind, the greater the security that the watch will be perfect of its kind. Yet again: The idea once there, he makes as many watches on the same type as he pleases. "But," you may say, "this illustration tells against this Theistic solution in two important points: first of all, the brass, steel, silver, &c., of which the watch is composed, do not pre-exist in the watchmaker's head; and, in the next place, the motion of Nature is intrinsic, whereas the motion of the watch is from without." To the first enstasis I make answer, first of all that the material out of which the watch and its contents are made is accidental, but that the *idea* of the material is in the artist's head beforehand. In the next place, the physical possession of such material, either in place of, or in addition to the ideal possession, would be an imperfection. Finally, there is this precise difference between the infinite artist and the finite; that the former produces both matter and form, whereas the latter produces the form only, and finds the matter ready to his hand. The second objection I answer as follows: There are even now eight-day clocks. There is nothing in the nature of things, allowing for future mechanical improvements, to render it improbable that we shall have clocks ere long going for seventy years, the life of man on the earth. In such case, those clocks would have their own intrinsic motion as long as man has. "Ye u may say, "but the clock was originally wound up by the watchmaker." True, I reply; and so was the universe by the Creator. If it were not so, how did motion first begin?

I desire to make one additional remark. There is no one who pretends to the name of a philosopher but will own, that of all the known works in the visible universe, man is incomparably the highest; so that the fullest, or rather the least incomplete and imperfect, expression of the Divine Essence is necessarily discoverable in Him. With these *data* before me, I own to an astonishment at the complaint which has been made by certain philosophizing writers of our day, that the old Theistic philosophy is at fault, because it inculcates humanitarian or anthropomorphic notions of God. Why, of course it does. If it did not so teach, it would *ipso facto* show itself to be a false philosophy. As the good Creator cannot become intuitively known by us in this present life, He reveals Himself in and through the works of His hands, and pre-eminently in and through man. Some dust has been thrown in our eyes by adducing from the sacred Scriptures such terms as the *anger*, the *repentance*, the *jealousy* of God—His *arm, hand*—God *seated, riding, walking*, &c. But what instructed child is there, who does not at once recognize that such expressions are metaphorical, and that between these and such terms as *spirit, substance, intellect, truth, will, good*, &c., in the application of each to God, there is an essential difference, even though it must be admitted that in neither case is the predication univocal? For in the one case the attribution is purely metaphorical; while in the other it is analogical, according to analogy of attribution of the second class.

I have purposely reserved till now a consideration of the *material* part, the remaining constitutive of an essence or metaphysical whole; because it has a close philosophical connection with the conceptual whole, which will next occupy our attention. The material part in any given essence is that which is indifferent in itself, and is differentiated by another, the formal part. Logically speaking, it is what has been called the proximate genus. Thus, *animal* in the porphyrian tree is the proximate genus of *man*. In itself indifferent to *man* or *brute*, it becomes differentiated by the addition of the specific difference, *rational*. Are these concepts objectively true? Is there anything really common to man and beast? Why, surely there are so many notes of resemblance, that some modern naturalists have maintained the evolution of man from a fish.[*] But if so, it is plain enough that there is a certain number of essential notes common to man and to beast which really exist, though not really existing save

---

[*] The lancelet, the lowest in organization of all vertebrates.

in both, and these notes, taken collectively, we term an *animal*. Such are, the possession of an animating soul, of faculties and organs of sense, of self-determined locomotion, and the like. Further: these souls are either rational or irrational; and these differences divide *animal* into two distinct specific groups, under the one or the other of which all animals are objectively ranged, and outside of which no animal ever has existed or can exist. Now, what does this mean? It means that, while man specifically differs from reptile, fish, fowl, and quadruped, he has nevertheless something really and truly in common with all these—a real objective basis of similarity. This is confirmed in a striking manner by the teaching of the Angelic Doctor, that the human embryo passes successively through the grades of vegetable, of animal, and finally of human life; which clearly evinces a certain generic unity of type, together with a unity of genetic evolution in each individual man. The question naturally arises: Whence this generic similarity? This question leads us straight to an examination of the conceptual or logical whole. Wherefore:

II. As touching the conceptual whole, I reply that it likewise has an objective value, and that it is founded on the fundamental connection and similarity which all finite things in common have with one another. But here I must interpose an observation or two, which will prove, if I mistake not, of great service to a clearer understanding of the two wholes, as well as of the main problem of this article. I have remarked before, that each universal may be regarded both as a metaphysical and as a logical whole, but under different respects; and I will now add, that this remark applies *in a way*, even to the ultimate species on the one hand, and to the *summa genera*—nay, to the transcendentals themselves—on the other. To put it somewhat differently: Each universal may stand sponsor to the mind for what is contained in it, or for the multitude of subjects (in a logical sense) contained under it. It may be considered as a whole of thought or as a representative whole. Whenever the *form* of the thought is predominant in the mind, the universal may be called either a logical or a conceptual whole—logical, if the form is exclusively considered; conceptual, if the form is considered in its essential relation to the matter—*i.e.*, the represented object of thought. As, however, a cognate line of abstraction and generalization necessarily connotes the primitive object of the intellect in such line; it is sufficiently obvious that the porphyrian tree and the Categories do not formally belong to logic proper, but rather to ideology. This is the reason why I have persisted in calling a universal, from this point of view, a logical or *conceptual* whole. To conclude these preliminary remarks: It behoves me to add a word touching the genetic relation of these two wholes. A child begins to think by transcendentals—that is to say, the primordial thoughts which it conceives are transcendentals. The first words it uses, independent of appellatives of affection and of indications of bodily wants, are such as *thing, good, one, pretty* (a form of the *beautiful*), and *true*. But in these young concepts the logical form is the principal, the representation the subordinate element. The reason of the one is, that the logical law is an inexorable concomitant of thinking, and the form is the law in act; consequently, there is no need of habituation. The reason of the other is, that the mind and senses of a child are raw at the beginning, intue and perceive things as it were in a fog, and consequently postulate time and habituation in order to get closer to, and to become more intimately cognoscitive of, their object. As time goes on and thought matures, first the more remote, then the nearer lines of demarcation offer themselves to observation; and thus the concept grows and the thought proportionably narrows, till it has reached the ultimate species, or complete representation of the essence. With what the youth ends, the philosopher begins. He reflects on the specific nature, and may be supposed to go upward. To resume the old instance: he ascends from *man* to *animal, living thing, body, substance, being*. But for him each universal, as he mounts, is a metaphysical not a conceptual whole. The eye of his mind is fixed on the contents, not on the containing form; so that he does his poor best to carry with him all the represented objects in lower spheres to the higher reality, which in turn occupies his analyzing powers, till he reaches the infinite heaven of the transcendentals, where reigns supreme in the natural order the queen of the sciences, metaphysics. Thus the transcendental concepts of the child are prominently logical, while the representations are vague, obscure, and lean; whereas those of the philosopher are metaphysical, and the representations are definite, clear, and full, as far as may be.

To resume our consideration of these generic universals: It will be remembered that by analysis of the specific nature of *man* we obtained the material part, or the proximate genus, *animal*, equally pertaining to man and brute. The reader will perceive, that I am following the *regressive* pathway of the philosopher rather than the primitive onward descent of the child; since, as I have said, I purposed to treat those universals as metaphysical wholes. Well, then, having philosophically determined all that is contained in the idea, *animal*, the philosopher compares this essential entity with plants and the entities generally which make up the vegetable world. By process of thought he discovers cer-

with the respective organs of each—and he conceives clearly and fully what is represented by the cognition, *living thing*. He then compares this conceptual yet real essence with the rocks, precious stones, fossils, soils, with gases and liquids, with sun, moon and stars, and finds fresh essential notes common to organized and unorganized substances; and thus he forms the philosophical concept of *body*. Such contemplations and observations take him through the book of Nature. Perhaps this genetic order of philosophical cognition was one reason why Aristotle recommends a study of physics, previously to beginning upon the metaphysical science. Hitherto, then, he has been investigating the essential nature of the multiform series of things in the visible universe—of the forms of organized and inorganic bodies; and he doubtless has not forgotten to make himself acquainted with the laws of quantity, that first and nearest property of material entities—with the laws of the measure of continuous quantity (geometry), and with the laws of the measure of discrete quantity (algebra and arithmetic). But now he passes beyond the realm of matter; and, comparing material entities or bodies with immaterial and spiritual, discovers still notes of an individual similarity and of an essential identity between the two, and conceives the foremost and noblest of the *summa genera*, that one which is in a sense the progenitor of the rest. "When Socrates was born, all the Categories were born with him." But he ventures yet one step higher. Comparing substance with the accidents of the remaining nine Categories, though he can find no common notes properly so called, yet he discovers an analogy of attribution more or less distant; and, pursuing the analogy, is plunged in a colourless undefined sea of essence, with its trinity of attributes or passions (as they are called), unity, truth, and goodness,—for beauty is the sunshine of truth,—wherein essence is formal principiant and existence act, on whose bosom rests in sleepless calm the integral universe, and whose waters glide through the narrowed shadows of the finite into the unruffled ocean of infinite Being.

What is the meaning of all this? Is it a mere conceptual dream? Have we passed out of the light of facts into the spectral land of ideal phantoms? I trow not. It has been seen that all through we never lose sight of the facts of experience; but these facts are mirrors that reflect, or rather, waters that mirror, the ideal. What, then, I repeat, is the meaning of all this? It means that each species bears the impress of its objective exemplar cause,—that species has fellowship with species, kind with kind, because the potentiality of primordial matter is indifferently one, and the forms march stately onward in their hierarchy of order, —that genus has homology with genus, because their prototypal idea has sprung from the intuition of one essence, and form part in the proportioned evolution of one homogeneous whole,—that the universe is the result of the ideal differentiation of unity,—that God, *the* Artist, is One. Thus the manifold becomes one in an ineffable harmony; and its light is the life of beauty. I cannot refrain from adducing here the authority of one who certainly cannot be accused of any prepossession in favour of the old philosophy: "Les sciences," he writes, "qui s'occupent de la nature organique reposent sur un fait primordial, sur lequel leur activité s'exerce d'une manière ou d'une autre. Ce fait consiste en ce que tous les types du règne animal et du règne végétal présentent entre eux une certaine ressemblance ou parenté, et forment, suivant le degré de cette parenté, un système co-ordonné qu'on appelle système *naturel*, précisément parce qu'au lieu de s'imposer artificiellement, bon gré mal gré, aux phénomènes concrets, il se présente comme un résultat de ces phenomènes eux-mêmes. . . . Mais ce fait"—viz., that Palæontology has revealed the development of the actual *flora* and *fauna* from very simple commencements—"ne semble nullement impliquer la nécessité de voir dans ce résumé du développement macrocosmique dans l'histoire microcosmique du germe individuel, autre chose que le lien d'une synthèse *purement idéale* de l'affinité systématique des types, au moins tant que nous ne trouverons pas ailleurs des raisons plus fortes pour l'admettre. Deux confirmations importantes viennent plutôt renforcer l'idée du lien purement idéal des rapports de parenté, savoir: d'abord le caractère *effectivement* idéal de la parenté des types dans le règne minéral et dans les œuvres de main d'homme, et ensuite l'entrecroisement successif des rameaux du système naturel, je veux dire la complexité des relations d'affinité dans chaque type."* I do not wish to make this learned and acute writer responsible for the meaning which I attach to his words. It may be that he had in his mind an exclusively subjective ideality; though I fail to discover the traces of such an opinion in his thoughtful essay. In particular, the argument included in the above passage (against the exclusive derivation of varieties of species from geneological evolution of a primitive unity), which is derived from the complex affinities of one and the same species, would lose much of its weight if the author's *ideal types* were so understood. Further: The confirmation deduced from human art seems to exclude any other sense than that which I have been hitherto developing, and to claim for the Supreme Artificer the conception of those ideal types which are the measure of the universe. However this may be, I here main-

---

* "Le Darwinisme." Par Edonard de Hartman. Traduit de l'Allemand par G. Guéroult. Paris: Germer Ballière et Cie. Ch. ii. pp. 10, Troisième édition.

tain, not without ample evidence of experience, that there are essential notes in common, which not only bind species with species, but genus with genus—notes which establish an affinity between the inanimate and animate kingdom, between organized and inorganic bodies; notes which are common even to body and spirit, apart from their interaction, and that this community of notes and these essential interlacings of affinities in species and genera are due to the impression of ideal types pre-existing in one creative intellect. The particular way in which the evolution of these divine prototypal ideas is effected within the sphere of matter and the sphere of spirit is another question, with which I have at present nothing to do.

Now after these lengthy prolegomena comes *the* problem of this paper. We have seen that there is a manifold antithesis between the logical or conceptual, and the metaphysical whole: *Is the synthesis of the two within the range of possibility?* Here is the difficulty. The metaphysical whole is the adequate expression of the essence of each individual species; and even in its definition includes only, as it were, virtually and fundamentally, affinity with a correlative species. Consequently, the number of actual species (for of possible species it imports not to make mention here) is the measure of the number of metaphysical wholes; and this, if we reckon the angels, is far beyond the count of human arithmetic. If, on the other hand, we turn to the conceptual whole, even as submitted to metaphysical investigation, we arrive at the ten Categories. Beyond this it is possible to go, but only at the expense of a logical whole; for, by help of analogy, we mount to the transcendental concept of *being*. Here, however, we are warned off from *unity*; for being has its three attributes or *passions* (as they are called), which are not included in the idea of being, albeit the idea of being is necessarily included in themselves. Hence, the transcendentals —the widest efforts of human thought—reckon as four. Wherefore, though in neither case is unicity attainable, yet there is an apparently invincible antithesis between the multiplicity of each. Again, there are two concepts of transcendental being. There is the logical concept of the child and of the uneducated man, in which the form of thought all but effaces the representation of the object; and there is the conceptual quasi-whole, or the cognition of the philosopher, in which the formal object is accurately analyzed and described, only because it cannot be defined. But both concepts are undifferential; and their representation of *first substances* (the primordial foundation of all human thought)— that is to say, of individual existing substances—minimized. Even when the transcendentals are cognized metaphysically by aid of reflex thought, when the human intellect struggles heroically after the nearest possible approach to the supreme unity of science; what is gained in height is lost in depth,—the universal engulfs the particular,—the higher one soars, the less and the more indistinctly can one see below—species and genera give place to higher generalizations,—and, in the transcendentals themselves, all the specific varieties of life and beauty, created multiplicity, are absorbed in a cloud-veiled, monotonous unicity of objective concept, which is not relieved by the necessary concomitancy of its three Passions. But the unicity even is imperfect; for *being* as a noun represents *essence*, as a participle represents *existence*; and between these two, though there is a transcendental relation, there is likewise an observable antithesis,— between themselves alike and their attributes. From the very constitution, therefore, of our mental structure, all the efforts of man to acquire and construct one universal science have been, as they ever must be, a failure. *Essence, existence, unity, truth, goodness* (as we men conceive them) do not represent to us even the order of the universe visible and invisible. Symmetry there is none, because symmetry is incompatible with intrinsic and extrinsic unicity; on the other hand, unicity of concept in a metaphysical whole does not supply the need, because it represents only an infinitesimal member of a vast, interlacing, genealogical tree. Once more: There remains another antithesis, among those mentioned in the earlier sections of this article. The metaphysical whole contains the least, but represents the most; the conceptual whole contains the most, and represents the least. The two are mutually opposed in their respective measures. One more remark : Both these wholes are intrinsically deficient. The metaphysical whole tends towards the singular and individual, but is debarred from attaining to it. *De singulis non datur scientia.* The conceptual whole tends towards unicity of objective concept, but is debarred from attaining it. The former fails in fulness; the latter, in completeness.

Once more, then, I ask: *Is the synthesis of the two within the range of possibility?* Certain it is, that the human intellect has an instinctive yearning after conjunction of the fulness of the singular with the completeness of the transcendental— a fact not to be explained by the mental unity of the thinker *only*. But its constant and painstaking efforts are so far in vain; though, in metaphysics, up to the point that we have as yet reached, it has distant glimpses of a conceivable synthesis. But we have not surveyed the entire realm of this queen among the sciences. The apex of metaphysics is natural theology; and in the one object of this latter—God, as discoverable by the unaided processes of human reason— metaphysic supplies the foundation of an en͏ ͏ ly real, though necessarily imperfect, synthesis. It remains to evolve this answer.

I. In the first place, then, I begin by remarking that a purely conceptual synthesis of these two wholes is impossible ; and by a purely conceptual synthesis I mean an identification, or an equation, of the two concepts as exhibited in ideology—concepts derived from, and limited to the finite. One reason for this is, that has never been attempted. It is true that it has been essayed by different forms of Pantheism ; but the invariable result should have taught its lesson. The effort has invariably ended in chaos. A Pantheistic god is never, never can be, individually one; he is at the utmost genealogically or collectively one. He is either the dead ancestor of a world of contradictions ; or he is a noun of multitude. But, in this case even, such diseased efforts of human thought postulate a theological foundation. There is an *à priori* reason why a purely conceptual synthesis is impossible, derived from the antagonism in order of thought between the two wholes. The metaphysical whole aims at a full representation of the singular or individual, and gets as near as it can ; whereas the conceptual (or logical) whole aims at the complete subordination of human concepts under one all-embracing idea, and gets as near as it can. But between the individual and the universal there can be no affinity of thought, but rather the bar of an eternal contradiction. This reason is confirmed by the consideration of the natural infirmity of the human intellect, which has no gift of bilocation. It cannot soar aloft, and at the same time, or rather by the same act, remain below. Its first act of abstraction and generalization shuts out from view the actual and concrete individual. As the mind extends its glance wider and wider, particular objects grow fainter and fainter in the dim perspective; till even the geometry of the universe of natures loses itself in the indefinite oneness of an obscure shadow that fills up the field of view. It cannot construct a panorama with the objects of its microscope. There may be angelic instruments that partially do this thing ; but they have not been lent to man.

II. Since, then, the human mind is insufficient of itself to effect this synthesis; it follows that, if the synthesis be possible at all, it must be the result not of any conceptual identification, but of the supremacy of one objective reality in which the synthesis is *really* discoverable. But,

III. The synthesis is *somehow* possible. This conclusion is established both in the subjective and in the objective order: subjectively, from the tendency of philosophic thought. The philosopher strives to commence from unity, and to develope into unity at last. He draws out his metaphysical system, as the geometer draws his circle, commencing from a point and to this same point returning for the completion of his figure; while there is one immutable, motionless, underived centre, whose radius is the measure of each point and the supreme reason and cause of the whole. I may perhaps be excused for adding, in order to complete the illustration, that the centre is not the circumference nor of it, but is its antecedent and sufficient generator. It is a patent fact, that the human mind yearns after unity—the unity of fulness and the unity of completeness in one—unity of each and unicity of the all. But a natural yearning is never in vain. The human will cannot will, or even practically wish for, the absolutely impossible. Accordingly, if the soul yearns after this synthesis; it must be somehow possible. It we turn our regard to the objective order, it will be found that there is (as has been already seen) a most complex intertwining, by apparent affinities and essential similarity, of species with species and of genus with genus; justifying a synthesis, which is ever reducing the number of differences and extending the essential union of natures in its concept, and thereby demonstrating by the facts of observation and experience that, as the universe sprung from unity, so in unity it is perfected.

IV. I now go on to show, that this synthesis of the two wholes is perfected in God, as made known to us in purely natural theology—that is to say, in the Being and Nature of God, as derived by the efforts of the unaided intellect from the material and immaterial creature; or, to put it in a slightly different form, from knowledge of ourselves and of the world around us,—the *ego* and *non-ego* of German speculation. This is of course tantamount to saying, that the forementioned conceptual antitheses are completely resolved in the true cognition of God, such as is afforded us in the later books of the "Metaphysics" of Aristotle. I will show this, first of all, in regard of the *numerical* anthesis between the two. Metaphysical wholes, as my readers may remember, are indefinitely numerous; but in God they are one. For their divine prototypes are the one intellect of God, necessarily in act—the one Divine idea which, like every other Divine perfection, in virtue of His infinite simplicity, is God Himself. Further: Through the imperfection of the human intellect, the metaphysical whole is arrested at a representation of the specific nature, and is impotent to represent the individual, or—to use the Aristotelian term—first substances. But in God individuality reaches its highest, its infinite expression. His is not only a unity, but unicity of essence; and in Him the ideal type of each individual, possible as well as actual, is overshadowed by, and antecedently contained in, His unity. So much for the metaphysical whole: Now for the conceptual whole. Here I have a reason for reversing the order of treatment. In the conceptual whole also, then, the human intellect by reason of its finite imperfection cannot arrive at complete unity. It is arrested at the ten Categories, for so long as it abides in the univocal; and if it ventures, under the guidance of analogy of attribution, up to the indeterminate concept of being, it is still confronted with five transcendentals—to wit, essence, existence, unity, truth, and goodness. But, again, in God the synthesis is completed; for in His Word, or expressed idea, substance and its accidents are supremely one. Hence it comes to pass, that the ten Categories are united in each actually existing substance. Once again : In God essence and existence are, by the necessity of self-derivation (so to speak), indescribably, infinitely one ; so that His essence *exparte rei* is His existence, and His existence His essence. His name is יְהֹוָה, ὁ ὤν, ὁ ἦν, ὁ ἐρχόμενος—*I am who am*—He who is, was, will be—and, as expressed in the tetragrammaton, the same in the past, the present, and the future; because, above all time in the *now* of His eternity, yet cognizant of all succession of time and of the multiform acts that are carried down, or will hereafter be carried down, the stream of history in the simple *now* of His eternity. He does not look down upon the past: He sees it. He does not foresee the future, He sees it. All things are *present* before Him with whom we have to do. Finally : In God being, in both its senses, is unity, truth, and goodness. For an infinite intellect in act, as it must be in order to be infinite, is infinite truth conceptual as well as ontological; and infinite will in act is infinite goodness, natural as well as moral—supreme object of desire, and supreme rule of finite action; and forasmuch as, by reason of the Divine simplicity, that which we formally understand by faculty *as such* is excluded because of its imperfection, as essence is objectively identical with existence, so intellect and truth and will and goodness are identical with essence and existence, and the former again—*exparte rei*—are identical one with another. Let us now turn to the antithesis between the two wholes as regards the measure of representation. After what has been already said, this part of the problem need not delay us long. Because God is the infinite ocean of essence, He is *fulness*; because He is the prototypal idea and sole first cause, He is *all*. Thus fulness and universality of representation, as of being, are unspeakably one. But of the manner of this synthesis it behoves me to speak more at length. Accordingly,

V. Let us consider *how* God is the fulness, and *how* He is the all, of Being. The artificer—to repeat what I have already remarked —must have the antecedent exemplar idea of his work in his intellect, and the power to realize his idea. In the case of the S e Artificer, there must of necessity be the prototypal idea e matter as well as of the form, and of the accidents as well as of the substance,—that is to say, of the whole; and He must likewise have the power of producing all—in other words, of creating his work. Now, let us take the instance of a man; because of the whole visible universe he has been made nearest to the likeness of God. He is made up of soul and body. His soul is an incomplete substance, because it is essentially created in order to inform the body. To this end, while it is in its nature spiritual, it has animal as well as spiritual faculties; though the former depend upon a special bodily organ for their existence *in act*. Further: Even the spiritual faculties of intellect and will are *properties* only of the soul, and find no place in its *essence*; albeit they are, unlike the lower faculties, rooted directly and exclusively in the soul. The final cause, or adequate object of the intellect, is truth; that of the will, goodness; that of all sensile faculties, a goodness proportioned to each; that of the imagination, beauty. Again: Man is endued with an immeasurably higher life than can be found in any other living thing of the visible universe—a life which will endure for ever after death. Yet again: Man claims a lordship over the rest of this earthly creation, which he unreservedly uses for the satisfaction of his own wants and enjoyment; for brute animals have no rights. Once more: Man acquires after a time intellectual and moral habits, which become a second nature—*e.g.*, justice, temperance, fortitude, prudence, truthfulness, generosity, wisdom, science, art. Finally: Man alone has the faculty of free-will; in other words, he has the faculty of choosing to act or not to act, to act this or to act that, according to the direction of his intellect, well or badly informed.

Now, I begin by remarking, that in man all these attributes have thus much in common, however they may differ among themselves, that they are all limited. There is always a possible *further* beyond. For instance, justice is first facultative, then actual, then habitual; and habit even is only an accidental quality of a faculty. But justice in act *only* is something beyond. Justice, moreover, that is substantial and really identical with the essence is something infinitely beyond. To sum up in a word: A finite entity cannot have an infinite attribute. I next proceed to observe, that of the human perfections some are simple perfections; others are mixed—that is to say, some are absolute perfections which remain universally such under any whatsoever conditions and circumstances; others again are only relative perfections attaching to some definite order. Thus, wisdom, love, justice, life, are absolute perfections; and some orders of being cannot possess them, only by reason of their natural imperfection. On the other hand, the vegetative and sensile faculties, body, the habit of temperance, are fections; for the three former are impossible to a purely spiritual nature, and a habit of temperance would be otiose and useless, where there are no passions to be restrained.

Now, all these attributes and real perfections must be in the Creator;—because He is their primordial efficient cause,—as they are in man; but not in the same way. (*a*) In the first place, all limit must be removed; and this is to know God *by way of negation*. He is infinite life, infinite wisdom, infinite love. He is not just, as man is just; but infinite justice. His justice is not facultative, is not habitual; because it is pure act. His justice is no accident or even accidental property; it is His essence, Himself. His justice and His mercy *ex parte rei* are not our justice and our mercy, since in us they are two habits of the will; in Him they are ineffably one, and one with the will, and all three objectively identical with the Divine nature. (*b*) In the next place, all absolute perfections are *formally* in God, or, to speak more accurately, are identical with the Divine nature. Thus God would not be God—*i.e.*, infinitely perfect,— if He were not spirit, life, omniscient, omnipotent, omnipresent, just, immutable, free of will, eternal without succession, love. After this sort we may be said to acquire a knowledge of God *positively* by way of *formal* predication; not, however, without negation of limit. (*c*) Again: All mixed perfections are *virtually* in God—that is to say, all that is in them of *being* is in God, to the exclusion of all imperfection which is privation of being. To take an instance from finite being: A vegetative soul is *virtually* included in an animal soul, and both vegetative and animal souls are *virtually* included in the human soul—that is to say, the human soul does all for its body, and beyond, which a vegetable and an animal soul could do if they were formally present; whereas their formal presence would be an imperfection. This may be called a knowledge of God *positively* by way of *virtual* predication; not, however, without negation of limit. Thus, God may be said to *see*, because His omniscient omnipresence embraces all, and infinitely more than all, which a pair of eyes and sense of vision can do for us; yet after an infinitely higher order of vision, in some such way as mental intuition transcends a sensile faculty that can energize only in a bodily organ. So God may be said in a sense to have the attribute of temperance, because He is infinitely just; and His justice would supereminently suffice, and abundantly more than suffice, to rule over emotions and passions, even if He could have them. These, however, He cannot have; for they too are mixed perfections. (*d*) Former remarks and instances will have prepared the reader for a fourth and last element in the natural t of God. He has, or rather is, whatever is truly predicated of Him, in infinite excess of eminence and perfection. He is supereminently just, He is supereminently wise, He is love in an infinite supereminence.

Thus, then, God is truly, though inadequately, known by His intellectual creature. He is known, not as He is in Himself, but as He is imaged in His visible and invisible universe. And this argnitive cognition is derived from a twofold—perhaps for completeness' sake I ought to say a threefold—order of relation of the creature to its Creator. He is known to us as efficient and exemplar cause; He is known likewise as final cause of His own handiwork. As efficient and exemplar cause, He is rather revealed in the metaphysical whole; as final cause, He is more formally recognized in the conceptual whole. As efficient cause, He is represented causatively; as exemplar cause, He is known in His impress on each creature. In the former, it may be said after a fashion, that the species is the term of His creative action; in the latter, the whole individual entity with all its properties and other accidents.

If this teaching of the Peripatetic doctrine be true—and if it be not true, let the gainsayer refute it—it follows, as a simple corollary, that there is no reality outside of God, which is not either formally or virtually, in both cases supereminently beyond all degree, within God likewise; it would be better to say, which is not either formally or virtually His own infinitely simple essence—*i.e.*, Himself, abstraction made of all whatsoever limit. The last clause suggests the true significancy of the remark made by them of old time, that we know most of God by the way of negation. For destroying all limit by negation, which is necessary in the conceptual transfer of every human or other finite perfection whether absolute (*i.e.*, pure) or mixed—every sort of even metaphysical composition included—the amazed intellect of man discovers, as it were in cloud, an unlimited ocean of essence which is also existence; and all finite concept is, as it were, paralyzed by the measureless reality. This is *how* we conceive truly, without comprehending—for how can the finite comprehend the infinite?—that our God is the fulness and the all of His universe, and an infinity beyond.

One more remark: By reason of the infinite simplicity of His being, in Him the fulness and the all are singularly one. There can be no distinction *à parte rei*, because there is no limit; for a distinction between two or more entities connotes a mutual limit. Further: Because, for the same reason, there cannot be two infinities, since in the hypothesis each must limit the other; it follows that in God there is the apex of perfect unity, which we call *unicity*. He is *singularly* one,

Thus, then, all the antitheses between the metaphysical and conceptual wholes are reduced to a wondrous unity; and the human intellect finds science, in the individual univocal concept of one supremest and all-inclusive Transcendental.

VI. Is, then, such conceptual synthesis possible in the actual order of things? I answer, *inchoatively* feeble human reason can know the synthesis enough for the purposes of true philosophy; nevertheless, it does not necessarily permeate all scientific thought, but becomes, after patient and often weary effort, the last, as it is assuredly the highest, object of philosophic contemplation. This seems to point to the fact that there is for us men a *beyond*, where somehow mere deduction shall give place to intuition, and where the clouds, which surround a light too brilliant for the eye of man in its present isolation from the empire of spirit, shall vanish before the infinite Glory of the Presence. It should further be observed, that this concept of our God, as I have described it, does not enter formally into the metaphysical and conceptual wholes; neither is the even virtual cognition of God necessary to the abstractions and generalizations, or other processes, of thought. What I here maintain is, that in this cognition of God these two wholes are perfected and united by a singular identity, and that it is the ultimate objective foundation of their ideal possibility.

VII. Without this cognition of God such synthesis is impossible; and all attempts to effect it must lead to inevitable error. Whatever theory of the genesis of the visible universe it may please men to construct or to adopt, however wild the exaggerations may be of the true doctrine of evolution; it must be admitted by all who hold to the objective reality of the world, that evolution presupposes the simple elements which enter into the constitution of all bodies. Now, modern chemistry has already certified to the existence of above sixty of such elements; and, as observation and experiment proceed in their work of careful analysis, the number seems to increase. At all events, we have above sixty essences or natures, which together form the protoplastic clay (so to speak), out of which the sensible universe was evolved. It is impossible to go back further, unless we introduce the first cause of these. But such a reality is objective, if anything; it cannot be subjective. To suppose anything subjectively anterior to the elements, is equivalent to supposing that these latter are compounds; and this is contrary to fact. So here we begin with more than sixty simple bodies without any *essential* bond of union, though provided with accidental powers of combination. We may physically reduce all known bodies to these; but in the midst of the composites we discern a division, which is absolutely irreducible to unity. I allude to that between inorganic and organized bodies. How is the chasm bridged over, that separates the two? So far as experience and observation go; life precedes organism, not organism life. But life is a new factor in the process of evolution. Not contented with remaining a formal cause of being, it becomes through its organs an efficient cause of being. Here is another serious division of the chain. How, out of such unpromising elements, can conceptual or logical wholes be constructed, much less one conceptual whole? By metaphysical abstractions and generalizations, say you. True; but what is the foundation of these, and what becomes of the differences? And when you have reached to transcendental being, what have you gained but the vaguest, most impotent, and altogether colourless notion, till the concept of God sustains and illumines it? And how can two such opposites perfect each other by an impossible union? Yet such have been the fruitless efforts of modern Pantheism. It has supposed a substantial *identity* between the metaphysical and logical wholes, and identified both with God. It has not resolved the antitheses in an objective Infinite—objective, I mean, to finite being—but it has deified the contradictions. It has made of finite an infinite, of compounds a simple, of collected bodies a spirit, of an indefinite number of real diversities an absolute unity, of the succession of time an indivisible and eternal present, out of a multiplication of limited spaces a limitless omnipresence. To illustrate: Let us look for a moment at Hegel's philosophy. He begins where sane metaphysic ends, but not *as* it ends. His theory is the ideology of the school turned upside down, and thereby drained of its contents.* He takes *being*, as it would seem, in the sense native to the intuition of a child; and what is there beyond? Nothingness. So Hegel assumes nothingness as his god in germ. Here I must interpose two observations. A negative concept is an immediate deduction from a positive concept; consequently, *not-being* presupposes, and is posterior both in order of concept and in order of nature, to *being*. In the second place, since all being is made out of *nothing*, according to this German writer; all being is an act of creation. But this creation is of a most miraculous kind; for not only does it exclude any pre-existing subject (which does not involve a metaphysical contradiction); but it excludes all efficient cause, so that being came out of nothingness, either by the intellect and will, or by the necessary self-expansion, of nothingness. After the

---

* Hegel seems to admit as much. In the preface to his "Logic" he writes: "Il est temps de transformer la science logique, qui constitue la vraie métaphysique, la philosophie spéculative par-"

appearance of being in this unexpected manner, it separates itself off into two main autitheses, *body* and *spirit*; and then these two continue to evolve in a twofold antithetical series, till we arrive at the existing specific natures in the Cosmos. But the work is not yet complete. This god has not concluded his growth. When beings (that is to say, finite beings) have exhausted their fullest possible development; then nothingness will have evolved into its inconceivable perfection, and the all in its specific completion will be the maturity of god. Thus, as by the touch of a magical wand, the sum of the finite is transformed into the simple unicity of the infinite. Remark, that this is a real, not a conceptual, cosmogony; and the god introduced is only the universe in a new dress, without the absolute perfection of individuality, and stripped, as he becomes more perfect, of an indefinite unity rising from the darkness of chaos. Banish *nothingness*, the primitive parent, from this cosmogony; and what remains? The metaphysical whole transformed into the conceptual, the conceptual into the metaphysical, a unicity of indefinitely numerous antitheses of being in the place of a real self-existent, all-surrounding, all-sustaining unicity of infinitely simple essence; the abstract idea of essence, as prescinding from existence, undifferentiated and only potential of differentiation, universal and, as a consequence, utterly incapable of existence, in place of the specific natures of the essences that inform the world of existing entities. The synthesis is a metaphysical impossibility, and therefore false. In truth, there can be no synthesis; because there are not two factors.

I will take another instance from the teaching of Spinoza. This eminent Dutch theorist is called by Professor Goldwin Smith "the arch-Pantheist." It seems to me that the title is an exaggeration; though it is not open to doubt, that Spinozism is one of the many forms of Pantheism. It would be obviously impossible to enter upon a full examination here of the entire system; but there is one central point round which it revolves, that will serve to illustrate my position. Spinoza does not mount up to the transcendentals like the German Pantheists, but pauses before the Categories, or *summa genera*. He assumes *substance* as his *point de départ*, and borrows from the Peripatetic philosophy its descriptive definition—viz., that substance is being that stands by itself (*ens per se stans*). Interpreting the words *stands by itself* to mean that *posits itself* or is *self-existent*; he naturally enough draws the inference that God is all substances, and *vice fversâ* that all substances are God. But the paraphrase is a false one. The descriptive definition was intended to mean, "Being that in such wise stands by itself as not to require any other entity as subject of inhesion." Let us trace Spinoza's definition (so called) to its ultimate logical issues. Self-existent being is but one—that is, God. Therefore, there is no other substance but God. What, then, becomes of that which has been hitherto called the Creation? Obviously it is not substance. Accordingly it must be a sum of accidents: *non datur medium*. But, if they are accidents, whose accidents are they? Accident (*ens entis*) is the accident of substance; but there is no other substance than God. Therefore, the conclusion is inevitable, that the works of Creation are simply the accidents of this *substantial* God. But these accidents cannot accrue from without; for this is excluded by the hypothesis. Consequently, they must of necessity be evolved from within. Thus, by another route we arrive at the same point; that the universe is the evolution of a germinal god. Such a theory is obnoxious to all the charges of inconsequence and self-contradiction, which have been already brought against Hegelianism; but, in addition, it exhibits certain philosophical difficulties proper to itself. In this connection I do well to repeat that all accident is not absolutely being, but *being of being*. It is a modification of substance; and aptitude of inherence is its nature, while actual inhesion in another—either directly or indirectly in substance—is its normal condition. Let us bear in mind, that Spinoza evidently understood these Aristotelian terms in an Aristotelian sense; for otherwise it might be urged that I am guilty of a *petitio principii* in what I am about to urge. I say, then, that this theory necessarily supposes, that the finite universe is a modification, or rather an indefinite series of modifications, of this fictitious god. Moreover, these modifications do not flow from the essence; otherwise, they would be properties. But, if properties, they would be inseparable from the substance in act; which would exclude any evolution or new generations in successions of time, and would admit the universe to a partnership in the unchangeableness of God—to say nothing of other inconsequences that will follow in the remaining hypothesis. If, then, the finite creation is not a property; it is an accident of this supposed god. Where is the primordial source of these accidents to be found? They do not flow from the substance, otherwise they would be properties; accordingly, they cannot be evolutions or developments of this substance, for evolutions or developments of substance must themselves be substance. Either, then, they are self-existent, or they are product of a higher cause that is not this unique substance. If they are self-existent; they are alone accountable for the imperfection of their being. But imperfection is limitation; and it is a metaphysical contradiction, that an entity should be efficient cause of its own limitation. Besides, a self-existent being presupposes nothing, in order of Nature to its own reality and its own existence. But accident essentially presupposes the priority of substance, at least in order of nature. So, then, these accidents and, as a consequence, their inhesion in this substance must of necessity be the effect of some cause which is not this substance. It follows, that all these modifications inherent in this substance, putatively divine—these, its multiform perfectionments, come to it from without and are created within it. What follows? Why, that this said god must be a real produced composite, made up of the created and the uncreated; and that, therefore, he must be half made. But again: In all real composition, such as exists between substance and its accidents, the component parts are prior in order of Nature to the composite, and are subject to the causality of him who is author of the composition. Therefore, this self-existent substance is subject to some prior cause; which is inconvenient. But these finite entities, at least of the visible universe, come and go, live and die, change from form to form, very often with degradation of type; so this marvellous god, the immutable and infinite, evolves or developes into death, change, transformation, degradation—all finite. Thus the infinite is perfected by the finite; the eternal and omnipresent, by the phenomena of time and space. Where the multitudinous personalities,—which, by the way, are accidents of substance in the hypothesis,—are supposed to go to, I know not. They are real absolute perfections, yet they disappear; so it must be concluded that, if this divine unique substance is supreme in its accidental perfection, from such perfection must be subtracted the not inconsiderable perfection of countless personalities. Here, likewise, there is a false synthesis of the metaphysical and conceptual wholes; for the conceptual whole is limited to one Category, and unity, truth, and goodness are subjected to the same limits; while the metaphysical represents the other nine Categories, which are mere accidental modifications of the conceptual whole—in other words, there are not two factors, and the two wholes are resolved into an impossible identity.

There remains one apparently considerable difficulty, which may prove an impediment to a recognition of the doctrine evolved in the present article; and with its solution I shall end. It may be urged that, unless we accept one of these pantheistic gods, it is impossible to maintain that God is the ultimate foundation, perfectionment, and unity, of the conceptual whole. Consequently, this boasted theological synthesis is a baseless dream. The *antecedent* is thus declared. If God is not purely subjective in relation to the universe of things, if He is something independent of and objectively distinct from it, then He is not universal higher than both and inclusive of both. Further: Aristotle in his "Nicomachean Ethics," speaking of happiness as man's supreme good, and proving its absolute sufficiency in itself, remarks that happiness " is the most desirable, when no addition is made; for if other goods are added to it, it is plain that it would become more desirable, by the addition of the smallest good." Consequently, *à priori*, God, if independent of finite being, would not be all-being and all-perfect; because the addition of the entity of even a worm would add to His being, and exhibit an additional perfection.

My answer to this difficulty will become clearer, if I take for my text the quotation from Aristotle. I might, indeed, have passed it by; since human happiness is not to be identified with God, even if the philosopher had represented God as the formal object of human desire. But a consideration of the passage with its two contexts will, I think, lead to a very different interpretation—an interpretation which contains in germ my answer to the difficulty. " Now, we define the absolutely sufficing," writes the Stagyrite, "to be that which, *taken by itself alone*, makes life desirable and *wanting in nothing*. And such we consider happiness to be; still further, it is the most to be desired, not as one of a series. For it is plain that, if reckoned as one of a series, it would become more desirable by addition of the least among the other goods; for the addition becomes an excess of goods, and the greater good is always preferable. Accordingly, happiness is something *perfect* and *absolutely sufficing in itself*."* Aristotle's argument is this. Happiness, in his definition of the term, is not the supreme good in a series, because then it would admit of addition; but it is the consummate good, including every good in itself, so that, taken by itself alone, it is absolutely self-sufficing, absolute, complete, wanting in nothing. Because happiness is all this, it does not follow that there are no other goods outside it, but only that these are virtually and eminently contained in it. So, after a similar manner, because God is the infinite Reality, infinite Essence, infinite Existence, the All of Being; it does not follow that there are no other finite existing essences outside Himself, provided that these are either formally or virtually, and supereminently, precontained in Himself. Now, the reality of every creature is precontained in God as their efficient and exemplar cause; and, on the other hand, it is metaphysically impossible

---

* τὸ δ' αὔταρκες τίθεμεν ὁ μονούμενον αἱρετὸν ποιεῖ τὸν βίον καὶ μηδενὸς ἐνδεᾶ. τοιοῦτον δὲ τὴν εὐδαιμονίαν οἰόμεθα εἶναι. ἔτι δὲ πάντων αἱρετωτάτην μὴ συναριθμουμένην, συναριθμουμένην δὲ δῆλον ὡς αἱρετωτέραν μετὰ τοῦ ἐλαχίστου τῶν ἀγαθῶν· ὑπεροχὴ γὰρ ἀγαθῶν γίνεται τὸ προστιθέμενον, ἀγαθῶν δὲ τὸ μεῖζον αἱρετώτερον ἀεί. τέλειον δή τι φαίνεται καὶ αὔταρκες ἡ εὐδαιμονία, ‑ πρακτῶν οὖσα τέλος.—*Nic. Eth.*, L. i, c. 5 in f.

that He should ever be their formal cause. As efficient cause, He has all in His hands infinitely, prior to their actual production; so that He gives that which He previously—to speak after the manner of men—possessed Himself. As formally exemplar cause, He is the prototypal idea of every individual, actual or possible, of the universe. As fundamentally exemplar cause, He is that infinite Essence whose imitability, outside, forms the real basis of the Divine pattern ideas. As infinite order, He prescribes by His free-will the physical laws that govern the Cosmos. Nor are the free acts of human history outside of Him; because, as the infinite Truth, these truths, like all others, are ever reflected in the light of His being to His infinite cognition—not as past or future to Him, though He knows them to be past or future to us in the flowing stream of time, but as ever present to the simplest *now* of His eternity, which is infinitely above, and inexorably excludes, temporal succession of every form and kind. *But* one point remains obscure. What about the real personality or supposit of every finite substance? How can this be in God? I answer that, as the personality of the rational, and the supposit of the irrational substances in creation are substantial modes, perfecting their subjects in a connatural incommunicability of themselves to another; they are necessarily contained, together with the substances, in their first efficient and exemplar cause. They are represented in the prototypal idea in their proper formality; and they are virtually and eminently contained in the Divine Personality.

From all this it follows, that *Being* cannot be predicated univocally of God and the creature, but by analogy of attribution of the second class, wherein God is the primary analogate.

THOMAS HARPER, S.J.

ART III.—LIFE OF ST. OLAF.

Passio et Miracula Beati Olavi. Edited from a Twelfth-Century Manuscript in the Library of Corpus Christi College, Oxford, with an Introduction and Notes by F. METCALFE, M.A., Fellow of Lincoln College, Oxford. Clarendon Press. 1881.

OUR Scandinavian neighbours have long shown a most enlightened zeal and activity in elucidating their native history and antiquities, and Mr. Metcalfe informs us that it was at the instance of Professor Gustav Storm, of the University of Christiania, he undertook to examine and edit a manuscript life of St. Olaf, King of Norway, preserved in the library of Corpus

Christi College, Oxford. The book in which this Life occurs belonged to Fountains Abbey, and was written early in the thirteenth century. Its contents are miscellaneous; some have been already published, but that part which regards St. Olaf had never hitherto been examined with care. This is an instance among many of the miserable effects of England's isolation from the rest of Christendom. When she cut herself off from the Catholic Church, she alienated herself in no small degree from the republic of letters also. Irreparable loss to history as well as to religion was occasioned by the immense destruction of manuscripts at the dissolution of monasteries, so feelingly described and lamented by Bale and Leland. But there are to this day many MSS. carefully preserved, yet unedited and unexamined, which would have been published long ago by foreign scholars could access have been had to them. Year after year our historical treasures are being brought to light; but theological treatises that should have been printed by Englishmen centuries since, and that would have been printed by the learned religious orders of the Continent, had not our English universities played the part of the dog in the manger, now lie unthought of.*

When the Bollandists, at the beginning of the eighteenth century, were occupied with the Life of St. Olaf, how gladly would they have commissioned one of their Fathers to copy the manuscript of Corpus Christi College, had it then been possible. After much search in various countries, the best Life of St. Olaf they could find was an imperfect copy of this very "Passio," but without name of author, and with no clue to its date or origin to give it authority. This they supplemented as well as they could from other sources. Now the English manuscript is a complete transcript, made in all probability immediately from the original, and that part which was not known to the Bollandists shows it to be the work of no less a person than Eystein or Augustinus, second Archbishop of Nidaros or Drontheim, who died in 1187. Its author, then, lived within a century of the death of the martyr king, and was archbishop in his royal city, where all traditions were fresh, and abundant documents and monuments preserved. He relates several miracles of which he was eye-witness—graces that

---

* Of course we are not speaking of the present time, since perhaps in no country are greater facilities given, or more courtesy shown to learned foreigners than in our own libraries. One who has gratefully spoken of this, and made good use of it in discovering some important writings of St. Anselm, remarks: "On ne saurait assez regretter que ces bibliothèques si riches aient été fermées à l'érudition catholique précisément à l'époque où elle possédait ses plus illustres représentants" (Le P. Ragey, dans "Les Annales de Philosophie Chrétienne"). Even in former times there were illustrious exceptions. The Bollandists acknowledge the courtesy of Dugdale.

happened to himself, and others into the truth of which he made personal investigation. He had the liveliest devotion to the royal apostle of his country, and it was he who planned and in great part built that magnificent cathedral of Drontheim, in which the relics of St. Olaf were enshrined for four centuries, until the gold and jewels were carried off by the Lutherans. Archbishop Eystein re-edited, with a supplement of his own, the "Passio et Miracula" already handed down in his church. He was moved to do this by gratitude. He says, very quaintly (p. 104), that, "since nobody is more near to a man than his mother's only son," he thinks it due to the martyr to declare the graces granted to himself, and then describes in a very graphic manner how he climbed the scaffold to inspect the new work in his cathedral, how a machine broke, and he fell and fractured his ribs against the edge of a vessel used for mixing mortar, and was carried off to bed; but how he felt impelled to be present three days later at the Mass on the martyr's feast, and was so perfectly healed during the procession that he was able to preach to the people.

We have, then, a MS. of the highest antiquity and greatest authority, as regards both St. Olaf and his cultus. Happily this unique manuscript has now found a competent editor. Mr. Metcalfe has not merely collated it carefully with such incomplete copies or fragments as are anywhere known to exist, he has illustrated its historical and geographical difficulties throughout in plentiful notes, and has accompanied it by sixty-three pages of introduction and several appendices. In the introduction he gives the history of the manuscript and of its author the archbishop, who was an exile in England for three years, and who may have himself brought with him his treatise, though it is also probable that it was sent to the monks of Fountains from the monastery they had established as an offshoot of their own in Norway sixteen years after their foundation. Mr. Metcalfe also gives a very animated and learned sketch of the life and martyrdom of St. Olaf, derived from vernacular Scandinavian sources, entering with zest into the poetical and legendary literature which gathered around his name. The combats of St. Olaf with Trolls and giants were passed over by the Bollandists with disdain, as *omnino vel conficta vel certe incredibilia.* It is a pity that our old learned biographers, while separating truth from mere legend, did not give some record of the latter, either for its intrinsic beauty or as a key to literature and monumental art. The labours of Scandinavian scholars during the last century and a half have cleared up many points that to the Bollandists were obscure or doubtful, and the present publication especially gives a much higher value to what was already published in the "Acta Sanctorum," by fixing its date and authenticity. Father Bosch complained that, though the evidence of the saint's ancient and wide-spread cult was clear, his acts were of such doubtful authority that one could not know what to affirm as certain. Mr. Metcalfe, on the other hand, writes :—

> For accuracy of detail, care in the chronology, and the remarkable way in which the various recensions of it correspond with each other, the Saga of S. Olaf stands foremost in the old historical literature of Norway before King Swerrir. This is unquestionably to be attributed to the fact that, directly after his death, a careful and complete oral account of his life was put together by some contemporary and well-informed Sagaman, and preserved by tradition, whole and intact, until it was committed to writing either at the instance of Are Frodi, or by that author himself. The basis of the account would of course be the verses of the King's scalds, relating his exploits. Such were Ottar the Black, and Sigvat, the latter of whom remained Court scald in the reign of his son Magnus. But much more is given in the Sagas than can be ascribed to these scalds.

For an account of these "exploits of the king" I must refer to the pages of Mr. Metcalfe. The account in Fleury, from whom Rorhbacher copies word for word, is quite inaccurate, Alban Butler is correct but scanty, the Bollandists are not accessible to many; yet if it were only for St. Olaf's connection with England, and the honour in which he was formerly held among us, an Englishman should welcome this opportunity of becoming familiar with his romantic story. In London no less than four parish churches were formerly dedicated under his invocation, and a fifth in Southwark, just below London Bridge, reminds us of the event by which his name became so famous with Londoners. That charming book, "The Chronicles of London Bridge," relates from Snorri Sturluson how the Norwegian Viking, aiding King Ethelred, pulled down the old wooden bridge upon the Danes. Those who have not read this story in the book just mentioned, or in one of the histories of London, may find it well told by Mr. Metcalfe. They will be reminded, too, that the hero was not yet King of Norway, much less a saint. He was but eighteen years old, and probably not yet a Christian. There are contradictory traditions about his baptism. One says that he was christened when three years old; the other that he became acquainted with Christianity in England, and was baptized and confirmed in Normandy. The discrepancy may easily be explained. If he was really baptized as an infant it was done to gratify the zeal of Olaf Tryggvason, who happened to visit the child's mother and stood godfather. But the baptism was followed by no Christian education and he was brought up as a mere heathen marauder. It was not till he was a young man that he made acquaintance with Christian doctrine, and his Confirmation by the Archbishop of Rouen might naturally have been thought, by those who knew only his general career, to have been immediately preceded by his baptism. Certainly from that period until his martyrdom zeal for justice and for Christianity was his ruling passion.

While I cannot speak too highly of Mr. Metcalfe's labours, I must make some reservation as regards the judgment he has passed on the saint's character. It seems to me that he is not altogether free from the ordinary Protestant itching to lay hands roughly on those whom the Church calls saints. He does not indeed, like Mr. Laing, call St. Olaf "the most bloodthirsty tyrant who was ever canonized;" nor does he think with the same writer that "never was a monarch opposed and cut off by his people on juster grounds." He protests against such language, and says that St. Olaf "may well be called a righteous and conscientious ruler." Yet he sees in the saint's repression of heathen abominations "violence and cruelty." "Like others before him and since," writes Mr. Metcalfe, "Olaf read the lesson of Christianity the wrong way. In him fanaticism is exemplified in its most cruel phase. But he acted according to his lights." To this judgment we must oppose first the testimony of contemporaries, and next the circumstances of the country as stated by Mr. Metcalfe himself. Certainly gentleness and clemency are the qualities most commemorated by those who lived near his own time. Florence of Worcester says that the turbulent nobles despised him "because of his simplicity and meekness, his equity and religiousness." Adam of Bremen "a very trustworthy historian," according to Mr. Metcalfe, writing about fifty years after his death "pays a very high tribute to St. Olaf's qualities as a Christian and a ruler. He states that King Olaf was constantly at war with Canute, but in the intervals of peace he governed his kingdom with judgment and justice. He made war upon the innumerable magicians, necromancers and other satellites of Antichrist. With him were many bishops and priests from England, by whose counsels he was guided in directing the affairs of the country." The Lutheran Torfœus says that, in his zeal for justice, "no one escaped unpunished, that penalties were inflicted without regard to rank or wealth, and that he had no regard to geometrical proportion." We are not sure whether these last words are meant for praise or blame. They are taken as fault-finding by the Bollandists, who rightly remark that if St. Olaf paid no respect to rank of persons, he paid great attention to degrees of guilt. He is said by ancient writers to have been severe to all men alike, but he was not severe to all crimes alike. What higher praise can be given to a ruler than that he procures the peace of the country and protects the poor and weak by strongly repressing powerful oppressors? That the conduct of such a man will be called by some bloodthirsty tyranny, by others zeal for peace and justice, is what we should expect beforehand; and the contradictory judgments passed on the conduct of rulers in our own time and country may well make us pause in denouncing as "cruelty and violence" what appeared zeal and justice to those who knew the nature of heathenism better than we can know it. However, if Mr. Metcalfe seems in the phrases above quoted to judge the saint harshly, he has himself written a most excellent vindication. "It had been the custom in Norway," he says, "before Olaf's time for the sons of great men to go marauding about, both in the country and out of the country, upon their own countrymen and on strangers—in short, to turn Vikings. These King Olaf resolved to put down, cost what it might. And if any of the aristocracy were proved to have committed such depredations they must suffer in life or limb. No offer of money, no entreaties could save them. As Sigvat sang:—

> He made the bravest lose his head
> Who robbed at sea and pirates led;
> And his just sword gave peace to all,
> Sparing no robber, great or small.

Such is the key to the whole transaction. He had caged and clipped the wings of the great birds of prey, and they turned and rent him with beak and claw." Much more Mr. Metcalfe has written to the same effect, and we are grateful to him for the light that he has thrown, as well as for the labour he has bestowed, on the life and character and influence of one of the Church's heroes.

In concluding this notice I would point out a passage in an old writer that throws some light on a very perplexing event in the life of St. Olaf. His son Magnus (called the Good) was illegitimate, and certainly born to him not only after his conversion and baptism, but after his marriage. On this the oldest authorities are unanimous, and the Bollandists admit it with sorrow as an example of human weakness and Divine clemency, naturally quoting the fall and repentance of David. Mr. Metcalfe gives only a few lines to this subject:—

William of Malmesbury [he says] recounts an ugly tale of his treatment of a poor captive, the English lady Elfildis, who became by him mother of the future King Magnus, of Norway. But the historian, while inveighing against the unbridled passion of the king, mentions that he was only acting according to the custom of the country, *pro more gentis suæ*. Matters of this sort would perhaps be looked upon with more lenient eyes by the Icelandic historians, according to whom, whatever indiscretions Olaf was guilty of in his Viking days, he was greatly altered for the better afterwards.

Thus far Mr. Metcalfe; but if the passage I am about to quote really refers to this matter, and be of any weight, though it will not establish the innocence of the king, it will prove that he was neither carried away by unbridled passions, nor acting with a lax conscience from heathen custom, and that, as compared with the sin of David, the fall of St. Olaf was light indeed. *He fell into sin once only and that from desire to have an heir to his throne.* The authority for this statement is Faricius, a monk of Malmesbury, like William, and his contemporary. In his life of St. Aldhelm this writer relates many miracles worked at his shrine, amongst others the following:—

For a long time after the cruel kings of the Danes and Norwegians devastated Britain, they carried off—as is the wont of barbarians— beautiful young girls. Among these was one very noble, named Helphildis, who by her beauty much pleased one of their leaders, so that putting away his lawful wife, as is the custom of that nation, he kept her as his concubine till his death, after which event she still remained in exile among them. Now the Archimandrite of the Danes, having no children, and desirous of an heir, though his wife was still living, having intercourse with this woman once only, begot a son. When this was known, the King, moved by pity because she was a stranger, and moved by the love of her offspring, for her safety and support, fearing his wife's anger, committed her to the keeping of a God-fearing bishop. The bishop, wishing to merit a reward from God, as well as the goodwill of his master, had the child honourably kept till he was weaned. After that the King died; and the mother, taking her child by night, sought security in flight, fearing to incur danger on the part of the surviving queen. Seven years later it became known to many that she was living in a remote country. Then the Danes sent for her to bring back her son that he might enjoy his father's throne. This was done; but the young king, having reigned only a year and a half, departed this life. Then Helphildis, considering her desolation, her past sorrows, and the misery that awaited her, resolved to return to her own country.*

---

* See "Acta Sanctorum," tom. vi. Maii. Vita II., S. Aldhelmi, sect. 25. Mr. Metcalfe gives no reference to the passage of William of Malmesbury to which he alludes, and I have not been able to find it. Is it possible that he refers by mistake to the passage of Faricius quoted above? The words, "pro more gentis suæ," quoted by him suggest the thought; for Faricius says that the first master of Helphildis," juxta gentis suæ morem," put away his wife and took a concubine. But this was not St. Olaf. Of him he says " quia carebat liberis, una tantum ingressus nocte, genuit filium."

What follows in Faricius does not concern St. Olaf. It is enough to say that Helphildis became paralyzed and was cured at the shrine of St. Aldhelm at Malmesbury. The monks there might have learnt her previous history from her own mouth, or from her attendants. Now I think there can be little doubt that this Helphildis is the same as the mother of Magnus. It is true that the Archimandrite mentioned by Faricius is said to be King of the Danes. It is true also that the son of Helphildis is said to have reigned only a year and a half, whereas Magnus returned from Russia in 1035 and died in 1047. Still the other circumstances correspond. The name of the mother of Magnus was Helphildis, and she was an English captive. Is it likely that there was at the same period another English captive of the same name, and mother of an illegitimate king of Denmark? Young Magnus was an exile in Russia for five years after his father's death, and was then called to the throne. Now there is no King of Denmark, of illegitimate birth, carried to a distant country at his father's death, while yet an infant, and after five or seven years recalled to be king, and dying so young as to leave his mother for many years childless; whereas Magnus of Norway was only eleven years old when crowned and twenty-three at his death. I conclude then that though Faricius may have confounded Denmark with Norway—which is no very strange confusion when Canute of Denmark claiming Norway as his own, and Magnus of Norway was also King of Denmark—yet he is really relating the history of the mother of St. Olaf's son. Perhaps it was out of reverence for the martyr's memory that he kept back his name. He may of course be also inaccurate in what he says of the intercourse between Olaf and Helphildis, yet he is quite as likely to be right as William of Malmesbury, who was fond of dressing up his stories, and who while inveighing against vice, shows a prurient desire to magnify its enormity and dwell upon its details. As I am not aware that this passage of Faricius has ever been noticed in connection with St. Olaf, I have thought it concerned the honour of the saint to call attention to it, since though it does not efface, yet it palliates, the one grievous blot on a dear and holy memory.

Mr. Hallam has recorded his opinion that there is nothing more tedious and profitless than reading the lives of the mediæval saints, except for the few fragments of secular history that may be fished up here and there from their depths. To my judgment the very reverse is the case. The secular history of barbarous times makes the heart sick. It is little else than a record of the wars, oppressions, cruelties, murders, and divorces of kings. The lives of the saints, on the contrary, cheer and console, not merely by presenting a spectacle of the few heroic men and women whom the world was not worthy," but by giving us glimpses of other and better phases of society, of those with whom the saint comes in contact during his life, and of those who throng to his tomb and shrine after death.

In the inspired Scriptures, the chronicles of most of the kings of Judah and Israel are summed up by the words, "He sinned and made Israel to sin." What a relief to come to the one perfect king, Josias, "who did what was right in the sight of the Lord, and turned not aside to the right hand or to the left," or to read the episodes of Elias and Eliseus. And in the life of Eliseus, what a charming glimpse we get of the faith and devotion of the humbler classes in the story of the little maid who served the wife of Naaman the Syrian, and spoke up so boldly about the merits of the prophet in her own country. From this point of view, the records of miracles, which are generally "skipped" by those who dip into the "Acta Sanctorum," are often little less interesting than the lives of the saints to which they are an appendix. I will give one specimen from the new matter not known to the Bollandists, and as so much interest has been taken lately in everything belonging to fisheries, I choose a miracle that will illustrate Norwegian fisheries in the twelfth century. It is Archbishop Eystein who writes:—

> I was one day in my church, when a youth told me, with every appearance of candour, that he had just come from the pagan parts (*i.e.*, from the extreme north), where a multitude of Christians had been passing the Lent in fishing.* After waiting for God's bounty for a long time in vain, they consulted as to what was to be done; for in that narrow strait of the sea, among those pagan solitudes, far from Christian habitations, they had been disappointed in their hopes of capture for three or four weeks, and were not only wearied but alarmed by their dearth of provisions. So one day, when the sea was being dashed furiously on the rocks, and the whole sky was dark with the tempest, and there seemed no prospect of calm weather, they implored the mercy of God and the intercession of St. Olaf, unanimously vowing that if God had pity on them they would send the best fish from each boat to the church of St. Olaf (*i.e.*, towards the construction of the cathedral of Christ Church, in which was the shrine of the martyr). The pagan Finns, who were also come for the fishing, hearing of the vow of the Christians, wished to be associated to it, but so that their idols should be no less honoured by their gifts than St. Olaf by those of the faithful. But as there can be no concord between Christ and Belial, the wretches were rejected in their error. The next morning the storm passed away with the darkness. The sea was calm,

---

* "Transacto quadragesimali tempore in piscatione convenerat." This would rather mean, began to fish after Lent, but as the writer says they fished several weeks and sent him their ex voto on the vigil of Easter, I have translated it otherwise.

and there was so great a multitude of fish, that the only complaint now was of the greatness of the draught. In this miracle was something still more miraculous. Though the pagans came every day with the Christians to the fishing, yet, contrary to custom, with all their arts they caught nothing. The few fish they took scarcely sufficed for necessary food. On the vigil of Easter, according to the vow of the Christians and the number of their ships, twenty-four large fishes were brought to us, together with the above account. But since in the worship of God, truth is above all things necessary, we put off publishing this matter, until we had come in the next summer to the borders of the pagans, and had made ourselves certain of the fact from those who had been eye-witnesses (p. 112).

From this story we learn, as Mr. Metcalfe remarks, that the famous winter fishery of the Luffodens was in full activity in the twelfth century; but we learn also something better—viz., the faith and devotion of the poor fishermen, the means by which such splendid cathedrals were erected, and the miraculous manifestations by which the heathen were taught to recognize the true religion. Many other illustrations of these and similar matters will be found in this volume. From the sources now opened, as well as from others we should gladly see an English life compiled of the saint who is the glory of Scandinavia, and who united in himself somewhat of the character of our own St. Oswald as royal apostle and martyr, and of our Alfred, in his romantic adventures and good legislation, and who, in Icelandic and Norwegian poetry, became a legendary hero like King Arthur in our own.

T. E. BRIDGETT, C.SS.R.

ART. IV.—ADRIAN IV. AND IRELAND.

Analecta Juris Pontificii. May–June, 1882. Paris.

THE author of the above treatise undertakes to prove that the privilege of coming to Ireland, so far from being granted to Henry II. by Adrian IV. was positively withheld by him. The statements and reasoning employed in support of this new theory appear to be absolutely endorsed lately by a writer in this REVIEW. His article in the last July number opens with the statement "that the Editor of the 'Analecta Juris Pontificii' has added fresh and almost conclusive evidence of the forgery" of the grant, and the last words in the same article are "that it is more than probable that Adrian in reality positively refused to be a party to the injustice."

While admitting neither injustice nor impropriety in the case, I have to say that I must form quite an opposite judgment to that of the "Analecta" and I proceed as directly as I can to give some of my reasons for such a judgment.

In the middle of the twelfth century Henry II. of England ascended the throne. The addition of Anjou and of the dukedoms of Normandy and Guienne to his English kingdom made him one of the most powerful monarchs in Europe. He was young, enterprising, and ambitious. Just as he ascended the throne, an Englishman, who took the name of Adrian IV., was crowned Pope. Henry judged the present a favourable opportunity of doing what several of his predecessors had contemplated—invading Ireland. That country was conveniently at hand, weak and miserably divided. Henry desired the Pope's consent to the invasion. Not that he expected any material aid from him: all he feared was positive opposition. It was for the Pope to decide who were to be admitted into or shut out from the family of European sovereigns. Such was the jurisprudence of the age. Whatever State placed itself under the protection of the Holy See might have defied the mightiest monarch. Hence Scotland, Wales, even England itself, were put under the protection of St. Peter. From the same feeling Reginald, King of the Isle of Man, placed his little kingdom as a feudatory under the protection of St. Peter and St. Paul and of the holy Roman Church, and promised to pay twelve marks yearly.

Donogh, son of Brian Boro, on being deposed by Irish princes, had gone to Rome in the previous century, carrying with him, it was said, the insignia of royalty and power, and transferred, before his death there, the sovereignty of Ireland to the Roman See. This has been an Irish tradition for centuries. But to guard against the possibility of a collision with Rome, from what had taken place or might take place, Henry II. thought it well to ask the privilege of invading Ireland. The occasion was favourable. Only three years previously a Roman legate presided at a National Council held at Kells for the remodelling of the hierarchy and the reformation of abuses in Ireland. The Pope was well acquainted with the irregularities that there prevailed. The country was as divided as 150 years previously, when the decisive battle at Clontarf had been fought. Good laws of course were passed from time to time, but a spirit of clanship interfered with their observance. The great want was a strong, controlling power which would make the laws respected through the land, and mould the several clans into the homogeneity of a nation. Henry sent an embassy of bishops to congratulate the Pope on his accession to the Papacy, and at the same time commissioned John of Salisbury to solicit leave for the invasion of Ireland.

The Pope, who loved John "as much as his mother or uterine brother," did not forget his earlier days as a poor scholar, but received Salisbury in the friendliest manner, and kept him for three months at Beneventum where the Papal Court was held. John of Salisbury returned with the required privilege and a gold ring as a symbol of the right with which Henry was invested to rule and reform Ireland. The project of invasion, however, was opposed by the Empress-mother and the barons. They dwelt on the rebellious spirit that prevailed in his continental dominions, and on the rival claims which others were preferring to the English throne. The privilege and ring of Adrian were kept in the castle of Winchester. This is attested by the Norman chronicles.* By-and-by the prevalent dissensions in Ireland took a peculiar turn. McMurrough, the dethroned King of Leinster, applied to Henry for aid in order to his restoration. Henry, being on the Continent and otherwise engaged, wrote to his subjects to aid McMurrough. The result was that some Anglo-Norman adventurers landed in Ireland in the year 1169, restored McMurrough and conquered Dublin, Waterford, Wexford, and Meath.

Henry II., hearing of the approach to Normandy where he then was, of Papal legates with a view of laying his dominions under interdict for his being implicated in the murder of St. Thomas A'Becket, thought well of retiring before them, and coming to England. In order to do something to propitiate Rome, and at the same time gratify his ambition, he prepared to go in person to Ireland, and carry out the reformation for which he had obtained a privilege from Pope Adrian. Though a fleet of 400 vessels carried mail-clad knights in hundreds and tens of thousands of archers, yet on landing in Ireland he made no movement of a warlike character in furtherance of the conquest of the country. He might have done so with the greatest success, in conjunction with those free lances who by themselves had already conquered the richest part of the country, from which they never have been driven. Nor was there a movement made by the native population. All were subdued in presence of the king. Not a sword was drawn; and to show that he came conscious of power and with a desire of using moral rather than physical means, he directed a national synod of bishops to be held in Cashel in the early part of the year 1172. Most of the Irish princes personally took the oath of fealty to Henry; and even Roderick O'Connor, supreme King of Ireland, having submitted by proxy, the Irish bishops had no difficulty in following his

* Besides their intrinsic marks of authenticity, the most competent authorities have pronounced these writings genuine. *Vide* Canciani, "Leges Barbarorum," &c., vol. iv.

example. They appended their signatures to the account of the synod and of the general submission to Henry II., which they transmitted to Pope Alexander III.

Henry, having learnt that the Papal legates before visiting him with ecclesiastical censures, were willing to give him a hearing, gladly hastened out of Ireland to Normandy for the purpose of exculpating himself of any participation in the murder of St. Thomas. He had the more confidence as he could appeal to his zeal in carrying out the mission in Ireland which he had sought from Adrian IV. The "Analecta" (p. 370) states that "it is beyond the reach of controversy there was not a word uttered at the Synod of Cashel about Adrian's grant." For this statement an atom of proof is not given. The very opposite is to my mind certain. There is reason for judging that the grant of Adrian was known to McMurrough inasmuch as he did what other princes in their mutual disputes had never done previously—apply for the interference of an English monarch. The several synods held immediately before the invasion would look as if the Church had been anxious to remove all grounds of complaint or foreign interference.

How could we expect that the bishops of a National Church, presided over by a Roman legate, would have assembled at the bidding of a foreign potentate coming as Henry did to the Irish, if he had not spoken of the authority and commission with which he was charged? Had he come beating down all opposition, and had he commanded individual bishops, with the sword at their throats, it is possible they would have been overawed. But considering the circumstances under which the bishops met, and that Henry lay under the imputation of abetting the murder of St. Thomas, it is unlikely that he spoke to the bishops, or that they would have obeyed in a matter touching spiritual jurisdiction, if he had not satisfied them as to his authority from Pope Adrian. One of the decrees of the synod enjoined that the ritual and liturgy of the Irish Church should thenceforth be modelled on the English form. Are we to suppose that the Irish Church surrendered its national customs and rites at the suggestion of a layman without an intimation of the Pope's will? If so, the Irish character appears quite different from what it was before or after under like circumstances. But if we could believe that the bishops as Celts forgot their tenaciousness of old customs, or their firmness as ecclesiastics, by moulding the national discipline at the will of a lay dictator, what of the Roman legate who presided at the council? Henry fled in terror from his own hereditary possessions, awed by the majesty and power of Rome as represented by foreign legates; and are we to believe that he dared to overawe and degrade that Roman power as represented in an Irish legate standing on his own mountain heath? Are we to suppose that the majesty of Rome was degraded in the pusillanimity of a legate in convening and presiding at a council without reference to him whose ambassador he was? Forbid the thought!

Furthermore, John of Salisbury, in a work which was in the hands of all, stated that twelve years previously he had received the privilege for Henry. For all these reasons I must believe, till I get strong proof to the contrary, that the grant of Adrian was fully made known; and a tittle of such proof has not been forthcoming.

Moreover, Pope Alexander III. on receiving an account of the Synod of Cashel wrote to King Henry, to the Irish bishops, and to the Irish princes. The Pope's letters, which are preserved in the "Black Book of the Exchequer," in reply to the bishops, allude to the signs of improvement and to the diminution of prevalent abuses as stated by them, as if a moral mission rather than a conquest had been the King's ambition. The letter to the Irish princes alludes to the peace and tranquillity which they would henceforth enjoy, as if unrest had been their curse. The letter to the King alludes to his sins, stating that as it was to obtain pardon for his sins he undertook the mission, so should he proceed in the same course for their further remission. On the other hand, Henry, so far from being proved guilty of the murder of St. Thomas, was declared innocent of any participation in it. This, coupled with services in the cause of order in Ireland, disposed the Pope the more to give a letter confirmatory of the privilege of Adrian. Henry was a changed man. Instead of supporting, as he had done, an anti-Pope against Alexander III., he swore fealty to him for his own crown, promised the redress of all grievances at home and to join in a crusade against the infidel abroad. The result was the confirmatory brief of Alexander III.:—"Inasmuch as things granted on good reasons by our predecessors are to be allowed, ratified, and confirmed, we, following the example of the venerable Pope Adrian, and looking to the realization of our own wishes, do confirm the donation of the kingdom of Ireland made by him to you: reserving to St. Peter and the Church of Rome the yearly revenue of one penny out of every house in Ireland as in England; and provided that the barbarous people of Ireland be reformed, &c."

As bearing on the genuineness of this document it may be observed that the letter written by Pope Alexander to the King on receipt of the account of the Cashel Synod, reminds him in the last paragraphs that the authority of the Roman Church over islands is, as he acknowledged, different from that over continents, and expresses a hope that the privileges of St. Peter would be cared for in said land. The Pope, writing a congratulatory letter to the King, could not decently do more than allude to the Peter pence and the King's own admission, in his letter to Pope Adrian, in applying for the privilege, of the Pope's more immediate authority over islands than over the mainland.

Now the adversaries who have to admit the genuineness of these letters must acknowledge that there is a delicate allusion, the more telling as made only by the way, to the main features in Pope Adrian's letter of grant. Then there is mention more than once of the atoning nature of the King's expedition to Ireland, which indirectly, but the more unsuspiciously on that account, brings out the motive which prompted the King as stated in his letter to Adrian, when he applied for the privilege of coming to Ireland— the very grounds on which the King had applied to Pope Adrian for the privilege. Previous and subsequent documents dwell on the unbridled licentiousness mentioned in Pope Alexander's letter.*

Moreover, the charge of eating meat in mid-Lent is glanced at in the letter. Now, one would think that this was a charge least likely to be made against the Irish, owing to their hereditary severity of discipline. Yet though not alluded to by any ecclesiastical historian, the charge is more or less borne out by original documents. The "Leabhar Breac" (p. 90) states that Lent began on the Sunday previous to Passion Sunday. This practice was limited probably either to a small district or a short period.

The charge of want of respect for ecclesiastical persons is fully sustained by contemporaneous authority. The Annals of the Four Masters come with their corroborative testimony. A synod was held in the year 1158, at Brimactigue. Twenty-five bishops attended, and the Papal Legate presided. The Church was endeavouring to ward off the impending blow on the nation by doing its own part. But how do its children co-operate? The Annalists inform us that while the Connaught bishops were on their way to the synod, they were plundered and beaten, and two of their followers killed by the soldiers of the King of Leinster. The bishops had to return home.

While the Pope, in his letter to the English monarch, congratulates him on conquering a kingdom which the Roman eagles never overshadowed, he delicately compliments the Irish princes on voluntarily submitting to his sway, the more so as he anticipated peace and order for their land, the want of which by internecine slaughter (*mutua cæde*), he deplored in his letter to

---

* "Velut effrenes per campum licentiæ ducerentur." Theiner, "Vetera Monumenta," ad an. 1290.

Henry,* and winds up by exhorting them to a loyal observance of the fealty which they promised on oath.†

The Pope, in writing to the Legate and Irish bishops, congratulates them on the nascent diminution of the prevalent abuses. The existence of these, he stated, was put beyond doubt by the bishops' letters, as well as by other authentic testimonies. In fact, the substance of the confirmatory letter of Alexander III. is given in his letters to the several parties; so that those who admit the genuineness of the latter cannot consistently deny that of the former.

I have dwelt on these documents not so much for the purpose of pointing out how they mutually support each other, as of showing the ground for anxiety on the part of the Holy See in regard to Ireland. It is idle to say that the Pope was misinformed on Irish affairs. It is no less idle to point to some worthy ecclesiastics who were Pope Adrian's teachers on the continent. Adrian's information, as Pope, was derived from the report of Cardinal Paparo, who presided at the National Synod only three years previously to the letter of privilege. Colgan, the author of "Acts of the Irish Saints," takes the same view of the situation. No one was better acquainted with the history of his country. The Order, of which he was a distinguished member, came to Ireland within fifty years of the coming of King Henry himself. Colgan inherited its earliest traditions, had unrolled before him every manuscript extant which told Ireland's story. He drew a picture of the glories of its ancient Church almost too bright, one would dream, to be realized on this side of the grave; still his estimate of the Ireland of the twelfth century corresponds with that of the Popes. He represents the nation as tottering to its fall, society as almost unhinged from dissensions, and the Church, once so glorious, as in a state of decay.‡ When the clannish elements offer no prospect of cementing into a nation; when the liberty of priest and bishop as such, as has been the case more than once, is hampered under any form of government; he is a public benefactor who restores to the Church and society the freedom and blessings for which they exist. In the mind even of an Irish Pope a change from a suicidal, elective monarchy to a hereditary form, not to speak of higher interests, might be a

---

* *Vide* "Regesta Nich. iv.," Ep. 155, "pacem inter eos solicite conservando."
† "Liber Scaccarii," fol. 96.
‡ "Acta Sanctorum Hiberniæ." "Et hæc misera reipublicæ facies stetit in suis promiscuis motibus donec regnum in se divisum et dissidiis excidio imminens tandem patuerit externis viribus et facilem Anglo sub-annum 1171 . . . . quibusdam tum populi proceribus eum adsciscentibus . . . . rei Catholicæ languentis."

rich compensation for a change of dynasty. And considering the development given to the arts and civilization under Norman rule, and the encouragement held out to holy and learned men —to the Lanfrancs and Anselms—Pope Adrian might very naturally calculate on the like good results from Norman sway in Ireland.

There are those who do not care to comprehend the quasi-feudatory relations to which the constitutional law of the Middle Ages gave rise in reference to the Pope and European States. If they will view society, then, not through the jurisprudence and the spirit which moulded and animated it, but in the light of the nineteenth century, let them at all events take a correct survey of its outward framework. In such a light let us view the social state of Ireland in the twelfth century. One would think that the Irish nation, after centuries of fierce struggle with the Northmen, who were eventually crushed in the year 1014, would sigh for repose or apply itself to the reconstruction of society and the cultivation of the arts of peace. But no: annalists tell us that in this very year a battle was fought between the sons of Brian Boroimhe. Allowing a hundred years to our countrymen to divide the spoils won from the Danes, to compose their own differences, and settle down to quiet work, let us confine our survey to the fifty years immediately preceding the privilege given by Adrian IV. Let our guides be no other than the native provincial annalists. Well, they inform us that the aim of the head kings—whether O'Briens, O'Neils, or O'Connors—was not to harmonize discordant elements, but to depose weak or obnoxious provincial kings, and substitute for them their own children or dependents. Fighting, plunder, harrying, and burning were the order of the day. Sacred buildings and consecrated persons were deemed fit objects of clannish outrage. In the year 1115 the stone church of Ardbreacan, " with its full of people," with many other churches, was burnt. The King of Connaught in 1121 made war on Desmond, and "preyed on the country and churches from Maghfemin to Tralee." Trim, with its churches, in 1128, was burnt. In the year 1131, the King of Fercall was burnt in the church of Raithin; and in 1133, Lusk, " with its full of people," was burnt, together with its relics.

When the dictates of humanity and the voice of religion were disregarded, we can easily imagine what a wreck was made of morality. In the year 1135, McMurrough, King of Leinster, forced the successor of St. Bridget, the Abbess of Kildare, from her convent, and compelled her to marry one of his followers. In the year 1153, just after Cardinal Paparo left Ireland, McMurrough carried away the wife of O'Rorke of Brefney; and what throws a more sickening light over the ghastly scene is that her unmanly brother suggested the unwomanly infidelity. During the fifty years through which we had the courage to wade, Irish annalists chronicle the deposition, with its disturbing consequences, of thirty kings or princes, the slaying of 113 lords or princes, and the fighting of 140 battles of a national or provincial character. Let us learn the effects of one of these from the Annals of the Four Masters. They tell us that in the year 1151 there was a battle between Munster men and Connaught men with the men of Meath and Leinster. Of the Munster men alone there fell in battle 7,000! But perhaps no less touching and eloquent is the remark of the annalist on the same year "that the lord of Luigne died on his bed; for he was under the laws of St. Ciaran."

This state of things continued down to 1155. Hence the annalists had to tell us that during the year 1154 four lords or princes were slain; that the fleet of Turlogh O'Connor swept the northern seas, plundering Tirconnell and Inishowen, with dreadful slaughter on both sides; that an army was led from the north by the O'Lochlain, who banished the O'Reilleys from the principality of Brefney, and destroyed the crops; that the said Turlogh O'Connor went on a predatory excursion, in which his son was slain; that a battle was fought between the O'Briens and people of Carlow, in which the chief of the O'Nowlans fell; that Tiernan O'Rorke led a devastating army into Leinster, plundering churches and the whole country; that the people of Melsinna were plundered by the great Melseachlan of Meath, and afterwards hunted with their chief into Connaught; that Desmond preyed on the Dalgais, and that the Dalcassians preyed on Desmond; that Deorah O'Flann put out the eyes of his son for assuming the lordship of Hi-Tuirtre; that Deorah himself was banished into Connaught by the O'Lochlan; and that the chief of Colleymore was done to death even at the very door of the church of Birr. Such was the programme gone through in one year.* With such evidence before us, how literally true appears the statement, which otherwise might be termed a poetic flight for the moment in the chronicler,"that all Ireland was a trembling sod;" and he might have added, with as much truth, that it was a vast human shambles. Was such a state of things to continue for ever?

The letter of privilege of Pope Adrian and the confirmatory one by Pope Alexander have been quoted by contemporaneous historians. The Pope who gave the letter confirmatory of the first privilege reproduces it substantially in his Pontifical letter, so that though there should have been no mention of these

---

* "Annals of Four Masters," sub an. 1154.

documents subsequently, yet we could not doubt the existence of the privilege. On the other hand, if we suppose every trace of these original documents had perished, as well as all allusion to them by contemporaneous writers, but that a constant, universal tradition prevailed, and one embodied into every variety of document, no unprejudiced person could avoid believing in the existence of the original grants.

But when the substance of the original privilege is preserved, even to the very words, and the testimonies of contemporaneous authorities are produced and corroborated by evidence furnished by Irish, English, and Roman documents, there surely are no grounds for reasonable doubt. It were to introduce universal pyrrhonism to doubt what so many various and widely scattered documents assert. Chronicles and Rolls of Parliament, collections of Councils from Labbe to Hefele, Cardinals as represented by Pole and Baronius, Nuncios speaking through Rinuccini,* Gallicans of whom Bossuet was mouthpiece, and who, when not able to deny the *privilege,* fiercely attacked the principles of which it was the outcome, Protestants represented by the learned Ussher, Bullaries of Pontiffs down to the latest edition, ecclesiastical historians from Natalis Alexander to Lingard— all agree in maintaining the authenticity of the privilege of Adrian. As a specimen of the allusions made to the letter of grant from Pope Adrian by subsequent Popes in their Bullaries, I select the following from Pope Paul IV., on the occasion of raising Ireland to the rank of a kingdom in the year 1153. "Ever since the Kingdom of England obtained the dominion of this island through the Apostolic See, the English Kings have had the custom of taking the title simply of lords of Ireland." That of lord is the very title which Adrian IV. recommended to be given to Henry II. This entry from the Bull of Paul IV. is taken from the latest edition of the Bullary. And with such evidence before them there are those who, while admitting the authenticity of the plays of Terence, or the "Anabasis" of Xenophon, affect to doubt that of the grant of Adrian!

The work at the head of this article is a treatise of 125 folio pages, and its aim is to establish that Pope Adrian, so far from countenancing the invasion of Ireland, positively opposed it in a letter written in the year 1159. The treatise includes articles and arguments of those who deny the authenticity of the grant. Though the writer in the "Analecta" affects to be confident that the evidence he has produced will at once destroy all belief in the asserted privilege of Adrian, still he undertakes to attack it piecemeal. While he is ready to come down with one fell swoop

* "Nunziatura," p. 256.

and take the position by storm, he does not disdain the slower method of sapping. Before stating, then, the novel theory in the "Analecta," I shall briefly notice the principal objections in it against the grant of Adrian.

The writer states that the privilege of Adrian speaks of Henry as *entering* Ireland, and contends that the word *enter* supposes the king already landed; and then concludes that the privilege was made out, not in the year 1155, but in 1172, when Henry was in Ireland and determined on entering or penetrating it. Without insisting that writers who describe Henry's first advent to Ireland as an *entrance*, I refer the writer to the true letter of refusal from Adrian as he states, and he will see (p. 379) that himself gives the word (*intrare*) and applies it to the invasion or entrance on the soil of Ireland: therefore the use of the word is no proof of forgery.

While his objection turns on verbal criticism, the learned bishop of Ossory, whose treatise the "Analecta" embodies, objects to the whole sentence and the idea connected with it. This illustrious writer (p. 378) states that the description of the barbarity of the country as sketched in Adrian's letter would suit the year 1172, that the country was not verging on barbarism in 1155, the year of the grant, but was in a flourishing condition, as Adrian could learn from Irish masters, and that three years' war from 1169 made the country in 1172 fit for the description given of it in Pope Adrian's letter.

I have said enough already on the awful state of the country in 1155. It is idle to put what the Pope might have learnt as a schoolboy in the balance against what he really learnt from his legates.

If in 1172 the country had fallen, as asserted, to such a state of barbarism, how is it that the Irish bishops stated that the evils were on the decrease? If the country was in such a flourishing state in 1155, how is it that we find the Connaught bishops hunted home from the National Synod? How is it that native annalists give such a description of 1154 as to make one's flesh creep in horror? How is it that the same description —"barbaries paganorum"—is given in what the "Analecta" contends to be the true letter?

The illustrious writer quoted in the "Analecta"(p. 371) objects to John of Salisbury's testimony, inasmuch as he had stated in the year 1160 that the ring of investiture given by the Pope was preserved in the public archives with the grant itself : " usque in hodiernam diem." The writer maintains that "the hand of the impostor is manifestly seen in this ' even to this day.'" The phrase, it is said, could refer only to a long period, and the period between the alleged grant in 1155 to 1160 was very short.

Firstly, the writer strains a point; for in my copy of the "Metalogicus" I do not read *usque* "all along or even," but "to this day," *ad hodiernam diem*. It is admitted that about the same length of time elapsed between the death of our Saviour and the Gospel of St. Matthew as intervened between the grant of Adrian and mention of it by John of Salisbury. Now St. Matthew, writing about the potter's field purchased with the thirty pieces of silver, states that the "field is called the field of blood even to this day"—an interval of about seven years (Matt. xxviii. 8).

Again (xxviii. 15), speaking of the bribes given by the Jewish priests to the soldiers, that they would say that Christ's body was stolen while they were asleep, the Evangelist says "that this word spread abroad even to the present day."

The case is made much clearer by the Acts of the Apostles (xxi. 31). St. Luke states that the Jews, seizing St. Paul, drew him out of the Temple, and that the doors were at once shut; and as they were about to kill him it was told to the tribune of the band. This happened in the year 58, and St. Paul, alluding to it in the Acts (xxvi. 21) in the year 60, said, in his memorable discourse before King Agrippa, "For this cause the Jews, when I was in the Temple, having apprehended me, went about to kill me; but by the help of God aided, I stand unto this very day." Thus the phrase is applied by the sacred writer to an interval of only two years.

It is made matter of objection in the "Analecta" (p. 370) that the remarks made by John of Salisbury, at the end of a metaphysical treatise, in reference to the grant of Adrian, look like an interpolation. These remarks occupy only a few short paragraphs. After finishing his treatise, and while contemplating the evils caused by schism, the great loss sustained in the death of his familiar friend, Pope Adrian, and his own grief at the sickness of his spiritual father, Archbishop Theobald, what wonder that John should indulge in a few reflections, should allude to the kindness of Pope Adrian in having given the privilege at his request, though, or perhaps because, that privilege was a dead letter in the castle of Winchester? Acknowledged on all hands as was his great familiarity with the Pope, still one might fear an exaggeration in the matter if he did not state that the ring and privilege had been brought to the King. And where is the matter for marvel that at the end of a book he left a note of sincere friendship, which delicacy prevented him from doing during the lifetime of the Pope?

Here is a case in point. Chevalier Artaud, while finishing the Life of Pope Innocent III.,* was quoting the testimony of

---

* L. B., p. 189.

Gregory XVI., as expressed in the "Triumph of the Church and the Holy See," in praise of Innocent, when news came of the former's death. He breaks off the life of Innocent, and gives a sketch of the Pontiff of whose death he had just heard, and thus blended the twelfth with the nineteenth century.

So again if we look into the "Leabhar Breac," we find that the Irish writer, after giving the martyrdom of St. John Baptist, and the legend of the Seven Sleepers, suddenly hears of the death of the Earl of Clanricarde, and at once forgetting the past, is thus absorbed in the world around him:—

And they are in affliction to-day in Clanricarde for the death of their chief and lord who died yesterday. This was Ulick, the first of the race of Ulick, who was styled earl, from the red earl down to this; and this lamentation is not without cause to them, for such was the goodness of that man, that they had no herdsman in charge of their cows and chattels; and it is the general saying of all that they know not how they shall be able to protect their chattels now that they know no way by which to escape, or asylum of retreat open to them, while wars press on them on all sides.

Now on the death of a petty chief the writer interrupted his narrative, and penned the obituary notice. Having no available space he wrote around the margin of the sheet. It was the natural expression of sadness and gratitude. No one suspects forgery in it, because it comes not in collision with any pet theory. But John of Salisbury, one of the finest characters morally and intellectually in the twelfth century, because he pays a tribute of gratitude and sorrow, not on a suspicious margin, but at the close of his book, to departed worth and friendship, is suspected of forgery!

Seeing the worthlessness of all previous objections against the grant of Adrian, the writer in the "Analecta" comes forward with the new theory. He produces a letter of refusal, maintaining that it has exclusive reference to Ireland, and argues naturally that if this be genuine, all previous letters of grant must have been forgeries. We agree with him that there is more than a casual similarity not only in idea but in the very words and whole sentences. It is contended that while the opening part of the Pope's letter of refusal is retained the body of the letter of grant is forged, and that the letter of refusal has been made the ground for the forged letter of grant. We are told that a letter of leave to invade Ireland was asked by Louis King of France and Henry King of England. The writer in the "Analecta" states that the letter of refusal written by Pope Adrian makes mention of a country whose initial letter was H, and that this stands for Ireland (Hiberniam), and not as all others who have noticed the matter state, for Spain (Hispaniam). The following is the part of the letter on which he grounds his theory :—

Adrian, bishop, servant of the servants of God, to our most dear son in Christ, Louis, the illustrious king of the Franks, health and apostolic benediction. Your majesty, very laudably and profitably, while anxious about spreading the Christian name on earth and laying up a reward of eternal happiness for yourself in heaven, are arranging to hasten into Spain with our most illustrious king of the English for the purpose of *subduing* the barbarity of pagans, and subjecting to the yoke and sway of Christians, the nations apostate and such as recoil from and receive not the truth. And you are busily engaged, in order that this work may have a happy issue, to gather together an army and all necessaries for the journey. But in order the more profitably to execute your project you ask the advice and favour of your mother, the holy Roman Church. . . . . It comes to this that it appears neither prudent nor safe to enter a foreign land without previously asking the advice of the princes and people of that land. You, however, as we have heard, without consulting the Church, princes, or people of that land are arranging to hasten thither, which you ought not attempt by any means without making certain of its necessity through the princes, and without being invited previously by them. Hence, as we heartily love your honour and advancement, and would have you attempt nothing of the kind without reasonable cause, we advise you by this letter to ascertain the will of the Church, its princes, and of its people, and take advice from them.

The writer grounds his argument on the above portion of the letter of Pope Adrian in the year 1159. For the first time, I suspect, people hear of a king of France having had any designs of conquest on Ireland, or that Ireland was sunk so low as to call for a crusade. It will surprise many to learn that an insignificant island would require the co-operation of two of the most powerful monarchs in Europe in order to introduce respect for law in Ireland, especially as a few thousand free-lances were sufficient in a few years subsequently to invade and make permanent acquisitions in Ireland. The ingenious writer does not inform us how the monarchs were to divide Ireland between them, or whether they were to return home on the accomplishment of their mission. He hints that King Louis was more religious than Henry, that Henry's views were more worldly, and that he made use of Louis in order the more readily to get the Pope's consent. I am afraid the writer gives Henry credit for a delicacy of feeling in making a request of his countryman, Pope Adrian, to which he has but very little claim. It is putting the case too strongly to assert that Louis was made the prime mover because Henry naturally feared that a Pope would be slow in acceding to the request of his fellow-countryman. One would think that Henry was not influenced by supremely supernatural views in his estimate of human things, and that he would naturally conclude that the Pope, so far as conscience would sanction it, would be disposed to accede to a request of a fellow-countryman and friend, and that he would reciprocate the feeling entertained towards him, and testified at his death.

It will, no doubt, sound strange to hear that leave should have been applied for in order to carry on a crusade in Ireland in 1159, when at this very time, according to the authorities of the "Analecta" (p. 378) Ireland was in a "flourishing condition." On the other hand, we know that in a Council held in the year 1148 decrees were passed with a view of preaching up a crusade against the Moors in Spain. This Council of Rheims was so representative, at which the Pope himself presided, that some historians have styled it a Plenary Council. The deliberations turned on Spain, and not a word about Ireland. In the year 1158 was founded in Spain the military Order of Calatrava, and that of Alcantara in the year 1156; and when in the year 1172 there was question of reconciling Henry II. to the Church, owing to his alleged complicity in the martyrdom of St. Thomas, one of the conditions for absolution was that he should undertake a crusade, if called on, against the Moors of Spain. All these circumstances lead to the belief, without evidence to the contrary, that the letter of Adrian referred to Spain rather than Ireland. The letter of Adrian was printed for the first time from an original manuscript in the year 1611 by Bongars, and while Spain is the country mentioned, not a word about Ireland. About thirty years afterwards it was published from another manuscript by Duchesne, and of Spain alone mention is made. Every subsequent historian, from Bouquet to Natalis Alexander, mentions Spain as the country in question.

The writer in the "Analecta" relies principally on internal evidence, while he claims the testimony of a contemporaneous chronicler. The continuator of Sigebert, he says, alludes to the preparations of Henry II. for invading Ireland in 1177. "Henry, King of England, puffed up with pride, and usurping things *not conceded*, striving for things he had no business to mind, prepared ships, and called together the soldiers of his kingdom to conquer Ireland." The "Analecta" italicizes the words "not conceded," to show that the king was setting about what was not conceded to him by the Pope. Now it is very questionable if the annalist, speaking of things not allowed in the year 1172, refers to what took place in the year 1159, when Henry was refused, as is asserted, leave to invade Ireland. There were many things done unlawfully during these twelve eventful years by Henry which the annalist could have referred to besides the alleged refusal of a grant twelve years before. Did not encroachments on the Church which led up to the martyrdom of St. Thomas take place? Could not the annalist have referred to these scenes as having taken place only the previous year? Could not the words " not conceded" (*non concessa*) mean something besides the refusal of a request in the ordinary sense? Frederick II. indulged in the very like usurpations as Henry II. The same Pope Adrian, writing to him on his encroachments on the spiritual domain, reminds him of the favour conferred on him when he received the crown at his own hands, and concludes with an advice and warning: " Come to your senses, then, we advise you. We fear lest your nobility, while grasping at what has not been *conceded*, lose what has been conceded."* Ecclesiastical historians have remarked that the words "conceded" and "not conceded" in the twelfth century in this connection meant what was "lawful and unlawful." Therefore the "Analecta" does not and cannot prove that the words of the annalist meant a refusal of a request.

But the writer may be more fortunate in his argument founded on the nature of the letter itself. He says that it supplies seven distinct points which prove that the letter could not apply to Spain, and ranges his argument under seven heads, while he devotes seven others to prove that the letter must refer to Ireland solely.

1. It is maintained that the Pope speaks of a "land" and not a kingdom. Spain had not only one, but three kingdoms, while Ireland was always spoken of officially as a land or country down to the sixteenth century.

But is it a fact that Ireland was never called a kingdom? Did not King John, in a very solemn document, speak of the "kingdom" of Ireland? He promised to pay 1,000 marks out of the kingdom of England and the "kingdom" of Ireland. The confirmatory letter of Alexander III. to Henry II. is a very official document; and in that the Pope, alluding to the grant of his predecessor, speaks of the kingdom granted to you (*regni vobis indulto*). Again, the same Pope, in a letter to Henry II., dated Sept. 20, 1172, congratulates him on having acquired a "kingdom." So, too, the agreement between Roderick O'Connor and Henry II. brings out the use of the word "kingdom" as applied to Ireland. For it is stated that Henry II. attached most firmly Roderick to himself by making his kingdom feudatory to himself. In the fourth year of the Pontificate of

* Labbe, col. 1149, " Resipisce, ergo, resipisce tibi consulimus ; . . . dum inconcessa *captas* ne concessa perdas."

Innocent III., he addressed the clergy of the cathedral churches of the *kingdom* of Connaught,* and advised them to respect the king's voice in their elections. Again, in the year 1221, Pope Honorius had to interpose between the Archbishop of Cashel and the English monarch. The Pope spoke of the various disputes in the kingdom of England and the kingdom of Ireland, and of the common law in England and that in the "kingdom" of Ireland. It would be impossible, as it is unnecessary, to refer to the numberless instances in which the word "kingdom" was applied to Ireland. It was applied by popes and princes in the most official communications.

On the other hand, the term "land" was applied to Spain. Thus the ecclesiastical historian, Bzovius, speaking† of the reconciliation of Henry II., says that one of the conditions was that he should go to free that "land" (Spain) from pagans. In good truth the Pope, in the letter under consideration, alluding to the unfortunate crusade to Jerusalem, speaks of the country as a "land" (*terra*), though ruled by the Mahommedan sovereigns. The Pope, in speaking of a country, considered it in its physical character, and abstracted from its form of government. He need not have considered whether it was a monarchy or not; whether it was a limited monarchy or otherwise. It was sufficient for his purpose to speak of the country, and abstract from its moral attributes. It is not true, then, as a matter of fact, that Ireland had been exclusively designated by "land" (*terra*) up to the sixteenth century; or that the term "kingdom" was exclusively applied to Spain. Why, without looking abroad, in the letter quoted by the "Analecta," the words "land" and "kingdom" are used indiscriminately (*prius necessitatem terræ per principes illius regni inspicias*). The Pope, in alluding to a country, found it convenient to abstract from its form of government. Thus Henry, son of Alphonsus, Count of Portugal, having defeated five Moorish kings in so many battles in the year 1139, was proclaimed King by the army. He was addressed as such by the Pope subsequently; but because the King of Castile would have him a dependant on his crown, he made a complaint at the Council of Rheims of his rights being trenched on by the Pope. The Pope explained by saying that, in giving him the title of King, he did not intend to curtail the rights of the Castilian crown. At all events, historical facts make it certain that neither the term "land" (*terra*) was applied exclusively to Ireland, nor that of "kingdom" to Spain.

2. It is maintained the country in question had a hierarchy capable of free deliberation, and of being consulted, a hierarchy

---

* Theiner, Ep. 226, Reg. an. v. Ep. 250.   † Tom. ii. p. 331.

which exercised influence on political questions. It is added that Spain was composed of two camps—one Christian and the other infidel. The Christians in the infidel part were not free to meet, and therefore the letter could not apply to that part, and that the Christian part did not require help.

There is confusion or inconsistency in the remarks of the writer in the "Analecta." He takes his stand in the Christian or infidel camp as it suits him. Could not the hierarchy in the Christian part have a voice in the affairs of their afflicted brethren? Was not there a Primate at Toledo? When the Kingdom of Portugal was established in 1139, did it not give rise to a question of the spiritual authority of Toledo? Could not the same happen on the acquisition of further territory from the Moors? Should not the writer in the "Analecta" remember that the Church does not surrender its rights even though they may be in abeyance through the temporary possession of them by pagans? Does she not daily give titles to her ministers in infidel districts—*in partibus infidelium?* Pope Nicholas claimed this very Spain as a feudatory, and as peculiarly belonging to St. Peter, though it had been for a long time in possession of the infidel.* Should not the Primate and the other bishops in like manner extend their views to the time when the Cross would replace the Crescent on even to Granada and the Straits of Gibraltar?

And touching the allusion to influence on political matters, could not the Spanish hierarchy have a voice in such questions? The Irish hierarchy had not a predominating influence. Owing to the divisions of the kingdom and the desolating influence of clanship, the Irish Church, to the detriment of nationality, was hampered in its action. Even in ecclesiastical matters where was the central power strong and constant and willing to see to the executions of canons however excellent? The earliest allusion in Irish documents which is made to the possession of Ireland by the English, connects it with the plundering of the property of a Cardinal who had come from Rome with certain instructions. For a long time the clergy, to their great relief, had been freed in Ireland from the necessity of joining the military expeditions of their chiefs; in fact the Irish clergy, except those cases in which the lay and ecclesiastical influence was centred in the same person, had little importance in civil questions.

The case was otherwise in Spain. The clergy of Spain had a strong title to such a privilege, if such it could be called. They contributed more largely to the public expenses than those in any

---

* "Proprii juris Sancti Petri fuisse licet diu a paganis occupatum." Ep. 7, lib. i.

other country in Europe. The learned Duchesne gives an interesting letter which Queen Blanche, mother of St. Louis, received. It describes a battle which had been fought between Christians and Saracens. The Abbot of Citeaux with the great captains led the van; all the bishops and clergy and religious orders were in the second rank.* The Order of Calatrava took its rise from the fact that the Abbot of Citeaux undertook its defence in the year 1158. King Alphonso gave to Martin, Primate of Toledo, the command of the army, and all his grandees as his council, and the result was that he returned full of booty and glory.† For these several reasons the writer in the "Analecta" might recognize more political influence in Spain than in Ireland in the year 1159.

3. It is maintained that "there were several princes, and not merely a single monarch in the country in question."

But Ireland was not singular in that respect. There were the princes of Arragon, Navarre, Portugal, and prince of Castile, who was styled by some, in courtesy, Emperor of Spain. It is said that the Pope would have known and mentioned the names of Spanish princes if there was question of them. But was the Pope to remember their respective names and titles? Was he to give the title of Emperor to one who did not own a fourth of Spain to the displeasure of the recognized Emperor? Was he, on the other hand, to disoblige the King of Castile by withholding from him a title which courtesy sometimes gave him? Therefore his not mentioning by name the princes nor their titles has not a shadow of proof that the Pope did not know them. He gave them the title of princes which was sometimes given even to Emperors.

4. The "Analecta" insists that the letter of Adrian required that the people should be consulted, and that it is to attribute great folly to the Pope to have the people of Spain consulted as to the necessity of foreign intervention.

The last answer would meet this assertion. The writer goes on the assumption that only those immediately under the Moorish yoke had a voice in the matter. Besides, if the writer throws his eyes down to the body of the letter he will see that the Pope attributed the reverses of a former crusade to the Holy Land to the neglect of the very means which he suggests (*inconsulto populo terræ*). When, then, Pope Adrian before preaching a crusade in favour of Spain, recommends the people to be consulted, we do not intend to charge him with *silliness*, but set down the advice to deep wisdom.

---

* "In secunda acie fuerunt omnes Episcopi et clerici et omnes ordines," l. iv. p. 447.
† "Mariana," lib. vii. ch. 28.

5. "It is stated that the great majority of the inhabitants professed Christianity, otherwise the Pontiff could not make mention of the Church of the land; for this leads us to suppose that the ecclesiastical hierarchy embraced the entire land, though some pagans and apostates remained but did not form a body or government; however, there is no question of a country tyrannized over by infidels against whom a crusade ought to be preached."

The writer of the above deals in assertions, and tries to reconcile the irreconcilable. How can paganism and apostasy be applied to Ireland? Suppose, if you will, any amount of barbarity in the Irish, how could they be called pagans and apostates? It is no fair explanation to say that they acted *as* apostates. The letter styles them simply apostates. Bad as the Irish may be allowed to have been, they were subject to Christian princes; how, then, with any truth could it be contemplated to subject them to the yoke of Christians? How, even on the supposition of savage habits of life, could the Irish be styled apostates? It has never been heard of that they fell away from Christianity. It has never been heard of that there were infidels during the twelfth century in Ireland " who rejected the faith." It is no answer to say that their lives if not their profession were pagan. The Pope, in a solemn document, calls the people—the entire people, for he makes no exception—apostates and pagans. What warrant is there for stating that they were in a minority? They were not few, they existed in hordes; they formed a nation, ay, nations (*gentes apostatrices*). And then the writer in the "Analecta" undertakes to show that this picture could not apply to Spain. He does so by asking us, " How could the Moors, not being idolaters, exhibit the qualities of pagans of whom Pope Adrian speaks. Where in Spain find apostates?" (p. 271.) And so the "Analecta" would have us seek for pagans and apostates in Ireland rather than in Spain! He judges the Moors, as not being idolaters, more removed than the Irish from paganism. It is too bad. It is to be feared that we do not attach the same meaning to paganism. The writer, it should be kept in mind, undertook to show that not only the terms of the letter applied to Ireland, but that also they could not apply to Spain. The Moors were pagans as understood in the twelfth century. If the writer looks into the *Corpus Juris Canonici* (" Decretals," lib. v. tit. vi.) he will see that Saracens and pagans are convertible terms. And in another passage it is stated that Christian writers call all those idolaters and pagans who never received the Christian faith (*Ibid.* ch. 10). Hence the Pope makes a distinction between those who received the faith and fell away (*Apostatrices*) from it, and those who refused to receive it. There were then apostates and pagans in the canonical sense. We are free to admit that the term "pagans" in its primary signification either with pagans before Christianity or with Christians in the sixth century did not apply to the Moors, but in using language we must understand it in its conventional sense; and that Mahommedans were called pagans in the twelfth century is beyond all reasonable doubt.*

The "Analecta" asks, where in Spain find apostates? Does the writer imagine that the original followers of the false prophet who crossed from the Arabian deserts were not reinforced in subduing and colonizing Africa and the south of Europe? Ought we not suspect that of the thousands taken captives of every age and condition some became apostates?

Where find apostates in Spain? Does the writer in the "Analecta" remember that after the first decisive battle with the Saracens in Spain, it was an apostate who headed the charge which led to the storming of the city and sacrilege of the church of Cordova? Does he forget a name familiar to poets, dramatists, and historians—that of Count Julian—in connection with apostasy, and the introduction of the Saracen Emir into Spain? Does he forget that, on the return of the same Emir to Damascus, young captives of both sexes, ranging from 18,000 to 30,000, followed in his train. While the alternative of ransom was given to the males, there was no choice but apostasy to the female captive.†

If the writer in the "Analecta" carefully peruses the office of "B. V. M. de Mercede," descriptive of the Spain of the twelfth century, he will change some of his views.‡ He will learn that the greater and richer part of Spain belonged to the Saracens, that they held innumerable Christians in savage bondage, that they were called pagans, and that the Christians were in extreme danger of apostatizing. And while this state of things continued for 500 years the "Analecta" asks, Where find apostates in Spain?

6. It is stated that the Pope expressed a doubt as to the necessity or utility of the crusade, and that therefore it must not have been intended against the infidels.

But it must be acknowledged at all events that there was a question of apostates. The people made no demand for help. There was no cry raised such as that by Peter the Hermit or St. Bernard, detailing the sufferings of the Christians. On

---

* Vossius' "Etymologicon," t. i. p. 420; Du Cange, "Med. et inf. Glossar."

† Gibbon, vol. ix. ch. 51.

‡ Brev. Rom., Sept. 24. "Innumeri fideles sub immani servitute, maximo cum periculo fidei abjurandæ .... felicior que Hispaniarum pars diro Saracenorum jugo .... fideles a potestate *paganorum*."

that account the Pope wished that Louis should have made himself acquainted with the immediate necessity of the crusade. That it was not necessary for checking an aggressive policy of the Saracens is made evident by the fact that the Christians were daily winning back their own; so that from being a handful cooped up in the mountain fastnesses, they had established four or five kingdoms at the end of the twelfth century. It would have been useful and desirable, indeed, to expel the infidel, but there was a question of the utility of the attempt to do so. As a proof of the risk to be incurred, the Pope reminded King Louis of the disasters that befell him and the Christian armies for not having taken proper precautions in the crusade to the Holy Land. It was a bitter but wholesome reminder to Louis. For we know that he saved his life only by his courage and climbing on a tree; and that he returned just ten years previously without having attained the object of the crusade. The Pope had reason to fear that a like result would come of the expedition into Spain. This was the more to be feared if the Christian armies entered it without an invitation or welcome from the Spanish Princes. They might have acted as the Greek Emperor Alexius, who is supposed to have supplied the Christians with treacherous guides and the Sultan with useful information about the plans of the Christians, while King Louis had a narrow escape from being taken prisoner by the Greek Emperor. This view of the matter brings again before us the absurdity of applying the letter to Ireland. A few thousand filibusters landed in Ireland, and Ireland in its divided state was unable to defeat them. How could there, then, have been any risk to two of the most powerful monarchs then in Europe in invading Ireland? Not so with Spain. Pope Adrian, who spent many happy days in the Monastery of St. Rufus, was well acquainted with it. He knew and told, what Napoleon afterwards to his cost learnt, that a small army was useless, and that the presence of a large was costly, hurtful to the feelings of the natives, and could subsist only with difficulty. To this the Pope alluded in his letter to King Louis.*

7. Under the last head of his argument, the writer in the "Analecta" states that there is no instance on record of a Pope refusing to preach a crusade against the infidel.

This reason does not prove what he undertook to prove, that the letter must have referred to Ireland. On the other hand, it may be said that the crusades were preached up because the Popes approved of them. Before this refusal there were only two

* "Ipsi vero principes et populus in tanto apparatu tuo si forte non incumberet gravarentur."

crusades, and of the disasters that befell the King and his army in the last crusade the Pope reminded him. Not only so, but he assigned as a cause of the disasters the not having consulted the princes of the land to which the Crusaders went. And even though there were a rule that the Pope as a general thing would sanction a crusade when called for, does he not give a sufficient reason in this letter for a departure from the rule?

The writer in the "Analecta," wishing to show that the letter does not apply to Spain, divides it into two camps—Christian and infidel; says there were no church, no bishops in the latter (p. 271), and that it were simply absurd to require the advice of bishops there on the necessity of an expedition. In the next sentence he asks, Would not King Louis have alluded to his father-in-law, the King of Castile, who asked the intervention, if he had written about Spain? In the first case it is supposed that the crusade was undertaken for that country, which had no bishops, or such as need not be questioned as to their feelings on the crusade; in the second supposition, the crusade was asked by those who had a hierarchy and a Christian ruler. It is illogical to take one's stand on contradictory grounds. It is unfair to avail of one supposition while claiming the benefit of a second whose force consists in ignoring the other. The writer, in supporting his theory, should let us know whether he speaks of the infidel or Christian part of Spain and stick to it. And even where he does so, he is hurried into inconsistency of another kind, which almost amounts to a change of sides. Thus (p. 264), in order to give us some idea of the substance of the Pope's letter, he refers to subjecting apostate *hordes* to the Christian yoke, and in endeavouring to fit the description to Ireland, says (p. 269) that though the Catholic hierarchy overspread the land, yet *some* pagans remained.

Behold another instance of confusion, or rather inconsistency. The writer asks (p. 355), Would King Louis require permission to help his father-in-law, the King of Castile, if there had been question of Spain? But he should remember that the permission and active co-operation of the Pope was required in the letter written to him, not for helping so much the King of Castile as King Louis himself, by preaching up the Crusade amongst his people, and indulgencing it, and by taking his kingdom under the protection of St. Peter during the Crusade. Moreover, his argument is intelligible only on the supposition that he is dealing with the Christian part of Spain, though when drawing out other heads he reasons on the assumption that there was question only of the infidel part. In fact, the writer does not give us a consistent view of his theory, nor does he himself appear to have more fixed views of it. So far as we can judge, his theory is unsubstantial; so much so, that without subjecting it to too much rough handling, one has only to look at it steadily and it vanishes.

The writer in the "Analecta," in his endeavour to build up an unsubstantial theory, has postulated a scaffolding which cannot be allowed him. He says that the letter of refusal from Pope Adrian to King Louis was consigned to the Castle of Winchester for two reasons: first, that the refusal should remain a secret, and that by-and-by it should serve as a model for a forged letter of grant. Well, it would appear more prudent to have destroyed the letter if the object had been to hush up all rumours of the refusal; and whoever was able to forge a part should have been able to forge an entire letter. How has our writer learnt that the letter of refusal was placed in Winchester? All who speak of Winchester in connection with it, state the letter was one of grant. But let this pass. The "Analecta" states the forged letter of grant was not to be produced till after the death of Louis VII., in 1180, as he was aware of the refusal of Pope Adrian, and would expose the forgery, and that the forged letters of grant were not made out till after the year 1188. If the letter was to be buried in profound secrecy in Winchester, how is it that we are told that the annalist of Anchin alluded to the refusal in 1171? The "Analecta" informs us on his authority that Henry was grasping at things not *conceded*, which, he told us groundlessly, referred to the refusal of Pope Adrian. If the forged letter were to be kept a secret till the death of Louis, why not have deferred the invasion likewise till then? If Henry II. shrunk from appearing to differ in words or writing from the wishes of the Pope, why was he not ashamed to do so by his acts in invading Ireland during the lifetime of King Louis? If Henry II. was at ease as regarded the French King after 1180, what of the reigning pontiffs? Rome has a long memory. Was not there in existence the original or a copy of Adrian's letter? Only thirty-eight years, a short period, elapsed from the supposed letter of refusal till the supposed forged letter of grant in 1188. Was there no fear or shame of the Roman Pontiffs? What would be thought at present of the man who would deny the establishment of the hierarchy in England thirty years ago by Pius IX., or who would assert that he made over the Irish nation to the French crown? Would the statement now pass without a protest from his successor, or a public comment if it could at all be deemed worthy of notice?

If Henry's plans required that the refusal of Adrian should not be made known, or that the false Bulls framed on it should not be published till the year 1188, why does Pope Alexander III. write to him in the year 1172, and congratulate him on having conquered a kingdom unapproached by the arms of imperial Rome? How account for the secret being kept at the Synod of Cashel? Then, again, we know that the letters of privilege from Popes Adrian and Alexander were published in Waterford, in 1175. But the writer in the "Analecta" says, on the authority of an illustrious writer, that there could not have been a synod in that year, and that Irish annalists make no mention of it. Why, the learned Ware in his " Annals" mentions the publication at a Synod in Waterford. So, too, does Gerald Barry. He came to Ireland only eight years after the publication, and he publicly stated that the letter of privilege was published at a synod of bishops in Waterford. How could he venture to state before all Ireland a fact as public if it did not take place? He could not deceive on a matter the truth of which was known to thousands, and stated by him in a book which was in the hands of all. He could not be disposed to deceive; for, according to the "Analecta," he honestly believed in the authenticity of the grant.

So much importance do I attach to Gerald Barry's statement, that I give up Irish authorities for him. The accurate Leland sets the publication of the privilege down to the year 1177. The old Irish "Book of the MacEgans," referred to by Dr. Keating, states that a Cardinal came from Rome with instructions in reference to the subjection of Ireland to England in the time of Donald O'Brien the Great. This would synchronize with 1177. Yet though either date would upset the theory in the "Analecta," I prefer the authority of Gerald Barry.

And why not a Synod of bishops possible in 1175? The "Analecta," when it finds Gerald Barry adverse, says, "It is useful to consult Hoveden, as he checks the other" (p. 287). Now, Hoveden assures us that there was a council held at Windsor on the Octave of St. Michael, at which King Henry appointed a bishop named Augustine to the diocese of Waterford. It was his first appointment in Ireland. The King recommended Augustine to the charge of St. Lawrence O'Toole, who, with Catholicus of Tuam, was negotiating terms for Roderick O'Connor, King of Ireland. The King directed that the consecration should be given by the Archbishop of Cashel. Now what was easier than for the archbishops to drop a line to their suffragans to meet them in Waterford, where Augustine was to be consecrated? The meeting in such circumstances would be more feasible than the famous Synod of Cashel in 1172. For Roderick had not then submitted personally or definitely, whereas the archbishops on the present occasion were after obtaining terms which were pleasing to Roderick. The meeting of bishops under the circumstances would have been more representative than that of Cashel. For at Cashel Armagh was not represented, nor indeed at Waterford. But there is this difference, that Gelasius being in Ireland could have been at Cashel, while blessed MacConcoille, being on his way to Rome, could not have been at Waterford. It is idle then to say that there is no authority for speaking of a meeting of bishops in Waterford in 1175.

And in this connection we are brought on another proof of the authenticity of Adrian's letter. How dare Henry intrude on the Irish Church without authority from Rome? How could he be thinking of appointing without jurisdiction a bishop to Waterford? Like an Attila or Tamerlane, he might have overrun the country, and have exacted an unwilling submission from an overawed populace, but the Church would have met him with a "non possumus." Within the recollection of persons still living the great Napoleon, whose conquering armies bivouacked in almost every capital in Europe, and who was keeping at the time the head of the Church in prison, could not prevail, in 1809, on the French bishops to give institution or consecration to the bishops designated by him. The Church was as jealous of its rights in the twelfth century as in the nineteenth. How could the Archbishop of Cashel give institution to one not duly appointed? In looking into the "Corpus Juris Canonici," I find that a Council in Rome, alluded to under the year 1170, was held in reference to the suspension of the Archbishop of Cashel[*] for too hastily consecrating a person intruded on the diocese of Ross. By-and-by, too, Innocent III. writes[†] to threaten or inflict censures on the Cashel metropolitan for not having acted quite canonically in regard to the consecration of a bishop. If, then, the archbishop did not escape censure in deciding according to his best lights, though not in strict conformity with the canons, on a disputed appointment, what had he not to fear for imposing hands on one sent over by the foreign invader? Necessity could not be pleaded for such a step. There was no need of such haste. The primate and his companions, who were after leaving for Rome, and who doubtless made the holy Father acquainted with the state of the Irish Church, might well be waited for. The archbishop nor the canons of the Church dare not receive the bishop elect without his producing credentials. Hence the propriety, if not necessity, of reading the privileges of Popes Adrian and Alexander, even though their contents were substantially known already. Henry felt the more anxious to have Alexander's confirmatory brief read, as his character was tarnished by the martyrdom of St. Thomas. As sovereign lord of the country, Henry was entitled, through the indulgence of the

[*] From the tenor of the decree in the "Corpus Juris," I suspect there is a mistake in the figures 1170.
[†] An. 111., Ep. 215.

Holy See, to the appointment to the bishopric of Waterford. How, then, reconcile, I again ask, the forgery of Papal letters, as asserted, in 1188 with the fact of their being published in the year 1175? How reconcile such a supposition with the enfeoffing John with the Lordship of Ireland at a Council at Oxford in 1177, by virtue of leave given by Alexander III.? If the letter of privilege had not been forged till after the year 1188, how is it or for what purpose did Urban III. give leave to Henry in 1183 to have his son crowned King of Ireland? Where was the need of forging Bulls to establish a title which was acknowledged, ay, and acknowledged to be hereditary? The favour which the Pope granted, though he refused the like favour to the Emperor of Germany, was not availed of, lest it might lead to a separation of Ireland from England. And, by-and-by, when Henry III. gave his son the Lordship of Ireland in order to make him a fit spouse for the Infanta of Spain, it was conditioned that Ireland should remain annexed to the Crown of England.*

Finally, the testimony of John of Salisbury is fatal to the theory in the "Analecta." He—one of the finest characters in the twelfth century—stated towards the end of 1159, that he himself, when on a visit to Pope Adrian at Beneventum, received for Henry the privilege from the Pope. This took place in the year 1155. This is not reconcilable with the theory that a letter of refusal was given in 1159. John of Salisbury stated in a book which was in the hands of all scholars, that he obtained the letter of privilege: this is not reconcilable with the plot which required that there should be no mention of the request made by Henry for leave to invade Ireland till after the death of King Louis in 1180. John of Salisbury then was not in the secret of the plot, for his statement is subversive of it, and, inasmuch as it unmasks the alleged forgery, is in favour of truth. The theory in the "Analecta," then, gives additional force to the evidence of Salisbury, just as the identity, so far as the matter allows, between the letter to King Louis and the letter of grant to Henry as regards Ireland, goes to show that Pope Adrian was the writer of both letters.

Now that the no-grant theory has been tested on its merits, we have only to assure its author that we have been not only fair but generous. We have pointed out that his statements are not borne out even by the evidence he adduces. Thus, while he rejects the letters written by Pope Alexander after the Synod of Cashel, and given in the "Black Book of the Exchequer," Dr. Moran, whose whole treatise he adopts as a *pièce justificative*,

---

* Artaud, "Lives of the Popes;" Brady, Inst. iv. 360; Hoveden; Lib. G. Lambeth.

admits their genuineness. He says John of Salisbury is not above suspicion, while Dr. Moran shrinks from such a charge. He admits, from the remonstrance of O'Neil, King of Ulster, that he and his Irish followers believed in the authenticity of the grant, while Dr. Moran states that the Irish nation always rejected it. The statements of the "Analecta," so far from being in harmony with evidence adduced in support of them, are not consistent with themselves. Thus the writer, p. 317, states King John would fear being badly received in Rome by Innocent III. if the tribute promised out of Ireland were not equal to the Peter-pence promised in execution of Adrian's Bull, yet in p. 316 he states that Innocent III. knew nothing of the Bull.

Alexander III. gave power to Henry to reform Ireland through those who were fit by faith, preaching, and conduct to do so; but the "Analecta," indignant at the idea that a layman should get such a commission, has only patience to ask (p. 308), "Is this tolerable?" Yet his own theory tolerates that Kings Louis and Henry should have such a commission, without any mention of the ministry of others.

The writer in the "Analecta," p. 308, states that Gerald Barry, in offering some devotional books written by him to Innocent III., took care, of course, to avoid being unmasked, "not to present the *expugnatio* which contained the Bull of Adrian," and yet he asserts (pp. 305, 310) that Gerald Barry honestly believed in the authenticity of the Bull.

In p. 351 he states that Baronius, in citing Adrian's Bull, draws for his information only "on such sources as William of Newbridge and Hoveden," and yet, p. 310, he asserts that "neither William of Newbridge nor Hoveden appears to have any knowledge of the Bull."

Besides these contradictions, there is a good deal of misrepresentation of the facts of history in the "Analecta." But as this article has already run to a considerable length, and as the misrepresentations concern not so much the false theory as the objections against the grant, I shall not dwell on them. My main object has been to test the new-broached theory. Contemporaneous history is revolutionized in order to make it conceivable, but it neither rests on any substantial foundation, nor hangs together consistently. And while, during the last 700 years, time has only added, year after year, fresh proofs of the authenticity of Adrian's privilege, making it more certain to our mind than the existence of Cæsar or Virgil, we venture to predict that before the lapse of many hundred years very few pages will be devoted to the discussion of the theory lately started in the "Analecta Juris Pontificii."

SYLVESTER MALONE.

Art. V.—THE EXPERIMENT OF FRANCE.

THREE years ago one of the principal admirers and champions in this country of the third French Republic, spoke of it as "the high water-mark of the democratic tide:" "a tremendous and prolonged political experiment, the ultimate success of which in France will lead to momentous results in the rest of Europe." These words, appropriate enough when they were written, are still more appropriate now. The tide has risen higher, the experiment has been carried further, and even those who are least inclined to prophesy when they are not sure, may advance a tolerably confident opinion, whither the "imperiosius æquor" is bearing the vessel of the State; what will be the issue of the French democratic venture. The present time, therefore, would seem to be opportune for the task which I propose to undertake in this article: to survey the present condition, and apparent prospects of public affairs in France, and to consider what lessons are thence derivable for ourselves.

On the fourth of September, 1870, the Second Empire fell, like so many of the Governments which have preceded it, before a Parisian mob, exercising "the sacred right of insurrection." The Third Republic still exists, but in a very different condition from that in which its chief founder left it. The veteran statesman, but for whose courage and sagacity it would have perished in its infancy, declared of it, "la République sera conservatice ou elle ne sera pas." Whatever the Republic may be, Conservative it certainly is not. In the month of March, 1882, seven hundred and eighty Communists sat down to a festive banquet in the Salle Favié to commemorate the events of March, 1871, and to take sweet counsel for the future. Red scrolls, bearing the names of the heroes the Commune delights to honour—Babœuf, Hébert, Raoul Rigault, Tridon, Varlin, Flourens, Delescluze, and Duval conspicuous among them—adorned the building, which moreover was garnished with banners, some displaying suitable texts, such as Blanqui's famous dictum, "Ni Dieu, ni maître," while others recalled "the memory of the thirty-five thousand Communists who were shot," or exhibited appropriate aspirations "Vive la République Sociale" and the like. The notorious General Eude was in the chair, and was supported by other Communistic warriors, Fortin, Beuillé, Granger, and Goix—who, it may be remembered, especially distinguished himself by presiding at Courts Martial; and the fair sex was well represented, Mademoiselle Louise Michel being conspicuous in a place of honour. The keynote of the oratory, which in due time set in, was that the Communists—such of them as General de Gallifet had left alive—had good reason to be satisfied with the course events had taken since their temporary defeat; that, in fact, their cause was slowly, but certainly, triumphing. They had clamoured for the amnesty of their confessors in Cayenne: they had obtained it. They had demanded the proscription of the Religious Orders: M. Ferry had gratified them. They had insisted upon the banishment of Christian teaching from the schools: M. de Freycinet had done their bidding. They had agitated for the abolition of the Concordat, and the withdrawal of the pittance solemnly guaranteed to the clergy by way of indemnity for the confiscation of ecclesiastical property in the First Revolution: these matters were then under the consideration of the Legislature. The practical conclusion expressed by Mademoiselle Michel was, that the ephemeral Governments, so rapidly succeeding one another, might be left to accomplish the decomposition of society (*la pourriture sociale*); for that underneath the putrescent body politic were the shoots of the Social Revolution: and the applause with which these utterances of the virago were received, sufficiently showed that in the opinion of her hearers she had well spoken. Certainly, the course of events during the last two years may be appealed to as justifying her confidence. The three main props of the social order still left in France are the Army, the Church, and the Magistracy, and all have been seriously shaken since the month of March, 1882. The Army has been subjected for months to the rule of a Minister of War whose sole title to fame is his violation of his *parole*, whose sole qualification for office, his eagerness to do dirty work which no other general officer could be found to undertake: its best administrative traditions have been outraged: its efficiency has been sacrificed to political jobs. The Concordat as yet remains, indeed, and the miserable stipends of the clergy are still grudgingly paid; but the war against Christianity has been vigorously carried on, even to the length of refusing to the dying in hospitals the consolations of religion. The long-threatened attack upon the magistracy has been made, and six hundred of the most learned, weighty, and trusted of French judges have been deprived of their office, the attendance of themselves or their families at public worship, their political opinions avowed or suspected, refusal to prostitute their judicial functions for the advancement of personal or party interests, being the reasons for their dismissal: reasons avowed by the Radical press with a frank cynicism which is a striking sign of the times.

Such are the main lines of French progress since the famous fourth of September, when the news of the terrible disaster at

Sedan, instead of rallying all Frenchmen round the common cause of the country, was hailed with fierce and monstrous gladness as the opportunity for the triumph of a party. But let us look a little more closely at the actual state of the public order in France. The supreme power is in the hands of the Chamber of Deputies. The men who sit there are the real rulers of the country. Consider, then, those five hundred and seventy-five sovereigns who so rapidly make and unmake Ministries, and control the external policy and internal administration of a great nation. The late M. Gambetta, whose angry words, at all events, had the ring of truth, spoke of them once as an assembly of *sous vétérinaires*. Not even their warmest admirers can in candour deny that the large majority of them are political adventurers of a very low type. Doctors without patients, lawyers without clients, authors without readers, cashiered officials, dishonoured soldiers—such is the stuff of which this sovereign legislature is largely made. M. Taine, writing of the First Republic, observes: "If it is true that a nation ought to be represented by its *élite*, France was singularly represented then. As assembly succeeds assembly, the political level falls steadily." These words are as true of the Third Republic as of the First. The existing Chamber is curiously like the Legislative Assembly of 1791. Nor is the return of such a body to be wondered at, if we consider the electorate. Universal suffrage prevails, and the first effect of universal suffrage, functioning in the political conditions which exist in France, and of which more will be said presently, is to swamp the higher intelligence and the wealth of the nation. The great majority of well educated and well-to-do Frenchmen, who in most countries would constitute the guiding element in the national life, *les classes dirigeantes*, the "men of light and leading," are what may be called Liberal Conservatives or Conservative Liberals; but these are effaced politically, and the sense of their effacement keeps them away from the electoral urns and from any participation in public affairs. The elections are determined in the urban districts by the artisans, and in the rural by the peasants —manipulated, of course, by the *délégués communaux* and the *délégués cantonaux*, the recognized wirepullers, with whom the candidate has to come to an understanding—and both these classes are the natural prey of the demagogue. The artisans in the large towns belong, almost to a man, to the *Intransigeant* or Irreconcilable faction; nor is this surprising. For years the *ouvrier* has been dazzled with visions of Socialistic and Communistic Utopias. And it is natural that he should burn to realize them. For years political agitators have trafficked in his worst passions—his greed, his envy, his hatred; and they have wrought a most disastrous change upon him. Think of the

French artisan as he used to be—as many, perhaps, who read these words can remember him—polite and amiable, sober and frugal, somewhat visionary, no doubt, in his political aspirations, —that was but the effect of the spirit of the age acting upon the perfervid Gallic temperament—but loyal to his *patron*, kind and helpful to his fellow-workmen, courteous to all the world, and, if not very devout, at all events not wanting in decent respect for *le bon Dieu;* one of the most charming types, in short, that modern civilization has produced. And now contemplate him as you may see him on almost any Sunday evening, in the Tivoli Wauxhall, or in some other large place of meeting in Paris, or in any great French city, listening greedily to inflammatory attacks upon the first principles of society; breathing forth threatenings and slaughter against capitalists, public functionaries, and priests; cheering the boldest utterances with a vehemence and heartiness which shows how deeply he has learnt the lesson of the demagogues who tell him that he is the only king, the only God; that he has a right to be rich, happy, and powerful; that the evil which he suffers is the result of unjust laws; that property is theft. The late M. Gambetta, upon a well-remembered occasion, described his constituents at Belleville as drunken slaves (*esclaves ivres*). It was a true saying. Slaves, in a sense, the great majority are and must always be. In the pathetic words of Victor Hugo, "Do what we will the lot of the great crowd, of the multitude, will always be relatively poor and miserable and sad; theirs is the hard work; theirs are the burdens to push, the burdens to drag, the burdens to carry."* Yes; what M. Louis Blanc called the *esclavage de travail* is a necessary element of human society. In this sense slavery is the lot of the *ouvrier*. But for the drunkenness he has to thank those who minister to him the deadly wine of the anarchical doctrines so well described by M. de Tocqueville: "la politique de l'impossible, la théorie de la folie furieuse; le culte de l'audace." And when once a taste for these things is contracted, it is as hard to cure as a taste for gin or for *absinthe*. It is in vain that statesmen like the late M. Thiers, after making a handsome competency by Revolutionary agitation, write beautiful books in defence of property. Heine was well warranted when he observed that the preachers of Communism use a language which the masses understand much more readily: "an universal language of which the elements are as easy as hunger, envy, and death." It is in vain that M. Grévy, anxious to complete in decent quiet his seven years' tenure of the Presidential chair, invokes "the great principles upon which rest public order and public tranquillity." "M. Grévy!"

---

* "Claude Gueu."

answer the orators of the Radical Clubs, "why in 1831 he was
one of the ringleaders of the mob that sacked the Archbishop's
Palace. Does it lie in his mouth to reproach his less lucky comrades?" It is in vain that M. Andrieux advocates "a policy of
conciliation," and the abandonment of the *guerre aux curés*.
He is immediately met with the rejoinder—" Were you not
among the keenest executioners of M. Ferry's decrees
against the Religious Orders? The very one who picked the
locks?" No; the politician who pleases the *ouvriers* is he who
is not open to the charge of being a *ventru*, an *arrivé*; who is
still lean and hungry, and who takes up Revolution as a career.
And when such an one appeals to the mob of great cities " to
continue the work of the giants of 1792," and to crown the
edifice by the emancipation of the *prolétariat*, he is received
with tumult of acclaim. It is curious and significant that a
workman will very seldom give his vote to an employer of
labour, however liberal or philanthropic: " Pourquoi mon
patron et pas moi?" he asks; that he will never give it to a
fellow operative, however trusted or intelligent: " Pourquoi
Ugène et pas moi?" he thinks. His favourite candidate is the
professional demagogue, copious in phrases and gesticulations, who
can most fluently repeat his pet shibboleths, and most vigorously
enlarge upon them. And this, too, is the favourite candidate of the
rural voters. Slow and patient as their own oxen, these sons of
the soil offer a singular contrast to their excitable and impetuous
brethren of the towns. But both classes are alike in preferring
the political agitator to any local notability. Of the seven
millions of adult males in France, five-and-a-half millions are
owners of real property. And these five-and-a-half millions of
peasant proprietors are often spoken of in this country as the
most conservative element in French society. This is one of
those half-truths by which opinion is governed, and which, as a
rule, are more misleading than whole errors. Conservative,
indeed, the French peasant proprietor is of one thing, and that
is his own petty property. He knows that the tenure by which
this is held dates from the First Revolution; that, so far as his
class is concerned, the effect of that great upheaval was to convert their copyholds, burdened with oppressive dues and the
feudal services of an outworn world, into freeholds. This is the
sum and substance of his knowledge of the history of his country;
and his dominant feeling is dread of any political movement which
may jeopardize his holding. The Revolution, especially as embodied in the first Napoleon, who curiously enough lives in his
memory as a lover of the people—

Napoléon aimait la guerre
Etson peuple, comme Jésus.

a song still popular in some districts declares—is the sole tradition which he cherishes; while the *ancien régime* stands for the symbol of all that is inimical to him. His intellectual horizon is the narrowest conceivable. His life is spent in incessant manual labour. The infinite subdivision of land, resulting from the Revolutionary Code, is an evil against which he finds no remedy save in the limitation of the number of his children. As a rule, he restricts himself to two. But even with two children he finds it hard to keep out of the hands of the village usurer. His five or six acres constitute a provision for only one son. To avoid a partition of his pittance of land, he must raise money to buy off the other. Hence it frequently happens that he is in the hands of the village Shylock, the most demoralized and demoralizing of tyrants. Doubtless, as a rule, the French peasant proprietor must be credited with the virtues of industry and frugality. Without them it would be impossible for him to live. But, on the other hand, he is given over to the spirit of utter selfishness, of complete indifference to all except the pettiest personal interests, of blind hatred and unreasoning fear of everything above his social and intellectual level, of abject meanness which no other peasantry in Europe displays in the same degree. And in politics he is the facile prey of the demagogue who can best play upon these passions. He is not apprehensive that Radicalism, in its extremest form, will touch his petty piece of land. The fine schemes for relieving of their wealth the millowner, the manufacturer, and the other capitalists most open to the indictment, that they toil not, neither do they spin, but live by the toiling and spinning of others, do not touch him. Nay, he dimly discerns that these measures would but carry forward for the benefit of other classes the same process of confiscation, whereby the nobles, the clergy, and the higher *bourgeoisie* were dispossessed for his benefit in the last century. Nothing is more utterly untrue than the allegation so commonly made in this country that the peasant proprietors of France are an impregnable barrier against Jacobinism. In political emergencies they are absolutely helpless. They have no principle of cohesion. They are a mere rabble, incapable not only of meeting, but even of understanding, any great crisis in the affairs of their country. They are driven to the ballot-box as sheep to the slaughter, at one time by the Government official, at another by the professional demagogue.

So much as to the electorate, to which France owes the five hundred and seventy-five sovereigns who constitute the Chamber of Deputies. And now glance at them as they sit there, grouped in their factions, and listen to the vapid sophisms, the stale platitudes, the gross personal insults and vulgar gibes which resound as their sterile debates proceed, and "quack outbellows quack." The five chief divisions of the professed supporters of the Republic are distinguished as the Left Centre, the Democratic Union, the Republican Union, the Radical Left, and the Extreme Left. And who that knows will be so audacious as to affirm that any one of these factions is dominated by any other thought than that of its own triumph—that is to say, the triumph of the members composing it? "Mais puisqu'ils ont le gouvernement de leur choix, qu'est-ce qu'ils demandent?" asks Rabagas; and Boubard answers: "A en être." Not "la patrie," but "le parti" is the supreme consideration. And "le parti," if analyzed, means, in the last resort, personal interest. Hence the absence of any real principle of cohesion in any of the Republican groups, nor are the other two in much better case. The Imperialists, from causes known to all the world, are as sheep having no shepherd. The Monarchists, who are ostensibly the most united are animated by the most discordant aspirations. One desiderates the *ancien régime*, the sort of monarchy the Comte de Chambord dreamed of, with the white flag and the *fleur de lys*, and nothing learnt or forgotten during the last hundred years; another, the monarchy imagined by the late M. Louis Veuillot, "a clerical monarchy" of that ardent polemist's peculiar type of "clericalism," rooting out "modern ideas" unsparingly, with "the sword of the Lord and of Gedeon," or, at all events, with some weapon for which that character is claimed; a third cherishes the ideal of M. de Broglie and M. Chesnelong, a monarchy at once Liberal and Christian; a fourth would prefer a monarchy of the Louis Philippe type—anti-clerical, slightly Voltairian, and Revolutionary enough to pose as the best of Republics; a fifth judges that no secure basis exists except universal suffrage, and demands a monarchy of the Napoleonic type, a Democratic Cæsarism with a Bourbon Cæsar. In the *Conciergerie*, in the year 1793, the prisoners condemned to death for attachment to the old order, formed several distinct parties, during the short interval between their sentence and their execution. Nothing save the guillotine, shearing off their heads into the same basket, could bring about a real fusion between them. It is an apt image of that irreconcilable contrariety among men, substantially in accord in their aims, which has characterized French politics ever since, and which has mainly contributed to place political power in the hands where it is at present lodged. The fierce democracy of the large French towns, divided almost infinitesimally in their constructive aspirations, are at all events united in their hatred of the actual social order, and in their eagerness to pull it down. It has been truly observed by Marr, in his well-known work on Secret Societies: "There is at least one flag under which the masses can be gathered, the flag of negation." " We are content"—this is the programme—" to lay down the foundation of Revolution. We shall have deserved well if we stir hatred against all existing institutions. We make war against all prevailing ideas of religion, of the State, of country, of patriotism. The idea of God is the keystone of a perverted civilization. The true root of liberty, of equality, of culture, is Atheism." There can be no question at all that these words represent, with substantial accuracy, the views of the Irreconcilable faction, which counts among its adherents the vast majority of the *ouvrier* class and which, in the present anarchy of French public life, possesses the signal advantage of knowing —at all events, to this extent—its own mind. The history of the last ten years in France is the history of the gradual gravitation of political power to this faction. The Governments which have succeeded one another so rapidly, have found in a *politique de complaisance* towards it, the only means of prolonging the days, few and evil, of their contemptible existence. M. Gambetta was right when, in the famous speech which so stirred the anger of M. Thiers, he saluted the advent to power of the *nouvelles couches sociales*. In the decade which has since passed away they have been gradually realizing their mastery, and with ever-increasing clearness have made it felt. The most recent elections in France are full of significance. Well-nigh everywhere the extremest Radicals—men whose programme is avowedly one of destruction and plunder—have been the favourite and the successful candidates; and the name of Thibaudin has been a name to conjure with: yes, Thibaudin has been hailed as the future "regenerator of society." The only effective power left in France is that supplied by popular passions—*passions de la cervelle et passions de l'estomac*—and supremacy belongs to the agitator who knows how most successfully to arouse them. Even in the rare cases in which men of good social position and approved antecedents present themselves to the electors, they are almost compelled to imitate the arts and to echo the phrases of the demagogue. " Who among us," asks M. Scherer, in one of the striking papers contributed by him last October to the *Temps*, " who among us, during the last election, did not blush for human nature on seeing how far the wisest and gravest citizen would descend to secure the success of a candidature?" But it is with them as with the necromancers of Eastern fable, who could evoke potent spirits but could not lay them; who found themselves the slaves of the terrible agencies they had hoped to use. What barrier exists against the mounting flood of Jacobinism? Patriotism? It has disappeared in partisanship. Public spirit? M. de Tocqueville told Mr. Senior in 1858—and his words are even truer now—that seventy years of Revolution had destroyed it; that only the most vulgar and selfish vanity and covetousness remain. Religion? It has been perseveringly exhibited by the propagandists of Atheism as the inveterate foe of popular liberties, the abject instrument of despotism; and some of its most zealous and prominent defenders, the late M. Louis Veuillot and his associates in the *Univers* conspicuous among them, have done their best to stamp indelibly that character upon it. The Senate? It exists but to surrender: *c'est son métier*. The Chamber? Split into factions warring against one another for office and the spoils of office, we may say of it, as Burke said of the National Assembly, that it has "a power .... like that of the evil principle to subvert or destroy; but none to construct except such machines as may be fitted for further subversion." That great body of well-trained civil servants, who, whatever we may think of the system which they carried out, represented all that was best in the traditions of French administration? They have largely disappeared since 1879, their place being taken by a host of needy and disreputable adventurers. The Magistracy? It has undergone the like fate. The Army—last unhappy refuge of order? Its permanent force is wanting in soldierlike qualities: its reserves are half trained and wholly undisciplined; *esprit de corps* among the men is a thing of the past:* the spirit of anarchy has been at work here too. There is nothing left to hinder the accomplishment of that social dissolution for which the Irreconcilables long. It is not merely residence within certain geographical limits and community of language and subjection to the same rule, of whatever type the Government may be, that make the aggregate of a vast number of individual men and women into a nation. No; to constitute a nation you must have common traditions, common feelings, common aspirations, common modes and ends of action. But in the present chaotic state of France all the bonds of thought are loosened, all classes are in antagonism, all interests are jarring and inimical. In every department of French life there is the odour, more or less pungent, which indicates how far advanced is that *pourriture sociale*, scented with delight by Mademoiselle Louise Michel two years ago. There is a convergence of signs that France is on the eve of a new '93, of a new Commune. "Be sure," said Talleyrand to Henry Greville, speaking of the horrors of the Jacobin conquest in the time of the First Revolution, "Be sure, that if we had the Republic back we should get the like events back with it, for the elements of them are always present."† To the

* See a very able article by Capt. Norman on "The French Army of To-Day," in the *Nineteenth Century* of November, 1883.
† "Leaves from the Diary of Henry Greville," p. 21.

same effect is the warning recently given to the world by one of the most accomplished and philosophic of French Liberals. "The Democratic Republic," M. Scherer tells us, "is bound, by the very law of its being, to make trial of Communism."

This, then, is the position, the prospect in France. What are we to learn from it? The only knowledge in politics, or in history, worthy of the name, is the knowledge why things are. Here, too, the dictum holds, "Savoir c'est connaître par les causes." Let us ascend the stream of time, and trace the antecedents of the present position of French affairs, and consider of what that condition is the outcome. The history of France for the last hundred years is, in its essence, the history of an abstract idea endeavouring to realize itself in fact. At a famous banquet, which took place at Dijon upon the eve of the Revolution of 1848, M. Ledru Rollin, speaking on behalf of himself and his political friends, said: "Yes, we are Radicals—ultra-Radicals, if you mean by that the party which seeks to unite to the reality of life philosophical abstractions, the great symbols of Liberty, Equality, Fraternity." And similarly, upon another occasion, he declared "To arrive at social amelioration through the political question ("passer par la question politique pour arriver à l'amélioration sociale") such is the course (marche) of the Democratic party."* This was the movement which in 1848 subverted the Monarchy of July, and which, checked for eighteen years by the Second Empire, and for five years by the Marshalate, is now victoriously bearing France before it. And this was the movement which, running subterraneously, but, as Royer-Collard describes it, "with full stream,"† throughout the period of the Restoration, swept away in 1830 the throne of Charles X. This was the movement which, first distinctly formulated in 1789, manifested itself in its logical results as a principle of action in 1791, and had full course until, on the 5th of October, 1795, Napoleon opposed to it those iron floodgates which more or less effectually held it in check for five-and-thirty years. To this great movement the French have given a name, the full significance of which is less appreciated among us than could be desired. They call it "the Revolution." Let us consider a little at large—it is worth while—what the Revolution really is.

The greatest man who adorned English public life during the eighteenth century discerned well what it was. His account of it, whatever deductions we may have to make here and there for rhetorical vehemence, has been happily called by its most recent

---

* "Histoire de la Révolution de 1848." Par Daniel Stern, p. 27.
† So Balzac in the "Deputé d'Arcis"—that graphic picture of French political life—speaks of "the permanent conspiracy" directed against the Government of Louis XVIII.

and philosophical historian "at once a literary masterpiece and a prophecy." Most curious and interesting would it be, did the occasion permit, to compare the picture drawn with such wealth of detail and laborious accuracy in "The Jacobin Conquest," with the large, bold outlines traced in the "Reflections on the French Revolution," and the "Letters on a Regicide Peace." It must, however, suffice here to point out that Burke, writing in the spirit of the seer—

> Fiery thoughts
> Do shape themselves within me more and more,
> Whereof I catch the issue—

finds both his best commentary and his most effective supplement in the vast psychological study of M. Taine. He saw, clearly enough, that the great change in France, the progress of which he watched so closely, was something more than a mere alteration in political arrangements, in public organization; that it was "a revolution of doctrine and theoretic dogma," bearing a great "resemblance to those changes that have been wrought on purely religious grounds, in which a spirit of proselytism makes an essential part." Now, human society reposes upon doctrines. Man acts because he believes. Without some faith— even if it be but in "the inalienable nature of purchased beef" —he could not act at all. What, then, is the faith, the doctrine, the dogma which underlies the Revolution?

Before answering that question let us look a little at the public order which the Revolution found and destroyed. Corrupt and outworn as it was, it rested upon certain definite principles. It had lived upon them for fourteen hundred years, and owed to them such vitality as it still possessed. And at the very root of them lay this conviction: that man, naturally of imperfect inclinations to good and of strong propensities to evil, is encompassed by duties, divinely prescribed, and resting upon the most august and momentous sanctions. Take that venerable document which so well sums up the fundamental religious and ethical conceptions unquestioningly received throughout Christendom, while Christendom was, "the Catechism or Instruction" prescribed by the Established Church of this country "to be learned of every person before he be brought to be confirmed by the Bishop." Duty is the keynote of it. It is nothing but an exposition of what the neophyte is "*bound* to believe and to do." It takes the child in the place in which it finds him: a Christian, and so under religious obligations; a human being, and so under obligations to his fellows of the race of man; a member of a family, and so under obligations to its head; a member of a body politic, and so under obligations to those set in public authority;

a member of a civil society, and so bound by the divine obligations attaching to his place in the same. Here is the fundamental doctrine of the old-world order which the Revolution found in its decadence and decrepitude: the doctrine of duty pervading the whole of man's existence, dominating every human being from the king to the peasant. Of course ethical ideas existed in Europe long before Christianity subdued it. But Christianity wrought a momentous change in them. Pagan antiquity conceived of the citizen as appertaining wholly to the State. But "the State itself had been founded upon a religion and constituted as a church. The religion which had brought forth the State and the State which maintained (*entretenait*) the religion, mutually upheld one another and constituted but one homogeneous whole; and these two powers, thus united, blended, formed one almost superhuman power, to which body and soul were alike subject."* Hence the law of society was the law of the individual, whence sprang his duties in every relation of life, and whence sprang his rights also; for the only rights of which antiquity knew were the rights of the citizen : of any abstract rights of humanity it knew nothing. Christianity changed all that by proclaiming another and a higher source of duty in the Divine Nature and the filial relation of man to It. This we may confidently affirm to be the primary, the essential dogma upon which it rests; and M. Renan is well warranted when he declares "l'idée de Jésus . . . . fut l'idée la plus révolutionaire qui soit jamais éclose dans un cerveau humain."† It was this idea which wrought slowly and imperfectly—for imperfection is the universal law of life—the greatest social revolution the world has ever seen; which freed the consciences of men from the yoke of Cæsarism, which raised woman from her degradation, as the sport of man's caprice, to moral and spiritual equality with him; which struck the fetters from the slave, and made of the rich the stewards of the poor. For it was by speaking to the sovereign, to the man, to the master, to the rich, of the duties attaching to them as spiritual and responsible beings, that all this was accomplished. The public order which gradually arose throughout Europe, on the ruins of the Roman Empire, was a vast hierarchy of duties, which, however grudgingly performed or brutally violated in countless instances, were everywhere undoubtingly recognized to be the divinely imposed laws of life; no more to be chosen by men or women, as Savonarola reminds the fugitive Romola, than birthplace or father or mother could be chosen, although they might choose to forsake them. And these duties were conceived

---

* "La Cité Antique," par Fustel de Coulanges, l. iii. c. 17.
† "Vie de Jésus," p. 125.

of as the source and the measure of human rights. It is indeed strictly true to say that the only right of man then recognized as inalienable and imprescriptible, was the right to do what he ought; and in the secure possession of this right human liberty was held to reside. This old-world view is well expressed by Milton. "The whole freedom of man," he writes, "consists either in spiritual or civil liberty. As for spiritual, who can be at rest, who can enjoy anything in this world with contentment, who hath not liberty to serve God and save his own soul ?.... The other part of freedom consists in the civil rights and advancement of every person according to his merit;"* such civil rights, such advancement, being his due as enabling him more fully and completely to use the talents entrusted to him by the "Great Taskmaster." It is this notion of divinely appointed, all-pervading duty, as the paramount law of life, which especially distinguishes the Middle Ages, and which is the source of all that is highest in them, and in particular of their liberties. Absolute monarchy, the all-absorbing, unrestrained despotism of Roman Imperialism, had no place among their political conceptions. The monarch was everywhere bound by pacts, solemnly recognized and sworn to, as a condition of his unction and coronation, and was hemmed in on all sides by free institutions; by the Universal Church, "the Christian Republic," as it was called; by universities, corporations, brotherhoods, monastic orders; by liberties and privileges of all kinds, which, in a greater or less degree, existed all over Europe. The Renaissance, which in politics, as in most other departments, was a mere plagiarism of antiquity, brought back into the world the idea of Pagan Cæsarism, and that idea, under one form or another, soon spread throughout the greater part of Europe. In France, especially, the doctrine of the omnipotence of the State, fostered by a servile clergy, attained proportions little, if at all, inferior to those prevailing in the antique world; and the will of the *Grand Monarque*—" transcendent king of gluttonous flunkies," if ever ruler deserved that description—became in practice the standard of religious obligation. In the emphatic language of Sainte-Beuve: "Sous Louis XIV. le culte du monarque etait devenue une démence universellement acceptée qui etonne encore par son excès." The king was again "a present Deity," and the obligation of passive obedience to him was well-nigh the only obligation really believed in. It was natural that this great idea of duty thus prostituted, and made a mere instrument of political slavery, should fall into discredit. It was not unnatural in an age when the great theistic conception brought into

---

* "Ready Way to Establish a Free Commonwealth."

the world by Christianity had lost its hold over the intellect of France—the most profoundly irreligious age the world has ever seen, perhaps—that the men who composed the National Assembly of 1789, and whose spiritual and intellectual masters had been Voltaire, Rousseau, and the Encyclopædists, should have sought another foundation whereon to rear the public order, to the construction of which they addressed themselves without the slightest misgiving as to their competency for the enterprise.

That foundation they obtained, as they thought, in the idea of human right, of certain political rights, imprescriptable, inalienable, attaching to man in virtue of his human nature. Ascertain these, said the Revolutionary legislators, and securely establish them, and you may with little difficulty make all things new. The world is out of joint: it is full of wrong and violence; and "the sole causes of public misfortunes and corruptions of Government are ignorance, neglect, or contempt of human rights."* Let us therefore solemnly expound these rights, "in order that the future claims of the citizens, being directed by simple and incontestable principles, may always tend to the maintenance of the constitution and the general happiness."† Accordingly they proceeded to set forth their Declaration of the abstract rights of humanity. This is the corner-stone, elect, precious, upon which they sought to rear the new political edifice, having first, as was necessary, made a clean sweep of existing institutions. I shall first consider their method, and then their application of it.

Their method has been happily described by Quinet as "social geometry, a kind of political mathematics," up to that time confined to the realms of speculation. They afford the first instance recorded in history of a number of men sitting down and saying, "Go to: let us reconstruct society upon *à priori* principles"—a gigantic task indeed, for which their qualifications were of the slenderest. A few men of conspicuous ability—a Mirabeau, a Talleyrand, a Barnave, had place among them. But the great majority were mere disciples of Rousseau, with no knowledge of men, or of affairs, or of anything beyond the dreams and speculations of their master; and may be said, as Aristotle said of the Sophists, to have professed political philosophy without in the least knowing what it is or wherewithal it is concerned. A few gaudy phrases, a few specious formulas, a few abstract ideas, an illimitable self-confidence, and an ebullient enthusiasm were their

---

* Preamble to "The Declaration of the Rights of the Man and the Citizen."
† *Ibid.*

equipment for the work of recreating society. The statesman, trained in the practice of public affairs and the traditions of government, had been wont to set himself to inquire, to calculate, to follow in advance, the working of any measure which he thought of introducing, bearing in mind the habits, the passions, the interests of the different classes, who, whether in greater or less degree, would be affected by it. Quite other was the method of the legislators of 1789, and of the Jacobins to whom the world owes the logical continuance of their work. To them their political axioms were all in all, applicable universally to the *individua vaga* of their theories; for all these were drawn upon one and the same pattern, and were conceived of as wanting nothing but liberty, equality, the rights of man, and the social contract. M. Taine has worked out the contrast, in an admirable page, which may, perhaps, fitly be given in English here, although my translation, as I am well aware, but dimly adumbrates the force and picturesqueness of the original.

When a statesman, who is not altogether unworthy of that great name, comes upon an abstract principle—such, for example, as that of the sovereignty of the people—he admits it, if at all, like every other principle, with the necessary qualifications (*sous bénéfice d'inventaire*). For that end he commences by picturing it to himself as applied and working in the world. And so, uniting all his own recollections and all the information he can get together, he imagines some particular village or borough or small town in the north or in the south or in the centre of the country, for which he legislates. Then, to the best of his ability, he represents to himself the people engaged in carrying out his principle—that is to say, voting, mounting guard, collecting their taxes, and carrying on their business. From these ten or twelve groups, with which he is familiar and which he takes as specimens, he draws conclusions by analogy regarding all the country. Clearly it is a difficult and doubtful operation. In order to be approximately exact, it needs rare talent for observation, and at every one of its steps exquisite tact; for the problem is to work out correct results from quantities imperfectly collected and imperfectly noted. And when a politician succeeds in this, it is through a delicate divination which is the fruit of consummate experience united to genius. Moreover, he proceeds in his innovation or reform with caution; almost always he makes preliminary trial of it; he applies his law only by instalments gradually, provisionally; he is always ready to correct, to suspend, to thin out his work, according to the good or bad success of his tentative application of it; and the condition of the human material which he has to handle is only apprehended by him, however superior his intelligence may be, after much manipulation. Just the opposite is it with the Jacobin. His "principle" is an axiom of political geometry, which is self-evident, for like the axioms of ordinary geometry it is formed by the combination of certain ideas, and its evidence compels the immediate assent of every mind which entertains together the two terms of which it is the sum. Man in general—the social contract, liberty, equality, reason, Nature, the people, tyrants—such are the elementary notions. Precise or not they fill the brain of the new sectary. Frequently they are there only as grandiose and vague words; but that does not matter. As soon as they are congregated in his mind they become for him an axiom, which he applies presently in its entirety upon every occasion and to all lengths. As to real men, he is not in the least concerned about them; he does not see them, he has no wish to see them. With eyes shut he casts in his own mould the human material which he handles. Never does it occur to him to picture to himself beforehand that shifting and complex material of peasants, artisans, bourgeois, curés, nobles, as actual life presents them, at their plough, in their lodging, in their place of business, in their presbytery, in their town house, with their inveterate beliefs, their masterful inclinations, their effective wills. Nothing of all this can enter or find a place in his mind; the avenues are blocked by the abstract principle which swells itself proudly out and takes up for itself all the room. If by the channel of eyes or ears actual experience drives in by force any inconvenient truth, it cannot find a home there : crying and bleeding though it be, he drives it away; nay if need be, he will take it by the throat and strangle it as a slanderer, because it gives the lie to a principle sacred from discussion and true in itself. Surely such a mind is not sound : of the two faculties which ought to pull equally together, one is smitten with atrophy, the other with hypertrophy. The counterpoise of facts is not there to balance the weight of formulas; overloaded on the one hand and empty on the other, the intellect is upset with violence in the direction to which it leans : and this is the incurable infirmity of the Jacobin mind.*

Such was the method of the men who made the Revolution. Let us now consider the principle to which they applied it. We may call that principle the sovereignty of the individual. That complete freedom or lawlessness—for they conceived the two things to be identical—is the natural condition of man, that all men are born and continue equal in rights, that civil society is an artificial state, resting upon a compact between the sovereign individuals, whereby the native independence of each is in part surrendered, in order to the attainment of certain ends, "that human nature is good, and that the evil in the world is the result of bad education and bad institutions"—"the central moral doctrine" of the Revolutionists, as Mr. John Morley correctly points out†—and that the will of the sovereign units residing in any territory, that is of the majority of them, expressed by their dele-

---

* "La Conquête Jacobine," p. 18.
† Morley's "Diderot," vol. i. p. 5.

gates, is the rightful and only source of law—these were to the legislators of 1789 prime political axioms. They took them for granted. They quite omitted to ask themselves, Are they true? And the generations that have come after have paid dearly for the omission. It is a profound saying of Novalis that "man consists in truth." But if you take a lie and make that the foundation of your political edifice, you do but build your house upon the sand: and when the rains descend and the floods come and the winds blow, fall it must, and great will be the fall of it. The conception of man in an extra-social or anti-social state is a dream. From the earliest glimpse of time which history discloses to us, he is, ζῶον πολιτικόν, as Aristotle calls him, a "political animal;" and the civil society, which is his normal state, is not a cunningly devised machine, but an organism, a body politic, or, in Burke's phrase, "the nation in its corporate capacity," the true end of which is freedom, by the education of the people in the principles and habits of self-government. Freedom, which is by no means the same thing as lawlessness—"to be free," according to Lord Mansfield's admirable dictum, "is to live under a government by law"—is not the point from which the human race starts, but the goal to which it slowly progresses. As a matter of fact, the unit of archaic society was the family, the head of which possessed despotic power over its members; and the history of social progress is the history of the evolution of the individual with his attributes of personal liberty and private property. It is untrue, then, that men are born free, and that the public order rests upon a compact whereby they sacrifice their natural liberty. It is equally untrue that they are born and continue equal in rights. Indeed, if you look at man from a merely secular standpoint, it would seem to be impossible to predicate of him any abstract rights at all. The theory concerning his rights, current in Europe until the French Revolution, rested, as we have seen, upon the conception of him as a spiritual being, bound to fulfil the supreme end of his existence. But if you regard him as an animated machine, apart from all question of any supposed supernatural destiny, which is the modern point of view, what possible rights can he have save such as are the creation of positive law? Whence can any other rights be derived? How can their existence be established? So far is equality from being in accordance with "the holy law of Nature," as Marat was wont to assert, that inequality is everywhere her rule, whether in the heaven above, where one star differeth from another in glory, or in the earth beneath, where the most startling variety exists in the endowments, mental and physical, of all sentient beings, or in the waters under the earth, the denizens of which range from whales to whitebait. Well did Vauvenargues warn his generation: "Il est faux que l'egalité soit une loi de la nature: la nature n'a rien fait d'égal : sa loi souveraine est la subordination et la dépendance." Yes; inequality is the law of human life, as of the whole universe. That men are born and continue equal in rights is the emptiest of fictions. Next as to the evil in the world: is it attributable solely, or even in greatest part, to bad education and bad institutions? as Rousseau and the Jacobins and Mr. John Morley teach us. Or is not that rather a perfectly nude hypothesis, to which the facts are quite as much opposed as they are to Calvin's theory of man's entire depravity? Experience of man, as he really exists, under any system of laws or education, is quite irreconcilable either with the optimist or the pessimist view of human nature; and if anything is clear from history it is that human nature has been, in all ages, pretty much what it is now; nor is there the slightest reason for supposing that it will be essentially changed so long as our race may continue to exist. While if from without we look within, the doctrine of the natural unalloyed goodness of man is the negation of that deep and most true instinct which in all ages, and in all times, has found expression of one kind or another: that sense of moral imperfection, that consciousness of indwelling evil, whereby man has been led to the idea of sacrifice, of ransom, of religion, of hope. False again is it that the will of the majority is the only standard of right or wrong: that, as Rétif asserted, amid the applause of his fellow legislators, "Whatever the people wishes is just." Coleridge has correctly observed, " It is not the actual man but the abstract reason alone that is the sovereign and rightful lawgiver." And he well adds, " The confusion of two things so very different is so gross an error that the Constituent Assembly could hardly proceed a step in their Declaration of Rights without a glaring inconsistency."*

The pretended axioms of the Revolutionary legislators were as false, then, as was their method. And the present condition of France is the natural, the inevitable result of their gigantic mistake. The dictum of the sovereignty of the individual, as they formulated it, if interpreted by the mob, must issue in anarchy; if interpreted by the leaders of the mob, in the despotism of adventurers, who, like the demagogue in the comedy, establish their tyranny in the name of freedom : " si vous me refusez le pouvoir absolu, comment, diable, voulez vous que je fonde la liberté?" The emancipation of the passions is the direct, the inevitable result of the effacement from the public mind of the idea of duty. "The only roots of the Revolution," said Camille Desmoulins—its *enfant terrible*—"are in individual self-love,

---

* "The Friend," vol. i. p. 267 (Pickering's edition).

from which springs the general interest." Now, where self-love is the sovereign law, and one recognized source of action, there is no room for patriotism. Without some such belief as "our common Christianity" supplies in this country, a belief in something higher and deeper than the visionary rights of the abstract man, in some laws such as the tragic poet speaks of, "unwritten and unchanging and Divine," and weighted with an obligation that no behest of any tyrant, one or many headed, can over-ride, men cannot be knit together in civil society. It is not the shallowness of the pedants, nor the vulgarity of the buffoons, who played their ignoble parts in the Constituent Assembly which are the main blots upon its proceedings: it is not the baseness and cruelty of the first Jacobins that are the damning features of the Revolution, although we may still reasonably echo Burke's protest against "the apotheosis of monsters whose crimes and vices have no parallel among men." The scurrility, the ignorance, the brutality which distinguished the movement were merely of its accidents. Its great fault is in its essence. It is a false dogma; and the whole history of France since 1789 is the history of that dogma seeking to realize itself in fact, and failing, because it is opposed to the nature of things. What is the net result of ninety-three years of Revolution in France? Take the formula of Liberty, Equality, Fraternity, which is its sacred and accredited symbol. How far have these abstractions been translated into fact? France is the country in the whole world where the hand of the State is most heavily felt in every department of human life: nowhere is the administration so ubiquitous and so autocratic. It is the natural result of the false conception of the public order which the Revolutionists learnt from Rousseau: of their master error in regarding Government as a mere engine of repression; an error which results practically in its conversion into a gigantic system of police, while the liberty of the subject, who is deluded into the belief that he is free because he possesses an infinitesimal share in the election of a Legislature, resembles the liberty of a ticket-of-leave man under perpetual *surveillance*. "Liberty," the late M. Gambetta declared in a famous speech, "is one of the prerogatives of power," and the dictum correctly expresses the Radical conception of it. The two main achievements of the party now in authority in France are the expulsion of the Religious Orders and the restoration to the State of the monopoly of education. Surely the proscription of whole classes of men and women, whose sole offence was their consecration of their lives to the service of others, is a strange instrument for working out civil and religious freedom; while the other measure to which the most earnest efforts (*efforts de prédilection*) of M. Ferry and his friends have been directed seems to have been aptly characterized in certain prophetic words written twenty years ago by one of the most thoughtful and sincere Liberals France has ever known, the late M. Laboulaye: "S'emparer des générations nouvelles pour façonner leur esprit au gré de la mode ou des passions du jour, c'est un abominable despotisme, c'est dépouiller l'homme du premier et du plus saint de ses droits."* Jacobin equality is as illusory as Jacobin liberty. The curse of aristocratic privilege recognized by law the Revolution, indeed, overthrew for good and all. Happy would France have been if its iconoclasm had stopped there. But no. It must make a *tabula rasa* of the past; it must throw down every institution which it found existing, until nothing was left save, on the one hand, a highly centralized State, and, on the other, millions of unrelated individuals, theoretically sovereign, virtually slaves. Absolute equality it has, of course, been unable to effect. Equality in property it has more than once aimed at. The boldest speculations of the most advanced Socialism and Communism of our own day were all anticipated by the original Jacobins. "We have destroyed the nobles and the Capets," urged Chaumette; "but there is still an aristocracy to be overthrown; the aristocracy of the rich." Tallien preached the same gospel of plunder, and proposed that owners of property should be sent to the dungeons as public thieves. Fouché—afterwards Napoleon's Duke of Otranto—when Proconsul at Antwerp, in "the year II. of the Republic," went so far as to decree "that all inferior citizens, old people and orphans should be lodged, clothed, and fed at the expense of the wealthy;" while St. Just, Barrère, and Robespierre, in many of their harangues, stigmatized opulence as a crime. Perhaps the only levelling proposal of the publicists of the First Republic which has as yet been unechoed by the levellers of our own day is that of one Armand, who demanded mental equality. This sage was certainly within his logic: he went to the root of the matter. The great, the perennial source of inequality among men lies in the difference of their intellectual constitution, and in the difference in the intensity of their desires: αἰὲν ἀριστεύειν καὶ ὑπείροχον ἔμμεναι ἄλλων is an aspiration deeply implanted in certain natures, and in it, when united with faculties adequate for its realization, is the primary cause of wealth, the motive power of civilization, the main factor of progress. "It is impossible to form a State all the members of which are alike. The parts which are to constitute a single organic whole must be different in kind."† So wrote "the master of those who know" two thousand

---

* "Le Parti Libéral," p. 67.
† Aristotle's "Politics," Book ii. c. 2.

years ago, and his words are as true now as they were then. Human nature itself must be changed before equality can be translated into fact. In France, at the present time, it is obviously theoretical only. There is no country where the same passion prevails for decorations. "The French care nothing for liberty: give them baubles and they are content," was the First Napoleon's judgment of them. Their is no country where official superiorities are so abjectly worshipped; there is no country in which the better sort are so tyrannously repressed: in which genius, and virtue, and religion, are so carefully excluded from public life. Lastly, if any fraternity reigns in France, it is certainly the fraternity of Cain and Abel. Nowhere is the antagonism of factions and classes so great: nowhere has individualism carried so far its dissolvent work. It is the necessary outcome of a system which establishes personal interest as the one law of society; which, in M. Renan's happy phrase, would seem to have been constructed for an ideal citizen who should begin life as a foundling and end it as a bachelor.

Enough has been said to indicate what we, in this country, have to learn from the great democratic experiment which has been so long tried in France, and with such results. In some sense it may be asserted, truly, that our progress during the present century has been parallel to that of France. Fifty years ago Chateaubriand wrote in his "Mémoires d'outre tombe:" "Europe is hastening towards democracy. The symptoms of the social transformation abound. The ancient society is perishing with the political order out of which it has come." That European movement of which the veteran statesman thus prophetically spoke has not been without large influence in this nation. Indeed, the changes wrought by it among us are so great that the Duke of Wellington judged even those of them which he lived to see, to amount to "a revolution in due course of law." It is not too much to say that we have realized all that the French Revolutionists have talked about. Our Government is carried on by statesmen whose title to office is that they possess the confidence of the nation, and to the nation at large direct appeal is made, in grave issues, by way of general election. We enjoy liberty, equality, fraternity, not as abstract ideas, but as concrete facts. Liberty of speech, liberty of the Press, liberty of worship, liberty of public meeting, educational liberty, testamentary liberty—we have them all. Equality exists; not in the state of dead level, but in the state of a free career to talent. No man's race or religion offers any bar to his advancement, political or social, according to his merit. Each has a fair entry into the combat of life, with those endowments, congenital and inherited, that belong to him. And if the race is to the swift, and the battle to the strong, if riches are to men of understanding, that is but in virtue of the universal law of the survival of the fittest which prevails, as elsewhere in the world, so in the tumult of those inimical interests which make up human society. Nor is this rivalry incompatible with true fraternity. The strife is honourable. The spirit in which it is carried on is the spirit of citizens, of warriors, not the spirit of sectaries, of assassins. National interests, county interests, municipal interests, and a thousand others, find Englishmen of all varieties of political opinion and religious creed meeting together for common ends with a brotherly readiness to give and take "which keeps our Britain whole within herself." The English State, as it now exists, may be properly called a democracy; for, as M. Scherer has well pointed out, " Democracy is not a theory or an institution which you establish and which you overthrow; it is a state of society issuing from the history of peoples and from the nature of things, the consequence of an industrial and intellectual development which, while giving the masses the consciousness of their power, has, at the same time, taught them how to use it." Yes, the English Constitution, as it lives and works, is a democracy in the true sense; in the truest, indeed, for nowhere else does the nation so directly control the government and the legislature. Nowhere else is public opinion so faithfully expressed and so potential in its expression. But how different a democracy from that which we see in France! What is the reason of the difference?

The main reason is that we in this country have never bowed down before the idol of absolute reason in politics; that we have been guided by experience, not by theory; by sense, not by sentiment. We have realized by an instinct what is the outcome of a thousand years of progressive liberty, the great truth so well stated by Hegel, that constitutions are not made but grow; that they are the outcome of the life of a people; and that solution of historical continuity is almost necessarily fatal to national vitality. And so we are content that our freedom should "slowly broaden down," and love to accomplish our reforms bit by bit, as the exigencies of the time appear to demand, securely indifferent to the requirements of abstract ideas. Thus, to take one example out of many, we have, more than once, widely extended the electoral suffrage, not in recognition of any supposed right to vote, inherent in "the sovereign individual," nor to satisfy the requirements of an imaginary "social contract," but upon the ground that the broader the foundation of the social edifice in this country, the greater will be its stability; that it is expedient to interest Englishmen as largely as possible in national affairs. Grave public questions lie before us—the Irish question, the question of Local Self-Government, in the widest sense, the question of the relations between Capital and Labour, which we may truly call "the condition of England question." And who can doubt that the solution of these questions will involve vast alterations in the body politic? In public life, as in individual, to live is to change. But the greatest problem of statesmanship is to combine duration with progress. And the example of France does not encourage us to relinquish the time-honoured method by which we have hitherto successfully solved that problem, and to betake ourselves to the "high *priori* road." Nor do the vast bulk of the people of this country, upon whatever side of party politics they may be ranged, exhibit the least inclination for such a new departure. As Mr. Escott has forcibly pointed out in a striking chapter of his well-known work, "the English masses look not to theories, but to facts." "They are not greatly occupied by or interested in constitutional discussions." "What the English multitude requires from the State is much what it requires from the private employers of its labour. It asks that it shall be fairly treated; that it shall not be the victim of any exceptional inferiority, disadvantage, or disqualification."[*] Such is the outcome, in the political order, of that quiet, steady practicality which is a main note of the English mind. Heine, in one of his letters, observes that "an Englishman loves liberty like his lawful wife." This is true. And the *doctrinaire* who would persuade him to give her a bill of divorcement, and to take in her place a Goddess of Liberty *à la Française*, must first solve the problem of transforming national character.

W. S. LILLY.

ART VI.—CHRISTENDOM IN IDEAL AND IN FACT.

1. *The Formation of Christendom.* By T. W. ALLIES. In Three Vols. London: Longman, Green, Longman. 1865-1875.
2. *Church and State, as seen in the Formation of Christendom.* By T. W. ALLIES. London: Burns & Oates. 1882.

TWO years ago at Cologne a famous testimony was rendered to the longevity of ideas. For centuries the shrine of the Three Kings stood forth in its unfinished splendour; the hand of the architect had long rested in its tomb, yet the conception of the architect lived on, awaiting the day of its complete realization, and at last the old crane gave way to the two

---

[*] "England," vol. ii. pp. 69-71.

matchless towers, which adorned with the finest art of the workman for the delight of the Divine Eyes, bear far up into the heavens the holy form of the cross. Every great work which has faith for its inspiration and its end, whether carried out in stone, in writing, in colour, or in music, points heavenwards as much as the spire of a cathedral, and testifies to the immortal aspirations of the human soul. There is, indeed, another sort of labour, fruitful for the hour but short-lived. No Tower of Babel is proof against the rust of time, and when men seek for the lasting testimonies of the world, the flesh, and the devil, their outcome leads to subversion and to a perilous negation. They are wanting in that which constitutes the essence of God; they tend to non-being.

I. A work which is being written in the very midst of us, will one day bear the same glorious testimony to the power of faith as Cologne Cathedral. We hope, indeed, that the author may be spared to bring his idea to the last stage of completion; that no crane, however time-honoured or cherished for its old memories, may rest upon the crown of his work. In its own time and day "the Formation of Christendom" is a reproduction, though a reproduction wise with the teaching and experience of eighteen instead of four centuries, of the book which more than any other, has moulded the feelings and minds of generations. In taking the City of God as his theme St. Augustine was responding to the intellectual need of the epoch, for at the break up of the Roman empire, the idea of the human *civitas* was in possession, and the great Father, looking upon visible things as the expression of invisible faith, turned the current of men's thoughts and aspirations towards the spiritual kingdom of which the mighty Roman empire had been only a figure. Who will deny the value of Eusebius' History of the Apostles and of the early Church, bare outline as it is of the great deeds which it records? Those annals need the comments of Christian philosophy, without which they fail to convey the whole meaning of the foundation of the spiritual kingdom. Our Lord's empire was to carry out and perfect the Roman *civitas*, to spread its dominion far beyond the old Roman boundaries, and to bestow a right of citizenship, from which no man was to be excluded save by his own fault. The greatness of Rome lay in her assimilating power. She took peoples as she found them, and moulded them by contact with her maternal civilization. When the majesty of that vast empire had been sufficiently before the eyes of men, then it disappeared, and made way for the spiritual πολίτεια for which God had used Rome as a preparation. As the signs and figures of the Old Testament are to the New, so is Christian philosophy to history. This was St. Augustine's work in his " De

Civitate Dei," for his inspired vision saw the force of the great idea which had then taken hold of the hearts and minds of men. During the first three centuries of the Christian era history had rendered one sound : the dominion of Rome; and the question was who was to succeed to the majesty of the Roman name. In our own day we have something analogous to the breaking up of an empire in the pending fall of the Turk. The question is one of the future, for though Christian sympathies may not favour the Crescent, who can foretell what the change may bring forth, or even what it indicates? Though the idea of a city or commonwealth is no longer a dominant one, St. Augustine's philosophy would still be what it was. He would view all the events and teachings of history as utterances of God, and as bearing in some mysterious way upon his spiritual kingdom, the great net which His divine Son spread over the whole earth. "This perpetual vision of faith, this eye of the heart centred upon the Unchangeable One, is the great mark of St. Augustine."[*] In these words the author has described the spirit of the Latin Father whom he has chosen for his type of a Christian, as uniting the best gifts of mind and heart, but in them also he gives us his own standing-point for the defence of Catholic truths. The production of Satan and of his offspring, heresy and unbelief, are filled with negation and invective: they live by what they deny. This book, on the contrary, announces by its title that it deals with a fact which is at once the growth and accomplishment of many centuries—a fact of which the mere existence is more than human philosophy can comprehend. The full exposition of a fundamental truth is thus its best defence, and the possibility of denial is removed there where the certificate of birth and well-being is held up to the broad light of noontide. In the matter of time Mr. Allies naturally has the advantage of St. Augustine; for if the " De Civitate Dei" was the production of the morning hours, "The Formation of Christendom" bears upon it the warmth and maturity of a summer day at its zenith.

In order to measure the work of the early Christian Church, a perfect apprehension of the heathen man, such as the most refined civilization had made him, is necessary; for the force of Christianity is seen in the powerlessness, morally speaking, of Paganism. It was the judgment of Bossuet, carried out and applied to every part of life : *tout était Dieu excepté Dieu lui-même*. The Roman citizen was in possession of every good thing which the world could procure, yet he was wholly wanting in moral strength and happiness. It has cost Mr. Allies years of study and research, not to make the assertion, but to prove it, as

---

[*] "The Formation of Christendom," vol. i. p. 207.

he does in a most exhaustive and masterly way. In his opening chapters he exposes the moral side of Heathenism, and the arms with which the Christian *civitas* conquered the world. " The consummation of the old world" was due to the obliteration of four great ideas. The abyss of misery in which their absence plunged men who were enjoying the highest pitch of civilization ever attained, is a negative testimony in favour of immortality. Religious rites, smoking altars, splendid temples, the multitude of false deities, who guarded, so to speak, all the avenues of human life, did not reveal the One for whom that society was pining away. Paganism was the forerunner of heresy, in that belief in it offered difficulties so insuperable to thinking men as to cause them, if not naturally pious, to give up all effort at grasping any superior power. Indeed, perhaps, it was the sign of piety among the Romans to worship publicly at shrines, and to hold all the while a private theory of religion, from which the gods were banished. The "immortal gods" were a name to cover the superstition which is born, if we may use the expression, of a want of faith. They were bound up with the fortunes of Rome, and were made to give their sanction to the abnormal growth of the State as a power which was gradually swallowing up all the marrow of individual lives. Thus are traced the birth and origin of the traditions of bureaucracy. Pure human reason, when unclouded by moral obstacles, must come to the knowledge of one God, but pure human reason is almost a fable. Where it exists there would be the implicit desire to acknowledge the Creator when revealed. The Romans were far removed from the light of pure reason. The passions of dominion, luxuriousness and immorality were rife, and without the dogmatic teaching of the Christian Church, even society must have perished. The nearest approach—and how feeble an approach!—to this fundamental doctrine, was Pantheism, but the Pantheistic First Principle appealed to the intellect only of the so-called philosopher; it filled no man's heart and regulated no man's private conduct.* Together, then, with the knowledge of God, the conception of His divine providence had been lost. The belonging to a powerful State constituted man's dignity; the individual soul was jostled in the crowd of human desires which all ended with this world. One of the distinguishing features of Our Lord's teaching was the worth of the individual, and this was the antidote divinely ordered for the preservation of a human

---

* As to Pantheism, compare St. Thomas' teaching on the natural power of man for gaining the knowledge of God : " Cum Deus sit suum esse, et quidnam sit nos lateat, hæc propositio, *Deus est*, per se nota secundum se est, licet non quoad nos, &c.—" Summa Theologica," Quæst. ii. Art. i.

society which slavery had accustomed to despise human life. The slave was no longer treated as a man, but as a thing, and it was this system of unlawful dependence which more than anything else had tended to banish the notion of personality. The Latin poet's *humanum paucis vivit genus* expressed tersely the spirit of slavery. But that human race, which was made for a few, was made only for this world in the eyes of the Roman. The hereafter of the slave, whose life was forfeited at his master's merest pleasure, was a matter of no sort of interest. The ruling spirits of Rome were to descend at best to a dim Hades, to be joined to the world-soul, or to cease to exist.* Thus the obliteration of the notion of God, our Creator and Rewarder, had brought about the most practical injustice. Slaves, who were society's beasts of burden, were to labour and suffer during this life's short day, and to be hurried out of existence whenever it suited their masters. The divine character of the new *civitas*, which in the midst of humiliation, persecution, and the contempt of the great, was being founded in the corrupt heart of old Rome, is abundantly proved by Mr. Allies in the course of his first volume. Since that foundation of the Christian Church, the world has again and again been exposed to the blight of corruption and to the advent of men who have used various remedies to cure the evil. Two eras, in particular, suggest themselves as periods of a mighty upheaving, which called forth arms very different to those used by the Apostles—human, not divine, treatment of the complaint. The Reformation was essentially a revolt against the "powers that be," and the French Revolution a struggle for the supposed *droits de l'homme*. The outcome of both these movements has been radicalism in the spiritual and social order. Yet what were the wrongs of the French peasant compared to those of the slave?

In order to restore the four ideas, for the want of which society was perishing, belief in one God, in Divine Providence, in the soul's personality, and in immortality, the Apostles took the individual man, and formed him anew after the likeness of the Crucified One, speaking of no rights save immortal ones, but suggesting new duties which were founded on charity, and the true conception of liberty as opposed to license.

Cicero and St. Augustine are given as types, the one of heathen Rome, the other of the ideal Christian. Of the former the author says: "If Cicero looked to human renown as his reward; if his hope began and ended with his dignity as a citizen and senator

* "The Formation of Christendom," vol. i. p. 129, where the words of Tacitus to Agricola are quoted: "If there be any place for the shades of the pious—if, as the wise will have it, *great souls* are not extinguished together with the body—mayest thou rest in peace."

of Rome; if he was unduly beaten down by adversity; if his private inner life was devoid of morality; and if the wide circle of his accomplishments excluded expressly the knowledge of a personal all-seeing God, the rewarder and punisher of men, and of a responsible soul in himself, these were not peculiarities in him, but the very air of the atmosphere which he breathed."*
St. Augustine profited by four centuries of Christian life, though Mr. Allies views him rightly as a man of higher natural order than Cicero. The "very air of the atmosphere which he breathed" was that of the earth no doubt, but chastened and purified by a current from above. If Cicero's death redeemed much that was little in his life, his conduct portrays in a most striking manner the weak points—we might say the innate weakness—of infidelity. It is characteristic of the man who has no God to possess no inner life, to live his life for the world and before the eyes of the world, to find no consolation in the presence of illness, and of sorrow, and death. All the comfort which Sulpicius had to administer over Tullia's funeral urn was marred by an *if—si quis etiam inferis sensus est*. Between the whinings of Cicero's wounded vanity and the pages in which Augustine tells the story of his life, between the death of Tullia and that of Monica, there is the difference of a divine revelation made known to the world by a kingdom which is not of it.

The gods of Paganism, numerous and unlovely though they were, represented both the deterioration of the human mind in consequence of moral obstacles and of the lack of a divine revelation, and the need which man has of seeking the aid of some power beyond his own. Even their marred rites dimly shadowed forth the great Sacrifice which was one day to answer all human needs, and ever afterwards to be daily renewed at the altar of the true God. A fragment of truth helped to nourish the blood and fire of the heathen sacrifices, and to keep the band of Vestal virgins; for the idea both of sacrifice and of virginity is a tribute from man in the state of Nature to the impress of the Creator's hand. We are at present less concerned with the value of bloody sacrifice amongst the heathens, which Mr. Allies has insisted upon largely in another part of his work. In this first volume, dealing with the foundation of the spiritual *civitas*, he develops what may be viewed as one of its corner stones, the new creation of marriage and the institution of the virginal life. This, again, was a heavenly ordained antidote to meet the outward character of the Pagan's course on earth, and to remedy the ravages which neglect of moral purity had caused to human society.

Here, too, Cicero is a typical man. In his mature age he procured a bill of divorce, gave up the wife whom he used to

---

* "The Formation of Christendom," p. 216.

address as *desiderium meum*, and married a rich young woman. The action of the Church was to build up again family life on the divine model of Nazareth, and to preach chastity in the married state by consecrating the sacrifice of virginity. What martyrdom was to the faith that confessorship was to purity, and it required no less a basis than the voluntary preferment of the Creator to the creature to found the traditions of Christian marriage and the Christian family.

The foundation of a kingdom implies a king and a system of legislation, but unlike the human country, this divine *civitas* was to possess no boundaries, to exclude no nationalities, to include all classes and ranks of men. In proving both the existence of the Christian Church from the time of our Lord, and the various ways in which it dealt with an old and corrupt civilization, that is, by the double example of holiness and suffering in the unity of one faith, Mr. Allies has written a work which is unanswerable in its testimony. The divine birth of the Church is a miracle, but it is only the beginning of her miraculous course through eighteen centuries, and the first, though not the least, important step in the ladder of positive controversy is the clear written witness to her cradle and the deeds of her infancy. It was fitting that as death begot life on the cross, so martyrdom should be the great battle in which the Church was to win her territory—human hearts—and the virginal life, the marriage which should raise her up sons and daughters.

The great fact, which Mr. Allies establishes in his first volume, from the evidence of contemporary documents and the moral influence of Christians on the world, is the task too great for any power but that of the Church of God—the "basing of natural society upon the Incarnation." The first important result has been dwelt upon: the foundation of the Christian family. The second is hardly less significant, and, in its Christian sense, was quite as novel to the Pagan: we allude to the work of education, or perhaps *training* more aptly expresses the action of the Church in imparting the heavenly treasures of the faith. None apprehended better than the Greeks and Romans the meaning and value of knowledge as a universal term applied to intellectual culture, and yet, to quote Cicero as an instance, who was more ignorant than they as "to the meaning of life itself, and the object for which it was given?"[*] The Church was to supply the necessary basis to Plato's ideal city, and it is this grand process which the author has in view in his second volume. The one idea, that of the growth and development of the City of God, runs like a leading thread through his work, just as the idea of the body

---

[†] Vol. i. p. 322.

of our Lord on the cross runs through the gothic nave and transepts of a great cathedral.

II. After bringing together the stones with which the building is to be erected he proceeds to the building itself. The medium by which the Church was to renovate society was the individual human heart, and, as in every process of grace, the growth would be slow, the seed-time seemingly contemptible, but the harvest magnificent. In his second volume the author applies what we believe to be a figure of his own, though based upon patristic teaching, to the Church. He speaks of the Body of Adam as contrasted with the Body of Christ, the one resting upon our first father, the other upon our Lord. To see the force of the divine and personal leadership of the Second Person of the Blessed Trinity, it is necessary to consider "the gods of the nations" at the time of the birth at Bethlehem. The Body of Christ was to counterbalance the Body of Adam, and as the figurative serpent in the desert, to heal and to save the stricken men who should turn to it in their desolation. The political unity of the Roman *imperium* was in sharp contrast to the aberrations of a polytheistic idolatry, which, with the one exception of Jewish monotheism, filled the world with its corrupt and wicked imaginings. In only one way did it bear a far-off testimony to the great Creator, in that it proclaimed man to have need of a power or agency higher than his own. History bears its witness to this significant fact: if man fall away from the service of God, he adopts the service of the devil. Worship he must have, whether he disguises it under the name of human intellect, or first cause, or world-soul. Many men now, as in the ancient world of Rome, sacrifice to their passions, and revive the old vices of paganism in resuscitating gods, who are as immoral as Jupiter or Venus, and as far removed from the source of all good.

Athens, the heart of intellectual life, and Rome, the centre of empire, are taken by the author as illustrations of the force and universality of polytheism. The false gods guarded every avenue of social, political, and private life; anger, greed, and immorality were set up on high for the adoration of human hearts, and under their emblems man was worshipping the arch-enemy of his race. That multitude of religious rites, whether in temple or in dwelling-place; that abject clinging to a crowd of unchaste deities; that utter want of moral sentiment noticeable in the heathen world, were an offspring of superstition which, in the Greek sense of the word, is fear of the demons. This it was which usurped the place of the chaste fear of God. The question as to how far human depravity had led to this universal superstition is naturally one of great importance, but beyond perversion of heart and intellect, Mr. Allies proves clearly that the supernatural phenomena occasionally connected with the heathen worship were due to diabolical agency. The consequences through long centuries of the Fall on the Body of Adam were set forth in the outward splendour yet inward penury of the Roman citizen. The worship of the gods did not bear the scrutiny of the intellect, but neither did they themselves call forth affection. The heart and mind of man not only required a deserving object to know and love, but both had been so long fed on fear of the demons that the work of the Church was a double labour of formation and reintegration. The powerlessness of mere legislation to produce moral results, or to stay the flood of moral depravity, proves, as nothing else could, the reason for a personal educator higher than man, who should speak with authority; but human wickedness itself bears witness to the fall of Adam. The solution given by the Christian faith of the "wonderful maze of polytheistic idolatry" was that this was simply the travail of the "Body of Adam carried out through thousands of years and fallen under a terrible captivity."* Just as the natural society rested on the headship of Adam, so did the spiritual on our Lord, the new Adam, and the parallel was to be carried out through all ages. As nationality had entered so largely into the worship of the gods, a wider bond was to unite the followers of our Lord: the name and character of Christian were to be more to them than the dearest ties of country or kindred. But more than this. As the sin of Adam had generated corruption in himself and his descendants, so the second Adam, infinitely holy, triumphed over sin and death, and bequeathed incorruptibility to His Body upon earth. Mr. Allies develops five analogies between the natural and the mystical body, but his meaning will be sufficiently illustrated by dwelling upon one. He says, then, founding his words on the Fathers and on St. Augustine in particular, that what the soul is to the human body, that the Holy Ghost is to this divine Body, whose presence in it, "as of the soul," gives to it unity and life.† How would St. Paul have treated men who not only would not hear the Church, but who declared her to be corrupt? Decay is the distinctive mark of the Body of Adam.

True to his character as the positive exponent of Catholic philosophy, the author points out the manner of teaching used by the Apostles and their successors as that which belongs to a body or society. The written word depended on the kingdom, not the kingdom on the written word; and the earliest proof of it was the method of our Lord Himself, who taught orally,

---

* Vol. ii. p. 59.   † Pp. 97, 99.

but wrote nothing. His heavenly doctrines were handed down by word of mouth, and written upon the hearts of men by the life-blood of his Apostles and first followers. The next example of this personal character of the divine society was the abolition of the Jewish Sabbath. Sunday, the day of our Lord's resurrection, is eminently the day made by the Christian Church, yet it is an institution not of her written but of her spoken teaching, and one which the whole Christian world has nevertheless accepted at her bidding. The third witness to the Gospel of the kingdom—for, as the author remarks, the Gospel *without* the kingdom is something very different—is the Roman Empire. All religions, even Jewish monotheism, save the one which was to bear witness to the truth, were taken under the protection of the great Roman peace. That one roused its suspicions and its jealousy precisely because of the royalty of its founder. Like the Jewish rabble, the Roman world wanted no king but Cæsar; and its witness to Christianity, as being the kingship of our Lord, was that of ten bloody persecutions. For besides the testimony of heroism even unto death, there is the testimony of hatred. When our own times become matter of history, the *Culturkampf* will as surely witness to the just claims of Christ's Body as the actual martyrdom of Catholic missionaries in the far East. What was the deep meaning of the word which has become a proverb, *deletum nomen Christianum?* The Christians followed a leader who proclaimed the foundation of a kingdom which should be in this world but not of it, and, like Herod, the Roman emperor was jealous of His sovereignty. The lie contained in that boast serves only to chronicle the powerlessness of deadly assaults when directed against the immortal Body of our Lord. It was nevertheless true that Christianity rested on principles which, "if carried out, would sweep away the whole fabric of polytheism on which the Roman State rested."* With the martyrdom of St. Peter and St. Paul began the proclamation of penal laws which were not repealed till the time of Constantine. Here it is that *deletum nomen Christianum* bears witness against itself. The greatest empire which the world has ever seen exerted all its sovereignty against the Christian people. A merely human institution would have been truly rooted out, but it was far otherwise with the city of God. Contact with the heavenly doctrines, which it proclaimed from the bleeding lips and in the torn members of its children, was its means of propagation. The example of Christians slowly undermined the vast fabric of Roman polytheism. During the last ten years of the reign of Antoninus,

* P. 193.

"Christian influences become unmistakable in their action upon heathen thought and society."* The struggle was one which all ages are repeating, and which the world is always ignoring: that of the united resources of wealth and might against the moral power of truth and goodness. The grain of mustard-seed had first been cast by the Apostles and their successors in the various cities of the empire; and the inward life and spiritual government of these centres offered a parallel to the civil liberties enjoyed by those on whom the Roman State conferred the right of citizenship. The seed grew to a tree in each city, and as a tree it ramified. With the third century the Church began to reap the harvest of her work of fashioning individual hearts. The Christian movement was gradually permeating all ranks of society, for no child of Adam was too lowly to contribute his part towards the new edifice of living stones. The successors of Augustus in the Empire had shown by their conduct that the happiness or misery, the liberty or the servility, which fell to the lot of the Roman people, depended upon the character of one man. From the period beginning A.D. 180 and ending in 222, three elements were noticeable, which were in sharp contrast to the opposite features displayed by the growing Christian society: a profound moral corruption, a disregard of civil rights, and an excess of cruelty. The extreme of dissoluteness and abject tyranny following upon the Empire's golden age announced the instability and innate weakness proper to the Body of Adam, as also the inherent littleness which accompanies mere human greatness.

But before coming to the contest with philosophy, which beset the Church from without, the first assault of heresy within her bosom enters naturally into the history of her philosophy, both because of the time and of the manner of defence adopted by Christian writers and apologists. When the last disciples of the Apostles had gone to their reward, and the legacy of tradition which had been handed down was in danger, humanly speaking, of being dispersed, the Gnostic error necessitated the clear defining of the nature of that legacy. The *Gnosis* was a knowledge not grounded upon faith, but based either upon philosophic science or a supposed intuition of truth, which, in fact, set up the individual reason as the highest standard of religious truth. In this point of view it was an incipient Protestantism, and, like Protestantism, it threatened "the whole existence and functions of the Church." The answer of the great Catholic champion, St. Irenæus, would also serve as a fitting apology against Luther, but more than this, "it is a complete answer to all heresy for ever."*

---

* P. 196.   † P. 271.

His grand argument is, that where the Church is, there also is the Spirit of God, and he thus meets the Gnostic error "that divine truth is acquired by the individual through some process of his own mind." The bearing of the first heresy on the Christian community is intensely significant, both as to date and as to the production through it of great doctors whose words should sound during all the ages of Catholic development. When the disciples of the disciples had died out, the attitude of Christian minds became altered, inasmuch as Christians perceived the need of "human learning, inquiry, and thought," turned upon the objects of their belief. Before all things it was necessary to define the nature and being of the Church as the organ which was to perpetuate the divine teaching, and this was done by overthrowing the denial of the divine headship and authority. Another point elucidated in the contest was the subservience of the Scriptures to the Church, or, in other words, to show that the Gospel of the kingdom is the work of the kingdom. The pages in which Mr. Allies develops the arguments of the three champions against Gnosticism can scarcely be surpassed in their pertinent setting forth of the principle of authority.

When we arrive at the "third age of the Martyr Church," we find the Empire, now become the prey of the strong Teutonic race, tottering, all but falling; the majesty of the Roman peace-seemingly departing; and society fluctuating between the fear of enemies beyond the borders and its own anarchy at home. The confusion of the Body of Adam—the representative, that is, of human society—is only equalled by the unity of the City of God. From the beginning of the Christian era down to the end of the third century, the author produces contemporary writers who bear witness to the organic unity of the Christian body. It was the basis of the whole structure, but a basis which had its root in divine power wielded on earth by the successor of St. Peter, whose primacy is likewise a matter of history. The foundation and preservation through the ever-changing tide of human things of a polity which embraced all countries and nationalities, was an unheard-of fact. "Stat crux dum volvitur orbis" is a motto which well describes the action of the Church amidst the fluctuations of human society; but the character of the Christian conflict against the Roman Empire was that of moral against worldly power. Rome held in her mighty hands civilization, luxury, the arts and enjoyment of life. She was a splendid *millionaire*, to know whom was to reign after human wise. Yet in the very heart of this all-powerful ruler a slight seed had been cast which was bearing greater fruit than that carried by the Roman legions. Another fact is brought out in the middle of the third century, and that is the cooling of Christian fervour, which was noted later on by St. Cyprian, after a terrible persecution had rekindled the fire of charity. It was a first instance of general decline, and God met it by a temporary consolidation of the decaying Roman power, as if the great heathen Empire had been a means for the forming and proving of His elect. It is a mark of Divine love when God allows the flail of suffering to winnow the chaff from the wheat as they lie together on the spiritual threshing-floor. After a reign of eighteen years, Diocletian, in the pride of successful power, ordered the fiercest and longest, though the last, of heathen persecutions. The Edict of Toleration closes the era of bloody struggle, but not the struggle itself. The conflict of Rome typifies the contest of the Body of Adam with the Body of Christ; there is a subtler and more perilous encounter, that of the human mind with the mind of Christ, which the author has set forth in his treatment of the Greek philosophy. "The thought of the world," of which Rome was the "golden head," belonged to the great Hellenic race. It is the revolt of human reason against the divine folly of the Cross, and as such belongs to all time.

Mr. Allies goes to the very fountain-head of Greek philosophy, tracing its course from its first representative, Thales, in the sixth century B.C. In its first stage it was evidently a seeking and using of the powers of Nature, a sort of natural religion which placed its centre of gravitation in one or other of the forces of the physical universe. It represented the results achieved by the human intellect, placed in very favourable circumstances as to region and climate, but cut off from the influence and traditions of Jewish monotheism. At the time of Thales and Pythagoras, the Greeks were without a religious system. They had the ancestral gods, who were good enough for the unthinking multitude, but who were despised by the speculative philosopher. He set himself earnestly to find out the causes of natural things, without referring them in any way to the will of the gods. From Thales to Socrates the universe occupied the energies of Greek philosophy, and its one significant result was the effort to attribute all things to one agency. Water, boundless matter, air, number, were in their turns regarded as the First Cause, and this reducing of the universe to a unity, however impersonal, satisfied the mere intellect better than the numerous gods of Olympus. Socrates introduced a change. He shifted the inquiry from the outward universe to man, as "a subject of logical thought and moral will," and this continued the bent of philosophy during the remainder of its course. The four principal schools of Greek philosophy are subjected to a thorough analysis, both in their teaching and their working. Plato based his philosophy not upon the Divine Being, but upon the being of ideas; his system did not reach the unlearned, and he frankly said that his intellectual God could not be attained by the unlettered multitude. Aristotle's standing-point was Nature, and his God a pure intelligence without power, who causes the world without being conscious of it. Plato's dualism was "God and Matter;" Aristotle's "God and the World." Amongst the true instincts of philosophy which seemed to resemble a natural forecast was the stress which each master laid upon oral teaching. The notion proper to them all was that of making disciples by oral training. They concurred in viewing writing as a subsidiary means of imparting a doctrine, which at best would need the explanation of a living educator. They rightly distrusted a dead letter, and Mr. Allies, by insisting on this point, has made philosophy—that best effort of the mere human mind—render a spontaneous homage to the divine Society of which it was in some sort a figure. In another sense, it shadowed forth the men who were one day to undermine the very basis of faith by undermining the principle of authority. The philosophers proved by their reason how gross were the fables of polytheism, how impure the Olympus of paganism; but they were far from enthroning as a sovereign the God of their conception. In reality His personality was as vague to the philosophic mind as was to that same philosophic mind the personality of a man after his spirit had crossed the threshold of death. The vague sort of First Agent, about whom they philosophized, did not possess the breath of life, nor any separate existence outside the mind of the individual conceiver. The proof of the finiteness of the philosophic God is that they one and all followed Plato's example, and "constructed no system of ethics in dependence on that conception which, if it be true, is of all-constraining influence, and is to the whole moral system what the law of gravity is to the material universe."* They could not bestow what they had not got—the almighty and infinite Creator of the universe; so, whilst they professed to believe in one God, they sacrificed the cock to Æsculapius, and the whole wisdom of their course on earth consisted in living according to Nature. The one result of philosophy was the conception of the human society "resting on the similarity of reason in the individual" which it brought out. Reason was the bond of citizenship in the human as faith was in the divine Society, and so far it was at least common to every son of Adam without regard to differences of people or nation. But this reason becomes a "relentless necessity" when the course of human things is viewed without the light of faith; for it fails to explain sorrow, sickness, and death, or to offer any sure hope of immortality.

---

* P. 469.

The Stoic remedy for dishonour, or weariness, or the intolerable burden of life was "the issue," simply because philosophy had no explanation of these things to offer. Its teaching, as viewed in the broad daylight which Mr. Allies has cast upon it, as the human counterpart to the Christian Church, is strangely significant. It expresses the whole measure of that which the human reason in its highest form was able to achieve. Its failure is no less important, recording, as it does, the necessity of a dogma, of a morality founded upon that dogma, and of a corresponding worship as the medium of both.

III. Having followed the course of philosophy during six hundred years, Mr. Allies, in the beginning of his third volume, contrasts with it the rise of the Christian Church : its foundation at Rome by St. Peter, who, in virtue of the divine authority, achieved in a few years what philosophy had been vainly striving after through fruitless centuries—a society based on oral teaching, independent of nationalities, consequently universal as human nature itself. As "Let there be light" is the divine word, which more than any other perhaps suggests the whole *arcanum* of creation, so that divine utterance, *Follow Me*, infused the breath of immortal life into Peter's kingdom. The great period of Greek philosophy, which was inaugurated by Thales, from whose time philosophy began to be viewed as distinct from religion, lasted a thousand years, and so at length became contemporaneous with the teaching of our Lord and of His Apostles, but at that date a new leaven was at work in it. A new star had had arisen in the East, whose light and warmth were radiating amid the dark places of the human reason, which, as far as any code of morality was concerned, had come to a standstill. Christianity revived philosophy, though it was to prove its ultimate downfall, or rather philosophy was, and is, the natural religion of man, and to the end of time it will prove the plank to which those who shrink from the folly of Christ will cling. In some aspects this third volume is the most opportune of the whole work on the formation of Christendom which has yet been published, because of the perfect analysis it presents of a combat ever old and ever new, as fierce in our own days amongst individuals as it was in the beginning of the Christian era amongst certain classes of men—that of the human reason against faith. Christianity caused the star of philosophy to pale, but it has not stopped the race of merely human philosophers, they who have turned away from the light and reached the stage of infidelity which is produced by vice not by ignorance.

Before the coming of our Lord four representative Greek philosophers had failed to set up a society. They were what Dissenters are to the Anglican Church, the uncomfortable witnesses to a want of divine power and life in their parent stem. At the time of our Lord three schools mainly represented Greek philosophy—the Stoics, Epicureans, and Sceptics; and of these the Epicureans were by far the most numerous. But the radiance, which the sun of the Christian teaching in the centre and heart of Paganism cast upon the workings of the human intellect exemplified in the Greek sects, produced the highest results in the natural order, the resuscitation of the old tenets under a softer garb, further efforts of the natural mind, which came to a riper maturity in virtue of its warmth. Mr. Allies is fond of illustrating a fact or principle in a person. Amongst others he has chosen Seneca, who was contemporary with St. Paul, as a type of the Neo-Stoic School, but he is more. Bearing witness as his writings do to the mysterious influence which had renovated the atmosphere of his sect, he constantly ignores its presence in his world, and remains what he was to the last—a worshipper of all that was good in Nature save Nature's King. The teaching of charity had produced natural kindness, which was based on the common possession of the reason. " When he (Seneca) termed the meanest slave fellow-man, friend, and even fellow-slave, and denounced cruelty inflicted on such an one as a wrong to humanity, he was using a language hitherto unknown."*

The words alone testified to this hidden influence, not the acts of the man. Seneca never proved his moral code in fire and water. As a minister of Nero his life was an utter contradiction to his teaching, nor did he even apply his philosophy to the prevention of the grossest crimes. He was perhaps the first of Eclectics, gathering the honey from all systems and leaving the gall behind; but his words, mere words as they are, prove that a radical change in thought and feeling had been at work, nor were these words the natural outcome of any teaching which philosophy had at any time propounded. The upholders of the law of Nature had recognized the beauty of Christian charity, and tried to inculcate from the common possession of reason in man that which our Lord enjoined upon His followers as children of one Father who is in heaven. They did as Seneca did: extolled brotherly love and kindness, and raised not a finger to prove either in their lives. The distinguishing feature of the first period of Greek philosophy had been its severance from religion, and at no time in its course had this characteristic been more marked than at its close. The moral code of philosophy in Seneca's day was fidelity to the law of Nature, and its sinners were the men who disobeyed it. Religion, properly so called, that is, polytheism, was left to the unlettered multitude, the

* Vol. iii. p. 90.

unthinking mass who would not trouble themselves to analyze
the basis of high Olympus. The heathen priest went through
perfunctory rites, but the philosopher, the expounder of the
natural law, was appealed to for the solution of all higher
questions. This feature was already very marked in Cicero's
time. His writing betokens slight regard for the "immortal
gods," the state of the case being that the philosopher considered
himself immensely superior to the popular belief, which,
though viewing it as a falsehood, he would not seek to root
out.

As the marked change in the language of philosophy to which
the teaching and writings of Seneca, of Epictetus, of Musonius,
and of Marcus Aurelius bear witness, was not produced by the
natural working of human philosophy, so its third and last
period bears upon it in like manner the reflection of the great
light which we know to have been Messiah's star. In the year
of A.D. 67 St. Peter and St. Paul had been martyred at Rome;
their sound was going forth into all the world, and that sound
was the divine revelation of the Son of God. The effect upon
philosophy of the forcible preaching of Christianity was to produce
one grand effort, which had for its object "to give a logical
and doctrinal foundation to heathenism, and so to reconcile
together popular belief with philosophic thought."* In the
beginning of the Socratic period of philosophy this had been its
line, though it soon ceased to be a true pursuit of wisdom,
a separation, that is, of truth from dross in its existing world.
Polytheism, and that form of it which flourished in Greece, was
debased with gross superstitions as to belief, and with foul
practices as to morality; but it still retained four fundamental
ideas, which, frequent as they are found to be among heathen
peoples, bear witness to a deep underlying truth, to a need which
they answered. These were prayer, sacrifice, oracles, and
mysteries. They suggest to Mr. Allies a striking analogy. He
considers that their existence in various nations of antiquity
points back to an original revelation, just as the comparative
grammar of the different Aryan nations tends to prove the
original Indo-Germanic language. In these four parts man
declared his belief that he was a creature, that he had need of
expiation, of authority, and of revelation. But philosophy,
instead of working this gold mine, had in its three principal
schools adopted negations of the primary truths which the
popular worship shadowed forth. " Far from purifying religion
of its corruptions, they had extinguished its essence, the sacred
fire of piety in the human heart, the human person's recognition

---

* P. 151.

of the Creator and Father of all."* In its last period philosophy in the garb of Neo-Pythagorean and Neo-Platonic tenets went back to its former traditions. Plutarch was the first representative of the Neo-Pythagorean school. His God was a pantheistic God, a constructor, not a creator of matter; but in two points, the reflection in his own mind of what he had taken from the Jew, Philo, he showed a very practical way of restoring the doctrine of the divine unity, and of maintaining the ancestral gods. He declared that the attainment of knowledge was an immediate gift of the Godhead, and not to be arrived at by merely human facilities, and he peopled the universe with intermediate powers who should work out God's high designs on man. He is a fit representative of the last stage of philosophy; for this attributing of semi-deification to intermediate powers or agencies exactly suited that heathen mind, whose whole ἦθος had been fed on the mythological fables, whose heroes, by a sort of dim anticipation of the communion of saints, were exalted to partial divine honours, as sons of the gods. Plutarch's monotheism raised neither enmity nor persecution, but rather procured him a post of honour from Trajan; whereas the same emperor ordered St. Ignatius to be cast to the lions for the sake of his Christian God. Besides this return to the ancestral gods, philosophy no longer showed itself hostile to the Empire. The movement which stirred it up from its innermost depths was an impulsion from without, and in the presence of a common enemy the Empire, Polytheism, and Philosophy joined hands. But if Plutarch's teaching was a so-called monotheism, which pandered to the popular taste by the admission of the Olympian gods as intermediate powers, and if his temper of mind was one of piety, Epictetus is the type of philosophy in another aspect. He, too, was a rigid monotheist, if the pantheistic world-soul may be so termed. His system dethroned the gods, but his kindliness attracted all men. Our author recognizes in him the "parent of modern Deism,"† the father of the race which never dies out, those who worship before all things and exclusively their "independent human reason." This is the sun of the system, and the pantheistic god is its planet; so that, although the outcome of philosophy under Septimius Severus is seen to have been the acknowledgment of one supreme God, the conclusion must be taken for what it is worth. The philosopher's god was made for his solar system, and followed it into being; whether the minor constellations, in the garb of the immortal gods, were tolerated or not was in reality a matter of small consequence, for they did not affect the pith of the question, that gospel of the

---

* P. 150. † P. 203.

human race which the united forces of heathenism were preaching over against the gospel of Christianity.

But the story of the mythical Apollonius of Tyana was to embody the heathen notions of a Christ, to give flesh and blood to the personification of the deified human nature. In this view Mr. Allies has rightly insisted on the fabulous history written centuries after the real Apollonius at the instigation of the Empress Julia Domna. Apollonius is a deified hero as far as circumstances and his own mission to mankind can make him one; he is not always, it is true, faithful to the law of nature, for he works wonders which are in opposition to it. Yet the Pagan ideal falls far short of the Christian conception in five particulars. Philostratus, the biographer of Apollonius, has the pantheistic notion of God and of the human soul, and Apollonius himself is given the heathen standing-point as to the task of philosophy, as to moral guilt, as to suffering, and as to the evil of matter. The character and working of the God-man had suggested this representation of a man-god, though throughout the work the Christian movement is absolutely ignored. "As a specimen of human nature in its highest condition, he was to bear a comparison with human nature as assumed by a Divine Person, in which fact the whole Christian revelation is summed up. The force of the simultaneous connection and contrast lies precisely in this, that Apollonius not only stood entirely on heathen ground, but represented *unassisted human nature.*"* Here is contained in three words that which constitutes the battle of a paganizing philosophy through all time: it is the battle of the mind of man against the mind of God; human reason against the folly of the Cross.

It was only one stage of the contest which terminated with Constantine, who, as Emperor, acknowleged the Christian religion by setting the Cross in his diadem. The star of philosophy as a body of opposition to the Christian Church, had paled before its divine radiance, and the spectacle which met the eyes of Constantine was one of powerlessness on the one hand, and of divine strength on the other. When all was said and done philosophy had only two admissions to show for its speculative reasonings now a thousand years old: it faintly grasped one Supreme God who was a purely immaterial intelligence, and the human soul as part of the same immaterial intelligence. Neither God nor soul was personal, nor was soul responsible when it came to be analyzed. The philosophical reformation of polytheism had been an attempt to prop up its falsehoods by a pantheistic unity, and it had consequently destroyed in thinking minds the habit and disposition of believing. It had upon it the

---

* P. 361. The italics are ours.

note of false reformations, which pull down and build not up.
Philosophy had not founded a society nor so much as a city, for
the independence of human reason was, and is, a dissolving
element. Constantine came to the throne with all the traditions
of Paganism and the Empire. He saw before him the edifice
which the Christian Church had been building by her own intrinsic strength, and he recognized in that society, which the
most fiery persecution was incapable of uprooting, the imprint of
the divine Hand, a unity in belief and working which was
beyond the power of man. Instead of the Pantheistic God the
Church had manifested the Incarnate God to the world; her
action was a double one, for whereas the philosopher had addressed
himself to the reason only, the Church based the action of the
intellect on that of the will, and her great medium was the One
Sacrifice offered to the one God in all lands. Belief, conduct,
and worship were the arms with which she, teaching in the name
of Our Lord, had conquered the heart of the world, and built up
an enduring society, one of whose principal tasks it ever will be
to fight the battle of faith against the independence of human
reason. She purified the parts of truth which a corrupt polytheism had retained. Her prayer, sacrifice, oracles, and mysteries
made saints where the false worship had used them for the
service of the devil.

IV. We have already remarked on the character of Mr. Allies's
work from its very beginning. It is one of positive controversy,
of setting forth the truth, and the results produced in the world
by the kingdom of truth. He now in his fourth volume comes to
a part of his scheme which is a further carrying on of the same
plan. The key-note of "Church and State" may be said to be
the divine origin of power. Further, the distinction between
the civil and the spiritual is traced back to Adam, and shown in
all the working of the Church down to the time when Constantine recognized the formation of the Christian people into a
kingdom. Adam's fathership of the human race was conferred
upon him directly by God. After the Fall he became a priest, for
sin imposed upon him the necessity of satisfaction; and Abel, son
of our first father, is recorded to have offered up bloody sacrifices
which were acceptable to God. Adam's fathership and authority
were not weakened by his sin, but he became a type of the new
Adam, and of the kingdom which he was to set up. Cain, on the
contrary, personified, as it were, the City of the Devil, in laying
murderous hands on Abel. His line was remarkable for human
skill and progress in the arts of social life. In the midst of the
desperate wickedness which brought about the Flood, the representative of the righteous line of Adam was reduced to one man,
Noah, like Adam, endowed with a double paternity, as the seed
of a double power. One man sufficed to maintain that which

was to be the means of propagation to both the orders which made up the race; marriage as the germ of the natural, sacrifice the germ of the divine society. Noah represented likewise the principle of authority or government, for God had made him the vicarious head of the human family, as discharging the duties of father and lawgiver in virtue of the divine commands. Babel was the first fruitless effort of independent human reason; the confusion of tongues was symbolical of the lost divine unity, and worked a double division on earth. Nationality, which corresponds to charity in the spiritual order, took its rise from the Tower on the ruins of the divine inheritance, but even in the debasement of nations and peoples who forsook the true God for the service of idols, four great goods are found, the impress of a thought higher than that of man. These "constituent principles" are the universal institution of marriage, the rite of bloody sacrifice, the instinct of society of which the development is civil government, and the alliance between civil government and religion. Thus, even variety of gods among the Gentiles did not eradicate the principle either of religion or of government. Both remained intact through all the aberrations of the human mind; the bloody sacrifice perpetuated the idea and need of expiation, and the reflection of the divine fathership was imaged out under the various forms of government everywhere adopted. But Abraham and his race had been chosen by God to form His people and to perpetuate His worship, and the descendants of the great patriarch transmitted the divine promises from generation to generation, till at the coming of the promised One, the Jewish sacrifice was offered up morning and evening to the true God, and the High Priest of the Old Law sat in the chair of Moses, preserving the bare outline of the idea of government and religion which the Messiah was to fulfil in all its plenitude. Whilst Gentilism bore the fourfold mark of the divine impress, the Jews alone maintained in its integrity the dominion of the spiritual over the temporal power. The Roman Empire in its abuse of domination had united the priesthood and the civil government in one person, and was the type in heathendom of that which Christian rulers without the Christian spirit have reproduced; the tyranny of Cæsar over the things of God. If the Jews, as the chosen people of the Old Law, may be taken to express the figure of what the reality was to be, then is their spiritual independence a fact, which the Christian people was to carry on and perfect. "Throughout all Gentiledom the sacerdotal authority had become the serf of the civil power, but to the Jews the worship of their God was in its own nature supreme."[*]

---

[*] Vol. iv. p. 80.

The representative of the two powers allied in one person, that is, the Roman governor of Judæa, Pontius Pilate, put to death One Who had come to found a spiritual kingdom, of which the Jewish high-priesthood had been only the figure. Our Lord died and rose again, and built upon His resurrection the divine power of His Church, which was to be independent of civil government, and to triumph over death even as His glorified Body had triumphed over the impotent walls of His sepulchre. The unquestionable testimony of facts proves that royalty and that kingdom as a sovereignty, not of this world though in it, and having for its aim the spiritual good of man. History proclaims it to be a royalty from the first, not the gradual development or growth of time, since supremacy was vested in one who received the keys of the kingdom from the Divine Founder. Both powers proceeded from God, but the spiritual as dealing with eternal interests has received a special divine confirmation all through the pages of human history. In it charity supplies the place of nationality; for all that which his country is to the natural man, the Church is to the Catholic. The question of the transmission of power, first by our Lord to St. Peter, and afterwards to the head of the spiritual body, has been rightly insisted upon by Mr. Allies. Four points are apparent in the whole mass of Scripture evidence, and, we may add, in the whole bent of tradition—its coming from above; its completeness; its unity; its independence of civil authority.*

From A.D. 29 to A.D. 325, as we have elsewhere seen, the growth of the spiritual kingdom may be likened to the grain of mustard-seed, which a divine Hand scattered into the bosom of the earth. During that time the Church was a secret power, working in the face of every kind of obstacle. The dark catacomb was a fitting emblem of her life of faith, for until the reign of Alexander Severus, not even the light of day was vouchsafed by the civil power to her worship. Her acts were to build up a Christian hierarchy which should form a Christian people, and he who gave impulsion and life to this work of formation was the successor of St. Peter. St. Clement, as Pope, calmed the dissension of the Church of Corinth, and in his letter, of which the full text has only just been recovered, to the Corinthian Church, he states emphatically his belief that the Christian succeeded the Mosaic order, or, in other words, that he himself carried on, as the reality does the figure, the high-priesthood and spiritual sovereignty of Aaron. "There is no strength without unity," was the cry of St. Irenæus and St. Ignatius, of Eusebius and Tertullian, who may be taken as men representative of the belief

---

* P. 175.

which was noted later on by St. Cyprian, after a terrible persecution had rekindled the fire of charity. It was a first instance of general decline, and God met it by a temporary consolidation of the decaying Roman power, as if the great heathen Empire had been a means for the forming and proving of His elect. It is a mark of Divine love when God allows the flail of suffering to winnow the chaff from the wheat as they lie together on the spiritual threshing-floor. After a reign of eighteen years, Diocletian, in the pride of successful power, ordered the fiercest and longest, though the last, of heathen persecutions. The Edict of Toleration closes the era of bloody struggle, but not the struggle itself. The conflict of Rome typifies the contest of the Body of Adam with the Body of Christ; there is a subtler and more perilous encounter, that of the human mind with the mind of Christ, which the author has set forth in his treatment of the Greek philosophy. "The thought of the world," of which Rome was the "golden head," belonged to the great Hellenic race. It is the revolt of human reason against the divine folly of the Cross, and as such belongs to all time.

Mr. Allies goes to the very fountain-head of Greek philosophy, tracing its course from its first representative, Thales, in the sixth century B.C. In its first stage it was evidently a seeking and using of the powers of Nature, a sort of natural religion which placed its centre of gravitation in one or other of the forces of the physical universe. It represented the results achieved by the human intellect, placed in very favourable circumstances as to region and climate, but cut off from the influence and traditions of Jewish monotheism. At the time of Thales and Pythagoras, the Greeks were without a religious system. They had the ancestral gods, who were good enough for the unthinking multitude, but who were despised by the speculative philosopher. He set himself earnestly to find out the causes of natural things, without referring them in any way to the will of the gods. From Thales to Socrates the universe occupied the energies of Greek philosophy, and its one significant result was the effort to attribute all things to one agency. Water, boundless matter, air, number, were in their turns regarded as the First Cause, and this reducing of the universe to a unity, however impersonal, satisfied the mere intellect better than the numerous gods of Olympus. Socrates introduced a change. He shifted the inquiry from the outward universe to man, as "a subject of logical thought and moral will," and this continued the bent of philosophy during the remainder of its course. The four principal schools of Greek philosophy are subjected to a thorough analysis, both in their teaching and their working. Plato based his philosophy not upon the Divine Being, but upon the being of ideas; his system

one sacrifice, the principle of jurisdiction was severely maintained from the first. Although the bishop was perfectly independent in his own diocese, he could not encroach upon that of another, nor perform even the duties of his episcopal office outside his sphere. For a long time the bishop was the guardian of the Holy Eucharist, which he dispensed, and then in course of time the system of parish churches and parish priests grew up, in subordination as complete to the bishop as the bishop's to the Holy See. It is evident that without one ruling force through the whole, the Church could never have built up her kingdom, nor, without internal and external unity, could she have attracted to herself powerful love or unquenchable hatred. Resting upon its priesthood, teaching, and jurisdiction, this spiritual fabric presented to St. Augustine in the fourth century an absolute proof of the Godhead of its founder, and with the light of its beauty before the eyes of his intellect, it is no wonder that the great father's dogma of dogmas should have been eminently the Church as the divine guardian of revealed truth.

The fact which is specially pertinent in " Church and State" is the organic growth of this divine *civitas* in perfect independence of the State. The Christian people were formed, indeed, under the hardest pressure from without, which proved all the more the abundant inner sap and life proceeding in them from a divine stem. The author has illustrated the independence of the Church's government by five points which he has gleaned from contemporary documents. That which concerns the election of her ministers is, if we mistake not, the first in importance. Power came to her from above, and consequently was never in the hands of the people; but as Moses had elected Aaron solely at God's command, so the princes of the Church, the perfect Priesthood of the New Law, were chosen not by popular suffrage, but by the institution of their own order and the confirmation of the Holy See. The first generation of Christians was formed during the first forty years of the Church's existence by oral teaching alone, and " by all this period the kingdom of Christ preceded the book in which we read at the distance of so many centuries the account of its origin."* Her independence as a living and teaching body is striking as to two points in which she resembled the child Jesus in the Temple at Jerusalem, of whom it is said that He grew in grace and truth, though He was from the beginning true God and perfect man. This double testimony to the vital power of the Church lies in the whole work of positive promulgation and the whole defence against error. The period of growth and formation, which terminated with Constantine, is crowned by the

* P. 319.

fuller exposition of doctrine, and the Council of Nicea is a brilliant illustration of the first solemn condemnation by which the Church preserved intact the treasure of the faith contained in our Lord's divinity. Five practices of the ante-Nicene Church proclaim her to have been, then, as now, a voice speaking with authority. The man who aspired to be admitted into the Christian body was put through a course of catechesis by question and answer. At an advanced age of his instruction, the use of a Creed was imposed for his acceptance. Few acts of constructive power are greater than that of putting together a Creed, because it involves the superiority of the Church over the Scriptures, of which it was the interpreter. Next came the dispensation of sacraments, which encompassed every important act of human life. The system of penance, again, testified to the living dispenser, as did the whole guardianship of the Holy Scriptures, which, if we may use the similitude, were surrounded by a court of honour every time they were submitted to the public gaze. The first Christians would have viewed with horror any frame of mind approaching to familiarity or free comment with regard to the writings which they believed on the word of the Church to be a divine charter.

The defensive attitude of the Christian *civitas* during the period which was crowned by the Council of Nicea, had to be maintained against enemies other than the whole force of Paganism. The conflict with Judaism threatened its unity at the outset; but Roman arms were the instruments for the fulfilment of the prophecy by which the centre of Judaism, the temple and city of Jerusalem, were destroyed, and the Christian Church was gradually recognized to be the power set up in the place of the ancient Holy of Holies. The holding of councils was the outward means of defence adopted by it, but the inner bond was the life of faith, resting, as we have seen, upon one Episcopate, nourished by one Sacrifice. In face of a body, which was at once the off-spring and the guardian of revelation, only two attitudes were possible to the human spirit : that of reason submitting itself to the teaching of faith, and that of reason taking of revealed truth what flattered itself while it rejected what it disliked. The one is the principle of orthodoxy, the other that of heresy, and we may add, of human philosophy.[*] It is the old lesson conveyed by St. Augustine in his commentary on the Psalmist's *Audi filia et vide*. During quite the first two centuries the Christian people followed out the first of these recommendations, and then began the era of its great doctors and great intellects, of the men who listened, and then were illuminated with light from on high. Of the time which immediately succeeded the Apostles the prin-

---

[*] P. 378.

cipal fruit was martyrdom. The Christian people consisted chiefly of the lower orders with a sprinkling of great names. Its ranks were in some cases recruited from heathen philosophy. Justin, Tatian, Athenagoras, Theophilus, Tertullian, Pantænus, and Clemens were attracted by the deep philosophy of Christian truth, and from enemies, became apologists. But besides Judaism and the whole influence of Gentiledom arrayed against it, there were the attacks of human reason from within, which were resisted by the means we have been describing. The ante-Nicene period was the progress from faith to knowledge, the *Audi filia*. The *Et vide* was to be realized by the epoch which was inaugurated by Constantine when he set the Cross in his diadem.

This great act of the first Christian Emperor is symbolical of the work of the Church which it attests. Were there no written documents of those first three centuries; if the catacombs had been destroyed together with the bodies of the martyrs; if the Gospel had been preached orally without leaving behind it the support of the Scriptures; history would still have to explain the fact which was involved in the Edict of Toleration. The Christian people had grown up into a kingdom, and the Roman world which had persecuted it, looked to be saved by it. A stone from the mountain without hands had upheaved it from its foundation: Cæsar refounded his empire on the power of the Cross. During the progress from faith to knowledge had been formed the Christian people, "that one miracle of Christ," which, according to St. John Chrysostom, "no heathen gainsayer could deny."[*] The witness of God had been miracles; the witness of man, martyrdom. Against the overweening power of the heathen State, which crushed and trampled upon individual rights, the spiritual *civitas* had set up a new basis of civil liberty; for the formation of the Christian conscience was to be the element of vital strength in an expiring society.

As a summing up of the work of the Church, and of the divine power which was in her, we may contrast the Apostolic College as it sat to nominate a successor to the traitor, Judas, and the three hundred bishops, who, at the voice of Peter's successor, flocked from all parts of the then civilized world, in order to meet the Arian heresy. The successor of Augustus, too, was there, not to control but to carry into effect the decision of the Church, and in so doing he set forth what should always be the action of the civil power. But, if as the representative of the old Roman power, he yielded to the Nicene Fathers and their Supreme Head, it was because the kingdom of Cæsar in his person had first recognized the Kingdom of Christ.

---

[*] P. 427.

May we be allowed to return to the analogy with which we began this review? The "Formation of Christendom" bears witness to the body of our Lord as does the mediæval cathedral, which was built in the form of a cross. These pages are the outcome of years of labour, which, no less than the aisle and transepts, all converge towards the one centre, the Divine Burden borne by the Tree on Calvary. To give Him a home on earth the one was built, whilst the book is written to establish the claims of His Kingdom in hearts of flesh. It is our earnest hope, then, that no crane rest on the summit of this work, but that in the perfection of all details, the fair towers may point to heaven, the eternal home of the City of God.

ART VII.—THE REVOLUTION IN THE SOUDAN.

1. *Report on the Soudan.* By Lieutenant-Colonel STEWART. Parliamentary Papers. Egypt, No. 11. 1883.

2. *The Story of Chinese Gordon.* By A. EGMONT HAKE. London: Remington & Co. 1884.

3. *Colonel Gordon in Central Africa.* By GEORGE BIRKBECK HILL, D.C.L. London: Thomas De la Rue & Co. 1881.

4. *Uganda and the Egyptian Soudan.* By the Rev. C. T. WILSON, F.R.G.S., and R. W. FELKIN, F.R.G.S. London. Sampson Low & Co. 1882.

5. *Les Missions Catholiques.* Lyon.

THE Dervish of the White Nile bids fair to establish at the sword's point his claim to be accepted as the long looked-for Guide or Latter-day Prophet of Islam. By a startling coincidence, the fourteenth century of the Hejra,[*] designated by venerable tradition as the era of the Mahometan Millennium, opened on the fatal November 2, 1883, when in the defiles of Kashgil, the army of Hicks Pasha came upon the hordes of its destroyer. That consummate disaster to England and Egypt, characterized with callous levity by a British Cabinet Minister, as "not necessarily an evil,"[†] is memorable for its moral, not

---

[*] The discrepancy with European chronology arises from the use in the Arabic calendar of the lunar instead of the solar year.

[†] Mr. Chamberlain at Newcastle-on-Tyne, January 15, 1884: "The defeat of the Egyptian forces in the Soudan is not necessarily an evil." See *Times*, January 16.

less than its material, consequences. The sign that Islam was looking for has been given to it, and the victorious Mahdi, thus punctually fulfilling the long tryst of ages, becomes a power in the Mahometan world.

The name, signifying "he who is guided aright," has been assumed by many Mussulman rulers, and with the earliest of the series is associated the belief in a hidden prophet destined to reappear on earth. Mohammed-bin-Hanifya, the son of the Prophet's son-in-law Ali, proclaimed Caliph under the title of Al-Mahdi, was believed to have escaped the ordinary lot of humanity, and to survive concealed on Mount Radwa, near Mecca, guarded by a lion and a panther. It is, however, the reappearance of the seventh and twelfth Imams, of whom the latter, Mohammed Abu'l Kasim, died in 879 A.D., that is looked for by the Ismailite and Shi'ite sects respectively.

Visionary as is the belief in these mythical survivals, it has given rise in Africa to two earlier revolutions, in their initial stages closely resembling the present movement.

It was after an obscure propaganda in the highlands of Barbary, that Abu-Abdallah, an apostle of the Ismailite sect, in the opening year of the tenth century, burst suddenly on the plains at the head of an army 300,000 strong, to lead his wild horsemen of the mountains, the self-styled "Cavaliers of Allah," to the gates of Tunis, and hurl the house of Aghlab from the throne of Kairewan. Obeid-allah-el-Mahdi, then proclaimed Caliph in the character of the seventh Imam redivivus, inaugurated by his reign, from 909 to 934, the Fatimite dynasty in Africa, and left his name to the once great city of Mahdiya, the emporium of the continent and port of Kairewan.

An equally momentous movement was initiated a century and half later, by the preaching of the Solitary of the Senegal, who from an island in that river first disseminated his tenets among the surrounding tribes, and founded the sect of Al Morabethun (dedicated to the service of God). The rude shepherds of the Sahara and wild mountaineers of Atlas, impelled to conquest by fanaticism, founded a city—that of Morocco—in 1062, and a little later an empire, that of the Almoravides, who from the throne of Granada ruled over north-eastern Africa and southern Spain.

The advent of the modern Mahdi, foreshown, in the belief of the Arabs, by the portent of the flaming sunsets conspicuously visible to them in October, 1883, is expected to herald the end of the world, preceded by the triumph, under his guidance, of reformed Islam. To conquer Egypt, then overthrow the degenerate Caliphate of Constantinople, and rule the universe from Mecca, is the ambitious programme of the meteor Prophet

of the Soudan, who threatens to launch his African proselytes
on the Valley of the Nile, with the irresistible momentum of a
Mahometan revival. The difficulties in the way of his advance
are, however, nearly as great as those which beset the path of
an army marching to attack him.

The question of the Soudan is indeed mainly a question of
communications, and its geographical isolation magnifies and
multiplies all the other difficulties it presents. Its vast area,
equal to that of Europe with the exclusion of the Russian empire, measures some sixteen hundred miles from its northern
frontier at Assouan to its southern near the Equator, and twelve
or fourteen hundred miles, across a line running east and west,
from the Red Sea to the extreme limit of Darfur. Thus, while
Khartoum is almost as remote from Cairo as London from St.
Petersburg, it is separated from Gondokoro, the principal post on
the White Nile, by 1,080 miles of river navigation. Nor do
these figures, representing linear distance alone, adequately
express the difficulty of transit between these points; since
Nature has here interposed special obstacles to communication.
A zone of fiery sand to the north is balanced by a zone of reeking morass to the south, both equally formidable barriers to traffic.

The first is crossed by that dreaded desert route across the
Nubian sands, along which England so recently followed in
thought her solitary knight-errant, thrilled with a sense of his
heroism and his danger. Here it was that an Egyptian detachment, marching to the conquest of Nubia, tempted from the
track by the mocking mirage, perished of thirst to a man. So
perilous, indeed, is the passage deemed, that it was once absolutely prohibited by a Government decree, rescinded only under
pressure from foreign consuls. The danger is emphasized to the
traveller's sight by the skeletons of camels strewing the tawny
sands at intervals, and lying thickest where the bitter wells of
El Murahd half-way across, occupy the basin of an extinct crater,
amid a scene that might have suggested one of the circles of
Dante's Inferno.

The alternative route, from Souakin on the Red Sea to Berber
on the Nile, is also a trying one, as it necessitates a camel-
journey of ten or twelve days. The girdling sands thus hem in
the Soudan on all sides with their fiery belt, cutting it off from
intercourse with the rest of the world.

The White Nile, on the other hand, the natural highway
between Khartoum* and the equatorial provinces, is liable to a

---

* There is in native parlance no Nile above Khartoum. The Bahr-el-
Abiad, or White River, extends thence to the Saubat junction, above
which it changes its name to that of Bahr-el-Djebel, Mountain River.

strange obstruction. Its sluggish stream, which in the 490 miles between Khartoum and Fashoda, has a fall of only 42 feet, disappears in some seasons beneath a floating marsh known as the *Sudd*, formed by accumulated growths of aquatic vegetation. Sir Samuel Baker's flotilla, which started from Khartoum before a strong northerly breeze in February, 1870, encountered this vegetable blockade, and only reached Gondokoro in April of the following year, after incredible toil in cutting canals through the matted overgrowth of cane and papyrus.

A more tragical fate overtook Gessi Pasha, who on his return from his successful campaign against the slave-traders, became entangled in the water-jungle, which surrounded the ships like a vast meadow. Provisions ran short, and the party experienced the last horrors of famine, the living preying on the dead. But 100 out of 550 survived to reach Khartoum after a three months' blockade, and the heroic leader, whose life was sustained at the time by small fish caught by his native servants, died at the end of a few months of the sufferings he had undergone.

Ismail Eyoub, when Governor-General in 1878, took up a party of soldiers to cut away the obstruction, and the final bursting of the dam is thus described by Gordon Pasha in one of his letters :—

At last one night the water burst the remaining part and swept down on the vessels, dragged the steamers down some four miles, and cleared the passage. The governor says the scene was terrible. The hippopotami were carried down screaming and snorting; crocodiles were whirled round and round, and the river was covered with dead and dying hippopotami, crocodiles, and fish who had been crushed by the mass. One hippopotamus was carried against the bow of the steamer and killed ; one crocodile, thirty-five feet long, was also killed. The governor, who was in the marsh, had to go five miles on a raft to get to his steamer. You can scarcely imagine the advantage of this opening to me. It took people eighteen months or two years to go to Gondokoro from here (Khartoum), and now it is only twenty-one days in the steamer.

It will be readily understood that on the present state of the Nile as regards the growth of the grass barrier, depends the possibility of relieving the garrisons in the extreme southern provinces.

It may be said that without the camel, the cushion-footed carrier of the desert, the Soudan would be absolutely inaccessible. Nowhere found in a state of Nature, though domesticated by man from the earliest ages, this wonderfully constituted animal can carry a load of 400 lbs. or 500 lbs., finding its rough pasturage on wiry grasses and prickly shrubs by the way, and only requiring to drink in summer every third or fourth, in winter every seventh or eighth day. Camel-breeding is one of the principal avocations of the Arabs, and as they supply these animals for transport, the local tribes practically command the various desert routes. The thoroughbred *deluls*, or saddle-dromedaries of Arabia, are beautiful creatures, with gazelle-eyes and silken coats, swift of foot, yet easy-paced as a rocking-chair. The *hygeen*, or riding-camel of Africa, is generally a rougher brute, with a jolting action very trying to the novice. Gordon Pasha, who in three years rode some 8,000 miles on camel-back, thus describes the effects of this form of locomotion:—

From not having worn a bandage across the chest, I have shaken my heart or my lungs out of their places; and I have the same feeling in my chest as you have when you have a crick in the neck. In camel-riding you ought to wear a sash round the waist and another close up under the arm-pits; otherwise all the internal machinery gets disturbed.

Ordinary pack-camels will travel from two and a half to three miles an hour, doing easily eight or nine hours a day, but good hygeens will go at double that pace. They are delicate animals, liable to many diseases, smallpox among others. The difficulty of military operations in the Soudan may be estimated from the fact that a horse can only cross the Korosko desert with an attendant camel as his water-carrier.

The climate of the Soudan is a still more formidable obstacle than its remoteness to its permanent occupation by foreigners. Arabs and Egyptians are decimated if long exposed to its effects, and few Europeans can survive many months' residence. Gordon Pasha lost nearly the whole of his foreign staff within a year, by death or invaliding, his Arab soldiers sickened in scores, and even he, though of a fibre like tempered steel, returned to Cairo a wreck after five years' service. The Austrian missions on the White Nile were perforce abandoned for the same reason, having in thirteen years lost fifteen out of twenty members by death, and two by total break-down in health. Physical geography is here a considerable factor in the social and political problem.

As regards soil and capabilities, the Soudan territories may be approximately classed under three heads—alluvial plains, swamplands, and desert. The first category, comprising the districts watered by the Abyssinian tributaries of the Nile, is the only one characterised by agricultural fertility. The province of Sennaar, called the granary of the Soudan, produces grain in such abundance that a camel-load of 500 lbs. may be bought for 3s. 6d., but for want of transport, it is often allowed to decay in the ground, while at famine prices in Suakin and Jeddah. Dhurra, a kind of millet, grows to such a height of stalk as to be on a level with the head of a man on camel-back; cotton flourishes on the rich loamy soil, and tobacco is successfully cultivated.

The great Equatorial sponge-lands, whose soakage feeds the river systems of the White Nile and Bahr-el-Gazal, form the next group of physically similar territories. The landscape of the Upper Nile has been sketched by many travellers, whose picture is not an attractive one. A sluggish ditch, fringed with gigantic canes or grasses, studded with floating isles of papyrus,* and overgrown with water-lilies and lotuses, whose seeds furnish a harvest to the natives, it rolls through a stagnant country of marsh and forest, beneath skies that are by turns reeking and scorching. A nightmare of Nature indeed seem these lands, where earth brings forth only strange and abnormal forms of life, and the very exuberance of creative energy breeds monstrosity, like the feverish activity of a sick brain. Gordon Pasha's letters—those most intimate utterances of a great spirit greatly tried—give a wretched picture of human existence in these regions:—

No one [he says] can conceive the utter misery of these lands—heat and mosquitoes day and night all the year round. Everything in this land is bitter, or astringent, or thorny or prickly. The nice green waving grass has silicious delicate hairs on it like spun glass and quite as sharp. Nice-looking turf has a seed like a crow's foot in it. You walk along, and think to pluck a handful of grass, and you get your finger cut to the bone.

Nor is his picture of humanity in these countries more favourable than that of Nature, for he found the inhabitants, devoid even of the parental instinct of the lower animals, ready to sell their children for a handful of grain, and rejoice in the bargain. He is, indeed, driven to exclaim at the mystery of their creation to lead a life of fear and misery night and day.

The principal tribes are the Shillouks, whose land is darkened by a perpetual smoke-canopy, from fires lit to keep off mosquitoes by night, and the sun by day; and the Denkas, owners of vast herds of cattle, which they bleed once a month, to feast on the boiled blood of the living animal, while they will starve rather than slaughter it. It will be seen that in such a country there is little to tempt colonization or traffic, and foreign intercourse in the shape of the slave-trade has only imported thither a worse barbarism and a more dreadful desolation.

The remainder of the Soudan, comprising the provinces of Darfur and Kordofan, with all the country between the Nile and the Red Sea to the north of the Atbara River, has more or less

---

* This great mushroom-headed rush, the ancient symbol of Upper Egypt as the lotus was of Lower, is no longer found below Khartoum, though it once grew as far north as Thebes.

the character of desert, though not everywhere to the point of absolute sterility. Through the whole of the two former territories* there is but one perennial stream, the Bahr-el-Arab; wells are few and far between, and the productiveness of the sandy soil is determined entirely by the annual rainfall. When this is copious, the plains of Kordofan are rich in corn and pasture; but drought is followed by famine, as in 1878-79, when, according to Mousignor Comboni's calculation, over an area thrice that of France, half the population perished. Water was then nearly as scarce as food, and was sold at the price of table wine in Europe. The missionaries of Kordofan, despite their own privations, did much to alleviate the sufferings of the people during this dearth.

In Darfur the water supply is still more scanty. The wells are thirty or forty miles apart, and even these are sometimes exhausted in the dry season, necessitating marches of three or four days without water. During the rains, they are supplemented by occasional surface-pools, which, however, foul with the ablutions of successive caravans, are reduced to what Gordon Pasha pithily calls, "a solution of blacks."

Water melons, grown in vast quantities, are in some districts the only form of liquid available during great part of the year; in others water is stored up in the hollow trunks of gigantic baobab trees, which are filled from the top and then sealed up, with a tap for drawing off the contents as required. These vegetable cisterns, with a diameter of twelve or fourteen feet, often contain a ton of pure sweet water, and the owner of seventy or eighty such trees is considered a rich man. Military strategy in Darfur is directed to the possession of the wells, cut off from which the enemy is driven by thirst to surrender.

The rains, which begin in June, and consist of a series of short but violent thunder-showers, continue till September, and clothe the desert with a brief glory of vegetation. The undulating waste, previously yellow with pale, dead grasses, is covered with the richest pasture, and the bare and thorny jungle is green with foliage and gay with blossom. Nature's jubilee is, however, the most trying time for man, as the rainy season is the least healthy.

Ostrich-feathers are the chief export of Darfur; as gum arabic, of the finest quality known to commerce, is of Kordofan. Produced by a prickly mimosa, from whose stem and branches it exudes in amber lumps, varying from the size of a cherry to that of an apple, the latter product furnishes loads for hundreds of camels which leave El Obeid every week for Dongola on the

---

* The name of Kordofan expresses this peculiarity—*Fan* meaning people, and *Khor* a stream running only in the rainy season.

Nile. A large increase in the price of this article must be looked for in Europe from the cessation of the supply from Kordofan, as it has remained ungathered in the disturbed state of the country.

The traffic of Darfur, consisting of some two or three very large caravans in September and January, follows the " Road of the forty days' march" from Kobbé to Siout. The commerce of the further west, which formerly pursued the same track, has recently been diverted to the route from Lake Tchad to Murzoukh and Tripoli.

It might have been thought that regions so uninviting and difficult of access would have remained exempt from foreign invasion, but such has not been the case. Arabia—prolific in humanity as barren of all other forms of life—from a very early age discharged her surplus population on the opposite shore of the Red Sea, whence the immigrants gradually penetrated to the interior, thrusting back the aborigines as they advanced. Hence the Bedouin fringe of Egypt, hemming in the narrow belt of sedentary inhabitants in the Valley of the Nile with a population restless and shifting as the sands of the desert. The subjection of these nomads to the authority of the Khedive is represented solely by the payment of an annual tribute, and they are otherwise independent under the rule of their hereditary sheikhs. Their migrations, prescribed by the change of seasons,* are confined within their own territories, strictly defined for each tribe. Unchanged since the dawn of history, they still squabble over disputed rights of pasture, like the herdsmen of Lot and Abraham, and still fight for precedence at the wells, as when Moses championed the daughters of Jethro against the Midianite shepherds. A hardy and warlike race, they leave agriculture, practised only in the cultivation of dhurra on a very limited scale, to their slaves and women, deeming plunder and fighting the only pursuits worthy of a man. Though indifferent to the ordinary practices of religion, it is a mistake to doubt its latent power of inflaming them to fanatical aggression—the form of piety most in harmony with their disposition. Brave in battle, and skilled in the use of the lance and shield, though little practised in that of firearms, those of the Red Sea border are physically a splendid race; and Mr. James, in a letter to the *Times* of December 10, 1883, says he has known one, in defence of his cattle, kill a full-grown lion with a single thrust of his spear.

---

* The appearance of the tsetse fly in a zone to the south of Khartoum during the rainy season drives the nomads to the north at that period, acting, Colonel Stewart says, as a tax collector, by bringing them within reach of the Government stations.

Two of the principal tribes in this region—the Bisharin, skirting the Nubian desert, and the Hadendoas, near the Abyssinian frontier—speak a language distinct from Arabic; and legend asserts the descent of the former from a Jewish colony sent by Solomon in the time of the Queen of Sheba. They are conjectured with more probability to have come from the islands of the Red Sea. The revolt of these tribes closes respectively the Souakin-Berber and Massowah-Kassala routes, for which they supply camel transport in ordinary times.

To the seventh and fourteenth centuries are traditionally referred the two most formidable Arab invasions of Central Africa. The Beni Omr, who led the van, settled first in the Sennaar district, but evidently extended their migrations westward, as the names El Hamr and El Homr are found throughout Kordofan and the Bahr-el-Gazal. The antiquity of the invasion of Darfur is proved by the existence there of armour, obviously of early Syrian manufacture. Shields, helmets, and cross-handled swords like those of the Crusaders are common, and some of these relics, presented by Gordon to the Khedive, and ascribed in native belief to the time of David, actually bore the date 280 of the Hejra.

The Arab and Negro races have in general remained distinct, the latter forming everywhere a sedentary and agricultural population, in contrast to the migratory and predatory habits of the former. The tenth parallel forms the southern limit of the Arab, defined by that of the camel, which will not live nearer to the equator; and the range of this animal is also coterminous with that of the Mahometan religion, which the immigrants everywhere carried with them.

To a large number of the wandering tribes of Kordofan is applied the generic name of Baggaras, derived probably from *baggar*, a cow, as these nomads being without camels ride horned cattle, and train even bulls to the saddle. They are inveterate slave hunters, and systematically make raids upon their negro neighbours to obtain prisoners for sale.

The Kabbabish, occupying the northern border of Kordofan, own vast herds of camels, some individuals possessing 2,000 or 3,000 head. They claim to be Maghrebbins, who from the neighbourhood of Tunis passed from oasis to oasis to their present locality. They are at constant feud with their neighbours the Hamr, who do battle against them in helmets and shirts of mail like knights of old. The Kabbabish furnish transport for the caravans from Dongola to El Obeïd, and their revolt closes this route.

Some of these tribes can put from 2,000 to 6,000 horse or camel-men into the field, but cannot conduct operations at a distance from their homes, whither they expect to return at the close of each campaign. The soldiers of the Mahdi are accordingly dismissed as soon as the immediate object contended for has been attained, instead of being kept permanently under arms.

History records but one epoch of comparative civilization in Central Africa, when, in the beginning of the last century, the kingdom of Sennaar, under a mixed Arab and negro dynasty, attained sufficient power and splendour to become the resort of learned men from Arabia, India and Egypt. Adlân, king of this country, in 1770 or thereabouts, sent an army across the White Nile to annex Kordofan, then occupied by scattered tribes without a central government. It fell an easy prey to Adlân's troops, but its conquest excited the jealousy of a neighbouring power, and Ibn Fadl, Sultan of Darfur, devoted himself to the organization of a permanent body-guard or standing army, with which he eventually defeated the forces of Adlân.

Kordofan, incorporated in his hereditary dominions, profited by the commercial prosperity of the ruling State, and became the highway of the traffic of the Soudan. Its people, lightly taxed, advanced in prosperity and civilization, and Syrian silks and Damascus cloths were bartered in the markets of Bara and El Obeid, for the crude riches of the heart of Africa.

But in an evil hour for the Soudan and the world at large, Mehemet Ali received glowing accounts of the rich and fertile regions beyond the deserts, and was shown by a French traveller the seeds of cotton indigenous there, confirming Pliny's account of the "wool-bearing trees of Ethiopia."

The conquest of the Soudan, undertaken in 1819, was signalized by an event of tragic horror. The leader of the expedition, the Viceroy's son, Ismail Pasha, fell a victim to the vengeance of the natives, who at Shindi set fire to a house in which he and his followers, while sleeping off the effects of a banquet, all perished in the flames.

Mehemet Ali's son-in-law, the terrible Achmet Bey, execrated under the name of the Defterdar, had meantime led a parallel expedition from Dongola into Kordofan, and encountered the natives at Bara, fifty miles to the north of El Obeid. Here they made a heroic stand, actually capturing the guns despite the dreadful havoc of their fire, and were only overpowered at last when mowed down in ranks by the steady fire of the infantry. The despair of the defeated warriors found utterance in the heart-rending shrieks of their women, who had accompanied them to the field to encourage them with their presence and their songs, and who now flung themselves on the ground tearing their hair in transports of rage and grief. About a thousand refugees found an impregnable asylum in the Djebel el Deir, a mountain with precipitous sides and a table summit covering an area of fifteen square miles. Here they were able to maintain their independence, as the chasms in the rocks supplied natural reservoirs of water, and their fields on the plain, though often laid waste, furnished their granaries with superabundant stores.

Dark days indeed came upon Kordofan under the rule of the Defterdar, until his cruelties passing the bounds of even Mehemet Ali's toleration, he rid himself by poison of his ferocious son-in-law.

The Egyptian government of the Soudan since its conquest has been a system of chartered brigandage. Governors who used their power solely for pillage, enforced their authority by means of a brutal soldiery, mostly unpaid, and living on the inhabitants as in an enemy's country, with all the amenities of African warfare. The unfortunate province of Fashoda has, according to Colonel Stewart's report, been permanently impoverished by the rule of one Selim-Bey-el-Kurdi, who, in addition to extorting large sums of money from the peasantry, sold many of them into slavery. Whole districts, moreover, along the Nile have been abandoned once more to the desert, in consequence of the heavy taxation of irrigating machinery. These are specimens of the fuel of accumulated wrong that feeds the present revolt.

Once, indeed, there was a three years' truce to oppression, and the Soudan from 1877 to 1879 enjoyed probably the best form of government possible to humanity, an absolute despotism, with Gordon Pasha as its autocrat. The spirit of his administration was summed up in the brief eloquence of his address to the applauding concourse at Khartoum, on his installation as Governor-General: "With the help of Allah, I will hold the balance level." Regardless of his own ease and comfort, he travelled incessantly through his vast dominions, inquiring personally into the grievances of the people, and redressing them whenever it was in human power to do so. Stern in chastising, as pitiful in relieving, he was the terror of tyrants and evil-doers, the hope and shelter of the poor and oppressed. Literature contains no nobler record of human aims and efforts than his Diary in Central Africa, registering for friends at home the self-communings of the solitary hero, alone in the wilderness with the barbarian.

No living man is known and loved over such wide tracts of the earth's surface; and in desolate Darfur, amid vast wastes unknown to Europe, the people still cry for his return, like abandoned children for that of their father. Mr. Felkin tells how his party were greeted in a remote village by joyous shouts of "Kurnek" the native corruption of his English title of colonel, and how the inhabitants, bitterly disappointed on finding that it was not, as they supposed, their beloved ruler returned, bade their visitors tell him, when they saw him, "that they wanted him, and he must come back to them."

To the brief interlude of justice during his *régime*, in contrast with previous and subsequent oppression, this far-seeing ruler attributes, in part, the present insurrection; and he himself warned the authorities that the old system could never safely be restored after the people had been taught to know a better. "There is no doubt," he wrote in 1879, "that if the Governments of France and England do not pay more attention to the Soudan, and see that justice is done, the disruption of the Soudan from Cairo is only a question of time. This disruption, moreover, will not end the troubles."

But Gordon Pasha in the Soudan had to combat an evil greater even than misrule and mal-administration. The slave-trade is, in truth, such an abyss of iniquity as to dwarf by comparison all other forms of crime. The conquests of Mehemet Ali gave an immense extension to this plague-spot of Central Africa, by opening up the Egyptian markets and Red Sea ports to the regions previously isolated by the unsettled state of the intervening country. Khartoum then became the great emporium of the traffic in humanity, and the countries of the White Nile and Bahr-el-Gazal its chief centres of operation. Here it was organized as a regular system of warfare, the armed escorts of the traders receiving a share of the captives in lieu of wages, while the cattle driven off at the same time were exchanged for elephant tusks with the friendly tribes. The slave-trade is thus a necessary adjunct to the ivory trade, under which name it shelters itself, and which depends for its profits on this more lucrative branch of commerce.

A set of lawless desperadoes, commanding numerous bands of armed followers, the slave-traders of Khartoum gradually became, in the outlying provinces, a power stronger than that of the State itself. Mapping out between them the country of the Bahr-el-Gazal, each chose a separate line of march to the interior, and defended it by a series of fortified camps, called zeribas. These stations, encircled with palisades and fences of thorn, were strong enough to defy attack, and to establish their owners' rule over the country, while the Bazingers, or slave soldiers, kidnapped as boys and trained to arms, furnished formidable garrisons. At the head of this confederacy of crime was a man whose career is a lurid romance.

If the name of Gordon be written in letters of light on the dark heart of Africa, that of Zebehr Rahama, the Black Pasha, is inscribed in characters of blood and fire across the same region. Born at Dongola, of a family which claims descent from the

Arabian Prophet, he early attained, by misdirected ability, to pre-eminence in his profession of iniquity. From his headquarters in the Bahr-el-Gazal a chain of thirty fortified posts carried the sway of this king of miscreants far into the centre of Africa, and an army of slave soldiers, superior to that of many European States, maintained his desolating rule over the intervening country.

His zeriba, resorted to by lesser slave-dealers to the number of 2,000 or 2,700 in a year, formed a mart where they could supply themselves with wares and provisions. Here Dr. Schweinfurth found him, in 1870, surrounded with a Court which he describes as little less than princely in its details. "Special rooms" (he says), "provided with carpeted divans, were reserved as antechambers, and into these all visitors were conducted by richly-dressed slaves. The royal aspect of these halls of State was increased by the introduction of some lions, secured, as may be supposed, by sufficiently strong and massive chains."

The quality of his troops, numbering some 10,000, may be judged from Gordon Pasha's description. "Had I said to them 'you shall be free' they would have scoffed at me, and it would have been taken as a sign of fear. Smart, dapper-looking fellows like antelopes, fierce, unsparing, the terror of Central Africa, having a *prestige* far beyond that of the Government—these are the slave-dealers' tools."

So powerful a subject was not likely to be very submissive to the remote and feeble Government of Cairo, and Zebehr attacked an Egyptian force sent into his country in 1869, and slew its commander, Hellali Bey. He next turned his arms against Ibrahim, Sultan of Darfur, the representative of a native dynasty of 400 years' standing. The Khedive, powerless to chastise the successful rebel, deemed it prudent to enter into partnership with him in his new enterprise, and sent a force under Ismail Eyoub, to co-operate in the campaign against Darfur. The result was the conquest of the province and its incorporation in the Egyptian dominions, the native ruler having been slain in battle with his two sons, who died gallantly defending their father's body with their long cross-handled swords. The title of Pasha, which in the Soudan usually decorates superlative rascality, was conferred on Zebehr Rahama, but did not satisfy his ambition. He aspired to the rank of Governor-General of the new province, and went down to Cairo, taking with him £100,000 to back his claim by bribery. He took other measures to secure his recall if these failed. Assembling his chiefs under a tree near Shaka, the slave-hunter's capital of Central Africa, he made them swear a solemn oath to obey his son Suleiman, and rise in rebellion whenever his orders to that effect should reach them. This compact, known as "the oath under the tree," was the origin of the great revolt of the slave-traders in the Bahr-el-Gazal.

The accuracy of Zebehr's calculation, that his services would be required for its repression, was justified by Nubar Pasha's offer to send him up to Gordon instead of the regiment demanded by the latter for the purpose. It seems he had offered Nubar to raise a revenue of £25,000 a year necessarily from the sale of slaves. But it was no Egyptian Pasha he had then to deal with in the Soudan, and the result of his conspiracy was the ruin of his cause. It was in July, 1878, that his message was received desiring that "the orders given under the tree" were to take effect, and his young son, Suleiman Bey, immediately proclaimed himself Lord of the Bahr-el-Gazal, driving out the Egyptian Vakeel and slaughtering the garrisons. The great slave-traders divided the Soudan provinces in anticipation between them, and boasted that they would plant their standards on the walls of Cairo. Joined by the Bedouin chiefs, whose rallying cry, "This is our land—we know no Effendina here," proclaimed their craving for independence, the rebels might have triumphed if only native officers had been sent against them. They were confronted instead by a military genius of no mean order, in the person of Gordon's Italian lieutenant, whose character is thus tersely summed up by his chief.

Romulus Gessi, Italian subject; aged forty-nine, short, compact figure; cool, most determined man. Born genius for practical ingenuity in mechanics. Ought to have been born in 1560, not in in 1832. Same disposition as Sir Francis Drake. Had been engaged in many petty political affairs. Was interpreter to Her Majesty's forces in the Crimea, and attached to the headquarters of the Royal Artillery.

With a force inferior to that of the enemy in numbers and discipline, their ranks moreover decimated by famine and disease, short of food and ammunition, in a country intersected by rivers and marshes, Gessi's heroic energy and resolution alone enabled him to fight and conquer in the teeth of all difficulties. He was at his last cartridge when the arrival of a small supply of ammunition enabled him to protract a gallant defence, and it was with his only remaining rocket that he fired Suleiman's stockaded camp in another crisis of the campaign. When the final blow was struck, he had but 300 men with whom to attack and surround the remnant of the enemy's force, still numbering 700, and occupying an entrenched position. He boldly sent to demand their surrender, and his envoy, penetrating to the young chief's tent at daybreak on the morning of July 15, 1879, woke him with a startling message, "The Pasha's salaams, and if you do

not lay down your arms in ten minutes you are all dead men."
The game of brag was played successfully, and Suleiman surrendered, but burst into tears on learning the weakness of the force that had surprised him. Young as he was, but four-and-twenty, he had signalized himself by many atrocities, and his last act had been to order in cold blood the butchery of four of his prisoners. Consequently, he met with no mercy from the victor, but was shot with ten others by Gessi's orders. Of his subordinate chiefs one may serve as a specimen,—Abdulgassin, spoken of by Gessi as "the hyena of these parts, who has massacred whole villages," and known also as the man who had baptized his flag in the blood of a little child, slaughtered to avert the omen of its overthrow when first displayed. In Suleiman's camp were found papers establishing his father's complicity in the revolt, but Zebehr, though tried in Cairo, was pensioned instead of punished, and received from the Khedive an allowance of £100 a month. Such is the history of the man whose name has recently been prominently before the public, first as the instrument of the Government in raising a force of Soudanese troops, and secondly, as one of those selected to accompany Gordon Pasha on his mission to Khartoum, an invitation declined by him on the ground of the blood-feud created between them by the execution of his son. His contemplated appointment to rule the Soudan, will, if persisted in, be an outrage on humanity. The joy of the population at Gessi's victory was, he says himself, a perfect delirium, and they hunted down the fugitive slave-traders and slaughtered them in hundreds. Forty thousand liberated captives were either restored to their homes, or planted in agricultural colonies throughout the country, and peace and prosperity were everywhere restored.

I had turned the country of the Bahr-el-Gazal into a garden, writes Gessi on Feb. 8, 1881. The people were all with me, and so I was able to discharge a large number of my soldiers. From all sides ivory, caoutchouc, and other products were brought in. A just government had done what seven-and-twenty thousand muskets had never been able to do—it had increased the revenue by tenfold.

But Cairo could not change its ways so quickly, and a reaction soon set in. Gordon Pasha was allowed to resign his post, and his lieutenant, Gessi, thwarted and hampered by his new superiors, had to do the same. The tragedy of his last voyage has already been told, and it was followed by his death at Alexandria a few months later. Thus things had slipped back into their old groove, and iniquity triumphed once more.

The scale of the slave trade in the Soudan may be judged from the fact that a third of the inhabitants of Darfur are believed to have been carried off, while the labour of the remaining population is almost exclusively devoted to supplying food and water to slave caravans in transit. The track of these dolorous processions is marked by the usual ghastly trophies, bleaching skeletons, many of them those of little children, and skulls which Gordon Pasha had piled in a grinning heap as a lesson to the population. Once passing one of these mementoes while riding with Yussef Bey, a noted slave-dealer, he said to him: "The inmate of that skull has told Allah what you and your people have done to him and his."

"I did not do it," was the Egyptian's reply; and the Englishman's rejoinder, "Your nation did, and the curse of God will be on your land till this traffic ceases."

But instead of reiterating the dreary details of these accumulated horrors, we prefer to tell the story of one of the victims—a very small one—the little negro boy Capsune, now in the service of Mr. Felkin, the English missionary. It is from the pages of the latter that we take the narrative of the infantine experiences of his *protégé*.

Young as the little exile is, he still remembers his home in a far-away land of running water and trees and flowers. Here he had kind parents, three·elder brothers, and a little white goat still fondly called to mind among the joys of his infancy. His father cultivated the ground, kept cows and sheep, which Capsune helped to look after, and grew cotton, to be spun and woven into the garments of the household. From this happy home and all his baby treasures, the little tender creature, barely three years old, was stolen by a party of cruel Dongolawi slave-hunters. With wonderful courage and intelligence he succeeded once in escaping and making his way home, but only to be recaptured, after his father and several of the men of the village had been slain in defence of their wives and little ones. After service with various masters, one of whom caused him to be whipped severely for an imaginary fault, he passed into the hands of an Arab trader, who was conducting a slave caravan through Darfur in June, 1879. During the march—one of such suffering that they were driven to eat grass for food, and suck the earth to allay thirst—a cry was raised that "Kurnek" was coming, and the dealers in abject terror tried to conceal their captives in the thicket, where, however, they were quickly discovered by the soldiers of Gordon Pasha. By "Kurnek's" orders food and, above all, water were given to them. "Children so thirsty," says the little narrator, "children very glad." Mr. Felkin, who tells his story, goes on as follows:—

Kurnek came from under the tree under which he had been sitting, and Capsune gazed with astonishment at the first European he had ever seen. The "white man's eyes" made the greatest impression on him, and he says, "I shake very much when I see eyes; eyes very blue, very bright, I think eyes can see through me, and when I see eyes I frightened, and think I finished to-day."

Strange that the "blue eyes" that had nothing but pity and ruth for him, and whose anger was all for his wrongs, should have inspired more terror than the tigerish eyes of his persecutors. It is of this little creature that Gordon Pasha says, in recounting his capture, that though under four years old he was so intelligent as to be able to give valuable information about the slave-dealers, and to whom he refers again a little later, as follows:—"Capsune never smiles—he has gone through too much bitterness to feel any joy." The small waif was made over to a master, on whose selection he was allowed to exercise a veto, and by whom he was kindly treated. Subsequently, coming into the possession of Slatin Bey, the Austrian Governor of Darfur, he was given by him to Mr. Felkin, and is now the devoted attendant of that gentleman's sisters. Humanity at large owes him a heavy debt of reparation for wrongs that can never be undone, and one may hope that the kindness of his present protectors may soften the memories of his dark past.

The power of the great slave-dealers was temporarily crushed by Gordon's repressive measures, but the system they represented retained its influence over the native mind. So closely is it interwoven with their social organization, that it is by its means that the Arab tribes pay their yearly tribute, the djellabs, or minor slave-dealers who accompany them on their raids, undertaking to satisfy the Government claim, in consideration of a certain number of prisoners of war. Those interested in the nefarious traffic have ranged themselves actively on the side of the Mahdi; Ilyas Pasha, Zebehr's father-in-law, the principal slave-dealer in El Obeïd, is his chief adherent in that town, and Osman Digna, his brother-in-law and lieutenant in the eastern provinces, belongs to the same profession. Thus the discontent of this powerful interest on the one hand, and popular resentment against a government at once oppressive and feeble on the other, were two elements of combustion ready-laid to produce the present explosion. But the spark of fanaticism latent in the Arab race was required to ignite the train, and the teaching of an obscure Dervish sufficed to enkindle it.

Mohammed Ahmed, now known to his adherents as the Seïd-el-Mahdi, was born some forty years ago on an island in the Nile opposite Dongola, the third son of a carpenter named Abdallah. Apprenticed early to his uncle, a boat-builder, near Sennaar, on the Blue Nile, he took umbrage at his relative's treatment of him, and ran away, to pick up a vagrant, semi-religious education at various free schools attached to the shrines of local saints. His secular studies were evidently but scanty, since, like most Dongolawis, he reads and writes with difficulty. Ordained a sheikh or faki in 1871, he aspired immediately to exceptional sanctity, and chose as his retreat a dry cistern in the island of Abba on the White Nile, about a hundred and fifty miles above Khartoum. Here his pious exercises, consisting of the usual Mahometan formulas, repetition of the names of the Deity and similar invocations, procured for him, not only a widespread reputation for sanctity, but substantial offerings from the faithful as well. Mohammed Ahmed became rich, and as it does not appear that his hermit vocation excluded the amenities of domestic life, he extended his influence by matrimonial alliances with the most powerful Baggara sheikhs, using freely the Mussulman privilege of divorce to enlarge his field of choice.

In May, 1881, he first proclaimed his mission in a letter to his brother sheikhs and fakis, and summoned them to join him at his island sanctuary. The various confraternities of dervishes, to an influential order of which he himself belongs, furnished a ready-made machinery for his propaganda, as they are organized as secret societies, with rites of initiation, grades of advancement, and vows of blind obedience on the part of the rank and file. They were, moreover, at this time smarting under a sense of grievance, as the subsidies, wisely granted them by Gordon Pasha, had been withdrawn as one of the economies of the Dual Control, and they contained all the elements of discontent furnished by a disestablished church. They joined Mohammed Ahmed in sufficient numbers to form a strong bodyguard, who, standing round him with drawn swords, defended him against a force of Egyptian soldiers sent, on August 3, to arrest him on his island. His next stronghold was in the mountains of Djebel Gadir, and here, in the following December, he inflicted a sanguinary repulse on the troops of Rashid Bey. In June, 1882, he gained a still more decisive victory over the main Egyptian army, under Yussuf Pasha, captured his camp at Djebel Geou, and annihilated a force 6,000 strong.

In September fortune seemed to have deserted him, for he encountered a crushing reverse in the repulse of three several assaults on El Obeïd, capital of Kordofan, with a loss of 10,000 men. He did not despair, however, but invested the town in due form, occupying the heights that commanded its approaches.

While engaged in this siege, his troops made prisoners, and brought to his camp, the Catholic missionaries of Kordofan, who, as the only Europeans brought into personal contact with him, furnish in their letters the most authentic particulars of his demeanour and surroundings.

The early history of the Mission of Kordofan, founded in 1873 by Monsignor Comboni, and confided to the Camillien Fathers of the Institute of Verona, has been told in a former number of this Review.* From its headquarters in El Obeïd it had established a colony at Delen, in the mountains of Djebel Nouba, amid the Noubas, a non-Mussulman population, believed to be a remnant of the early Christians of Nubia, driven southward before successive Arab invasions. Here a marauding band of insurgents appeared on the 15th of September, 1882, sacked the chapel and buildings, divided as booty, to the inexpressible grief of the missionaries, the boys and girls trained in their schools, and carried off as prisoners two priests, two lay-brothers, and three nuns, forming the whole staff of the Mission. They left the valley amid the lamentations of the inhabitants, and after a weary march of nine days, during which they were subjected to many indignities, reached the Arab camp before El Obeïd. Surrounded on their arrival by a fierce crowd of fanatics, who reviled and execrated them, they expected nothing less than instant death as the price of their refusal to repeat the Mussulman formula—*La iláh, ila Alláh, na Mohammed rasul Allah.*

Conducted after a brief delay to the headquarters of the Mahdi, they found themselves in presence of a man of about forty, described as tall and slight, with a black beard, a reddish-bronze complexion, and a sympathetic expression of countenance. These personal gifts are dwelt upon by his adherents in the language of Oriental hyperbole, and they declare that "he is always smiling, and his face is resplendent as the full moon. His form is as of the sons of Israel, and on his right cheek is a *khal* (wart) and other marks, which are written in the books of the Holy Law."† The missionaries were minutely interrogated by him as to their aims and intentions; but with a delicacy of feeling, scarcely to be looked for in such a quarter, he shrank from openly proposing apostasy to them, and confined himself to reading, by way of example, from a book, the story of some Christian potentate who had embraced Islam. After this mild hint they were confided to the care of a Greek renegade, by name Georgi Stambuli, who constituted himself their guardian and protector, even offering to pay a large sum for their ransom. Fully expecting, however, that their martyrdom was only deferred, great part of the night was passed in preparations for death, and a paper in the form of

---

* DUBLIN REVIEW, April, 1881, "Catholic Missions in Central Africa."
† Letter published in the Soudan correspondence of the *Times*, September 19, 1883, addressed to the Muslim officers of the garrison of Khartoum, by Iskander Bey, and Sheikh Yussuf Mansour, ex-Egyptian officers, signing themselves "auxiliaries of the Mahdi."

a testamentary document signed by all was confided to Georgi for transmission to Europe. Father Louis Bonomi, the Superior, describes their experiences of the next day in a letter published in *Les Missions Catholiques*, May 25, 1883:—

In the morning we were awakened by the sound of a military bugle and a great drum. Troops under arms assembled from all quarters, each division following the banner of its own chief. We believed an assault on the town was intended, but it was only a review of the forces. Soon after the *Seïd* appeared in the midst of his army riding on a white camel, with a young lad on its croup, who held an expanded umbrella over his head. From our position we commanded the whole plain in front of El Obeïd, on which were assembled not less than 25,000 men, about 10,000 of them armed with firearms.

Georgi told us that a similar review took place every Friday. It was then about eleven o'clock, and at that moment a detachment of soldiers appeared, and bade us follow them, as the *Seïd* was awaiting us in the centre of his host. We exchanged thoughts in a look, and having confided to Georgi our little testament, and a relic of the True Cross we had saved from pillage, we followed our guardians whose escort was by no means superfluous. The crowd surged round us, howling, menacing, hideous with hate and fury, and our satellites were forced at every step to defend us from the lances and sabres turned against us.

We went along, reciting the prayers for the dying, and returning thanks for the honour conferred on us in being allowed to die for the faith. The *Seïd* was waiting for us near the Catholic cemetery, whither we had so often brought our departed brethren to their last home. The act of contrition recited, and absolution given, we presented ourselves at last before the *Seïd*.

"*God lead you to the truth !*" said he.

Since these words signified nothing but what was good, we made a gesture of assent. The *Seïd* requested us to move on, placing himself behind us, so as to protect us from the fury of the crowd. Arrived at the foot of the hill where he had his abode, he repeated the same words and left us. We did not know what to think of all this, particularly as he had himself desired his followers to replace their swords in their scabbards.

We were not long left in doubt, for one of the principal chiefs rode up to us, stopped us rudely and said, "Which, will you turn Mussulmans or die?"

"Death first," we all replied.

He repeated the question, and on our refusal turned his rein and rode off.

Nevertheless they met with no further molestation; food was provided for them at the Mahdi's headquarters, and Georgi was eventually allowed to shelter them under his roof. Here they suffered, during the remainder of the siege, only such incidental hardships as are inseparable from a rude camp-life, to which unfortunately two of the sisters and a lay-brother succumbed in the course of a few weeks.

After the fall of El Obeïd, on January 19, 1883, the survivors were reunited to their companions within the walls, numbering six individuals—a priest, Don Paolo Rosignoli, a cleric, and four sisters, one of whom, a native of the country, has since reached Cairo. Assigned quarters in a fortified camp outside the walls, they have continued to reside there unmolested, the Mahdi having forbidden his followers to injure or insult them under pain of strangulation. Their constancy evidently inspired him with admiration, for he frequently held them up as an example to his adherents, saying, "See how these infidels remain steadfast in their false belief, while many of you have so little confidence in me." He is also reported to be often seen in friendly converse with the fathers, especially with Father Louis Bonomi. As the sum of £2,000, demanded by him for their ransom, has been collected and forwarded to him by Herr Hansal, the Austrian Consul in Khartoum, we may soon hope to hear of their release.

A letter from Mgr. Sogaro, Vicar Apostolic, published in *Les Missions Catholiques*, April 20, 1883, gives interesting details of the capture of El Obeïd, as narrated by one of its inhabitants. Its seems that when provisions began to run short after a four months' blockade, the garrison mutinied, and signalled to the enemy, who swarmed into the ditch and over the ramparts. The occupation was effected with perfect order, but Mohammed Ahmed, with a subtlety worthy of an Oriental brain, contrived to secure the booty for his treasury both from the rapacity of his followers and from the lawful possession of its owners. Bidding all the inhabitants repair to a camp without the walls, taking with them nothing but their bedding, he had them searched at the gates and despoiled of the property, which, as he foresaw, they gave him a pretext for confiscating by disobedience of his orders. The spoil was then lodged in the fortress, while further searches were set on foot for hidden treasure in the tombs, the wells, and the drains.

The capture of El Obeïd, in addition to that of Bara, effected some days previously, rendered the Mahdi master of Kordofan, of which the destruction of Hicks Pasha's force confirmed him in the possession. His recognition by English authority as sovereign of that province raises him from the status of a rebel to that of a monarch, and is one of the many unforeseen results of a policy shaped by circumstances instead of controlling them.

The story of recent events in the Soudan is indeed the story of the Sibylline books, each lost opportunity doubling the cost of future retrieval. An additional brigade sent to Hicks Pasha before his march into Kordofan, might have averted the disaster of Kashgil—an army could scarcely have counteracted its results. Perhaps, all things considered, it was as well that the authorities in Cairo were too prudent or too craven even to attempt it. A single regiment landed at Suakin in December might have saved Sinkat and Tokar; a British expedition sent in February was in time, indeed, to assert the honour of English arms, but not to effect any strategic purpose. Will the future bring a correspondingly heavy advance in the price to be paid for order in the Delta itself?

Even the intervention of General Gordon, the moral reserve of England, may, it is to be feared, have been invoked too late, and his mission scarcely promises success, though, facilitated by the fact that his action has been in the direction of accelerating rather than staying the revolution in progress. Moreover, whatever may be the form of government he ultimately establishes, it must for a long time depend for its stability on his personal influence. The public, which received a momentary shock on the appearance of a proclamation from him, interpreted at first as a sanction of the slave-trade, was somewhat relieved by his subsequent explanation, restricting its application to domestic slavery, a mild form of servitude inextricably identified with the habits of the people.

The relief of the remote garrisons of the Equatorial Province, numbering some 2,000 men, under Emin Bey, of the Bahr-el-Gazal, where Lupton Bey, an old officer of Gordon's, is reported blockaded at Meshera-el-Rek, with a force of 900 men, and of the Sennaar district, is dependent on the reopening of the water-ways of the Blue and White Niles.

Meantime Abdil Shakoor, son of the late Sultan of Darfur, has started to resume possession of his hereditary dominions, but his success is problematical, as the smaller garrisons were, by the last accounts, surrendering to the rebels, though Slatin Bey, governor of the province, still held out at Fasher, the capital.

The future of Egypt is gravely compromised by the violent disruption of her southern provinces, and by the establishment of the champion of the church militant of Mahometanism so near her frontier. The Mahdi, now quiescent at El Obeïd, like a wild beast in his lair, may start into renewed activity as soon as the rainy season—June to October—by increasing the available supply of water, shall have rendered the movements of troops possible. He could then march on Dongola by the caravan-route, leaving Khartoum a hundred miles to the east, and once on the Nile would be within striking distance of Egypt Proper. The danger would be increased were he supported in his movement, as has been sometimes predicted, by Mohammed-es-Senoussi, the powerful sheikh of the Tripolitan Sahara, who, though himself a *soi-disant* Mahdi, might be contented to waive his pretensions in favour of his rival. Their coalition would threaten the very existence of Egypt, which would be girt by the uprising of the Deserts as with a ring of fire.

These are, perhaps, remote contingencies, but they deserve to be borne in mind, since they are of vital interest to the people of this country. For amid the shifting aspects, the thronging confusion, and the bewilderingly rapid movement of contemporary events, one certainty looms up with growing clearness on the horizon of the future—that England, with faltering steps, indeed, and many hesitations and misgivings, despite divided counsels among her rulers, and factious clamour from a section of her population, is slowly and awkwardly blundering into empire on the banks of the Nile, as she has done on those of the Indus and Brahmapootra.

E. M. CLERKE.

Art. VIII.—THE DWELLINGS OF THE POOR.

1. *How the Poor Live.* By G. R. SIMS.
2. *Homes of the London Poor.* By OCTAVIA HILL. London: Macmillan & Co. 1883.
3. *The Bitter Cry of Outcast London.* 1883. London: James Clarke & Co.
4. *Labourers' and Artisans' Dwellings.* By the Marquis of SALISBURY, K.G. (*The National Review*, November, 1883.) London: W. H. Allen & Co.
5. *Labourers' and Artisans' Dwellings.* By the Right Hon. J. CHAMBERLAIN, M.P. (*The Fortnightly Review*, December, 1883.) London: Chapman & Hall.
6. *Homes of the Poor.* By the Right Hon. Sir R. A. CROSS, M.P. (*The Nineteenth Century*, January, 1884.) London: Kegan Paul & Co.
7. *Digest of the Artisans' and Labourers' Dwellings Improvement Acts* (Sir R. A. Cross's Acts). London: Eyre & Spottiswoode.
8. *Digest of the Artisans' and Labourers' Dwellings Acts* (Mr. Torrens' Acts). London: Eyre & Spottiswoode.
9. *Digest of Provisions as to the Removal of Nuisances* (Metropolis).

The Dwellings of the Poor. 415

10. *Digest of the Labouring Classes' Lodging-houses Acts.*
London : Eyre & Spottiswoode.

WHEN in His divine presence, the claims of the poor were once urged, our Saviour said, "the poor ye have always with you," implying thereby a commission, a prophecy, and a promise; a commission to His followers to care for the poor, a prophecy that there should never be wanting those upon whom His disciples might lavish their love, and a promise that the charity bestowed upon His poor would be accepted by Him as charity to Himself. That prophecy has been abundantly fulfilled; and to His saints have never been lacking opportunities for superhuman exertions in the cause of God's poor. Civilization, it is true, looked forward to falsifying the prophecy, and yet speaks of the social evil of their existence as a thing to be deplored, or still better to be forgotten, as it cannot be cured. Socialism even now prophesies the extinction of poverty by the abolition of wealth, but Christianity regards the poor not as an evil to be exterminated, or a pest to be avoided, but as a divine trust to be nourished for Christ's sake.

By a vigorous effort of will civilized London had succeeded in forgetting its poor, notwithstanding the obtrusiveness of the presence of poverty which horrifies the foreign visitor. Not that there have been wanting earnest and active men who have had the good of the poor at heart, men of high position who have taken a personal interest in their concerns, men who have influenced legislation for their good, and men who have lived and worked among them and for them. But society had nothing in common with such men ; if it knew or heard of them, if it regarded them as harmless, though eccentric, enthusiasts, and the poor for whom they cared voted it uninteresting if not repulsive. It had no objection to going to a ball or a bazaar for the benefit of a hospital, because the process involved no very offensive reminder of the unpleasantnesses of poverty, but for a really interesting object of solicitude it found greater attractions in a South-sea Islander or Red Indian, whose troubles had a touch of picturesqueness, than in a street arab, whose most prominent characteristic was dirt. The poor went their way, and the rich theirs, widely divergent; and those who had the care of the poor at heart laboured on through many difficulties with a success which, though real, was out of proportion to what they hoped to achieve.

Such was the position of affairs in the middle of last year. We had in April of that year quoted in these pages the words of Ozanam, "that Christians should interpose between the two camps" (of poverty and wealth), and we had then no anticipation of the excitement into which one of those camps would shortly be thrown by learning the proximity of the other. Later on in the year a journalist made an exploring expedition to the slums, accompanied by an artist, and published the result in a weekly illustrated paper. Then a Nonconformist body, wishing to obtain funds for the erection of mission halls, published a harrowing account of an inspection of some bad courts, which was followed by a paper in a review from the pen of a noble marquis. This fired the train; the excitement at once became intense, and great was the astonishment of Belgravia and Mayfair at the discovery of Whitechapel and Seven Dials. Exploring parties were at once organized, spies sent out, and those who were reputed to know the lie of the enemy's country, policemen, sanitary inspectors, and priests, were in great request. The reports of special commissioners were read with avidity, committees were formed, the press made coin out of the question, and forgotten companies republished their prospectuses. No stories were too sensational for belief, no disclosures too appalling; princes, ministers, and noble ladies visited localities commonly frequented only by the priest or the police; terrible tales were current of great personages being arrested by mistake, their zeal in the cause having taken them, shrouded in mysterious cloaks, to places usually frequented only by pickpockets and vagabonds.

To those of us who have the interest of the poor deeply at heart, there is something at once grotesque and sad in all this; grotesque in the surprise of the awakening, sad in the deepness of the past sleep, and sad in the little promise of improvement for the future. For we cannot conceal from ourselves that this excitement is of a passing type, a fashion of the moment; we dare not expect that it will produce in the wealthy any lasting care or real labour for the good of the poor; we can only hope that some few may be stirred to exertion, and must endeavour to turn any energy that has been aroused into a useful channel. With this end in view we propose here to briefly review the discussion of the past few months, and then to pass on and deal in greater detail with the present condition of the homes of the poor; what has been done in the past for their improvement, and what suggestions can be made for the future.

The work which has the honour of being first in point of date of the publications which have recently called attention to this subject is the series of papers[*] by Mr. G. R. Sims, which appeared in the *Pictorial World*. Besides the merit of priority, they have also such merits as are due to a dramatic touch and a sympathetic heart, but from the circumstances of their publication

---

[*] "How the Poor Live."

in the weekly numbers of an illustrated paper, they naturally lack any of the requisites of a careful and elaborate consideration of the subject. The same objection applies to the work published by the London Congregational Union.*

This work created more stir than any of the others, excepting, perhaps, the article by Lord Salisbury in the *National Review*. It opens with a naïve admission of the inadequacy of the dissenting bodies to reach the poor. "Whilst we" (the London Congregational Union) "have been building our churches and solacing ourselves with our religion, and dreaming that the millennium was coming, the poor have been growing poorer, the wretched more miserable, and the immoral more corrupt."† We are forcibly reminded, by this sentence, of Mrs. Oliphant's "Minister of Salem Chapel" drinking tea with the deacons and utterly ignorant of the poor of "Wharfside." "It is easy," it goes on, "to speak of the encouraging reports published by missions, reformatories, refuges, temperance societies; of theatre services, midnight meetings, and special missions. But what does it all amount to?"‡ About as much, we presume, as the reports of Protestant missionary societies in India or South America. The expectation raised by this exordium is disappointed by the conclusion of the pamphlet; for after touching on details of the most harrowing description, the Congregational Union announces its intention of erecting, in the three worst districts which they have been able to find, three commodious mission halls !

The articles by Lord Salisbury, Mr. Chamberlain and Sir Richard Cross are more careful attempts to deal with the question from the point of view of the statesman and legislator. Lord Salisbury recognizes the important fact that the action of the Peabody Trustees and Artisans' Dwelling Companies have benefited only the classes earning twenty-three shillings a week and upwards, and that no provision has yet been made on a large scale for those whom he conjectures to be a still larger number whose earnings fall short of that amount.§ When he goes on to deal with the prospect of this larger class he is not so satisfactory, preferring apparently to leave the matter to be dealt with by individual exertion rather than by legislative enactments. We venture to think that this conclusion is hardly satisfactory in the mouth of a legislator ; it at all events proves the utter inability of statesmen, however well disposed, to cope with the difficulties of the situation. We shall revert to the subject later on.

Mr. Chamberlain gives some interesting though discouraging

---

* "The Bitter Cry of Outcast London." † *Ibid.*, p. 4.
‡ *Ibid.*, p. 4. § *National Review*, No. 9. p. 309.

details of the work of improvement in provincial towns, especially in Birmingham, but he is still less satisfactory in his conclusions. Whether or not there be any attempt in his article to make political capital out of the question (which we cannot say is so apparent to us as it seems to have been to some), it is, of course, no part of our present purpose to consider, but, to whatever end the article may have been written, its conclusions strike us as the result of a somewhat superficial consideration of the subject. For example, the writer has certainly not grasped the full effect of either Sir Richard Cross' or Mr. Torrens' Acts, and he makes various suggestions, as we shall point out later in detail, which are covered by those enactments.

Lord Salisbury suggests that employers of labour should provide for their workmen's dwelling accommodation ; but though this may be practical in new towns, it is out of the question in London.* This Mr. Chamberlain rightly points out, but he goes on to say in italics : " *The expense of making towns habitable for the toilers who dwell in them must be thrown on the land which their toil makes valuable, and without any effort on the part of the owners.*" Surely this is no more than a *tu quoque* from the employer of labour to the landowner.

We turn to Sir Richard Cross with a feeling of greater confidence in his judgment. He has given much care and attention to this question ; he is the author of three Acts, those of 1875, 1879, and 1882 respectively, dealing with it, and he treats of the matter without any of the heat or prejudices of party feeling. He very rightly points out the distinction made by Lord Grey between prohibiting bad houses and providing good ones; he goes on to urge that very efficient measures should be taken to prohibit the bad ones, but when we come to the difficult question of providing good houses, we are disappointed to find that even he has no adequate suggestions to offer.

What a different atmosphere breathes in the pages of Miss Octavia Hill's work ! No doubts, no questions there, but plain straightforward statements; " I have done this," " I am doing that," and full confidence in the future of her work. We shall have so frequently to allude to it again that we will not do more here than say that Miss Hill's book is a republication of her articles in magazines dating from 1866 to 1872, collected in 1875, and now republished in 1883. The digests of Acts of Parliament are those which were recently prepared by the Local Government Board for the use of local sanitary authorities, and accompanied the much-talked-of circular of Sir Charles Dilke to the local boards.

---

* Sir R. Cross seems inclined to the same idea. *Nineteenth Century*, No. 83, p. 162.

Having thus briefly mentioned some of the more important works which have brought this question before the public, we must proceed to our consideration at greater length of the question itself. As we said at the outset the subject is not so new as some of those, who have written and talked about it recently, appear to think; not so new certainly as the newly awakened intelligence of society would make believe. "It is strange to find," says Sir R. Cross, "from these writings and speeches, that many have either forgotten or been ignorant of much that has already taken place in legislation and administration, and that some even appear to look upon this as a new question brought forward now for the first time."* On the contrary, as Lord Salisbury says at the outset of his article, "the condition of the dwellings of the wage-earning classes has occupied public attention" (he speaks here as a legislator), "and many efforts have been made to improve them; but very much still remains to be done, and, in spite of the exertions that have been made, the question in some of its aspects becomes more urgent every day."† This paragraph states concisely the true position of the case.

"Much has been done;" new streets, public buildings—the New Law Courts, for instance—and railway extensions have cleared considerable areas of bad dwellings; other areas have been condemned and cleared under Sir R. Cross' and Mr. Torrens' Acts, their sites being now either occupied by model dwellings or still vacant. "Much remains to be done," for overcrowding has greatly increased in the remaining low neighbourhoods, and many houses and streets, which were formerly decently habitable, have fallen into decay and descended in the social scale.‡

Sir Charles Dilke considers that of the localities visited by him several cannot be said to have improved in the last quarter of a century, a few have retrograded, and some have improved; he gives on the whole a slight balance in favour of improvement.§ This is not a very brilliant result of the past twenty years of hard work. Moreover, it is quite certain that during the same period the wealth of the upper classes has increased, the comforts of the middle classes have advanced perhaps still more, whilst the advantages which have been given to the artisan class during the same time have been very considerable. Many of these advantages were intended no doubt at the time of their grant to benefit the poorer classes also, and some of them may to a certain extent have done so; but it will

* *Nineteenth Century*, No. 83, p. 150.
† *National Review*, No. 9, p. 301.
‡ This statement, which we know from experience as the correct, is confirmed by a letter we have received from the agent of one of the largest London landowners.
§ Speech to deputation from the Mansion House Council.

be generally admitted by impartial persons that by far the lion's share of the plunder has gone into the pockets of the artisan.

Lord Salisbury cites the figures given by the Chairman of the London School Board. The children in three schools "came from 1,129 families. Of these, 871 families had only one room to live in."* Our own experience confirms this. We have visited a number of the families of children attending one of the large Catholic schools in Central London, and in no case do we remember to have found the families occupying more than a single room. Take a single street: starting from the end, at the first house there is a shop, in the shop itself is the bed in full view, whereon the proprietor takes her rest, and in the shop also sleep her two sons. We have visited every house in that street, and we do not recall an instance of a family occupying more than one room, except in a house which is the property of a philanthropist. In one case certainly, where a family of several generations, including the grandmother and infant children, was in occupation of a room about nine or ten feet square, there was a sort of small cupboard in addition with a bed in it. The next room to this was of yet smaller dimensions, and occupied by two young men and their sister. In another house a portion of the landing was partitioned off for the accommodation of an old lady and her son who had been turned out of a condemned area. In another house in the same street, in a room about twelve feet by nine feet, live a woman, her two grown-up daughters, her sons of sixteen and fourteen years old, a little granddaughter and a niece. The family is most respectable, they do not object to the overcrowding, and they pay 3s. 6d. for the room, which has a hole two feet square in the floor.

"It is difficult to exaggerate the misery which such conditions of life must cause," says Lord Salisbury, " or the impulse which they must give to vice."† His lordship might have added that the dangers which beset the young from being boxed up in such narrow limits with thieves and vagabonds, and worse, are inconceivable. "Many places," as we have said elsewhere, " which were exclusively criminal quarters, have, in consequence of overcrowding, been penetrated by respectable poor." And if the poor are too respectable to be contaminated by their neighbours, what can we say about their children or their children's children? "Is it wonderful," asks Mr. Chamberlain, "that from time to time are heard murmurs of discontent, and even of impatient anger? What manner of men and women must these millions of paupers be" (not necessarily "paupers," but, perhaps, he writes, loosely for " poor"), " if they can see without repining or resentment the complacent exhibition of opulence and ease which is

---

* *National Review*, No. 9, p. 305. † *Ibid.*, p. 304.

for ever flaunted in their faces within a few hundred yards of the noisome courts and alleys in which they huddle for warmth and shelter, without a single comfort, and in hourly anxiety for the barest necessaries of life?"*

Such is the problem with which we are confronted, and for which we have to endeavour to find a remedy. "All parties are now at one," says Mr. Chamberlain, "as to the existence and serious nature of the disease—none have hitherto found a specific for its cure. The field is open to experiment and discovery, and every contribution which may lead to a practical solution should be cordially welcomed from whatever quarter it may proceed."†

There are, however, many difficulties to be dealt with by the way. Perhaps the most serious is to be found in the attitude of the poor themselves. As servitude begets slavishness, and the gaol-bird loves his prison-house, so fresh air and wholesome cleanliness are poison and death to the dwellers in the slums. It is this rock on which great government schemes and wholesale philanthropic undertakings are wrecked; it is this which disheartens legislators who are nobly bent on reform in these matters, and which has to so great an extent defeated the objects of Sir Richard Cross' and Mr. Torrens' Acts.

You cannot persuade the family who occupy a miserable attic, endeared to them as home, to quit it for your brand-new dwellings with their whitewash and their bare square rooms. The love of home descends from the palace to the cellar; "be it ever so humble," or ever so unhealthy, "there's no place like home." You will find it also equally difficult to convince these people that dirt does not produce warmth, that fresh air is pleasanter than stuffiness, that the road is not the natural receptacle for refuse, and that a black ceiling is not more homely than a white one.

The next evil is the system of tenure; the ground landlord leases to a middleman who in his turn lets off the separate rooms. Not infrequently the middleman does not collect the rents himself, but employs a third person, who has to make yet another profit out of the hapless tenants. When a third person is employed, his only object is to get in the rents, and he is certainly not paid to point out where improvement is required. The middlemen, as a class, have the name of being extortionate, overbearing, and inconsiderate; but, to give the devil his due, we must admit that this very often is not the case; that middlemen are often, when their tenants are ill or out of work, very forbearing in the matter of rent. This, as Miss Octavia Hill has pointed out,‡ is

---

* *Fortnightly Review*, No. CCIV., New Series, p. 761.
† *Ibid.*, p. 763.   ‡ "Homes of the London Poor," p. 26.

one of the greatest curses of the present system. She instances a man who was a small tradesman, without capital to spend on improvements, who lost large sums through the bad debts of his tenants. Had he been more careful to collect his rents punctually, and to demand them effectually where they were withheld, as is most often the case, without good cause, he would have been able to spend money on improvements, and, at the same time, have been a richer man himself. She has another good story of an undertaker who owned some houses, and who, on being asked about bad debts, admitted their existence, but added, by way of explanation, "It is not the rents I look to, but the deaths I get out of the houses." The fact is, that the dishonest poor take great advantage of these indulgent landlords, and so honest men have to pay higher rents to make up for it. So far from its being the case that a lady fared worse at the hands of her tenants than the bugbear middleman in the case in question, Miss Hill, by an insistance upon the punctual payment of rent, was able to make these same dwellings habitable and to have a fair profit into the bargain, without any increase of rent.*

Another cause of difficulty, hitherto, has been the indifference of the local authorities. Sir Charles Dilke has pointed out the ample powers vested in the sanitary authorities, which have been very little used, and he gives it as his opinion that in only one parish in London have those powers been exercised to their full extent.† "The vestries," says Mr. Chamberlain, "often in the hands of cliques, and chosen at elections which excite no public interest, are largely composed of small house-property owners, who cannot be expected to be enthusiastic in putting the law in force against themselves."‡

We are not here concerned with the moral that Sir William Harcourt draws from these facts, that a central Municipal Government would create a greater interest in the elections;§ but the facts were admitted by him. A case in point came to our own knowledge in which the sanitary inspector turned a family out of their rooms, in exercise of his ample authority, not on account of its unhealthiness, but for the admitted reason that they had not paid their rent.

Lord Grey, however, says that there is not sufficient evidence to support a general charge of wilful inactivity against the local authorities, and Sir R. Cross considers that the evidence given before

---

* "Homes of the Poor," p. 26.
† In Chelsea. Sir C. Dilke's speech to the delegates from the Mansion House Council.
‡ *Fortnightly Review*, No. CCIV., New Series, p. 766.
§ Sir William V. Harcourt to the delegates from the Mansion House Council.

the Committee of 1882 bears out this opinion.* Granting for a moment that this may be the case, it will be admitted that, from what cause it matters not, the Acts have not been enforced by the persons whose province it was to enforce them, and that consequently we have yet to have what benefits may accrue from the proper carrying out of their provisions. But in spite of the assertions of so grave authorities as Lord Grey and Sir Richard Cross, we are afraid we cannot acquit the vestries of blame. It may be perfectly true that evidence is not forthcoming at Royal Commissions on this point, because vestrymen's tongues are tied, but we have it on the personal assurance of members of vestries, that very great scandals might be brought to light on this subject if only anyone among the vestrymen were in a position of independence and could speak without fear of the persecution which would inevitably follow.

Such, then, are some of the difficulties that present themselves to block our progress at the outset. How they may be eventually overcome, and how the condition of the homes of the poor may be amended, we must now proceed to discuss; and, in the first place, we shall consider for a moment what has been the result of attempts at reform in the past, and what guidance these attempts give us in our plans for the future.

In the first place, we must notice the Acts at present in force with regard to unsanitary dwellings. These may be classed under three heads. The first are the *Acts for the Removal of Nuisances*: the Nuisances Removal Act, 1855 (18 & 19 Vict., cap. 121); the Sanitary Act, 1866 (29 & 30 Vict., cap. 90, Part II.); and the Sanitary Law Amendment Act, 1874 (37 & 38 Vict., cap. 89). The scope of these Acts is to give to the local authorities (the Commissioners of Sewers in the City of London and the vestries and district boards of works in the rest of the Metropolis) powers to order the removal of nuisances, and, in the event of the notice being disregarded, to institute proceedings before the justices. Nuisances as defined by these Acts include "any premises, drains, ashpits, &c., in such a state, any animal so kept, and any house so overcrowded, as to be a nuisance or injurious to health." With these we may class *the Labouring Classes' Lodging-houses Acts*, a series of Acts passed in 1851, 1866, and 1867, which have been, we believe, practically dead letters. The second are what are known as *Mr. Torrens' Acts*—namely, the Artisans and Labourers' Dwellings Act, 1868 (31 & 32 Vict., cap. 130); the Artisans and Labourers' Dwellings Act, 1868, Amendment Act, 1879 (42 & 43 Vict., cap. 64); and the Artisans' Dwellings Act, 1882 (45 & 46 Vict., cap. 54, Part 11.). And the third are *Sir Richard Cross' Acts*—the Artisans and

---

* *Nineteenth Century*, No. 83, p. 155.

Labourers' Dwellings Improvement Act, 1875 (38 & 39 Vict., cap. 36); the Artisans and Labourers' Dwellings Improvement Act, 1879 (42 & 43 Vict., cap. 63); and the Artisans' Dwellings Act, 1882 (45 & 46 Vict., cap. 54, Part I.) These two sets of Acts empower the authorities named in them to clear away unsanitary dwellings; the radical difference between them is that Sir Richard Cross made the Metropolitan Board of Works the authority for the carrying out his Acts, whilst Mr. Torrens placed the powers given by his in the hands of the local authorities as defined by the Nuisances Removal Acts.

"If the powers given by the Nuisances Removal Acts had been fully and continuously enforced," says Sir R. Cross, "we should probably not have had much to complain of now, so far as isolated houses and simple streets are concerned;"[*] but as regards larger areas, he goes on to say, these could only be dealt with by such an Act as his of 1875. The results of these Artisans' Dwellings Acts are now pretty well known; in the City of London alone £210,000 has been lost in enforcing them; on the schemes promoted by the Metropolitan Board of Works £1,250,000 is estimated to have been lost.[†] The Act of 1882, however, which prevents evasion of the clauses relating to compensation for unsanitary dwellings under the old Acts, and takes away the 10 per cent. compensation on compulsory purchase (given by the Lands Clauses Act, 1845) in the case of dwellings unfit for habitation, will to a great extent remedy these defects, though Mr. Shaw-Lefevre still anticipates a certain amount of loss on the transactions under these Acts. In view of the serious difficulties and losses incurred in enforcing Sir R. Cross's Acts, the Metropolitan Board of Works have been compelled to refrain from further operations.

It remains to consider the operations of the companies which have been formed to take advantage of the clearances made under the powers given by these Acts. Of these there are a considerable number—"The Metropolitan Association for Improving the Dwellings of Industrious Classes," and "The Improved Industrial Dwellings Company," and Sir Sydney Waterlow's Company, are among the most important. These companies have been very generally a financial success, paying fair dividends and affording good accommodation for the rents, for the most part providing from two to four rooms for each family at rents varying from 5s. to 10s. a week. "But," says the Trades' Council, "the one apparently insurmountable objection governs all these buildings in a greater or less degree. It is of little use to the ordinary artisan or labourer, or to the poor class, to look with longing eyes

---

[*] *Nineteenth Century*, No. 83, p. 156.   [†] *Ibid.*, p. 158.

at the superior domestic advantages of some of these systems of dwellings professedly erected for his use, if these are placed beyond the reach of his purse." "This," as Lord Salisbury says, "is the real knot of the difficulty."* We are compelled to include amongst this class of buildings which are above the pocket of the poor, the houses erected by the Peabody Trustees. Cut off as they are from any necessity for a parsimonious economy, compelled to earn no more than 3 per cent., treated with consideration by all the authorities, and with unexampled opportunities of doing an excellent work, the Trustees yet have not provided a class of dwelling at all suited for the class which we have no doubt Mr. Peabody was especially desirous to assist. This is the more to be regretted as their example will naturally tend to deter others from embarking money in any scheme of a similar character; where failure has attended such exceptional advantages, it may safely be predicted of any less favoured attempts.

There is one further attempt which has been made in the past to which we must allude before we reach the constructive portion of this paper; we mean the work initiated by Miss Octavia Hill. How highly Miss Octavia Hill is spoken of by those who should know best the value of her work we need not say; Sir R. Cross speaks of her as a great benefactor, "who sets a noble example well worth the following." Both Lord Salisbury and Sir R. Cross are loud in their praise of her, partly, we venture to think, in order to justify their desire to shift the *onus* of the work upon voluntary assistance; but whilst we need not follow them in their conclusion, we must heartily acquiesce in their premises. Miss Octavia Hill, at all events, stands alone in the position of having dealt with this problem in a manner successful from every point of view. It is, however, only just to Lord Salisbury and Sir R. Cross to say that Miss Hill herself expresses her convictions very fully on the necessities of voluntary labour. "I do not believe that this difficulty will ever be met except by a good deal of volunteer work." .... "I am certain you can hunt the poor about from place to place, rout them out from one place and drive them to another, but you will never reach the poor except through people who care about them and watch over them."†
"I say very deliberately that management is the greater difficulty [than finance]. How it can be met by the watchful and wise helpfulness of volunteers" her book shows.‡

What then is this wonderful panacea which has found a remedy where the highest authorities have been at fault? It is difficult

* *Nineteenth Century*, p. 162.
† Report of House of Commons Committee. See also *Nineteenth Century*, No. 83, p. 154.
‡ "Homes of the London Poor," preface to edition of 1883.

accurately to define it; in fact, Miss Hill, on being asked, was unable to give any other explanation than "that it requires the minutest personal supervision of details. The system which she and her associates have followed is to take some court where the buildings are out of repair and inhabited by a dense and neglected population, and to purchase the leases of the houses as occasion offers. *She collects the weekly rents herself*, which gives her the opportunity of making the acquaintance of the inmates; and the object she thenceforth pursues is to improve the tenants with the tenements, repairing the rooms, and persuading the inmates to preserve them, and to take, where necessary, two rooms instead of one.* As time goes on, and necessity arises, she rebuilds the houses on the simplest possible model, with the necessary sanitary appliances of the strongest make, but without uncalled-for decoration or elaboration.

It is no doubt her system of management which is the secret of her success; for she so identifies herself with her tenants as to make the payment of rent a pleasure. Her bookkeeping is simple but excellent; she puts down on one side the aggregate of the weekly rents, on the other the necessary outgoings for ground rent, rates, taxes, and insurance; she then deducts five per cent. interest on capital, and the balance is available for repairs. She makes her tenants understand that their punctuality in payment will be the gauge of the available balance at the year's end, and she so far succeeds as to make them take a lively interest in the prospect of a fair surplus. When necessary repairs are paid for, there is often enough left to provide an extra cupboard or odd bit of work for the most punctual among the tenants. Arrears she strictly guards against, being convinced of the evils which we mentioned earlier as being entailed by bad debts; and she rarely, except in cases of illness, has any arrears on her books; and illness she endeavours to provide for by inducing her tenants to subscribe to a sick fund. We were a little taken aback by being informed by one of the most successful of Miss Hill's associates, that she always insists upon her tenants pawning some of their goods if ready money is not forthcoming. On explanation, however, it becomes obviously equitable, because not only do these people readily pawn their property when they require money for their own purposes, but they very often invest their spare cash in the purchase of superfluous furniture and clothes for the purpose of laying by for a rainy day. The same lady told us that these purchases are carefully selected with a view to their ultimate destination—the pawnshop; and that she found it impossible to convince her tenants of the advantage of putting money into the savings bank. They

---

* *National Review*, No. 9, p. 315.

fail to see that by their favourite process they lose interest on money when they have it, and have to pay high for it when they want it. We need not here dwell on the many other directions in which Miss Hill's activity has found scope for the benefit of her tenants; the playgrounds, the class rooms, the coffee rooms, the drying grounds and recreation rooms, besides the thousand and one kindly and useful things which can be done by one who knows her people's every want, and is daily watching over, encouraging and assisting, them.

We have said enough to convince our readers that nothing has been said in praise of Miss Octavia Hill's system beyond its legitimate deserts; it is indeed one of the most practical and beneficial forms of charity; for in place of pauperizing, it encourages thrift, sobriety, honesty, cleanliness, and habits of self-control and self-reliance. In considering the lines on which we should work in the future, very large account must be taken of her work, because she alone has already succeeded; though we shall point out presently the impossibility of an absolute reliance upon volunteer exertions.

So much for the past; we have seen the course of this agitation, we have glanced at the existing evils, we have considered the difficulties that have to be dealt with, and the attempts hitherto made for dealing with them; and we must now go on to deal with that part of our paper which treats of reform in the future.

We approach this subject with diffidence; it is easy to cry out about the evils, to re-echo "the Bitter Cry," it is easy to denounce the inactivity of vestrymen, or to lament the want of success of legislators, but it is difficult, most difficult, to say where the mistake of the past has been, or to propose anything which shall commend itself to the sense of the public as feasible, and, at the same time, as efficient to cope with the almost insurmountable obstacles which block the way of improvement. The difficulty of adequate suggestions is confirmed by the utter absence of any satisfactory proposal hitherto, notwithstanding the thorough threshing out of the subject in the public press. When we turn to Lord Salisbury and Mr. Chamberlain, or even to the maturer wisdom of Sir Richard Cross, we are struck with the sudden blight which seems to come over their ideas when they begin to recommend methods of relief.

We must, however, glance for a moment at their recommendations *seriatim*, and for this purpose we will set them down in order, concisely, indicating the author by an initial, and proceed to make a few observations on them afterwards. Their suggestions then, briefly, are:—

(1) Easy access to the suburbs (S.).
(2) To enforce existing Acts (R. C.).

(3) To encourage investors to put their money into improvement schemes (R. C.).

(4) Voluntary effort (S. & R. C.).

(5) That employers of labour should provide accommodation for their labourers (S.).

(6) To fine owners of unsanitary dwellings (J. C.).

(7) To deduct a fine for nuisances at the discretion of the arbitrator, on compulsory purchase of property (J. C.).

(8) To enable the authorities to close bad houses without being compelled to acquire them (J. C.).

(9) To enable the authorities in carrying out a scheme under Cross's Acts to acquire any property without compensation, and to levy the cost of the scheme upon the owners of property within a given area (J. C.).

These are the principle suggestions made by the legislative writers on the subject; we may add that Sir Richard Cross insists generally upon improved administration in preference to legislation. The first of these suggestions has not the advantage of novelty, and probably no scheme for railway extension in the suburbs will pass through Parliament without very stringent provisions for workmen's trains. Whether, however, greater advantages than those already secured will be obtainable is open to question; indeed the Great Eastern Railway is said to have been at considerable loss in consequence of the very low price for which workmen can travel on that line. There is, moreover, this to be remembered, that there are very large classes of the poor to whom it is indispensable to be within easy reach of their work. Even for those who are able to live in the suburbs, the additional hour at either end of a long day's work spent in getting to and fro must be a pretty severe tax.

Of suggestion (2) we shall speak again; it is excellent, of course, but Sir Richard goes into no detail of the manner in which it should be carried out. Suggestion (3) is vague, and Sir Richard again gives no clue as to what encouragement he proposes to give to investors. When we come to our own suggestions in the matter, we shall point out the manner in which this suggestion should be carried out. Suggestion (4) is the mainstay of both Lord Salisbury and Sir Richard Cross. It is, however, one thing to hold up your hand for volunteers, and another thing to get them just when you wish; for philanthropists, like poets, "*nascuntur, non fiunt;*" and it is, moreover, questionable how far the country, having got into a mess, can ask individuals to give their time and money towards getting it out again. As we have before said, however, the best authorities are agreed in thinking that some volunteer help is essential; how far it may be legitimately made use of, and to what extent it will be necessary to call for it, we shall consider hereafter.

Suggestion (5) is disposed of by Mr. Chamberlain; it is tempting, but in London hopeless.

Mr. Chamberlain's suggestion of fining owners (6) is an extension of the principles of Sir Richard Cross's Act of 1875; it is, however, not clear whom he intends by "owners," and the word is probably used by Mr. Chamberlain without an exact appreciation of the kinds of tenure prevalent in this class of property. Lord Grey considers that owners should be held responsible for the condition of their property, and defines owners to mean "the immediate lessor to the tenant," thereby generally excluding the class of owners probably intended by Mr. Chamberlain—the ground landlords. The proposition as defined by Lord Grey, Sir R. Cross considers as impracticable, and if our reading of Mr. Chamberlain's meaning is correct, it would, in the present state of tenure, be unjust. Suggestion (7) does not take sufficiently into account the operation of the Act of 1882, which deducts from the valuation of unsanitary houses an amount equivalent to the value of the repairs which ought to have been carried out; and it is moreover contrary to the opinion of Sir Charles Dilke, who considers very rightly that the Act of 1882 should have a much longer trial than it has at present had before any amendment can be made in the systems of compensation. Suggestion (8) is superfluous; the powers it desiderates being already given by the existing Acts.

Mr. Chamberlain, in a series of suggestions which we have placed together under the heading (9), would give fuller powers to the authorities in carrying out a general scheme of improvement, by enabling them to take any land, beside that covered by condemned dwellings, for the purposes of the scheme, without compensating the owners. Without doubt the owners of well-kept property would object to such a course, and their objection would no doubt be well grounded; the only possible justification being that public policy necessitated sacrificing the good with the bad for the general benefit; and we doubt whether such a justification could be maintained, except, perhaps, in the case of a single house surrounded by unsanitary dwellings, but such cases are probably rare.

It will be seen that no new departure in legislation is anticipated in any of these proposals; they aim mainly at slight extensions of the existing Acts, or at the improved administration of those Acts, to which must be added the urgent appeal made by both Sir R. Cross and Lord Salisbury to individual exertion. Having mentioned them here, we shall embody any of them which appear useful or practical in what we are now going to say upon the subject of reform.

There is now no question that reform is needed; this is admitted by all, and the appointment of a Royal Commission to inquire into the subject, approved as it has been by universal acclamation, leaves no further room for doubt upon the point. It therefore remains to accept Mr. Chamberlain's invitation, and to set down in some details the method by which we believe the remedy will be provided.

And here we must subdivide our subject into two parts, and speak of, first, immediate reforms, which must be provided at once, and are, as we propose, but temporary in their character; and, second, a deferred but final and enduring reform, which will require time for the carrying out.

Like Sir Richard Cross, we find our immediate and first reform in the better administration of the existing law. We demand no legislation upon the subject, being convinced that for our present and temporary purpose the existing Acts give sufficient powers. The operations under Sir Richard Cross's Acts are, we believe, at present suspended, and in the meantime we do not wish to see these Acts put into operation. We may here explain, lest our readers should have forgotten, that Sir Richard Cross's Acts are those which empower the Metropolitan Board of Works to clear unsanitary areas. We would go farther, we would say that at the present time we should like to stay the operations under Mr. Torrens's Acts, which give similar powers to vestries and district boards. Our reason is this: whilst we fully admit the desirability of clearing unsanitary areas, we consider that these clearances should be gradual, and that adequate provision should be made for the evicted tenants. We shall show in our second subdivision the method in which we should like to see these clearances effected. At present, however, no such provision is made for evicted tenants. Many of the evils of overcrowding have arisen from these indiscriminate evictions, either for improvements or under the Acts, as we have already pointed out; and until such provision is made no more clearances should be allowed. We quite admit that many streets will have to be condemned—we hope to see all unsanitary quarters disappear—but it must be in a regular and orderly manner, as we shall point out hereafter. In the meantime, however, in consequence of Sir Charles Dilke's circular, the vestries are on the alert, and are condemning unsanitary dwellings right and left. *This must be stopped at once,* or the results will be disastrous in the last degree.

The portion of Sir Charles' letter on which we should lay most stress for our present purposes is that relating to the Nuisance Removals Acts. Let these Acts be strenuously enforced, whether by renewed vigour on the part of the local authorities, or by the energetic action of private individuals. Here, indeed, we have an excellent opportunity for that public-spirited charity which

Lord Salisbury invokes. There has already been formed a Central Sanitary Aid Committee, and local committees in connection with it have been formed, or are being formed, in every part of London, and these committees will, we are convinced, perform an excellent work. By means of short abstracts of the Acts and pamphlets giving the leading points of sanitary essentials and obvious sins against health, they instruct those whose work or charity takes them amongst the poor in the alphabet of sanitation. They point out defects that the tenant should remedy, and simple rules of health; they show the matters in which landlords are to be held responsible, and they afford a ready means of enforcing the law in this respect. They take from the individual visitor the odium of bringing defaulting landlords to book, a task which is generally beyond the reach of the average visitor; he (or she) simply has to report the defect to the committee, and the committee notifies the fact to the sanitary authority, and, if necessary, enforces the notice by an appeal to the law.

We have already alluded to Mr. Chamberlain's indictment of the vestries, and to Lord Grey's and Sir Richard Cross's opinion, that it is not borne out by any proven examples. We have pointed out that the charge of gross and wilful neglect of duty from interested motives is a difficult one to substantiate, but at all events we have it on the authority of Sir Charles Dilke, that the neglect of duty, from whatever motive, is an actual and almost universal fact. Whether the authorities which may be constituted to deal with these matters by the London Municipal Reform Bill, if and when it becomes law, will have a keener sense of duty remains to be proved; at present, however, we are in these matters in the hands of vestries and district boards of works, and in lieu of anything better we must exert ourselves to bring these bodies to their senses. We are told on excellent authority of a vestry in the East-end which holds its meetings in a public-house, where the members have to pay their footing by ordering liquor for their colleagues; whilst the practical control and nomination of the vestrymen is in the hands of the keeper of a house of immoral repute. In such a case we can readily imagine the vestrymen reading the Local Government Board's admonitions with more amusement than profit, and we can picture the leer with which the clerk reports to the President of the Board that the district requires no improvement in the matter of removal of nuisances. It will, we think, be wiser not to rely too much upon the passing of the London Reform Bill, but to work strenuously to obtain the election of really suitable men upon local boards as at present constituted. It is no doubt difficult to induce gentlemen to associate with some of those who seem to be leading men upon them; if, however, some would sacrifice themselves for the public good, a great deal of useful reform might be effected in a quiet way. The interest taken in the elections is *nil*, the least vigour shown in enlisting voters would secure the return of desirable candidates, were such forthcoming, and there should be surely no difficulty in finding respectable men who would be willing to sacrifice a little time for the public benefit. At present, however, gentlemen are in so small a minority that they can be howled down by the disreputable, and the small tradesmen fear the petty annoyances to which they are open if they dispute the will of the *clique*. We are not here concerned directly with these matters, but think it desirable to lay some stress upon the improvement of the tone of vestries as a salutary step towards reform.

Public opinion has now been sufficiently educated upon the subject to condemn any wanton *laches* on the part of the authorities, and a few well-established cases of neglect, if reported to the press, might do some good in keeping up the interest. Between the pressure of the Local Government Board and the public indignation, the sanitary authorities will be probably goaded into activity, and there seems no question that they will for the moment exercise some vigilance in the matter. We must not let that wakefulness slumber; and we must guard against the danger of activity—wholesale condemnations. We place the greatest stress upon the enforcement of the Nuisances Removal Acts, as the only ready method of relieving glaring and present evils. They do not, of course, touch the worse difficulty of overcrowding. The pressure of overcrowding, as we have said before, is becoming more intense, and will become much more so if this blind and wholesale clearance is to go on. It must be relieved, but the relief can only be gradually attained. We must not expect, therefore, to suddenly jump from overcrowding into ease and comfort. We are going to point out directly how this can be brought about by easy stages, at present, and for immediate relief. We are reduced to two suggestions; first, as it has been put up with so long, that it should be borne for a brief space longer; secondly, that those who can should adopt Lord Salisbury's suggestion of a migration to the suburbs.

Had those terrible artisans' and Peabody's dwellings never been erected in Central London, the crush would not have come to such a crisis. It is no use, however, to regret them now. We can only say let nothing more be done for artisans in London. We see with sorrow several large artisans' dwellings at this moment being erected on the sites of the homes of the poor. Let the building of any more such houses be stopped at once. The better class of artisans can well afford to live in the suburbs. They get there, for the rent of a couple of rooms in the Peabody dwellings, a decent cottage, with even a strip of garden. Let them go there by all means. They can much more easily bear the extra cost of the journey.

The very large class who are bound to be within easy access of the markets or their work must be accommodated. No provision has been made for them hitherto. They have had to give place, on the contrary, to those who could have been as well provided for elsewhere. No impetus is needed in the direction of providing cottage accommodation in the suburbs. The speculation of builders will do all that is required; only the builders should be carefully overlooked to see that they do not, as they are only too prone to, run up worthless and flimsy structures which will rapidly become as dangerous to health as the worst we have now to deal with. The best terms possible must be made with the railway companies for the provision of workmen's trains. As we have before said, Parliament appears fully alive to this necessity and the advantages already secured in this direction go probably as far as the railway companies will endure.

One word for the owners—that is, as Lord Grey has it, the immediate lessors to the tenant. We do not see that there is need for further legislation. It might be well to fine them, as Mr. Chamberlain suggests;* but, as this would require further legislation, we are content to leave them to the mercy of the present law, which, if properly enforced, will compel them to put their houses in order. Such, then, are our views as to the immediate and temporary relief. Enforce the Nuisances Removal Acts, work up your Sanitary Aid Committees, improve and instruct the vestries and district boards of works; let the powers for condemning houses and clearing sites, under Mr. Torrens's and Sir Richard Cross's Acts, be for the time being suspended; cheapen your workmen's trains, and take people into the suburbs, but erect no more artisans' dwellings on the grand scale.

Our second and lasting remedy is another and a larger matter, and we submit it for what it is worth. We have seen that the greater lights are at fault here; they twinkle and are obscured. they give us no steady and certain guidance through the shoals. It remains for us to offer without apology a suggestion which at all events possesses the merits of not being too timid and of being founded on certain and admitted premises.

Let us remind ourselves for a moment of the problem we have to deal with. It is admitted on all sides that the slums and rookeries must go, whilst ample powers exist for their removal; it remains to consider how the people who are evicted are to be

* *Fortnightly Review*, No. CCIV., New Series, p. 775, and see above.

provided for. But whilst, as Lord Grey points out, "the State has the same right to *prohibit* the use of unsanitary houses as to prohibit the sale or use of unwholesome meat or drink; on the other hand, the same cautious rules must apply in dealing with the poorer classes as to *providing* any such necessaries of life out of State or local aid, whether the matter in hand be food and clothing or be sanitary dwellings."* We are bound to admit that it is inexpedient for the State to enter into competition with builders, and that any such action would probably be attended with disastrous failure. But we must bear in mind that the State has already taken action in this direction by practically, so far as greater London alone is concerned, subsidising the Artisans' Dwelling Companies to the extent of £1,250,000. By purchasing land at 17s. a foot, and selling it to the companies at 3s. 4d. a foot, the Metropolitan Board of Works has to all intents and purposes made the companies a present of the difference. It is not for us to say whether or no this is a proper expenditure of public money: the thing is done; in dealing, however, with the housing of the poorer classes, we may fairly expect that a certain proportionate consideration will be shown by the State to those who take the matter in hand.

In the work before us there is a commercial and there is a philanthropic side: we propose to keep them apart; for though in some few instances finance and philanthropy may be successfully united, as by Miss Octavia Hill, we have a great suspicion of their harmonious blending on a large scale. One of Miss Hill's largest and most successful imitators has placed all her financial concerns in the hands of independent companies, and we believe this to be the most prudent course except in exceptional circumstances.

We propose, then, to entrust the financial transaction to the hands of a large company with a capital of at least £2,500,000, which will probably have to be increased. The directors would have to be men of the highest standing in order to give exceptional credit to the undertaking. Of the original capital, £1,250,000, a sum corresponding to that expended on the artisans' dwellings, should be subscribed by the State, whether by the Metropolitan Board of Works or the Treasury would be a matter for Government to determine. That £1,250,000 would, however, not be thrown into the gutter as the former was; it would simply be invested on first-class security, and would, if required, pay 3 or 3½ per cent. As, however, the former money was simply given away and this is only lent, we question whether the authorities should require interest at all. The State contribution would at all events stand

* *Nineteenth Century*, No. 83, p. 151.

on a separate footing, and should not under any circumstances pay more than 3½ per cent., whilst the remaining £1,250,000 required to make up the original capital will have to be subscribed by the public, and should, as we shall show directly, pay at least 4 per cent. The authority contributing public money should have the right of nominating a proportion of the directorate, in order to safeguard State interests, the subscribers electing the remainder. The company so constituted should be incorporated by special Act of Parliament, and the powers given to the Metropolitan Board of Works for acquiring bad neighbourhoods should, subject to proper control by that Board or by some other competent authority, be given by the Act to the company.

The Artisans' Dwellings Companies, with the aid of £1,250,000 of public money, have dealt with 42 acres of land, and we propose that the company should with a similar subsidy deal with an equal area. If further operations become necessary, it will be matter for consideration what share, if any, of public money should be asked for; experience will enable the company to decide whether or no it will be able to carry on its transactions without State assistance. When we come to statistics we are very much at a loss for data, and Miss Octavia Hill is unable to furnish us with any figures on which to base generalizations; as she very truly says, the circumstances of each case make a very great difference. We therefore cannot guarantee our figures, but can only say that they are based on the best authorities, and are as nearly accurate as our materials render it possible.

The cost of land purchased by the Metropolitan Board of Works has, according to Mr. Chamberlain, been 17s. a square foot, in consequence of the enormous compensation given; the land would have fetched, on the same authority, 10s. a foot for commercial purposes. Mr. Shaw-Lefevre states that had the purchases of the Board been made under the rules of the Act of 1882, the loss of £1,250,000 would have been reduced to £400,000—that is to say, the Board would have purchased at 8s. a foot. This tallies pretty accurately with Mr. Chamberlain's estimate, for, if the land be purchased by arbitration without compensation, and subject to deduction for want of repairs, we may well suppose, on a comparison with his figures, that 8s. a foot is about its value.

We presume, then, that the Company acquires its land at the cost of £17,424 an acre; and that for every acre it acquires it sets aside about half an acre for roads and open spaces, and builds on the remaining half. We assume that the cost of building would be about the same as the prices paid by the Artisans' Dwelling Companies, but we think it ought to, and would probably, be much less. In the absence, however, of reliable data, we must allow for the same cost, and we arrive at a total cost, for forty-two acres purchased and twenty-one covered with buildings, of £2,411,808. When we come to rents we are in a still greater difficulty, but must go upon received figures. We consider that the normal rents should be, for one large room, 2s. 6d. per week, and for two rooms, 4s. Miss Octavia Hill has a capital system of building rooms upon a lobby in such a way that they can readily be let in single, double, or three rooms, as the case requires. We see no objection to a single large room being occupied by a man, his wife, and small children; when the family grows up two rooms would be desirable. For the class of people we are dealing with, more than two rooms would, under any circumstances, be a superfluous luxury. For the enormous class earning 25s. a-week, and less, 2s. 6d. rent is enough, no man with £500 a year prudently lives in a house of over £50 a-year rent, and we think that that proportion is the correct one ; and as the children grow up to wage-earning age another room can be taken. Such rents would, of course, be an immense boon to the poorer classes, who now have to pay from 3s. 6d. to 5s. for a single small room. We calculate that these rents would earn £148,512 per annum on our twenty-one inhabited acres, out of which we allow £59,404 for repairs, losses, and expenses, and have an available balance of £89,108 for interest. If $3\frac{1}{4}$ per cent. has to be paid for the State loans, it will absorb £38,125, leaving £50,981 to pay 4 per cent. on the subscribed capital, with a balance of £981. For every deduction of interest on the State loan we have a corresponding increase of interest on the subscribed capital.

We estimate that by our scheme the Company would benefit 47,140 persons, or about double the number assisted by the Artisan Companies. The clearances would be effected, and the buildings erected gradually, and it would be the aim of the Company to provide the evicted tenants with immediate accommodation.

So much for finance; for philanthropy we should give ample scope. It has been said that "The Bitter Cry" is a mis-nomer, because no complaint is heard from those who live in these wretched tenements, and it is our own experience and that of all others who know the poor that they do not really feel the evils we see. We should therefore organize a Society of ladies and gentlemen to interest themselves in our tenants, to stand to them in the position of Miss Octavia Hill, and to educate them in decent and healthy living. We should allow ample space in the basements for recreation and club-rooms, and the open spaces could be utilized for playgrounds. We should, if possible, get the ladies and gentlemen to collect the rents in the same manner as

Miss Octavia Hill does, for though the Company would not benefit pecuniarily by the transaction, as, of course, they would pay the volunteers the same percentage as the ordinary collectors-yet it would reap all those moral advantages which we have before said result from Miss Octavia Hill's work. The percentage on rents is always given by Miss Hill, and by all others who work on her lines, as it makes the matter a business one. We do not propose to go into further detail here about this side of the question, we have already said enough to convince our readers of Miss Octavia Hill's success, and for further information we cannot do better than refer to her " Houses of the London Poor."

Such is our suggestion to meet the present evils; we have heard of no other at all adequate to the urgency. We have had a quarter of a century of patching, and are informed, by the best authorities, that little or no advance has been made. You may follow Lord Salisbury and Sir Richard Cross by continuing the patchwork, and will meet with as much success as in the past. You might even give Mr. Chamberlain his way, and if thought desirable, hang a few landowners, but we question whether much good would come of that. You may call in your philanthropists, but they may not come; if they do come to call, will you ever have them in sufficient numbers to meet the crisis? We have indicated what we believe to be the maximum of philanthropic assistance which may be safely relied on. For ourselves, we are content to go on patching until something better offers; shall we have to wait until the people take the matter into their own hands and forcibly occupy the houses in Grosvenor Square or Belgravia?

HENRY D. HARROD.

ENCYCLICAL OF POPE LEO XIII. TO THE BISHOPS OF FRANCE.

Venerabilibus Fratribus Archiepiscopis et Episcopis Galliæ

LEO PP. XIII.

VENERABILES FRATRES, SALUTEM ET APOSTOLICAM BENEDICTIONEM.

NOBILISSIMA Gallorum gens, multis in rebus pace bellove praeclare gestis, singularem quamdam sibi comparavit in Ecclesiam catholicam laudem meritorum, quorum nec interitura est gratia, nec gloria consenescet. Institutis christianis, praeeunte rege Clodovaeo, mature susceptis, hoc sane perhonorificum fidei pietatisque testimonium simul et praemium tulit, ut *primogenita Ecclesiae filia* nominaretur. Ex eo tempore, Venerabiles Fratres, saepe maiores vestri ad magnas res et salutares vias sunt divinae ipsius providentiae adiutores: nominatim vero ipsorum est nobilitata virtus in vindicando ubique terrarum catholico nomine, in christiana fide ad barbaras gentes propaganda, in liberandis tuendisque sanctioribus Palaestinae locis, ut non sine causa vetus illud vim proverbii obtinuerit, *gesta Dei per Francos*. Atque his rationibus contigit, ut fideli animo sese pro nomine catholico devoventes, in societatem gloriarum Ecclesiae aliquo modo venire potuerint, et complura publice privatimque instituere, in quibus eximia vis religionis, beneficentiae, magnanimitatis cernitur. Quas patrum vestrorum virtutes Romani Pontifices Decessores Nostri maiorem in modum probare consueverunt, reddendaque pro meritis benevolentia, non semel ornare Gallorum nomen laudibus voluerunt. Amplissimae quidem illae sunt, quas Innocentius III. et Gregorius IX., magna illa Ecclesiae lumina, maioribus vestris tribuebant: quorum prior in epistola ad Archiepiscopum Rhemensem, *regnum Franciae*, ait, *praerogativa quadam diligimus caritatis, utpote quod prae ceteris mundi regnis Apostolicae Sedi ac Nobis obsequiosum semper extitit et devotum :* alter vero in epistola ad sanctum Ludovicum IX., in regno Galliae, *quod a devotione Dei et Ecclesiae nullo casu avelli potuit, nunquam libertas ecclesiastica periit, nullo unquam tempore vigorem proprium christiana fides amisit : quin imo pro earum conservatione reges et homines dicti regni sanguinem proprium fundere et se periculis multis exponere minime dubitaverunt.*—Parens autem naturae Deus, a quo mercedem virtutum recteque factorum utique in terris accipiunt civitates, multa Gallis ad prosperitatem largitus est, laudes bellicas, pacis artes, gloriam nominis, imperii auctoritatem. Quod si oblita quodammodo Gallia sui, munus a Deo demandatum aliquando defugiens, maluit infensos spiritus adversus Ecclesiam sumere, tamen summo Dei beneficio nec diu nec tota desipuit. Atque utinam funestos illos religioni ac civitati casus, quos proximiora aetati nostrae tempora pepererunt, sospes evasisset! Verum posteaquam mens hominum novarum opinionum imbuta veneno, auctoritatem Ecclesiae passim coepit reiicere infinita libertate ferox, cursus praeceps, quo proclive erat, factus est. Nam cum mortiferum doctrinarum virus in ipsos hominum mores influxisset, humana societas huc magnam partem sensim evasit, ut omnino desciscere a christianis institutis velle videatur. Ad hanc perniciem per Gallias dilatandam non parum valuerunt superiore saeculo quidam insaniente sapientia philosophi, qui christianae veritatis adorti sunt fundamenta convellere, eamque philosophandi rationem inierunt, quae excitata iam immodicae libertatis studia vehementius inflammaret. Proxima fuit eorum opera, quos rerum divinarum impotens odium nefariis inter se societatibus coniunctos tenet, quotidieque facit opprimendi catholici nominis cupidiores: an vero maiore, quam uspiam, in Gallia contentione, nemo quam Vos, Venerabiles Fratres, iudicare melius potest.

Quapropter paterna caritas, qua universas gentes prosequimur, sicut alias Nos impulit ut nominatim Hiberniae, Hispaniae, Italiaeque populos, datis ad Episcopos litteris, convenienter temporibus ad officium cohortaremur, ita nunc ad Galliam suadet mentem cogitationemque convertere.—Ea enim molimenta, quae diximus, non Ecclesiae solum nocent, sed ipsi quoque sunt perniciosa et funesta reipublicae; propterea quod fieri non potest ut prosperitas civitati comitetur, virtute religionis extincta. Et sane ubi vereri Deum homo desiit, maximum iustitiae tollitur fundamentum, sine qua bene geri rem publicam vel ipsi ethnicorum sapientes negabant posse: neque enim satis habitura dignitatis est auctoritas principum, neque satis virium leges. Plus apud unumquemque valebit utilitas, quam honestas: vacillabit incolumitas iurium, malo custode officiorum poenarum metu: et qui imperant, facile in dominatum iniustum, et qui parent, levi momento in seditionem et turbas delabentur.—Praeterea quia nihil est in rerum natura boni, quod non bonitati divinae acceptum referendum sit, omnis hominum societas, quae a disciplina et temperatione sui abesse Deum iubeat, quantum est in se, divinae beneficentiae adiumenta respuit, planeque est digna, cui caelestis tutela denegetur. Itaque quantumvis opibus firma et copiis locuples esse videatur, gerit tamen interitus sui in ipsis reipublicae visceribus inclusa semina, neque spem habere potest diuturnitatis. Scilicet gentibus christianis, non fere secus ac singulis hominibus, tam est inservire Dei consiliis salubre, quam deficere periculosum; eisque illud plerumque accidit, ut quibus temporibus fidelitatem suam erga Deum vel Ecclesiam studiosius retinent, in optimum statum naturali quodam itinere veniant; quibus deserunt, excidant. Has quidem vices in annalibus temporum intueri licet; earumque domestica et satis recentia exempla suppeterent, si vacaret ea recordari quae superior vidit aetas, cum procax multorum licentia tremefactam Galliam funditus miscuit, rem sacram et civilem eodem excidio complexa.

Contra vero haec, quae certam civitatis ruinam secum ferunt facile depelluntur, si in constituenda gubernandaque tum domestica tum civili societate catholicae religionis praecepta serventur. Ea enim sunt ad conservationem ordinis et ad reipublicae salutem aptissima.

Ac primo quidem ad societatem domesticam quod attinet, interest quam maxime susceptam e coniugio christiano sobolem mature ad religionis praecepta erudiri; et eas artes, quibus aetas puerilis ad humanitatem informari solet, cum institutione religiosa esse coniunctas. Alteras seiungere ab altera idem est ac reipsa velle, ut animi pueriles in officiis erga Deum in neutram partem moveantur: quae disciplina fallax est, et praesertim in primis puerorum aetatulis perniciosissima, quod revera viam atheismi munit, religionis obsepit. Omnino parentes bonos curare oportet, ut sui cuiusque liberi, cum primum sapere didicerunt, praecepta religionis percipiant, et ne quid occurrat in scholis, quod fidei morumve integritatem offendat. Et ut ista in instituenda sobole diligentia adhibeatur, divina est naturalique lege constitutum, neque parentes per ullam caussam solvi ea lege possunt. Ecclesia vero, integritatis fidei custos et vindex, quae, delata sibi a Deo conditore suo auctoritate, debet ad sapientiam christianam universas vocare gentes, itemque sedulo videre quibus excolatur praeceptis instituisque inventus quae in ipsius potestate sit, semper scholas quas appellant *mistas* vel *neutras*, aperte damnavit, monitis etiam atque etiam patribusfamilias, ut in re tanti momenti animum attenderent ad cavendum. Quibus in rebus parendo Ecclesiae, simul utilitati paretur, optimaque ratione saluti publicae consulitur. Etenim quorum prima aetas ad religionem erudita non est, sine ulla cognitione adolescunt rerum maximarum, quae in hominibus alere virtutum studia, et appetitus regere rationi contrarios solae possunt. Cuiusmodi illae sunt de Deo creatore notiones, de Deo iudice et vindice, de praemiis poenisque alterius vitae expectandis, de praesidiis caelestibus per Iesum Christum allatis ad illa ipsa officia diligenter sancteque servanda. His non cognitis, male sana omnis futura est animorum cultura: insueti ad verecundiam Dei adolescentes nullam ferre poterunt honeste vivendi disciplinam, suisque cupiditatibus nihil unquam negare ausi, facile ad miscendas civitates pertrahentur.

Deinde illa saluberrima aeque ac verissima, quae ad civilem societatem vicissitudinemque iurium et officiorum inter sacram et politicam potestatem spectant.—Quemadmodum enim duae sunt in terris societates maximae, altera civilis, cuius proximus finis est humano generi bonum comparare temporale et mundanum, altera religiosa, cuius est homines ad veram illam felicitatem perducere, ad quam facti sumus, caelestem ac sempiternam, ita gemina potestas est; aeternae naturalique legi obedientes ambae, et in rebus quae alterutrius ordine imperioque continentur, sibi singulae consulentes. Verum quoties quidquam constituti de eo genere oporteat, de quo utramque potestatem, diversis quidem caussis diversoque modo, sed tamen utramque constituere rectum sit, necessaria est et utilitati publicae consentanea utriusque concordia; qua sublata, omnino consecutura est anceps quaedam mutabilisque conditio, quacum nec Ecclesiae nec civitatis potest tranquillitas consistere. Cum igitur pactis conventis inter sacram civilemque potestatem publice aliquid constitutum est, tunc profecto quod iustitiae interest, interest idem rei publicae, concordiam manere integram ; propterea quod sicut alteri ab altera praestantur officia mutua, ita certus utilitatis fructus ultro citroque accipitur et redditur.

In Gallia, ineunte hoc saeculo, posteaquam ingentes illi, qui paulo ante fuerant, motus civiles terroresque conquieverant ipsi rerum publicarum rectores intellexere, haud posse melius fessam tot ruinis civitatem sublevari, quàm si religio catholica restitueretur. Futuras utilitates opinione praecipiens Pius VII. Decessor Noster, voluntati primi Consulis ultro obsecutus est, facilitate indulgentiaque usus tanta, quanta maxima per officium licuit.—Tunc de summis capitibus cum convenisset, fundamenta posita sunt tutumque iter munitum restituendis ac sensim stabiliendis rebus religiosis opportunum. Et revera plura eo tempore ac posteriore aetate prudenti iudicio constituta sunt, quae ad incolumitatem et decus Ecclesiae pertinere videbantur. Permagnae exinde perceptae utilitates, tanto pluris aestimandae, quanto gravius in Gallia omnia sacra essent antea prostrata et afflicta. Publica dignitate religioni reddita, plane instituta christiana revixere: sed mirum quanta ex hoc facto in prosperitatem civilem bona redierunt. Etenim ex turbulentissimis fluctibus vixdum emersa civitas, cum vehementer tranquillitatis disciplinaeque publicae firma fundamenta requireret, ea ipsa quae requirebat, oblata sibi a religione catholica percommode sensit : ita ut appareat, illud de concordia ineunda consilium prudentis viri populoque bene consulentis fuisse. Quare, si ceterae rationes deessent, tamen omnino eadem caussa, quae tunc ad pacificationem suscipiendam impulit, nunc deberet ad conservandam impellere. Nam inflammatis passim rerum novarum studiis, in tam incerta expectatione futurorum, novas discordiarum caussas inter utramque potestatem serere, interiectisque impedimentis beneficam Ecclesiae prohibere aut remorari virtutem, inconsulta res esset et plena periculi.

At vero hoc tempore huius generis eminere pericula non sine sollicitudine et angore videmus: quaedam enim et acta sunt et aguntur cum Ecclesiae salute minime congruentia, posteaquam nonnulli infenso animo instituta catholica in suspicionem invidiamque adducere, eaque civitati praedicare inimica vulgo consueverunt. Neque minus sollicitos anxiosque habent Nos eorum consilia, qui, dissociandis Ecclesiae reique publicae rationibus, salubrem illam riteque initam cum Apostolica Sede concordiam serius ocius diremptam vellent.

Nos quidem in hoc rerum statu nihil praetermisimus, quod tempora postulare viderentur. Legatum Nostrum Apostolicum, quoties oportere visum est, facere expostulationes iussimus: quas qui rem publicam gerunt prono se ad aequitatem animo accipere testati sunt.— Nos ipsi, cum lata lex est de collegiis sodalium religiosorum tollendis, animi Nostri sensa litteris consignavimus ad dilectum Filium Nostrum S. R. E. Cardinalem Archiepiscopum Parisiensium datis. Simili modo, missis superiore anno mense Iunio ad summum rei publicae Principem litteris, cetera illa deploravimus, quae saluti animorum nocent, et Ecclesiae rationes incolumes esse non sinunt. Id vero effecimus tum quod sanctitate et magnitudine muneris Nostri apos-

tolici permovebamur, tum quod vehementer cupimus ut accepta a
patribus et maioribus religio sancte inviolateque in Gallia conservetur.
Hac via, hoc ipso tenore constantiae certum Nobis est rem Galliae
catholicam perpetuo in posterum defendere.—Cuius quidem officii
iusti ac debiti Vos omnes, Venerabiles Fratres, adiutores strenuos
semper habuimus. Revera sodalium religiosorum coacti dolere vicem,
perfecistis tamen, quod erat in potestate vestra, ne indefensi succum-
berent, qui non minus de re publica quam de Ecclesia meruerant.
Hoc autem tempore, quantum leges sinunt, in eo evigilant maximae
curae cogitationesque vestrae, ut probae institutionis copia suppeditet
iuventuti: et de consiliis quae adversus Ecclesiam nonnulli agitant,
non praetermisistis ostendere, quantum ipsi civitati essent allatura
perniciem. Atque has ob caussas nemo iure criminabitur, aut aliquo
Vos respectu rerum humanarum duci, aut constitutae reipublicae
adversari: quia cum Dei agitur honos, cum salus animarum in dis-
crimen adducitur, vestrum munus est harum rerum omnium tutelam
defensionemque suscipere.—Pergite itaque prudenter et fortiter in
episcopali munere versari: caelestis doctrinae praecepta tradere, et qua
sit ingrediendum via in tam magna temporum iniquitate populo
demonstrare. Eamdem omnium oportet esse mentem idemque pro-
positum, et ubi communis est caussa, similem in agendo adhibere
rationem. Providete ut nusquam scholae desint, in quibus notitia
bonorum caelestium officiorumque erga Deum diligentissime alumni
imbuantur, et discant penitus Ecclesiam cognoscere eidemque dicto
esse audientes usque adeo ut intelligant et sentiant, omnes
labores, eius caussa, patibiles putandos. Abundat Gallia praestan-
tissimorum hominum exemplis, qui pro fide christiana nullam ab sese
calamitatem, ne vitae quidem ipsius iacturam deprecati sint. In ipsa
illa perturbatione, quam commemoravimus, viri invicta fide perplures
extiterunt, quorum virtute et sanguine patrius stetit honos. Iamvero
nostris etiam temporibus virtutem in Gallia cernimus per medias insidias
et pericula satis, Deo iuvante, se ipsam tueri. Munus suum Clerus
insistit, idque ea caritate, quae sacerdotem est propria, ad proximorum
utilitates semper prompta et sollerti. Laici viri magno numero fidem
catholicam profitentur aperto impavidoque pectore: obsequium suum
certatim huic Apostolicae Sedi multis rationibus et saepe testantur:
institutioni iuventutis ingenti sumptu et labore prospiciunt, necessi-
tatibus publicis opitulantur liberalitate et beneficentia mirabili.

Iamvero ista bona, quae laetam spem Galliae portendunt, non conser-
vanda solum sed etiam augenda sunt communi studio maximaque
perseverantia sedulitatis. In primis videndum est ut idoneorum virorum
copia magis ac magis Clerus locupletetur. Sancta sit apud sacerdotes
Antistitum suorum auctoritas: pro certo habeant sacerdotale munus,
nisi sub magisterio Episcoporum exerceatur, neque sanctum, nec satis
utile, neque honestum futurum.—Deinde necesse est in patrocinio
religionis multum elaborare lectos viros laicos, quibus cara est communis omnium mater Ecclesia, et quorum cum dicta tum scripta
tuendis catholici nominis iuribus magno usui esse possunt. Ad optatos
autem fructus maxime est conspiratio voluntatum et agendorum

similitudo necessaria. Profecto nihil magis inimici cupiunt, quam ut dissideant catholici inter se : hi vero nihil sibi magis quam dissidia fugiendum putent, memores divini verbi, *omne regnum in seipsum divisum desolabitur.* Quod si, concordiae gratia, necesse est, quemquam de sua sententia iudicioque desistere, faciat non invitus, sperata utilitate communi. Qui scribendo dant operam, magnopere studeant hanc in omnibus rebus animorum concordiam conservare ; iidem praeterea quod in commune expedit malint, quam quod sibi : communia coepta tueantur ; disciplinae eorum, quos *Spiritus Sanctus posuit Episcopos regere Ecclesiam Dei*, libenti animo pareant, auctoritatemque vereantur; nec suscipiant quicquam praeter eorumdem voluntatem, quos, quando pro religione dimicatur, sequi necesse est tamquam duces.

Denique, quod facere in rebus dubiis semper Ecclesia consuevit, populus universus, Vobis auctoribus, obsecrare obtestarique Deum insistat, ut respiciat Galliam, iramque misericordia vincat. In ista fandi scribendique licentia pluries est divina violata maiestas, neque desunt qui non modo beneficia Salvatoris hominum Iesu Christi ingrate repudiant, sed etiam impia ostentatione profiteantur, nolle se Dei numen agnoscere. Omnino catholicos decet hanc sentiendi agendique pravitatem magno fidei pietatisque studio compensare, publiceque testari, nihil sibi esse Dei gloria prius, nihil avita religione carius. Ii praesertim qui alligati arctius Deo, intra monasteriorum claustra aetatem degunt, excitent nunc sese ad caritatem generosius, et divinum propitiare numen humili prece, poenis voluntariis, suique devotione contendant. His rationibus eventurum, Deo opitulante, confidimus, ut qui sunt in errore resipiscant, nomenque Gallicum ad genuinam magnitudinem revirescat.

In his omnibus, quae hactenus diximus, paternum animum Nostrum, Venerabiles Fratres, et amoris, quo universam Galliam complectimur, magnitudinem recognoscite. Nec dubitamus quin hoc ipsum studiosissimae voluntatis Nostrae testimonium ad confirmandam augendamque valeat salutarem illam inter Galliam et Apostolicam Sedem coniunctionis necessitudinem, unde nec pauca, nec levia in communem utilitatem bona omni tempore profecta sunt.—Et hac cogitatione laeti, Vobis, Venerabiles Fratres, civibusque vestris maximam caelestium munerum copiam adprecamur : quorum auspicem et praecipuae benevolentiae Nostrae testem Vobis universaeque Galliae Apostolicam benedictionem peramanter in Domino impertimus.

Datum Romae apud S. Petrum die VIII Februarii a. MDCCCLXXXIV, Pontificatus Nostri Anno Sexto.

LEO PP. XIII.

Science Notices.

Cometary Collisions.—The possibility of our earth encountering a comet in its path has often been mooted of late. Some have ventured to predict the most alarming consequences from such an event. It may be well to hear what so eminent an astronomer as Professor Young, of Princetown, has to say on the matter. In an article contributed to the *North American Review*, he enters into the whole question of astronomical collisions. The earth, he holds, is certain to collide with a comet at some time or other, though the intervals may be as far distant as is represented by once in fifteen million years. There are three comets whose paths intersect the earth's orbit, and should they ever pass the point of crossing at the same time as the earth, a supposition by no means improbable, a collision must occur. These three comets are Biela's, Tempel's, and the comet of 1862. But so far as we are concerned, any consequence of such a collision to us must depend on the nature of the cometary nucleus. Is the comet's head solid or gaseous? An attempt has been made to estimate the density of the nucleus from the magnitude of the glowing envelope that streams around the head. Were this an atmosphere like our own we could calculate the amount of gravity necessary to hold this in equilibrium. It would result from such a calculation that the cometary nucleus may in some cases be a ball of iron some 100 miles in diameter. The encounter with such a mass of metal would produce upon the earth a widespread destruction too terrible to picture. Were the cometary nucleus to consist of but a ton or two of solid matter the results upon our globe from such a collision would be most disastrous, far exceeding those of any volcano or earthquake. It is pleasant to learn from Professor Young that the grounds on which such calculations have been made are pure assumptions. He seems satisfied that a comet is throughout only a cloud of dust and vapour—a mere smoke-wreath. All that may be expected from an encounter with such a body would be a brilliant display of shooting stars, affording a magnificent spectacle for over an hour in duration. This is a teaching more consoling even than that of the late Sir J. Herschell, who contended that the solid contents of any comet might be carted away in a waggon of ordinary dimensions; for the impact of even so much matter moving at planetary velocities would be by no means pleasant to contemplate.

Recent Extraordinary Sunsets.—The after-glow which has been so remarkable a feature of the last few months is by no means an unusual phenomenon. But it may be questioned whether we have on record any outburst of the kind equalling in brilliancy and duration that which of late "has sanctified our mortal day." The well-known poem of Wordsworth, "Had this effulgence disappeared with flying haste," doubtless refers to a similar phenomenon. To account for the appearance of these radiant skies is not at all an easy matter, and scientific men are by no means agreed upon the cause. There are some who hold with Mr. N. Lockyer that the volcanic eruptions of Krakatoa have poured so vast a quantity of volcanic dust into space as seriously to interfere with the rays of the sun. Professor Piazzi Smith professes to see in it nothing but the presence of an unusual amount of aqueous vapour in the upper regions of the atmosphere. A more probable explanation has been offered by Mr. Ranyard, that the earth passed through a region of the heavens more than ordinarily rich in the dust that we know is so widely distributed in space. In the meantime Professor Langley has added considerably to our knowledge by his researches into the existence of dust-clouds in regions where they would be least likely to be found. On the volcanic wastes of Etna, where the air is as clear as anywhere in the world, the telescope showed the air to be full of minute dust particles. Professor P. Smith, from the Peak of Teneriffe, saw these strata of dust rising to the height of over a mile, and so dense that they frequently hid a neighbouring mountain. On Mount Whitney, in Southern California, Professor Langley ascended a height of nearly 15,000 feet for the purpose of studying such phenomena. But even here, in these snow wastes, he looked down upon a kind of dust ocean, some 6,000 feet deep, which was invisible from below. It is interesting to note that the light reflected from this dust-cloud was clearly red, and thus the fact is established that dust-clouds possess the property of absorbing all rays but the red. The Professor has come to the conclusion that there is a permanent dust-cloud enclosing the whole planet to a depth of three miles, and not improbably to a height even greater.

Since this is the more habitual condition of the atmosphere, we shall look here in vain for the explanation of the unusual displays of late. Nor does the aqueous vapour theory offer a more hopeful solution, for there is no evidence to show that aqueous vapour has of late been in any marked excess in the air. There remain then the volcanic dust and the cosmic dust theories. One rather fatal objection to Mr. Lockyer's view that the Krakatoa eruptions are at the bottom of the mystery, lies in the fact that the remarkable sunsets were first observed in the island of Trinidad, almost a hemisphere's distance from Java, within seven days of the date of the volcanic disturbance. Now it is hardly conceivable that any air current could convey the dust at such unheard-of velocity to a point some 12,000 miles away. Mr. Ranyard's view, that the phenomenon is due to the passing of the earth through a region of space unusually rich in cosmic dust, is therefore left in possession of the field.

The Cholera Commission.—The German and French Governments have issued Scientific Commissions to study the real nature of the dreaded disease of Cholera. It is not to the credit of our rulers that England, which suffers more through India than any other European nation, should have shown herself indifferent to the prosecution of such researches. The whole history of biological research during the past few years is favourable to the theory that every contagious or epidemic disease is the product of some germ specifically constituted to induce it. The researches of M. Pasteur into the diseases of the silkworm and splenic-fever are now classical. The brilliant manner in which he arrested and stamped out these contagious diseases of animals warrant us to hope that a similar method of procedure will be equally successful in the terrible maladies which hurry off so large a section of mankind. The method in short is this: to discover first the micro-organism that is peculiar to each disease, and then by different series of breedings and generations to rob the organism of the dangerous quantity of its virus. The germ thus shorn of half its terrors may be introduced into the blood to produce a mild form of the disease, and the human subject after this can confidently expect a freedom from any further attacks. Three contagious diseases, small-pox, chicken-cholera, and splenic-fever, have of late been treated on this principle and with most satisfactory results. It is not too much to hope that patient research may yet succeed in discovering the specific germ of other contagia and bring the whole question within the sphere of one grand beneficent law. For this purpose Dr. Koch, the chief of the German Commission, started for Egypt during the late cholera epidemic there, but he was unfortunately too late. The crisis had passed, and nothing is more curious in the pathology of these diseases than the abrupt disappearance of the germs from the system when the critical point has been rounded. He therefore decided to transfer the sphere of his labours to Calcutta, where the general death-rate is as high as 10 per 1,000 from cholera. His fifth report has been received, and he believes that he has discovered the special *bacillus* which is the root of all the mischief. He has tried to inoculate animals with this germ, but so far without result. A later telegram announces that the Commission has succeeded in discovering the same *bacillus* in the water tanks of the city. This is an important discovery, and may give us the clue to the mystery. It has long been felt that water in some manner or another conveyed the disease, but it was a mere surmise and required proof. It will now be easy to test the matter in the most thorough manner, and we may be sure that rigorous researches will be made. It will be an honour to the German Commission beyond all praise or reward, should they succeed in ridding the cholera plague of some of the terrors that its outbreak now inspires.

Arctic Exploration.—The expenditure of men and of money upon Arctic research has during the past twelve months produced nothing but barren and disappointing results. It was confidently put forward last year that the interior of Greenland, if properly explored, would be sure to reveal wonders for the benefit of the whole civilized world. Baron Nordenskiold last July directed an expedition from the west coast of Greenland. The party pushed forward in an easterly direction upon sledges and reached an altitude of 5,000 feet above the sea. The line of march was one continuous slope upwards, and all hopes of smiling valleys nestling beneath the snow-clad peaks had soon to be abandoned. The Esquimaux pushed on some 1,000 feet higher, but found nothing but a desert of ice and snow, the breeding ground of glaciers.

The Dutch expedition in the Straits of Waygatz, consisting of the two ships, the "Varna" and "Dymphna," have had some perilous and fruitless adventures.

The party from the "Varna" were obliged to leave the ship in haste, and encamp upon an iceberg; but the berg opened an enormous crevasse between them and their ship, and threatened them with instant destruction. Fortunately, the opening closed over, and the expedition had barely time to recover their instruments and provisions from on board when the "Varna" was crushed by the ice. They took refuge on the "Dymphna;" but the latter, having broken its screw, could not escape from the pack. After a variety of adventures, they reached home about the end of October; and we learn that, nothing discouraged by its ill-success, the expedition is shortly to start again.

The British Government has placed the "Alert" at the disposal of the United States navy, to form part of the expedition that will set out in April in search of the American explorers of 1881. It may be remembered that a party from the United States joined the International Polar Expedition of 1881, that was to beleaguer the frozen zone, and extract from it its long-cherished secret. It is needless to speak of the exhausted crews that returned baffled and defeated in the enterprise. All interest is now centred upon the American party, some twenty-five in number, of whom no news has been received for two years. There is only too much reason to fear that another sacrifice of brave lives has been added to the dark roll of Arctic disasters. It is true that the Esquimaux last year reported them all well, but we fear their evidence is not of the trustiest character. Unless they have penetrated farther north than any previous explorers, they could hardly have been missed for two years by the number of ships and whalers that pass and repass in the summer season. Their fate has naturally roused much interest, and the act of our Government in offering the "Alert" to join the relief expedition is felt to be at once graceful and humane. The "Alert" will join the three vessels—the "Thetis," the "Bear," and "Hope"—all three of which will be equipped by the American Government. It is hoped that the expedition will be ready to start in April next, and every one will echo Lord Aberdare's words when referring to the disaster in his annual address to the Royal Geographical Society:—

Such a fate [he said] happening to any people would be sure to evoke our warm regrets; but the feeling is heightened when we remember with how keen a sympathy the American people have ever followed the disasters of British adventurers in the Arctic seas, and how generous and untiring have been their efforts to carry relief to the sufferers as long as the slightest chance remained of their being still in the land of the living.

Three Generations Contrasted.—The difference of habits, especially in the matter of hard drinking, between the present generation and our great-grandfathers, is a matter of constant remark. The "four-bottle man," who was so conspicuous a figure in the last century, is now as extinct as a Plesiosaurus; in fact, we have come to ask with amazement how their constitutions could stand the strain of such habitual excess? It would almost seem as if they were little the worse physically for all their port-drinking, and we very little the better for our abstinence. This question is now in a fair way of being solved by some researches made by Mr. F. Galton, and communicated to *Nature*, January 17, of this year. Mr. Galton was fortunate enough to discover, in an old-established firm of wine merchants, a register of weights of their customers, dating back as far as 1740. These registers were kept for the amusement of their *habitués;* and the principal noblemen and gentry of the kingdom, who patronized the firm, have left behind them a pretty continuous record of their weights from year to year. As the dates of the birth and death of the nobility are easily learned, Mr. Galton was inspired to compare the different weights of our aristocracy for the last three generations. The results are certainly striking. Those born between the years 1740 and 1770 very rapidly came to their prime; at forty years of age they acquired their maximum weight of 184 lbs. From this age a steady decline of weight sets in. Those born between the years 1770 and 1800 touched their maximum weight of 184 lbs. at the age of fifty; and then, up to eighty years of age, the curve of weight shows a steady decline. The most remarkable features are presented by the group born between 1800 and 1830. No decline whatever of weight is exhibited throughout their eighty years of life; they steadily and regularly increase in weight from twenty years of age up to eighty. The line of weight connecting these two years, instead of exhibiting a curve of rise and fall as in the preceding generations, is now one continuous straight line, and a maximum weight of 186 lbs. is reached at eighty years of age. These facts are not only curious but welcome. Temperance advocates will be able to point many a moral with such figures as these. The longevity of our modern statesmen is thus shown to be no accidental occurrence, but the result of some well-established causes. The world as a whole will be a gainer from the matured judgments, the ripe experience, of the green old age which will be a more familiar feature of a generation characterized by habits of temperance.

Notices of Catholic Continental Periodicals.

GERMAN PERIODICALS.
By Dr. BELLESHEIM, of Cologne.
1. *Katholik.*

THE January number of this periodical has an interesting contribution on a recent Essay by the Commendatore de Rossi, on "Pope Liberius." The great Roman archæologist has fortunately found in a manuscript volume, belonging at present to the Imperial Library of St. Petersburg, a poem of much value as illustrating the history of the Roman Church during the fourth century. The MS. originally belonged to the Abbey of Corvy, passing afterwards to the Benedictine house of St. Germain-des-Prés, Paris. Besides other Latin poems it contains a collection of inscriptions gathered by a French monk of the time of Charlemagne, during a visit to Rome. Curiously, the author, in putting together these inscriptions of churches or catacombs, follows exactly the order in which pilgrims were wont to visit the Roman sanctuaries. Hence De Rossi argues that the collection was intended to serve pilgrims as a guide. The remarkable poem which will henceforth claim the attention of theologians and archæologists is composed of fifty-four hexameters. Its Latinity does not belong to the classical period, but, breathing as it does the style and spirit of the oldest Christian inscriptions, an archæologist would hesitate to ascribe it to a period later than the fourth century. It speaks (25, 26) of a Pope "Electus fidei plenus summusque sacerdos, Qui nivea mente immaculata papa sederas." Speaking of his education and virtues the poet styles him "Sine felle columbam," and says in another place, "Parvulus utque loqui cœpisti dulcia verba, Mox scripturarum lector pius factus." The Pope, it will be noted, is styled "sacerdos." During the sixth and seventh centuries the Popes were called "Pontifices" and the inscriptions on their tombs of the period immediately preceding have the title "Præsul;" the simple appellation "sacerdos" belongs to the fourth century. Siricius (385–398) is praised thus: "Magnus meruit sedere sacerdos." S. Damasus, too, eulogises his predecessor S. Melchiades as "Vixit qui in pace sacerdos." Next to the title of "sacerdos" the mention of the office of "lector" merits notice: the Pope of our poem is praised for having fulfilled well this office. This affords another argument for dating the poem at the fourth century; for it was precisely at that period that lectors accompanied bishops to synods, acting there as stenographers or secretaries. Siricius was secretary to Liberius, and followed him to Milan. From the sixth century the "lector" gave way to the "cantores," who gradually obtained great influence. Then also the Pope of this poem is praised in highest terms as defender of the Nicene faith in the course of which he was victorious, in a Synod, in uniting to the Church most determined opponents. The remarkable verses deserve inserting:—

> Electus fidei plenus summusque sacerdos,
> Qui nivea mente immaculatus papa sederes,
> Qui bene apostolicam doctrinam sancte doceres
> In synodo, cunctis superatis victor iniquis
> Sacrilegis Nicaena fides electa triumphat.

This, taken in conjunction with the last part of the poem, where the Pope is described as opposing the Emperor, who summons him to side with the Arians, scarcely admits of any interpretation if it be not referred to the great Liberius. The result of De Rossi's essay is a vindication of Liberius's orthodoxy. I may add that Professor Döllinger's statement of the so-called case of Liberius in his "Papstfabellen" is totally at variance with our eulogistic poem; whilst Cardinal Hergenröther's exposition of it is in as complete harmony.

Another article in the same number describes the introduction of Protestantism into the dukedom of Cleves, and the opposition to it of Duke William. Protestant historians generally exaggerate the influence of Erasmus at the court of Cleves. The Duke, though fond of certain liturgical innovations, strongly defended Catholic doctrine.

2. *Historisch-politische Blätter.*—The February issue contains a notice of a very noteworthy work by Dr. Schmitz, a priest of the archdiocese of Cologne, entitled "Die Bussbücher und Bussdisciplin der Kirche nach handschriftlichen Quellen dargestellt. Mainz, 1883." Only a few years ago, Father Palmieri treated the same topic, examining it, however, chiefly from a dogmatical point of view. But he corrected numerous misconceptions, perpetrated by even modern theologians, who have been too ready in following unquestionedly the learned Morinus. Dr. Schmitz treats the subject as a historian. He draws our attention to the *libri pœnitentiales*, a large number of which, and of rituals, have rewarded his researches into the chief libraries of Rome, Naples, Bologna, Munich, Paris, London, and Dublin. A prominent place must be given to the "Pœnitentiale Arundel" in the British Museum, now for the first time published. But we have here besides this, other valuable liturgical books, which throw new light on the principles by which the Church has been guided in her public penitential discipline, and in the administration of the sacrament of penance. Dr. Schmitz brings into due prominence the influence and authority of the Holy See on the development of penitential discipline. A powerful witness to this influence is borne by a hitherto unknown "Pœnitentiale Romanum" which he has had the great good fortune to discover in the Vallicellana, Rome. Whilst this last was invested with official authority, the Penitentials which had their origin in England and Germany are, as it were, of a private character. The author dwells upon the vast difference between the

two. He also shows that the Anglo-Saxon *libri pœnitentiales* in large part cannot be ascribed to the authors whose names they bear. In the last part of Dr. Schmitz's work we see the *libri pœnitentiales* giving place gradually to the systematic collections of canon law, from Gregory IX. to Clement V. There was a manual of practical guidance for confessors, the "Canones Astesani," collected by a Friar Minor of Asti, in Piedmont, in 1320 (which Dr. Schmitz has also discovered in the Vatican Library); and for two centuries it was largely used by the clergy, lapsing into disuse only with the new departure begun by the Council of Trent. Dr. Schmitz's book is founded on wide and successful research, and will take a permanent and high place in the literature of canon law and liturgy.

The March issue of this periodical has a notice on "Die Echtheit der ignatianischen Briefe auf's neue vertheidigt von Dr. F. Funk. Tübingen, 1883." Dr. Funk comes forward for the second time as a stout defender of the genuineness of the Epistles of St. Ignatius of Antioch. In this new work he is chiefly opposed to the modern non-Catholic critics, and his arguments go to prove the opinion, nearly universal with Catholic theologians, that the short text of the Ignatian Epistles is the genuine production of that great bishop and martyr. The reader's attention may well be called to those chapters in which Dr Funk treats of the constitution of the Church and the heretical movement in St. Ignatius' time, and also of the saint himself. Dr. Funk's edition of the Ignatian Epistles, which he brought out three years ago, is the best critical edition. In his new work he shows himself to be one of their most able defenders.

3. *Stimmen aus Maria Laach.*—Father Baumgartner, having returned from a journey to Iceland, Sweden, and Russia, intends to give the readers of the *Stimmen* his impressions. He begins in this last issue with an article on Upsala. He takes us back to the great Catholic period in the history of this remarkable town, and gives a graphic account of the foundation of the University and the status of the Church at the advent of the Reformation. Pope Sixtus IV., by a Bull of February, 1477, founded the University of Upsala, and gave it the same privileges as those enjoyed by Bologna. The Cathedral of Upsala is described as one of the finest specimens of Catholic art in the north. In picturing the state of clergy and people of Sweden at the period named, Father Baumgartner appeals to an unimpeachable witness. This is the present Protestant Archbishop A. N. Sundberg, who, seven years ago, on the occasion of the fifth centenary of the University of Upsala, published the "Life of Jacob Ulfssohn," the Archbishop of Upsala, who received the Bull of Sixtus IV. just mentioned. According to Archbishop Sundberg, the Catholic Archbishop of the fifteenth century was not only a brilliant patriot and a protector of art and science, but also a saintly prelate. Nay, the Protestant biographer does not hesitate to put forth views on the work done by the Swedish clergy of those Catholic times, and the devotion of the people to the Church, which are totally at variance with the historical misconceptions too often perpetuated by non-Catholic writers, who

are content to repeat the oft-repeated fiction, and either forget or are afraid to consult original sources and documents. Archbishop Sundberg strangely enough dwells largely in his book on the subjects of preaching and Indulgences; and he very successfully shows that the Catholic priest of that period faithfully discharged his duty, and that on the other hand the people were sufficiently instructed as to the nature and value of Indulgences. Father Baumgartner's article is well worth reading.

4. *Historiches Jahrbuch der Görresgesellschaft.*—Dr. Schmid, of Tübingen, gives us the third portion of his study on the reform of the Calendar in the reign of Gregory XIII. He is chiefly concerned in the present contribution with the opinions given by the Universities of Padua and Louvain. These valuable notices, gathered from Roman archives and libraries, now appear, for the most part, for the first time. Foremost in introducing the "Reformed Calendar" was S. Charles Borromeo, who was aided in this by his Vicar-General (Cardinal Allen's well-known friend), Owen Lewis, through whose exertions a cheap edition of the Calendar was printed at Milan. Dr. Schmid mentions also the negociations which passed between the Holy See and the Eastern Churches as to their adopting the reform.

Father Esser, O.P., contributes an erudite dissertation on the "Ave Maria," indicating definitely the periods during which the several portions of this prayer were added. In its present form the "Ave Maria" may be traced back to the sixteenth century.

ITALIAN PERIODICALS.

La Civiltà Cattolica, 2 Febbraio, 1884.

The Properties of the Church.

IN an article thus entitled, which has appeared in a recent number of the *Civiltà Cattolica*, the writer, when treating of the unity of the Church, makes a digression for the purpose of considering an hypothesis which is not devoid of interest. After showing that the unity of the Church subsists in and is maintained by the oneness of its Supreme Head, which Head is Christ, represented by His Vicar, how unity of faith is preserved by unity in teaching, and how that teaching cannot be one if the Supreme Teacher be not the ultimate appeal—in other words, infallible in his judgments regarding faith and morals, as is the Roman Pontiff—he observes that it may be asked whether this property of the Church be the exclusive privilege of that which Christ founded, or whether there was previously anything similar or analogous thereto among true believers. Now, it is certain that under the written law—that is, among the Hebrew people—there was something similar, for, besides the order of simple Levites, there was the order of priests, descended from Aaron, and, amongst them, the high priest, whom all were bound to obey. The high priest was therefore among the Israelites the bond of unity in worship, and, according to the most probable opinion, he was even infallible in his dogmatic decisions.

The question, then, can only regard the so-called state of nature wherein the moral and religious conduct of man was governed by the dictates of natural reason, and by the primitive revelation preserved traditionally in families. Religion at that time was, properly speaking, domestic. Every father of a family was priest in his own house, and to him his first-born son succeeded. And yet the writer thinks it by no means improbable that even then, besides this domestic priesthood. God had ordained the institution of a public and, so to say, universal priesthood, which should preside over the regulation of external worship and should be, as it were, an intermediary for the manifestation of such precepts as God from time to time was pleased to add to the natural law. He believes that the first who was invested with such an office was Abel, and the last, Melchisedech, who had no successor, on account of the almost universal lapse of men into idolatry.

This is, of course, a simple conjecture, but in support of it there is no slight amount of Scripture evidence. In the fourth chapter of Genesis we are told that "*after many days*" Abel and Cain offered a sacrifice to the Lord, and the Lord gave Abel the preference, which so excited the anger of Cain that he slew his brother. Now, what is the meaning of this sacrifice offered after a considerable lapse of time? We cannot believe that Adam, and, to speak of no other, that the just and holy Abel had never before offered sacrifice to God. It was therefore, in all probability, an extraordinary sacrifice, having some religious object, in which the two brothers were placed in competition; and might not this have been with a view to the selection of one of them for some exalted office, the exclusion from which of Cain, who was the elder, was the source of his envy and resentment? We may reasonably conceive that office to have been the public and universal priesthood indicated above. Moreover, we are told that the Lord gave to Adam Seth as a substitute for Abel. But a substitute in what sense? Of one son for another? At that time, however, Adam must have had many sons, and he must have had many more subsequently. After the murder of Abel, Cain said to the Lord, "Every one that findeth me shall kill me." There must therefore have been many men upon the earth already. And soon after, it is said that Cain built a city, which must certainly have been peopled with his own descendants. Accordingly the substitution of Seth for Abel cannot be understood as the mere substitution of one son for another, but would seem to have regarded the replacing of him in the supposed office of a public and universal priesthood. This idea receives confirmation from what follows—viz., that to Seth was born a son whom he called Enos, who "began to call upon the name of the Lord." But had not the name of the Lord been invoked by Adam long before, as well as by his son Abel, not to speak of his other descendants, who assuredly must have continued obedient worshippers of God. In what, then, did this invocation differ from previous invocations? In all probability it was the institution of public rites and ceremonies, which Enos would have had no title to establish but for some pre-eminence in priestly dignity over the other fathers of families.

Again, in the seventh chapter of his Epistle to the Hebrews, the Apostle, quoting Psalm cix. 4, repeats the declaration that Christ was a priest for ever according to the order of Melchisedech, and he proceeds to represent the priesthood of Melchisedech as superior to that of Aaron, seeing that he and the whole Levitical priesthood paid him tithes in the person of their father Abraham, who, although he had the promises, allowed himself to be blessed by Melchisedech; upon which the inspired writer makes this comment—that " without all contradiction that which is less is blessed by the better." But what does all this mean, inasmuch as the patriarch Abraham was himself a priest and offered sacrifices to God? In reply we shall be told that the priesthood of Melchisedech represented the priesthood of Christ. No doubt; but wherein? In that he offered to God a sacrifice of bread and wine, which were figures of the Eucharistic Sacrifice. But the priesthood of Christ was also figured by the sacrifice of Aaron, the victims offered being typical of the bloody Sacrifice of the Cross, by which man's redemption was accomplished. Looking then only at the types, why does the Apostle affirm that the priesthood of Christ was according to the order of Melchisedech rather than according to that of Aaron? All difficulty is removed if Melchisedech be regarded, not simply as a priest, but as a high priest—" Summus sacerdos tuus Melchisedech," as the Church calls him in the canon of the Mass, and high priest, not of one particular people alone, as was Aaron, but of all believers. Then, indeed, the whole thing becomes at once intelligible. Aaron, in the person of his father Abraham, justly paid homage to Melchisedech as to his superior; and Christ is a priest according to the order of Melchisedech because He resumed, although in a more sublime manner, the universal priesthood which had ceased in Melchisedech, and resumed it as the Eternal Son of God, without beginning and without end, the which was figured in Melchisedech, who is introduced to us in Holy Scripture as having "no genealogy, having neither beginning of days nor end of life, but, likened unto the Son of God, continueth a priest for ever."

Journalism.

In the same number of the *Civiltà Cattolica* we have the third of a series of articles on Journalism which have appeared in its pages. The present article treats in particular of the discouragement which Catholic journalism has to contend with on the part of good and well-meaning persons, who can be little aware of the mischief they do by their bitter criticisms and unsparing complaints. Catholic journalists, after doing their best to content the public, seeing themselves repaid in this coin at the hands of even pious and learned men, either fling up their occupation in despair, or, if they persevere, write much less well than if they had met with more charity and forbearance. In short, Catholics treat their journalists far worse than the Revolutionists treat theirs, for whom they habitually exhibit a marked esteem, while, on the contrary, it is not rare to see writers who are deserving of all honour for their labours and persevering exertions in the cause o religion, reduced by Catholics to such a degree of public discredit that their sworn enemies could not have wished them any worse treatment. The result of this proceeding is that Catholic journalism not only cannot make itself respected by the Revolutionary party, but does not even succeed in winning the esteem of the bulk of sincere Christians, who are led to think that, after all, there is very little to choose between one journal and another, so that they may as well take a Liberal newspaper as one of those styled Catholic.

This species of practical indifference, which has widely spread among the mass of Christians in regard to the selection of newspapers, if not checked, will speedily work the ruin of all morality and religion among the Italian population. It is sufficient to allude to the grossly immoral stories appended to the above-mentioned journals, which form the chief attraction in the eyes of youthful readers, to prove what their corrupting influence must be. Fathers of families leave these newspapers carelessly on their tables, and their young daughters of sixteen or seventeen eagerly peruse them, simply on account of these abominable appendages, in which the filthiness of vice is invested with attraction by the charm of romance. The disgusting reports of trials and other cognate subjects, the Voltairian cynicism with which suicides are recorded, and the like, become a fruitful source of contamination and evil example to persons of all classes and all ages; while the insulting and blasphemous language towards all that appertains to God and our holy religion is rapidly undermining the faith of thousands. Satan has never wielded a more potent and destructive weapon than journalism, and we have only to open our eyes to see that its un-Catholic portion, including that which represents the so-called moderate party, the most dangerous perhaps, because more insidious, is the main source of modern religious indifference. Hence we can readily appreciate the wisdom and prudence of the bishops in stringently enjoining the faithful to abstain from the perusal of bad newspapers, which practice, as the Bishop of Bruges, in conformity with maxims laid down by him in concert with the other Belgian prelates in 1858, declared, is forbidden by the natural, the divine, and the ecclesiastical law; the fathers, mothers, and superiors who do not hinder it becoming accomplices in the spiritual ruin flowing therefrom. The which prohibition the immortal Pius IX. confirmed by apostolic authority in his letter of June, 1871, to the Cardinal Patrizi, Vicar of Rome. Through the breach of Porta Pia a muddy stream of pestilential journals had burst into the Eternal City, all directed to the same object, that of drowning in unbelief the centre and heart of the Christian religion. This letter inhibited the reading of certain journals printed in Rome, and that under pain, not of venial sin only, but of grievous sin.

Juridically considered, this act of the Holy Father regarded the

Roman people alone. But under a moral aspect, as a direction and guide to conscience, it may certainly be extended to all the faithful, and be received as condemnatory of the habitual perusal of journals written in a similar spirit of hostility to religion and morality elsewhere. There are, of course, exceptional cases where a perusal of such journals may be necessary, but apart from these, the writer considers that the excuse pleaded by many of the necessity of keeping up their knowledge of current affairs is a mere pretext, since it is notorious that all that is needful for even men of business to know is, generally speaking, to be found in all the journals, Catholic as well as Liberal. (The writer, we must remember, is speaking of Italy.) The truth is, men are ashamed to be seen with a so-called clerical journal in their hands, lest the nickname of *codino* should be applied to them. If Catholics would combine in a practical obedience to the injunctions of the Holy Father and the Bishops—if, for instance, the Catholic Committees of the *Opera dei Congressi* would cause their seventy thousand associations to abstain, along with their families, from buying and reading bad journals; if the *circoli* of Catholic youth, the associations for Catholic interests, the conferences of St. Vincent of Paul, and the numerous confraternities existing in every corner of Italy, would do the same; if the Franciscan Tertiaries, who may be reckoned at some hundred thousand, would unite with these in stigmatizing a practice so abhorrent to the spirit of their holy rule, and all these several classes would labour to enlist adherents beyond their own circles—the writer is ready to pledge himself that of the 1,378 bad periodicals existing in Italy in January, 1883, two-thirds would very shortly be obliged to quit the field, for they live on day by day chiefly by the money furnished them by people who are nevertheless "devout to the Madonna and the Saints."

But abhorrence and repudiation of evil journalism must be accompanied by the love and encouragement of the good, for it is sad to note the low ebb, in point of number alone, to which want of support has reduced Catholic journalism in that Catholic land. A few figures will serve to prove this. Of 159 daily papers published in Italy only 23 profess Catholic principles. Milan, out of 141 daily and other periodicals, has only eight good ones; Turin, only 15 out of 94; Naples but 9 out of 120; Florence, including the *Civiltà Cattolica*, which may be said to be a guest, only 6 out of 79. Rome itself, the richest as would be expected in periodicals, has, out of 200, scarcely 30 which are fit reading for Catholics. These disgraceful statistics speak volumes.

FRENCH PERIODICALS.

Revue des Questions Historiques. Janvier. Paris: 1884.

THIS is an excellent number, but we must confine ourselves to a very brief mention of one or two articles. "Arnold of Brescia," by the Abbé E. Vancandard, deserves mention. The author is already favourably known in connection with the epoch of which he treats by his work "Abélard, sa doctrine, sa méthode et sa lutte avec S. Bernard," published three or four years ago. He remarks justly that Arnold of Brescia divided public opinion about himself as much in his own day as he does in ours. The celebration of his centenary in 1882 evoked at least as much eulogy as it did blame. We did not forget on which side the Holy Father spoke. The Abbé Vancandard's article is a new attempt to show, by most recent evidence, that the opinion too widely held, that Arnold was a fine patriot, a martyr, and the rest of it, must be held in defiance of history. The conclusion of his article, which we may usefully put first, runs thus:

But now, what judgment ought we to pass on this famous reformer? Some historians vie with each other in exalting him as an apostle of the pure gospel and a friend of liberty. We must be allowed to hold aloof from such enthusiasm. They may celebrate as much as they like the private virtues of Arnold, his austerity, his continence, even (so far as it was sound), his zeal for the reform of the church—we are ready to subscribe to all such merited eulogy. We unreservedly admire the disinterestedness of which he gave proof all through life. We even wish to believe that his intentions were pure, at least at the beginning of his undertaking. But the work of a reformer is a thing which is judged less by the good faith of the reformer himself than by the end he strives after, the means which he uses, and the result which he achieves. Now the end aimed at by Arnold were twofold; to strip the clergy of their temporal possessions, and to hand these on to the German Empire which had now become an universal empire. And if the first part of this programme pleases many moderns, the second, it seems to us, ought certainly to merit their condemnation. The means used by Arnold were of no better sort. The call to insurrection needs to be a weapon raised against the Papacy before men call it an evangelical weapon. Lastly, in what did his efforts, culpable or unwise, all result? In ruin and desolation. Every step of Arnold, as S. Bernard said, was marked by troubles and disaster. In a word, this celebrated religious and political reformer has rendered service neither to the church nor to his country. Let who will honour the rebel monk. Neither Catholics nor the friends of true patriotism can join in his apotheosis.

The author insists on this last point, that (apart from Catholic sentiments) the political aspirations of Arnold were mistaken:—neither liberal nor patriotic, and quite other than would be acceptable to true lovers of Italy, and to very many of his present-day admirers. The article, extending over sixty pages, contains very much in proof of the author's conclusions. The writer points out that the historical movement in favour of Arnold of Brescia, which was inaugurated by the Jansenist Guadagnini, prevailed in Germany, Italy and France (and we may add is at least the popular view in England) until the appearance, in 1868, of Pertz' "Historia Pontificalis." This work drew anew the attention of students on Arnold, and resulted in two great works—that of Giesebrecht in Germany, in 1873, and of Giacintho Gaggia in Italy, in 1882. On this work, chiefly together with the "Life of the Emperor Frederick," by Otho, the Abbé Vacandard found his study of Arnold of Brescia—which we recommend to the attention of students of history.

In another article, "Le moine Roger Bacon et le mouvement scientifique au xiii. siècle," the Abbé C. Narbey traces the defects which gave the stamp of "erring nature" to the great gifts of Roger Bacon, his antipathy to Albert the Great, and the real kindness and encouragement shown him in his studies by his own superiors and brethren. The author gives an interesting sketch of Bacon's studies, discoveries, and mathematical deductions, and he ranks his genius high; but shows that he owed much to the Arabians, and to even his own contemporaries.

Notices of Books.

A Catholic Dictionary: containing some Account of the Doctrine, Discipline, Rites, Ceremonies, Councils, and Religious Orders of the Catholic Church. By WILLIAM E. ADDIS, Secular Priest, and THOMAS ARNOLD, M.A. London: Kegan Paul & Co. 1884.

WE are disposed to think that, since Butler's "Lives of the Saints," there has not appeared in the English language any Catholic work so important as this. English Catholic literature, though not as rich as it ought to be, has produced not a few books which will live—in theology, sermons, Saints' lives, metaphysics, and asceticism. One or two of our writers are simply in the very first class of their countrymen, and their books have exercised, and will exercise, an influence which cannot be estimated. But here we have a book, admirably planned and carried out, which takes in the whole range of Catholic information. Now, Catholic information is exactly what everybody is constantly wanting. Priest and layman, the gentle and the simple, Catholics and non-Catholics, are continually wanting to inquire about some detail of Catholic doctrine or ritual, of Catholic names or Catholic things; and any book which, even imperfectly, supplies such a want as this is sure, not only to be bought up, but to influence a whole generation widely and deeply.

It may be said at once that the compilers have given us not only a comprehensive, but an exceedingly valuable book. Considering the scale of the Dictionary—some 900 pages, double columns—the amount of information is enormous. Some of the more important articles, such as "Christ," "Church," "God," "Holy Order," "Sacrament," and "Holy Trinity," are miniature treatises, full of learning and reference, admirably condensed, and yet smoothly and eloquently written. The preacher in a hurry for a scriptural or patristic text, the missioner with an inquiring convert in hand, or the theological professor who wishes to have a handy synopsis of a wide subject, will be equally grateful to Father Addis—for we suppose this class of articles must be credited to his pen. There is a special value in these more elaborate theological and patristic articles of the Dictionary, because they are evidently not second-hand matter, but are the fruit of the writer's own reading. The magnificent article on the "Trinity," for example, with its completeness of scriptural and patristic detail, makes us regret that the author cannot dedicate more of his time to subjects which he is so well fitted to treat.

But perhaps it is in minor doctrinal points and phrases, and in the unfailing explanation we everywhere meet of much used but little understood words, that the general value of the Dictionary will be most felt. The ordinary Protestant seems utterly unable to find out Catholic meanings for himself; and his friend, the ordinary Catholic, who really does understand a good deal, finds it very warm and distressing work to formulate semi-theological definitions off-hand. A book of reference to which they can turn in an argument about fasting, prayers for the dead, or indulgences, will be much prized. We cannot but think that this Dictionary comes not a week too soon. There is a great deal of explanation and definition going on in our elementary schools. The very difficult work of putting doctrine and ritual into words which will produce some impression on the "standards" and the "gallery" is being carried on without any undue diffidence by nuns and pupil-teachers; and, with all their goodwill, it is very hard for them to find the right words, or the right historical explanations, for everything. The staff of every elementary school ought to make a formal petition to its manager to keep a copy of this Catholic Dictionary in an accessible place. A ready reference to its pages would teach them, without loss of time, what to say about ceremonies, vestments, ecclesiastical usages, feasts, religious orders, and many other things. And there is many a Christian household who, in their moments of reunion, very naturally fall into discussion about a coming festival or a point of Church discipline. It used to be said, by the men of a generation just passing away, that in regard to doctrine, discipline and liturgy, "everything" was to be found in the Notes to Alban Butler's "Lives." The assertion is not so very much exaggerated. But this Dictionary will now be a rival to the Notes. And as those who use a dictionary are generally impelled by a sort of fascination to go on reading it, and to keep turning from one heading to another long after the primary impulse has exhausted itself, we may expect to find, in a few years, that a race will have sprung up of terribly well-informed Catholics, who will have formed themselves on their "Addis and Arnold." The prospect may not be reassuring on all sides; but perhaps they may become a stay and a support to much-interrogated persons (editors, for instance), and may undertake to answer the letters in the papers.

Seriously, however, the Dictionary is a very great boon, and the Catholic body may be deeply thankful that such competent hands have been induced to take it up. It is little to say that we had nothing of the kind before. We had not only no Catholic Dictionary, but we had to put up with the blunders and misrepresentations of books like the

"Church Dictionary" of Dr. Hook, a work to which Protestants and even sometimes Catholics were driven to refer in the absence of any other. It is needless to say that a book which has been carefully read by the Rev. Father Keogh, of the London Oratory, and bears the *imprimatur* of the Ordinary, is entirely safe and free from all important errors.

The article called "English Catholics" is one of the best, and also of the longest, in the work. With its clear and succinct detail and its exact dates, it brings out in the most striking manner the dramatic story of English Catholicism since 1534. The writer speaks without any partisan bias, but states facts in the soberest terms. We need not say that there are several burning "domestic" questions capable of being raised in regard to the behaviour of Kings, Popes, and the English Catholics themselves. We never saw a paper on the subject in which dignified moderation combined with historical fidelity is better maintained than in this. The author writes very severely of James II.; but we entirely follow him here. The end of the paper is rather hurried and meagre. Some account of the exact attitude taken by English Catholics and the Holy See in the affair of Emancipation would have been desirable, seeing the numerous misrepresentations so often made in this matter. A few dates and details as to legislation, efforts at legislation, and political attacks on Catholicism since 1829, would have been useful. The writer does not even use the historic word "Papal aggression," or give the date of the "Titles Act" or of its repeal.

A corresponding article on American Catholics would have given satisfaction in the United States, where the Dictionary ought to be as warmly received as in England. But, after all, even a dictionary has its limits of capacity.

The treatment of subjects coming under the name Religious Orders is, perhaps, as satisfactory as that of other portions of the work. The articles "Dominicans," "Franciscans," and "Jesuits," are carefully and fully done. That on "Benedictines," however, is excessively meagre. Writing, as they do, for English-speaking readers, the compilers should surely have remembered that such words as "Benedictine," "Abbot," "Prior," "Cathedral Prior," "Cellarer," &c., are interwoven in English literature, and require a special attention on the part of Catholic interpreters in order to remove false ideas. The "Cathedral Prior" is not mentioned at all, or perhaps only once in passing; and the connection of the Benedictines with the cathedrals and parishes of England might well have been given in some detail. Indeed, a somewhat more complete treatment of matters connected with the early and mediæval English Church would not be out of place in a second edition. Few subjects are more attractive to non-Catholics, or possess a more genial power of leading minds to the faith, and few are less understood or more utterly ignored by the ordinary middle-class Englishman.

The articles on Our Lady are very good, on the whole; but we miss any reference to the very early and striking evidence of cultus afforded by the Catacombs, as detailed, for instance, in Von Lehner's " Marienverehrung in den ersten Jahrhunderten."

We have noticed other omissions and some few mistakes, but for the moment it is better to confine ourselves to welcoming this excellent work and recommending it to every one who wishes for a serviceable guide in all that relates to the Church of Christ.

Memoirs of James Robert Hope-Scott, of Abbotsford, D.C.L., Q.C. With Selections from his Correspondence. By ROBERT ORNSBY, M.A. Two vols. London: John Murray. 1884.

THE interest of these two volumes is very various. The late Mr. Hope-Scott was one of the Anglicans associated in the historic Oxford movement: he was a parliamentary barrister of the first rank; he was connected by marriage and by friendship with the family of Sir Walter Scott, and with that of the Dukes of Norfolk; and he was one of the noblest and most engaging characters which it has been any one's privilege to know. In the pages of Professor Ornsby's well-executed and admirably written biography we again come across the men and the scenes, so often described, of a period which is now receding into history, but which will stand out in more heroic proportions as it recedes. Mr. Hope-Scott was not a clergyman, though at one time he was urged to take Orders. He became a Fellow of Merton in 1833, the year in which was begun the publication of " Tracts for the Times." He does not, however, seem to have entered into Tractarian views for some years after that date. He was brought up in Low Church ideas, like one of his intimate Oxford friends, Mr. Gladstone; and when, in early days, they went together to hear Chalmers and Rowland Hill, neither of them thought that he was in any way compromising his principles. It was in 1837 or 1838 that he first sought out John Henry Newman and asked for his acquaintance. But he lingered outside the fold for some years after Newman. It was on Passion Sunday, April 6, 1851, that Mr. Hope-Scott and Mr. Manning (now the Cardinal Archbishop) were received into the Church at Farm Street, by the Rev. Father J. Brownbill, S.J. Of the Anglican Church he writes a few months later:—" I can safely say that I left her because I was convinced that she never, from the Reformation downwards, had been a true Church" (i. 84). Of the years during which this conviction was maturing in his mind we have most attractive memorials in Mr. Ornsby's pages. There is a considerable correspondence with all the Anglican leaders, and besides letters of Mr. Hope-Scott's own, we have many hitherto unpublished of Newman, Gladstone, Keble, and Manning. They chiefly refer to the startling and sensational ecclesiastical events of the time—Oxford College Reform, Mr. Gladstone's " Church and State," the Jerusalem Bishopric, Tract XC., and the cases of Mr. Ward, of Mr. Oakeley, and Dr. Hampden. There is much interest in them all; and they bring out the earnestness, the genius, and the sweetness of the character of the subject of the memoir. But he was not a man who took advice, or even asked for it, in things that regarded his interior doubts or convictions. We cannot in these pages follow the progress of his mind from truth to truth, from light to light. Indeed, the effect of these volumes, on the whole, is to impress the reader much more with what Hope-Scott's friends thought about him than with what he shows himself to be by any performance of his own. His own letters, and the extracts from his papers, and the verses which are here printed, are clever, and more than clever; they are emphatically worth preserving, and worth printing. But they give us little insight into the man whom Mr. Gladstone describes as "the most winning person of his day," and of whom his friend Cardinal Newman said, at Farm Street, in the presence of his mortal remains, "I know that his departure hence has made the heavens dark to me." But those who knew him and came under the spell of his strong and magnetic personality are likely to treasure every word which brings him back to their memory.

There are numerous passages which we should be glad to quote from these very attractive pages. Mr. Hope-Scott's own letters during the early part of his life, before he had joined the Church, are interesting personally, and contain some things of public or abiding value. He wrote with clear and masterly effect upon every subject which he took up, and sometimes with real eloquence. Mr. Ornsby gives lengthy extracts from an article he wrote in the *British Critic* in 1840, on "Magdalene College Statutes." The article is one long and able plea for the revival of the old quasi-conventual character of the Oxford College foundations. There could be no better illustration of the character and position of the writer at that moment. It portrays a mind filled with ecclesiastical and mediæval ideas, sighing after a race of priestly scholars or scholarly priests for the Anglican Church, and anxious to do his best to keep out of the University that "Liberalism" which at first was, perhaps, the chief enemy the Tractarian leaders thought they had to dread. The following passage is full of the flavour of the Oxford revival of half a century ago. He is speaking of the religious effect of the old Oxford collegiate life :—

To be every moment subject to a sudden command for some common object; to be forced every now and then into the practical business of life; to be obliged to attend to dress and to punctuality in hours; to have no choice but to associate with men of equal or superior ability every day; and, above all, to be brought continually under the influence of a choral service, and thus when the heart is narrowed to some trifling object, to have it roused and expanded, whether it will or not, into a sense of God's presence, of the communion of saints, and of the nothingness of all knowledge which does not point towards heaven, are surely not expedient things alone, but where they may be had, necessary, and in all ways most desirable (i. 188).

Of Mr. Hope-Scott's professional success, Mr. Ornsby gives an interesting account. As this success was gained almost wholly within the walls of the committee-rooms of the Houses of Parliament, it does not admit of being illustrated with any degree of completeness; but on every hand there is a *consensus* of testimony that he was one of the foremost parliamentary barristers of the day. He had the good luck to begin his career with the beginning of the railway fever—a golden time for parliamentary barristers. One who well knew him, Mr. H. L. Cameron, writes:—

> The secret of his great success at the bar, beyond his intellectual power, lay, I think, in a peculiar charm and fascination of manner—a manner which could invest the driest and most technical matters with interest, and compelled the attention of the hearers. . . . . The melody of his voice was, to me, one of his greatest attractions. Then again, what a noble presence! and that goes a long way at the bar. I can look back, and see now, as he used to walk into his room to attend some consultation, how vigorous, handsome, and stately he always appeared (ii. 104).

During the time that Parliament was sitting his life was one of harassing and incessant work, under which his splendid constitution gave way at last. He would rise, in London, between five and six, and make himself a cup of coffee. He then "went through his devotions," as Mr. Ornsby puts it; a much more serious thing than "saying his prayers" in the fashion that some less busy and less occupied people are fond of following. His biographer commemorates the black ebony crucifix, which his first wife had held when dying, which used to stand on his table. After his prayers, he read his brief, mastering it with great rapidity, making notes as he went. Even at this early hour clients would seek him out, and before he appeared at breakfast he would have given an attentive audience to more than one anxious promoter of "improvements" or solicitor for a new railway. He would breakfast at eight, and by half-past nine he would be on his way from his private residence, or from Norfolk House, to his chambers. Here he attended consultations, varying in length from five to ten or fifteen minutes. Public business began in the Lords at eleven, in the Commons at twelve. From eleven till four he went from committee to committee; his speeches would be made, his examinations and cross-examinations carried through, and all the diverse business of half a dozen different cases conducted with a calmness that was never ruffled, a clearness which nothing could confuse, and a carefulness which no labour could weary. From four to six there were more consultations in chambers; and when at last he reached home and had dined, exhausted nature would assert herself and he would sleep for an hour or two. At ten he read his night prayers, and it was not long before he was in bed.

It is needless, as far as most of our readers are concerned, to say that Mr. Hope-Scott was a thorough Catholic, both in mind and practice, in intellect and in heart. He was, as his biographer says, a man of great faith, great earnestness, and the most sincere intention to obey the will of God. His busy life seldom allowed him, during the business season, to attend a week-day Mass or receive Holy Communion. But at Abbotsford he communicated two or three times a week. He would say the "Angelus" as he mounted the stairs to a committee-room at Westminster. He had intense devotion to the Blessed Sacrament. St. Michael is stated to have been his favourite saint, after Our Lady and St. Joseph. Among books of devotion he preferred the "Missal" and the New Testament. The services he rendered to Catholicism—why will Mr. Ornsby always say *Catholicity?* —are difficult to reckon. His biographer enters into interesting details on this subject. For these, and for the sermon of Cardinal Newman, the memorial letter of Mr. Gladstone, and many other matters, the reader must be referred to the Life itself. Mr. Hope-Scott died in London on the evening of April 29, 1873. He was strengthened by the Holy Sacraments and by the Holy Father's benediction; and he died with the praise of the most holy will of God on his lips, embracing the crucifix. "Happy soul!" cries out his friend, John Henry Newman, "who, being the counsellor and guide, the stay, the light and joy, the benefactor of so many, yet hast ever depended simply, as a little child, on the grace of thy God and the merits and strength of thy Redeemer!"

La Messe. Études archéologiques sur ses Monuments. Par CH. ROHAULT DE FLEURY, continuées par son fils, GEORGES ROHAULT DE FLEURY. 4to. Vol. I. Paris: Morel et Cie. 1883.

THE worthy son of a worthy father, M. Georges Rohault de Fleury has thrown his untiring energy and his wide erudition, already manifested in many noble volumes due to his pen and pencil, into a work which, by its monumental character, the importance of its subject, and its supreme interest for Catholic archæology, must surpass and crown all his previous labours. The handsome quarto before us, with its hundred and odd finely engraved plates, must be succeeded by several similar volumes before the weighty task which it commences is complete. The laborious amassment of his vast material, no less than its logical and lucid arrangement; the clear and carefully drawn illustrations, reflecting the most conscientious accuracy; the collation of countless authorities, Jew and Gentile, Christian and Pagan, orthodox and heretical; and last, but not least, the spirit and intention of the author, combine to produce a work which is a tribute to faith and an honour to archæology. But it is best to let M. de Fleury speak for himself of the work to which he has set his hand, and which was left unfinished by his father :

The task is one I cannot refuse. Nothwithstanding its weight, I am bound to take it up for the honour of that sacred memory to which it is my sweetest solace to render pious homage. I am bound to take it up especially to follow out my father's thought to glorify the Church, in my humble sphere, and by marshalling the monuments of its history to offer some arguments to its defenders. Ever beset as she has been by the world's hatred, the Catholic Church has rarely seen her enemies attain such a pitch of audacity and persistent virulence as animates them to-day. My father considered that in the contest waged against her it was the duty of devoted sons to rally round her, and employ their energies in her defence. It is in obedience to this brave intention that I accept the task by which it may be fulfilled.

Our adversaries have imprudently made their attacks upon the ground of history where science every day offers them fresh checks; they must be followed up and pursued to the foot of the monuments which now emerge from the soil, unexpected auxiliaries of Truth. Archæology is becoming more and more a science of religion. It cements the history of the Church through nineteen centuries into one block which nothing can disintegrate. In consulting, for my work, the countless labours which during the last fifty years have found a place in monographs or in the multitude of modern European reviews, I have been struck with the unanimity of religious convictions therein manifested, and which I explain by the saying of a learned architect: " I was incredulous : my art has given me belief."

For a work of this kind (writes M. de Fleury in another paragraph), the author is nothing; the monuments are everything, and themselves record their own history. Our work has been merely to arrange them as in a kind of museum, keeping as far as practicable aloof from the domain of liturgiology, which has already been so exhaustively treated by so many great men, and confining our work to "la liturgie monumentale," which has hitherto received too little attention.

After this avowal, which reveals the humble and patient nature of the true antiquary, we would not quarrel with M. de Fleury if we could; the more, however, we examine his work, the more we find we could not quarrel if we would.

The most useful way to notice the important work before us in the limited space available will be to give the scheme of the whole.

First comes the text of the Mass copiously annotated; this is followed by the iconography of the holy sacrifice at every epoch, including Mass in the catacombs, as represented in a veiled and symbolical way in the times when discovery led to persecution and death; then Mass after the triumph of the Church; then the clearer and more literal pictures of the august rite painted in the Carlovingian period; and finally, to complete the unity of the record from Calvary to almost our own time, the mediæval representations of the Holy Sacrifice.

After these general pictorial records of the Mass, the author proceeds to details, beginning with the seat and centre of worship, the altar. Next after altars come naturally the screens and ciboria, which are indeed but parts of the altar, and the tabernacles for the Holy Eucharist; then the confessions or repositories of relics, the chair occupied by the depositary of God's word; the ambo, or desk, from which the Holy Scripture was read; and the enclosure of the choir, so important in the history of liturgy. An investigation into the choir and the early form of the church or basilica concludes the portion of the work dealing with the immovable objects. Next come the portable utensils employed in the Mass—portable altars, chalices, pattens, cruets, &c.; missals, torches and candles, censers, &c.; then the alb, chasuble, mitre, &c.; and lastly, to crown and complete the work, a study of the Saints of the Mass.

The plates, which occupy almost half the bulk of the volume, are drawn in the exact and scientific spirit of the architect, rather than the picturesque inaccuracy which too often characterizes the ordinary illustrator's work. M. de Fleury's very numerous plates of engravings, which give not only general views of the objects in perspective, but also supply precise plans, sections, elevations, and measurements, as well as careful drawings of details on an enlarged scale, warrant and inspire full confidence in the conscientiousness and industry of the author, who is himself the artist. These plates indeed seem the ideal of what archæological illustrations should be.

The altar, to which this first volume is devoted, is traced with an abundance of illustration through its various forms from the primitive domestic table to the *cippi*, transported as trophies into the Christian temple, to the time of Charlemagne, and the rich ornamentation with which they were covered, and then to the subsequent elongation of their form. M. de Fleury's fine and delicate plates of the superb golden altar frontals preserved at Milan, Aix-la-Chapelle, and the Hôtel Cluny in Paris, will doubtless prove to many readers, who have gazed with admiration on the originals, welcome reminders of those works of religious art which seem almost miraculously to have escaped the cupidity of centuries. Scarcely less interesting are the gilt elaborate altars preserved at Copenhagen and at Stockholm, and, going back to a still earlier date, the author's account of the Roman *cippi* used as altars, and marked with the Chi Rho monogram. Most remarkable, perhaps, of all is the circular altar at St. Étienne, Besançon.

To trace the altar (remarks M. de Fleury) not only through the Middle Ages, but up to the primitive times of Christianity, is to prove that Mass has always been said from the days of the Apostles, and that to justify Calvin's abolishment of it, history must be effaced. When in the Rimini altar we find beneath the sacred slab a casket of relics, and even the three grains of incense usually placed with them in our own day, such a discovery bears wonderful testimony to the constancy of our liturgical traditions.

We hope to notice the succeeding volumes of the work in future numbers of the Review.

Cathedra Petri; or, the Titles and Prerogatives of St. Peter and of his See and Successors, as described by the Early Fathers, Ecclesiastical Writers, and Councils of the Church, &c. By C. F. B. ALLNATT. Third Edition. London: Burns & Oates. 1883.

IT is superfluous to recommend a book which recommends itself, and which has already approved itself, to the Catholic public on the one hand, and been tried in the furnace of controversy on the other. The high merit of the book is undoubted, and we may be quite sure that it has secured a lasting place in our literature. It is because of its great value that we should like to see the book absolutely perfect. Very little pains are needed to secure this, and we venture to subjoin a few instances of possible improvement.

The most defective part, so far as we have seen, is the Appendix headed "St. Peter at Rome." Three questions at least seem in our judgment to be confused, which are nevertheless quite distinct, and in regard to which Protestants have taken distinct positions. They are these—Was St. Peter ever at Rome? Did he found the Roman Church? Was he actually Bishop of that Church? There are of course subsidiary questions, as to the length of his episcopate, &c. But our point is that eminent Protestant scholars, who do not dream of doubting St. Peter's martyrdom at Rome, nevertheless stoutly answer the second and third questions in the negative.

Then, again, the old maxim that the half is often more than the whole, is verified in controversy as much as anywhere else. We should wish the words of the Fathers to be translated literally; the version, indeed, can scarcely be too literal, provided it is plain English, and no opening should be left for the charge that too much is made of patristic dicta. Thus, we object altogether to the version given of the words of St. Ignatius (p. 70), προκαθημένη τῆς ἀγάπης—"presiding over the covenant of love." This quite possibly may be what the saint meant, but it is not what he said, and should not be set in inverted commas. Still more do we dislike the translation of Tertullian (de Pudic. i.) —Pontifex scilicet maximus quod est episcopus episcoporum—"The Bishop of Bishops, which is equivalent to the Sovereign Pontiff." Tertullian writes crabbed Latin, and the most has been made of his inversions of style in the exigencies of the Eucharistic controversy. But we are quite unable, in spite of Kenrick, whose authority is alleged (p. 116), to believe in such an inversion as this. And what is gained by such torture of the words? Other details of scholarship might be mentioned. For example, if the Peshito text of Matt. xvi. 18 is given at all, it should be given correctly. As it is, in the five short Syriac words given in Roman characters (p. 6) there are three mistakes, two of which involve gross offences against grammar. By the way, why does Mr. Allnatt write Peschito? This is a form which Germans rightly use, because they naturally express the "sh" sound common to Syriac and English by "sch." But we have no need to imitate them. "Peshito" and "Peshitto" exactly represent two legitimate Syriac forms, the latter being preferable. But these are small blots in a book which lays all English Catholics, and indeed all theological scholars, under a heavy debt of gratitude.   W. E. ADDIS.

Obituary Notices of the Friar-Preachers, or Dominicans, of the English Province from 1650. By the Rev. C. F. RAYMUND PALMER, O.P. London: Burns & Oates. 1884.

NOT many months have passed since we called our readers' attention to the "Necrology of the English Benedictines," edited by a monk of that congregation; and now it is our pleasing duty to say a word or two about a similar but much briefer contribution to post-Reformation English Catholic history, the "Obituary Notices of the English Dominicans." Father Palmer begins by a few introductory notes on the old English province of the Black Friars, which consisted of some fifty-five houses in all, and which revived for a brief space in Mary's reign, when the old house of Canons at St. Bartholomew's, Smithfield, was refounded for the children of St. Dominic. After the death of Father Hargrave (1560), the last Prior of Smithfield and Vicar-General of the English province, the order of the Preaching Friars had scarcely an existence in England for above fifty years, when in 1622 the Master-General of the Order reorganized the affairs of the few English Fathers, and united them into a congregation of the Order. But the complete establishment of the English Dominican province was not brought about till some years later, when Father Philip Thomas Howard, afterwards a Cardinal, of the noble family of Norfolk, founded the convents of Bornhem and Vilvorde, in Flanders, for friars and nuns respectively. The latter house was afterwards removed to Brussels, and, after various migrations subsequent to the French Revolution, the community found a settled home at Carisbrooke, in the Isle of Wight.

The convent of Bornhem was destined to fill a very useful place in the little English Catholic world. Its community was distinguished for its regularity, and many of its members bore a high reputation for learning and piety. A secular school, much patronized by our forefathers of the eighteenth century, was taught by the Fathers; a college for higher studies for the Dominicans themselves was opened in the University of Louvain, and thus a high standard of literary and theological culture was maintained in the English province. Like the other regulars, the Dominicans took their share in the labours and dangers of the English mission. There were often six or seven of the Fathers in London alone, at one or other of the ambassadors' chapels or in private families; but the principal sphere of their work was in the northern counties, where many missions and chaplaincies were served by them. And, when the history of the progress of Catholicity in England comes to be written, it will be no small honour to the small English family of St. Dominic to have established the first Catholic chapels since the Reformation in such important centres as Leeds, Leicester, and Coventry.

Brief as is Father Palmer's latest contribution to our knowledge, it is full of interest to those who can read between the lines and appreciate the force of the dry facts which he puts on record. When the English Franciscans have found their chronicler, and when the scattered notices of the labours of the few English members of the Carmelite Order in this country have been gathered together, we shall be in possession of materials for an interesting chapter in any future edition of the "Monasticon Anglicanum."

Acta Sanctorum Octobris (Tom. XIII.). Paris: Palmé, 1883.

THIS latest instalment of the great collection of the "Acta Sanctorum" needs no commendation from us. To say that the Bollandist Fathers of the Society of Jesus have given another volume to the world, is only to say in other words that a fresh proof has been afforded of, a new monument raised to the piety, industry, research, and critical acumen of the learned children of St. Ignatius. The introductory memoirs of Fathers Joseph Van Hecke, Edward Carpentier, and Henry Matagne, convince us moreover that in the nineteenth century as in the thirteenth, saints may be engaged in writing the lives of Saints.*

The present volume treats of the holy personages whose feasts fall on the last three days of October, and the brief period embraces representatives of the holiness of the Church Catholic in almost every part of Christendom, and every age of the world. An ancient martyrology from Berne, now printed for the first time, prefaces the saints' lives, and by comparison with other accessible old martyrologies will afford much curious and valuable information.

Of the longer biographies of foreign saints, those of Blessed Alphonsus Rodriguez, temporal coadjutor of the Society, of the Cistercian nun, Blessed Ida of Louvain, and of Blessed Dorothea, a widow and recluse of Quidzin in Prussian Poland, will probably be found of the greatest interest to students of hagiography. Ascetical writers, too, will be able to gather much from the lives of the above-named holy personages—much that is striking and of great value, as affording an insight into the workings of grace and the dealings of the Holy Spirit with interior souls. The similarity of many things in the career of Blessed Dorothea of Quidzin with what we know of a modern servant of God, the Venerable Anna Maria Taigi, the Roman matron, is very striking. Her domestic troubles, her life of drudgery, her influence over others, especially men (their "spiritual sons" form a remarkable group in both cases), above all, the frequency of her revelations, make the German saint of the Middle Ages a very prototype of the illuminated soul whose memory is still green in the Holy City.

Of more special interest to us are the lives of the English and Irish saints which are given in this volume. One of these is St. Eadsy, or Eadsin, the friend of King Cnut and St. Edward the Confessor, who from being Royal Chaplain became successively Chor-Bishop of St. Martin's and Archbishop of Canterbury. Before he would accept the primatial See he would be enrolled as a monk among the brethren of the Cathedral monastery; and King Cnut marked his approval of the Canterbury monks for giving a welcome to his chaplain by bestowing upon them—though tourists and summer residents may not be aware of the fact—the town of Folkestone. Another Archbishop of Canterbury whose life is given is St. Aethelnoth, the eighth monk of Glastonbury who governed the English Church. He it was who brought to England and reposed in the great Abbey of Coventry the arm of St. Austin of Hippo, which he had purchased at Pavia for a hundred talents of silver and a talent of gold. The notes on St. Arilda, a virgin martyr of Kington, near Thornbury-on-Severn, Gloucestershire, afford an instance of the care and research bestowed on little-known saints. Strange to say, the name of St. Arilda, whose

---

* In Lect. 2, Noct. in festo S. Bonaventuræ, in Brev.

body was translated to St. Peter's Abbey, Gloucester, does not appear in the history and chartulary of that monastery. The other English saints discussed are the holy anchorites of Croyland, SS. Cissa, Egbert and Tatwin, companions of St. Guthlac; and the hermits of Thorney, SS. Tancred, Tothred, Tova, Huna, and Herefurth.

The same careful elucidation of contemporary history, the same laborious care in fixing a date or a name or an obscure locality, which distinguishes the above memoirs, will be found to give new light to the histories of the three Irish saints, SS. Colman, Foillan, and Ernach, whose memory is honoured in the last days of October.

Commenta Reformationis Lutheranæ ex Tabulariis Secretioribus S. Sedis. 1521-1525. Collegit, Ordinavit, Illustravit PETRUS BALAN, Prælatus Domesticus S. D. N., Eques Torquatus I. K. Ordinis Francisci Josephi. Ratisbonæ: Pustet, 1884.

THIS important collection contains not less than 266 documents gathered from the secret archives of the Vatican. They refer to the period of the beginning of the Reformation, the first document belonging to the year 1520, whilst the last one gives a letter written by Clement VII. in 1525 to the Archbishop Elector of Mainz. Some documents inserted in the collection were indeed known before, but in a text either mutilated or corrupted. Hence Mgr. Balan may claim the merit of having published genuine texts of letters throwing new light on the means employed for the propagation of the Lutheran movement. The texts restored from the Vatican originals are chiefly letters written to the Vice-Chancellor Cardinal Medici by the Nuncio Aleander, from the Diet of Worms in 1521. Numerous corruptions, and inaccuracies connected with the text of some of Aleander's letters as published from a codex existing in Trent by the "old Catholic" Professor Friedrich, are now corrected. And yet it may be said that Mgr. Balan's work falls short of what might have been expected from him. He has supplied the work with an index; but the few footnotes are quite insufficient for elucidating the text. The importance of theological questions referred to in the documents, as well as the vast number of the most influential persons of that agitated time who frequently figure therein, would demand the help of footnotes on nearly every page—at least to make the text easily intelligible.

Attention may be called to Leo X.'s letters to the Christian princes, urging them to resist the new heresy, the instructions given to Nuncio Aleander for the Diet of Worms, the famous letters of Aleander on the appearance of Luther in Worms, Luther's examination before the Emperor and the Estates, and the letter of King Wasa to Hadrian VI. These valuable documents combine to bring into prominence the unremitting zeal of the Holy See in opposing the heresy of the Augustinian monk of Wittemburg, and the base character of the means adopted for securing the victory to the Reformation. Also several documents concerned with England seem to deserve mention. There is a letter of Henry VIII. to the Archbishop of Mainz, urging him "Lutherum istum, a Christo rebellem, nisi resipiscat, una cum hæretica ausis libellis funditus delere ignique servandum credere" (229). There is also a letter of Clement VII. to Cardinal Wolsey, admonishing him to protect the Church in England (349). In a third letter written by Pacius from Richmond to Leo X., occurs Bishop Fisher of Rochester, whose sermon "habitum Londini astantibus triginta (ut minimum dicam) hominum milibus," on the very day on which Luther's writings were publicly burnt, was forwarded to the Pope. I conclude by remarking that ecclesiastical history from 1521 to 1526 has now to be written on the basis of Balan's documents. They are also a striking testimony to the treasures unveiled to students of history by the opening of the Vatican Archives by Pope Leo XIII.   BELLESHEIM.

Life of the Ven. Servant of God, Clement Maria Hofbauer, Vicar-General of the Congregation of the Most Holy Redeemer. By Father R. P. MICHAEL HARINGER, Consultor-General of the Congregation. Translated by Lady HERBERT. New York and Cincinnati: Pustet & Co. 1883.

THIS is the life of a Redemptorist priest who joined the new congregation two years before the death of St. Alphonsus; and who spreading it north of the Alps into the Prussian-Polish and Austrian provinces, reproduced in his own life a striking likeness of the mind and heart of his founder. Consequently, the biography is full of the Redemptorist spirit from beginning to end. It derives interest also from the fact that when Father Clement Hofbauer was declared Venerable in 1864, many persons were still living who had known him intimately, and their testimony and letters bring up to our days the record of heroic sanctity and miracles such as too often appear to belong only to saintly lives many generations distant from our own.

Father Clement Hofbauer's life extended from 1751 to 1820. He began as a baker's boy; he ended as the apostle of Vienna. From childhood it was his one dream to devote his life to the service of God in the priesthood. He chose a trade that would leave him time for study; and while he was carrying his bread-basket through the streets of Znaim, or baking in the monastery of Bruck, or working at Vienna at the sign of the Iron Pear, he was labouring with his books as soon as his manual work was done. Two years of his youth were passed in hermit life, one at Mühlfrauen, the other near Tivoli; but he found no rest until at Rome he entered the Redemptorist church by one of those unexpected acts of Providence which we call chance. He was the first foreign novice of the new congregation, and with the companion of his pilgrimage he made his religious profession in 1785 and was ordained the same year, being then at the age of thirty-three. When St. Alphonsus at Naples heard of the desire of the two German novices to found a house some day beyond the Alps, he answered with prophetic foresight: "God will not fail to promote His glory by their means. Their mission, however, will be different from ours. In the midst of the Lutherans and Calvinists, among whom they will be placed, the Catechism will be more necessary than preaching. These good priests will do a great work; but they will have need of greater light."

The "great work" of Father Hofbauer had chiefly Warsaw for its scene until 1808, when through the enmity of a faction of the French army the consent of the King of Saxony was obtained to an edict expelling the Fathers from the city, and they were dispersed and their church-doors sealed up, very much in the manner of the expulsions in Paris not long ago. Father Hofbauer took refuge in Vienna, deprived of community life and so hampered by Government restrictions that he only afterwards in secret received one novice. In Vienna, by the policy of Joseph II., religion had been reduced to a system of moral maxims, political prudence, and empty and neglected churches; Father Hofbauer's position was like that of a priest under the Culturkampf. But exiled and restricted as he was, this became the most fruitful period of his life. He saw in his position as confessor to the Ursulines, a possible influence over a great educational centre, for the convent numbered a thousand of the poorer classes in its schools, beside higher day schools and an institution for the training of schoolmistresses. This was only part of his sphere of work; his love of the poor led him to give several hours of the morning once or twice a week to hearing their confessions in a poorer quarter of the town; his evenings were spent in the midst of a crowd of young men of every class, who had learned to frequent his room as a place of meeting and conference where recreation was to be found as well as spiritual help; and even his short rest was often sacrificed when he spent night after night beside the dying. At the time of the Congress of Vienna, when the protection of Catholic interests was confided to Helferich and Baron von Wamboldt, specially chosen for the work by Cardinal Consalvi, they found in Father Clement Hofbauer an adviser who knew the situation thoroughly; and though the Redemptorist in his humble lodging received no public credit for his share in the labour, it was to him that the credit was due for the defence of Catholic interests at the Congress; every day Helferich came to consult him, and the memoranda he presented had all been drawn up by Father Clement. A very clear picture of this "apostle of Vienna" is given by the chapters that tell of his simple and earnest sermons, when the crowd filled the church and waited in the street; his love for the poor, and especially for the *pauvres honteux;* his zeal for the splendour of ritual in those churches that had been empty and neglected; his maxims and characteristic devotions, all full of the spirit of St. Alphonsus. The frontispiece, which has great merit as a portrait engraving, does not give us a better idea of his appearance than the book gives us of Father Clement's character.

It is to be regretted that so interesting a little work should be full of what we must call curiosities of printing; "$\frac{1}{2}$ 11" is at least original for an hour of the day, and so are such novelties as "a 1000 pretexts were found to prevent Father Clement's journey." The translation bears marks of hurry, for which, however, we receive some amends in a translator's preface, giving a sketch of the spread of the congregation in Great Britain since 1848, and very striking statistics of its work. At present there are 122 members in the English province, including New South Wales. The number of missions and retreats given is already between three and four thousand; and the number of converts made nearly seventeen thousand. Father Frederick de Held, the founder of the English province, was one of the first to enter the noviciate after Father Clement Hofbauer's death; he had been one of the young men who frequented the evening meetings in his room at Vienna. "I was eighteen," he wrote, "and studying philosophy at the University of Vienna, when, by the kindness of Father Springer, I had the good fortune of becoming intimately acquainted with that great servant of God, Father C. Hofbauer. At the very first sight of him, he inspired me with such confidence that I chose him at once as my confessor, and constantly went to visit him in the evening." This closely links the work of the English Redemptorists with the subject of the biography.

La Terre Sainte. II. Partie. Liban, Phénicée, Palestine Occidentale & Meridionale, &c. Par VICTOR GUÉRIN, Chargé des Missions en Orient, &c. Paris: E. Plon & Cie. 1884.

IN our number for April, 1882, we noticed the first volume of this magnificent folio. All the praise we then gave both the text and the illustrations may readily be extended to what now lies before us. Those of our readers who have seen the panorama of splendid scenes unfolded before them in the first volume, representing the chief scenes in Judea, Samaria, and Galilee, will need no further word in praise of this volume, which completes the series. Here we get no less picturesque glimpses of the Lebanon, Phœnicia, and Western Palestine from Acre southwards—first to Carmel, then to Cæsarea, to Ascalon of the Crusaders, to Hebron, through the wilderness to Engaddi, and on to the southern shores of the Dead Sea.

The author's text through all these scenes is marked by the same scholarship and the same clearness of style as we noted in the former volume. His descriptions of the various localities still derive a great charm from the light which his archæological lore enables him to throw on the Scripture texts connected with them. This, however, is by no means all their attraction. M. Guérin has a power of graphic description and an eye for the beauties of Nature, and it is no small praise to say that his descriptions often effectively supplement the charming sketches of the artists who "illustrate" him. Besides this, he never fails to give us fuller information than we have anywhere else met concerning the present condition of religion in the various towns and villages. This feature, so noteworthy in the former volume as regards the "Holy Places," is scarcely less so in this as regards, especially, the Lebanon. Thus, also, Beyrout is placed before us with such details as are most interesting. We are told something of the zealous work being done there by the Sisters of Charity, and of several other orders; also by the Capuchin Fathers, and particularly by the Jesuits. *Apropos* of the magnificent establishment of the Jesuit Fathers, he tells us that " to contend more successfully at Beyrout, against Protestant influence, which grows apace, seconded as it is, at the same time, by England, America, and Prussia, they have transferred thither their College from Ghazir." Here the Fathers have a printing establishment, where they print books in twelve Oriental languages. " It is, without doubt, the best-appointed printing press in the East." To the college and seminary is soon to be joined a school of medicine, when the whole will bear the name of the University of St. Joseph. Then we further learn that the Maronites have not a few churches here, and that Mgr. Deba, their archbishop, has finished building a college, and is commencing a cathedral, and that Greeks, both Catholic and schismatic, have schools and churches. The author notes, too, here as always without any acrimony, the work being done by Protestants—the American Mission with "a very fine college and school of medicine, and an observatory;" the English with their schools, and the Prussians with a hospital and orphanage.

A succinct, but equally erudite and interesting, account of Sinai and Egypt concludes the volume; dealing, not indeed strictly with "La Terre Sainte," but closely connected with the people whose special possession the Holy Land was, and with their preparation for it and long-protracted entry into it. This portion of the work, supplementary to its main purpose, has proved, to us at least, as full of information and interest as any other. Certainly the sketches, whether by pen or pencil, of Petra, and of the hills, valleys, and ancient convents of Sinai, are of such romantic and wild grandeur and old-world character as makes them intensely interesting. In this portion of the work, too, the Old Testament references are frequent, and the help gained therefrom is considerable. We have here, therefore, a work of a great traveller and *savant* on the land that to us is *the Holy* Land, written in a graceful and attractive style, and with the reverence and from the point of view of an educated Catholic. First-rate artists have profusely illustrated its pages with some of their best work. Lastly, the eminent publishers have deserved well for the many external advantages of type, &c. The result is a book that deserves to become a great favourite. No finer gift-book could be chosen for scholar or friend.

Life of Antonio Rosmini Serbati, Founder of the Institute of Charity. By GABRIEL STUART MACWALTER. Vol. I. London: Kegan Paul & Co. 1883.

THIS important work ought to have been noticed before. There is always, however, something unsatisfactory in reviewing a first volume of a biography, and the difficulty is the greater in the present instance, that the life of the great servant of God here related is of significance comparatively slight during its earlier years, and only becomes remarkable when he has published his well-known philosophical works, and is before the world as a founder and a reformer. Mr. Macwalter writes a rather militant preface, in which he draws a parallel between the "persecutions" which have beset Rosmini and the misunderstandings which had to be endured by St. Augustine, St. Thomas of Aquin, and St. Ignatius. But there is no trace of any persecution in the present volume. We are presented with a rather diffuse but interesting and well-written account of Rosmini's family, childhood, studies, vocation, and ordination to the priesthood.

We quote the following passage, both as a specimen of the volume, and as relating an interesting occurrence in Rosmini's life:—

One of the least frequented streets in Rovereto in those days was an avenue called *Terra*, in which persons of wealth and rank had residences carefully railed in or walled off from "noisy business." While passing homeward slowly, thoughtfully, and all alone through this quiet street, one evening after a "philosophical excursion" with Don Orsi and his pupils, young Rosmini allowed his mind to speculate freely on a variety of things. Now his attention was held by one mental object, and now by another. Suddenly he perceived that each object was far from being simple. "On the contrary," said he, when explaining the circumstances to Don Paoli, "each object appeared to me in itself a group of many objects. But, on looking more closely into the matter, I saw that these, instead of being many objects, should have been called many determinations of one object, more universal and less determinate—their common container. Then, by repeating on this object the very analysis I had applied to the others, I found that it was itself in the same condition, and that when divested, by means of abstraction, of those less definite determinations which it still retained, it appeared to me as a new object, still more universal and less determinate than the former. I say new in reference to my intuition (because I had not as yet looked at its new aspect), but not as being new in itself; for it was the container not only of the object which my mind had under analysis, but also of the others that had been previously analyzed. But by continuing this process I discovered that, no matter what the point of departure might be, I was invariably brought to the most universal object—*Ideal Being*—destitute of all determinations whatever, so that I found it no longer possible to abstract anything from it without annihilating thought, and at once I saw that this object was the *universal container* of all the objects on which my mind had already rested. I then undertook the process of verification. This consisted in seeking to discover which determinations of *indeterminate being*, were the first possible, and then which came next, and so on, to the last. By these means I discovered that synthesis brought up again before my intellectual vision all those objects which analysis had caused to disappear gradually from it. Then it was that I became convinced that indeterminate *ideal being* must be the first truth, the first thing seen by immediate intuition, and the universal means of all acquired knowledge, whether perceptive or intuitive" (pp. 88–90).

Whether this discovery was one which ought to call up in an admiring biographer references to Newton and Watt is a matter into which it may be possible to inquire on a future occasion.

Synopsis Philosophiæ Moralis, seu Institutiones Ethicæ et Juris Naturæ secundum principia philosophiæ scholasticæ, præsertim a. Thomæ, Suarez et De Lugo methodo scholastica elucubratæ a JULIO COSTA-ROSSETTI, Sacerdote Societatis Jesu. Oeniponte: Rauch. 1883.

IN the preface of this elaborate and closely reasoned work the author tells us that it originates from the Encyclical on the restoration of scholastic studies; it contains the substance of lectures given in the college of the Society to which the author belongs. He has adopted the scholastic method, but combines it with undeniable elegance of Latin. The title of the volume suggests the author's principal aim. He wishes to vindicate Catholic truth against modern erroneous juridical theories, and to establish the intimate and indissoluble connection between right and morals, between morals and religion. Hence, to a large extent, the book is devoted to destroying the so-called positivism of right, or that theory which wantonly proclaims civil law to be the public conscience. The "Synopsis," which is a volume of not less than 820 pages, is divided into five parts; which treat respectively on (1) the general principles of morality; (2) the accurate idea of right as based on the teachings of the Fathers; (3) the family; (4) society; (5) international law. I would particularly direct attention to the dissertations on the family and on society, as embodying questions which are daily discussed—or rather grossly misrepresented. The author's expositions of the origin of civil society and of the power of the Sovereign are most interesting. In three indices (p. 562) he ingeniously compares the theories of Rousseau, Suarez, and James I. of England; and there needs no laboured effort to bring out the immense difference between Rousseau and Suarez. The same must be said about Bellarmine. But, on the other hand, it cannot be denied that the greatest writers of the Society of Jesus in our day, as Taparelli and Liberatore, do not commit themselves unreservedly to the theory expounded by Bellarmine and Suarez. On the contrary, they teach the immediate derivation of the Sovereign's power from God. The last chapter, which treats "de jure gentium," is all the more worth reading that the boundaries dividing nations one from another are in our days all but entirely removed, and the wonderful inventions of the century seem to establish a "familia gentium" not in the least thought of by our forefathers. BELLESHEIM.

A Familiar Introduction to the Study of the Sacred Scriptures. In a Series of Fourteen Letters Addressed to a Young Lady left an Orphan at an Early Age; with the Addition of a Copious Appendix, relating in a more general manner to Education and the Study of the Sacred Scriptures. By the Rev. HENRY FORMBY. London: Burns & Oates. 1884.

THE "copious appendix" which is mentioned on the above title-page, and which occupies considerably more than one-third of the whole book, is made up of "four sermons addressed to young ladies" and "considerations addressed to teachers." We mention this as leading up to the remark which strikes us at once on turning over these pages—a remark which is not at all necessarily unfavourable— viz., that the book is not an "Introduction" to the Sacred Scriptures in the sense which is now recognised and familiar. Dr. Dixon's "General Introduction," Gilly's "Introduction générale et particulière," to speak only of Catholic manuals, will at once occur as examples of a multitude of similar works. The present work is not an introduction in that sense: it would have been, we think, more happily entitled "A Familiar Exhortation." As an "Introduction" supplying any *apparatus* for practical application to the Sacred Volume it is not even intended: as an earnest exhortation to practical study it is excellent and opportune. We could have wished, for our own part, that the author had not addressed his letters to that orphan young lady, nor failed to say anything of the example of the Blessed Virgin for boys; because what is good in the book is quite as useful for boys and young men.

The fourteen letters of which the body of the work is composed are occupied with drawing attention to the charm that may be found in the study of the Scriptures by even the young compared with the charm attending works of fiction: and the solid wisdom that will naturally result from the one study as contrasted with the too frequently conspicuous folly and danger attendant on the other. The most striking letters are those in which the author shows the character of the Christ in both Testaments, and also the character of the "true Blessed Mary of the Scriptures" as contrasted with the "glittering and imaginary" delineations of the Blessed Virgin which too often pass for her "life" or her "example" with sentimental readers and authors. In such passages as the exposition of the "Magnificat" at page 28, or, still more particularly, the explanation of the titles in the litany, "Ark of the Covenant" and "Tower of David," the author shows samples of those treasures new and old which are to be drawn from such study of the sacred books as he so earnestly pleads for.

*** As the above lines are being revised for press, we hear to our great regret of the death of the much-esteemed author of the work they review. At this last moment we can only make space for a brief line to the memory of one who, besides his zeal in priestly duty, deserved well of the English Catholic public by his arduous literary labours—more particularly, perhaps, by some of the least pretentious of them—*e.g.*, by his excellent Bible and Church History Series for the Young—an educational help of permanent value. R. I. P.

The Christian Brothers: their Origin and Work. With a Sketch of the Life of their Founder, the Venerable Jean Baptiste de Salle. By Mrs. R. F. WILSON. London: Kegan Paul, Trench & Co. 1883.

THIS admirable work deserves far more lengthened consideration than is at our disposal this quarter. Not that it calls for criticism: quite the contrary. But it is concerned with a topic which, beyond many others, is of present-day interest: the views of the Church as to the duty of providing education for working and lower classes, and her efforts to fulfil the duty. It is concerned with this topic not by way of theorizing and declaiming; but it places before us the work achieved by the Christian Brothers since their humble beginning in the last quarter of the seventeenth century to the present day. France was the cradle-land of the Christian Brothers, and the authoress is specially concerned to show that they have long understood the educational difficulty of France, and have long worked effectually in the direction of solving it. She speaks warmly of their self-sacrifice, their gratuitous services, the marked success of their scholars, "not only in examinations in elementary knowledge, but also in the higher branches of education—music, drawing, mathematics, geometry, mechanics, natural science, &c.;" and last, but not least, the confidence of the French people in them and their love for the Brothers, who in turn have given the most striking proof that could be given of patriotism and devotion to their country. "Such are the men," she indignantly adds, "whom the powers that be at this present time in France would banish (if they could) from the country; out of whose hands they would take (if they could), at an enormous cost to the nation, the education of the people." And this French statesmen would do precisely from hatred of Christianity—for this is the Brothers' only crime: they are Christians, and will not banish Christ from their schools; their lives, their garb, their whole bearing witness to their faith in Christ. This is the real and only cause; for these Christian Brothers are not even priests, and are forbidden by their Founder to even learn Latin themselves, lest the temptation to aim at the sacerdotal office or to allow their schools to become higher grade schools should ever spoil their educational mission to the poor and working classes. Mrs. Wilson twits the modern Liberals with foolish presumption in claiming for themselves the credit of alone seeing the need and the duty of extending education among the working and lower classes. She shows that only a century ago it was the anti-clericals in France who opposed the efforts of the Church for such elementary education. That the Founder of the Christian Brothers understood the needs of the classes and responded to them with an organization which has been crowned with a century of success, and is still equal to the task demanded of it; that this organization is able (as is true of many other Orders) to do the task with facilities and with chances of success denied to any remunerated labour; that the Government of France is wicked, or foolish, or both, in thwarting and rejecting the proffered help of such men. Detailed proofs of these assertions should be sought in the interesting pages of this book. Mrs. Wilson tells clearly and pleasantly her story; we thank her warmly for a useful and opportune book. The career of the Venerable Founder is told with much simplicity, but so as to show the working in his life of a true divine vocation to the work which he accomplished. Her book will, we trust, be widely read by many besides Catholics; its perusal is well calculated to do good to the cause of religion and of Christian education even in England.

True Men as we Need Them. A Book of Instructions for Men in the World. By the Rev. BERNARD O'REILLY. (Laval.) New Edition. Dublin: M. H. Gill & Son. 1883.

THIS volume emanates from the pen of the author of the "Mirror of True Womanhood," and as far as its purpose permits is arranged on a similar plan. Its main idea is to define and hold up for example to men a high standard of morality. In a series of didactic instructions, copiously illustrated by telling examples, it shows how true men in the world may by courage, manliness, and grace attain to a high standard of Christian perfection. Special instructions are addressed to statesmen, professional and business men, as well as to men and youths in every home relation. It is a fairly good specimen of a class of books of which we have by far too few—*interesting* books, with a moral and practical aim that are nevertheless not strictly books of spiritual reading.

Repertorium Oratoris Sacri: containing Outlines of Six Hundred Sermons. Compiled by the REV. HERMAN HUESER, D.D. New Edition. In three volumes. Dublin: M. H. Gill & Son. 1883.

THE enterprising Dublin publishers have done for this the same good office they recently did for another useful American work —the translation of Alzog's Church History—they have reprinted it and brought it out at a price less than one-half of the price of the American edition. We have not seen this last, the original, edition, of the "Repertorium," but we may say that the cheaper reprint is defective in no essential of a serviceable book. The type is large and clear, and as far as we have been able to test the fact, the printer's reader has been careful with his work; the paper is strong and white, and the binding also strong and neat; for a book of frequent reference we should say, that further elegance would be to the detriment of its usefulness. It is much to be hoped therefore that Messrs. Gill & Son, will find such a sale for these volumes as will repay them and encourage them to place other useful works within the reach of a modest purse.

The nature of the "Repertorium" may be briefly indicated: it is a collection of outlines of sermons, of which it contains a total of six hundred. They are outlines or *résumés* of sermons by the more celebrated preachers of different times and nationalities: we have Marchant, S. Thomas of Villanova, S. Bonaventure, even S. Thomas Aquinas, S. Alphonsus Liguori, &c. &c.; we have also a host of more modern writers, Ventura, Campadelli, Zollner, Reinecker and others too numerous to detail. Choice of sermons appears to have been fairly well made. There are several outlines for each Sunday and Feast of the year, besides several series for Lent, month of May, and various Octaves and Novenas. The outlines are so far filled in as to give besides the points, a sufficient amount of useful matter, arguments, texts and the like; they are thus to a certain extent substantial—there could not at least be a famine in the land on any Sunday morning or other occasion, if the young preacher had these outlines by him. We should think that they will be found really a boon where sermons are many and leisure small; they supply the embarrassed orator with as much as a book of the sort ought to offer; plans, texts and *some* matter—leaving, very properly, the manner, treatment, style, to his own talent or at least to his own efforts. Without at least that much of *himself* no speaker can be natural or effective.

A Course of Philosophy, embracing Logic, Metaphysics, and Ethics. A Textbook for use in Schools. Second Edition, revised and enlarged. By the Very Rev. A. LANAGE, C.S.C. Baltimore: John B. Piet & Co. 1883.

THIS unpretending volume is intended as a Text-book for a lecturer on Logic and Metaphysics. The author is one of those much-to-be-commiserated professors who are ordered by the ruling powers to compress a course of philosophy into a single year. Nay, he seems to have been even worse off than this, for he tells us that he "had been entrusted" (who was the scholastic or ecclesiastical Pharoah that gave such an order ?) "with a class in which, *besides philosophy*, we were to teach *other matters* in one scholastic session of *five months*." Much may be excused in a Text-book elaborated under conditions like these. As it is, the book is not lively reading. It assumes, of necessity, almost the form of a vocabulary, or dictionary of terms; detailed and consecutive exposition or reasoning is rare, and rival theories are dismissed in the briefest possible manner. We do not forget that the book is meant to be merely the bare outline which a professor would fill in by word of mouth. Considered in this light, the manual will no doubt prove useful. The writer follows the scholastic or Thomist school. It is to be noted, as a sign of a certain backwardness in our Catholic schools, that the Darwinian and Spencerian "evolution" theories are utterly passed over. As these theories, now so widely accepted, have rendered obsolete many stock arguments, such as the usual form of the proofs of the existence of God from motion and design, have changed the common conceptions of material substance, and have made it necessary to restate, in the most careful way, the argument for the soul's spirituality and individuality, we could well spare the pages devoted to Epicurus and Spinoza for a few lucid paragraphs on the difficulty of the day.

Historical Portraits of the Tudor Dynasty. By S. HUBERT BURKE. Vol. IV. London: John Hodges. 1883.

THE long task which Mr. Burke set himself to fulfil in giving the public a truer knowledge of men and manners under the Tudors than it had previously possessed has been at length accomplished, and we must congratulate both the author and his readers on the way in which it has been performed. The work was undoubtedly a somewhat difficult one. To begin with, the ground was in part already occupied, and, we need not say, occupied by a rival force. The prejudices of three centuries of Protestantism had to be dislodged, and truer if newer notions to be popularized, before the victory can be said to have been won. But it has been won—at least, in great part. What the historical records published under the direction of the Master of the Rolls, what the calendars of State Papers, what the researches of conscientious specialists have done for the inner circle of readers and students, that Mr. Burke has endeavoured to do for the outside public, which likes to have its ideas presented to it in an attractive, ready-made sort of way. Mr. Burke brought to the work an earnest determination to find out the truth, the whole truth, and nothing but the truth, and when found to make a note of it, and tell it, with more or less picturesqueness of detail, to those whose leisure, means, or taste might be insufficient to help them to form their ideas at first hand from the original documents now so profusely offered to public inspection by the custodians of the national archives. Mr. Burke is not a blind partisan—who could be nowadays?—of all the sayings and doings of the so-called Catholic party of the Tudor period; he has his remarks, and very severe ones sometimes, on the shortcomings, political and religious, of not a few whose religion was but too often a cloak for political intrigues or interested partisanship. Even the clergy, nay, especially the clergy, of the last generation of Catholic England come in for a large amount of hostile criticism, which facts and references show to be only too well deserved. Perhaps Mr. Burke does not make sufficient allowance for the difficulties of the times; for the great force of the intellectual movements of the day, the chaotic state of European polity, the religious revolutions over so great a part of Europe; all which must have unsettled the minds of men, whether clerks or lay folk. But apart from any divergence of view on this or other topics between ourselves and Mr. Burke, and apart from the slight inaccuracies and occasional contradictions to which the treatment of so long a period necessarily exposes a writer, the work is well done. The broad outlines of the various reigns are given not so much in their political aspect as in their influence on home affairs; and then, in unfolding, page by page, the strange careers of bold men, the cruel fortunes of upright and true men, the varied but almost uniformly unhappy inner life of the country during the sixteenth century, Mr. Burke has a fine opportunity for that mingling of grave with gay, of pregnant fact with graphic description, which gave a character to his earlier volumes. To him, and to all who labour to unveil truth, remove prejudice, and make us more familiar with the past, we wish a lasting success and a wide circle of readers.

Lives of some of the Sons of St. Dominic. First Series. By a Father of the same Order. New York: D. & J. Sadlier & Co. 1883.

THIS handy little volume, partially a reprint from magazines and newspapers, comprises clear and concise accounts of seven sons of the Dominican Order—viz., Jordan of Saxony, Antony Neyrot, James of Ulm, Giles of Santarem, Bertrand of Sarrigne, all of whom are beatified; and of Bartholomew of the Martyrs, and Lewis of Granada, whom the Church has declared Venerable. Though primarily meant for Dominican Tertiaries, the volume (mostly compiled from the Bollandists) will naturally appeal to all Catholics.

The Parables of Jesus. A Methodical Exposition. By SIEGFRIED GOEBEL, Court Chaplain in Halberstadt. Translated by Professor BANKS, Headingley. Edinburgh: T. & T. Clark. 1883.

IT is natural for an English reader to begin this book with very strong prejudice against it. Any one who feels much interest in New Testament studies is pretty sure to be familiar with the work of Archbishop Trench on the same subject—which is the fruit of varied learning; breathes throughout a singularly devout and profoundly Christian spirit; and is characterized none the less by sobriety of interpretation and well-balanced judgment. The exposition before us is far less attractive, and we were inclined at first to consider it dull and lifeless. And dull it certainly is, by comparison with Dr. Trench's work; yet we believe that no intelligent reader who takes the trouble to peruse it carefully will regret his pains. It furnishes a real complement to Dr. Trench. Goebel does nothing to illustrate the parables from general literature; he gives nothing like those passages from the Fathers which Dr. Trench selects with a skill which is simply masterly, and which are invaluable to the preacher. But, on the other hand, Goebel has merits of his own. He sticks close to the Greek words, and discusses the text and its meaning with minute care. The labours of German scholarship are diligently used, but the author never for a moment fails to show the independence of his own judgment, and the careful way in which he has thought out each part of the matter for himself. Often of course we should decline to follow him in his conclusions. We cannot, *e.g.*, believe that in the parable of the wicked vine-dressers the words ἀπέστειλεν ἄλλους δούλους πλείονας τῶν πρώτων (Matt. xxi. 36) can possibly mean "he sent other servants higher than the first." Of the references given in proof that πλείων in the New Testament ever bears such a meaning, Heb. xi. 4 is the only one which comes near the point, and even that does not touch it. The idea of "more in quantity" when applied to things, insensibly passes into that of higher worth, but there is no connection between the idea "more in number" applied to persons, and that of "higher in rank." Still Goebel is often instructive, and the very fact that he shows such careful attention to the minutiæ of exposition, and such a steady determination to hammer out the clear sense, is of itself a stimulating example to the student. It teaches how to go to work. Then the very titles chosen may sometimes arrest attention. such, *e.g.*, as the "parable of the divers soils," for the familiar "parable of the sower." Another special excellence is the manner in which the parables are connected with the great periods in Christ's ministry. Far more attention is given to the grouping of the parables than we find in Trench. The introduction, though too brief, is sound and sensible. We ought to add, perhaps, that the book before us represents the highest Protestant orthodoxy. We can only express in conclusion our earnest hope that the book may be carefully studied by many of our own clergy. The knowledge of the Bible is surely the most necessary of all knowledge for us; nor is there any Biblical study which yields a speedier return to the pastor than the study of the parables. W. E. ADDIS.

The Revision Revised. Three Articles reprinted from the *Quarterly Review*. To which is added a Reply to Bishop Ellicott's Pamphlet, including a Vindication of the Traditional Reading of 1 Timothy iii. 16. By JOHN WILLIAM BURGON, B.D., Dean of Chichester. London: John Murray. 1883.

WE are glad to see that the Dean of Chichester has yielded to the solicitations of his friends and published, in one volume, his slashing criticisms on the Revised Version. This volume forms a worthy sequel to Dean Burgon's masterly defence of the last twelve verses of St. Mark's Gospel, which he published, as he reminds us, just twelve years ago. That work has been ignored, but never answered, by the Dean's opponents. Certainly, Dean Burgon deserves the thanks of all who value the integrity of the New Testament for his courage in protesting against the rash conclusions of the Revisers, and in appealing from the over-confident decisions of modern editors to the "consentient voice of Catholic antiquity." There are but few men who would have had at once the courage and ability to do what Dean Burgon has done. In his special department of textual criticism he is second only to Dr. Scrivener, with whom he is in substantial agreement. Nor can there be much doubt in the minds of impartial judges but that the Dean has done what he meant to do—spoilt the Revision, and prevented it from ever taking the place of the old English version. He has certainly made good his charge that the Revisers exceeded their instructions, that they made needless alterations which are not improvements, that in place of revising an old translation they have constructed a most fallacious Greek text. The Dean sums up in one sentence what he thinks of the Revision—that it is "the most astonishing as well as the most calamitous literary blunder of the age." The ten years' labour of the Revisers has resulted in a "wholly untrustworthy performance, full of the gravest errors from beginning to end, and constructed throughout on an entirely mistaken theory"— a theory for which Drs. Westcott and Hort are held responsible, who built their new Greek text almost entirely on the Vatican

Codex. Dean Burgon's condemnation of this new theory of textual criticism is immensely strengthened by the opinions of Dr. Scrivener, just published in the last edition of his "Plain Introduction." Dr. Hort's system, Dr. Scrivener says, is "entirely destitute of historical foundation," and "entails such consequences as to make it hopelessly self-condemned."

Another special point of interest in the volume is Dean Burgon's answer to Dr. Ellicott, which now appears for the first time. The Dean's prolonged attack upon the Revisers has ended in a hand-to-hand conflict with their chairman, the Bishop of Gloucester and Bristol. The battle-ground is Dr. Ellicott's own choice—the oft-disputed reading of 1 Tim. iii. 16. The Bishop is for the relative pronoun masculine, the Dean maintains θεός to be the right reading. No such controversy has been seen since the days of Porson and Travis. Dean Burgon reminds us of Porson. And of Dr. Ellicott we may say what Dr. Scrivener says of Archdeacon Travis—"'impar congressus Achilli,' no match at all for the exact learning, the acumen, the wit, the overbearing scorn of Porson." We cannot refrain from giving just one sample of the Dean's polemical style :—

You flout me: you scold me: you lecture me. But I do not find that you ever *answer* me. . . . . Denunciation, my Lord Bishop, is not argument; neither is reiteration proof. And, then, why do you impute to me opinions which I do not hold, and charge me with a method of procedure of which I have never been guilty? Above all, why do you seek to prejudice the question between us by importing irrelevant matter, which can only impose on the ignorant and mislead the unwary? Forgive my plainness, but really you are so conspicuously unfair—and at the same time so manifestly unacquainted (except at second-hand, and only in an elementary way) with the points actually under discussion—that were it not for the adventitious importance attaching to any utterance of yours, deliberately put forth at this time as Chairman of the New Testament body of Revisers, I should have taken no notice of your pamphlet (p. 370).

After reading this and many similar passages, it is amusing to find the Dean saying in his dedication, "In handling certain recent utterances of Bishop Ellicott, I considered throughout that it was 'the textual critic,' not the successor of the Apostles, with whom I had to do." And in the preface he requests that the volume may be taken as "a sample of how Deans employ their time, the use they make of their opportunities!" The outcome of the controversy seems to be this, that the Bishop is left with only one uncial MS., the "Codex Sinaiticus," and one solitary version, the Gothic, and "*perhaps two cursive copies;*" whilst the Dean claims four uncials (A, K, L, P), 296 cursives, three versions (Harkleian, Georgian, and Slavonic), and upwards of twenty Greek Fathers. No doubt a better case could be made for the Vulgate reading "quod," than for the masculine pronoun which the Revisers preferred. But whatever may be the opinions of critics on this disputed reading, it must be acknowledged that Dean Burgon has spared no pains in his researches throughout the libraries of Europe, and has thus added considerably to the list of known manuscripts. His book contains a list and description of fifty-six additional Codices of St. Paul's Epistles, and forty-six additional copies of the "Apostolus." Many of them belong to the Ambrosian Library at Milan, some to the Vatican, and others were found in the Basilian monastery, at Crypta-Ferrata, near the ancient Tusculum. A couple of these newly found MSS. throw a new light on a curious story told by Liberatus of Carthage in the sixth century, about the Patriarch Macedonius II. being expelled from his See for falsifying 1 Tim. iii. 16. The account in Liberatus ("Breviarium") is this:— "At this time, Macedonius, Bishop of CP., is said to have been deposed by the Emperor Anastasius on a charge of having falsified the Gospels, and notably that saying of the Apostle, 'Quia apparuit in carne, justificatus est in spiritu.' He was charged with having turned the Greek monosyllable ος (*i.e.*, qui) by the change of a single letter (ω for ο) into ως—*i.e.*, 'ut esset Deus apparuit per carnem.'" Hincmar, Archbishop of Rheims, in the ninth century, understood this to mean that Macedonius changed ος into θεος. And this is the version of the story adopted by Dr. Ellicott, who thus, to use Dean Burgon's phrase, "As a Christian Bishop, swells the Socinian chorus of the unbelieving school who have revived and embellished the silly story, in order, if possible, to get rid of a text which witnesses inconveniently to the Godhead of Christ." That this could not be the true explanation of what Liberatus said was abundantly clear. Both Cornelius a Lapide and Cotelerius, in the seventeenth century, shrewdly conjectured that at the time of Macedonius there must have been codices which had ος θεος in this place, and that the Patriarch was falsely charged by the Eutychian Emperor of changing ὅς into ὡς. And yet there was no manuscript then known which bore witness to such a reading. Now two such manuscripts have been found—one at Crypta-Ferrata, the other at Paris by the Abbé Martin. This, as Dean Burgon says, "is new," and it is important; for it both explains an historical difficulty and breaks down a Socinian argument.

Dean Burgon expresses a wholesome contempt for modern critics, who never collate a manuscript or verify a reference, who

invent their facts and deliver themselves of oracular decrees, on the sole responsibility of their own inner consciousness. I know but too well [the Dean adds] how laborious is the scientific method which *I* advocate. A long summer day disappears, whilst the student—with all his appliances about him—is resolutely threshing out some minute textual point. Another, and yet another bright day vanishes. Comes Saturday evening at last, and a page of illegible manuscript is all that he has to show for a week's heavy toil. *Quousque tandem?* And yet it is the indispensable condition of progress in an unexplored region that a few should thus labour, until a path has been cut through the forest, a road laid down, huts built, a *modus vivendi* established.

Our parting wish to Dean Burgon, the doughty champion who "hits so hard and so straight to defend the integrity of the deposit," is that he may be spared for many a summer yet, and that his long laborious days be not a few. And the high compliment which the

Dean pays to our great Catholic authorities, Vercellone and Ceriani, calling them "giants in textual criticism," is fully earned by himself. Like a giant, long may he delight to run his course!

A New English Dictionary on Historical Principles; founded mainly on the Materials collected by the Philological Society. Edited by JAMES A. H. MURRAY. Part I. A—ANT. Oxford: Clarendon Press. 1884.

A DICTIONARY which has taken thirteen hundred persons twenty-seven years to prepare, and for which this body of labourers has collected some three millions of quotations out of five thousand different authors, is an undertaking which is not unlikely to startle the "general reader." Perhaps the ordinary "writer" ought to be still more deeply impressed, for that personage can never be made to understand nice distinctions of words and phrases; yet, when we begin with about sixteen closely printed quarto columns on the word "A," we must be prepared to find out a good many new facts about our own language. It is to be feared that a too prolonged study of Dr. Murray's researches will tend to unsettle the spelling of unripe scholars, and to still further confuse the ideas of modern critics as to what is "elegant" English and what is not. Seriously, however, this is a very valuable and most important work. There is nothing like it in the English language—that need hardly be insisted upon—and it bids fair to surpass in many respects both Littré and Grimm. The present instalment (A—ANT) is of 352 pp. triple columns. No indication is given by the editor as to how long the whole work will be, or at what rate the parts may be expected to issue.

More Leaves from a Journal of a Life in the Highlands, from 1862 to 1882. London: Smith, Elder & Co. 1884.

"HER Majesty's Journal," of which this book is a continuation, is calculated to make her subjects more intimately acquainted with her personal character. No "Journal" was ever so simple, so natural, and so unaffected. There is nothing of royal pomp or State about it except in a "significant phrase here and there," which is, however, just as natural as the rest; for the life of a Sovereign, even in these days of little ceremony, must affect habits of thought and expression. The pages here printed have a pervading tinge of melancholy. The death of the Prince Consort colours the whole book. In the presence of the Queen's genuine grief criticism is silent, and one forbears to say a word about Prince Albert's character or merits. The death of the Prince Imperial is mourned with touching pathos, and the loss of many humbler friends, from John Brown downwards, finds an affectionate record in Her Majesty's notes from day to day. There is interest of a genuine sort, though it may not be deep, in the Queen's descriptions of scenery and houses, of her rooms and accommodation in various journeys, of the incidents of the journeys themselves, and of the varying circumstances of the immutable afternoon tea. There is a good deal of "religion" in the book, and the late Dr. McLeod is introduced to the reader at considerable length; but the only occasion on which Her Majesty pleads guilty of unroyal impatience is under the infliction of a prolonged "address to the Deity," delivered during a heavy rain by the local minister at the unveiling of the Prince Consort's statue at Aberdeen.

A Commentary on St. Paul's Epistles to the Corinthians. By JOSEPH AGAR BEET. Second Edition. London: Hodder & Stoughton. 1883.

THIS learned work deserves special notice, for it combines two peculiarities not often found together. It is a thoroughly English Commentary, and yet one that speaks both fairly and kindly of the Catholic Church. We are so accustomed to translations from the German that it is quite refreshing to notice the work of a genuine English scholar, and to find that without being inferior in learning it surpasses foreign works in clearness and method. In fact, the Rev. Mr. Beet is to be congratulated on his success as an expositor, understanding as he does exactly what a reader wants in a commentary— much knowledge and copious reading condensed into small compass. The analysis of each chapter is most carefully done, and the sequence of thought clearly shown. Another special feature of Mr. Beet's method is the stress he lays on the Evidences of Christianity and the undesigned coincidences which overthrow the objections of modern scepticism. Mr. Beet's theological views on certain points are in contradiction to the teaching of the Catholic Church, and for that very reason we appreciate the more his kindly tone and his scrupulous fairness. In one place he speaks of his

"sincere affection for our brethren of the Roman Church, with whom I hope to spend eternity in the one Universal Church above," and he acknowledges "our deep obligation to that Church for preserving the light of Christianity, often obscured but still burning, during the long night of the dark ages." And of the Catholic version of the Scripture he says " that it rests upon a purer text than does our Authorised Version: of sixty corrections of the Greek text, accepted by the revisers and all recent editors, forty-one were already incorporated in the Rheims version" (p. 541).

Nor does Mr. Beet allow any *odium theologicum* to hinder him from doing justice to his opponent's case. When discussing the Catholic teaching of the Real Presence, he is careful to use the Church's own language as found in the Council of Trent. He is not afraid to go to approved Catholic authors, or to say what he thinks of them. For instance, he says:—

The Roman Catholic doctrine is defended with great ability, candour and devoutness in the "Symbolik" of Moehler. This last work I strongly commend to Protestant theologians. Only by a study of the best writings of those who differ from us, can we understand their opinions and correctly estimate our own (p. 209).

To enable our readers to form an opinion for themselves of Mr. Beet's terse and suggestive style of commenting, we will quote a part of what he says on St. Paul's "stake for the flesh":—

A humiliating malady is suggested by its divine purpose, the word *gives* suggests that it was not inborn, or if inborn afterwards greatly aggravated. Paul's prayer implies that its removal was conceivable. It therefore cannot have been a memory of past sin. Christ's refusal implies that it was not sinful; and so does Paul's resolve to boast in it. These indications suggest severe and recurrent and painful bodily ailment, which Paul recognized as a work of Satan but also as a gift of the kind forethought of God, and which seemed to hinder his apostolic activity... Certainly it was something calculated to counteract any lofty self-estimate which the rapture might create. The above is the oldest explanation of the verse. It was held probably by Irenæus (bk. v. 3); and certainly by Tertullian ("On Modesty," c. xiii.); a "pain," as they say, of ear or head, and it is that given by most modern expositors. Purely inward temptations, either sensual (Roman Catholic writers), or spiritual (Luther), would hardly have been matter of boasting; while the former contradicts 1 Cor. vii. 7, and the latter the word *flesh*. Outward persecutions (Greek Fathers) would be hardly sufficiently personal" (p. 459).

Mr. Beet has an interesting and copious dissertation on St. Clement's first Epistle to the Corinthians, which has the honour of a place in the Alexandrian Codex. Not only is the letter most interesting in itself, but it is at once an important corroboration of St. Paul's Epistles and a refutation of the modern notion of Pauline and Petrine antagonism. From the letter it is apparent that St. Clement, the successor of the one and the fellow-labourer of the other, knew of no such difference between the great Apostles, or he would certainly not have quoted them as an example in a letter to the Corinthians to rebuke them for their quarrels. All doubt about the authenticity of St. Clement's letter must surely cease now that fresh MSS. evidence has been produced. Mr. Beet gives an interesting account of this :—

No other copy (except the Alexandrian Codex) was known until in A.D. 1875 there was published at Constantinople by Bryennios, Metropolitan of Serræ, a cursive MS. found in a library at Constantinople and containing entire, among other writings, both Epistles of Clement. The next year, among some MSS., purchased from Paris for the Library of the University of Cambridge, was found a Syriac MS. of the New Testament, containing, after the Epistle of Jude and before that to the Romans, the two Epistles of Clement. The heading of the former is "The Catholic Epistle of Clement, the disciple of Peter the Apostle, to the Church of the Corinthians," and at the foot we read "Here ends the First Epistle of Clement, which was written by him to the Corinthians from Rome." The latter is called simply "The Second Epistle of Clement to the Corinthians." The MS. bears a date corresponding to A.D. 1170.

We have, then, to thank the Rev. Mr. Beet for his excellent Commentary, and to express the hope that he may be able to accomplish his intention of explaining the other Epistles of the Great Apostle.

little too long, but they are all that could be wished in simplicity, directness, accuracy of language, and interest of style.

3. Although this small book is entitled "Spirit of St. John the Baptist," the holy precursor's name never occurs in it except on the title-page. It consists of sixty or seventy pages of very warm "fine writing," addressed first of all to worldlings in general, and then to young women and young men specially, on the frivolity and sinfulness of life. The intention of the writer is excellent; what she says is very true, and the advice given is very good. It is a pity that grotesque phrases and a painfully strained style should go so far to spoil the book.

4. A Dominician book on the Rosary, containing more than a dozen fully developed "methods" of making meditation on the fifteen Mysteries. There is no "imprimatur," but, as far as we can see, it is accurate, useful, and edifying.

5. The translation of the "Children's Manual" of Thomas à Kempis is anonymous, but it appears with the sanction of the Cardinal Archbishop of Dublin. Of the treatise itself most readers will be inclined to say that it is disappointing. There is nothing in it which specially refers to children, except perhaps the opening sentences. We have a string of somewhat disconnected reflections, very pious, and sometimes vigorously expressed, but we miss the broad sweep, the searching stroke, and the marvellous "distinction" of the "Imitation." The translation is fairly done. But how shocked would Thomas have been to know that his dear Latin word "pauper" was to be translated in the nineteenth century by an English word with such associations as *pauper!*

6. The four well-known devotional books here named have been republished by Messrs. Burns & Oates at the price of sixpence each. The form is handy but not too small, the type excellent, and the get-up serviceable. We recommend them strongly to the clergy for purposes of distribution.

7. The Bishop of Ossory's name is sufficient by itself to recommend the prayer-book which he has compiled. Messrs. Browne & Nolan have sent it out in a most attractive form, handsomely printed on good paper, and bound with a view to its being thoroughly well used. Looking through it we find devotions of every kind, and forms of prayer and meditations suited for all. The "Calendar" at the beginning contains the names of all the Irish national saints whose feasts are kept. In an Irish prayer-book like this, we are somewhat surprised that the verse in Father Faber's well-known hymn, "Shall win our country back to Thee," is not altered as it usually is when sung in Ireland. And may we venture to remonstrate with the translator of Thomas of Aquin's prayer after Communion for leaving out "jucunditas consummata," one of the fine "notes" by which the prince of the schools describes the effect on the soul of the Beatific Vision.

8. A short selection of useful forms of prayer, such as are more generally required. Many will consider it an advantage that the Litany of Loreto, the "Miserere," the "Veni Creator," and other devotions which the Church uses in her public offices are here given in Latin.

9. The author of "Paillettes d'Or" thinks that the devout soul, to do good, often only needs "to be advised," or, perhaps, we should say to be "reminded." Hence this thin book, which is meant to be a sort of Guardian Angel's voice for each day and each hour. It seems to be meant specially for young girls, and they could not do better than get it and use it. The very first monition, for Monday, will be found, we fear, rather *gênant*—" Retain a smile on your lips even when you are alone ;" but there is nothing so hard as this in the rest of the book. The "Visits to the Blessed Sacrament" are pleasing and suggestive.

10. The Calendar prefixed to this Almanack, or rather which constitutes the body of the little work, is very interesting, giving, as it does, the feast or commemoration of the Blessed Virgin which is kept on each and every day of the year throughout the Church. We notice some omissions; for instance, the celebration of the Most Pure Heart on the 8th of February, which is the national feast of the daughters of the Ven Père Eudes; and reference might have been made to the fact that Our Lady, under the title of the Immaculate Conception, is the patroness of most of the dioceses of England. There are one or two dissertations in the latter half of the Almanack which are edifying, if not always trustworthy. We trust that the prophecy stated to have been made to Gavin of Dunbar, Bishop of Aberdeen, that he was "the last bishop of that city who should be saved," may be considered to have lapsed since the restoration of the Scottish hierarchy.

11. The Rev. Father Coleridge says, in the preface to this new volume from his pen, that it seems to be a part of the office of St. Paul to present to the Church the causes, the significance, the effects and the divine reasons of the great Sacrifice of the Cross. He has therefore written forty considerations on the Passion, making each of them a commentary on some passage of the Apostle, or on a passage of the Gospels or the Psalms, which the words of St. Paul lend themselves to interpret. The book is not a meditation on the Passion itself; it is a manual of spiritual reading on the Passion in its relation to the Sacred Heart, to God, the soul, sin, the angels, personal suffering, death, penitence, hell, the Church, the virtues, and almost everything connected with man's salvation. This brief description will suffice to show the reader, who is acquainted with this eminent spiritual writer, how excellent a book they have here for the season of Lent and Passion-tide.

12. The "Soldier's Guide" is far from being a book of devotion or mere spiritual reading. It is full of practical hints and instructions for the Catholic soldier in India—as to religion, temperance, his family, thrift, &c. One admirable feature is the excellent collection of edifying stories or examples.

13. An anonymous brief account, very well condensed and extremely touching, of sixteen names connected with Manchester, or Lancashire, who suffered for the Faith from 1584 to 1746.

14. Really devotional and wise books on Purgatory are not so common that we can afford to pass over this one without commenda-

1. *Alice Riordan; a Tale for the Young.* By Mrs. J. SADLIER. Dublin: M. H. Gill & Son. 1884.
2. *The Castle of Roussillon.* Translated from the French of Mme. Eugénie de la Rochère by Mrs. J. SADLIER. Dublin: M. H. Gill & Son. 1884.
3. *The Knout; a Tale of Poland.* Translated from the French by Mrs. J. SADLIER. Dublin: M. H. Gill & Son. 1884.
4. *Mary Queen of Scots; a Tragedy in Three Acts.* By M. QUINN. London: R. Washbourne. 1884.
5. *Ethelreda; a True Story for the Young.* By BETTY. London: R. Washbourne. 1884.
6. *Twitterings at Twilight.* By T. S. CLEARY. Dublin: M. H. Gill & Son. 1883.

THE original story by Mrs. J. Sadlier appeared first with success in the *Boston Pilot*; and its character is told when we explain that its heroine is a dressmaker's apprentice, and that, as the preface says, it "bears its moral on every page." Of the two translations from the same hand, though their merit is almost level, the "Castle of Roussillon" will please young folks best; the very title of the other is somewhat too grim for a story. The style and spirit of both stamp them unmistakably as translations; and we cannot help being, as old writers would say, "exercised in mind" by the multiplication of foreign work whose originals are not striking or famous. Have we not many Catholic writers, the translator herself amongst the number, able to supply our young readers with original fiction; and is there not a disadvantage to our own writers in this introduction of foreign books of only ordinary merit? The original story and the two translations are all brilliantly bound in the style dear to the sight of prize winners; of course "Alice Riordan's" experience is mostly intended for girls of her rank in life.

"Mary Queen of Scots" is an excellent subject for a play that convent girls will enjoy. How they will manage the "Executioner" and the "English Earls," we leave to themselves; their wits will be able also to rectify the Queen's inadvertence in calling her maid-of-honour "ma mignon"—an indifference to gender which Mary Seton hardly deserved even for saying she would rather be a warrior. Our writers of historical plays for boys and girls would do well to look through Elizabethan poetry, and through reprints of colloquial prose, such as occur in the "Troubles of our Catholic Forefathers;" and they would escape from that stilted style which is the besetting defect of school dramas.

"Ethelreda" is a very little unpretending book, finely printed in large type, so that young readers will run quickly through a saint's story. It is prettily told; one does not look for precise historical accessories in such a trifle; the spirit and purpose are both true, and the general impression left is beautiful enough to cover the defects, especially if this be a first attempt.

Verses, chiefly of the average merit of magazine poetry, are published

under an ill-chosen title as "Twitterings at Twilight." One is
reminded of Aubrey de Vere's constant vision of Nature's symbols of
the ritual of worship, in the verses about the trees in the rain bowing
their heads under baptismal waters, and the sun looking out to give
the revivified earth a blessing. The religious thought of a Catholic
is everywhere, and there are many bits far too good for the unfortunate title. Wit is not absent; the best sample is the address
" To Noll in Bronze, as he appears *outside* Trinity College, Dublin."

> In vain by hapless Fortune led,
> You taxed your matchless thriftless head
> To tempt the world to give you bread—
>   They'd give you none;
> But for your safe support when dead
>   They raise a stone.
>
> *   *   *   *   *
>
> Yet e'en unto this day, poor Noll,
> Are those within the learned hall
> Who do not quite forgive you all
>   Your kindly failings;
> You're still, although without their wall,
>   Within *their railings*.

Creed of the Day. By HENRY COKE. In Three Series of Letters.
London: Trübner & Co.

IN these three series of letters Mr. Coke applies himself to the task
of investigating the question "Is there any God? or what
Evidence have we of His Existence?" his method being to collect the
opinions of "our ablest thinkers recent and present," and so to set
forth "the conclusions of the age we live in." We have carefully
looked through his volumes, and we gladly testify to the wide reading,
serious thought and honesty of purpose which they manifest. But
as to his conclusions—well, they remind us of a chapter in one of our
great humorists, a conclusion where nothing is concluded. Anything
like extended criticism of Mr. Coke's work would be impossible for
us here, so great is the range of the topics which he discusses. We
will only observe that his first series of letters, in which he deals with
Revelation, seems to us almost valueless as a contribution to the great
controversy which it handles, because of his manifest ignorance of
Catholic faith and its accredited expositor, while his second series,
which is devoted to Rational Theology, is radically vitiated by his
want of acquaintance with Catholic philosophy. The third series, in
which he discusses Transcendental Theology, is far and away the
best, and his refutation of Materialism is, in some respects, very
skilfully framed and very cogently urged. But upon the whole the
impression left upon us by his pages may be well expressed in certain
words of Leibnitz: "On a grande raison de récrier sur la manière
étrange des hommes qui se tourmentent en agitant des questions mal-
conçues. Ils cherchent ce qu'ils savent, et ils ne savent pas ce qu'ils
cherchent."—(" Nouveaux Essais," L. ii. c. 21, § 14.)

BOOKS OF DEVOTION AND SPIRITUAL READING.

1. *The Most Beautiful among the Children of Men.* Meditations upon the Life of Our Lord Jesus Christ. By Mrs. ABEL RAM. With a Preface by the CARDINAL ARCHBISHOP OF WESTMINSTER. London: R. Washbourne. 1884.

2. *The Dawn of Day, First Prayers and Meditations for the Young.* Compiled from approved sources. London: Burns & Oates.

3. *The Spirit of St. John the Baptist.* London: R. Washbourne. 1884.

4. *Short Meditations to aid Pious Souls in the Recitation of the Holy Rosary.* Translated from the French. By a Member of the Order of St. Dominic. New York: F. Pustet.

5. *Manuale Parvulorum.* By THOMAS À KEMPIS. Translated into English. Dublin: M. H. Gill & Son. 1884.

6. *Missal for the Laity. Key of Heaven. Garden of the Soul. The Following of Christ.* (Messrs. Burns & Oates's Sixpenny Edition). London: 1884.

7. *The Catholic Prayer-book and Manual of Meditations.* Compiled by the RIGHT REV. PATRICK F. MORAN, Bishop of Ossory. Dublin: Browne & Nolan. 1883.

8. *A few Flowers from the Garden.* London: Burns & Oates.

9. *A Friendly Voice; or, the Daily Monitor.* By the author of "Golden Sands." Translated from the French. London: R. Washbourne. 1883.

10. *Our Lady's Almanack for the Year of Grace,* 1884. By the author of the "Pilgrim's May Wreath." Manchester: (St. Francis's, West Gorton).

11. *The Baptism of the King.* Considerations on the Sacred Passion. By HENRY JAMES COLERIDGE, S.J. (Quarterly Series). London: Burns & Oates. 1884.

12. *The Catholic Soldier's Guide during his Stay in India.* By FATHER GEORGE WENINGER, S.J. Bombay, *Examiner* Press. 1883.

13. *Memorials of a few who Suffered for the Catholic Faith.* (Diocese of Salford.)

14. *Entretiens spirituelles sur les Ames du Purgatoire.* Par un Religieux expulsé. 2me. ed. Marseille: Société Anonyme de l'imprimerie Marseillaise, 1883. London: Richardson & Son.

15. *Growth in the Knowledge of Our Lord.* Meditations for every day in the year. Adapted from the French of the Abbé DE BRANDT. By a "Daughter of the Cross." Vol. V. London: Burns & Oates. 1883.

16. *A Treatise on the True Devotion to the Blessed Virgin.* By the Ven. LOUIS MARIE GRIGNON DE MONTFORT. Translated by F. W. FABER, D.D., of the Oratory. With a Letter to his Clergy by the Lord Bishop of Salford. Third edition. London: Burns & Oates; New York: Catholic Publication Society Co.

17. *The Life and Teaching of Jesus Christ.* By NICOLAS AVANCINO, S.J. Two vols. (Quarterly Series.) London: Burns & Oates. 1883.

18. *The Divine Ideal.* By F. M. Dublin: Duffy & Sons.

1. A book of descriptive meditation on the Life of Our Lord, such as we have here should be welcomed by mothers and by all who are trying to teach young children the first steps in mental prayer. The writer faithfully follows the Gospel narrative, but endeavours to make it more striking to young minds by suggesting, in picturesque but restrained language, the scenery, the grouping, the season, the hour, and other circumstances. This is an excellent idea. It is true that the same "picturesque" presentment of a Gospel scene which pleases and moves one heart will often simply repel another; and it is true, also, as we need not say, that those who are habituated to meditative prayer for the most part find that very little "composition of place" is enough for them. But that is no reason why there should not be a wide field for a book like this. We could not have a better description of it than in the exquisite words which Père Chocarne has written to the author: "Un tableau qui parle, une verité sortant d'elle-méme du texte sacré, un bon mouvement du cœur, une aspiration vers le bein, le beau, le divin; tout cela en quelques lignes qu'ont le charme, la douceur, la suavité de la voix d'une mère à l'oreille de son fils—voilà votre livre." The devotion of a child is of the kind which easily kindles in the presence of an epithet a scene or a vivid description; and if such devotion is not very deep, yet it is true and real enough, it will lead to what is deeper. The writer has taken very great pains to make her descriptive commentary accurate and not misleading; and she is careful to indicate what is merely legend or pious belief. The reflections, aspirations, and resolutions which accompany each of the seventy-one scenes from Our Lord's life, have a simplicity, a directness, and a warmth which make them admirably suitable for children.

2. This little manual is for children of a more tender age than the one just noticed. It bears no date, but as the "imprimatur" is of 1862, we presume this is a new edition. Nothing could be better than the prayers for morning and evening, and for Mass, with their simple "rubrics," to help the little one of four years old to nine to understand as he goes along. The meditations are even better. They may be a

m. The "expelled religious" who has written it does not give his
ume; but he is evidently a man of devout heart and an accurate
ieologian besides. The work is divided into five parts. The first
insists of "spiritual entertainments," that is, devout elevations of
ie soul to God, on the subject of Purgatory, each ending with a
rayer or offering on behalf of the Holy Souls. The second treats of
pparitions, and the third of Purgatory itself. In the fourth we have
short treatise on Indulgences, and in the fifth a description of the
"Heroic Act" of Charity. The book contains a very large number
rf stories, most of which are sober and edifying; they will be found
useful by preachers and catechists.

15. This is the fifth volume of this useful and admirably edited
book of Meditation. As we have already mentioned the former
volumes, we content ourselves with drawing attention to its appearance.

16. A new edition of the Ven. Grignon de Montfort's treatise on
the Blessed Virgin, translated by Father Faber, hardly calls for notice.
But the present issue is excellently printed and cheaply issued, and
is enriched with a Letter by the Bishop of Salford, to whom, indeed
the publication of the present edition is owing.

17. Father Coleridge, in his preface to these two handsome volumes
of Meditation, says that the present translation was made, some years
ago, from a German version of Father Avancino. Those who desire
to have a manual of solid and not too lengthy considerations, will find
here what they want. As to the method of using books of this kind
they cannot do better than read carefully the excellent remarks made
by Father Coleridge in the preface already referred to.

18. Some readers may have a taste for the sentimental style and
slipshod English of this well-intentioned production. For ourselves,
we confess we find it wearisome and, in parts, repulsive. In consequence, inaccuracy, tawdriness, obscurity, and straining after fine
writing are hardly compensated for by unmistakable piety, and a
certain capacity for appreciating the late M. Nicolas.

BOOKS RECEIVED OF WHICH NOTICES HAVE TO BE HELD OVER THROUGH WANT OF SPACE.

"Exposé de la Doctrine Catholique." Par P. Girodon, prêtre.
Two vols. Paris: Plon.

"Richelieu et la Monarchie absolue." Par le Vicomte G. D'Avenel.
Two vols. Paris: Plon.

"Spicilegium Dogmatico-Biblicum." Auctore Josepho Corluy,
S.J. Tomus I. Ghent: Poelman.

"Essays and Leaves from a Note-Book." By George Eliot.
Edinburgh and London: Blackwood.

"Historical and Biographical Sketches." By the late Most Rev.
John McHale, D.D. Dublin: Gill & Son.

"The Works of Orestes A. Brownson." Collected and arranged by Henry F. Brownson. Vol. III.—Philosophy of Religion. Vol. IV.—Heterodox Writings. Vol. V.—Controversy (I.) Detroit: Thorndike Nourse.

"Conrad Vallenrod." An Historical Poem. By Adam Miskiévitch. Translated by M. H. Dziewiski. London: Richardson & Son.

"Young and Fair." By Vossian. London: Burns & Oates.

"Maud Hamilton; or, Self-will and its Consequences." By M. A. Pennell. London: Richardson & Son.

"The Little Gipsy Girl." The "Comedy of Convocation" on Mount Parnassus. Composed at St. Mary's Convent, York. London: Burns & Oates.

"Handbook of the Law and Practice in Sales from Landlord to Tenant in Ireland." By George Fottrell, junior, and John George Fottrell, Solicitors. Dublin: Gill & Son.

"Biblical Thesaurus." By the Right Rev. J. Hellmuth. London: Hodder & Stoughton.

"Our Next Leap in the Dark." By Earl Fortescue. Ridgway.

"A Funeral Discourse read at the Burial of Marcia Lady Herries." By Father Gallwey, S.J. London: Burns & Oates.

"Luther's Jubilee." By A. J. Christie, S.J. Dublin: Gill & Son.

"Pierre Olivaint." From the French of Paul Féval. London: Burns & Oates.

"The French Revolution of 1792." By T. G. MacCarthy. Dublin: Hodges.

"A Latin Letter to His Holiness Pope Leo XIII." By T. W. Mossman, D.D. London: John Hodges.

"The Threshold of the Catholic Church." By the Rev. J. B. Bagshawe, D.D. Shilling edition. London: R. Washbourne.

"A Review of Hume and Huxley on Miracles." By Sir Edmund Beckett, Bart. London: S.P.C.K.

"The Theory and Practice of Teaching." By Rev. E. Thring, M.A. Cambridge University Press.

"Folk-Lore of Shakespeare." By Rev. T. F. Thistleton Dyer, M.A. London: Griffith & Farran.

"Life of St. Mildred, Abbess of Minster in Thanet." London: R. Washbourne.

"Life of Elizabeth Lady Falkland." By Lady Georgiana Fullerton. London: Burns & Oates.

"Characteristics of Christianity." By Stanley Leathes, D.D. London: Nisbet.

"The Old Religion." By William Lockhart, B.A. London: Burns & Oates.

"Mary Queen of Scots and her Marriage with Boswell." Revised, &c. By Hon. Colin Lindsay. London: Burns & Oates.

INDEX.

ACTA SANCTORUM OCTOBRIS, *noticed*, 468.
Adalbold, St., at Douai, 154.
Addis, W. E., and Arnold, T., Catholic Dictionary, *noticed*, 458.
———— Notices by, 466, 482.
Adrain IV. and Ireland, 316; Letter of, on Spain, 329.
Alexandria, Foundation of Patriarchate of, 95.
Allies, T. W., Formation of Christendom, 366; Church and State, 385.
Allnatt, C. F., Cathedra Petri, *noticed*, 466.
Amé, St., Sanctuary of, at Douai, 165.
"Analecta" on Pope's grant of Ireland, 325; on supposed refusal of Ireland, 328.
Anchin, The Legend of, 168.
Animalcules, persistence of, 204.
Arctic Exploration, 446.
Armada, The, and Alexander Farnese, 88, *seq.*
American Independence and "Liberty," 68.
Augustine, St., type of ideal Christian, 370.
Avancino, N., S.J., Life and Teaching of Christ, *noticed*, 492.

BALAN, Mgr., Monumenta Reformationis, *noticed*, 470.
Barry, Rev. W., Dreizehnlinden, 245.
Beet, J. A., Commentary on Corinthians, *noticed*, 487.
Bellesheim, Dr. A., Geschichte der K. Kirche in Schottland, *noticed*, 221; Notices by, 206, 235, 449, 470, 476.
Brandt, Abbé de, Growth in Knowledge of our Lord, *noticed*, 492.
Bridgett, Father, Life of St. Olaf, 307.
Brownbill, J., Principles of English Canon Law, *noticed*, 229.
Burgon, Dean, on value of old Codices, 188; the Revision Revised, *noticed*, 483.
Burke, S. Hubert, Historical Portraits of Tudor Dynasty, Vol. IV., *noticed*, 480.

CAMUS, E. le, Vie de Jesus Christ, *noticed*, 236.
Celtic remains at Douai, 152, *seq.*
Chalcedon and the Copts, 97.
Cholera Commission, The, 445.

Christendom, in Ideal and in Fact, 366; formation of, 367; work of in the heathen world, 368; and Pagan Philosophy, 380.
Church, disorders in the, 24; the Body of Christ, 373, *seq.*; and State, Analysis of, 385.
Cicero, the type of an ideal Pagan, 370.
City of Our Martyrs, The, 149, *seq.*
Cleary, T. S., Twitterings by Twilight, *noticed*, 489.
Clerke, Miss E. M., Madagascar, Past and Present, 117; Revolution in the Soudan, 392.
Cochin, A., Les Espérances Chretiennes, *noticed*, 231.
Coke, Henry, Creeds of the Day, *noticed*, 490.
Coleridge, Father, The Baptism of the King, *noticed*, 491.
Cometary Collisions, 444.
Copts, The, 93; history of, 94; origin of name of, 98; persecution of, by Mahomedans, 99; character of, 101; state of religion and education among, 103; the three Liturgies of, 105; faith of, in the Sacraments, 106; rigorous fasts of, 109; state of clergy of, 110; Franciscan missions among, 111; Jesuit missions among, 112; Monks and Monasteries of, 113.
Corbey, poetic description of, 255.
Costa-Rosetti, Fr., Philosophia Moralis, *noticed*, 476.

Dawn of Day, *noticed*, 491.
Delplace, L., S.J., Wycliffe and the Primacy, 23.
Devas, C. S., Groundwork of Economics, *noticed*, 237.
Dioscorus, 97.
Divine Ideal, *noticed*, 492.
Douai, The City of our Martyrs, 149; historical account of, 152; St. Adalbold at, 154; St. Riotrude and her children at, 155; sieges of, 158; material growth of, 163; treasures of, 164; St. Amé at, 165; religious orders in, 167; commercial activity of, 169; trade of, with England, 172; decadence of, 174; university of, 176; British Colleges and Convents at, 179; taken by French, 183.
Doyle, Canon, Principles of Religious Life, *noticed*, 224.
Dreizehnlinden, 245; greatness of, 248; difficult theme of, 253; analysis of, 254; utility of, 268; critique of, 269; *see* Weber, F. W.
Drinking: Three Generations Contrasted, 448.
Dwellings of the Poor, 414;

Education, Secular, 1; change of English Government regarding, *ibid.*; Government recognition of Catholic claims to, 5; Government buys entrance into Catholic schools, 8; interference with religious, 12; rights of State in, 14; rights of parents in, 19.
Egypt, Conversion of, 95; Mahomedan Conquest of, 98.
Electrical Progress, 203.
Entretiens sur les Ames du Purgatoire, *noticed*, 491.
Etheldreda, *noticed*, 489.

Euclid, The Imperfections of, 203.
Eusebius of Cæsarea, and Vatican and Sinaitic Codices, 194; value of authority of, 197.
Eutychianism of the Copts, 95.
Experiment of France, The, 344.

FARNESE, ALEXANDER, 81; Loyalty of to Philip II., *ibid.*; life of, 82; with Don John in Netherlands, 83; succeeds him, 85; and the Prince of Orange, 86; Philip's treacherous conduct towards, 88; death of, 91.
Fleury, C. Rohault de, La Messe, *noticed*, 464.
Formby, Rev. H., Introduction to Sacred Scriptures, *noticed*, 476.
Forster, C. D., Law of Compensation under Holdings Act, *noticed*, 242.
Fourbin d'Oppède, M. de, La B. Delphine de Sabran, *noticed*, 232.
France, The Experiment of, 344; main lines of political progress in, 345; Chamber of Deputies in, 349; causes of present position of affairs in: the Revolution, 353; method of Revolution, 357; net results of Revolution, 362; progress of, contrasted with that of England, 364.
Franciscan Missions in Egypt, 111.
French Revolution, 68, 343; artisan past and present, 347.
Friendly Voice, A, *noticed*, 491.

GERMANUS, Dr. G., Reformatorenbilder, *noticed*, 230.
God, the Synthesis of the two Wholes, 296; How "Being" can be predicated of, 307.
Goebel, ., The Parables of Jesus, *noticed*, 482.
Gordon in the Soudan, 402.
Grandidier, Alfred, and Madagascar, 122.
Guérin, Victor, La Terre Sainte, Part II., *noticed*, 473.

HALLAM, Mr., on the reading of Saints' Lives, 314.
Hamilton, Sir Wm., System of Logic, 279.
Haringer, Fr., Life of Ven. C. M. Hofbauer, *noticed*, 471.
Harper, Rev. Thomas, S.J., from Logic to God, 273.
Harrod, H. D., The Dwellings of the Poor, 414.
Henrici, Prof., on Mathematical Teaching, 202.
Henry II., Grant of Ireland to, 317; contemporary evidence of, 324; the "Analecta" against, 325.
Hueser, Rev. H., Repertorium Oratoris Sacri, *noticed*, 479.
Hymn Book, The Parochial, *noticed*, 233.

IRELAND, state of at time of Henry II., 317; Grant of to Henry, 319.
Irish Bishops and Princes, Letters of Alexander III. to, 320.

JESUIT Missions and Seminary in Egypt, 112.
John Baptist, The Spirit of St., *noticed*, 491.
Jullien Père, Visit to Coptic Monasteries, 114.

KEMPIS, Thomas à, Manuale Parvulorum, *noticed*, 491; Following of Christ, *noticed*, 491.

LANAGE, V. Rev. A., Course of Philosophy, *noticed*, 480.
Langdale, Mr., Efforts of, for Catholic Education, 5.
Leo XIII., Encyclical of, to Bishops of France, 438.
"Liberals," Changing Watchwords of, 63; "Liberty and Property Defence League," and the, 65.
"Liberty," Laisser-faire and Legislation, 62; various meanings given to, 67; principle of and expediency, 71; principle of and "popular" government, 73; real nature of political, 75.
Lilly, W. S., The Experiment of France, 344.
Liturgy, The Coptic, 105.
Lives of some Sons of St. Dominic, *noticed*, 482.
Logic to God, from, 273.
Logical and Metaphysical wholes, 273; antithesis between, 275; in abstractions and generalizations, 281; in intuitions, 282; objective value of, 289; synthesis of, possible, 293; synthesis of, perfected in God, 294.

MACCARTAN, Rev. E., Reminiscences of Rome, *noticed*, 234.
Mackey, Rev. H. B., Four Essays on St. Francis de Sales, *noticed*, 233.
Mackinlay, Rev. J. B., The City of Our Martyrs, 179.
MacWalter, G. S., Life of A. Rosmini Serbati, *noticed*, 474.
Madagascar, Past and Present, 117; description of, 118; discovery and history of, 122; rise of the Hovas, 127; English missionaries in, 130; French occupation, 130; persecution of Christians, 131; letter of Radama II. to the Pope, 135; baptism of Ranavàlona II., 139; social organization of the Hovas, 140; language, 143; superstitions, 145; history of Catholic missions in, 147.
Mahomedan Conquest of Egypt, 98.
Malone, Rev. S., Adrian IV. and Ireland, 316.
Manning, H. E., Cardinal, The Eternal Priesthood, *noticed*, 218.
Mary, The B. Virgin, Coptic Devotion to, 105.
Mary, Queen of Scots, a tragedy, *noticed*, 489.
Maurand, St., at Douai, 157.
Meditations on the Rosary, Short, *noticed*, 491.
Memorials of a few who suffered for the Faith, *noticed*, 491.
Merry England, Vol. I., *noticed*, 243.
Mill, J. S., on "Liberty," 68.
Missions in Egypt, Franciscan, 111; Jesuit, 112.
Montfort, Ven. G. de, Treatise on Devotion to the Blessed Virgin, *noticed*, 492.
Moran, Bishop, the Catholic Prayer Book, *noticed*, 491.
Murray, J. A. H., New English Dictionary, Part I., *noticed*, 486.

NETHERLANDS, Don John and Alexander Farnese in, 83.

New Testament Vaticanism, 186; Dean Burgon against, 188; serious issue involved in, 190; the reductio ad absurdum of Protestantism, 201.

O'Brien, R. Barry, Fifty Years of Concession to Ireland, *noticed*, 241.
Olaf, St., Life of, 307; authorship of MS., 308; Editor's judgment of criticized, 311; a perplexing event in, 312.
O'Reilly, Rev. B., True Men as we need them, *noticed*, 479.
Ornsby, R., Memoirs of J. R. Hope Scott, *noticed*, 461.
Our Lady's Almanack for 1884, *noticed*, 491.

Palmer, Rev. C. F. R., Obituary of Friars Preachers, *noticed*, 467.
———— W., Narrative of events connected with publication of Tracts for the Times, *noticed*, 229.
Periodicals, *noticed*, French, 214, 456; German, 206, 449; Italian, 209, 452.
Philip II., Character of, 81, *seq*.
Poor of London, present interest in, 415; testimony to state of, 417; indifference of local authorities about, 422; Acts to ameliorate condition of, 423; suggestions for efforts of relief, 427.
Prayer Books, various, *noticed*, 491.
Prehistoric Footprints, 204.
Primacy, Roman, Wycliffe's teaching on, 27, 36, *seq*.

Queen's, The, More Leaves from a Journal, *noticed*, 486.

Ram, Mrs. A., Most Beautiful of Children of Men, *noticed*, 491.
Rictrude, St., 155.
Rochère, E. de la, Castle of Roussillon, *noticed*, 489.

Sadlier, Mrs. J., Alice Riordan, *noticed*, 489; The Knout, *noticed*, *ibid*.
Schopenhauer, A., The World as Will and Idea, *noticed*, 240.
Science and Religion, 205.
———— Notices, 202, 444.
Secular Education, 1.
Shuttleworth, Sir James Kay, on Secular Education, 3.
Sickel, Th., Das Privilegium Otto I., *noticed*, 235.
Sinaitic Codex, History of, 192.
Soudan, Revolution in the, 393; difficulties of communication in, 394; tribes of, 397; conquest of, 401; Gordon Pascha's popularity in, 402; slave trade in, 406; Catholic missions in, 410; recent events in, 402.
Spencer, Mr. Herbert, and "Liberty," 69.
Stock, St. George, Attempts at Truth, *noticed*, 238.
Sunsets, Recent Extraordinary, 444.
Synnott, N. J., Liberty Laisser-faire and Legislation, 62.

Theistic Philosophy, anthropomorphism of, 288.

Theology, Natural, the Apex of Metaphysics, 294.

UNIVERSALS, Genesis and objective value of, 280.

VATICAN Codex, Extravagant esteem of, 187; Dean Burgon's opinion of, 189; history of, 190; related to Sinaitic Codex, 193; mistakes of, 195.
Vaticanism, New Testament, 186.

WEBER, F. W., Life of, 245; becomes a Physician, 247; translates Tennyson, 248; estimate of his "Dreizehnlinden," *ibid. seq.*
Weninger, Fr., The Soldier's Prayer-Book, *noticed*, 491.
Wilson, Mrs. R. F., The Christian Brothers, *noticed*, 477.

END OF VOL. XI.

PRINTED BY BALLANTYNE, HANSON AND CO.
LONDON AND EDINBURGH

BURNS & OATES' NEW LIST.

Books for the Month of May.

Month of Mary. By the Rev. Father Beckx, General of the Society of Jesus. Translated from the German. (Ready 15th of April.)

	£	s.	d.
Book of the Holy Rosary: a Popular Doctrinal Exposition of its Fifteen Mysteries. By the Rev. H. Formby. Embellished with 36 full-page illustrations. Cloth, elegantly bound. Reduced from 10s. 6d. to net	0	5	0
Children of Mary. Select Narratives for the Young. Cloth extra gilt	0	2	0
Child's Month of May	0	0	6
Father Faber's Translation of De Montfort's True Devotion to the Blessed Virgin. Cloth	0	2	0
Little Book for Mary's Month. Compiled and adapted for the use of our Blessed Lady's Sodalists and other Liegemen of Her Dower, as England is called. Blue cloth	0	1	0
Lourdes Month of May. From the French of Lasserre	0	2	6
Cloth	0	3	0
Mary in Sorrow and Desolation	0	1	0
Calf	0	4	0
Mary Magnifying God.—May Sermons. By Rev. Father Humphrey, S.J. New edition	0	2	6
May Carols, or Ancila Domini. By Aubrey de Vere. Third edition, enlarged, cloth, gilt, with frontispiece	0	5	0
With photos., gilt edges	0	7	6
May, Tickets for, per packet	0	0	4
Miniature Life of Mary for every day of the Month. Compiled by H. S. Bowden, of the Oratory. Cloth	0	0	6
Gilt	0	1	0
Music and Hymns for the Month of Mary, in 'Hymns for the Year' and Music	0	2	0
Month of Mary. By Rev. Fr. Muzzarelli, S.J. Consecrated to Mary Most Holy, with Exercises in Sunday Flowers of Virtue. Cloth	0	1	0
Oratory Month of May	0	0	1
Pilgrim's May Wreath. By Rev. F. Thaddeus, Stratford. Second edition. Blue cloth	0	2	6
Rosary Hymns and Music for Children	0	0	2
St. Alphonsus' Month of Mary	0	1	0
Cloth	0	1	6
Virtues of Mary. Second edition	0	2	6
Visits to the Altar of Mary	0	0	9

Granville Mansions, 28, Orchard Street, London, W.,

Books for the Month of May.

	£	s.	d.
Husenbeth, Very Rev. Provost (D.D., V.G.):			
Apparition of the Blessed Virgin at Pontmain	0	1	6
Life of Blessed Virgin Mary. Translated from the French of the Abbé Orsini. With Eight full-page illustrations. Cloth extra	0	3	6
Legends of Our Lady and the Saints. New edition. Tastefully bound in blue cloth, extra gilt	0	3	6
May Pageant, A: a Tale of Tintern. By Father Caswall. Second edition	0	2	0
May Chaplet, A, and other Verses. By Rev. Kenelm Digby Beste, Priest of the Oratory of St. Philip Neri. Blue cloth, gilt	0	4	0
May Papers; or, Thoughts on the Litanies of Loreto. By the Rev. J. Purbrick, S.J. Third edition	0	2	0
Mary, Glories of. By St. Alphonso Liguori. Edited by Bishop Coffin. The best and only complete English edition. New edition, cloth ...	0	3	6
With Frontispiece, cloth	0	4	6
Also in better bindings.			
Mary, Star of the Sea; or, a Garland of Living Flowers culled from the Divine Scriptures, and woven to the honour of the Holy Mother of God. A Story of Catholic Devotion. By the Author of 'Mount St. Lawrence.' New edition	0	5	0
Our Lady's Dowry; how England won and lost that Title. By the Rev. T. E. Bridgett, (C.SS.R.). Second edition. With Four illustrations by H. W. Brewer	0	9	0
Our Lady's Manual of the Sacred Heart. Cloth	0	2	0
Red or gilt edges	0	2	6
Calf	0	5	6
Morocco	0	6	6
Gilt	0	7	6
Sacrum Septenarium; or, The Seven Gifts of the Holy Ghost. By the Rev. H. Formby. In cloth, neat, red edges	0	3	6
Summer Talks about Lourdes. By Miss Caddell, Author of 'Never Forgotten,' &c. ... ... 1s. 6d. and	0	2	0
Twelve Visits to Our Lady and the Heavenly City of God. By Rev. Fr. Rawes, D.D.; S.H.G. Third edition	0	0	8
Or in 1 volume, Visits and Devotions, neat cloth	0	3	6

Granville Mansions, 28, Orchard Street, London, W.,

French Books for May.

Mois de Marie, par le R. P. Jacolet, S.J., traduit par le P. Blot, relié en chagrin, tranche dorée ...	0	2	6
Mois de Marie de la Jeunesse Chrétienne, par l'Abbé Dumax	0	1	0
Mois de Marie Paroissial, par M. l'Abbé Laden ...	0	2	6
Mois de Marie de Notre-Dame de l'Immaculée-Conception de Siez, par M. l'Abbé Cauval ...	0	1	6
Mois de Marie Invoqués sous le titre de Notre-Dame du Saint Sacrement. Extrait des écrits du R. P. Eymard	0	1	6
Mois de Marie des Mères Chrétiennes, par le R. P. Huguet	0	1	6
Mois de Marie des Paroisses et des familles Chértiennes, par l'Abbé Ricard ...	0	2	0
Mois de Marie Pratique, par M. l'Abbé Peyre ...	0	1	6
Mois de Marie des Fleurs, par le R. P. Fonteneau ...	0	1	0

NEW WORKS—IN THE PRESS.

NEARLY READY.

SUAREZ ON THE RELIGIOUS STATE.

A Digest of the Doctrine contained in his Treatise, "De Statû Religionis."

By Rev. W. HUMPHREY, S.J.

Three vols., pp. 1250, cloth. Royal 8vo, £1 10s.

Life and Glories of the Great Patriarch, St. Joseph. Taken, by permission, from the Italian of Dom Antonio Vitali. By Edward Healy Thompson, M.A.

Life of Father Baptiste Muard, Founder of the Benedictine Preachers of the Sacred Heart of Jesus and Mary. Being Vol. ix. of the "Library of Religious Biography." Edited by Edward Healy Thompson, M.A.
This life will be enriched with materials supplied by the Reverend Fathers of Buckfast Abbey.

"Divine Office:" from the French of l'Abbé Bacquez, of the Seminary of S. Sulpice, Paris. Edited by the Rev. Father Taunton, of the Congregation of the Oblates of S. Charles. With an Introduction by H.E. the Cardinal Archbishop of Westminster.
The above work—deservedly popular in France, where it has already passed through Four Editions—is now for the first time presented to English readers.
The Price will be 6s.; per post, 6s. 4d.

Stonyhurst Illustrated. By Alfred Rimmer, Author of "Ancient Streets and Homesteads," "Our Old Country Towns," "Pleasant Spots round Oxford," &c., &c. Imperial Quarto. Embellished with about Forty Illustrations of the College, surrounding Country, Treasures, Relics, &c. Price £1 1s. per copy. An *Edition du Luxe* will be published, of 100 copies only, on extra paper, bound in morocco, and the illuminated letters will be coloured, either by, or under the superintendence of the author, in exact imitation of the original. These copies will be numbered and signed, price £3 3s. Orders now received.

Works of S. Francis de Sales. Translated into the English language by the Rev. H. B. Mackey, O.S.B., under the direction and patronage of the Right Rev. Dr. Hedley, O.S.B.
Vol. II. *The Love of God.* Founded on the rare and practically unknown English translation, of which the title-page is as follows: A Treatise on the Love of God, written in French by B. Francis de Sales, Bishop of Geneva, and translated into English by Miles Car, Priest of the English College of Doway. 1630.

Granville Mansions, 28, Orchard Street, London, W.,

NEW BOOKS.

Newman's (Cardinal) Works. Complete in 36 volumes, Half-bound in Calf. The set £14 0s. 0d. net.

Manning's (Cardinal) Works. Complete in 14 volumes, Half-bound in Calf. The set £6 0s. 0d. net.

Faber's (Father) Works. Complete in 12 volumes, Half-bound in Calf. The set £5 0s. 0d. net.

Parochial Hymn-Book. Containing Music and Words. Compiled by the Rev. A. POLICE. Demy 8vo, Cloth, 6s. 6d. net. Words for ditto, price 1s. net.

Growth in the Knowledge of Our Lord. Meditations for Every Day of the Year, exclusive of those for Festivals, Days of Retreat, &c. Adapted from the Original of ABBE DE BRANDT. By a "Daughter of the Cross." This work bears the "Imprimatur" of his Eminence the Cardinal Archbishop of Westminster, and has received the approbation of his Lordship the Bishop of Salford. Complete in 5 vols., 7s. each.

New Parish Priest's Practical Manual: A Work useful also for other Ecclesiastics, especially for Confessors and Preachers. By JOSEPH FRASSINETTI, Prior of St. Sabina, Genoa. Translated from the Italian by WILLIAM HUTCH, D.D., President of St. Colman's College, Fermoy. Crown 8vo, printed on extra superfine paper, price 6s.

Spiritual Exercises according to the Method of St. Ignatius of Loyola. By Father ALOYSIUS BELLECIO, S.J. Translated from the Italian Version of Father ANTHONY BRESCIANI, S.J., by WILLIAM HUTCH, D.D., President of St. Colman's College, Fermoy; Author of "Nano Nagle: Her Life, Her Labours, and their Fruits," &c., &c. Second edition, 18mo, cloth, gilt lettered, 2s. 6d.

Lacordaire's Conferences:—Jesus Christ—God—God and Man. Translated from the French, with the Author's permission. New edition, 1 vol., 6s.

Joys and Sorrows of Human Life. Cloth, extra gilt, 1s. 6d.

The Sixpenny Missal for the Laity. Containing the Masses of the Sundays and Festivals of the Year. Neatly bound in cloth, red edges, gilt lettering, 6d.; roan, 1s. 6d. and upwards.

Obituary Notices of the Friar-Preachers, or Dominicans of the English Province. From the Year of Our Lord, 1650. Compiled by Rev. C. F. Raymund Palmer, O.P. 1s. 6d.

Uriel; or, The Chapel of the Angels. By the Author of "Lady Glastonbury's Boudoir," "The New Utopia," &c. Cloth, 4s.

Grantley Manor. A Tale. By Lady G. Fullerton. New edition. Cloth, 3s. 6d.

Liguori on the Redemption. New edition. Cloth, 2s. and 3s.

Sanctuary-Boys' Illustrated Manual. By Rev. James A. McCallen, S.S. Cloth, red edges, net, 4s.

Children's Pictorial Mass-Book. Cloth, gilt lettering, 1s.; cloth, red edges, extra gilt, 1s. 6d.

Luther. By W. H. Anderdon, S.J. 1s.

Life of St. Aloysius Gonzaga. Edited by Edward Healy Thompson, M.A. New edition. Cloth, gilt lettered, 5s.

Familiar Introduction to the Study of the Sacred Scriptures. By Rev. H. Formby. 2s. 6d.

Granville Mansions, 28, Orchard Street, London, W.

NEW BOOKS.

From the Crib to the Cross. Meditations for the Young. With a Preface by the Very Rev. Father Purbrick, Provincial, S.J. Translated, with the Author's permission, from the French of "De la Crèche au Calvaire." 4s.

Baptism of the King, The. Considerations on the Sacred Passion. By the Rev. H. J. Coleridge, S.J. Quarterly Series. 7s. 6d.

Life of Lady Falkland. By Lady G. Fullerton. Quarterly Series, 5s.

Mary Queen of Scots and her Marriage with Bothwell. Seven Letters to the *Tablet*. Revised, with a Preface and Notes and a Supplement, by the Hon. Colin Lindsay. Cloth, 2s.

Catechism made Easy. Being an Explanation of the Christian Doctrine. By the Rev. H. Gibson. Third edition, 2 vols. Cloth, 7s. 6d.

Liguori on the Mysteries of the Faith, the Holy Eucharist, the Blessed Sacrament, &c. New edition, cloth, 3s. 6d.; cheap edition, 2s.

Young and Fair. A Tale to while away a waste hour for Juveniles. By Vossian. Fancy cloth, 5s.

Footprints: Old and New; or, A Nun's Mission. By L. Y. B., Author of "The Queen's Lieges," "Lost or Sold," etc., etc. Fancy cloth, 7s. 6d.

Last Loaf, The. A Temperance Drama. 6d.

Wine Cup, The. Do. 6d.

Pierre Olivant. From the French of Paul Féval. 3d.

Old Religion. By the Rev. W. Lockhart. New edition, 5s.

Sketches of the Life of Mgr. de Mazenod, Founder of the Order of the Oblates of Mary Immaculate. In 2 vols. By the Rev. R. Cooke (O.M.I.).
Vol. I. treats of the Missionary Labours and Travels of Members of that Society in Canada, Labrador, Red River Regions, British Columbia, &c., &c.
Vol. II. in Texas and Mexico, in Great Britain and Ireland, in Ceylon, Natal, &c., &c. 8vo cloth; the 2 vols. reduced to 10s.

Apostolic Brief on Perseverance in the Use of the Rosary, The. By our Holy Father Pope Leo XIII. Followed by the three Decrees by the Bishop of Salford. 2d.

A Pastoral Letter in Spiritual Reading. By the Lord Bishop of Salford. 3d.

Clifton Tracts. New Edition. Cloth extra; complete in two vols., 9s.

Martin Luther; or, A Reply to the 10th November, 1883. 3d.

Excerpta ex Rituali Romano pro Administratione Sacra-mentorum. Convenient size for pocket. Cloth, gilt edges, 4s. 6d. net.

Catholic's Latin Instructor in the Principal Church Offices and Devotions. For the Use of Choirs, Convents, and Mission Schools, and for Self-Teaching. By the Rev. E. Caswall, of the Oratory. New and complete edition. Cloth, red edges, 3s. 6d.

Granville Mansions, 28, Orchard Street, London, W.,

Dramas suitable for Young Ladies, etc.

	£	s.	d.
Little Gipsy Girl, The: a Drama. Arranged from an old French story	0	1	0
"Comedy of Convocation" on Mount Parnassus	0	0	6
Festival of Corpus Christi, The. A Floral Drama. Composed by a Sister of Mercy. Cloth	0	1	6
Fire of London, The; or, Which is Which. A Play in Three Acts. By Lady Georgiana Fullerton	0	0	6
Germaine Cousin: The Shepherdess of Pibrac. A Drama. By Lady Georgiana Fullerton	0	0	6
Heiress of Elshamstowe, The. A Drama in Three Acts	0	1	6
Isabel de Lisle; or, The Fruits of Pride. A Drama. 64 pp.	0	1	6
King Rodolpho's Will. A Drama in One Act, with Prologue. By Rev. H. C. Duke. Wrapper	0	1	3
Mercy's Conquest; a Play in One Act. By A. Allen	0	0	3
Mystery Play, A. With Songs and Music, for Girls' Schools, in Four Acts. The Presentation of the Blessed Virgin, at the age of seven years, in the Temple. By the Rev. H. Formby	0	1	6
Passion Play of Ober-Ammergau, The, with Complete Text. Translated for the first time from the German. By M. F. Drew. Wrapper ...	0	2	0
Cloth	0	3	0
Short Easter Mystery Play, A. By Rev. H. Formby. The Company of the Holy Women Companions of Jesus. A Drama, with Chorus and Music	0	1	0
Youthful Martyrs of Rome. By Canon Oakley. New edition. Cloth	0	1	8

DRAMAS, NEW AMERICAN.
ALL PRICES MARKED NET.

Irish Heroine, The. A Drama in Five Acts. By the Rev. J. De Concilio. 1s.

Julia; or, The Golden Thimble. A Drama for girls. In One Act. Adapted from the French by Mrs. J. Sadlier. 1s.

Foundling of Sebastopol, The. A Drama. By W. Tandy, D.D. 2s.

Fanny Allen, the first American Nun. A Drama in Five Acts. By Maria Josephine. 1s.

Mary Beatrice and her Step-daughters, the uncrowned and the crowned. An Historical Drama. By the Authoress of "The Life of Catherine McAuley," etc. 2s.

Marie Antoinette. An Historical Drama. By the same Authoress. 2s.

Secret, The. A Drama. By Mrs. J. Sadlier. 1s.

House on the Avenue, The. A Drama in Five Scenes. By Winnie Rover. 2s.

Double Triumph, The. A Drama in Two Acts. Dramatised from the Story of Placidus in the "Martyrs of the Coliseum." By the Rev. A. J. O'Reilly, D.D. 2s.

Deaf Mute; or, The Abée de l'Epée. An Historical Drama in Four Acts. Translated from the German. 2s.

A Dialogue between the Faculties of the Soul. Translated from the French of Madame de Stolz. By Mrs. J. Sadlier. 1s.

Breton Cottage; or, A Mother's Curse. A Drama in Three Acts. By J. A. Guyet. 1s.

Orphan Sisters; or, Pupils of the Common School. A Drama for Girls. In One Act. By a Catholic Clergyman. 1s.

Knights of the Cross, The. A Sacred Drama in Three Acts. By a Franciscan Brother. 2s.

Granville Mansions, 28, Orchard Street, London, W.

NEW AMERICAN BOOKS.

(All prices marked NET.)

An Apostolic Woman; or, The Life and Letters of Irma le Fer de la Motte. With a Preface by M. Léon Aubineau. Translated from the French. Fancy cloth, 6s.

Baron of Hertz: A Tale of the Anabaptists. From the French of Albert de Labadye. Cloth, 5s.

Church of the Parables and True Spouse of the Suffering Saviour. By Joseph Prachensky, S.J. Cloth, 3s. 6d.

Cross and the Shamrock; or, How to Defend the Faith. An Irish-American Catholic Tale of Real Life. Written by a Missionary Priest. Fancy cloth, 5s.

Father Drummond and his Orphans; or, The Children of Mary. By Mary C. Edgar. Cloth, 2s.

Father Oswald: A Genuine Catholic Story. (Premium Library Series.) Cloth, 3s.

Glimpses of Pleasant Homes: A few Tales for Youth. By a Member of the Order of Mercy, Authoress of "The Life of Catharine McAuley," &c. Cloth, 5s.

Joseph Haydn: the Story of his Life. Translated from the German of Franz von Seeburg, by the Rev. J. M. Toohey, C.S.C. Cloth, 6s.

Journal of Eugénie de Guérin. Edited by G. S. Trebutien. Cloth, 6s.

Life and Letters of Madame Swetchine. By Count de Falloux, of the French Academy. Translated by H. W. Preston. Cloth, 5s.

Mary, the Model Child; or, First Fifteen Years of Mary Immaculate. By Rev. Alfred Mornin, Author of "The Life of the Curé d'Ars." (Excelsior Library Series). Cloth, 4s.

Pearl. By Kathleen O'Meara. Fancy cloth, 5s.

Pearl in Dark Waters: A Tale of the Times of Blessed Margaret Mary. By the Author of "Tyborne," "Dame Dolores," &c. Cloth, 3s.

Stray Leaves from a Passing Life: and other Stories. Cloth, 5s.

The Flemmings: A True Story. By Mrs. Anna H. Dorsey. (Notre Dame Series). Cloth, 5s.

Granville Mansions, 28, Orchard Street, London, W.,

Month of Mary.

BURNS AND OATES

HAVE A LARGE ASSORTMENT OF

STATUES

OF

"OUR BLESSED LADY,"

WITH AND WITHOUT THE HOLY CHILD.

In Composition, Plain, or Decorated; from 6 in. to 72 in. high.

Photographs and Prices on application.

VESTMENTS.

Low Mass Vestment, Roman or French form, plain, and well lined, in any colour, for Missions ... ... £2 : 10 :
Do. superior, lined merino or alpaca ... ... £4 10s., £6, £8, and 10 : 0 :
Do. ribbed silk or fine damask silk ... ... £6 10s., £9, £12, and 15 : 0 :
Do. imitation cloth of gold, lined alpaca or merino ... ... 4 : 10 :
Do. cloth of gold, half fine ; half fine do., lined silk ... ... £6, £8, and 10 : 0 :
Do. cloth of gold, trimmed with fine gold laces and lined with silk
 £12, £15, and 20 : 0 :
Do.   do.   embroidered ... ... £25 to 50 : 0 :

The Gothic vestment may be reckoned to cost one-third more than a Roman c French vestment of similar material.

Burns & Oates have much pleasure in announcing that they are no\ the sole London representatives of

HARDMAN, POWELL & CO.,

OF BIRMINGHAM,

Metal Workers, Silversmiths, Gas Fitters, Ironworkers,

MEDALLISTS, ENAMELLERS, ENGRAVERS,

PLATERS & GILDERS, STONE & WOOD CARVERS, &c.

Illustrated Price Lists forwarded post free.

Granville Mansions, 28, Orchard Street, London, W.

LAMPLOUGH'S PYRETIC SALINE,

EFFERVESCING AND TASTELESS;

Forming a most Invigorating, Vitalising and Refreshing Beverage. Gives instant relief in **Headache, Sea or Bilious Sickness, Constipation, Indigestion, Lassitude, Low Spirits, Heartburn, Feverish Colds**; prevents and quickly relieves or cures the worst form of *Typhus, Scarlet, Jungle, and other Fevers; Prickly Heat, Smallpox, Measles, Eruptive or Skin Complaints, and various other altered conditions of the Blood.*

The Testimony of Medical Gentlemen has been unqualified in praise of LAMPLOUGH'S PYRETIC SALINE, as possessing most important elements calculated to restore and maintain health with perfect vigour of body and mind.

Dr. Turley.—'I found it act as a specific, in my experience and family, in the worst form of Scarlet Fever, no other medicine being required.'

Dr. S. Gibbon (formerly Physician to the London Hospital).—'Its usefulness in the treatment of disease has long been confirmed by medical experience.'

Her Majesty's Representative, the Governor of Sierra Leone, in a letter of request for an additional supply of the Pyretic Saline, states:—'It is of great value, and I shall rejoice to hear it is in the hands of all Europeans visiting the tropics.'

Dr. Morgan.—'It furnishes the blood with its lost Saline constituents.'

Dr. J. W. Dowsing.—'I used it in the treatment of Forty-two Cases of Yellow Fever, and I am happy to state I never lost a single case.'

Rawul Pindee, Punjaub, India, 28th March, 1871.—'Solely from the ascertained merits of your preparation in the Fever-stricken Districts by which we are surrounded, we firmly believe that the use of your Pyretic Saline will do more to prevent Fever than all the Quinine ever imported can cure.'

In Patent Glass-Stoppered Bottles, 2s. 6d., 4s. 6d., 11s., and 21s. each.

LAMPLOUGH'S CONCENTRATED LIME JUICE SYRUP,

A perfect luxury—forms, with the addition of Pyretic Saline, a most delicious and invigorating Beverage.
In Patent Glass-Stoppered Bottles, at 2s. and 4s. 6d. each.

H. LAMPLOUGH, 113, HOLBORN HILL, LONDON, E.C.

OLDRIDGE'S

SIXTY YEARS' SUCCESS.—The best and only certain remedy ever discovered for preserving, strengthening, beautifying, or restoring the Hair, Whiskers, or Moustaches, and preventing them turning Grey. Sold in bottles, 3s. 6d., 6s., and 11s., by all chemists and perfumers, and at 22, Wellington Street, Strand, London, W.C. For Children's and Ladies' Hair it is most efficacious and unrivalled.

STOWMARKET.

Mission of Our Lady of Seven Dolours, Stowmarket, Suffolk.

WE are still in the poor little IRON SHED, 24ft. by 12ft. Please help to continue building and to finish the school-chapel in this poorest of the poor missions of this poverty-stricken diocese. I make this appeal with the SPECIAL APPROVAL of the Right Rev. Arthur Riddell, Lord Bishop of Northampton, who has already blessed all who may assist.

SIR,—When the "Word was made Flesh, and dwelt amongst us," the shepherds came, and the Magi came; the stars of heaven, the beasts of the field, and the fruits of the earth, had their ambassadors at the Court. When the Bishop of our souls would say his first Mass, a man was found who heard the voice of the master, and prepared an altar in his upper room, and furnished it as best he could. All the world knows it. The shepherds, the Eastern Kings, the man the apostles met at the gate of the city, are household words with thousands who never heard of Cæsar or Cyrus, or the thousands of others who have staked their lives and perished in the attempt to write their names on the remembrances of men. And better far, the names of those holy ones are well known to the angels, and the countless multitude before the throne, for they can read them in the Sacred Heart of Our Lord, and who would not wish to share in their deeds, and their reward? To-day there is an upper room here, but unfinished and unfurnished. Are there no shepherds to be found to give of their herds, no wise men to give of their gold, that this place may be finished and made less unfit for "the Word made Flesh" to dwell amongst us? Is there no man with a pitcher "to hear what the master saith," and prepare for the Pasch in the upper room? Are there none of your many readers who would wish to help in so great a work? Surely all heaven must envy us the power to administer to the wants and needs of our God.

The names of the benefactors of to-day may not be written in the Gospel, but the angels and saints, and souls saved by their means will know them, when it will no longer be in the power of the inhabitants of Bethlehem to refuse shelter to the Mother and the Child; when the day of God's silence is over, and His turn is come to say to the benefactors Come, and to the malefactors Depart. Surely, Sir, many among the thousands of the readers of your very valuable Review will see, read, and give help.

Yours truly,

FRANCIS J. WARMOLL.

www.ingramcontent.com/pod-product-compliance
Lightning Source LLC
Chambersburg PA
CBHW031939290426
44108CB00011B/607